The History of
Children's Literature

ELVA S. SMITH'S

The History of Children's Literature

A SYLLABUS WITH
SELECTED BIBLIOGRAPHIES

Revised and enlarged edition by
MARGARET HODGES
and
SUSAN STEINFIRST

American Library Association · Chicago 1980

Library of Congress Cataloging in Publication Data

Smith, Elva Sophronia, 1871-
    Elva S. Smith's The history of children's literature.

    Includes index.
    1. Children's literature, English—Bibliography.
2. Children's literature, English—History and criticism—
Bibliography.   3. Children's literature, American
—Bibliography.   4. Children's literature, American
—History and criticism—Bibliography.   5. Children—
Management—History—Bibliography.   6. Parent and
child—History—Bibliography.   I. Hodges, Margaret, joint
author.   II. Steinfirst, Susan, joint author.   III. Title.
Z2014.5.S57   1980 [PN1009.A1]   010   79-28323
ISBN 0-8389-0286-3

Designed by Harvey Retzloff
Composed by Modern Typographers in Linotype
    Caledonia
Printed on 50# Antique Glatfelter, a pH neutral stock,
by the Chicago Press Corporation,
and bound by Zonne Bookbinders, Inc.

CONTENTS

To our students and teachers

PREFACE

In 1937, when THE HISTORY OF CHILDREN'S LITERATURE was first published, the author and compiler, Elva Sophronia Smith (1871–1965), had been teaching the history of children's literature for many years. She had come to Pittsburgh as a young woman, a student in the Training School for Children's Librarians, the first school of its kind. She later became head of the Boys and Girls Room at Carnegie Library of Pittsburgh, where the training school was housed, and associate professor in the school itself.

Elva Smith brought to her work a keen intelligence and a consuming interest in children's literature. She worked in close partnership with Frances Jenkins Olcott, director of the training school, and in the introduction to her syllabus gives Miss Olcott credit for the purchase, about 1907, of an outstanding collection of rare books for children. It was Elva Smith who made the greater use of the collection, since it formed the basis for her landmark work, *The history of children's literature: a syllabus with selected bibliographies.* The quality of the collection may be judged from a comment made by d'Alté Welch on a visit to Pittsburgh: "I wonder if people here know what treasures they have in this collection." The core collection, still intact, is now known as the Olcott-Smith Collection.

The 1907–8 *Circular of information concerning the training school for children's librarians* mentions income ($7000) from an endowment given by Andrew Carnegie for the support of the school and for the development of "a special reference library." This may refer to the Olcott-Smith Collection. Elva Smith's introduction to *The history of children's literature* identifies the source of the purchase as Charles Welsh, a retired member of the English publishing firm Griffith, Farran, Okeden and Welsh. The firm had occupied quarters near the site of John Newbery's Bible and Sun in St. Paul's Churchyard, London, and it carried on the publishing interests of the Newbery family. Charles Welsh himself was the author of a biography of John Newbery, *A bookseller of the last century.* Welsh was also a member of a group of English bibliophiles who called themselves "Ye Sette of Odd Volumes" and as their "chapman" wrote occasional pieces, privately printed, on rare books for children and on the history of children's literature. He came to the United States in 1895 and was acknowledged here as an authority on children's literature. He worked on the annotated bibliography of Harvard's great collection of chapbooks, wrote various articles setting standards for children's literature, and edited numerous sets of books recommended for young readers. It is not known exactly when or how during this period he sold the Olcott-Smith Collection to the Training School for Children's Librarians in Pittsburgh.

Elva Smith included in her bibliographies a large number of references to sources available in other libraries. Some of these sources were brief and are now difficult to locate. When she retired in 1944, she was anticipating the need for a revised edition; one copy of the first edition is full of her penciled marginal notations for additional sources. Since that time, a flood of books and articles has appeared on the history of children's literature. Many acknowledge Elva Smith's admirable contribution to the subject through her scholarly *History*. The first edition laid the groundwork for much of the work done later by others, but nothing similar in form and substance has appeared.

The intention of this edition is to be useful to the researcher preparing a dissertation or scholarly article, to the teacher on either the undergraduate or the graduate level, to the student who wishes to read widely in specific phases of the history of children's literature, and to the librarian who sees a need to expand a collection in this field or to examine a current collection for important out-of-print titles. The latest date for the titles here is 1977.

The selection for this edition includes most of Elva Smith's sources and adds many new ones that throw light on historic backgrounds, issues, and persons in the history of children's literature. These have been chosen because they measure up to one or more of the following criteria: they are generally available in large libraries that offer interlibrary loans; they make fresh, valid contributions and are not merely rewritten from earlier sources; they are in themselves well-written pieces of prose; their format, illustrations, maps, photographs, or facsimilies bring out the color and flavor of a period in children's literature; they include valuable bibliographies; in the case of editions intended for children, they have distinctive style and illustrations of high quality. Where possible, the date of first publication is given. Many later editions listed by Elva Smith are omitted here. The present editors have listed without annotations a few sources that they have been unable to examine personally.

The Training School for Children's Librarians became the Carnegie Library School, from which came another scholarly graduate and teacher, Elizabeth Nesbitt, coauthor of *A critical history of children's literature*, another landmark in the field. Miss Nesbitt's teaching owed much to the intellectual and material resources inherited by those who followed Elva Smith in Pittsburgh. In 1964, after further expansion and changes, the School became the Graduate School of Library and Information Sciences at the University of Pittsburgh. (In 1979 the name was changed to School of Library and Information Science.) Throughout seventy-five years of the school's existence, and through all periods of change, the course in the history of children's literature has remained a special feature of study in the field of library service to children.

Elva Sophronia Smith was born on April 28, 1871. It seems appropriate to date the preface to the first revised edition of her *History of children's literature:*

Pittsburgh, Pennsylvania
April 28, 1980

FROM THE INTRODUCTION
TO THE FIRST EDITION

As here presented, the period covered is from the sixth century to the close of the nineteenth, but the study is limited to England and America except in cases where a foreign author was directly influential in the English or American development, as was Madame De Genlis, "le plus gracieux et le plus galant des pédagogues."[1] Traditional literature—fable, myth, and folk tale—is likewise excluded, except for the bibliographical history of such epochal collections as those of Perrault and Grimm. In Anglo-Saxon times and for several centuries thereafter, children's books were inseparable from schools and education, but since the days of John Newbery and the development of general reading interests the production of children's books has increased to such an extent that textbooks have become differentiated from other literature. They now constitute a class within a class, a group so large and distinctive that it has not been found possible to continue its history in the later periods within the time limitations of the course.

Children's periodicals make up another interesting group; but, though a few of the more important are noted, their complete story is not attempted. The illustration of children's books is one of the most fascinating aspects of their history and some of the "high spots" in its evolution from early times to the twentieth century have been touched upon, but more detailed study of illustrative processes and individual artists could be added to advantage. There are other alluring bypaths which cannot be followed too far in a short course but which may be suggested for further exploration. Because of correlation with other library school subjects— book selection, the history of books and libraries, storytelling, with its study of source materials—there are cases where only special aspects of topics are indicated. Any topics which thus overlap may be omitted or amplified, according to the needs and judgment of those using the outlines and lists.

For convenience the general subject is divided into sections or units representing, usually, special periods. Historical headings are frequently used, but these are not to be construed too literally with exacting limitations of time. It is necessary to segregate groups of books if the qualities and characteristics which differentiate them from others are to be determined and defined, but literary periods have a

1. Saint-Beuve, C. A. *Causeries du lundi.* Garnier Frères, [18–?], v.3, p. 20.

way of merging indistinguishably one into another. As Miss Repplier has so aptly said, "Nothing is so hard to deal with as a period. Nothing is so unmanageable as a date. People will be born a few years too early; they will live a few years too long. Events will happen out of time. The closely linked decades refuse to be separated."[2] To illustrate, hornbooks were in use for some three hundred years. Chapbooks, especially characteristic of the eighteenth century, came into existence earlier and were still being printed in the nineteenth. Lear's *Book of nonsense* was published in 1846; *Laughable lyrics,* in 1876. In these and similar cases authors and books have been placed in the period or with the group to which they have seemed most naturally to belong; but, as already indicated, changes in arrangement are easily possible if a different grouping appears more logical to the instructor. Some periods are particularly interesting for study, that of John Newbery, for example, and the so-called "happy half century" (approximately 1775 to 1825), and these naturally are stressed; but others are also important links in the chain and cannot be neglected. A few outstanding writers, those most typical of a given era, are usually singled out for detailed study, other authors are considered more briefly; many have of necessity been omitted.

In order to trace the genesis of types of books—primers, for instance—it may be necessary to go back through time for their beginnings and it may also be desirable to note changes and developments in later periods than the one being studied. It is usually advisable to consider the work of an individual author as a whole, although this procedure may affect strict historical sequence. As an aid, therefore, in keeping a chronological point of view the section bibliographies have been supplemented by a short selected list of books arranged in the order of first publication.

The bibliographies are limited for the most part to the resources of the Carnegie Library of Pittsburgh and the Carnegie Library School, but a few books from other collections have been included. With two or three exceptions, however, all books mentioned have been seen and examined and most have been used with students. Comparatively few of the early children's books from the special collection in the Pittsburgh School have been listed, as it has seemed inexpedient, except in special cases, to note books which might not be generally available. Some writers have been unduly prolific—Mrs. Sherwood, Jacob Abbott, and Samuel G. Goodrich, to mention but three. Full lists of their work seemed another unwarranted expansion of the bibliographies and only a few typical books have therefore been included. The references given, it is hoped, will be helpful for suggestions, but it is assumed that additions and substitutions will be made as needed, according to the interests of instructor and students and the resources accessible.

For some children's books, such as the *Divine and moral songs* of Isaac Watts and the poems of Ann and Jane Taylor, there have been many editions, English and American, since their first publication. For other books, such as Miss Alcott's *Little women,* there are a number of modern editions in print. The whole question of editions is complicated and no attempt has been made to trace or enumerate the earlier issues or to list all that may be in print at the present time. The editions specified are generally those available in Pittsburgh, but they are not in all cases the only editions that have been used or always the ones most desirable. Facsimiles

---

2. *A happy half-century, and other essays.* Houghton, 1908, p.VII.

of early editions are preferable for teaching purposes to original copies of later editions. However, if the original content and format have not been altered, late editions may sometimes be found quite satisfactory. Modern editions, even though form and illustrations differ, may need to be used for text if others are not accessible, and they are often useful for comparison. Sometimes also, they contain introductions which are helpful.

As the early books for children are associated in the bibliographies with those of later days, the same form of entry has been followed and no attempt has been made in the transcription of title pages to follow the originals with the typographical fidelity required for such a volume as Rosenbach's *Early American children's books.*

To the lists of suggested children's books have been added biographical, historical, and critical references. Some of these will be recognized as indispensable sources of information; others, more specialized, will be optional, depending upon the length of courses and other conditions. For some of the more recent authors, such as Kipling, only a few references are given, as there is a wealth of material which is easily obtainable if desired. A number of valuable new books bearing on the subject of children's literature, such as the study of Thomas Day, by George Warren Gignilliat,[3] have been published in recent years. These are of importance in giving fuller or more accurate information than was available previously and for new interpretations of authors and their work, but earlier contributions are still useful for the contemporary point of view and for the atmosphere and spirit of other periods. Kenneth Grahame, in an address included in his *Life, letters, and unpublished work,* emphasized the need of "a proper recognition of the special contemporary appeal which almost every good writer has for his own actual contemporaries, the subtle *liaison,* the bond between themselves and their actual contemporaries only, and never between the writer and later generations." Critics of today, he says, "should recognize the force of this contemporary appeal and its reality, and in judging past work, should try and make themselves as contemporary as possible, so to speak, in the hope that they too may catch some faint vibration of the particular thrill."[4] Although his remarks did not refer to children's literature they are applicable; for this "contemporary appeal" or "incommunicable thrill" must needs be taken into account in the criticism or estimate of such writers as Charlotte Yonge and such books as *The heir of Redclyffe.*

Occasionally references may duplicate each other to some extent, but with large classes it is desirable to have a number of books that can be used at one time; also it is sometimes necessary to provide substitutes at short notice if one is largely dependent upon circulating collections and the preferred books are not available when needed.

General reference books, such as *The dictionary of national biography,* have not been included. Other valuable aids, which could not well be noted, include sales catalogs, pictures, and clippings. Collections of these once started will grow surprisingly and will often prove most useful. Periodical and other references will naturally be added as they appear. For example, *The tradition of Boethius; a*

---

3. *The author of Sandford and Merton; a life of Thomas Day, Esq.* Columbia University, c1932.

4. Chalmers, P. R. *Kenneth Grahame; life, letters, and unpublished work.* Methuen, [1933], p.289, 298.

study of his importance in medieval culture, by H. R. Patch, recently published by the Oxford University Press, should be of interest in the early historical period and *The Horn Book Magazine* for May-June, 1936, contains three articles of importance in this connection, two of them treating of Kipling,[5] and the third of Jane Andrews.[6] The annotations are descriptive rather than critical. They were added to the lists from time to time, most of them to indicate the point of view of the author of the book or to facilitate ready reference to special topics. Uncredited quotations are from the article or book annotated. Many of the books listed include bibliographies which are useful when additional references are needed for special topics. Although the content of the bibliographies is determined by the topical outlines the arrangement differs to some extent. The outlines are detailed and points are arranged in a logical order for class discussion. In the bibliographies entries may be grouped under inclusive headings to avoid undue expansion of the lists; also names of individual authors used as headings are arranged alphabetically under a main head or a subhead, this plan having been found more convenient for practical use.

The end of the Victorian epoch seems a fitting point to bring to a temporary close a study of the evolution of books for children. The turn of the century brought little noticeable variation; for authors of the eighties and nineties were continuing their work. *The Wouldbegoods* appeared in 1901 and Kipling's *Just so stories* in 1902. As one looks backward, however, over the last three decades striking contrasts are apparent. The changes in the social and economic life of the people, the international contacts resulting from the European war, studies in child psychology, new educational theories and methods, more critical reviewing of children's books, new processes in printing and illustration, the establishment of children's rooms in public libraries and special departments in publishing houses —these and other causes have resulted not only in a greatly accelerated production but in a new literature for children differing from the old in subject, literary method, format, and illustration. These books with their many innovations and their varying content, a reflection of the complexity and diversity of interests today, are a major problem in book selection of the present time, and they will constitute the next important chapter in the history of children's literature when time shall have given perspective.

One result of the various influences contributing to the development of children's literature in this first third of the twentieth century has been the increased interest in the subject among different groups, as evidenced by the books and articles written in the last few years, the catalogs of special collections that have been published, and the number of book exhibits that have been held by associations and libraries. The courses that have been added to the curricula of many educational institutions also indicate a growing recognition of the value and importance of a knowledge of children's books, both those of today and those of yore. The latter may be of interest simply because they are curious and quaint, or because of the contrasts between new and old.

The study of origins and influences is, to many, particularly fascinating. Why, for example, were early books written in question and answer style? Were the

5. "The wisdom of Baloo: Kipling and childhood," by Helen E. Haines; "Kipling and his publishers," by Margaret Lesser.

6. "Jane Andrews: her books and her school," by Ethel Parton.

miniature books of the John Newbery period a mere accident? How did the modern school primer derive from a religious manual? Why did the literary annuals spring into such prominence in the second quarter of the nineteenth century?

The side lights thrown on the social history of different epochs are almost equally fascinating. The occupations and diversions, the manners and morals, the modes of thought, the attitudes of parents and writers toward the young—these are reflected in children's books. Mrs. Trimmer, for instance, insists that children should understand that her *Fabulous histories* are "a series of fables, intended to convey moral instruction applicable to themselves," and she introduces the "mockbird," properly a native of America, into her English story "for the sake of the moral."

Not only the moralities, but the proprieties, are strictly observed. Mrs. Benson considers the proposal that eleven-year-old Harriet mount a stepladder to look into a robin's nest as "rather an indelicate scheme for a lady" and Miss Edgeworth's little Patty, who falls down stairs, decently covers her ankle with her gown. The good French governess introduces the children in her care to a "rational toy-shop" where there were neither whips nor horses, dressed dolls, nor baby-houses; but instead cabinets for minerals, materials for the making of baskets and other useful articles, small looms, and printing presses. In *Tales of the castle*, the children are taken to the country where they are weaned from their fondness for fairy lore by stories related in turn by their mother and grandmother. It is surprising at times to note how frequently the wheel of progress brings uppermost some supposedly outdated attitude or method so that the old seems new and the new is old. This is not the place for further illustration, but the subtitle of Mr. Darton's *Children's books in England,* "Five centuries of social life," is an indication of the importance as well as the interest of this phase of study.

And finally, as Charles Welsh says, "to study, however briefly, some of the oldest and best tried books, and to try to define the qualities to which they owe their permanent hold on the child mind, will be useful as a means of comparison, and perhaps as furnishing some standards of value."[7]

ELVA S. SMITH

February, 1935

---

7. *The Library,* 11, new ser. 1:314 (June, 1900).

General Bibliography

BOOKS

Andreae, Gesiena. The dawn of juvenile literature in England. Amsterdam: H. J. Paris, 1925.
For the most part a study of the eighteenth century. Emphasizes the new conception of childhood and the deepening awareness of its significance.

Andrews, Siri, ed. The Hewins lectures, 1947–1962. Boston: Horn Book, 1963.
Introduction by Frederic G. Melcher. "A series of annual papers on the writing and publishing of children's books in New England's fertile years."

Arbuthnot, May Hill, and **Zena Sutherland.** Children and books. 4th ed. Glenview, Ill.: Scott, Foresman, 1972.
A text for the study of children's literature with guides and full bibliographies. Chapter 4, "Children's literature: history and trends," p. 82–101, carries the subject to the twentieth century and includes a chronological list of milestones in books, from *Aesop's fables*, 1484, to *The wind in the willows*, 1908.

Avery, Gillian E. Nineteenth century children: heroes and heroines in English children's stories, 1780–1900. [London]: Hodder, [1965].
Adult attitudes toward children as revealed in the writing of late Georgian and Victorian writers. Includes two chapters on fairy tales.

Barry, Florence Valentine. A century of children's books. New York: Doran, 1923; reprint: Detroit: Singing Tree, 1968.
The period studied is the eighteenth century. "Notes and extracts," p. 224–49, supplement the text, and there is a "Chronological list of children's books from 1700 to 1825," p. 250–57.

Bayne-Powell, Rosamond. The English child in the eighteenth century. New York: Dutton, 1939.
Partial contents: Theories on education; Children's books; Some children in 18th century fiction.

Bodger, Joan. How the heather looks. New York: Viking, 1965.
Chapters on the English background of Randolph Caldecott, Arthurian legends, and other landmarks in the history of children's literature. The format is a lively account of a visit by the author's American family to the scenes and sites of the books.

Brigham, Clarence S. Fifty years of collecting Americana for the Library of the American Antiquarian Society 1908–1958. Worcester, Mass.: American Antiquarian Society, 1958.
Included among the notable collections at AAS are children's books, schoolbooks, imprints to 1820, and miniature books.

Caroline M. Hewins, her book: containing *A mid-century child and her books* by Caroline M. Hewins and *Caroline M. Hewins and books for children,* by Jennie Lindquist. Boston: Horn Book, 1954.
Includes a reprint of *A mid-century child and her books* and an appreciation of Caroline Hewins as a pioneer in library service for children. Her *Books for the young,* 1882, gave rules for "How to teach the right use of books," reprinted here.

Commire, Anne, ed. Yesterday's authors of books for children. v. 1. Detroit: Gale, 1977.
Subtitle: "Facts and pictures about authors and illustrators of books for young people, from early times to 1960." Gives information about the subjects' personal life, career, writings, adaptations made from the writings. Also extensive excerpts from autobiographical writings, in "Sidelights." Bibliographies. An invaluable resource.

Cruse, Amy. The Victorians and their reading. Boston: Houghton, 1935.
Shows "what books, good and bad, were actually read by the Victorians during the first fifty years of the Queen's reign." "Books from America" and "A young Victorian's library" are useful chapters.

Darton, Frederick Joseph Harvey. "Children's books," *Cambridge history of English literature,*

v. 11, p. 366–87. Cambridge: Cambridge University Press, 1966.
Includes a fine bibliography.

———. Children's books in England: five centuries of social life. 2d ed. Cambridge: Cambridge University Press, 1958.
A highly literate survey covering the books written for or adopted by children from the days of Caxton to the end of the nineteenth century. Valuable bibliographies with each chapter and a list of "some books of general and specific interest published since 1932."

Davidson, Gustav. First editions in American juvenalia and problems in their identification. Chicago: Normandie House, 1939.
For the librarian as well as the collector. Includes bibliographic data.

Doyle, Brian, ed. The who's who of children's literature. New York: Schocken, 1968.
Includes widely read writers as well as those who are "approved." Mostly English and American, but some writers whose work has been translated into English are included. Photographs. List of "principal annual awards in British and American children's literature." Bibliography for individual authors and illustrators.

Eastman, Mary Huse, comp. Index to fairy tales, myths and legends. 2d edition, rev. and enl. Boston: Faxon, 1926.
A guide to sources and parallels with two supplements, 1937 and 1952.

Fadiman, Clifton. Party of one: the selected writings of Clifton Fadiman. Cleveland: World, 1955.
Includes essays on Mother Goose, Lewis Carroll, and Edward Lear, by a master of English prose.

Field, Carolyn W., ed. Subject collections in children's literature. New York: Bowker, 1969.
Consultants: Virginia Haviland, Elizabeth Nesbitt, for the National Planning Committee for Special Collections, Children's Services Division, American Library Association. A guide to collections grouped by subject, a directory of locations, and names of librarians in charge of the collections. Includes a bibliography of publications about the collections.

Field, Louise Frances Story (Mrs. E. M. Field). The child and his book: some account of the history and progress of children's literature in England. 2d ed. London: Wells Gardner, Darton, 1892; reprint: Detroit: Singing Tree, 1968.
From Anglo-Saxon days to Victorian times. Includes chapter entitled "Some illustrators of children's books."

Fisher, Margery. Who's who in children's books: a treasury of the familiar characters of childhood. New York: Holt, 1975.

First published in England. Arranged by names of characters in English and American fiction for children. Fairly extensive outlines and critical commentary on the books in which the characters appear.

Gottlieb, Gerald. Early children's books and their illustration. New York: Pierpont Morgan Library; Boston: Godine, 1975.
Written in connection with an exhibit at the Morgan Library in 1975. Lavishly illustrated and with commentary on 225 books from a third- or fourth-century Aesop to *Le petit prince*. Bibliography.

Green, Roger Lancelyn. Tellers of tales: British authors of children's books from 1800 to 1964. Rewritten and rev. ed. New York: Watts, 1965.
In well-written and informative notes, a British scholar discusses a wide range of authors. Lists of each author's works for young readers, dated. Also sources for information about the authors.

Halsey, Rosalie Vrylina. Forgotten books of the American nursery: a history of the development of the American story-book. Boston: Goodspeed, 1911; reprint: Detroit: Singing Tree, 1969.
Contents: Introductory; The play-book in England; Newbery's books in America; Patriotic printers and the American Newbery; The child and his book at the end of the 18th century; Toy-books in the early 19th century; American writers and English critics.

Haviland, Virginia, comp. Children and literature: views and reviews. Glenview, Ill.: Scott, Foresman [1973].
Essays and other writings selected to "make readily available both the historical background and the broad range of subjects and issues covered in a library science or teacher education course in children's literature."

Hazard, Paul. Books, children & men. Translated by Marguerite Mitchell. 4th ed. Boston: Horn Book, 1960.
First published in 1944, this is a landmark in the study of the history of children's literature and of famous books adopted by children.

Hewins, Caroline M., comp. Books for the young: a guide for parents and children. New York: F. Leypoldt, 1882.
The first important library list of books for children. The compiler was one of the outstanding figures in library service and literary criticism of children's books.

———. A mid-century child and her books. New York: Macmillan, 1926; reprint: Detroit: Singing Tree, 1969. Also included in *Caroline M. Hewins: her book*, edited by Jennie D. Lindquist, p. 1–76. Boston: Horn Book, 1954

Memories of Mother Goose, Maria Edgeworth, Jacob Abbott, and *Uncle Tom's cabin;* also a facsimile of *Peter Piper's alphabet.*

Hürlimann, Bettina. Three centuries of children's books in Europe. Translated and edited by Brian W. Alderson. Cleveland: World, 1968.
First published in Zurich, 1959. Especially useful for the editor's comments and booklists added "to show how certain European children's books have been received in this country [England] and to provide references to English translations which are currently available."

Ireland, Norma Olin. Index to fairy tales, 1949–1972, including folklore, legends, and myths in collections. Westwood, Mass.: Faxon, 1973.
Continues the Eastman index (see above).

James, Philip. Children's books of yesterday. Edited by C. Geoffrey Holme. London: The Studio, 1933.

The studio special autumn number. Covers children's books from Comenius to the end of the nineteenth century, with facsimiles of pages from chapbooks, battledores, and colored books.

Johnson, Edna, Evelyn R. Sickels, and **Frances Clarke Sayers.** Anthology of children's literature. 4th ed. Boston: Houghton, 1970.
Illustrated by Fritz Eichenberg. Excellent introductions and bibliographies for chapters on nursery rhymes, fables, folk tales, myths and legends.

Jordan, Alice M. From Rollo to Tom Sawyer and other papers. Boston: Horn Book, 1948.
An authority long connected with her work at the Boston Public Library writes on nineteenth-century American books for children. Most of the chapters appeared first in *Horn book magazine.*

Kunitz Stanley J., and **Howard Haycraft,** eds. Junior book of authors. New York: Wilson, 1934.
Subtitle: "an introduction to the lives of writers and illustrators for younger readers from Lewis Carroll and Louisa Alcott to the present day. Illustrated with 260 photographs and drawings. With an introduction by Effie L. Power." Includes a "Children's almanac of books and holidays," compiled by Helen Dean Fish and originally published by Frederick A. Stokes in pamphlet form with a cover in color, "obtainable" at twenty-five cents.

Meigs, Cornelia, et al. A critical history of children's literature. Rev. ed. New York: Macmillan, 1969.
First published in 1953. A landmark, in which four authorities—Cornelia Meigs, Anne Eaton, Elizabeth Nesbitt, and Ruth Hill Viguers—trace the chief social trends influencing writers whose books have been written for or adopted by children from earliest times to the present. Includes folklore of the British Isles.

Miller, Bertha Mahony, et al., comps. Illustrators of children's books, 1744–1945. Boston: Horn Book, 1947; reprint, 1961.
Contains ten essays, including "Illustrated books for children before 1800" by Anne Eaton. Also includes brief biographies of about eight hundred artists and bibliographies that list examples of the artists' works. Bibliography of the authors whose works were illustrated, and other supplementary material that makes this an indispensable source.

Moore, Annie E. Literature old and new for children; materials for a college course. Boston: Houghton, 1934.
Includes chapters on Mother Goose, folk tales and fairy ways, fables, myths, early books for children, and Hans Christian Andersen.

Muir, Percival H. English children's books, 1600 to 1900. New York: Praeger, [1954]; London: Batsford, [1969].
A short history of children's books, each chapter ending with a checklist and postscript of bibliographic material. Includes harlequinades, books made with paper dolls or with movable parts. "List of illustrated books to 1800." Based on the Bussell collection and the National Book League Exhibition of 1946. Generously illustrated.

Nietz, John A. Old textbooks: spelling, grammar, reading, arithmetic, geography, American history, civil government, physiology, penmanship, art, music, as taught in the common schools from colonial days to 1900. Pittsburgh: University of Pittsburgh Press, 1961.
A history, with facsimiles and charts.

Palgrave, *Sir* **Francis Turner.** "Antiquities of nursery literature," in his *Reviews, essays and other writings,* v. 2. Cambridge; Cambridge University Press, 1922.
Reprinted from *The quarterly review,* January, 1819. The author says, "The man of letters should not disdain the chap-book, or the nursery story." He connects English tales with those of Europe and with Teutonic myth.

Quayle, Eric. The collector's book of children's books. New York: Potter, 1971.
Describes works from the late sixteenth century to the present with illustrations from the author's own collection of books. *Contents:* Juvenile incunabula; 18th century children's books; Fairy, folk tales and fantasia; Books of instruction, natural history and travel; Poetry and nursery rhymes; Stories—before 1850; Stories—1850 and after; Boys' adventure stories; Periodicals, annuals, and penny dreadfuls; Miscellania; Toy books and moveable books.

Rosenbach, Abraham S. Wolf. Early American children's books, 1682–1840: the private collection of A. S. W. Rosenbach, on exhibition at

the New York Public Library. New York: New York Public Library, 1927.
Text is useful as a résumé. Four reproductions.

———. Early American children's books, with bibliographical descriptions of the books in his private collection. Portland, Me.: Southworth Press, 1933; reprint: New York: Kraus, 1966.
Foreword by A. Edward Newton. Lists 816 items, arranged chronologically, 1682–1836, from a great private collection. Full bibliographical data with notes of location and other important descriptive detail. Includes biographical notes on authors, copious facsimile illustrations, indexes, and bibliography.

Salway, Lance, ed. Collections of children's literature: a guide to collections in libraries and other organizations in London and the home counties. Birmingham, England: Library Assn., Youth Libraries Group, 1972.

Sloane, William. Children's books in England and America in the seventeenth century: a history and checklist, together with *The young Christian's library,* the first printed catalogue of books for children. New York: King's Crown Press, Columbia University Press, 1955.
Describes books that amused and instructed the young reader. Points out the role of folklore for children in this period before the tales of Perrault had been translated. Gives a chronological annotated list of the books mentioned with locations of copies. Includes a facsimile of *The young Christian's library.*

Smith, Elva Sophronia. History of children's literature: a syllabus with selected bibliographies. Chicago: American Library Assn., 1937.
An invaluable aid to teachers of the history of children's literature including many references to early sources omitted in the present revised edition.

Targ, William, ed. Bibliophile in the nursery: a bookman's treasury of collectors' lore on old and rare children's books. Cleveland: World, 1957.
A collection of essays by notable historians and bibliophiles, including Darton, Hazard, the Opies, and others. Facsimile illustrations and bibliographical footnotes.

Tassin, Algernon. "Books for children," *The Cambridge history of American literature,* v. 2, p. 396–409. New York: Putnam, 1918.
A survey. Bibliography, p. 631–38.

Thwaite, Mary F. From primer to pleasure in reading: an introduction to the history of children's books in England, from the invention of printing to 1914 with an outline of some developments in other countries. 2d ed. London: Library Assn., 1972.
Intended as an "introduction to the more scholarly and detailed histories of literature." Readable and useful. Chronological table and bibliography.

Townsend, John Rowe. Written for children: an outline of English-language children's literature. Rev. ed. Philadelphia: Lippincott, 1975.
First published in England. A historical survey, generously illustrated, from Caxton to modern times, with critical analysis of social forces, authors and illustrators of English-language books for children.

Tuer, Andrew W. 1000 quaint cuts from books of other days including amusing illustrations from children's story books, fables, chapbooks. London: Field & Tuer; New York: Scribner & Welford, 1886; reprint: Detroit: Gale, 1968.
Old woodcuts printed from original blocks, including some from early chapbooks.

Whalley, Joyce Irene. Cobwebs to catch flies: illustrated books for the nursery and schoolroom 1700–1900. Berkeley: University of California Press, 1975.
First published in England. "A study of the illustrated educational books which were used to instruct children during their earliest years, in the home rather than the school." Over 150 book illustrations. Extensive bibliography.

Wilson, Albert E. Penny plain, two pence coloured: a history of the juvenile drama. London: Harrap, 1932.
Foreword by Charles B. Cochran. Discusses the art work and presentation of "the most fascinating offshoot of the British drama." Includes lists of publishers and plays, a bibliography and index.

PERIODICAL ARTICLES

Allen, Carolyn A. "Early American children's books at the American Antiquarian Society," *Horn book magazine* 52: 117–31 (April, 1976).

The introductory chapter of d'Alte Welch's *Bibliography,* reprinted here as an article, "is virtually a catalog of the Society's collection." Illustrated with facsimile pages of texts and woodcuts.

"Collections of rare children's books: a symposium: parts 1–6," *Library journal* 63:20–21, 105–7, 192–93, 360–62, 452–53, 535–37 (January 1–July 1, 1938).

Descriptions of outstanding collections by Valta Parma, Library of Congress; David Davies, Huntington Library, San Marino, California; Wilbur Macey Stone, private collector; Elva Sophronia Smith, Carnegie Library School, Pittsburgh; Mary Helen Kidder, Hewins Collection, State Historical Society Library, Hartford, Connecticut; and Anne Carroll Moore, New York Public Library, New York City.

Curtis, John Gould. "Saving the infant class from hell," *Scribner's magazine* 86:564–70 (1929).

Individual examples, setting forth the dire consequences of Sabbath breaking and other juvenile delinquencies, are used to illustrate the Sunday school literature of the nineteenth century.

Dodd, Catherine Isabel. "Some old school-books," *The national review* 45:1006–14 (1905).

Describes typical books from the time of Aldhelm and Bede to the early part of the nineteenth century.

Erisman, Fred. "American regional juvenile literature, 1870–1910: an annotated bibliography," *American literary realism* 6:109–22 (Spring, 1973).

Fadiman, Clifton. "The case for a children's literature," *Children's literature* 5:9–21 (1976).

Traces the history of children's literature, dating its inception from Perrault rather than from Newbery.

Fish, Helen Dean. "The charm of the old fashioned story: about some books written for our grandparents," *Horn book magazine* 2:27–34 (March 1926).

A review in depth of E. V. Lucas's *Forgotten tales of long ago* and *Old fashioned tales;* discusses Maria Edgeworth, Mrs. Sherwood, and the Taylor sisters.

Grey, Jill E. "Historical study of children's books," *History of education society bulletin* 7:23–31 (Spring, 1971).

Gumuchian, Kirkor. "From piety to entertainment in children's books," *American scholar* 10, no. 3:337–50 (Summer, 1941).

A notable bookseller of Paris writes on didactic as opposed to fanciful books.

Hürlimann, Bettina. "Fortunate moments in children's books," *Top of the news* 29:331–50 (June, 1973).

The fourth May Hill Arbuthnot lecture; describes seven European episodes in the best of children's books that seem to the author typical and significant. Comments on Grimm, Spyri, Brunhoff, Hoffman.

Jordan, Alice M. "Children's books in America: the first 200 years," *Horn book magazine* 10:9–19 (January, 1934).

An appreciative review of *Early American children's books* and *Children's books of yesterday.*

———. "Children's books today and yesterday," *More books* (Boston Public Library) 3:333–40 (1928).

An overview covering chapbooks, battledores, and other types of books for instruction and amusement. Includes discussion of publishers of early children's books and modern rare book collectors.

———. "Children's classics," *Horn book magazine* 23:8–28 (January–February, 1947).

Discusses particular editions and in a bibliography recommends sixty classics from Aesop to Wyss.

———. "The dawn of imagination in American books for children," *Horn book magazine* 20:168–75 (May–June, 1944).

Credits Hawthorne with the influence that led children away from Peter Parley and Jacob Abbott. Extensive discussion of Christopher Pearse Cranch and his fanciful tales.

———. "Early children's books," *More books* (Boston Public Library) 15:185–91 (1940).

Lists and describes fifty books from the rare book department of the Boston Public Library and shows the significance of each in the history of children's literature.

Library Association. Youth Libraries Group. "Collections of early children's books," *Library association record* 68:261–62 (July, 1966).

Indicates the number of volumes in each collection of seventeen British libraries, the period covered, whether books are for loan or for reference only, and any special features of the collections. Subsequent lists have been planned.

Margaret Miriam, Sister. "Children's books that have shaped the past," *Catholic library world* 34:348–52 (March, 1963).

A careful choice of important titles, including a number of books adopted by children.

Nesbitt, Elizabeth. "The early record," *Horn book magazine* 47:268–74 (June, 1971).

A lecture delivered for the Fall Festival of Children's Books, Carnegie Library of Pittsburgh, 1970. Shows how children's books of lasting beauty, import, and appeal helped to bring about the start of library service for children at the turn of the century. A tribute to the great names in children's literature, laying special stress on *Alice in Wonderland.*

Osborne, Edgar. "Children's books in the nineteenth century," *Junior bookshelf* 2:62–67 (January, 1938).

By a distinguished bibliophile and donor of the Osborne Collection of Early Children's Books.

———. "Children's books to 1800," *Junior bookshelf* 4:15–22 (October, 1939).

A discussion of trends in books for children from the period before printed books to the period of controversies concerning instruction and amusement.

Peabody journal of education 19, no. 3 (November, 1941).

An entire issue devoted to books: (1) a series of authoritative articles presenting various phases of children's literature and (2) "The high school library of science for 1940–41," by H. H. Webb; includes "Early American magazines for children" by M. F. Alstetter, "Penny plain, tuppence colored" by R. E. Cundiff, and "Some significant firsts in children's literature" by E. N. Saucier.

Quayle, Eric. "Juvenile incunabula," *Wilson library bulletin* 46:326–34 (December, 1971).

A book collector suggests 1700 as the date before which any books for children can be called "juvenile incunabula" and picks out some important examples.

Rayward, W. Boyd. "What shall they read? A historical perspective," *Wilson library bulletin* 51:146–62 (October, 1976).

A survey of the attitudes shown toward children in books written and recommended for them from the Middle Ages to the late twentieth century.

Salmon, Edward. "Literature for the little ones," *The nineteenth century* 22:563–80 (1887).

———. "Should children have a special literature?" edited with an introduction by Lance Salway, *Signal* 11:94–101, 111 (May, 1973).

Reprint of an article originally published in *The parent's review* in 1890. Defends contemporary literature for the young, drawing attention to the gap between the cheap magazines and the worthwhile books. Makes a plea for inexpensive editions of Henty, Kingston, and Ballantyne. The author wrote *Juvenile literature as it is* (1888), an important book on the subject.

Stone, Wilbur M. "Children's books of long ago," "Flowery and gilt," "Pinafores and pantalettes," *Saturday review of literature* 5:762–63, 810–12, 864–65 (1929).

Viguers, Ruth Hill. "Margin for surprise: reflections on the pursuit of excellence in books for children," *Bulletin* (New York Public Library) 66:519–34 (October, 1962).

The reviewing of children's books from the post–Civil War period to the present. An Anne Carroll Moore Lecture delivered in the New York Public Library.

Walker, Caroline Burnite. "The beginnings of a literature for children," *Library journal* 31:107–12 (1906).

Paper presented at a meeting of the Children's Librarians Section of the American Library Association, July, 1906. It traces the evolution of children's literature from the time of Watts and includes a selected list of books to illustrate the subject.

Welsh, Charles. "The children's books that have lived," *The library* 11, n.s. 1:314–23 (1900).

A short survey of children's literature with special emphasis on chapbooks and the work of John Newbery.

———. "The early history of children's books in New England," *New England magazine* 26, n.s. 20:147–60 (1899).

Focuses on Mother Goose and on Sunday school books. A good résumé.

———. Some notes on the history of books for children," *The Newbery House magazine* 3: 218–26, 336–43, 428–71, 599–613 (August–November, 1890).

Contents: Prior to the invention of printing; Block books and early printed books; The middle period, 17th and 18th centuries; Close of the 18th and beginning of the 19th centuries. A valuable article.

Wilson library bulletin 50, no. 2 (October, 1975).

Entire issue is devoted to "Children's literature collections and research libraries." Articles by ten authorities written with the aim of encouraging library directors to "examine more closely their own collections and seek answers to the obvious questions about purpose and conflict of effort within and without their respective institutional programs."

Worthing, Sarita M. "Preserving the old: historical collections of children's books in California libraries," *California librarian* 36:12–15 (July, 1975).

Brief descriptions of some collections with notes on their origins, most important holdings, various types of books, and locations within buildings.

Zweigbergk, Eva von. "Aims and ideals reflected in children's books," *Bookbird* 6, no. 3:3–14 (1968).

A Swedish critic of children's literature looks back on the lessons that earlier ages wished to teach through books and ponders the present and future.

PERIODICALS

Children's literature. Philadelphia: Temple University. Published annually.

Formerly *Children's literature: the great excluded* (v. 1–3; Storrs: University of Connecticut, 1972–74). Includes essays emanating from the Modern Language Association Group on Children's Literature and the Children's Literature Association. Some of the authors are authorities in the history of children's literature and articles often cover material hard to find elsewhere.

Children's literature in education: an international quarterly. New York: APS Publications. Published in one volume, four issues a year.

Each issue offers well-qualified writers and major articles, usually including one or more subjects of interest to students in the history of children's literature.

Horn book magazine. Boston: Horn Book. Published six times a year in February, April, June, August, October, December.

Frequent articles on writers of the past and on antiquarian interests, all by outstanding authors and authorities.

Junior bookshelf: a review of children's books. Thurstonland, Huddersfield, England. Published six times a year.

Articles about children's books, authors, and illustrators, frequently retrospective.

Phaedrus: an international journal of children's literature research. Published at Marblehead, Mass., for *Phaedrus* (Fairleigh Dickinson University). Published twice yearly.

Frequent articles of interest to teachers and students in the history of children's literature, antiquarians, and collecting specialists. Lists dissertations, books, articles, meetings, and collections of importance to research.

Signal: approaches to children's books. South Woodchester, Gloucestershire, England: Thimble Press. Three issues per year.

"Signal reprints" edited with an introduction by Lance Salway have been a valuable contribution, offering important articles of criticism or biographical sketches by major writers of the past.

ANTHOLOGIES ILLUSTRATING THE HISTORY OF CHILDREN'S LITERATURE

Blishen, Edward, comp. Oxford book of poetry for children. New York: Watts, 1963.

An outstanding compilation, illustrated by Brian Wildsmith. Almost all of the sixty-two poets included here are pre-twentieth century.

Haviland, Virginia, and Margaret N. Coughlan. Yankee Doodle's literary sampler of prose, poetry and pictures. New York: Crowell, [1974].

Subtitle: "being an anthology of diverse works published for the edification and/or entertainment of young readers in America before 1900." Selected from the Rare Book Collections of the Library of Congress and introduced by Virginia Haviland and Margaret N. Coughlan. A handsome volume, profusely illustrated.

Hodges, Margaret, ed. Tell it again: great tales from around the world. New York: Dial, 1963.

Excerpts mostly from the nineteenth-century authors whose work became part of English-language children's literature in the original or through translation. Includes Hans Christian Andersen, Phoebe Cary, Charles Dickens, Alphonse Daudet, Lafcadio Hearn, W. H. Hudson, Rudyard

Kipling, Henry W. Longfellow, Carlo Lorenzini, Johanna Spyri, Louise de la Ramée.

Lucas, Edward Verrall, comp. Another book of verses for children. London: Wells Gardner, Darton, 1907.

Illustrations by F. D. Bedford. "Prince Dorus" by Charles Lamb and "Dame Wiggins of Lee" are included. There are ten selections from *The daisy* and other books by Mrs. Turner. Peter Parley and Mrs. Ewing are also among the old-time authors represented.

———. A book of verses for children. London: Chatto, 1897.

About two hundred old proverbs, nonsense rhymes, ballads, and story-poems.

———. Forgotten tales of long ago. London: Wells Gardner, Darton, 1906.

With illustrations by F. D. Bedford. A companion volume to *Old fashioned tales*. It contains twenty stories, all but three representing the period 1790–1830.

———. Old fashioned tales. London: Wells Gardner, Darton, 1905.
Illustrations by F. D. Bedford. Nineteen stories representing writers of the late eighteenth and early nineteenth centuries. Includes *The history of little Jack,* by Thomas Day, and selections from Maria Edgeworth, Alicia Catherine Mant, Mrs. Sherwood, Mrs. Barbauld, Mary Lamb, and Jacob Abbott.

Scudder, Horace Elisha, ed. The children's book: a collection of the best and most famous stories and poems in the English language. Boston: Houghton, 1909.
Partial contents: A few songs; The book of stories in verse; The book of familiar stories.

Smith, Elva S., comp. Good old stories for boys and girls. Boston: Lothrop, 1919.
Includes selections by Mary Howitt, Lydia Maria Child, Jane Taylor, Jean Ingelow, and Phoebe Cary.

Tappan, Eva March, comp. Old fashioned stories and poems. (The children's hour, v. 6) Boston: Houghton, 1907.
Contents: Old-fashioned stories; Poems and rhymes; Stories in verse.

Tuer, Andrew White, comp. Pages and pictures from forgotten children's books. London: Leadenhall Press, 1898–99.
Collection of facsimile pages from children's books published between 1788 and 1830.

———. Stories from old-fashioned children's books. London: Leadenhall Press, 1898–99.
Taken in part from picture books, magazines, books of manners. Arranged in chronological order, 1767–1827. Title pages and "Odd cuts" are reproduced.

Watt, Homer A., and **Karl J. Holzknecht,** comps. Children's books of long ago: a garland of pages arranged. New York: Dryden Press, 1942.
With facsimile reproductions and excerpts from nineteenth-century texts.

CATALOGS AND BIBLIOGRAPHIES

American Antiquarian Society. Exhibit of American children's books printed before 1800. Worcester, Mass.: American Antiquarian Society, 1928.
List of books with a foreword.

Aubrey, Doris, comp. The Wandsworth collection of early children's books. Catalogue. London: Wandsworth Public Libraries, 1972.

Bateson, F. W., ed. "Children's books," *Cambridge bibliography of English literature* (Cambridge University Press) 2:553–66; 3:561–79 (1940).

Blanck, Jacob N. Peter Parley to Penrod: a bibliographical description of the best-loved American juvenile books. New York: Bowker, 1938; reprint: Cambridge, Mass.: Research Classics, 1961.
Exact and complete descriptions of books noted as landmarks or favorites in children's literature published in the United States from 1827 to 1926.

Brewer, Henry L. Rare children's books. (List no. 7) New York: Henry L. Brewer, 1941.
Brewer was a pioneer specialist in old and rare children's books. He gives short descriptive notes and an interesting record of early activities.

British Museum. An exhibition of early children's books. London: Trustees of the British Museum, 1968.
The catalog for the museum's first display of children's books, all published before the "upsurge of remarkable children's books" that came after 1850. Includes annotations for 107 books. Cover title: *Children's books.*

Crouch, Marcus, ed. Books about children's literature: a booklist prepared by the Committee of the Youth Libraries Group. London: Library Assn., 1966.
A partial bibliography "useful to students as a working tool, giving briefly the principal books which are reasonably accessible in [England]." A revision of a 1963 bibliography.

Good, David, comp. A catalogue of the Spencer collection of early children's books and chapbooks: presented to the Harris Public Library, Preston, by J. H. Spencer, 1947. Preston, England: Harris Public Library, 1967.
With an introduction by Percy H. Muir. The collection includes seventeen hundred books, 1665–1930.

Gumuchian et Cie. Les livres de l'enfance du xve au xixe siècle 2v. Paris: En vente à la librairie Gumuchian & Cie., [1931?].
In effect a history of children's literature from the fifteenth to the nineteenth century, vol. 1 consisting of over 6,251 annotated entries; vol. 2 of facsimiles showing title pages, illustrations, binding, etc., some in color. Prefaces for both volumes by Paul Gavault. Bibliography in vol. 1.

Haviland, Virginia, et al. Children's literature: a guide to reference sources. Washington, D.C.: Library of Congress, 1966.

—— with the assistance of **Margaret N. Coughlan.**
Children's literature . . . . First supplement,
Washington, D.C.: Library of Congress, 1972.
Especially useful for this study are chapters
entitled "History and criticism"; "Books and
children."

Miller, Bertha Mahony and **Elinor Whitney,** comps.
Realms of gold in children's books. Garden City,
N.Y.: Doubleday, 1929.
The fifth edition for *Books for boys and girls:
a suggestive purchase list,* previously published by
the Bookshop for Boys and Girls, Women's Educational and Industrial Union, Boston. The preface by Caroline M. Hewins, p. ix–xii, deals with
early publishers of children's books, and there is
an introductory article, "Five centuries of children's books," p. 1–12. Though the catalog is a
modern purchase list, the notes for special types
of books and for individual authors and illustrators may also be useful. The introduction appeared
in *Publishers weekly,* March 2, 1929, p. 975–79.

Morrill, Edward, & Son, booksellers. American
children's books. (Catalogue six) Boston: Edward
Morrill & Son, [1941?].
A list covering many types of books, 1723–1939.
Some entries are not in Rosenbach. Also includes
games and novelties inspired by children's books.
Annotations and bibliography unusually rich in
information.

Muir, Percy H., comp. Children's books of yesterday: a catalogue of an exhibition held at 7 Al-
bemarle Street, London, during May 1946. London: published for the National Book League,
[1946].
With a foreword by John Masefield, poet lau-
reate. An annotated list of an exhibit that included
alphabet books, readers and other schoolbooks,
nursery rhymes and other verses, fiction, games,
and books illustrated by noteworthy artists.

Opie, Iona, and **Peter Opie.** Three centuries of
nursery rhymes and poetry for children: an exhibit held at the National Book League, May,
1973. London: National Book League, 1973.

Philadelphia. Free Library. Children's books, reference and research collections of the Free
Library of Philadelphia. Philadelphia: Free Library of Philadelphia, 1962.
An illustrated brochure with brief information
about the Rosenbach collection, 1682–1836; the
collection of children's books published after 1836;
the Elizabeth Ball hornbook collection; the American Sunday-School Union collection; the folklore
collection, and collections of work by Kate Greenaway, Beatrix Potter, Arthur Rackham, Howard
Pyle, and A. B. Frost.

Pierpont Morgan Library. Children's literature:
books and manuscripts: an exhibition, November
19, 1954, through February 28, 1955. New York:
Pierpont Morgan Library, 1954.

An annotated list with a bibliography. Includes
schoolbooks, ABCs, fables and fairy tales, nursery
rhymes, poetry, and moral tales.

Pittsburgh. Carnegie Library. Catalogue of books
in the Children's Department of the Carnegie
Library of Pittsburgh. Pittsburgh, 1909.
An author list with bibliographic information
and annotations for twenty-five hundred books.
Fine subject index and a title list. With a New
York City Board of Education catalog, this was
used for the basis of the first *Children's catalog,*
1909.

——. Children's reading: a catalog compiled for
the home libraries and reading clubs conducted
by the Children's Department of the Carnegie
Library of Pittsburgh. Pittsburgh, 1905.
At head of title: American Library Association.
Publishing Board. A pioneer catalog used as a
source for *Children's catalog.*

Quaritch, Bernard, Ltd. Catalogue 464: rare and
valuable early schoolbooks (15th, 16th & 17th
centuries) and books relating to early education. London: Bernard Quaritch, 1932.
Lists and describes 342 editions of Asham, Comenius, Lily, Euclid, hornbooks, etc.

Rosenbach, Abraham S. Wolf. Early American
children's books, 1682–1847: the private collection of A. S. W. Rosenbach. Philadelphia:
Free Library of Philadelphia, 1928.
List of books in exhibit held in the Free Library of Philadelphia.

St. John, Judith, ed. The Osborne collection of early
children's books, 1556–1910: a catalogue. Toronto: Toronto Public Library, 1958.
With an introduction by Edgar Osborne. A
landmark in the bibliography of children's literature. Chronological list of editions; illustrators,
engravers, publishers, booksellers, printers are
listed. A supplement lists additions to the collection, 1542–1910, published in a souvenir booklet,
May, 1964.

Sargent, John F. Reading for the young: a classified and annotated catalog, with an alphabetical
author-index. Boston: published for the American Library Association Publishing Section by
the Library Bureau, 1890–96. 2v. in 1.
Includes a supplement, 1891–95, and subject-
index to the complete work, compiled by Mary
E. Sargent and Abby L. Sargent. Books are classified by subject, and twenty-five periodicals are
listed.

Schatzki, Walter. Old and rare children's books.
(Catalogue no. 1) New York: Walter Schatzki,
1941; reprint: Detroit: Gale, 1974.
The books offered for sale include ABCs, *Orbis*

pictus, the moral tale, games, picture books, and other types. Illustrated with twenty-six plates.

Schiller, Justin G., Ltd. Chapbook miscellany: Rollo to Rebecca; juvenile temptations; a paper menagerie; the children's hour. New York: Justin G. Schiller, 1970.
Four issues constituting vol. 1 (all published); illustrated and detailed listing of rare children's books, antique games, and related juvenilia, including numerous titles in *Peter Parley to Penrod.*

———. Catalogue 29: Children's books from four centuries including original drawings, manuscripts, and related juvenilia. New York: Justin G. Schiller, 1973.
Detailed and descriptive bookseller's catalog listing nearly seventeen hundred items. Illustrated.

Scribner. First editions of juvenile fiction 1814–1924. (Catalogue 107) New York: Scribner Book Store, Rare Books Department, 1936.
This sales catalog, prepared by David Randall, was one of the earliest rare book catalogs on juvenile literature and gives detail and annotations for 334 items. It ranks in importance with Gumuchian and Schatzki.

Southern Connecticut State College Library. The Carolyn Sherwin Bailey collection of children's books: a catalogue. Researched, compiled, and edited by Dorothy R. Davis. New Haven: Southern Connecticut State College Library, 1967.
Describes about 1,880 books from a collection of over 3,000, primarily English and American, 1657 to 1930. Includes biographical notes on authors.

Stone, Wilbur Macey. Four centuries of children's books. Boston: Boston Public Library, 1928.
A loan exhibit from Stone's private collection. The collection was also shown at the Newark (N.J.) Public Library during 1928.

United States. Library of Congress. Rare Book Division. Children's books in the Rare Book Division of the Library of Congress: author/title and chronological catalogs. 2v. Totowa, N.J.: Rowman & Littlefield, 1975.

Victoria and Albert Museum. South Kensington Library. Victorian children's books, selected from the library of the Victoria and Albert Museum. London: Victoria and Albert Museum, South Kensington Library, 1973.
Catalog of an exhibit.

Welch, d'Alté A. A bibliography of American children's books printed prior to 1821. Worcester, Mass.: American Antiquarian Society, 1972.
Considered to be one of the great bibliographical contributions of our time. The introduction by the author gives a chronological history of eighteenth-century books for children in America. Collections of American children's books are listed. Includes an invaluable chronological index of printers and publishers.

Welsh, Charles. On coloured books for children: [a paper] read before the Sette [of Odd Volumes]; with a catalogue of the books exhibited. London: C. W. H. Wyman, 1887.
Half title: "privately printed opuscula issued to the members of the Sette of Odd Volumes, no. XIII." "A catalogue of the coloured books for children, past and present," p. 27–47.

———. On some of the books for children of the last century, with a few words on the philanthropic publisher of St. Paul's Churchyard: a paper read at a meeting of the Sette of Odd Volumes, with a catalogue of the books exhibited. London: Griffith, Farran, Okeden & Welsh, 1886.
Half title: "privately printed opuscula issued to the members of the Sette of Odd Volumes, no. XI." "A list of the books exhibited," p. 27–104.

SUPPLEMENTARY REFERENCES

Child Life

Ariès, Philippe. Centuries of childhood: a social history of family life. Translated from the French by Robert Baldick. New York: Knopf, 1962; reprint. Random (Vintage), 1962.
The definitive study of childhood in which Ariès traces the evolution of the family and the image of the child. His theory that the concept of childhood was unknown in the Middle Ages, though now disputed, has been the cornerstone for most historical studies on childhood to the present time.

Avery, Gillian. Childhood's pattern: a study of the heroes and heroines of children's fiction, 1770–1950. London: Hodder, 1975.

Avery uses children's books of her chosen period to depict the attitudes of adults towards children and changing assumptions about the place of young men and women in society.

———. Nineteenth century children: heroes and heroines in English children's stories, 1780–1900. [London]: Hodder, [1965].
This work concentrates on "the attitude of the writer toward his readers, the changing nature of the fictitious child, the different demands made upon him, and the adult ideals of behaviour in the young," illustrated especially by the fairy tale and the domestic tale.

Bayne-Powell, Rosamond. The English child in the eighteenth century. New York: Dutton, [1939].
This book covers educational theory, as well as eighteenth-century dame schools and charity schools, children's toys and books, games and amusements, and children's needlework and handicrafts.

Beales, R. "In search of the historical child: miniature adulthood and youth in colonial New England," *The American quarterly* 27: 379–98 (October, 1975).
An excellent, scholarly article that refutes the theory that colonial parents treated their children as "miniature adults" and that adolescence was absent in colonial New England.

Bedford, Jessie (*pseud.* Elizabeth Godfrey). English children in the olden time. London: Methuen, 1907; reprint: Folcroft, Pa.: Folcroft, 1977.
Partial contents: Nursery lore; The church and the children; Tales of wonder; Nurture in kings' courts; Some royal children; Concerning pedagogues; Educational theories; The superior parent. Scattered through the text are many reproductions of old paintings that picture children.

———. Home life under the Stuarts, 1603–1649. New York: Dutton, 1903.
"This study of seventeenth century life makes no attempt to draw an ideal picture of the times, but simply tries to gather from letters, diaries, or chance references in contemporary writings some notion of the ordinary life of every day in homes for the most part of the cultivated classes."—introduction.

Byrne, M. St. Clare. "Childhood and education," in her *Elizabethan life in town and country*, p. 176–97. London: Methuen, [1925].
Discusses the notion of the precocious child and the treatment of schoolboys in the Elizabethan period.

Cable, Mary. The little darlings: a history of child-rearing in America. New York: Scribner, [1975].
"With a view of separating the truth from legend, this book proposes to trace the history of American ways with children."—preface. Pt. 1 covers the colonial period: the seventeenth and eighteenth centuries; pt. 2, the nineteenth century; and pt. 3, the twentieth century.

Calhoun, A. W. The social history of the American family. Cleveland: A. H. Clark, 1918.

Chrisman, Oscar. The historical child. Boston: Badger, 1920.
This is an early book in the field of "paidology" (the scientific study of the child). Includes a study of the child in ancient and medieval Europe and in the early years of the United States.

Coveney, Peter. The image of childhood. Rev. ed. Baltimore: Penguin, 1967.
A study of childhood as presented mainly in nineteenth- and twentieth-century literature written for adults. The author studies, in particular, writings about childhood by Blake, Wordsworth, Coleridge, Dickens, George Eliot, Butler, and Twain.

———. The poor monkey: the child in literature. London: Rockliff, 1957.
Original title and printing of *The image of childhood* (above).

de la Mare, Walter. Early one morning in the spring; chapters on children and on childhood as it is revealed in particular in early memories and in early writings. New York: Macmillan, 1935; reprint: New York: Octagon, 1975.
A presentation of childhood "by way of recollection."

de Mause, Lloyd, ed. History of childhood. New York: Psychohistory Press, 1974; New York: Harper Torchbooks, 1974.
Essays on the history of childhood. A systematic review of the attitudes and practices of parents towards their children. Takes a psychoanalytic approach.

Earle, Alice Morse. Child life in colonial days. New York: Macmillan, 1899; reprint: Folcroft, Pa.: Folcroft, 1974.
Primarily a record of the life of children in the American colonies, with comparisons of conditions in England during the seventeenth and eighteenth centuries. Numerous illustrations. Partial contents: Schools and school-life; Hornbook and primer; School books; Manners and courtesy; Religious books; Story and picture books.

———. Customs and fashions in old New England. New York: Scribner, 1894.
Although this is not primarily about childlife in New England, there are several references to the hornbooks and texts read by the children.

———. Home and child life in colonial days. Edited by Shirley Glubok. New York: Macmillan, 1969.
This is an abridgment of Earle's *Home life in colonial days* and *Child-life in colonial days*. Lavishly illustrated.

Fleming, Sandford. Children and Puritanism. New Haven: Yale University Press, 1933.
A classic text that considers the role of the child as defined by adult Puritans.

Garland, Madge. The changing face of childhood. New York: October House, 1965.
A beautiful volume that traces the adult conception of childhood and childhood preoccupations through paintings and sculpture. There are sections on children's learning, books, toys and games, pets, dolls, dress, and food.

Gloag, John, and **C. Thompson Walker.** Home life in history: social life and manners in Britain, 200 B.C.–A.D. 1926. New York: Coward, 1928.
The purpose of this book is to show "as closely as possible representative examples of home life in Britain from the days of the pre-Roman British princes to the first quarter of the 20th century."

Goodsell, W. A history of the family as a social and educational institution. New York: Macmillan, 1915.
Concerns Europe and America.

Greven, Philip. Patterns of child-rearing, religious experience, and the self in early America. New York: Knopf, 1977.
The author's material is "the ill-documented, nearly inaccessible interaction between child-rearing, family life, religious affiliation and political conviction in the period between 1630 and 1780, with a few follow-ups in the 19th century."—*New York Times* book review, February 5, 1978.

Hewins, Caroline Maria. A mid-century child and her books. New York: Macmillan, 1926; reprint: Detroit: Singing Tree, 1969. Also included in *Caroline M. Hewins: her book,* edited by Jennie D. Linquist, p. 1–76. Boston: Horn Book, 1954.
The first section gives revealing glimpses of family life in the mid–nineteenth century. The second is a delightfully reminiscent account of the books Caroline Hewins read and enjoyed as a child, books that influenced the tastes and pursuits of later life. "Peter Piper's alphabet" is added, and there are reproductions of title pages and illustrations.

History of childhood quarterly: the journal of psychohistory.
This journal began with the Summer 1973 issue.

Hole, Christina. English home-life, 1500–1700. London: Batsford, [1947].
Divided into two periods, 1500–1700 and 1700–1800, this book deals with several aspects of family life, including child rearing and schooling. Includes a bibliography.

Homan, Walter Joseph. Children and Quakerism. Berkeley: University of California Press, 1939.
Partial contents: Children in the thought and life of the early Friends; The education of children before 1737; The religious experiences of children; Children and Quakerism.

Horn, Pamela. The Victorian country child. Kineton, Warwick, England: Roundwood Press, 1974.
A study of the "average" country child, most likely the son or daughter of a farm worker. This book "seeks to trace day-to-day experiences of youngsters who were often deprived of the material possessions which are nowadays regarded as essential for contented life."

Jackson, Annabel Huth. A Victorian childhood. London: Methuen, 1932.

Jones, G. B. "Childhood in literature," *The school librarian* (London) 23: 295–300 (December, 1975).
Reviews the attitudes of certain adults towards children, especially those of Lord Chesterfield, William Blake, Dylan Thomas, Louis MacNeice, Henry James, Richard Hughes, and Edmund Gosse.

Keddie, Henrietta (*pseud.* Sarah Tytler). Childhood a hundred years ago, with chromos after paintings by Sir Joshua Reynolds. London: M. Ward, 1876.

Kett, Joseph. Rites of passage: adolescence in America, 1790 to the present. New York: Basic Books, 1977.

Kiefer, Monica. American children through their books, 1700–1835. Philadelphia: University of Pennsylvania Press, 1948.
"This study is an attempt to trace the changing status of the American child in the Colonial and early national periods as it is revealed in juvenile literature."—introduction. Bibliography of primary and secondary sources, p. 230–43.

Kuhn, Anne L. The mother's role in childhood education: New England concepts, 1830–1860. New Haven: Yale University Press, 1947.
The purpose of this fascinating study is "to portray the mother's educational role, not as it actually was, but as it was seen through the eyes of a group of socially minded New England writers."

Larcom, Lucy. A New England girlhood. Boston: Houghton, 1889.
Written by the editor of *Our young folks.* Contents: Up and down the lane; Schoolroom and meeting-house; The hymn-book; Naughty children and fairy tales; Old New England; Glimpses of poetry; Beginning to work; By the river; Mountain friends; Mill girls' magazines; Reading and studying.

Lockhead, Marion. Their first ten years. London: Murray, 1956.
A detailed description of the Victorian nursery, divided into three sections: early Victorian (1837–1850), mid-Victorian (1850–1875), and late Victorian (1875–1900). Each section has a chapter on books.

————. Young Victorians. London: Murray, [1959]. Using the same format as above, the author covers the years of the child's life from age ten to nineteen.

Mackarness, Matilda Anne Planché. Children of the olden time, with preface by J. R. Planché. London: Griffith, 1874.
Covers Anglo-Saxon times to the early nineteenth century; topics treated include schools and books. Although the book was written for children, the subject matter is of value to others. Text illustrations from illuminations, paintings, and early prints.

McClinton, Kathleen Morrison. Antiques of American childhood. New York: Bramhall, 1970.
Includes chapters on children's dress, schoolbooks and schooling, books read for amusement, furniture, dishes, needlework, outdoor and indoor games, and toys. Bibliography, p. 340–43.

Morgan, Edmund S. The Puritan family. Boston: Boston Public Library, 1944; rev. and enl. ed.: New York: Harper & Row, 1966.
Contents: Puritanism and society; Husband and wife; Parents and children; The education of a saint; Masters and servants; The family in the social order; Puritan tribalism.

Pearson, Lu Emily. Elizabethans at home. Stanford, Calif.: Stanford University Press, 1957.
This is a synthesis of materials available about Elizabethan domestic life. Includes chapters on fathers and mothers, the education of children, sons and daughters. Also includes a bibliography.

Pinchbeck, Ivy, and **Margaret Hewitt.** Children in English society. 2v. London: Routledge & Kegan Paul, [1969, 1973].
Vol. 1 covers the period from Tudor times to the eighteenth century, vol. 2 from the eighteenth century to the Children Act of 1848.

Plumb, J. H. "Children, the victims of time," in his *In the light of history,* p. 153–65. Boston: Houghton, 1973.
A superb essay that traces the attitudes towards children from "the beginnings of the modern world" (the Renaissance) through the nineteenth century. The author then concludes, "the difference between the life of a sixteenth- and late nineteenth-century child is so vast as to be almost incomprehensible."

————. "New world of children in eighteenth century England," *Past and present* 67:64–95 (May, 1975).

Roe, Frederic Gordon. The Georgian child. London: Phoenix House, 1961.
Includes chapters on toys, games, hobbies, manners and punishment, dress, school, amusement, as well as a chapter entitled "Books, chapbooks, and broadsheets," p. 69–83.

————. The Victorian child. London: Phoenix House, [1959].
Contents include chapters on the nursery, toys, games, and hobbies, dress, manners and punishment, "Books, bloods, and comics," school, holidays and entertainment.

Sharp, Evelyn. The London child. London: John Lane, [1927].
Presents and contrasts the well-to-do and poor child in London, c1880. There is a section called "In the children's library."

Slater, Peter G. Children in the New England mind: in death and life. Hamden, Conn.: Shoe String (Archon), 1977.

Stuart, Dorothy Margaret. The boy through the ages. London: Harrap, 1926.
Chapters 6 and 8–12 deal with the life of boys in England. Interspersed among the prose sections are original poems, and the illustrations from contemporary sources are many and varied.

————. The girl through the ages. London: Harrap, 1933; reprint: Detroit: Singing Tree, 1969.
Aims "to give a vivid and faithful picture of the typical child in each age and setting, outward aspect, early environment, sports and studies." Well illustrated.

Wishy, Bernard. The child and the republic: the dawn of modern American child nurture. Philadelphia: University of Pennsylvania Press, [1968].
"Wishy explores the 19th century views of child nurture, home care, and religious life, exploiting the contradictions of a culture that is . . . radically at odds with itself, putting man against man, fathers against sons, man against God, nature and society." Bibliography, p. 182–201.

Wood, Robert. Children, 1773–1890. London: Evans, 1968.

Education

The books listed below cover the whole range of the history of education in England and America. Any history of education that is confined to one period, for example, Leach's *Schools at the Reformation* or Barnard's *History of English education from 1760,* is included in its proper chapter.

Armytage, W. H. G. The American influence on English education. London: Routledge & Kegan Paul, 1967.
Discusses in part the impact of American mass education on English education.

———. Four hundred years of English education. 2d ed. Cambridge: Cambridge University Press, 1970.
"Sketches the historical determinants of English educational endeavours over the last 400 years, and [their] development around certain recognizable turning points."—introduction.

Atkinson, Carroll, and Eugene T. Maleska. The story of education. Philadelphia: Chilton, [1962].
An ambitious book that "attempts to relate the major events and forces that have affected American education since Colonial days."—preface. Pt. 1 covers educational history since the beginning and in Europe; pt. 2 is concerned with the evolution of education in America.

Barnard, John, and David Burner. The American experience in education. New York: Watts (New Viewpoints), 1975.
"This anthology includes some of the more recent and provocative writings on the best of American education."—preface. Partial contents: Education of the households and schools of Colonial America, by Lawrence A. Cremin; Growing up in a rural New England, 1820–1840, by Joseph Kett; The American child as seen by British travelers, 1845–1935, by Richard L. Rapson; American school books in the 19th century, by Ruth Elson; Racial teachings in the 19th century, by Ruth Elson; John Dewey's contribution to education, by Oscar Handlin.

Bayles, Ernest E., and Bruce L. Hood. The growth of American educational thought and practice. New York: Harper, 1966.
The author says that the need for still another text on the history of education comes from the portrayal of "the thinking through [of] the subsequent stages of American educational growth to, and even beyond, the mid-twentieth century." This book covers Puritanism, Comenius, John Locke, the American early national period, Rousseau, Pestalozzi, Herbart, Froebel, Thorndike, and progressive education.

Bernier, Normand R., and Jack E. Williams. Beyond beliefs: ideological foundations of American education. Englewood Cliffs, N.J.: Prentice Hall, 1973.
Selects diverse ideologies and shows how each helped formulate the bases for our modern educational system. The chapter on Puritanism, p. 188–235, is particularly interesting and relevant.

Best, J. H., and Robert Sidwell, eds. The American legacy of learning: readings in the history of education. Philadelphia: Lippincott, 1967.
Includes readings from original sources from the colonial period (1607–1789), the national period (1789–1877), and the era of expansion (1877–1960).

Brubacher, John S. A history of problems in education. New York: McGraw-Hill, 1947.
The basis of organization of this work is not chronological, but problem oriented. Covers educational aims, politics and education, nationalism and education, economic influences on education, philosophy of education, educational psychology, methods of instruction, curriculum, religious and moral education, formal and informal education, elementary education, and public and private education.

Butts, R. Freeman. A cultural history of education. New York: Macmillan, 1947.
Original publication of *A cultural history of Western education* (listed below).

———. A cultural history of Western education, its social and intellectual foundations. New York: Macmillan, 1955.
Proceeds from the "beginnings of culture and education in the Eastern Mediterranean" to the twentieth century.

——— and Lawrence A. Cremin. A history of education in American culture. New York: Holt, 1953.
Uses the chronological approach, from 1600 through the mid–twentieth century.

Carpenter, Charles. History of American schoolbooks. Philadelphia: University of Pennsylvania Press, [1963].
A general portrayal of American textbooks "as a requisite accompaniment, a picture of the pioneer-day school system." There are sections on primers, readers, grammars, rhetorics, and foreign-language books, arithmetics, spelling books, literature texts, elocution manuals, handwriting and copy books, school histories, general science texts, physiologies, and geographies.

Clarke, Martin Lowther. Classical education in Britain, 1500–1900. Cambridge: Cambridge University Press, 1959.

Cordasco, Francesco, and William W. Brickman. A bibliography of American educational history: an annotated and classified guide. New York: AMS Press, [1975].
Includes a "Historiography of American education," and a section on elementary education and curriculum by Robert Chasnoff.

Cremin, Lawrence A. The American common school: an historical conception. New York: Teachers College Press, Columbia University, 1951.
In the foreword, George Counts calls this work, "A brilliant study into some of our educational conceptions and institutions," in which Cremin (1)

relates "the origin of the common school to the play of social forces and ideas agitating the young republic," and (2) demonstrates, through "abundant documentation, that the 'founding fathers' of the common school understood the relationship between education and political systems."

Curtis, Stanley James. History of education in Great Britain. London: University Tutorial Press, 1948.
Traces the development of all types of English schools from the Middles Ages to 1940.

de Montmorency, James Edward Geoffrey. State intervention in English education: a short history from the earliest times down to 1833. Cambridge: Cambridge University Press, 1902.
Traces the relationship between education and the state from Saxon times to the nineteenth century.

Edwards, Newton, and **Herman G. Richey.** The school in the American social order. Boston: Houghton, 1947.
Pt. 1 is about the school in colonial society; pt. 2 describes the school and the emergence of the democratic national state, 1776–1860; pt. 3 covers the school in modern society, through the nineteenth century.

Elson, Ruth. Guardians of tradition: American school books of the nineteenth century. Lincoln: University of Nebraska Press, 1964.
Puts forth the theory that adult values, beliefs, and concepts are to be found in children's schoolbooks of the nineteenth century. Includes a long bibliography of texts discussed, p. 349–414.

Freeman, Ruth S. Yesterday's school books. Watkins Glen, N.Y.: Century, 1960.

———. Yesterday's schools: a looking glass for teachers of today. Watkins Glen, N.Y.: Century, 1962.
Contents: The colonial schools; Early district schools; Pioneer common schools; Pioneer school activities; "Modern" district schools; Training for daily life; School equipment.

Good, Harry G. A history of American education. New York: Macmillan, 1956.
Covering the period from the Puritan schools, this "deals especially with the public school as an instrument of public policy."

Hazlitt, William Carew. Schools, school-books and schoolmasters: a contribution to the history of educational development in Great Britain. London: J. W. Jarvis, 1888.
Covers the history of education through the seventeenth century. There is an emphasis on sixteenth-century humanist texts.

Herbst, Jurgen, comp. The history of American education. (Goldentree bibliographies in American history) Northbrook, Ill.: AHM Publishers, [1973].
This bibliography includes divisions for general works, the colonial period, the period from the Revolution to Reconstruction, and America in the urban age.

Jarman, Thomas Leckie. Landmarks in the history of education: English education as part of the European tradition. London: Cresset, 1951.
"The history of education in England is traced as part of the historical development of European education, from its origins in ancient Greece to the modern practice of education for all."—preface.

Johnson, Clifton. Old time schools and school books. New York: Macmillan, 1904; reprint: New York: Dover, 1963.
The introduction to the Dover edition was written by Carl Withers. This charming history of early American schools and texts spans the period to roughly 1850. Includes many illustrations.

Karier, Clarence J. Man, society, and education: a history of American educational ideas. Glenview, Ill.: Scott, Foresman, 1975.
"Not a definitive history," but an "interpretive study of certain American ideas . . . limited to those systems of ideas which have given form and purpose to educational practice in the United States."

Katz, Michael B., ed. Education in American history: readings on social issues. New York: Praeger, 1973.
Divided into six sections on special interests, such as education and early American society, class, culture, and family in the origins of public education.

Lawson, John. A social history of education in England. London: Methuen, 1973.
The first concern of this book, the author states, is the history of education itself, "the question of who, at different times, was being educated, by whom, how, and to what ends. . . ." "The book seeks to explore consistently two themes which widen the context of discussion—first, changes in population structure and distribution, and secondly, the extent and functions of literacy." Covers the period 1600–1975. "Select bibliography," p. 471–75.

———. A town grammar school through six centuries; history of Hull Grammar School against its local background. London: Oxford University Press for the University of Hull, 1963.
This study "aims to illustrate the general history of the English endowed grammar schools through a particular study of one of them—the six-hundred-year-old grammar school of Hull, which, if not typical of all of them, reflects the history of many." —preface.

Livengood, William W., comp. Americana, as taught to the tune of a hickory stick. New York: Women's National Book Assn., 1954.
Introduction by Mary Ellen Chase. "Includes sheaves of material from popular elementary schoolbooks of the past." Facsimiles and extracts from readers, spellers, arithmetics, geographies, and U.S. histories.

Mark, H. T. Outline of the history of educational theories in England. Syracuse, N.Y.: C. W. Bardeen, 1899.
English educational theory as determined by English literacy and historical development.

Mathews, Mitford M. Teaching to read—historically considered. Chicago: University of Chicago Press, 1966.
This covers beginning reading methods through the present day.

Medlin, William K. The history of educational ideas in the West. New York: Center for Applied Research, [1964].
Shows how the ideas, educational theories, and aspirations of the Jews, Greeks, Romans, the early Christians and medieval scholars, the Renaissance and the Reformation, the Enlightenment and the philosophers and naturalists of the eighteenth and nineteenth centuries have affected the "aims and contents" of today's education.

Monroe, Paul. The founding of the American public school system: a history of education in the United States from the early settlements to the close of the Civil War. 2v. New York: Macmillan, 1940.

Morrison, Henry Clinton. The evolving common school. Cambridge, Mass.: Harvard University Press, 1933.
The Inglis Lecture, 1933. A discussion of the common school, what the author calls "the heart of our school system in the 19th century, at least in its social and civil purposes, as distinguished from cultural, eruditional, and professional purposes."

Nietz, John. Old textbooks: spelling, grammar, reading, arithmetic, geography, history, civil government, physics, penmanship, art, music, as taught in the common schools from colonial days to 1900. Pittsburgh: University of Pittsburgh Press, 1961.
Well-illustrated, classic study of eighteenth- and nineteenth-century textbooks.

Noble, Stuart Grayson. A history of American education. New York: Rinehart, [1954].

Rippa, S. Alexander. Education in a free society: an American history. New York: McKay, [1967].

A chronological account of American educational history as a vital aspect of social history, "with topics organized around dominant patterns of educational thought."—preface.

Rodgers, John. The old public schools of England. London: Batsford, [1938].
Contents: Early schools; The 14th and 15th centuries; The reign of Henry VIII (1509–1547); The reign of Edward VI (1547–1553) and the reign of Mary (1553–1558); The reign of Elizabeth (1558–1605); The 17th century; The 18th century. With many photographs.

Ryan, Patrick J. Historical foundations of public education in America. Dubuque, Iowa: William C. Brown, [1965].
Ten chapters, one for each great historical period: ancient, Greco-Roman, early Middle Ages, scholastic, Renaissance, Reformation, colonization, Enlightenment, industrial period, and 1900s. Traces for each period developments in curriculum, educational methodology, and school administration.

Smith, Frank. A history of English elementary education, 1760–1902. London: University of London Press, 1931; reprint: Fairfield, N.J.: A. M. Kelley, 1970.
"A valuable history for English and European influences on American educational practice."—Cordasco, *Bibliography*, p. 42.

Smith, Joan K., and **L. Glenn Smith.** The development of American education: selected readings. Ames: Iowa University Press, 1976.
Pt. 1 covers the European and colonial background; pt. 2 describes some nineteenth-century developments. Uses mainly secondary sources.

Stephens, W. R., and **William van Til,** eds. Education in American life: selected readings. Boston: Houghton, [1972].
A book of readings from primary sources. Pt. 1 covers European transplants in colonial America, 1620–1776; pt. 2, the search for the new America, 1776–1900; and pt. 3, urbanization of American education, 1900 to the present.

Thayer, V. T. Formative ideas in American education: from the colonial period to the present. New York: Dodd, 1965.
Pt. 1, "Formative ideas in American education take shape," covers the seventeenth and eighteenth centuries' contributions to education, especially those of John Locke. Pt. 2, "Philosophy and science give character to education," is concerned with economic and social changes in the nineteenth century and the impact of the theories of evolution and psychology. Pt. 3, "Conflicting conceptions of education in the 20th century," is about the theories of Dewey and Thorndike.

Vassar, Rena L. Social history of American education. 2v. (Rand McNally education series) Chicago: Rand McNally, [1965].

Uses primary sources. Vol. 1 covers education from colonial times to 1860; vol. 2 covers 1860 to the present.

Welter, Rush. Popular education and democratic thought in America. New York: Columbia University Press, 1962.

An analysis "not of the American commitment to education in its entirety—a task that would stagger the imagination of anyone even superficially familiar with American thought—but of the idea of education in its essentially political applications and function."—introduction.

Folklore in the History
of Children's Literature

In the 1937 edition of Elva Smith's *History of children's literature,* there is no section covering folklore. Some individual titles are given, such as *Adventures of Ulysses,* which is listed with other writings of Charles Lamb. The heading "Fairy stories" comes under "Chapbooks." The Comtesse d'Aulnoy and Charles Perrault are credited as the authors of books with the title *Fairy tales,* but there is no general coverage of fairy tales as a subject. Myths and epics are missing. This was certainly not due to lack of interest on the part of Elva Smith. During her years as head of the Boys and Girls Room at Carnegie Library of Pittsburgh, she was responsible for several bibliographies, ranging in length from twenty-two to thirty-five pages: *Stories from the Iliad and the Odyssey,* 1912; *Stories from the Greek Myths,* 1912; *Stories from the Norse,* 1914; and *Stories from the Ballads of Robin Hood,* 1924. Folklore was also a strong element in the numerous collections of which she was coeditor with Alice Isabel Hazeltine. If, with few exceptions, her *History of children's literature* confines itself to literature written for children by known authors, it may be that Elva Smith considered folklore to be too vast a subject for coverage within one volume. She would have been right, and the judgment is even more correct today.

Folklore, that body of oral tradition that includes myths and many types of folktales, takes the whole world for its province and originally was not meant for children. Bards, scops, minstrels, and storytellers performed for adult audiences, whether in castles or cottages. Children might or might not have been present also. Today the serious study of folklore belongs more to the fields of anthropology, psychology, and adult literature than to literature for children. Still, it has been decided that some attempt should be made in this revised edition of Elva Smith's work to include a subject that has been of preeminent importance in the lives of children. Folklore now receives special attention in all major publications on the history of children's literature.

This section limits itself to the folklore of the English-speaking people in the British Isles, including Ireland, and in America. Even with this limitation, many of the books chosen for listing are bibliographies that only point the way for further study. It may be assumed that folktales from most of the ethnic groups immigrating to the United States have found their way into collections and picture books written in English and intended for children. An example is *Folklore from Africa to the United States* by Margaret N. Coughlan of the Children's Book Section, Library of Congress. This splendid bibliography demonstrates the wealth of material available. A single section in a *Syllabus with selected bib-*

liographies cannot adequately select from the excellent retellings of folktales for children that have long been published and continue to appear in greater numbers each year.

Instead, the focus here is on some of the important types of tales, indigenous or imported, that have become part of literature for children in the English language. Writers, editors, and publishers are given credit for noteworthy titles that influenced children's reading and thinking. Aesop's *Fables,* for instance, are of great antiquity but became a special treasure of English-speaking children through Caxton's publication of the fables in 1484. *Arabian nights entertainments,* translated into English from the French of Antoine Galland in the early years of the eighteenth century, was quickly adopted by children, who devoured the countless editions from that time onward. Similar decisions have been made in this section for dates at which other bodies of folklore became part of children's literature in the English-speaking world. In a few cases, particularly attractive or otherwise important editions of recent date are called to attention. It is hoped that this scheme, supplemented by the liberal use of the listed bibliographies, will be useful for the study of folklore as a part of the history of children's literature.

Under "General references," some names and titles have been chosen as essential for a guide to the past in folkloristic studies and to the sources of the most significant work now being done, especially in the English language. An important part of that work is the building of folklore collections in public, school, college, and university libraries.

In choosing books for folklore collections, teachers and librarians need familiarity with original or early sources. They also need a discriminating taste. The art of retelling folktales has a long and honorable history, and the tales do need to be retold for each generation. Even adults today cannot be expected to feel the excitement felt by the young Keats on first looking into Chapman's *Homer.* But retellings vary greatly in quality. Joseph Jacobs in England and Richard Chase in America are examples among writers with a broad and intimate knowledge of original sources, revealed in their notes. They also had a mastery of contemporary English and a fine ear for the sounds of spoken language. As a result, their tales still have the life and color that attract children. Other retellings are less successful, their language wooden and ordinary, sometimes including inappropriate modern slang. In an ill-conceived effort to woo a juvenile audience, the original spirit may be distorted out of all recognition.

Yet a tale as originally transcribed by a collector is often fragmentary and lacking in the plot structure that would make it interesting to anyone beyond the narrow realm of the folklorist. Therein lies the art of retelling. The great retellers from Perrault onward have consciously, and sometimes admittedly, shaped and refined the stories they collected. Frau Viehmann's tales did not reach the printed page without the strong imprint of the Grimms' style upon them. Finally, from French, German, Icelandic, Norse, or other languages, stories must pass through the process of translation into English before they can reach the English-speaking child. One needs to compare the translations of the Brothers Grimm by Mrs. E. V. Lucas in the nineteenth century and by Wanda Gág in the twentieth, both excellent in their craft, to understand the subtleties of the art.

The field, then, is vast and demanding, but great opportunities and great pleasure await both teacher and student in the field of folklore as a part of the history of children's literature.

GENERAL REFERENCES

Bettelheim, Bruno. The uses of enchantment: the meaning and importance of fairy tales. New York: Knopf, 1976.

A child psychologist explores the value of fairy tales in the emotional development of children.

Bonser, Wilfrid. A bibliography of folklore, as contained in the first eighty years of the publications of the Folklore Society. London: W. Glaisher for the Folk-Lore Society, 1961.

A classified subject-index to studies published in *Folk-lore record, Folk-lore journal, Folk-lore,* and *Extra publications.* Includes folklore of the British Isles, folklore of other countries and races, calendar customs, religious folklore, and folklore in literature and art.

Brunvand, Jan Harold. Folklore: a study and research guide. New York: St. Martin's, 1976.

A reference guide for anyone interested in folklore study and research. Surveys major bibliographical resources—books, journals, monograph series, bibliographies, and other reference works—and provides lively, detailed, and thoroughly practical advice on choosing and conducting a research project and preparing a formal paper.

Bulfinch, Thomas. The age of chivalry, or, legends of King Arthur. Boston: S. W. Tilton, 1858.

———. The age of fable, or stories of gods and heroes. Boston: Sanborn, Carter & Bazin, 1855.

———. A book of myths: selections from Bulfinch's *Age of fable.* New York: Macmillan, 1942.

Intended for children. Illustrated in black and white by Helen Sewell.

———. Legends of Charlemagne, or, romance of the Middle Ages. Boston: S. W. Tilton, 1862.

———. Mythology: the age of fable, or, stories of gods and heroes. Garden City, N.Y.: Doubleday, 1948.

Illustrations by Federico Castellon. Many editions of Bulfinch's writings have appeared in America since first publication.

Cook, Elizabeth. The ordinary and the fabulous: an introduction to myths, legends and fairy tales for teachers and storytellers. London: Cambridge University Press, 1969.

Pays tribute to the importance of folklore from Greek and northern mythology and from Arthurian and Celtic tradition. Compares various tellings of tales and shows how to present them "so that they become part and parcel of children's lives."

Eastman, Mary Huse. Index to fairy tales, myths and legends. 2d ed., rev. and enl. Boston: Faxon, 1926.

Over a thousand books of folklore indexed by title with "see" and "see also" references as guides to varying titles. Includes a subject index and a section entitled "Geographical and racial lists for story tellers."

——— ———. Supplement. Boston: Faxon, 1937.

——— ———. 2d supplement. Boston: Faxon, 1952.

Hamilton, Edith. Mythology. Boston: Little, 1942.

An important modern contribution by an authority retelling Greek, Roman, and Norse myths in the differing manners of "the very different writers [e.g., Hesiod, Ovid, the Elder Edda] from whom our knowledge of the myths comes." Longer tellings are supplemented by "The less important myths"(p. 411–23) and "Brief myths arranged alphabetically" (p. 424–40).

Ireland, Norma Olin. Index to Fairy Tales, 1949–1972, including folklore, legends and myths, in collections. Westwood, Mass.: Faxon, 1973.

A continuation of Eastman's *Index to fairy tales.* The sources indexed include many collections of tales from the British Isles and Ireland.

Leach, Maria, ed. Funk and Wagnalls standard dictionary of folklore, mythology, and legend. 2v. New York: Funk & Wagnalls, 1949–1950.

"A representative sampling of the gods of the world, the folk heroes, culture heroes . . . dances, ballads, folksongs . . . festivals and rituals . . . games and children's rimes, riddles . . . witchcraft, omens, magic charms and spells . . . and the supernatural beings of folk belief and story."

Opie, Iona, and **Peter Opie.** The classic fairy tales. London: Oxford University Press, 1974.

Introduction covers the nature and study of fairy tales and the early collections and gives special attention to Perrault, d'Aulnoy, de Beaumont, the Grimm brothers, and Andersen. Extensive analysis of twenty-four tales. Outstanding bibliography.

Quinnam, Barbara, comp. Fables from incunabula to modern picture books: a selective bibliography. Washington, D.C.: Library of Congress, 1966.

Of special interest to students of children's literature is the chronological arrangement of "Indian and related fables," "Aesop," "La Fontaine," and "Krylov."

Thompson, Stith. The folktale. New York: Dryden, 1946.

One of the foremost scholars in the field discusses the universality and forms of the folktale, traces the spread of types of tales in the Western world, analyzes the folktale as a part of American Indian culture, and defines a variety of folktale studies. Includes important bibliographies and two indexes of tale types and motifs.

————, ed. Motif-index of folk-literature. Rev. and enl. ed. Bloomington: Indiana University Press, 1955–1958.
A classification of narrative elements in folktales, ballads, myths, fables, medieval romances, exempla, fabliaux, gest-books, and local legends. A monumental work with which teachers should be familiar.

Tolkien, J. R. R. Tree and leaf. Boston: Houghton, 1965.
A scholar of early English literature and language contributes a long essay, "On fairy-stories," and a tale, "Leaf by Niggle," which illustrates the points made in the essay.

Wells, Evelyn K. The ballad tree: a study of British and American ballads, their folklore, verse, and music, together with sixty traditional ballads and their tunes. New York: Ronald, 1950.
The author of this book has chosen what is pertinent for the student or the casual reader at the beginning of ballad study. Emphasizes the British ballads of the Child collection. Considers the relationship of ancient ballads with modern folk songs. There are vivid sketches of Francis James Child and Cecil Sharp. "The ballad and the nursery" has special interest for students of children's literature. Bibliography. Indexes.

Yearsley, Percival M. The folklore of fairy-tale. London: Watts, 1924; reprint: Detroit: Singing Tree, 1968.
"An account . . . to form a clear understanding of the true nature and meaning of the fairytales . . .," mostly from the British Isles. A scientific discussion with samples of various types of tales.

FOLKLORE AS ENGLISH LITERATURE

Aesop

Adams, Frederick B., Jr. "The Codex Pithoeanus of Phaedrus," *Horn book magazine* 41:260–66 (June, 1965).
The director of the Pierpont Morgan Library gives the history of a ninth-century manuscript of Aesop's fables and traces the evolution of editions in both verse and prose from the earliest collection made by Phaedrus to James Thurber's *Further fables for our time.*

Aesopus. Aesop: five centuries of illustrated fables. Selected by John J. McKendry. New York: Metropolitan Museum of Art, 1964.
The introduction states that "the fables of Aesop are the only text that has been illustrated so often, so diversely, and so continuously that the history of the printed illustrated book can be shown by them alone."

————. Aesop's fables: a new translation by V. S. Vernon Jones. London: W. Heinemann; New York: Doubleday, 1912; reprint: New York: Watts, 1967.
G. K. Chesterton's introduction compares Aesop with Uncle Remus and analyzes the reasons for Aesop's being "more obviously effective than any other fabulist." Illustrations by Arthur Rackham.

————. Fables. London: Scolar Press, 1976.
Limited facsimile edition. Introduction by Edward Hodnett gives credit to Caxton, whose "edition of his own translation from the French version of Julien Macho first gave currency to the *Fables* in English." Includes 186 woodcuts commissioned by Caxton and modeled on those in a German Aesop.

————. The fables of Aesop, as first printed by William Caxton in 1484. Edited by Joseph Jacobs. 2v. London: D. Nutt, 1889.
Vol. 1 gives a history of the Aesopic fable with a chart showing the "Pedigree of Caxton's Aesop," and a "Synopsis of parallels." Indexes. Vol. 2 gives Caxton's text, including his misprints. Glossary.

————. The fables of Aesop, selected, told anew and their history traced by Joseph Jacobs. London and New York: Macmillan, 1894; reprinted: New York: Schocken, 1966.
Illustrated by Richard Heighway. Preface by Joseph Jacobs, folklorist of the late nineteenth century, gives a "short history of the Aesopic fable." Also includes the "Pedigree of Aesop" and "a series of notes, summing up what is known as to the provenance of each fable."

Miner, Robert. "Aesop as litmus: the acid test of children's literature," *Children's literature: the great excluded* 1: 9–15 (1972).
Traces translations and editions of Aesop from the earliest to the present day and notes the salutary influence attributed to the fables by scholars and literary notables.

Nolen, Eleanor Weakley. "Aesop in the Library of Congress," *Horn book magazine* 14:311–15 (September, 1938).
Describes copies of the earliest editions in this important collection, from the Greek text of 1480 and Latin text of 1487 to the French of 1786.

Arabian Nights

Arabian nights entertainments. Selected and edited by Andrew Lang. London and New York: Longmans, 1898.
Based on the Galland translation and illustrated by H. J. Ford.

———. New edition with decorations by Vera Bock. New York: McKay, 1946; London: Longmans, 1951.
A foreword by Mary Gould Davis notes that this edition omits several of Lang's original selections and adds "Ali Baba" and "Prince Ahmed."
Traces the spread of *The Arabian nights* through translations into several Western languages.

The Arabian nights: tales of wonder and magnificence. Edited by Padraic Colum. New York: Macmillan, 1951.
Illustrated by Lynd Ward. Based on a translation from Arabic into English by Edward William Lane, except for "Ali Baba" and "Ala-ed-Din," which are translated from the French of Antoine Galland.

The Arabian nights, their best-known tales. Edited by Kate Douglas Wiggin and Nora A. Smith. New York: Scribner, 1909.
Illustrated by Maxfield Parrish. Ten stories adapted from Scott's and Lane's editions.

Gerhardt, Mia I. The art of storytelling: a literary study of the *Thousand and one nights*. Leiden: E. J. Brill, 1963.
Recommended as a guide to the study of *The Arabian nights*, the most famous contribution from the Middle East to literature for English-speaking children.

Mozley, Charles. First book of tales of ancient Araby. New York: Watts, 1960.
Seven tales beautifully illustrated and well retold for easy reading.

Ballads

Child, Francis James. English and Scottish popular ballads, from the collection of Francis James Child. Edited by Helen Child Sargent and George Lyman Kittredge. 2v. Boston and New York: Houghton, 1880.
Became a ten-volume definitive edition based on the Child collection at Harvard, where American studies in the oral literary tradition began.

Malcolmson, Anne, ed. Song of Robin Hood. Boston: Houghton, 1947.
Music arranged by Grace Castagnetta. Designed and illustrated by Virginia Lee Burton. Preface gives notes on the traditional airs used here. Text and illustrations are closely linked in the manner of illuminated manuscripts.

Manning-Sanders, Ruth, ed. A bundle of ballads. Philadelphia: Lippincott, 1959.
A collection of sixty-three ballads sung by minstrels of the Middle Ages. Some words have been modernized "without losing any of the original flavor and vitality." Words only. Illustrated in black and white. Glossary.

Percy, Thomas, *bishop of Dromore.* Ancient ballads; selected from Percy's collection, with explanatory notes, taken from different authors, for the use and entertainment of young persons. London: Vernor, Hood & Sharpe; J. Harris; Exeter: W. Wilson for E. Upham, 1807.
A selection from Bishop Percy's 1765 publication of *Reliques of ancient English poetry.* Credited "by a lady." With plates.

———. The boy's Percy. Edited and with an introduction by Sidney Lanier. New York: Scribner, 1912.
Subtitle: being old ballads of war, adventure and love from Bishop Thomas Percy's *Reliques of ancient English poetry;* together with an appendix containing two ballads from the original Percy folio ms." Fifty illustrations from original designs by E. B. Bensell.

Pittsburgh. Carnegie Library. Stories from the ballads of Robin Hood, with lists of other ballads to tell and to read aloud. Pittsburgh: Carnegie Library, 1914; 2d ed., 1924.
"The source books are arranged with the original or old versions standing first, followed by other sources in the approximate order of their literary value or usefulness." Second edition also lists "Stories from other old ballads," p. 24–26.

Ritson, Joseph, ed. Robin Hood: a collection of all the ancient poems, songs and ballads now extant. . . . 2v. Edinburgh: Nimmo, 1887.
A preface gives the supposed historical anecdotes of the life of the legendary outlaw. With eighty wood engravings by Bewick and nine etchings by A. H. Tourrier and E. Buckman.

Serraillier, Ian. Robin and his merry men: ballads of Robin Hood. New York: Walck, 1969.
A companion volume to the author's *Robin in the greenwood.* Four ballads retold in verse form. Illustrated in black and white and in color by Victor G. Ambrus.

Beowulf

Crossley-Holland, Kevin, trans. Beowulf. New York: Farrar, 1968.
Suitable for young adult readers. An introduction by an Oxford scholar, Bruce Mitchell, summarizes the story of the poem, gives the probable date and place of composition of the manuscript in the British Museum, and discusses the meaning and effect of the poetry.

Laurence, M. P. J. "Heritage and Heorot," *Junior bookshelf* 19:125–28 (July, 1955).
Points out the value, importance, and beauty of the Anglo-Saxon epic, *Beowulf*, especially in the version for children, *Beowulf the warrior* by Ian Serraillier.

Nye, Robert. Beowulf, a new telling. New York: Hill & Wang, 1968.
Illustrated by Alan E. Cober. A free interpretation which gives credit to translations by a number of earlier scholars, 1837–1958.

Riggs, Strafford. The story of Beowulf retold from the ancient epic. (Junior Literary Guild) New York: Appleton, 1933.
The first important retelling for children. Outstanding decorations by Henry C. Pitz. Foreword by Charles J. Finger notes the survival and discovery of "a solitary manuscript" of the Anglo-Saxon epic.

Serraillier, Ian. Beowulf the warrior. New York: Walck, 1961.
Retold in spirited verse, as readable as prose.

Sutcliff, Rosemary. Beowulf. New York: Dutton, 1962.
The plot stays close to the original with a few interpretations added. Cadenced sentences give this retelling in prose the spirit of the ancient poetic version. Drawings by Charles Keeping.

Tolkien, J. R. R. "Beowulf: the monsters and the critics" (The Sir Israel Gollancz memorial lecture), in *The proceedings of the British Academy* 22. London: Oxford University Press, 1936.
A reassessment of *Beowulf* not as epic but as "a contrasted description of two moments in a great life, rising and setting . . . youth and age, first achievement and final death."

Fairy, Folk and Heroic Tales, Myths

Alger, Leclaire Gowans (*pseud.* Sorche Nic Leodhas). Heather and broom. New York: Holt, 1960.
The author has a unique position as a reteller of Scottish folktales for children. This is the first of a number of collections, all distinguished for individual traits that "do not instantly suggest counterparts from other countries." Contains eight "seanachie stories" told to the author in America. Her introduction explains how seanachie stories were handed down from generation to generation.

Asbjörnsen, P. C., and **Jorgen I. Moe.** East of the sun and west of the moon: twenty-one Norwegian folk tales. Edited and illustrated by Ingri and Edgar Parin d'Aulaire. New York: Viking, 1938.
Illustrations faithful to the Norwegian spirit. Translation based on "an old Norwegian edition, Dasent's translation and [the d'Aulaires'] own translation."

———. Norwegian folk tales. Translated by Pat Shaw Iversen and Carl Norman. New York: Viking, 1960.
Thirty-five stories in a translation by an American Fulbright scholar and "a devoted Norwegian folklorist." Illustrations by Erik Werenskiold and Theodore Kittelsen, who also worked with Asbjörnsen and Moe.

———. Popular tales from the Norse. Translated by Sir George Webbe Dasent. Edinburgh: Edmondston and Douglas, 1859; new ed.: Edinburgh: D. Douglas, 1903; reprint: London: Bodley Head, 1969.
The new edition has a memoir by Arthur Irwin Dasent and an introductory essay by Sir George Webbe Dasent, the Oxford scholar whose work stimulated English interest in Norse and Icelandic studies. Publisher's note mentions that the second edition included thirteen "Ananzi" stories, "drawing comparisons between these West Indian stories and tales from Germany, India, Norway and Egypt." This edition gives fifty-one stories.

Briggs, Katharine M. The fairies in tradition and literature. London: Routledge, 1967; Chicago: University of Chicago Press, 1967.
Shows the influence of English folklore as seen in literature. Also brings out parallels in the folklore of other countries. This is a survey from medieval times to the present, examining fairy types, fairy beasts and plants, regional differences, contacts between humans and fairies.

———. The personnel of fairyland: a short account of the fairy people of Great Britain for those who tell stories to children. Oxford: Alden, 1953; reprint: Detroit: Singing Tree, 1971.
Makes careful distinctions among numerous types of fairies known in the British Isles. Includes tales; a dictionary of fairies, p. 189–226; and a list of selected books with stories suitable for telling.

———, ed. Dictionary of British folk tales in the English language. Part A: Folk narratives. 2v. London: Routledge, 1970. Part B: Folk legends. 2v. Bloomington: Indiana University Press, 1970; London: Routledge, 1971.
A notable set of four volumes. Tales are told exactly as originally reported or summarized. Obscure dialects are translated. An enormous and fascinating collection drawing on a vast variety of sources.

——— and **Ruth L. Tongue,** eds. Folktales of England. (Folktales of the world series) Chicago: University of Chicago Press, 1968.

Foreword by Richard M. Dorson traces the history of "folklore science," chiefly in England. Includes ninety-two brief tales arranged by type, a glossary, an extensive bibliography, an index of motifs, and an index of tale types.

Colum, Padraic. The island of the mighty: being the hero stories of Celtic Britain retold from the Mabinogion. New York: Macmillan, 1924.
Eliminates nonessential matter, simplifies names, condenses and rearranges parts of the original text, holding closely to the Guest translation of *The Mabinogion* (see below).

Gayley, Charles M., ed. The classic myths in English literature and in art. Boston: Ginn, 1893. Rev. and enl. ed. New York: Ginn, 1911.
Based on Thomas Bulfinch's telling of the myths in *The age of fable* and "adapted to the needs of the classroom." Later edition copiously illustrated in black and white with drawings of statuary, friezes, and paintings, this book quotes appropriate passages from English literature, chiefly from poets who used myths for their subjects.

Green, Roger Lancelyn. "Andrew Lang in fairyland," *Junior bookshelf* 26:171–80 (October, 1962).
A biographical sketch that pays tribute to Lang as folklorist, author of "the finest prose translation of the Iliad and the Odyssey," and collector and occasional reteller of the stories in the Color fairy book series.

Grimm, Jakob Ludwig Karl, and **Wilhelm Karl Grimm.** The complete Grimm's fairy tales. New York: Pantheon, 1944.
A complete edition based on the translation of Margaret Hunt, with 212 illustrations by Joseph Scharl. Introduction by Padraic Colum connects the Brothers Grimm with the whole tradition of storytelling. A "Folkloristic commentary" by Joseph Campbell (p. 833–64) provides scholarly insight into the work of the Brothers Grimm, the types of stories, the history of the tales, the question of meaning.

———. German popular stories and fairy tales, as told by Gammer Grethel. Revised translation by Edgar Taylor. London: G. Bell, 1888.
From the collection of M. M. Grimm. Illustrations from designs by George Cruikshank and Ludwig Grimm. The first English translation was published by C. Baldwyn in 1823.

Guest, Lady Charlotte, ed. The Mabinogion, translated with notes. London: B. Quaritch, 1877.
Translated from a part of one group of narratives in the Welsh manuscript known as *The red book of Hergest.*

Hartland, Edwin S., ed. English fairy and other folk tales. London: W. Scott, 1890; reprint: Detroit: Singing Tree, 1968.

Introduction (p. vii–xxvi) explains the editor's division of stories into groups: nursery tales; sagas, including historical and local; giants, fairies, the devil and other goblins, witchcraft, ghosts; drolls.

Hays, May B. "Memories of my father, Joseph Jacobs," *Horn book magazine* 28:385–92 (December, 1952).
A biographical sketch showing Jacobs as family man, folklorist, researcher, and member of the circle of Burne-Jones, Rossetti, Lang, Kipling, and others.

Hazeltine, Alice Isabel, comp. Hero tales from many lands. New York: Abingdon, 1961.
Selected by a distinguished teacher, this is an excellent source for tellings traditionally familiar to English-speaking children. Includes hero tales from Greece, England (*Beowulf* and others), Ireland, and Wales.

Hull, Eleanor. Celtic fairy tales. New York: Putnam, 1892.

———. Cuchulain: the hound of Ulster. New York. Crowell, n.d.
Draws together the tales about Cuchulain with imaginative style and continuity.

———. The Cuchullin saga in Irish literature, being a collection of stories relating to the hero Cuchullin, translated from the Irish by various scholars. Compiled and edited with introduction and notes, by Eleanor Hull. London: D. Nutt, 1898.

Jacobs, Joseph, ed. English fairy tales. New York: Putnam, 1891.
Skillful retellings intended for children. Valuable "Notes and references" give sources, parallels, and remarks for each story.

———. More Celtic fairy tales. New York: Putnam, 1893.

———. More English fairy tales. New York: Putnam, 1894.

MacManus, Seumas. Hibernian nights. New York: Macmillan, 1963.
Illustrated by Paul Kennedy. A significant preface "About storytelling." Padraic Colum's introduction pays tribute to MacManus as writer and storyteller.

Meigs, Cornelia. "The deepest roots," in Meigs et al., *A critical history of children's literature*, p. 3–11. Rev. ed. New York: Macmillan, 1969.
A fine résumé of British folklore, briefly analyzed for its regional traits.

Morris, Kenneth. Book of the three dragons. New York and Toronto: Longmans, 1930.
A Welsh hero tale, written in lyrical prose and given an impressive format with memorable illustrations by Ferdinand Huszti Horvath.

Perrault, Charles. Perrault's complete fairy tales. Translated from the French by A. E. Johnson and others. New York: Dodd, 1961.
Illustrated by W. Heath Robinson. Includes eight tales translated from Perrault's versions. Three others, "The ridiculous wishes," "Donkeyskin," and "Patient Griselda," are paraphrased. Also includes "Beauty and the beast" by Mme. Leprince de Beaumont; "Princess Rosette" and "The friendly frog" by Mme. d'Aulnoy.

———. Popular tales. Edited from the original editions by Andrew Lang. Oxford: Clarendon, 1888.
A translation into English by Robert Samber was published in 1729.

Sutcliff, Rosemary. The hound of Ulster. New York: Dutton, 1963.
A retelling of the Cuchulain saga of the Red Branch heroes descended from the Celtic gods.

Thomas, William Jenkyn. The Welsh fairy-book. New York: Stokes, 1908; reprint: London: Philip Allan, 1935.
With illustrations by Willy Pogany. Includes eighty-three stories. Notes on Welsh pronunciation.

Tregarthen, Enys. Piskey folk: a book of Cornish legends. Collected by Elizabeth Yates. New York: Day, 1940.
A chief source for tales from Cornwall, retold by a Cornish folklorist. Photographs of the places associated with the stories. Glossary of Cornish words.

Yeats, William Butler, ed. Fairy and folk tales of Ireland. New York: Macmillan, 1973.
A foreword by Kathleen Raine explores the possibility that belief in fairy folk may persist in the collective unconscious mind of people like the Celts in spite of the civilizing influences of Christian faith and modern times. Appendix, "Classification of Irish fairies," by W. B. Yeats.

———. Fairy and folk tales of the Irish peasantry. London: Walter Scott, 1888.
The intense nationalism of the Young Ireland movement was reflected in this collection.

Young, Ella. Celtic wonder tales. New ed. New York: Dutton, 1923.
Stories of the gods told in poetic prose. Decorations by Maud Gonne.

AMERICAN FOLKLORE AS LITERATURE

General References

Botkin, Benjamin A., ed. Treasury of American folklore: stories, ballads, and traditions of the people. New York: Crown, 1944.
Foreword by Carl Sandburg. "Most important single volume of American folklore to date . . . . Extremely valuable reference tool because of source details, cross-index and encyclopedic coverage of well-known material."—*Library journal.*

Brunvand, Jan H. The study of American folklore: an introduction. New York: Norton, 1968.
Defines terms and categories and gives a survey of ballads, riddles, tales, songs, drama, dance, games, music, architecture, dress, food.

Carmer, Carl. "American folklore and its old-world backgrounds," in *Compton's pictured encyclopedia and fact-index,* p. 291–306. Chicago: Compton, 1975.
Illustrated and with an outstanding bibliography.

Ramsey, Eloise, and **Dorothy M. Howard,** comps. Folklore for children and young people. (Bibliographical series, v. 3) Philadelphia: American Folklore Society, 1952; reprint: New York: Kraus, 1970.
Pt. 1: Books for children and young people, covers folk tales, folk rhymes, folk songs, and singing games, legends and sagas, and literary uses of folklore. Each section suggests basic sources and relevant materials. Pt. 2: Selected sources for teachers, has similar divisions, a section useful to storytellers, one on folk arts and crafts, and a list of important periodicals on folklore. Appendix 2 gives an excellent list of out-of-print books that should be preserved.

Ballads

Carmer, Carl. America sings: stories and songs of our country's growing. New York: Knopf, 1942.
Illustrated in color by Elizabeth Black Carmer, this combines tales of American folk heroes with songs from various geographical regions.

Sandburg, Carl. The American songbag. New York: Harcourt, 1927.
Songs from every section of the country, particularly representative of a wide variety of work songs. Each song is introduced with a note about

the source. Widely considered to be a significant contribution to the history of American folklore.

Sharp, Cecil J. English folk songs from the Southern Appalachians. Edited by Maud Karpeles. 2v. New York: Putnam, 1917.
Comprising 273 songs and ballads with 968 tunes, including 39 tunes contributed by Olive Dame Campbell. Map and bibliographies.

Hiawatha

Longfellow, Henry Wadsworth. The song of Hiawatha. Boston: Houghton, 1890; facsimile reproduction: Chicago: J. G. Ferguson, 1968.
This edition is of special interest for its illustrations by Frederic Remington. His detailed pen-and-ink drawings on almost every page preserve the appearance of objects used by various Indian tribes. The poem relates Indian myths and legends surrounding the epic figure of Hiawatha, using the meter of the Finnish *Kalevala*. The work therefore stands as an epic of American origin.

————. Boston and New York: Houghton, 1911.
With illustrations and designs by Frederic Remington, Maxfield Parrish, and N. C. Wyeth, which give this edition special value.

Schoolcraft, Henry Rowe. The myth of Hiawatha, and other oral legends, mythological and allegorical, of the North American Indians. Philadelphia: Lippincott; London: Trübner, 1856.
Published immediately after the first appearance of *The song of Hiawatha* and dedicated to Longfellow, who had acknowledged his indebtedness to Schoolcraft's studies in Indian folklore. "These legends and myths are . . . versions of oral relations from the lips of the Indians" reproduced with additional legendary lore in revised form.

Folk and Tall Tales, Legends

Blair, Walter. Tall tale America: a legendary history of our humorous heroes. New York: Coward, 1944.
Includes Captain Stormalong, Jonathan Slick, Mike Fink, Davy Crockett, Johnny Appleseed, Mose the New York fireman, and Paul Bunyan.

Brookes, Stella Brewer. Joel Chandler Harris: folklorist. Athens: University of Georgia Press, 1950.
Pt. 1 traces the development of Harris into an eminent folklorist and creator of Uncle Remus. Pt. 2 analyzes the stories by type: trickster tales, tales of other "creeturs," myths, the supernatural, proverbs, dialect, songs. Includes an article by William Owens, "Folk-lore of the southern Negroes," from *Lippincott's magazine*, December, 1877, which first focused Harris's attention on Negro folklore. Bibliography.

Chase, Richard, ed. Grandfather tales: American-English folk tales. Boston: Houghton, 1948.
The editor has "taken a free hand in the retelling of 25 stories from North Carolina, Virginia and Kentucky." An appendix traces origins of the tales through sources that include Sir George Dasent, Joseph Jacobs, Grimm, and Aarne-Thompson's *Types of the folk tale.*

————. The Jack tales. Boston: Houghton, 1943.
Subtitle: "told by R. M. Ward and his kindred in the Beech Mountain section of western North Carolina and by other descendants of Council Harmon (1803–1896) elsewhere in the southern mountains; with three tales from Wise County, Virginia." Preface describes and pays tribute to these storytellers. In an appendix, Herbert Halpert, Indiana University, acknowledges the author's scholarly contributions to American folklore. Sources and parallels, p. 189–200. Glossary of Appalachian usage.

Coughlan, Margaret N. Folklore from Africa to the United States: an annotated bibliography. Washington, D.C.: Library of Congress, 1976.
The foreword by Virginia Haviland points out that "some of these black (or Afro-American) tales have become as much a part of the heritage of American children as has classic folklore derived from European sources. . . . The purpose of this bibliography is to reveal original sources of African tales and to trace their relationship to stories carried to the West Indies and the American South. . . ." Divided by geographical areas with "Studies and collections for adults" distinguished in each case from "Collections for children."

Dorson, Richard M. Buying the wind: regional folklore in the United States. Chicago and London: University of Chicago Press, 1964.
A large collection with many types of tales arranged by region. Extensive bibliography and indexes.

Harris, Joel Chandler. Brer Rabbit: Uncle Remus stories adapted by Margaret Wise Brown. New York: Harper, 1941.
Pictures by A. B. Frost redrawn for reproduction by Victor Dowling.

————. Nights with Uncle Remus: myths and legends of the old plantation. Boston and New York: Houghton, 1883.
A large collection based mostly on African folklore brought to the United States by blacks in slavery.

————. Uncle Remus: his songs and his sayings. New and rev. ed. New York: Appleton, 1895.
The first edition to appear with illustrations by A. B. Frost.

Leach, Maria. The rainbow book of American folk tales and legends. Cleveland: World, 1958.

Lively illustrations by Marc Simont. "Fun for browsing . . . valuable for reference . . . useful for special storytelling, and helpful for study of the origin and meaning of the variety of stories." —Virginia Haviland.

Life treasury of American folklore, by the editors of *Life*. New York: Time, 1961.

Arranged by types of Americans from the period of the explorers to modern times. A large collection of stories briefly told. Contains "A regional guide to American folklore" (fold-out map in color) and extensive glossary and index, helpful in identifying "persons, places and events in American folklore."

Ullom, Judith C. Folklore of the North American Indians: an annotated bibliography. Washington, D.C.: Library of Congress, 1969.

North American Indian culture areas are the basis for a grouping of source books and children's editions with full annotations. Facsimile illustrations in black and white.

The Anglo-Saxon Period

During the fourth century A.D., a wave of nomadic peoples, the Huns, swept from north central Asia across Europe, driving before them Germanic tribes who, toward the end of the fifth century, reached England. These tribes were themselves a relatively uncivilized people. They waged war against the Britons, who fought under the leadership of a Romanized Christian later known to legend as Arthur. Finally the invaders settled and established their own rule. The Angles had small kingdoms in East Anglia, Mercia, and Northumbria. The Saxons held sway in Sussex, Wessex, and Essex. Most of the defeated Britons gradually withdrew to Scotland, Wales, Ireland, and Brittany, taking with them their civilization, a blend of Roman and Christian influences overlying ancient Celtic traditions.

Inevitably some of these influences and traditions were absorbed by the Anglo-Saxons. The refinements and ceremonies of Christian missionaries and later churchmen made themselves felt, and England began to take on a special character, a mingling of the Germanic, the Roman, and the Christian Celtic, in ways of life and in language. Monasteries opened or reopened, becoming centers of civilized living and in many cases beacons of learning. The Venerable Bede told of a school set up by King Sigebert as early as 635 where students were taught Holy Writ, the arts of ecclesiastical poetry, astronomy, arithmetic, Greek, and Latin. At each center, one name tends to stand out as teacher, leader, and writer of school books; Aldhelm, Bede, Alcuin, Alfred the Great, Ælfric—their names span the Anglo-Saxon period.

Aldhelm was abbot at Malmesbury in Wiltshire during the seventh century, when learning among the Anglo-Saxons was scarce at best. It was a time when the Celtic monasteries alone kept learning alive and at a high level. From Celtic scholars the English were to learn how to write and illuminate beautiful manuscripts.

The Venerable Bede came from Northumbria where Celtic learning was strong. From the age of seven, Bede was trained in monasteries on the east coast near the Scottish border. There he had the advantage not only of good masters but also of rich libraries.

Alcuin too was a Northumbrian, educated at York, which had the finest library north of the Alps. Alcuin's fame reached the emperor Charlemagne, who persuaded him to come to his court at Aachen in order to establish a school. This school was followed by others for children of all classes within Charlemagne's empire.

In ninth-century England, after the Danish invasions, King Alfred too believed in educating all classes of children, earning the right to be called "Great," not only for his power of command and genius in administration but also because, as his statue at Wantage proclaims, "he found learning dead, and he restored it."

The savage Danes had indeed killed learning in Anglo-Saxon England. They destroyed the monasteries and burned their books and records. For this reason, our ideas of monastic schools are far from complete. It is even more difficult to get a clear picture of the children who attended schools in Anglo-Saxon days. We do know that children of prosperous families dressed like small counterparts of their parents, wearing belted tunics of bright blue or scarlet, woven of fine wool or linen. A cloak fastened with a gold brooch might cover the tunic in cold weather, and leather sandals or boots protected the feet. It was the Venerable Bede, in his *Ecclesiastical history of the English nation,* who gave us the beguiling picture of two of these children, taken as slaves to Rome, where they were seen by Pope Gregory I. On hearing that they were Angles, the Pope said, *"Non Angli sed Angeli."*

Bede wrote of a child he knew who was sent to school in a monastery at the age of three. One can sense the sympathy the best schoolmasters felt for students, some of whom were so very young. There are, for instance, touches of humor in the *Colloquy* imagined by Ælfric of Winchester at the end of the Anglo-Saxon age. The *Colloquy* is a conversation between a master and his pupils about the kinds of work a man might do. It was a form of writing obviously devised to make learning easier and more entertaining for children.

Verse was another form of writing widely used to make learning more enjoyable. Numerous anthologies of Anglo-Saxon poetry are available. Such collections have the advantages of brevity and accessibility while offering a broad range of selections. But today's teacher should try above all to find translations that convey the strength, vitality, and dignity of the original writings. It is these qualities that help to explain why children before the Norman Conquest listened to poetry and learned much

of it by heart, and why Anglo-Saxon studies are alive today. *Beowulf* may be taught as part of the heritage left to children's literature by the Anglo-Saxons, since this poem is generally thought to have been written down in the eighth century from its folklore sources.

For the student of children's literature, the chief impression of the Anglo-Saxon period will probably be of the great masters who founded schools and wrote the first schoolbooks for English children. Through records of their lives and through their writings, still in print a thousand years later, the reader can see these teachers as men of keen minds and broad vision. They have been called "saints and scholars." The human side of their personalities is equally attractive. The first of them to write a book especially for the young was Aldhelm, abbot of Malmesbury, who used to dress as a gleeman and stand on a bridge where people passed near the church. There he sang songs and ballads to attract the faithful to come to worship. We see the Venerable Bede writing or translating no less than forty-five books for his students in the monastery at Jarrow, and by an effort of will living on, still at work in his cell, until with his final breath he dictated the last words for his translation of Saint John's Gospel. We read the noble words of King Alfred revealing his beneficent spirit as he urged the bishops to see to it that the village priests allowed the little children to come to school freely.

A bibliography has been added here, under "Individual writers and educators," for one great figure, Boethius, who was not an Anglo-Saxon scholar but a Roman philosopher and statesman. His *Consolation of philosophy,* written in prison, was one of the most popular of all school texts and was one of the books that King Alfred put on his list of those "which are most needful of all men to know." No study of the Anglo-Saxon period would be complete without at least a nodding acquaintance with Boethius and *The consolation of philosophy.* King Alfred himself translated this book into the English of his day, and, like most of the other Anglo-Saxon writings referred to in the following bibliographies, it is easily available today, translated into modern English.

OUTLINE

I. Historical background
  A. Schools in England coeval with introduction of Christianity
  B. The mission of Saint Augustine
  C. Founding of school at Canterbury
  D. Monasteries as literary centers
II. Anglo-Saxon schools
  A. Connection with monastic or ecclesiastical institutions
  B. The song school and the grammar school; functions of each
  C. The curriculum
    1. The seven liberal arts
    2. Grammar; what it included, and its importance
      a) Donatus
      b) Priscian
    3. Value of colloquial Latin
  D. Method of teaching
  E. Need and use of textbooks
III. Revival of learning under King Alfred
  A. Restoration of monastery and other schools
  B. The court school
  C. Views on the education of children
  D. Use of vernacular in elementary teaching
IV. Early educational books and their makers
  A. Aldhelm, bishop of Sherborne (639?–709)
    1. Fame as English singer and Latin poet
    2. Theological and literary writings
    3. *De septenario*
      a) Significance of dialogue form
      b) Educational value of riddles and puzzles

B. The Venerable Bede, Jarrow (673?–735)
  1. Personality as shown in writings
  2. Informational treatises; sources and range of interests represented
  3. Importance in transmission of Latin learning.
  4. *The ecclesiastical history of the English nation*
C. Alcuin, scholar of York and master of the palace school of Charlemagne (735?–804)
  1. Dialogues on grammar, rhetoric, and dialectics·
  2. *Treatise on orthography*
  3. *Disputation with Pepin*
  4. *Propositions . . . for whetting the wit of youth* (attributed to Alcuin)
D. Alfred the Great (849–99)
  1. Translations into the vernacular
  2. The "Epistle to the bishops," preface to Alfred's translation of Pope Gregory's *Pastoral care*
  3. Translation of Boethius's *Consolation of philosophy*
E. Ælfric the Grammarian, Winchester (955?–1020?)
  1. Anglo-Saxon writings
  2. Schoolbooks
    a) Anglo-Latin grammar
    b) Vocabulary; arrangement
    c) *Colloquy;* Anglo-Saxon gloss
      (1) Theme, method, and primary purpose
      (2) Value for pictures of everyday life in England

LIFE AND LITERATURE

Anderson, George K. The literature of the Anglo-Saxons. Rev. ed. Princeton, N.J.: Princeton University Press, 1966.
A lively, readable, and complete literary history with a full bibliography on every aspect of Anglo-Saxon life and literature.

The Anglo-Saxon chronicle. Translated and edited by G. N. Garmonsway. Rev. ed. London: Dent; New York: Dutton (Everyman), 1954.
Presents in compact form all the vernacular chronicles from the time of the arrival of the Anglo-Saxons to 1154. Bibliography.

Blair, Peter Hunter. An introduction to Anglo-Saxon England. Cambridge: Cambridge University Press, 1956.
A short and readable history.

Cambridge History of English Literature. v. 1. The Cambridge book of prose and verse in illustration of English literature, from the beginnings to the cycles of romance. Edited by Sir A. W. Ward and A. R. Waller. Cambridge: Cambridge University Press, 1967.
"A selection of passages to illustrate the first volume of Cambridge history of English literature."—preface. See especially chapter 3, "Early national poetry," for *Beowulf;* chapter 4 on Caedmon, the riddles; chapter 5 on Gildas, Aldhelm, Bede, and Alcuin; chapter 6 on King Alfred.

Cook, Albert S., and **Chauncey B. Tinker.** Select translations from Old English prose. New York: Gordian Press, 1968.
Includes the Venerable Bede, the *Old English chronicle*, the works of King Alfred, Boethius, Ælfric, Alcuin.

Crossley-Holland, Kevin, trans. and ed. The battle of Maldon and other Old English poems. London: Macmillan; New York: St. Martin's, 1965.
Informative introductions precede each selection. Beautiful translations.

Duckett, Eleanor Shipley. Anglo-Saxon saints and scholars. New York: Macmillan, 1947.
Includes chapters on Aldhelm of Malmesbury and Bede of Jarrow. The style is informal and in the spirit of Bede, who was advised to write "very simply, that humbler students may also know of these truths."

"A father's instruction," in *The Exeter book: an anthology of Anglo-Saxon poetry, presented to Exeter cathedral by Leofric, first bishop of Exeter 1050–1071,* edited from the manuscript with a translation, notes, introduction, etc., by Israel Gollancz, pt. 1, p. 300–5. London: Kegan Paul, Trench, Trübner, 1895.
A poem, possibly of the time of Aldhelm, representing a father's instructing his son.

Field, Louise Frances Story (Mrs. E. M. Field). "In the cradle," in *Bibliophile in the nursery,* edited by William Targ, p. 38–105. Cleveland and New York: World, 1957.
Abridged from the first 135 pages of Field's *The child and his book,* still one of the best sources on the subject.

Grohskopf, Bernice. From age to age: life and literature in Anglo-Saxon England. New York: Atheneum, 1968.
Includes selected translations of prose and poetry from the Old English period, 500–1066 A.D., and gives the historical and literary background needed to understand the literature. Special sections on the Venerable Bede, Alfred the Great, and Ælfric.

Hassall, W. O., comp. How they lived: an anthology of original accounts written before 1485. Oxford: Blackwell, 1962.
Has excellent illustrations, which, like the text, are taken from contemporary sources.

Hieatt, Constance B., trans. and comp. Beowulf and other Old English poems. New York: Odyssey, 1967.
Includes Beowulf; The battle of Maldon; The wanderer; Deor. Simple translations into modern English prose. Bibliography.

Hodgkin, Robert Howard. A history of the Anglo-Saxons. 3d ed. 2v. London: Oxford University Press, 1952.
An authoritative history with many illustrations. Covers the period through the age of Alfred. Chapter 9, vol. 1, "The golden age," has sections on Aldhelm and Bede. Chapter 17, vol. 2, is a scholarly and readable discussion of King Alfred's role in "the restoration of order and learning."

Keenan, Hugh T. "Children's literature in Old English," *Children's literature: the great excluded,* 1:16–20 (1972).
Gives examples of Old English verse that children learned and quotes passages from Ælfric's *Colloquy,* "designed to teach students Latin . . . by dialogues between students and teacher."

Lester, G. A. The Anglo-Saxons: how they lived and worked. Chester Springs, Pa.: Dufour Editions, 1976.
Describes the organization of Anglo-Saxon society and gives brief accounts of how its members lived, played, worked, worshiped, spoke, wrote, and fought. Bibliography.

Quennell, Marjorie, and **C. H. B. Quennell.** Everyday life in Roman and Anglo-Saxon times, including Viking and Norman times. Rev. ed. New York: Putnam, 1961.
Intended for boys and girls but useful also for teachers and advanced students because of its excellent handling of detail in text, in profuse illustration, and in index. Bibliography.

Raffel, Burton, trans. and ed. Poems from the Old English. 2d ed. Lincoln: University of Nebraska Press, 1964.
The translator has taken some justifiable liberties with the texts.

Sellman, Roger Raymond Stanley. The Anglo-Saxons. London: Methuen, 1959.
Brief coverage of six centuries, from the first tribal migrations to the Norman conquest: history (with maps); social customs; useful survey of learning and cultural contributions under the Celtic church; later schools; Bede, Caedmon, Gildas, King Alfred, and others. Selected bibliography.

EDUCATION

Field, Louise Frances Story (Mrs. E. M. Field). "Before the Norman conquest," in her *The child and his book,* p. 10–35. 2d ed. London: Wells Gardner, 1892; reprint: Detroit: Singing Tree, 1968.
Useful as a résumé. There are brief extracts illustrating the work of Aldhelm, Ælfric, and other writers.

Gardiner, Dorothy Kempe. "Saxon times," in her *English girlhood at school,* p. 13–32. London: Oxford University Press, 1929.
The topics treated are: The influence of France; The northern abbesses; Women scholars in southern England; The first palace-schools; Tenth century to the Conquest; The early teaching of embroidery.

Hodgkin, Robert Howard. A history of the Anglo-Saxons. 2v. Oxford: Clarendon, 1952.

From the time when the Angles and Saxons were first mentioned among the tribes of Germany to the death of Alfred. For a background of the life of the people in England, see vol. 1., p. 201–44; the Roman mission to the English, p. 257–81; Aldhelm, p. 321–26; Bede, p. 347–55; the restoration of order and of learning under Alfred, vol. 2., p. 599–631; "Alfred the man and his message," p. 670–95. Chronological tables, maps, and many illustrations.

Leach, Arthur Francis. The schools of medieval England. London: Methuen, 1915.

A history of English schools from the establishment of the grammar school at Canterbury about 598 to the reign of Edward VI. The first six chapters, p. 1–95, constitute an interesting and important contribution to the subject of Anglo-Saxon education. The headings are as follows: Our oldest school, Canterbury; The Greek and Roman models; Theodore of Tarsus and Aldhelm of Winchester; The schools of Northumbria, Bede and Alcuin; Alfred the Great and the school of Winchester; The schools from Edward the Elder to Edward the Confessor. Illustrations reproduced from manuscripts and other original sources.

Stuart, Dorothy Margaret. "The Anglo-Saxon boy," "Birds' Latin," in her *The boy through the ages,* p. 113–33. London: Harrap, 1926.

References to Bede, Ælfric, Aldhelm, Alcuin, and King Alfred; also interesting illustrations, including pictures of a bone writing tablet and an Anglo-Saxon school.

———. "In the dark ages," in her *The girl through the ages,* p. 76–94. London: Harrap, 1933; reprint: Detroit: Singing Tree, 1969.

Chiefly useful as a picture of life in Anglo-Saxon times, but notes briefly the training of girls in convents and the education given the daughters of Charlemagne and Alfred.

Ælfric the Grammarian

Ælfric. "Dialogue between a teacher and pupils," in *Readings in English history drawn from the original sources* edited by Edward Potts Cheyney, p. 69–72. Boston: Ginn, 1922.

Extract in modern English from Ælfric's *Colloquy.*

BIOGRAPHY AND CRITICISM

Hurt, James. Ælfric. (Twayne's English authors series, v. 131) New York: Twayne, 1972.

Chapter 5, "The *Grammar* and the *Colloquy,*" p. 104–19, is of special interest to students of children's literature.

Westlake, John S. "From Alfred to the Conquest," in *Cambridge history of English literature,* v.

1, p. 114–29. Cambridge: Cambridge University Press, 1963.

Discussion of Ælfric's writing from a literary point of view.

White, Caroline Louisa. Ælfric, a new study of his life and writings. Boston and New York: Lamson Wolffe, 1898; reprint: Hamden, Conn.: Shoe String (Archon), 1974.

A scholarly work, of which chapters 1–6 on the life, works, and influence of Ælfric are most useful.

Alcuin

Duckett, Eleanor Shipley. Alcuin, friend of Charlemagne: his world and his work. New York: Macmillan, 1951; reprint: Hamden, Conn.: Shoe String (Archon), 1965.

For the general reader. See "Alcuin in York," p. 3–36, and "The Frankish court and school," p. 83–117, focusing on Alcuin as scholar and teacher.

Mullinger, James Bass. The schools of Charles the Great and the restoration of education in the ninth century. London: Longmans, 1877; reprint: New York: Stechert, 1932.

Contents: Introduction; Charles the Great and Alcuin, or, The school of the palace; Alcuin at Tours, or, The school of the monastery; Rabanus Maurus, or, The school at Fulda; Lupus Servatus, or, The classics in the ninth century; John Scotus Erigena, or, The Irish school. Awarded the Kaye prize of the University of Cambridge in 1875 and published in London in 1877.

West, Andrew Fleming. Alcuin and the rise of the Christian schools. New York: Scribner, 1920.

"A sketch of Alcuin in his relations to education. . . . Based mainly on a study of Alcuin's writings." Scholarly and interesting. See especially "The educational writings of Alcuin," p. 89–116. An earlier edition was published in 1892.

Aldhelm

Field, Louise Frances Story (Mrs. E. M. Field). "Before the Norman conquest," in her *The child and his book,* p. 16–22. 2d ed. London: Wells Gardner, 1892; reprint: Detroit: Singing Tree, 1968.

A pleasing picture of Aldhelm as a person, partly drawn from one of his letters. Also outlines the various forms of writing used by Aldhelm to attract and teach the young.

Alfred the Great

Alfred the Great. The whole works of Alfred the Great. 3 pts. in 2v. Edited by J. A. Giles. Lon-

don: Bosworth & Harrison, 1858; reprints: London: Methuen, 1947; New York: Scholarly Press, 1976.
Includes preliminary essays illustrative of the history, arts, and manners of the ninth century.

BIOGRAPHY AND CRITICISM

Besant, Sir Walter. "Alfred as educator," "Alfred as writer," in his *The story of King Alfred,* p. 140–62. New York: Appleton, 1924.
Includes the "Epistle to the bishops," which forms the preface to Alfred's translation of Pope Gregory's *Pastoral care.* This is particularly valuable for the picture it gives of the conditions of the time and for the views on education presented.

Duckett, Eleanor Shipley. Alfred the Great. Chicago: University of Chicago Press, 1956.
Chapter 6, "King Alfred and his scholars and teachers" (p. 106–28) is a pleasant introduction for the general reader.

Mapp, Alf Johnson. The golden dragon: Alfred the Great and his times. La Salle, Ill.: Open Court, 1974.
Chapter 10, "King's English," is an easily read account of King Alfred's contributions to English learning and literature. Extensive bibliography.

Bede

Beda Venerabilis. Bede's ecclesiastical history of the English nation. Translated by J. Stevens. London: Dent, 1954; New York: Dutton (Everyman), 1954.
In his introduction, David Knowles explains Bede's right to be called "the father of English history" and "a born storyteller" whose stories "have passed from the folio to the schoolroom and from the schoolroom to the nursery." Includes a life of the Venerable Bede by J. Stevens (1723), revised with notes by L. C. Jane (1903).

BIOGRAPHY AND CRITICISM

Thompson, A. Hamilton, ed. Bede, his life, times, and writings: essays in commemoration of the twelfth centenary of his death. New York: Russell & Russell, 1966.
Notable scholars writing in the cultural tradition. "The life of the Venerable Bede," p. 1–38, by the Rev. C. E. Whiting, is a good introduction to the subject. Bibliography.

Boethius

Boethius, Anicius Manlius Severinus. The consolation of philosophy. Arundel and London: Centaur Press, 1963.
The translation by the anonymous I. T. (1609). An introduction by William Anderson gives credit to Boethius as having laid down the basis for the trivium and quadrivium, the educational curriculum that was to be followed from his time (480–524) throughout the Middle Ages. See in this edition Boethius's note "To the young gentlemen readers" (p. 23).

———. ———. (Library of liberal arts) Translated with introduction and notes by Richard Green. Indianapolis, Ind.: Bobbs-Merrill, 1962.
An introduction gives a biographical sketch and analyzes the lasting importance of Boethius as philosopher and poet.

———. King Alfred's version of the *Consolation* of Boethius, done into modern English. Oxford: Clarendon, 1900. Introduction by W. J. Sedgefield.

BIOGRAPHY AND CRITICISM

Barrett, Helen Marjorie. Boethius: some aspects of his times and work. Cambridge: Cambridge University Press, 1940; reprint: New York: Russell & Russell, 1965.
Includes biographical chapters on Boethius, followed by a critical analysis of *The consolation of philosophy* and some extracts in Latin and in English.

Rand, Edward Kennard. Founders of the Middle Ages. Cambridge, Mass.: Harvard University Press, 1928.
The chapters of this book were delivered as lectures before the Lowell Institute of Boston. See "Boethius, the first of the scholastics."

Stewart, Hugh Fraser. Boethius: an essay. London: W. Blackwood, 1891; reprint: New York: Burt Franklin, 1974.
Chapter 3 (p. 55–80) summarizes the five books of *The consolation of philosophy,* written by Boethius in prison and destined to become a standard textbook in English schools from Anglo-Saxon times through the Middle Ages.

Taylor, Henry Osborn. Classical heritage of the Middle Ages. 3d ed. New York: Macmillan, 1911.
Provides a summary of the philosophy of Boethius.

The Feudal Age

For the purpose of this study, the Feudal Age is given a wide span and includes the Middle Ages. It begins with the Norman Conquest, includes the Hundred Years War, and ends with the Wars of the Roses. The literature of the Middle Ages takes its shape from feudalism. With William Caxton, who in 1476 introduced printing into England, it becomes the focus for contemporary manners. Caxton can be seen as a figure who helped to lead the English-speaking people from the Feudal Age to the Tudor period and the Renaissance.

The Feudal Age was a time when the influence of the Romans and of later Nordic invaders faded and the more sophisticated language and life of the conquering Normans was superimposed upon older patterns of speech and custom. Among the British people, however, ancient memories remained, and traditional stories were still told. The earliest written versions of Celtic and British folktales and ballads now extant date from the era following the Norman Conquest, when monastery libraries recorded in manuscript the oral traditions surrounding the revered figures of saints and mythical heroes.

We may rightly picture the child of the Middle Ages as having no books of his or her own and no access to books except for the familiar Donatus or other textbooks kept on the desk of the schoolmaster. But educational opportunities were spreading almost without benefit of books. Schools in noble houses accepted a favored few, grammar schools were opening for boys from the middle class, and the talented, hard working, and ambitious, regardless of class, could find places in the monastery schools and song schools, which trained candidates for the religious life. Girls of noble families were generally taught at home by a governess or tutor.

Far more children were sent to grow up as apprentices to a master of a trade, with little chance for book learning. For these young people, the oral tradition was still the chief door to literature. This literature now included tales that had traveled from Britain to France and, after the Conquest, returned to England with the Normans, embroidered and refined. It also included drama, both sacred and profane, which children watched with their elders in churchyards and town squares where guilds produced miracle and mystery plays. The players worked from written texts, which still exist, but for the audiences the plays were part of the oral tradition. *Guy of Warwick* and *Bevis of Southampton* were tales with English themes but incorporating echoes of European adventures and the Crusades. Children learned rules of courtesy and good manners orally, in rhymed couplets, easily remembered, and these rules added polish to a society that was embracing the ideals of chivalry.

Geoffrey Chaucer (1340?–1400) is the first of the two great names that dominate the literature of the Feudal Age. Chaucer did not write for children, except in his *Treatise on the astrolabe,* which he wrote for his son, Lewis. But *The Canterbury tales* are full of folklore and legendary stories, some of them taken from the *Gesta Romanorum,* already known by children of Chaucer's day. His versions of these tales were to be adopted by and adapted for children of future generations.

The fifteenth century, the last century of the Feudal Age, began with the birth of Sir Thomas Malory (1400?–1471). Like Chaucer, Malory did not write for children, but he too drew from the deep well of British and Norman folklore. Children already knew, through the tellings of bards and minstrels, the Arthurian legends that Malory transcribed in the English language and that were edited by William Caxton as one book, *Le morte d'Arthur.* It is the single medieval romance that survives as a living book today, and it has been the source for innumerable retellings for children in collections and in colorful volumes of separate tales.

OUTLINE

I. The Norman conquest; its effect upon language and literature

II. Anglo-Norman schools
   A. Monastic, cathedral, and parish schools
   B. Rise of endowed grammar schools
     1. Opening of opportunities to middle class
     2. Relation to universities
     3. School life
       a) "The birched schoolboy"
   C. Education at the king's court and in noblemen's houses
     1. Kind of training received and its purpose
     2. Value of training: "Manners makyth man"
     3. Contrast with ideals of the church schools

III. Educational books of the 11th, 12th, and 13th centuries
   A. Latin and French reading books and vocabularies
     1. Neckam's *De utensilibus* (12th century)
     2. De Garlandia's *Dictionarius* (13th century)
     3. Walter de Biblesworth's *Phraseologia* (late 13th century)
   B. Scientific treatises and books of general information
     1. Anselm's(?) *Elucidarium* (11th century)
     2. Neckam's *De naturis rerum* (12th century)
     3. *Elucidarium magistri alani* (13th century)
     4. *De proprietatibus rerum* of Bartholomæus Anglicus or De Glanvilla (13th century)

IV. The Donatus or Latin grammar
   A. Manuscripts, 15th-century block books, and printed editions
   B. Literary references to the Donatus

V. Rhymed treatises on manners and morals
   A. *Stans puer ad mensam*
   B. *The boke of curtasye*
   C. *How the good wiff taugte hir dougtir*
   D. John Russell's *Boke of nurture*
   E. Symon's *Lesson of wysedome for all maner chyldryn*
   F. *The babee's book*
   G. *Book of curtesye*
   H. Hugh Rhodes's *Boke of nurture*
   I. *The schoole of vertue*
   These rhymed treatises originated on the Continent before the invention of printing. They began to appear in England about 1430. They are extant in both manuscript and printed forms, and the last two noted date from the sixteenth century. This section, therefore, overlaps the next period division, but it seems desirable to disregard individual dates and to consider the books of demeanor in one group in connection with feudal training for knighthood.

VI. Ballad and romance literature
   The origin and development of medieval romance and folk ballads has been treated under "Folk tales and ballads." Although they have their origins earlier, attention should be called to them again as an important part of the literature known to children during the Feudal Age.

VII. Geoffrey Chaucer (1340?–1400)
   A. Historical background in 14th-century England
   B. Structure of *The Canterbury tales*
   C. Characters of *The Canterbury tales* as reflections of 14th-century life
   D. A selection of tales adapted for children
   E. *Treatise on the astrolabe*

VIII. Sir Thomas Malory (1400?–1471)
   A. Historical background in 15th-century England
   B. Influence of the times on the life of Malory
   C. Malory's ideals as reflected in *Le morte d'Arthur*
   D. Caxton's edition of 1485 and the Winchester manuscript
   E. Later translations and retellings, especially those for children

LITERATURE

Brockman, Bennett A. "Children and literature in late medieval England," *Children's literature*, 4: 58–64 (1975).
Gives examples from medieval literature in which children are seen as reading to themselves or reading aloud. Points out evidence of some medieval attitudes toward children.

———. "Medieval songs of innocence and experience: the adult writer and literature for children," *Children's literature: the great excluded*, 2:40–49 (1972).
Compares twentieth-century stories for children with works read by children of the late Middle Ages.

Clarke, Sidney W. The miracle play in England: an account of the early religious drama. London: W. Andrews, 1897; reprint: New York: Haskell House, 1964.
Written "to give an account of the manner in which the people at large entered into the spirit of the performances and to tell how they presented and embellished their plays."

Goodrich, M. E. "Childhood and adolescence among thirteenth century saints," *History of childhood quarterly* 1:285–309 (Autumn, 1973).
A study showing how tales told of the saints as children reflected patterns of medieval life and "personified the ideals of the age."

Haskins, Charles Homer. The Renaissance of the twelfth century. Cambridge, Mass.: Harvard University Press, 1933.
Discusses "the Latin classics and their influence . . . the new knowledge of the Greeks and Arabs and its effects upon Western science and philosophy, and the new institutions of learning, all seen against the background of the century's centres and materials of culture."—preface.

Jacobs, Joseph, ed. The most delectable history of Reynard the fox. London and New York: Macmillan, 1895; reprint: New York: Schocken, 1967.
Illustrated by W. Frank Calderon. Philip Rieff's introduction shows how the beast epic of the Middle Ages symbolized "the violence inherent in winning."

Komroff, Manuel, ed. Tales of the monks from the *Gesta Romanorum*. (The library of living classics) New York: Lincoln MacVeagh, Dial, 1928.
The earliest English translation was published about 1510–1515. This collection of 181 stories shows the source of many tales known by children of the feudal age.

McMunn, Meradith Tilbury, and William Robert McMunn. "Children's literature in the Middle Ages," *Children's literature: the great excluded*, 1:21–29 (1972).
Examines the evidence that children's literature was synonymous with adult literature at this period.

Malcolmson, Anne. Miracle plays. Boston: Houghton, 1956.
Seven medieval plays adapted for modern players, with an introduction explaining the spirit, language, and method of production. Glossary of medieval words and expressions.

Marchalonis, Shirley. "Medieval symbols and the *Gesta Romanorum*," *The Chaucer review* 8:311–19 (Spring, 1974).
An essay showing how the popular *Gesta* were used by medieval writers for didactic purposes, twisting the usual significance of animal or other symbols to bring out unexpected meaning in the tales.

Schofield, William Henry. English literature from the Norman Conquest to Chaucer. New York and London: Macmillan, 1906.
There are sections on "Beast-fables, beast-epics and bestiaries," p. 330–37, and "Didactic works," p. 418–34; also brief references for Alexander Neckam, Bartholomaeus Anglicus, and other writers. The introduction notes the changed conditions of the new epoch and the peculiar literary characteristics of the period. "Chronological table," p. 458–65; "Bibliographical notes," p. 466–86.

Thoms, William John. The old story books of England. Westminster [London]: J. Cundall, 1845; reprint: New York: Johnson, 1969.
The editor, who coined the term *folk-lore*, used traditional English sources for this compilation of tales and ballads, including *Guy of Warwick* and *Bevis of Southampton*.

Vising, Johan. Anglo-Norman language and literature. London: Oxford University Press, 1923.
Indicates the effect of the Norman Conquest upon the English language, and outlines the general types of literature of this period. Also contains a detailed catalog of works from the twelfth century to the fifteenth.

Westwood, Jennifer. Medieval tales. New York: Coward, 1968.
Translated and adapted from Chaucer, the legends of the Round Table, and the French *chansons de geste*, this collection has illustrations in black and white conveying the flavor of the Middle Ages.

EDUCATION

Barstow, Allen M. "The concept of the child in the Middle Ages: the Ariès thesis," *Children's literature* 4:41–44 (1975).
Calls attention to a controversial study claiming that life in the Middle Ages was insensitive to childhood and that family life hardly existed as a social concept.

Bedford, Jessie (*pseud.* Elizabeth Godfrey). "Nurture in kings' courts," in her *English children in the olden time*, p. 82–98. London: Methuen, 1907.
Popular account of the training in courtesy and knighthood, and of the books of demeanor.

Coulton, George Gordon. "Monastic schools in the Middle Ages," *Contemporary review*, p. 818–28 (June, 1913).
The author throws doubt on the theory that nunneries and monasteries took significant numbers of pupils for schooling, except for those who expected to enter the religious life and for a limited number of the nobly born.

Field, Louise Frances Story (Mrs. E. M. Field). "Books from the Conquest to Caxton, 1066–1485," and two following chapters, in her *The child and his book*, p. 36–111. 2d ed. London: Wells Gardner, 1892; reprint: Detroit: Singing Tree, 1968.
The chapter "Manners makyth man" covers *Boke of curtasye, Stans puer, Boke of nurture, School of vertue.*

Gardiner, Dorothy Kempe. "From the Conquest to the Black Death," "The Black Death to the Reformation," in her *English girlhood at school*, p. 48–113. London: Oxford University Press, 1929.
Account of the treatise of Walter of Biblesworth, p. 63–64; of *The boke of the knight of La Tour-Landry*, p. 91–95.

Leach, Arthur Francis. The schools of medieval England. London: Methuen, 1915.
Partial contents: The schools from Lanfranc to Becket; University colleges, collegiate churches, and schools; The era of school statutes; The Black Death and Winchester college; The almonry or choristers' schools in the monasteries.

McMunn, William Robert. "The literacy of medieval children," in *Children's literature* 4: 36–41 (1975).
The author recapitulates material from his earlier "Children's literature in the Middle Ages" and concludes that "a large number of medieval children of all classes could read and enjoy the writings that were available to them."

Orme, Nicholas. English schools in the Middle Ages. London: Methuen, 1973; New York: Harper, 1973.

"Formal education at the lower levels . . . [in] English schools from the mid-12th to the mid-16th century." Chapters on the curriculum and on student life are of special interest. Maps. Photographs. Bibliography.

Parry, Albert William. Education in England in the Middle Ages. London: W. B. Clive, 1920; reprint: New York: AMS Press, 1975.
First published as a thesis approved for the degree of Doctor of Science in the University of London, 1920. An analysis of types of schools, their organization, curricula, and methods of teaching. Includes a record of the origins of the great public schools.

Plimpton, George Arthur. The education of Chaucer: illustrated from the schoolbooks in use in his time. London: Oxford University Press, 1935.
See especially the chapter "Elementary education," p. 18–92. Reproduction of pages from early primers, the *Donatus*, the *De proprietatibus rerum*, and other manuscripts.

Riggio, Milla B. "The schooling of the poet: Christian influences and Latin rhetoric in the early Middle Ages," *Children's literature* 4: 44–51 (1975).
Shows how the rhetorical schools of the third through sixth centuries exerted a stultifying influence on the style of writers and produced "a sodden mass of highly artificial, highly imitative poetry" in later centuries.

Stuart, Dorothy Margaret. "In feudal Europe," "In the later Middle Ages," in her *The girl through the ages*, p. 95–136. London: Harrap, 1933; reprint: Detroit: Singing Tree, 1969.
Reference to *How the good wife taught her daughter*, p. 133.

————. "The medieval boy," and "Thus Wykeham willed," in her *The boy through the ages*, p. 159–86. London: Harrap, 1926.
Refers to *The babees book, Urbanitatis*, and other rhymed treatises.

EDUCATIONAL AND INFORMATIONAL BOOKS

The Donatus, or Latin Grammar

De Vinne, Theodore Low. "The Donatus, or, boy's Latin grammar," in his *The invention of printing*, p. 254–63. New York: Francis Hart, 1876.
The *Donatus*, so-called for the Roman grammarian of the fourth century, served as a basic text in schools from early Anglo-Saxon times. The manuscript was superseded in the fifteenth century by the block book, and the reference gives

an interesting account of the elementary grammar in this form.

Donatus, Aelius. The *Ars minor* of Donatus, for one thousand years the leading textbook of grammar. (Studies in the social sciences, and history, no. 11). Translated from the Latin, with introductory sketch by Wayland Johnson Chase. Madison: University of Wisconsin Press, 1926.

Pays tribute to the influence of Donatus upon "(1) the learning of Latin, (2) the form that Latin grammars have taken in the modern age, and (3) the terminology of the grammars of various vernaculars of Western Europe, especially English." The text follows in Latin and in English.

Latin and French Readers, Primers, Vocabularies, and Books of General Information

Hazlitt, William Carew. "Vocabularies, glossaries and *nominalia*," in his *Schools, school-books, and schoolmasters*, p. 32–37. 2d ed. New York: Stechert, 1905.
Describes briefly the Latin-French treatise *De utensilibus* of Alexander Neckam, the works of Johannes de Garlandia, and the Anglo-Gallic *Phraseologia* of Walter de Biblesworth.

James, Montague Rhodes. "The bestiary in the university library," *Bulletin* (Aberdeen University Library) 6:529–31 (1928).
Brief account of the origin of the bestiary, as well as a description of the Aberdeen ms. Five full-page reproductions are inserted.

Littlehales, Henry, ed. The prymer; or lay folks' prayer book. (Early English Text Society publication no. 105) London: Kegan Paul, Trench, Trübner, 1895.
The text of the common medieval *Prayer-book* taken from a manuscript of about 1420–30. In the English of the period, when it was required reading for children as well as adults.

Physiologus. "Physiologus," in *The epic of the beast*, translated with an introduction by James Carlill, p. 153–250. London: Routledge, [1924?].
Allegorical animal tales presenting early religious conceptions. They were widely read in the Middle Ages and there are extant manuscripts in Latin, High German, Anglo-Saxon, Old French, and other languages.

Robinson, James Harvey. "Mediaeval natural science," in his *Readings in European history*, v. 1, p. 438–44. Boston: Ginn, 1904.
Extracts in modern English from *De naturis rerum, De proprietatibus rerum,* and other medieval treatises.

Wright, Thomas, comp. Anglo-Saxon and old English vocabularies, v. 1. 2d ed. London: Trübner, 1884.
Vocabularies from the twelfth to the fifteenth century, including a metrical vocabulary and a pictorial vocabulary. The introduction discusses the different types, their value and use, and outlines the topics treated by Alexander Neckam, Johannes de Garlandia, and Walter de Biblesworth.

Treatises on Manners and Morals

Book of the Knight of La Tour-Landry, compiled for the instruction of his daughters. London: Trübner for the Early English Text Society, 1868.
Introduction and notes by Thomas Wright. A fourteenth-century book written by a French nobleman for his daughters: ". . . a compilation of moral precepts, with advice on religious and social conduct, supported by stories illustrating how women should and should not behave." Originally translated into English and printed by Caxton at Westminster, 1484.

Caxton's book of curtesye, printed at Westminster about 1477–1478 A.D. (Early English Text Society publications extra ser. no. 3) Edited by F. J. Furnivall. London: Trübner, 1868.
This "lytill newe Instruccion" to a "lytle childe, to remove him from vice & make him follow virtue," was written by a disciple of Lydgate and is addressed to "Lytill John."

Furnivall, Frederick James, ed. The babees book, Aristotle's *A B C*, Urbanitatis, Stans peur ad mensam, The lytille childrenes lytil boke, The bokes of nurture of Hugh Rhodes and John Russell, Wynken de Worde's *Boke of keruynge*, The booke of demeanor, The boke of curtasye, Seager's *Schoole of vertue*, &c, &c, with some French and Latin poems on like subjects, and some forewords on education in early England. (Early English Text Society publications original ser. no. 32) London: Trübner, 1868.
Half title: "Manners and meals in olden time."

———. Early English meals and manners. . . . London: Kegan Paul, Trench, Trübner, 1904.
The poems and treatises included are reprinted, with one exception, from *The babees book, &c.,* published for the Early English Text Society in 1868. This edition does not include Hugh Rhodes's *Boke of nurture,* nor the French and Latin poems.

Rickert, Edith, ed. The babees book: medieval manners for the young: done into modern English from Dr. Furnivall's texts. (The new medieval library) London: Chatto, 1908.
Contents: Introduction; The babees book; The *A B C* of Aristotle; Urbanitatis; The little children's book; The young children's book; Stans puer ad mensam; How the good wife taught her daughter; How the wise man taught his son; John Russell's *Book of nurture*; The book of courtesy; Symon's *Lesson of wisdom for all manner children*; Hugh Rhodes's *Book of nurture*; Francis Seager's *School of virtue*; Richard Weste's *School of virtue,* the second part, or, *the young scholar's paradise*; Notes.

Symon. "Lesson of wisdom for all manner of children," in *A book of verse for children,* com-

piled by Edward Verall Lucas, p. 153–55. London: Chatto, 1897.
Includes 48 of the 102 lines with modern spelling: The closing lines of "The birched schoolboy" are given in the notes, p. 333.

Welsh, Charles. "Some notes on the history of books for children," *The Newbery House magazine* 3: 221–26, 341–42 (1890).
Notes on the books of good manners and courtesy. Includes an extract from *The babees book* and facsimile of one of the pages.

INDIVIDUAL WRITERS

Geoffrey Chaucer

Chaucer, Geoffrey. The Canterbury tales: special edition for young readers. New York: Golden Press, 1961.
Illustrated by Gustaf Tenggren. A selection of tales retold in modern prose, notable for the color and flavor of the illustrations. A page of Chaucer's "Prologue" is given in the style of an illuminated manuscript.

———. Chanticleer and the fox. Adapted and illustrated by Barbara Cooney. New York: Crowell, 1958.
The *Nun's priest's tale* in an adaptation from Robert Mayer Lumiansky's translation. A Caldecott Medal book.

———. A taste of Chaucer: selections from the Canterbury tales chosen and edited by Anne Malcolmson. New York: Harcourt, 1964.
An introduction gives a biographical sketch of Chaucer seen against the background of his times. The "Prologue" and nine of the Canterbury tales are in verse close to Chaucer's own text. Connecting passages by the editor explain characters and tales. Illustrated in black and white. Glossary and notes.

Farjeon, Eleanor. Tales from Chaucer: the Canterbury tales done into prose. New York: Jonathan Cape & Harrison Smith, 1930.
A graceful prose version, following closely the text of Chaucer's verse form. Illustrated in color. Intended for young readers.

BIOGRAPHY AND CRITICISM

Brewer, Derek. Chaucer in his time. London: Nelson, 1963.
England in the Middle Ages, its famous men and turbulent history as a background for the life and work of Chaucer. Illustrated in black and white with photographs and contemporary works of art.

Chute, Marchette. Geoffrey Chaucer of England. New York: Dutton, 1946.
An outstanding biography of Chaucer. An excerpt from the second chapter, "Geoffrey Chaucer goes to school," has been included in *Bibliophile in the nursery*, edited by William Targ (see "General Bibliography").

Jambeck, Thomas J., and Karen K. Jambeck. "Chaucer's *Treatise on the astrolabe*: a handbook for the medieval child," *Children's literature: the great excluded* 3:117–22 (1974).
Quotes liberally from a little-known work written by Chaucer for his son and showing in its style "not only Chaucer's awareness of his son as a child but also his concern for an appropriate pedagogical discipline."

Sir Thomas Malory

Malory, Sir Thomas. The boy's King Arthur. Edited for boys by Sidney Lanier. New York: Scribner, 1917.
A new edition of this classic with N. C. Wyeth's splendid illusrations omits "some minor passages and introductory matter—all the greater tales, those of Arthur, Launcelot, Tristram, Gareth, Galahad, Percival, and the Holy Grail, being retained."

———. King Arthur and his knights: selected tales. Edited and with an introduction and notes by Eugene Vinaver. Rev. and enl. ed. Boston: Houghton, 1968.
The introduction comments on Malory's sources and style. Critical studies on the tales are listed. *The tale of the death of King Arthur* has been added to those in the first edition, published in 1956.

———. Le morte d'Arthur. London: Scolar Press, 1976.
A limited facsimile edition of Caxton's 1485 edition with introduction by Paul Needham, published in association with the Pierpont Morgan Library. This is "the most famous version and the first in English prose of all the legends which have collected about King Arthur. It is the only true English epic."

———. ———. Edited by H. Oskar Sommer. London: D. Nutt, 1889–91.
Caxton's text, reprinted page for page, line for line. Also includes an essay on Malory's prose style by Andrew Lang.

———. ———. New York: Heritage, 1955.
Subtitle: "the story of King Arthur & of his noble knights of the round table written by Sir

Thomas Malory, first printed by William Caxton, now modernized, as to spelling and punctuation, by A. W. Pollard, illustrated with wood engravings by Robert Gibbings." A handsome edition with lavish decorations in black and white.

————. The works of Sir Thomas Malory. Edited by Eugene Vinaver. 3v. Oxford: Clarendon, 1947.
The text of the Winchester manuscript with scholarly annotation and glossary by the leading authority on Malory. Thoroughly indexed.

Pyle, Howard. The story of King Arthur and his knights. New York: Scribner, 1903.

————. The story of the champions of the Round Table. New York: Scribner, 1905.

————. The story of Sir Launcelot and his companions. New York: Scribner, 1907.

————. The story of the grail and the passing of Arthur. New York: Scribner, 1910.
Noteworthy retellings for children, enhanced with magnificent illustrations by the author.

BIOGRAPHY AND CRITICISM

Altick, Richard D. "The quest of the knight-prisoner," in his *Scholar adventurers,* p. 65–85. New York: Macmillan, 1950.
Traces for the general reader the search made by scholars to find "the real Malory."

Ashe, Geoffrey. King Arthur in fact and legend. Camden, N. J.: Nelson, 1971.

A history of Arthurian legends from the earliest records to modern versions. Discusses sites in the British Isles traditionally connected with Arthur. An appendix identifies characters in the legends. Generously illustrated. Useful background for a study of Malory.

Hibbert, Christopher. The search for Arthur. New York: American Heritage, 1969.
Arthurian legend compared with the known facts surrounding the early "commander in the battles." Richly illustrated with photographs, maps, and works of art, both ancient and modern. Bibliography and index.

Hicks, Edward. Sir Thomas Malory, his turbulent career: a biography. Cambridge, Mass.: Harvard University Press, 1928.
Based on research in the Public Record Office in London, this is the first biography of the man who wrote "the greatest of English prose romances."

Hodges, Margaret. Knight prisoner: the tale of Sir Thomas Malory and his King Arthur. New York: Farrar, 1976.
A biography, slightly fictionalized, connecting all the currently known facts of Malory's life with themes and characters of the *Morte d'Arthur.* Intended for the secondary-school reader.

Vinaver, Eugene. Malory. Oxford: Clarendon, 1929.
Using his previous detailed studies of the French manuscript sources, the author establishes a new view of Malory's achievement and puts together all the facts known at the time of Vinaver's writing.

Tudor Times, the Renaissance, and the Reformation

Printing, like the Renaissance, came late to England. It was probably between 1380 and 1420 that a primitive, secretly practiced form of printing emerged in Holland. Whether or not it was invented by Coster or others does not matter for, as Warren Chappell has said, "The quality of the early Dutch type making and printing still extant is so markedly inferior to Gutenberg's, that the possibility of a few years' priority is less important than Gutenberg's results."[1]

William Caxton, businessman and sometime diplomat, became aware of the art when he

1. *A short history of the printed word* (New York: Knopf, 1970), p. 5.

was living in Bruges. He learned to print in Cologne, and in 1473–74 produced in Bruges the first book printed in English. About 1477 he came back to England and began printing at his shop in Westminster. It is hard to categorize the types of books printed by Caxton: he printed religious books and texts, books of hours, traditional romance literature and ballads, a book of manners, Aesop's *Fables*, and various works of English and foreign authors that might not have survived without him. Of the 106 books printed by Caxton, he translated 28 to 30.

Most historians concur that Caxton tended to cater to the tastes of aristocrats (indeed, they were the very people who bought the books) and that he was only a mediocre writer and translator and an even more mediocre printer. Contemporary opinion sees him taking a place in history as a propagator of the English language and as a disseminator of English and foreign literature.

The impact of printing on all aspects of English life was, of course, incalculable. It has been said that the Reformation could not have occurred without the printed word, for such information reached much greater numbers of the reading public and with much greater speed than was ever possible with manuscripts. Henry VIII, in an attempt to make religion uniform, had primers and other religious texts printed and, in 1538, he ordered every parish priest to purchase the newly printed English Bible and place it in every parish church.

For this period, it is difficult, if not impossible, to separate religion from education. The monks who dominated education during feudal days had let it fall into the hands of the secular clergy. Henry, however, firmly believed that the domination of England included domination of the church, and that entailed domination of education. Under Henry, education became an instrument of political and religious policy. Influenced by Luther, Henry believed that the new Church should promote a new system of education controlled by secular power. Aside from dissolving the chantry foundation schools and setting up his own (the extent of the damage of this act is hotly disputed in the literature), Henry provided

his own set of texts as mentioned above. Edward and Elizabeth continued Henry's policies. Mary, of course, made many changes in the texts.

When we speak of children's "literature" at this point in history, we are confined in the main to religious books and texts. In the fifteenth and sixteenth centuries, three types of these texts existed: the hornbook, the A B C, and the primer.

The hornbook was the first "book" that the child touched or held. It was small, paddle shaped with a handle, and most often made from wood, although hornbooks were also fashioned in silver, copper, lead, ivory, and, sometimes, gingerbread. Called a hornbook because of the sheet of horn that protected the printed page from the child's hands, it contained an invariant text: the alphabet, often preceded by a cross (the Christ's cross), the syllabary, and the Lord's Prayer.

The child learned his letters in the hornbook, passed on to the A B C book, and then went on to the primer. The distinction between the A B C book and the primer is hazy: both had religious texts, but the primer had a longer set of prescribed prayers and was considered, says Anders, "a more advanced, and generally much larger book."[2] Bradshaw describes the A B C book as an "elementary book for children, containing the alphabet and the Lord's Prayer, with other elementary religious matters necessary for a child to know."[3] Both A B Cs and primers were published by public authority (the hornbook was licensed also) and were subject to modification "according to the temper of the time." From the Register of the Stationers' Company, which dates as far back as 1510, we know that thousands of these little A B C books were printed, although only four complete and several incomplete are extant. One is the *B A C* [sic] *bothe in Latyn and Englysshe*, printed in 1538 by Thomas Petyt, and another is William Powell's *ABC*, published

2. "The Elizabethan ABC with the catechism," *The library*, ser. 4, 16:34 (1935–36).
3. "On the ABC as the authorized schoolbook in the 16th century," in his *Collected papers* (Cambridge: Cambridge University Press, 1889), p. 334.

in 1547. A third extant A B C was printed by John Day in 1553.

The primer has medieval origins. Its source is the book of hours, originally intended as a private devotional to help the layman pray either at home or at church. Invariably, the primers' contents included specific prayers to be said at certain hours during the day. The earliest books of hours, intended for adults, of course did not contain alphabets. The first *Horae* for the use of children was printed in Paris in 1514 by an English publisher, and it contained, in addition to the prayers, an alphabet. Henry VIII authorized a whole set of primers for adults and children carrying his own religious message.

By the end of this period, grammar schools in towns and rural parishes provided for what we would call an elementary school education. A fairly universal curriculum was reached at this time, and most children at the age of five were entered in schools to learn "The A B C, Primer, Catechism and such other English books whereby they may attain to the perfect reading of the English tongue."[4] Although education was limited to those who could afford it (most schools charged tuition), it is noteworthy that, under Elizabeth, noblemen began for the first time to send their children to schools instead of educating them at home.

There is a fascinating influx in the sixteenth and seventeenth centuries of educational theories, spurred on by Erasmus and the other humanists who advocated such "radical" theories as placement of local schools under public control, humane treatment of students, and promotion of the "good society." John Colet's school at St. Paul's was directly influenced by Erasmus and the other humanists, and all the pedagogical writers of the next two centuries felt its impact.

The works of Coote, Hoole, Mulcaster, Hart, Brinsley, and finally, Comenius—whose great work for little children, *The orbis pictus,* is considered the first "picture book" published for children—dealt with teaching methods. Even those who wrote mainly for adults, produced texts for children to exemplify their methods. By the seventeenth century, the child had begun, under the guidance of these and other educators, to become an individual capable of learning and taking a place in the society at large.

Texts with alphabets and religious materials dominated children's literature. Aside from a few broadsides and ballads, Aesop's *Fables,* *Reynard the fox,* Chaucer's *Tales,* the *Morte d'Arthur* and a few romances, popular literature was still being handed down orally rather than in print. It would take another one hundred years for these romances to reach the masses in print. A true children's literature was yet to come.

4. Quoted in Kenneth Charlton, *Education in Renaissance England* (London: Routledge & Kegan Paul, 1965), p. 100.

OUTLINE

I. The introduction of printing into England
   A. William Caxton (1422?–91)
      1. Early life
      2. Literary pursuits and early translations
      3. Development of interest in printing
      4. Earliest printed works done in Bruges with Colard Mansion
      5. The Westminster press and its earliest works
      6. Character of publications
   B. Wynken de Worde (d.1534?)
   C. Other presses
   D. Examples of early printed books
      1. *Mirrour of the world* (Caxton)
      2. *Reynard the fox* (Caxton)
      3. *Fables of Aesop* (Caxton)
      4. *Book of curtesye* (Caxton)
      5. *Dives pragmaticus* (Thomas Newbery) (Other examples may be added if desired.)

II. The Renaissance
   A. Secularization of life
   B. New attitude toward learning and scholarship; influence of the humanists
   C. Taste for Hellenic culture
   D. Interest in educational theories
   E. Effect upon educational curricula and methods

III. Educational developments
   A. Primers and A B C books

1. Primers
   a) Origin and development
   b) Derivation of the name
   c) Content
      (1) Hours of the Blessed Virgin, litany, etc.; variations in manuscript and printed versions
      (2) Determined and limited by authority of the church and crown
      (3) Leaf giving alphabet and syllabarium
   d) Evolution in language and style
   e) Illustration
   f) Use
      (1) As devotional manuals for laypeople
      (2) As elementary reading books for children
   g) The forerunner
      (1) On the one hand, of *The book of common prayer*
      (2) On the other hand, of the modern school primer
2. A B C books
   a) Distinction between A B C books and primers
   b) Content
   c) Primary purpose and educational use
3. Henry VIII's reform primers and A B C books
   a) *A goodly primer* (1535)
   b) *The manual of prayers, or, the prymer in English* (1539)
   c) *King Henry's primer* (1545)
4. *The B A C bothe in Latyn & Englysshe* (1538?)
5. Unauthorized primers
   a) Content
   b) Influence in the spread of dissent
   c) Examples
B. Hornbooks
   1. Period of use
   2. Literary references
   3. Description
   4. Significance of the Christ cross
   5. Varieties
   6. Use
   7. Words conferred on the English language
      a) Crisscross
      b) Ampersand
C. Representative educators and their books
   1. The influence of Erasmus (1466?–1536)
   2. English classical scholars and educators
      a) Sir Thomas More (1478–1535)
      b) Thomas Linacre (1460?–1524)

   c) John Colet (1467?–1519) and St. Paul's School
   d) William Lily (1468?–1522) and his grammar
   e) Roger Ascham (1515–68) and his *Scholemaster*
3. Later educators; their theories and their books
   a) Richard Mulcaster (1530?–1611); Merchant Taylors' School, St. Paul's School
      (1) *Positions* (1581)
      (2) The first part of the *Elementarie, which entreateth chefelie of the right writing of our English tung* (1582)
   b) John Brinsley, fl. 1663
      (1) *Ludus literarius, or, the grammar schoole* (1612)
      (2) *Pueriles confabulatiunculae* (1617)
      (3) *The posing of the parts, or, a most plaine and easie way of examining the accidence and grammar by questions and answers* (1630)
      (4) *Corderius dialogues, translated grammatically* (1653)
         (a) Purpose and value
   c) Edmund Coote, fl. 1597; Free School, Bury St. Edmunds
      (1) *The English schoole-master* (1596)
         (a) Basic principles
         (b) Reasons for popularity
   d) Charles Hoole (1610–66?)
      (1) *New discovery of the old art of teaching school* (1660)
      (2) *Visible world* (1659)
         (a) Translation of the *Orbis sensualium pictus* of Comenius
      (3) *Common accidence*
         (a) Lily's grammar "ordered" in method more agreeable to children's capacities
      (4) Terence, *Plays*
         (a) Translated into English by Hoole
4. Comenius (1592–1670)
   a) The *great didactic*; its fundamental principles
   b) *Janua linguarum reserata* (Gate of tongues unlocked)
   c) *Orbis sensualium pictus* (1658)
      (1) Character and purpose
      (2) Translations
      (3) Reasons for popularity
      (4) Child's first picture book
   d) *Schola ludus*

WILLIAM CAXTON AND THE INTRODUCTION OF PRINTING

Adamson, John William. "The extent of literacy in England in the fifteenth and sixteenth centuries: notes and conjectures," *The library*, ser. 4, 10:163–93 (1929–30).

Adamson's article refutes the theory that literacy during the fifteenth and sixteenth centuries was limited primarily to nobility; this view had been widely held until Adamson published.

Altick, Richard. The English common reader: a social history of the mass reading public. Chicago: University of Chicago Press, 1957.

Chapter 1 deals with the period from Caxton's press to the eighteenth century. By 1477, Altick estimates, one-third to one-half of the people were literate, although books were the possession chiefly of the more prosperous members of the middle class in the sixteenth and seventeenth centuries.

Aurner, Nellie Slayton. Caxton, mirrour of fifteenth-century letters: a study of the literature of the first English press. London: P. Allan; Boston: Houghton, 1926; reprint: New York: Russell & Russell, 1965.

Caxton, as author and editor, seen among his patrons and helpers. Appendixes include bibliography on Caxton; a list of his publications in chronological order, giving various editions and reprints; and a reprint of Caxton's prologues, epilogues, and interpolations. Illustrated.

Bennett, H. S. English books and readers 1475 to 1557, being a study in the history of the book trade from Caxton to the incorporation of the Stationers' Company. Cambridge: Cambridge University Press, 1952.

"It endeavours to establish what was the cultural situation when Caxton began to print, . . . to consider Caxton's work as a bridge between the manuscript era and the age of print, . . . and this leads to a detailed study of the work of his immediate successors in stabilizing and developing the new craft."—introduction.

———. English books and readers 1558 to 1603, being a study of the book trade in the reign of Elizabeth I. Cambridge: Cambridge University Press, 1965.

The object of this book is "to make a survey of the whole of printed matter . . . in the hope of showing the ways in which the printer put at the disposal of readers a wealth of matter touching almost every side of their daily life, both intellectual and practical."—introduction.

———. English books and readers 1603–40, being a study of the history of the book trades in the reigns of James I and Charles I. Cambridge: Cambridge University Press, 1970.

This work endeavours "to examine the number and variety of books which were published between the death of Elizabeth I and 1640 . . ." and "to investigate the different kinds of audiences the books hoped to interest."—introduction.

Blades, Rowland Hill. "Who was Caxton?" *The library* 14, ser. 2, 4:113–43 (1903).

This short study takes most of its information from William Blades' biography of Caxton, but it differs in its view of Caxton's earlier printing efforts at Cologne and Bruges.

Blades, William. The biography and typography of William Caxton, England's first printer, 2d ed. London: Trübner, 1882.

Trübner originally published this work in 1861–63 in two volumes as *The life and typography of William Caxton, England's first printer, with evidence of his typographical connection with Colard Mansion, the printer at Bruges*. In 1876–77, this was published in a single volume, revised and reissued, as *The biography and typography of William Caxton*. The 1861–63, two-volume edition was reprinted in one volume by Muller (London) in 1971.

Most scholars concur with Deacon (below) that Blades' work is the "first serious biography of Caxton in modern times . . . . It . . . supplied the solid framework on which all subsequent students of Caxton have based their own researches." The book is flawed, limited, and sometimes based on flimsy evidence, but its achievements, according to Pollard (below), are (1) that it proved the typographical connection between Caxton and Colard Mansion, (2) that it traced the works in chronological sequence according to type used in printing, and (3) that it set a bibliographical model for future studies. The corrective to Blades, says Pollard, is Duff's *William Caxton* (below).

Blake, Norman Francis. Caxton and his world. London: André Deutsch, 1969.

This biographer discusses Caxton's life—setting out fact from fiction and critically evaluating his work as publisher, editor, and translator—from both fifteenth- and twentieth-century points of view. Appends a list of Caxton's publications arranged alphabetically.

———. England's first publisher. New York: Barnes & Noble for Harper & Row, 1976.

Written for the quincentenary of the beginning of printing in England. It is a difficult book dealing with the technical aspects of Caxton's book production, meant to complement Blake's earlier work (see above), which attempts to cover the literary aspects of Caxton's publications. Contains a chronological listing of Caxton's books.

Buhler, Curt Ferdinand. William Caxton and his critics: a critical reappraisal of Caxton's contributions to the enrichment of the English language. Syracuse, N.Y.: Syracuse University Press, 1960.

Discusses the variations of the English language that existed in the fifteenth century and concludes that the language became fixed through the works of Caxton and other English sixteenth-century printers.

Byles, A. T. P. "William Caxton as a man of letters," *The library,* ser. 4, 15: 1–25 (1934).

Deals primarily with the literary aspects of Caxton but characterizes him as a businessman and a manipulator of the reading public who catered especially to the tastes of his aristocratic readers.

Childs, Edmund Lunness. William Caxton: a portrait in a background. London: Northwood, 1976.

This competent biography deals with Caxton—the diplomat, the courtier, the printer—in London, Bruges, and Westminster. Beautifully illustrated.

Deacon, Richard. A biography of William Caxton: the first English editor, printer, merchant, and translator. London: Muller, 1976.

An excellent study of Caxton; summarizes many contemporary scholars' theories that he was a greater linguist and editor than printer or publisher: "in effect a schoolmaster for adults . . . and not a scholar."

Duff, Edward Gordon. Early English printing: a series of facsimiles of all the types used in England during the XVth century, with some of those used in the printing of English books abroad. London: Kegan Paul, Trench, Trübner, 1896.

Includes essays on Caxton, Wynken de Worde, and several others. Also has a series of facsimiles of all typefaces used in England in the fifteenth century. Plates 1–12 are reproductions from the books of Caxton and de Worde.

———. Fifteenth century English books: a bibliography of books and documents printed in England and of books for the English market printed abroad. London: Oxford University Press for the Bibliographical Society, 1917.

Precedes Pollard's *Short title catalogue* (below) as a compilation of all known English incunabula. Lists 431 items with short descriptions and collations. Also includes facsimiles.

———. William Caxton. Chicago: The Caxton Club, 1905.

Short essays on Caxton's life and work at Bruges and Westminster. Has a list of his books, with collations. Also includes facsimiles. An exquisite book.

Dunlap, Joseph R. William Caxton and William Morris: comparisons and contrasts. London: William Morris Society, 1964.

Compares the men, their printed works, and their similar and dissimilar views and tastes; concludes that "both Caxton and Morris were of the stature of men whom other men follow: Caxton influencing the direction the English language was to take; Morris showing the relevance of art to all aspects of life including book production."

Field, Louise Frances Story (Mrs. E. M. Field). "Some early printed books," in her *The child and his book*, p. 172–86. 2d ed. London: Wells Gardner, 1892; reprint: Detroit: Singing Tree, 1968.

Good analysis of *Myrrour of the worlde.*

Harnett, Cynthia. Caxton's challenge. Cleveland: World, 1960.

A charming, fictionalized account of Caxton and his workshop. Intended for children.

Jackson, Holbrook. William Caxton, the first English printer. Berkeley Heights, N.J.: Oriole, 1959.

Knight, Charles. William Caxton, the first English printer: a biography. London: Charles Knight, 1844.

———. The old printer and the modern press. London: John Murray, 1854.

The first book is an early fictionalized, and sometimes incorrect, account of Caxton and his press. It was revised and reissued in the second book as pt. 1. Pt. 2 is concerned with the publishing industry from Caxton's time to the nineteenth century, with special emphasis on cheap, popular literature.

McMurtrie, Douglas C. "The first printing in English," in his *The book: the story of printing and bookmaking*, p. 216–29. New York: Oxford University Press, 1943.

An excellent summary with a fine bibliography.

Meigs, Cornelia. "The multiplying leaves," in Meigs et al., *A critical history of children's literature*, p. 22–32. Rev. ed. New York: Macmillan, 1969.

Discusses Caxton's books read by children.

Moran, James. Wynken de Worde. London: The Wynken de Worde Society, 1960.

Nickels, Sylvie. Caxton and the early printers: a Jackdaw. London: Jonathan Cape, 1968.

A jackdaw is a series of facsimiles on a given subject used as a teaching aid with high school students. This one includes facsimiles of Caxton's work, illustrations of a printing press, etc.

Painter, George Duncan. William Caxton: a quincentenary biography of England's first printer. London: Chatto, 1976.

For bibliophiles and researchers.

Plomer, Henry Robert. A short history of English printing, 1476–1900. 2d ed. London: Kegan Paul, Trench, Trübner, 1915.
The first seven chapters cover Caxton, de Worde, Thomas Berthelet, and John Day.

———. William Caxton (1424–1491). Boston: Small, Maynard, 1925.
This early biography is strongly biased by Plomer's contention that Caxton was motivated by "an overmastering love for his country," his piety, and his strong will.

———. Wynken de Worde and his contemporaries from the death of Caxton to 1535. London: Grattis, 1925.

Pollard, Alfred W. "Printing in England, 1476–1580," in his *Fine books,* p. 204–23. London: Methuen, 1912.
Discusses Caxton and other early English printers.

——— and **G. R. Redgrave.** A short title catalogue of books printed in England, Scotland, and Ireland and of English books printed abroad, 1475–1640. 3v. London: Oxford University Press for the Bibliographical Society, 1926; reprint 1963.
Includes abridged entries of all "English" books printed up to 1640 and in the collections of the British Museum, the Bodleian Library, the Cambridge University Library, and the Henry E. Huntington Library. Essential for research in English incunabula.

Putnam, George Haven. "William Caxton, and the introduction of printing into England, 1412–1492," in his *Books and their makers during the Middle Ages,* v. 2, p. 101–48. New York: Putnam, 1896.
Indicates "the influences from which Caxton derived his interest in literary undertakings, and the sources from which he secured his training as a printer, with some reference to the character of his publishing undertakings." Includes a list, with notes, of the works identified as Caxton's.

Ricci, Seymour de. A census of Caxtons. Oxford: Oxford University Press for the Bibliographical Society, 1909.
Useful in this connection chiefly for its table of contents listing the books printed at Bruges and at Westminster. Frontispiece from an old engraving and facsimiles of pages showing typefaces used.

Roberts, W. Wright. "William Caxton, writer and critic," *The bulletin of the John Rylands Library* 14: 410–22 (1930).
Concludes that he was not a scholar, but a "shrewd and dogged disseminator" who "gave them Chaucer and Malory."

Smith, George. William de Machlina: the primer on vellum printed by him in London about 1484 . . . with facsimiles of the wood cuts. London: Ellis, 1929.
An essay about this printer who was contemporary with Caxton, with facsimiles of the existing leaves of the primer. A beautiful, rare book.

Stuart, Dorothy Margaret. "William Caxton: mercer, translator and master printer," *History today* 10: 256–65 (April, 1960).
An excellent, concise, unbiased summary in this English journal, presents Caxton and his press in historical perspective.

Thwaite, Mary F. From primer to pleasure in reading. 2d ed. London: Library Assn., 1972.
The chapters entitled "Printing" and "Romance and traditional literature" deal with the influence on printing of what became children's literature and also discuss the romance literature published by Caxton and the Robin Hood ballads printed by de Worde.

Wells, James. William Caxton. Chicago: Caxton Club, 1960.
A long essay primarily about the life and times of William Caxton, "with emphasis on the times." Wells places Caxton historically as a person who lived in a period of significant changes, i.e., the end of church monopoly, the end of serfdom, the depletion of half the population by Black Death, the establishment of English as a legal language, the rise of the middle class.

Winship, George Parker. William Caxton: a paper read at a meeting of the Club of Odd Volumes in Boston, Massachusetts, in January, 1908. London: T. J. Cobden-Sanderson at the Doves Press, 1909.

———. William Caxton and his work: a paper read at a meeting of the Club of Odd Volumes in Boston, Massachusetts, in January 1908, with a letter from the author. Berkeley: Book Arts Club, University of California, 1937.
The first book, now a collector's item, has been reprinted with a letter from Winship restating his views, which concluded, "Not only did he print the first English book and introduce the art of printing into England, but he also did as much as anyone has ever done to establish the English language as a vehicle for literary expression."

EARLY PRINTED BOOKS

Books Printed by Caxton

AESOP

Aesopus. The book of the subtyl historye and fables of Esope which were translated out of Frenshe in to Englysshe by William Caxton. Westminster: W. Caxton, 1484.
This original version is available on microfilm. Many of the books listed in the *Short title catalogue* have been microfilmed.

Caxton's Aesop. Edited with an introduction and notes by R. T. Lenaghan. Cambridge, Mass.: Harvard University Press, 1967.
The scholarly introduction includes discussions of the Aesopic tales in the Middle Ages, of editions of Aesop that preceded Caxton's, and a comparison of Caxton's prose. Has a glossary and several woodcut facsimiles. Prepared from microfilm copies of Caxton's 1484 editions in the Royal Library at Windsor, the British Museum, and the Bodleian Library.

The fables of Aesop, as first printed by William Caxton in 1484, with those of Alfonso, and Poggio, now again edited and induced [sic] by Joseph Jacobs, 2v. London: D. Nutt, 1889; reprint: New York: Burt Franklin, 1970.
An early scholarly analysis and comparison of Caxton's *Aesop* with earlier versions.

BOOKS ON MANNERS

Book of courtesye. Westminster: W. Caxton, 1477–78 [?].

The book of good manners. Westminster: W. Caxton, 1487.
Available on microfilm. Caxton printed it in 1487, Pynson in 1494, and de Worde in 1507. All on film.

Caxton's book of curtesye, printed at Westminster about 1477–78. Edited by F. J. Furnivall. (Early English Text Society publications: extra ser. no. 3) London: Trübner, 1868.
Same as *Book of courtesye* above. This reprinting includes "two MSS. copies of the same treatise."

REYNARD THE FOX

The history of Reynard the fox. Westminster: W. Caxton, 1481.
Caxton's first printing was his own translation of the Dutch text of 1479.

———. (English Scholars' literature of old and modern works. v. 1) Edited by Edward Arber. London: the editor, 1878.
This is an accurate reproduction of Caxton's 1481 text. Inadequate introduction.

The history of Reynard the fox, translated and printed by William Caxton in 1481. Edited with an introduction and notes by Donald B. Sands. Cambridge, Mass.: Harvard University Press, 1960.
An edition of the first printing of Caxton's translation of the middle Dutch version. In modernized spelling and punctuation. The long introduction summarizes "all the best and all the modern studies devoted to Reynard as the hero of a comic beast epic." Includes a complete bibliography of "1) all modern printings of Reynard and Reynaert together with pertinent studies, 2) major editions and translations of continental beast epics, and 3) studies of Caxton as a literary figure."

The history of Reynard the fox, his friends and his enemies, his crimes, hairbreadth escapes and few triumphs: a metrical version of the old English translation with glossorial notes in verse by F. S. Ellis. London: D. Nutt, 1894.
"Upon the edition printed by Caxton in 1481 and worthily reproduced at the Kelmscott Press in 1892, this present version is founded."–p. viii. "Devices" by W. Crane.

Other Early Books

Fox, John (*or* Foxe, John). Actes and monuments of these latter and perillous dayes, touching matters of the Church. . . . London: John Day, 1563.
The complete manuscript is available on microfilm. The book was published under this title until 1761, when it was published under the title, *Book of martyrs, containing an account of the sufferings and death of the Protestants in the reign of Queen Mary the First . . . Originally written by Mr. John Fox and now revised and corrected with a . . . preface by . . . Mr. Madan* (London: John Fuller, 1761).

Hakluyt, Richard. The principall navigations, voiages and discoveries of the English nation, made by sea or over land . . . within the compasse of these 1500 yeeres . . . London: G. Bishop and R. Newberie, 1589.

———. Principal navigations of the English nation. 8v. New York: Dutton (Everyman), 1907–9.
Introduction by John Masefield. Cornelia Meigs considers this the first adventure story for children.

Mirrour of the world. Westminster: W. Caxton, 1481.
Available on microfilm.

———. Edited by Oliver H. Prior. (Early English Text Society publications, extra ser. no. 110) London: Kegan Paul, Trench, Trübner, 1913; reprint: London: Oxford University Press, 1966.

Translated by Caxton in 1480 from a French prose version of the *Image du monde,* a compilation from various Latin sources. It is the first work in English to have been illustrated.

Newbery, Thomas. A booke in Englysh metre, of the great marchaunt man called Dives Pragmaticus, very preaty for children to rede, wherby they may the better and more readyer rede and wryte wares and implementes, in this world contayned. London: A. Lucy, 1563.

———. ———. in *Fugitive tracts written in verse which illustrate the condition of religious and political feeling in England and the state of society there during two centuries.* 1st ser. London: privately printed, 1875.
Preface by Henry Huth.

———. ———. Manchester: The University Press, 1910.

Reproduced in facsimile from the copy in the John Rylands Library. Introduction by P. E. Newbery and remarks on the vocabulary and dialect, with a glossary by H. C. Wyld.

Plutarch. The children's Plutarch: tales of the Greeks, by F. J. Gould. New York: Harper, 1910.

———. The children's Plutarch: tales of the Romans, by F. J. Gould. New York: Harper, 1910.

———. The lives of the noble Grecians and Romanes, compared together by . . . Plutarke of Chaeronea. Translated from the French by T. North. London: T. Vautroullier & J. Wight, 1579.

———. Plutarch's lives. Translated by Sir Thomas North. Edited by W. H. D. Rouse. 10v. London: Dent, 1898–99.

EDUCATION

Adamson, John William. Pioneers of modern education, 1600–1700. London: Cambridge University Press, 1905.
Partial contents: The new philosophy; The school-room in the early seventeenth century; Bacon and Comenius; The great didactic; The new pedagogy in London and in Germany; A successful schoolmaster: Hoole.

Baynes, Thomas Spencer. "What Shakespeare learnt at school," in his *Shakespeare studies,* p. 147–213. New ed. London: Longmans, 1896.
Interesting discussion of the probable course of instruction in Stratford grammar school during the years when Shakespeare was a pupil.

Bedford, Jessie (*pseud.* Elizabeth Godfrey). "Concerning pedagogues," "Educational theories," in her *English children in the olden times,* p. 135–50, 215–25. London: Methuen, 1907.
References to the *Catechism* of Dean Colet, Lily's *Grammar,* and the *Orbis pictus* of Comenius.

———. "Some lesson-books," "Public Schools," in her *Home life under the Stuarts, 1603–1649,* p. 31–65. New York: Dutton, 1904.
Refers to hornbooks, *The English schole-master* of Edmund Coote, Lily's *Grammar,* and other books. Popular in treatment.

Brown, John Howard. Elizabethan schooldays: an account of the English grammar schools in the second half of the sixteenth century. Oxford: Basil Blackwell, 1933.
Chapter 4, p. 68–88, deals with the curriculum. There are nine illustrations, including a page of Lily's *Grammar* reproduced from the edition of 1574.

Byrne, Muriel St. Clare. "Childhood and education," in her *Elizabethan life in town and country,* p. 176–97. 2d. ed. rev. London: Methuen, 1934.
What was taught and how it was taught. Makes note of the educational ideas of Mulcaster and Brinsley and quotes from original sources.

Cambridge history of English literature. v. 3, Renascence and reformation. Edited by A. W. Ward and A. R. Waller. New York: Putnam, 1909; reprint: Cambridge: Cambridge University Press, 1967.
Chapter 1, p. 1–27, "Englishmen and the classical renascence," covers Erasmus, Linacre, Colet, Lily, More and Elyot; chapter 3, p. 54–62, "Dissolution of the religious houses," discusses the new educational theories; and chapter 19, p. 475–99, "English universities, schools and scholarship in the sixteenth century," is concerned with Ascham and Mulcaster.

———. v. 7, Cavalier and Puritan. Edited by A. W. Ward and A. R. Waller. Cambridge: Cambridge University Press, 1911.
Chapter 14, "English grammar schools," p. 368–88, notes the transition from the scholastic to the humanistic theory of education and includes mention of St. Paul's, Christ's Hospital, and the Merchant Taylors' School.

Charlton, Kenneth. Education in Renaissance England. London: Routledge & Kegan Paul, 1965.
Argues against Leach's theory (see below) that education was dealt a death blow when Henry VIII dissolved the chantry schools and concludes that "the period was . . . one in which it was

realized that education could serve the welfare of the community just as much as the political and religious interests of a sovereign."

"Dalyaunce," in *Come hither: a collection of rhymes and poems for the young of all ages.* Compiled by Walter John de la Mare. London: Constable, 1923.
Fragment of an old play, *Mundus et infans,* written about 1500 and printed by Wynken de Worde in 1522. "The lines need a slow reading to get the run and lilt of them. . . . But the boy, Dalyaunce, if one takes a little pains, will come gradually out of them as clear to the eye as if you had met him in the street to-day, on his way to 'schole' for yet another 'docking.' "

Davies, William J. Frank. Teaching reading in early England. London: Pitman, 1973.
Chapter 3, p. 32–57, summarizes the types of schools at this time—song schools, guild and chantry foundations, grammar schools. Chapter 5, p. 89–122, is concerned with the A B C, the hornbook, psalter, primer, and books of pedagogy for teachers of reading.

Davis, William Stearns. "Concerning the pains of schooling," in his *Life in Elizabethan days,* p. 107–20. New York: Harper, 1930.
The chapter indicated describes school life in terms of the concrete, with mention of the hornbook and of Lily's *Grammar.* Other chapters of special interest are, "Concerning books, authors, and printing" and "Concerning the politer learning."

Field, Louise Frances Story (Mrs. E. M. Field). "Educational reform, 1510–1649," in her *The child and his book,* p. 136–72. London: Wells Gardner, 1892; reprint: Detroit: Singing Tree, 1968.
Deals with the influence of Erasmus on the English educators from Colet to Milton.

Gardiner, Dorothy Kempe. English girlhood at school. London: Oxford University Press, 1929.
Chapters 8 through 12 deal with the Renaissance and various aspects of sixteenth- and seventeenth-century education of girls.

Hazlitt, William Carew. "Schools and school-books in the Tudor period," in his *Schools, schoolbooks and schoolmasters,* p. 101–49. New York: Stechert, 1905.
Among the topics treated are the influence of Erasmus and Sir Thomas More, the foundation of St. Paul's by Colet, and Lily's *Grammar.*

Laurie, Simon Somerville. Studies in the history of educational opinion from the Renaissance. Cambridge: Cambridge University Press, 1903.
"Writing concisely, yet adequately for his purpose [the author] passes in review the opinions and methods of representative exponents of edu-

cation from the Renaissance onwards, with much valuable criticism by the way."—*Contemporary review,* 1903. Includes chapters on Ascham and Comenius.

Leach, Arthur Francis. Educational charters and documents, 598 to 1909. Cambridge: Cambridge University Press, 1911.
To be used for source material illustrating educational development. Includes "The re-foundation of Canterbury Cathedral and grammar school, 1541," p. 452–71; "Statutes of Westminster School, 1560," p. 496–525; "Hoole's grammar school curriculum, 1637–60," p. 530–34. See also the "Introduction," p. xlii–lii.

————. English schools at the Reformation, 1546–8. London: Constable, 1896; reprint: New York: Russell & Russell, 1968.
Although the hypothesis set forth by this classic text on education in England—that Henry VIII and Edward VI destroyed monastic education by the Chantry Acts—is now disputed, this work still contains excellent descriptions of the different types of schools in existence during the sixteenth century.

————. "The fifteenth century and humanism," "Henry VIII and the schools," in his *The schools of medieval England,* p. 235–332. London: Methuen, 1915.

Moberly, Charles Edward. "The revival of classical learning, 1390–1509," in his *The early Tudors,* p. 79–101. New York: Scribner, 1921.
Account of the founding of St. Paul's School.

Nelson, William, ed. A fifteenth century school book. Oxford: Clarendon, 1956.
Subtitle: "From a manuscript in the British Museum (MS. Arundel 249)." This is an excellent example of Tudor *vulgaria,* so named because it consisted of "vulgar" or colloquial matter. Used by teachers of Latin grammar for students to translate from English to Latin. This material contains insights into school life in the fifteenth century.

Plimpton, George Arthur. The education of Shakespeare, illustrated from the school books in use in his time. London: Oxford University Press, 1933.
Contents: Teachers in Shakespeare's day; Courses of study in Shakespeare's day; The textbooks of Shakespeare's day. The book describes, and is illustrated from, books in the author's own collection (now at Columbia University). Included is a primer Plimpton dates to the fourteenth century.

Quick, Robert Hebert. Essays on education reformers. New York: Appleton, 1890.
Authorized edition as rewritten in 1890. Partial contents: Effects of the Renascence; Renascence tendencies; Ascham; Mulcaster; Comenius.

Rowse, Alfred Leslie. "Education and the social order," in his *The England of Elizabeth: the structure of society,* p. 489–538. New York: Macmillan, 1951.
A concise summary of the types of schools and prevailing educational theories in Elizabethan England.

Simon, Joan. Education and society in Tudor England. Cambridge: Cambridge University Press, 1966.
This work argues against Leach's theory, and, in fact, maintains that state intervention in English education began at the Reformation and not during the nineteenth century.

Stuart, Dorothy Margaret. "In Tudor England," "In the seventeenth century," in her *The girl through the ages,* p. 157–91. London: Harrap, 1933; reprint: Detroit: Singing Tree, 1969.

———. "The Renaissance boy," "A child of the Chapel Royal," in her *The boy through the ages,* p. 187–208. London: Harrap, 1926.
Dean Colet's school is discussed.

Timbs, John. "Progress of education," in his *School-days of eminent men,* p. 48–109. London: Lockwood, 1864.
Education of each sovereign, foundation of important schools, educational customs. See also note on primers and hornbooks, p. 140–44, and "anecdote biographies" of Caxton and Sir Thomas More, p. 150–52.

Watson, Foster. The English grammar schools to 1660: their curriculum and practice. Cambridge: Cambridge University Press, 1908; reprint: London: Frank Cass, 1968.
This classic text in English education traces the "development of the teaching in the English Grammar schools from the time of the Invention of Printing up to 1660. It is a history of the practice of the schools . . . in distinction from the history of the theories of educational reformers."—preface. Of special interest are the chapters on medieval elementary instruction, the elementary schools in 1547–1660, and the hornbook, primer, and A B C.

———, ed. English writers on education, 1480–1630: a source book. Gainesville, Fla.: Scholars' Facsimiles and Reprints, 1967.
Originally published as *Notices of some early English writers on education* by the United States Government Printing Office in U.S. Department of the Interior annual reports for 1901–4, under the aegis of the U.S. Commission of Education.
Introduction by Robert O. Pepper. A fascinating compendium of early educators' writings, with brief biographies and explanatory notes, done in chronological order. Includes Erasmus, Elyot, Vives, Lily, Ascham, More, Coote, and others.

———. The old grammar schools. Cambridge: Cambridge University Press, 1916.
Discusses such topics as the founders, church control, religious observances, curriculum, conditions of entrance, school hours.

Primers and A B C Books

Anders, H. "The Elizabethan A B C with the catechism," *The library,* ser. 4, 16:32–48 (1935–36).
Discusses the relationship of the A B C book to the hornbook and the primer. Includes facsimiles of several sixteenth-century primers. Includes as a "Biographical note" a representative list of "historically important" A B Cs and primers.

Birchenough, Edwyn. "The prymer in English," *The library,* ser. 4, 18:177–94 (1937).
Discusses mainly the derivation of the primer and its use for religious instruction with adults. Birchenough traces the alterations made in the text during the reigns of Henry VIII and Elizabeth I.

Bradshaw, Henry. "On the A B C as an authorized schoolbook in the 16th century," in his *Collected papers,* p. 333–40. Cambridge: Cambridge University Press, 1889.
Gives briefly the results of researches into the history of the A B C.

Burton, Edward, ed. Three primers put forth in the reign of Henry VIII. Oxford: Oxford University Press, 1834.
Contents: *A goodly primer,* 1535; *The manual of prayers, or the prymer in English,* 1539; *King Henry's primer,* 1545.

Butterworth, Charles C. "Early primers for the use of children," *Papers* (The Bibliographical Society of America) 43:374–82 (October–December, 1949).
Historical account of how the primer (originally used by adults) and the A B C converged into a teaching tool for children. Discusses specifically primers in use in the sixteenth century in Latin, Latin and English, and English, with emphasis on Petyt's 1538 primer.

———. The English primers (1529–1545): their publication and connection with the English Bible and the Reformation of England. Philadelphia: University of Pennsylvania Press, 1953.
A scholarly study of the development of the primer from the book of hours to Henry VIII's authorized primers. Includes a discussion of primers with A B Cs. Contains a complete chronological listing of primers and books of hours, as well as bibliographies of materials on the history of primers and related subjects. This is the standard authority on the English primer.

Field, Louise Frances Story (Mrs. E. M. Field). "A B C," in her *The child and his book*, p. 112–85. 2d ed. London: Wells Gardner, 1892; reprint: Detroit: Singing Tree, 1968.
An excellent summary of the history of the A B C, primer, and hornbook as teaching tools.

Ford, Paul Leicester. "Introduction," in his *The New-England primer: a history of its origin and development*, p. 4–12. New York: Dodd, 1897.
Treats of the unauthorized primers and A B C books and of their effect in the spread of dissent.

———. ———. in his *The New England primer: a reprint of the earliest known edition*, p. 8–16. New York: Dodd, 1899.

Krapp, George Philip. "Bible and prayer book," in his *The rise of English literary prose*, p. 256–70. London: Oxford University Press, 1915.
Traces the development of the English prayer book from the primer or lay folks' service book. The content of the early primers is indicated.

Littlehales, Henry, ed. English fragments from Latin medieval servicebooks, with two coloured facsimiles from medieval prymers. (Early English Text Society publications, extra ser. no. 90) London: Kegan Paul, Trench, Trübner, 1903.

———. The prymer, or, lay folks' prayer book (with several facsimiles). (Early English Text Society publications, no. 105, 109) 2 pts. in 1v. London: Kegan Paul, Trench, Trübner, 1895–97.
"On the origin of the prymer," by Edmund Bishop, is included in pt. 2.

Shuckburgh, E. S., ed. The B A C [*sic*], bothe in the Latyn & Englysshe, being a facsimile reprint of the earliest extant English reading book. London: Elliot Stock, 1889.
Believed to have been published about 1538. The original is preserved in Emmanuel College, Cambridge, England. The preface, p. v–xii, includes a royal injunction indicating the use of such A B C books as the one reproduced. Introduction by E. S. Shuckburgh.

Siegenthaler, David, ed. The primer set furth by the kinge's maiestie & his clergie (1545). Delmar, N.Y.: Scholars' Facsimiles and Reprints, 1974.
A facsimile of the authorized primer of Henry VIII with an introduction.

Steinfirst, Susan. "The origins and development of the ABC book in English from the Middle Ages through the 19th century." Ph.D. diss. University of Pittsburgh, 1976.
Traces the evolution of the form and content of the ABC "book."

Hornbooks

Chargin, Madeleine. "The hornbook in America," *Horn book magazine* 16:280–86, 357–66 (July–August, September–October, 1940).
Although this book gives some history, its main thrust is on the hornbook brought to America by the Puritans.

Folmsbee, Beulah. A little history of the hornbook. Boston: Horn Book, 1942.
Brief but detailed description of the methods for making hornbooks and battledores, and a list of titles using the word *hornbook*. Bibliography.

New York Public Library. The hornbook. New York: New York Public Library, 1927.
Describes a collection of thirty-three hornbooks given by James C. McGuire to the New York Public Library. Foreword by McGuire. The list of hornbooks was prepared by Paul D. Bailey. The frames are described with considerable detail so as to present the variations in general design and ornamentation. The printed sheets have been separated from the frames and dispersed or worn out, and so they are not described. Ten of the hornbooks are pictured.

Plimpton, George A. Marks of merit, together with an article on the hornbook and [its] use in America. Boston: Ginn, 1916.
Reprinted from an address before the American Antiquarian Society. Using his own collection of twenty-four hornbooks (now in the Butler Library, Columbia University), Plimpton exemplifies his history. Emphasis is on hornbooks brought to America.

Shaffer, Ellen. "The horn book: an invitation to learning," *Horn book magazine* 47:85–91 (February, 1971).
An excellent summary of the hornbook's history and uses. Splendidly illustrated with early engravings of people using hornbooks and with pictures of some hornbooks from the collection of the Free Library of Philadelphia.

Shepard, Leslie. The history of the horn book: a bibliographic essay. London: Rampant Lion for the Broadsheet King, 1977.

Tuer, Andrew W. The history of the hornbook, with three hundred illustrations. 2v. London: Leadenhall; New York: Scribner, 1896; 1v., London: Leadenhall; New York: Scribner, 1897; reprint: 1v., New York: Benjamin Blom, 1968.
The original, now a collector's item, contains a total of seven facsimile hornbooks and battledores. The reprint, a facsimile edition, has none. This invaluable, though at times confusing, study of the printed alphabet is, indeed, as Elva Smith pointed out in her original text, "a treasure house of information."

INDIVIDUAL EDUCATORS AND THEIR WORKS

Roger Ascham

Ascham, Roger. The scholemaster, or, plain and perfite way of teachyng children, to understand, write and speake, the Latin tong . . . . London: John Daye, 1570.

————. The schoolmaster (1570). Edited by Lawrence V. Ryan. Ithaca, N.Y.: Cornell University Press for the Folger Shakespeare Library, 1967.

BIOGRAPHY AND CRITICISM

Ryan, Lawrence V. Roger Ascham. Stanford, Calif.: Stanford University Press, 1963.
Ryan characterized Ascham not as a brilliant thinker, but as a popularizer of widely held Renaissance ideals and educational theories. His *Scholemaster* influenced education for a hundred years. Chapter 11, p. 250–86, analyzes the text in historical perspective. Notes and index. No bibliography.

Tannenbaum, Samuel Aaron, and Dorothy Tannenbaum. Roger Ascham: a concise bibliography. New York: privately printed, 1946.

John Brinsley

Brinsley, John. A consolation for our grammar schooles, or, a faithfull incouragement for laying of a sure foundation of all good learninge in our schooles. London: Richard Field for Thomas Man, 1622.

————. ————. New York: Scholars' Facsimiles and Reprints, 1943.
Introduction and bibliographical notes by Thomas Clark Pollock. A reprint of a copy in the New York Public Library.

————. Ludus literarius, or, the grammar schoole: shewing how to proceede from the first entrance into learning to the highest perfection required in the grammar schooles. London: for Thomas Man, 1612.

————. ————. Edited with an introduction and bibliographical notes by E. T. Campagnac. Liverpool: The University Press, 1917; London: Constable, 1917.

John Colet and St. Paul's School

BIOGRAPHY AND CRITICISM

Dark, Sidney. Five deans: John Colet, John Donne, Jonathan Swift, Arthur Penrhyn Stanley, William Ralph Inge. New York: Harcourt, 1928.
The chapter on Colet, p. 15–54, considers him as a typical representative of the English Church in the years immediately before the Reformation and points out his relation to the movements and reaction of his time.

Knight, Samuel. The life of Dr. John Colet, dean of St. Paul's in the reigns of K. Henry VII and K. Henry VIII, and founder of St. Paul's School. New ed. Oxford: Clarendon, 1823.
Subtitle: "with an appendix, containing some account of the masters and more eminent scholars of that foundation and several original papers relating the said life."
Articles on the founding of St. Paul's, the educational views of Colet and Erasmus, and accounts of the books prepared for the pupils. Material on endowments, statutes, and inscriptions also included.

Lupton, Joseph Hirst. A life of John Colet, D.D., dean of St. Paul's and founder of St. Paul's School, with an appendix of some of his English writings. London: G. Bell, 1887.

Marriott, Sir John Arthur Ransome. The life of John Colet. London: Methuen, 1933.
Calling Colet a "zealous reformer," Marriott outlines his life and concludes that the founding of St. Paul's School was his crowning achievement. Includes an appendix on the modern school (1933) and a good, basic bibliography. Illustrated.

Seebohm, Frederic. The Oxford reformers: John Colet, Erasmus, and Thomas More, being a history of their fellow-work. 3d ed., rev. and enlarged. London: Longmans, 1887.
First printed in 1867. Chapter 9, p. 154–77, is entitled "The foundation of St. Paul's School." The statutes are appended.

Comenius

Comenius, Johan Amos (*also* Komenský, Jan Amos). The great didactic, now for the first time Englished with introductions, biographical and historical by M. W. Keatinge. London: Black, 1896.
Same as *Opera didactica omnia*, listed below. A later edition by Keatinge has the title *The great didactic . . . with biographical, historical and critical introductions*. 2 pts. in 2v. London: Black, 1907–10.

————. Opera didactica omnia. Amsterdam, 1657.

————. Orbis pictus. Syracuse, N.Y.: C. W. Bardeen, 1887; reprint: 1967; facsimile ed.: Detroit: Singing Tree, 1968.
Plates and Latin text from the edition of 1658. Text for English translation from 1727 edition.

————. Orbis sensualium pictus. Nuremberg, 1658.

————. Orbis sensualium pictus . . . a work newly written by the author in Latine and High Dutch,

. . . & translated into English by Charles Hoole. London: 1659.

In Latin and English. No publisher is given for 1659. Abel Swall is given for a 1689 edition. Hoole's translation is entitled *Comenius's Visible world or a picture and nomenclature of all the chief things that are in the world*.

———. ———. Sydney, Australia: Sydney University Press, 1960.

Facsimile of the third London edition (1672).

———. Porta linguarum reserata et aperta . . . (The gates of tongues unlocked and opened). Translated by T. Horn. London: M. Sparkes and T. Slater, 1631.

This was also published under the title *Janua linguarum reserata* in London in 1643 (no publisher given).

———. The school of infancy: an essay on the education of youth during their first six years, to which is prefixed a sketch of the life of the author. Translated by Daniel Benham. London: W. Mallalieu, 1858.

This was originally written in Czech. Comenius translated it into German and published it in 1633. Approximately twenty years later, it was published in Latin.

———. ———. Edited with an introduction by Ernest M. Eller. Chapel Hill, N.C.: University of North Carolina Press, 1956.

An excellent introduction clearly explains Comenius's educational "plans" for children through the age of six. Written as a textbook and guide for mothers of young children, the work explains Comenius's basic principles of education.

———. Selections. Paris: UNESCO, 1957.

Issued in commemoration of the third centenary of the publication of *Opera didactica omnia*, 1657–1957. Introduction by Jean Piaget, who states that "the real problem is to find in Comenius' writing . . . not what is comparable with modern trends, to the neglect of the rest, but what makes the vital unity of the thinking of the great Czech specialist in theory and practice; and to compare this with what we know and want today." Selections from *The great didactic* and others included.

BIOGRAPHY AND CRITICISM

Davidson, E. W. "*Orbis pictus*: Comenius' contributions to children's literature." Ph.D. diss., Catholic University of America, 1958.

Keatinge, M. W. Comenius. New York: McGraw-Hill, 1931.

Contents: Life of Comenius and his educational view; *The great didactic*; Aims in education; Pages from Comenius's textbooks.

Kožik, František. John Amos Comenius, 1592–1670. Translated by Sylvia R. Fink-Myhre. Prague: SNTL, 1958.

A biography with many illustrations of the places where Comenius lived and worked. Written to celebrate the 300th anniversary of the first edition of the *Orbis pictus*.

Laurie, Simon Somerville. John Amos Comenius, bishop of the Moravians: his life and educational works. Boston: W. Small, 1885.

Discusses his pansophic and educational theories and concludes, "His real merits in language lie in the introduction of the principle of graduated reading-books, in the simplification of Latin grammar, in his founding instruction in foreign tongues on the vernacular, and in his insisting on method in instruction." Includes a bibliography of Comenius's educational works.

Munroe, James Phinney. "Comenius: the revolt against feudalism," in his *The educational ideal*, p. 68–91. Boston: Heath, 1895.

Brings out, briefly and concisely, the principles and methods of Comenius and indicates his contribution to the educational ideal.

Rood, Wilhelmus. Comenius and the low countries: some aspects of life and work of a Czech exile in the seventeenth century. Amsterdam: Van Gendt; New York: Abner Schram, 1970.

Concerns Comenius's plans for the reform of educational system and his pansophic views. Bibliography on p. 257–68.

Sadler, John Edward. Comenius. London: Collier-Macmillan, 1969.

An excellent, concise work dealing primarily with Comenius's educational theories. Chapters entitled "Curriculum," "Methods of teaching," and "Instruments of education" are particularly useful. A bibliography of works by and about Comenius is appended.

———. J. A. Comenius and the concept of universal education. New York: Barnes & Noble, 1966.

Touches on Comenius's concepts concerning books and schools for the very young child. The section on textbooks for the elementary school child is good. Bibliography.

Spinka, Matthew. John Amos Comenius: that incomparable Moravian. Chicago: University of Chicago Press, 1943.

Uses Comenius's autobiographical notes to present "the entire scope of Comenius' interest and activity—pedagogical, ecumenical, and pansophic." Includes a bibliography.

Young, Robert Fitzgibbon, ed. Comenius in England. Selected, translated and edited with an introduction, and tables of dates by R. F. Young. London: Oxford University Press, 1932.

Subtitle: "the visit of Jan Amose Komenský

(Comenius), the Czech philosopher and educationist, to London in 1641–42; its bearing on the origins of the Royal Society, on the development of
the encyclopaedia, on the development of the
Indians of New England and Virginia, as described
in contemporary documents."

Edmund Coote

Coote, Edmund. The English scholemaister,
teaching all his schollars, of what age soever the
most easie short & perfect order of distinct read-
inge & true writinge our English tonge. London:
R. Jackson & R. Dexter, 1596.
For a fascinating account of the publishing record of this book, see " 'The English Schoolmaster,'
Dexter v. Burby, 1602" by W. W. Greg, *The library,* 4th ser. 23:90–92 (September–December,
1942).

———. ———. Menston, England: Scolar Press, 1968.
A facsimile with introduction.

Erasmus

Erasmus, Desiderius. "The child's piety," in his
The colloquies, translated by N. Bailey, edited,
with notes, by E. Johnson, v. 1, p. 86–99. London: Turner, 1878.
Dialogue between Erasmus and Gaspar, a boy,
presumably of St. Paul's as he refers to "that
honestest of men, John Colet . . . who instructed
me when I was young in these Precepts."

———. The education of a Christian prince. Translated by Lester K. Born. New York: Columbia
University Press, 1936; reprint: New York: Octagon, 1965.
First published as *Institutio principis Christiani,*
in 1516, by Froben. This is the first English translation. Includes "an introduction on Erasmus and
on ancient and medieval political thought."

BIOGRAPHY AND CRITICISM

Woodward, William Harrison. Desiderius Erasmus concerning the aim and method of education. Cambridge: Cambridge University Press,
1904; reprint: (Classics in education no. 19)
New York: Teachers' College Press, Columbia
University, 1964.
Includes excerpts from several of his educational treatises. With biographical notes and a
summary of his educational theories. Reprint has
an introduction by Craig R. Thompson.

Charles Hoole

Hoole, Charles. A new discovery of the old art of
teaching schoole, in four small treatises. London:
J. T. for Andrew Crook, 1660.

———. ———. Edited with bibliographical index by
E. T. Campagnac. Liverpool: The University
Press, 1913.

———. ———. Menston, England: Scolar Press, 1969.
Facsimile.

———, trans. J. A. Comenius's *Visible world,* or,
a nomenclature and pictures of all the chief
things that are in the world, translated by
Charles Hoole for the use of young Latin scholars. London, 1659. No publisher given for first
edition. 12th ed. London: S. Leacroft, 1777.

William Lily

Lily, William. A shorte introduction of grammar,
generally to be used in the Kynges Maiesties
dominions, for the bryngynge up of all those that
entende to atteyne the knowledge of the Latine
tongue. London: Thomas Wolf, 1548.
This is the English part of a two-part grammar
written by Lily and Colet, the second half of
which was in Latin. Originally entitled *An introduction of the eyght partes of speche, and the
construction of the same . . .*, it first appeared in
1542. There is a copy in the British Museum. It
was the authorized grammar.

———. ———. New York: Scholars' Facsimiles and
Reprints, 1945.
Introduction by Vincent J. Flynn. This is a
facsimile of the Folger Shakespeare Library copy
published by Berthelet at London in 1567.

Richard Mulcaster

Mulcaster, Richard. The first part of the elementarie which entreateth chefelie of the right writing of our English tung. London: T. Vautrollier,
1582.

———. ———. Menston, England: Scolar Press, 1970.
Facsimile edition.

———. Mulcaster's elementarie. Edited with an introduction by E. T. Campagnac. Oxford: Clarendon, 1925.
Facsimile edition.

———. Positions wherein those primitive circumstances be examined, which are necessarie for
the training up of children, either for skill in
their booke, or health in their bodie, etc. London T. Vautrollier, 1581.

———. ———. reprint: London: Harrison, for Henry
Bernard and R. H. Quick, 1887.
Facsimile edition.

Puritan Literature:
The Seventeenth Century

The Puritans gained parliamentary power and social influence in England at the beginning of the seventeenth century. They sought a true reformation in the Church, demanding purity in the worship of God—hence the name Puritan. By the time of Elizabeth's death in 1603, Puritans represented the largest group in the Church of England.

Puritanism has been defined as Calvinism in the extreme. At its core was an intense religiosity. "Nothing," says William Sloane, "in our own diffuse civilization holds quite the pivotal position, the centrality, which religion held in seventeenth century England and America. To man's relationship with God all the other circumstances of his life were peripheral."[1]

Children figured predominantly in Puritan theory. Treated as miniature adults, they were not excluded because of age from the depravity of man that resulted from the Fall. Children were by nature evil and in need of salvation, just like adults. Besides being evil, Puritans were considered to have been born ignorant but with the capacity both for attaining knowledge and for overcoming evil. Evil and ignorance could be overcome by education.

The Puritans ascribed extraordinary power to education. They believed it was the duty of government to bring free public education to all children. In England, nationally established and supported education was seriously considered but was put aside during the civil war. After the war, despite persecution, the Puritans persisted in bringing education to tens of thousands of children who otherwise would have been denied it.

Education began with the hornbook, the authorized A B C, and the primer. To these was added the catechism, a summary of Christian principles in question-and-answer format. It was used to test the learner in Christian doctrine. The catechism, also authorized, was a popular work, and Maunsell's *Catalogue of books* (1595) lists no fewer than sixty different editions.

The most important religious text was, of course, the Bible, which embodied for the Puritan the whole of revealed truth. It was incorporated as a teaching tool in 1604. The Bible formed the core of Puritan theology, and urgency to teach children and adults to read can be traced to the Puritans' desire that the Bible be read universally.

While children were taught to read at schools, the center of learning began to shift to the home as the Bible became the center of family religious life. It was at home that all members of the family read aloud from the Bible, morning and night, in family prayer sessions.

Aside from educational books, William Sloane has identified 261 items published for children from 1559 to 1710. He has put them in three categories: (1) traditional or folk materials, (2) books of good manners, and (3) religious books; the first group was "condemned," the second "esteemed," and the third "extolled." Folktales were not allowed into Puritan households at all and, with some exceptions, did not appear in print until the eighteenth century.

There were enormous numbers of religious books prepared for children. These books were meant to inspire good conduct and teach children to live and die as noble Christians. All literature for children was tinged by the concept of the precocious, pious, impossible child who knew all there was to know at the age of four or five and then died young, being too perfect for life on this earth. An extreme example of this type of religious book is James Janeway's *A token for children: being an exact account of the conversion, holy and exemplary lives, and joyful deaths of several young children* (1671?). Janeway's book and other martyrologies were based on John Fox's *Book*

1. *Children's books in England and America in the 17th century* (New York: King's Press, Columbia University Press, 1955), p. 12.

of martyrs, originally published under the title *Actes and monuments . . . touching matters of the Church* (1559?). Though not written for children, it was considered a most desirable book for them and it was widely read by young people.

Another "desirable" book of the seventeenth century was Abraham Chear's *A looking glass for children* (1672), which contained the justly famous lines:

> When by spectators I am told,
>   What beauty doth adorn me,
> Or in a glass when I behold
>   How secretly God did form me.
> Hath God such comeliness bestowed
>   And on me made to dwell,
> 'Tis pity, such a pretty maid
>   As I should go to Hell.

The first part of John Bunyan's *Pilgrim's progress* appeared in 1678. Though not written or intended for children (Elva Smith did not include it in her *History*), it belongs to them today "by right of annexation." Children, des-

perate for reading material, merely discarded the religion and took the story. By the later seventeenth and early eighteenth centuries, almost every literate child knew it.

Bunyan's only work written for children—known in the seventeenth century as *A book for boys and girls, or, country rhimes for children,* and in the eighteenth as *Divine emblems, or, temporal things spiritualized*—is a typical Puritan book meant for children's amusement and not-so-gentle instruction. Heavily moralistic and religious, it is considered a dreary affair by most historians today.

Another typical Puritan work, *A little book for little children* (12th ed., 1702) by Thomas White, describes lives of martyred children and ends with the rhetorical question, "Now you have read all these stories of holy Children, do you long to be like them? Why should you not love God as well and as much as they?"

Aside from exemplary biographies, the Bible, and Bible histories, the child was also permitted to read sermons and books of courtesy.

PURITANS IN AMERICA

The Puritans who came to America brought with them a religious life that was predominantly somber, with chief emphasis on the emotion of fear. The doctrine of God's wrath was central to New England preaching. Within a very rigidly defined framework of theology, children were considered merely smaller editions of the adults. And it is now believed that this intense theology had a decidedly adverse effect on the children.

Despite their emotional abuse of children for the sake of religion, the American Puritans, like the English, believed in a strong family and in education. Parents were obliged by law to educate their children at home and at school. In 1647, Massachusetts provided for the establishment of free reading schools, because it was "one chief project of that old deluder, Satan, to keep men from knowledge of the Scripture."[1] In most New England states, every town of

100 households or more was required by law to provide grammar school education for all children.

As in England, learning to read the Bible was the goal of Puritan schools. And like his European counterpart, the colonial child learned his A B Cs at home, usually from a hornbook—many of which were brought to the colonies with their crosses carefully blotted out. Catechisms were published here and used by American children. John Cotton's *Spiritual milk for Boston babes. In either England. Drawn out of the breasts of both testaments, for their souls nourishment but may be of like use for any children* was published first in England in 1646 and was incorporated into the *New England primer.*

1. Massachusetts Laws of 1648. Quoted in Edmund Morgan, *The Puritan Family* (rev. ed.; New York: Harper, 1966), p. 88.

After the catechism, the Puritan child moved on to the *New England primer* which, next to the Bible, was the most widely used book in New England. Although its origins are obscure, most historians assign its authorship to Benjamin Harris, an English Puritan printer who fled England and settled in Boston. In 1679, Harris had written a tract called *The Protestant tutor*, which contained several elements of the *New England primer*. An entry in the registers of the Stationers' Company in England shows us that one Master John Gaine in 1683 entered a title *The New England primer or milk for babes*. However, an entry in the register only indicated *intent* to print. No copy exists earlier than a Boston copy of 1727, but newspapers advertised it as early as 1686.

The *New England primer* was basically a book of religious instruction. It contained an invariant body of material, including several alphabets, one of which was the famous "Rhyming alphabet" that begins with the couplet, "In Adam's fall,/We sinned all"; the story (with picture) of John Rogers, who was burned at the stake while his wife and ten children looked on; a catechism (either John Cotton's or the *Westminster shorter catechism*); and the *Dialogue between Christ, youth, and the devil*, a poem about tempted youth. Later editions had more secularized material and included several poems, including Isaac Watts's "Cradle hymn," which begins, "Hush, my dear, lie still and slumber,/Holy angels guard thy bed"; and the poem that begins, "Now I lay me down to sleep. . . ."

Aside from the *Primer* used as a text, American Puritan children read Janeway's *Token for children . . .*, to which Cotton Mather added a section entitled, *A token for the children of New England, or, some examples of children, in whom the fear of God was remarkably budding before they died; in several parts of New England; preserved and published for the encouragement of piety in other children*, which, Alice Morse Earle has pointed out, "out-Janeways Janeway."

The most widely read book in America, as in England, was the Bible, and Puritan children read through it and memorized long portions of it. In the eighteenth century, several abridgments were made especially for children.

Seventeenth-century Puritan children's literature was unique. No other literature has ever rivaled it for singleness of purpose and concept. Gloomy, heavily doctrinaire, dreary, filled with "painful stories of morbid conditions of childhood"[2] and multitudinous martyrdoms, it was a literature created solely to redeem children's souls from the consequences of Adam's fall.

2. Mrs. E. M. Field, *The child and his book* 2d ed. (London: Wells Gardner, 1892), p. 199.

OUTLINE

d) Method of teaching the moral lesson
    (1) Verses to illustrate: "On the rising of the sun," "Meditations upon an egg," "Upon the frog," "Upon a penny loaf"
e) Value considered as poetry
    (1) Verses to illustrate: "Upon the swallow," "Of the child with the bird at the bush"
f) Comparison with other poetry of Bunyan
g) Importance of book
C. The New England primer
  1. Use of primers for religious instruction and elementary lessons in reading
  2. Benjamin Harris; his life and character
  3. *The Protestant tutor*
  4. Early editions of the *New England primer*
  5. Distinctive features
    a) Alphabet; significant omission of the Christ cross
    b) Syllabarium
    c) Lord's Prayer and Apostle's Creed

d) Alphabet of lessons for youth
e) Rhymed alphabet
    (1) Variations in different editions
f) John Rogers's exhortation; its history
g) Catechism
    (1) Westminster Assembly's shorter catechism
    (2) John Cotton's *Spiritual milk for babes*
  6. Other features and minor variations in different editions
  7. Influence in American life
D. Early Bible abridgments for children
  1. The importance of the Bible to the Puritans
  2. Several early editions
    a) *The Holy Bible in verse* by Benjamin Harris (1698)
      (1) Publishing history in England and America
    b) *A curious hieroglyphic Bible . . . for the amusement of youth* (1788)
      (1) Printed by Isaiah Thomas

THE PURITAN SPIRIT

Bedford, Jessie (*pseud.* Elizabeth Godfrey). Home life under the Stuarts, 1603–1649. New York: Dutton, 1903.
A description of seventeenth-century life as drawn from letters, diaries, and references in contemporary writings.

Dowden, Edward. "Puritanism and English literature," "John Bunyan," *Contemporary review,* July, 1899; reprint: in his *Puritan and Anglican studies in literature,* p. 1–34, 232–78. London: Kegan Paul, Trench, Trübner, 1900.
The first article presents very fairly the dominant ideas of Puritanism and shows how they affected the literature of the seventeenth century.

Earle, Alice Morse. Child life in colonial days. New York and London: Macmillan, 1899; reprint: Folcroft, Pa.: Folcroft, 1974.
Articles on aspects of babyhood and childhood, dress, school life, discipline, precocity, toys, games, religious training, etc. Thorough.

———. Customs and fashions in old New England. New York: Scribner, 1893; reprint: Williamstown, Mass.: Corner House, 1969; paperback reprint: Rutland, Vt.: C. E. Tuttle, 1971.
Chapter entitled "Childlife," p. 1–36, is invaluable for the student of this period.

———. Home life in colonial days. New York and London: Macmillan, 1898; reprint: New York: Macmillan, 1969.
Reprint entitled *Home and child life in colonial days,* edited by Shirley Glubock. A fascinating account, with photographs, of various aspects of colonial life.

Fleming, Sandford. Children and Puritanism: the place of children in the life and thought of the New England churches, 1620–1847. (Yale studies in religious education, v. 8) New Haven, Conn.: Yale University Press, 1933.
Chapter 6 deals with the conditions and doctrines responsible for the attitude of the churches toward children, and chapter 8 with children's books.

Furlong, Monica. "The Puritans," in her *Puritan's progress,* p. 23–46. New York: Coward, [1975].
An excellent synopsis of Puritan theory with a brief discussion of some Puritan writings.

Hanscom, Elizabeth Deering, ed. "Of the training and education of youth, both around the family altar and in institutions of learning," in her *The heart of the Puritan,* p. 83–118. New York: Macmillan, 1917.
Selections from letters and journals.

Kiefer, Monica. American children through their books, 1700–1835. Philadelphia: University of Pennsylvania Press, 1948.
This study attempts "to trace the changing status of the American child in the colonial and early national periods as it is revealed in juvenile literature."—introduction. Although the study begins in 1700, several Puritan religious and colonial secular works are discussed.

Lenski, Lois. Puritan adventure. New York and Philadelphia: Lippincott, 1944.
A fictitious but well-researched account of life in New England in the mid-seventeenth century. Intended for children.

Lodge, Henry Cabot. "A Puritan Pepys," in his *Studies in history,* p. 21–84. New York: Houghton, 1884.
A review of the Sewall diary. Some of the extracts and comments are useful in illustrating the Puritan character and spirit, particularly p. 34–37, 43–47, 52–55. For the attitude toward children and children's literature, see p. 31–43.

Miller, Perry. The New England mind: from colony to province. Cambridge, Mass.: Harvard University Press, 1953.
Classic, scholarly history of seventeenth-century New England.

——. The New England mind: the seventeenth century. Cambridge, Mass.: Harvard University Press, 1939; reprint, 1954.
Covers the period to 1660.

——. The Puritans. New York: American Book, 1938.
This classic text of the Puritan period includes a general introduction ("The Puritan way of life" and "The Puritans as literary artists") and "Readings from the Puritans." Of special interest are the section of readings on education, p. 695–727, and Miller's prefatory remarks.

Morgan, Edmund Sears. The Puritan family: essays on religion and domestic relations in seventeenth-century New England. Boston: Trustees of the Public Library, 1944; rev. and expanded ed.: New York: Harper Torchbooks, 1966.
Originally appeared in *More books* (Boston Public Library, 1942–43). A scholarly study of the Puritan family. Of interest especially are the chapters "Puritanism and society," "Parents and children," "The education of a saint," "The family in the social order," and "Puritan tribalism."

Scudder, Horace Elisha. "In English literature and art," in his *Childhood in literature and art,* p. 128–33. New York: Houghton, 1894.
Brings out the Puritan attitude toward children.

Slater, Peter Gregg. Children in the New England mind: in death and life. Hamden, Conn.: Shoe String, 1977.
Based on his dissertation entitled "Views of children and of child-rearing during the early national period," University of California, Berkeley, 1970.

Storrs, Richard Salter. "The Puritan spirit," in his *Orations and addresses,* p. 409–56. Boston: Pilgrim Press, 1901.
An oration delivered before the Congregational Club, Boston, in 1889. Considers the Puritan spirit in its broader aspects and points out its essential elements.

Stuart, Dorothy Margaret. "In the seventeenth century," in her *The girl through the ages,* p. 178–97. London: Harrap, 1933; reprint: Detroit: Singing Tree, 1969.
Educational opportunities for girls and women in Puritan England are outlined.

Trevelyan, George Macaulay. "Puritanism," in his *England under the Stuarts,* p. 57–71 (*History of England,* edited by Sir Charles Oman, v. 5) 15th ed. London: Methuen, 1930.
This book as a whole gives a good background for the political and social life of the period. The chapter named indicates the influence of Puritanism on the general community and on literature.

Wendell, Barrett. "The earlier Puritanism," "The later Puritanism," in his *The temper of the seventeenth century in English literature,* p. 207–66. New York: Scribner, 1904.
Aims to give an understanding of the Puritan character and the Puritan spirit.

——. "Some neglected characteristics of the New England Puritans," *Annual report* (American Historical Association) 1891, 1892, p. 243–53; *Harvard Monthly,* April, 1892; also in his *Stelligeri, and other essays concerning America,* p. 45–62. New York: Scribner, 1893.
Discusses the Puritan doctrine of election and the special traits that characterized the religious leaders, with special reference to Cotton Mather.

LITERATURE FOR CHILDREN

Altick, Richard. "From Caxton to the eighteenth century," in his *The English common reader.* Chicago: University of Chicago Press, 1957; Phoenix Books, 1963.
Describes Protestantism in general and Puritanism in particular as a "book religion." A brief description of secular literature and a definition of the reading public are given.

Bedford, Jessie (*pseud.* Elizabeth Godfrey). "Under a cloud," in her *English children in the olden time,* p. 197–214. London: Methuen, 1907.
Among the books noted are *A new book for children* by George Fox "the younger" and Janeway's *Token for children.*

Darton, Frederick Joseph Harvey. "Hell-fire tales," "Exemplary compilations," in *The Cambridge history of English literature*, v. 11, p. 409–13. New York: Putnam, 1914.
Describes briefly Bunyan's *Book for boys and girls*, Thomas White's *Little book for little children*, and another book with the same title, the authorship of which is uncertain.

———. "The Puritans: 'good godly books,' " in his *Children's books in England: five centuries of social life*, p. 53–69. 2d ed. Cambridge: Cambridge University Press, 1958.
For James Janeway, see p. 54–58; John Bunyan, p. 65–68. Contains complete bibliographical information on Bunyan's *Divine emblems*.

Eames, Wilberforce. Early New England catechisms: a bibliographical account of some catechisms published before the year 1800, for use in New England. Worcester, Mass.: Charles Hamilton, 1898; reprint: Detroit: Singing Tree, 1969.
Read, in part, before the American Antiquarian Society, at its annual meeting in Worcester, October 21, 1897. Catechisms were forerunners of the *New England primer*. This scholarly bibliography includes an introduction and chronological listing of catechisms by town, as each New England town had its own catechisms printed. Concord, Salem, and Boston were the first, dating from 1646.

Earle, Alice Morse. "Books and book-makers," in her *Customs and fashions in old New England*, p. 257–88. New York: Scribner, 1893.
Printing in the colonies. Especially Stephen Daye's *Bay psalm book*, other psalm books, and some secular works.

———. "Religious books," in her *Childlife in colonial days*, p. 248–63. New York: Macmillan, 1899; reprint: Folcroft, Pa.: Folcroft, 1974.
Includes discussion of the works of Bunyan, Fox, Cotton Mather, Janeway, Jonathan Edwards, Michael Wigglesworth, Thomas White, and others. Also considers anonymous Puritan works as well as Bible abridgments and various lives of Jesus.

Field, Louise Frances Story (Mrs. E. M. Field). "The fear of the Lord and of the broomstick," in her *The child and his book*, p. 186–214. 2d ed. London: Wells Gardner, 1892; reprint: Detroit: Singing Tree, 1968.
Indicates the "new aspect of childhood" in the Puritan period and describes many of the books provided for children, including Thomas White's *Little book for little children* and Bunyan's *Book for boys and girls*.

Gottlieb, Gerald. Early children's books and their illustration. New York: Pierpont Morgan Library; Boston: Godine, 1975.

This extensively illustrated catalog has scholarly descriptions of early readers, primers, religious books, and emblem books.

Halsey, Rosalie Vrylina. "Introductory," in her *Forgotten books of the American nursery*, p. 3–18. Boston: Goodspeed, 1911; reprint: Detroit: Singing Tree, 1969.
Brief account of the literature thought suitable for children in early Puritan days, with special reference to John Cotton's *Milk for babes*, Cotton Mather's *Token for the children of New England*, and his *Good lessons for children*.

Jacobus, Lee A. "Milton's *Comus* as children's literature," *Children's literature: the great excluded* 2:67–72 (1973).
The masque, first performed in 1634, is described as "drawing on archetypes and becoming itself a model, if not type, which influenced literature for children in later ages."

Meigs, Cornelia. "Compass of the world," "Three tales of travel," in Meigs et al., *A critical history of children's literature*, p. 32–40, 43–52. Rev. ed. New York: Macmillan, 1969.
These chapters deal with John Fox, *Pilgrim's progress*, and Puritan literature.

Muir, Percy. English children's books, 1600–1900. New York: Praeger, [1954]; London: Batsford, [1969].
The section on the Calvinists is a good synopsis of Puritan theory and writing. Discusses in depth Bunyan, Janeway, Chear, and Crouch.

Repplier, Agnes. "Little pharisees in fiction," in her *Varia*, p. 85–108. New York: Scribner, 1897.
Reprinted from *Scribner's magazine*, December, 1896.

Rosenbach, Abraham S. Wolf. Early American children's books. Portland, Me.: Southworth Press, 1933; reprint: New York: Dover, 1971.
The earliest book in Rosenbach's collection is dated 1682 (*The rule of the new-creature*); however, he lists several early eighteenth-century Puritan religious works, including a Janeway *Token* (one of two extant copies), John Cotton's *Spiritual milk for Boston babes*, and Keach's *War with the devil*. Rosenbach's introduction to his catalog is fascinating.

Sinanoglou, Leah. "For of such is the kingdom of heaven: childhood in 17th century English literature." Ph.D. diss., Columbia University, 1971.
Traces the Puritan concern for "real" children through several seventeenth-century Puritan writings for adults.

Sloane, William. Children's books in England and America in the 17th century: a history and checklist, together with *The young Christian's library*, the first printed catalogue of books for children. New York: King's Press, Columbia University Press, 1955.

This is the primary scholarly work on children's literature in the seventeenth century. Sloane identifies 261 works published for children between 1559 and 1710, mostly in England. Appended is a chronological, annotated list of the books cited.

Welch, d'Alté A. A bibliography of American children's books printed prior to 1821. Worcester, Mass.: American Antiquarian Society and Barre Publishers, 1972.

Originally published in six parts in *Proceedings* of the American Antiquarian Society. A–C, April, 1963; D–G, October, 1963; H, October, 1964; I–O, October, 1965; P–R, April, 1967; S–Z, October, 1967. Although the bibliography lists no seventeenth-century works, it does cover several Puritan books printed in the first quarter of the eighteenth century. An excellent, scholarly introduction, "A chronological history of American children's books," is included.

Welsh, Charles. "The early history of children's books in New England," *New England magazine* 26, new ser. 20:147–60 (1899).

Good résumé.

Pious Memories

Chear, Abraham (*pseud.* P. H.). A looking-glass for children. London: R. Boulten, 1673.

Subtitle: "being a narrative of God's gracious dealings with some little children; recollected by H. Jessey in his lifetime. Together, with sundry seasonable lessons and instructions to youth, calling them early to remember their Creator: written by A. Chear. The second edition, corrected and amended. To which is added many other poems . . . by A. Chear. All now faithfully gathered together for the benefit of young and old." Chear added some poems to the basic work of the martyred Henry Jessey (died 1663). The oft-quoted verse of Chear's that was included contained the lines: "'Tis pity, such a pretty maid/As I should go to Hell."

Crouch, Nathaniel (*pseud.* Robert Burton). Winter-evening entertainments. 6th ed. London: A. Bettesworth & C. Hitch, 1737.

——. The young man's calling. London: T. James, 1678.

——. Youth's divine pastime. 3d ed. London: published for Nathaniel Crouch, 1691[?].

Crouch wrote under the initials R. B. and used the pseudonyms Richard and Robert Burton. Percy Muir said of him, "His contributions are not remarkable by late standards. . . . Nevertheless, he forms a landmark, however tawdry and disreputable, in the evolution of children's reading, and,

without exaggerating his importance, his significance is evident."—*English children's books, 1600–1900,* p. 33.

Fox, John (*or* Foxe, John). Actes and monuments . . . touching matters of the Church. London: John Day, 1563.

Known as *The book of martyrs.* "After the Bible itself, no book so profoundly influenced early Protestant sentiment as the *Book of Martyrs.*"—James Miller Dodds, *English prose.*

——. Fox's book of martyrs. Edited by William Byron Forbush. Philadelphia: Winston, 1926.

Reprinted because "to keep in print this Protestant classic has seemed to the present publishers an important duty. . . . The special contribution of this work to Protestant thought has been to keep alive spiritual freedom."—preface.

Janeway, James. A token for children; being an exact account of the conversion, holy and exemplary lives, and joyful deaths of several young children. London: Dorman Newman, 1672.

This book met with great favor and was many times reprinted.

——. A token for children. The second part. Being a farther account . . . of several other young children, not published in the first part. London: Dorman Newman, 1672.

——. ——. Being an exact account of the conversion, holy and exemplary lives and joyful deaths of several young children . . . To which is now added, a token for the children of New England . . . Preserved and published for the encouragement of piety in other children. Boston: Nicholas Boone, 1700.

This is the first American edition. It contains both parts of Janeway's *Token* with the supplementary part that was written by Cotton Mather. Virginia Haviland, in speaking of a later American edition, says "an account of youthful piety, in tune with the doctrine of original sin, this is the first of the few narratives that were available to 18th century children in America and undoubtedly the most widely read children's book in the Puritan age."—*Yankee Doodle's literary sampler . . .,* p. 11.

——. A token for children. (Classics of Children's literature, 1621–1932) New York: Garland, 1977.

A facsimile edition of the first two parts. With a preface by Robert Miner.

White, Thomas. A little book for little children. 12th ed. London, 1702.

A "ghastly compilation" (Percy Muir) that warns children against ballads and foolish books.

BIOGRAPHY AND CRITICISM

Mozley, James. John Foxe and his book. New York: Macmillan, 1940; London: Society for Promoting Christian Knowledge, 1941.

A long, scholarly biography written "to reassign him greatness." Includes four chapters from the *Book of martyrs,* two portraits of Fox, and a list of his minor writings.

Editions and Abridgments of the Bible

Harris, Benjamin. The holy Bible in verse. Boston: John Allen, 1717.
The first Bible designed for children was written in England in 1698 by Benjamin Harris. The Pierpont Morgan Library owns the only copy extant of the 1724 John Allen edition. It is pictured on p. 85 of the Morgan Library catalog entitled, *Early children's books and their illustration.*

———. ———. Edited and reproduced by Wilbur Macey Stone. Worcester, Mass.: American Antiquarian Society, 1935.
Seven facsimile pages.

Stone, Wilbur Macey. The thumb Bible of John Taylor. Brookline, Mass.: The LXIVMOS, 1928.
Early British and American editions and translations of "one of the outstanding classics of juvenile literature." Nine facsimile pages.

Winship, George Parker. The first American Bible. Boston: D. B. Updike at the Merrymount Press for Elias E. Goodspeed, 1929.
Subtitle: "a leaf from a copy of the Bible translated into the Indian language by John Eliot and printed at Cambridge in New England in the year 1663. With an account of the translator and his labors and of the two printers who produced the book. Limited edition of 150 copies.
In his introduction, Winship says that, although the first American published work was the *Bay psalm book,* this Bible is the first "real American work."

INDIVIDUAL WRITERS

John Bunyan

Bunyan, John. A book for boys and girls, or, country rhimes for children. London: printed for N. P. [Nathaniel Ponder], 1686.
Gottlieb calls this the first emblem book for children, and the only book Bunyan wrote directly for children. When first published in 1686, it had the title given above. The first edition is of "formidable rarity," the British Museum and Harvard having the only two copies extant. The first edition was not illustrated, nor was any before 1707. In 1724, a shortened version was published under the title, *Divine emblems, or, temporal things spiritualized* . . . (see below). The original contained seventy-four "meditations" or similes, in verse, with a characteristic preface and "an help to children to learn to read English."

———. ———. London: Elliot Stock, 1889.
Subtitle: "being a facsimile of the unique first edition published in 1686, with an introduction giving an account of the work, by John Brown."

———. ———. Edited by E. S. Buchanan. Boston: American Tract Society, 1928.
A more modern edition, which does not take the place of the facsimile above. Twelve color illustrations.

———. "A book for boys and girls, or, temporal things spiritualized," in his *Works,* edited by George Offor, v. 3, p. 746–62. London: Blackie, 1858.
This is the title of the editions of 1701 and 1707. The 1724 edition, as noted above, had the new title, *Divine emblems, or, temporal things spiritualized* and contained only forty-nine facsimiles.

———. Divine emblems, or, temporal things spiritualized, calculated for the use of young people, adorn'd with cuts suitable to every subject. London: John Marshall, 1724.
In the British Museum. The Pierpont Morgan Library owns a 1790 edition.

———. Grace abounding to the chief of sinners, or, a brief and faithful relation of the exceeding mercy of God in Christ, to his poor servant John Bunyan . . . whereunto is added, a brief relation of his call to the work of the ministry. London: George Larkin, 1666.
Written in Bedford jail in 1666, this is Bunyan's spiritual autobiography, which aims, in Henri Talon's words, to "edify the brethren from whom he was separated." Though not a children's book, it is included here because of its use to Bunyan scholars and students of the Puritan period.

———. The pilgrim's progress. London: for Nath. Ponder, 1678.
Subtitle: "from this world to that which is to come, delivered under the similitude of a dream, wherein is discovered, the manner of his setting out, his dangerous journey, and safe arrival at the desired countrey [sic]."
Although *Pilgrim's progress* was not written for children, it was eagerly read by them and has become a children's classic. According to Richard Greaves, "It continues to be translated into European, African, and Asian languages and dialects, and in England still sells about 10,000 copies annually."

———. ———. New York: Payson & Clark, 1928.
A reprint of the first edition of 1678 from the British Museum copy.

———. ———. London: Elliot Stock, 1895.
Subtitle: "as John Bunyan wrote it: being a fac-simile reproduction of the first edition published in 1678." Introduction by John Brown.

———. ———. New York: Dodd, [1968].
Includes an introduction to the book and a note on the William Blake designs by A. K. Adams, together with an essay on John Bunyan by Thomas Babington Macaulay. Sixteen pages of illustrations, including reproductions of the frontispiece and eight designs for the first part by William Blake.

———. ———. New York: Heritage, 1942.
Subtitle: "delivered under the similitude of a dream, by John Bunyan." Illustrated with water-colors by William Blake. Blake made twenty-eight sketches for *Pilgrim's progress,* although some were never published and few survive. This edition and the one by Dodd, Mead are noteworthy among modern editions, especially for their Blake illus-trations.

———. ———. London and New York: Oxford University Press, 1904, 1959.
With a biographical introduction and new index. Illustrated by George Cruikshank.

———. ———. London and New York: H. Frowde, 1903.
Illustrated with twenty-five drawings on wood by G. Cruikshank from the collection of Edwin Truman. Biographical introduction by Edmund Venables, a Bunyan scholar. This book is a reprint of the second edition of the first part. Indexes. Both this and the Oxford University Press edition are noteworthy for the illustrations.

———. ———. London: Strahan, 1880.
With 100 illustrations by Frederick Barnard and others. Engraved by the Dalziel Brothers. This magnificent book is "an edition de-luxe printed on special handmade paper, with proofs of illustrations on Japanese paper." Five hundred copies were made.

———. ———. Edited with an introduction by Roger Sharrock. Baltimore: Penguin, [1965].
A good, modern critical edition introduced by a notable Bunyan scholar.

———. ———. Boston: Wilde, [1950].
Subtitle: "John Bunyan's story rewritten for young people by Wade C. Smith." Intended for children.

———. ———. Retold and shortened for modern read-ers by Mary Godolphin [*pseud*]. New York: Stokes, 1939.
Exquisite, black-and-white illustrations by Rob-ert Lawson with Godolphin's nineteenth-century text in her typical "one-syllable" rendition. Much abridged and intended for children.

———. The works of that eminent servant of Christ Mr. John Bunyan. 2v. 3d ed. London: printed for W. Johnson & W. & C. Dilly, 1767.
On title page: "to which are now added, the *Di-vine emblems,* and several other pieces, which were never printed in any former collection. With a recommendatory preface, by the Reverend George Whitefield." A splendid folio edition of the com-plete works. Vol. 1 includes *Grace abounding, Pilgrim's progress,* and some minor works; and vol. 2 contains the *Holy war* and *Divine emblems.*

BIOGRAPHY AND CRITICISM

Bedford (England) Public Library. Catalogue of the John Bunyan Library. (Frank Mott Harrison Collection) Bedford: Bedford Public Library, 1938.
A listing of 800 items by and about Bunyan. An important listing of editions of each work is of use.

Brown, John. John Bunyan: his life, times, and work. Boston and New York: Houghton, 1885. New and revised tercentenary edition edited by Frank Mott Harrison, 1928; reprint: Hamden, Conn.: Shoe String (Archon), 1969.
Brown was one of Bunyan's successors in the ministry of Bedford church and had access to many manuscript sources. This work is considered the earliest and one of the most comprehensive of Bun-yan biographies, though it is now believed to have been superseded by later scholarly works. Still a basic, standard text from which scholars begin.

Coats, Robert Hay. "John Bunyan as a writer for children," *Westminster review* 176:303–7 (1911).
Has special reference to Bunyan's *Book for boys and girls,* though there is some discussion of the general character of children's reading in the seventeenth century.

Freeman, Rosemary. "John Bunyan: the end of tra-dition," in her *English emblem books,* p. 204–28. New York: Octagon, 1966.
In this scholarly work on the English emblem book, Freeman states that Bunyan wrote the first emblem book for children and that this has had critical importance because it directed the conven-tion into the channel in which it was ultimately to survive. Analyzes the bibliographical changes.

Froude, James Anthony. Bunyan. New York: Har-per, 1880.
An early biography. No bibliography.

Furlong, Monica. Puritan's progress: a study of John Bunyan. New York: Coward, 1975.
Two chapters devoted to *Pilgrim's progress,* p. 92–125. An excellent biography that attempts to analyze how the man thought, what made him

write what he did, and how his religion influenced him.

Greaves, Richard L. An annotated bibliography of John Bunyan studies. Pittsburgh: Clifford E. Barbour Library, Pittsburgh Theological Seminary, [1972].
Very complete bibliography listing biographical and reference works, editions published in Bunyan's lifetime, notable editions of his important works, selected works on seventeenth-century literature, background materials, etc.

————. John Bunyan. (Courtenay studies in Reformation theology, v. 2) Abingdon (Berks.): Sutton Courtenay, 1969.
Bunyan's theories exemplified in his writings. Greaves concluded he was "a Bedfordshire tinker with the vision of Paul, the conviction of Luther, and the commitment to freedom of Milton."

Harrison, Frank Mott. A bibliography of the works of John Bunyan. Oxford: Oxford University Press for the Bibliographical Society, 1932 (for 1930).
A critical bibliographical account of Bunyan's works with collations. Known existing copies of first editions listed. A long biographical introduction.

————. "Editions of *Pilgrim's progress*," *The library* 4th ser., 22:73–81 (June, 1941).
Harrison has a record of more than 1,300 edition and reprints. Discusses the diversity of editions and the rarity of certain ones. Includes Catholic editions, abridgments, adaptations, dramatizations, and imitations.

————. John Bunyan: a study in personality. London: Dent, 1928; reprint: Hamden, Conn.: Shoe String (Archon), 1967.
Emphasizes Bunyan's personality and ideas as reflected in his writing.

Ivimey, Joseph. The life of Mr. John Bunyan, minister of the gospel at Bedford. London: Button & Burditt, 1809.
An early, flawed biography. Includes a bibliography.

Lindsay, Jack. John Bunyan: maker of myths. London: Methuen, 1937; reprint: Port Washington, N.Y.: Kennikat Press, 1969.
A standard biography, somewhat critical.

Macaulay, Thomas Babington. "John Bunyan," in his *Critical and historical essays*, selected and introduced by Hugh Trevor-Roper, p. 130–45. New York: McGraw-Hill, 1965.
Written in December, 1831, this essay has been printed often and widely. Macaulay wrote it in response to Southey's introduction to his edition of *Pilgrim's progress* (see below). Macaulay noted

the revival of interest in and popularity of Bunyan, and he concluded, "Though we are not afraid to say that there were many clever men in England during the latter half of the seventeenth century, there were only two minds which possessed the imaginative faculty in a very eminent degree. One of these minds produced the *Paradise Lost*, the other the *Pilgrim's Progress*." It is noteworthy that Macaulay, Southey, Browning, and others manifested typical late-Victorian interest in Bunyan. It has been suggested that the reason for this is that his life and work was not unlike the evangelical tradition of English Christianity at that time.

Sharrock, Roger. John Bunyan. London and New York: Hutchinson's University Library, [1954].
A standard biography, which Richard Greaves calls "sound and scholarly."

Southey, Robert. The pilgrim's progress, with a life of John Bunyan. London: John Murray, 1830.
Includes a long, admiring essay.

Talon, Henri Antoine. John Bunyan. London: Longmans, Green for the British Council and the National Book League, 1956.
A short essay by a French scholar. He gives a psychological interpretation of *Grace abounding* and *Pilgrim's progress*. Includes a selected bibliography of Bunyan's collected editions and separate editions, as well as some lists of critical and biographical studies.

————. John Bunyan: the man and his works. Translated by Barbara Nall. London: Rockliff, 1951.
First published in 1948 under the title *John Bunyan—l' homme et l'oeuvre*. A standard biography in which the author says that "Bunyan incarnates the Puritan spirit at its best and most durable; its gravity, its solemn approach to life, its taste for endeavor."

Tindall, William York. John Bunyan: mechanick preacher. New York: Columbia University Press, 1934.
All scholars consider this one of the best Bunyan biographies. It is Tindall's theory that "John Bunyan was a typical mechanick preacher and that his writings owe their nature both to the social, economic and sectarian condition of their author and to the literary conventions of a numerous company of mechanicks."

Venables, Edmund. Life of John Bunyan. London: W. Scott; New York: T. Whittaker, 1888.
Another late Victorian biography.

White, Alison. "Pilgrim's progress as a fairy-tale," *Children's literature: the great excluded* 1:42–45 (1972).
Compares *Pilgrim's progress* to Tolkien's *Lord of the rings*. The author calls the Bunyan work "an evangelical fairy tale."

Winslow, Ola Elizabeth. John Bunyan. New York: Macmillan, 1961.

In a section on *A Book for boys and girls,* p. 190–97, Winslow writes that seventeenth-century children, brought up to believe that the main business of life was to prepare for death, would have turned to these emblems with delight, even though they are highly moralistic and religious.

Winterich, John T. "John Bunyan and the *Pilgrim's progress,*" in his *Books and the man,* p. 123–40. New York: Greenberg, 1921; reprint: in *Bibliophile in the nursery* edited by William Targ, p. 208–22. Cleveland: World, 1957.

A sympathetic biography of Bunyan and a description of the writing of *Pilgrim's progress.* Details the whereabouts of the eleven extant copies of the first edition (seven in America, four in England), all of which have been found since 1850.

EDUCATION

The New England Primer

The New-England primer. Edited by Paul Leicester Ford. (The book lover's library of early American literature) New York: Dodd, 1897; reprint: (Classics in Education, no. 13) New York: Teachers' College, Columbia University, 1962.

Subtitle: "a history of its origin and development, with a reprint of the unique copy of the earliest known edition and many facsimile illustrations and reproductions." Reprint lacks some photoengravings and woodcuts in original. Appendixes: Reprint of the *New English tutor*; Reprint of Roger's *Exhortation unto his children*; Cotton Mather's *Plea for catechising*; Clarke's *Saying the catechism*; Reprint of the *Holy Bible in verse*; Bibliography of the *New England primer*; Variorum of the *New England primer.* Though we now believe the *New England primer* to have been published earlier than Ford assumed (about 1678), "his introduction still remains the best introduction to the *Primer,* its antecedents in England, and its successive versions in the New World, and the 1727 edition of the *Primer,* which Ford reprinted is still the earliest extant copy."—introduction to the 1962 edition.

———. New York: Dodd, 1899.

Subtitle: "a reprint of the earliest known edition, with many facsimiles and reproductions, and an historical introduction." Does not contain the appendixes of the earlier edition.

The New England primer. Boston: Ginn, 1900.

Subtitle: "twentieth century reprint." Facsimile reproduction from an original published in Boston sometime between 1785 and 1790. The last leaf of the original is missing, and this page is reproduced in modern type. The title page reads, "The New-England primer enlarged; Or, An easy and pleasant guide to the art of reading; adorn'd with cuts; to which are added the Assembly of Divines and Mr. Cotton's catechism, &c."

———. Hartford, Conn.: Ira Webster, 1843.

Subtitle: "improved for the more easy attaining the true reading of English." Reprint of the 1777 *New England primer* reprinted by Edward Draper in Boston. It includes a picture of John Hancock at the front and several of Dr. Watts's poems.

The New England primer improved. Philadelphia: King & Baird, 1856.

Subtitle: "an easy and pleasant guide to the art of reading; to which is added the assembly's shorter catechism." Cover dated 1857.

———. New York: Munsell, 1885.

Subtitle: "for the more easy attaining the true reading of English, to which is added the Assembly of Divines and Mr. Cotton's catechism." Another facsimile reprint of the 1777 edition.

———. New York: S. Babcock, n.d.

Subtitle: "for the more early attaining of the true reading of English to which is added the Episcopal and the Assembly of Divines' catechism; embellished with cuts."

CRITICISM

Carpenter, Charles. "*The New England primer,*" in his *History of American schoolbooks,* p. 21–34. Philadelphia: University of Pennsylvania Press, 1963.

Discusses the origin of the *New England primer* and its contents.

Cohen, Daniel A. "The origin and development of the *New England primer,*" in *Children's literature* 5: 62–65. (1976).

Part of a series of articles entitled *Shaping the national character,* this one discusses the obscure origins of the *Primer,* links it with Benjamin Harris's *Protestant tutor,* and considers the entry of John Gaine in the Stationers' Register in London in 1683.

Ford, Worthington Chauncey. "*The New England primer,*" in *Bibliographical essays: a tribute to Wilberforce Eames,* p. 61–66. Cambridge, Mass.: Harvard University Press, 1924; reprint: Freeport, N.Y.: Books for Libraries, 1967.

The seventeenth-century primer, in evolving from the totally religious primer of the Middle Ages, has become a "school book, but with the religious feature still dominant." Ford disagrees with Cohen in that he sees a large difference between Harris's *Protestant tutor* and the *New England primer,* calling the former a political tract and the latter a schoolbook. Ford also thinks that Gaine printed the first *New England primer* in England about 1683.

Heartman, Charles Frederick, comp. *The New-England primer* issued prior to 1830. New York: Privately printed, 1916.
Subtitle: "a bibliographical check-list for the more easy attaining the true knowledge of this book; embellished with thirty-seven cuts, and now revised, greatly improved, and arranged in two alphabets, with preface, introduction, and indexes." With a long introduction. Heartman believes that six million *Primers* were printed between 1680 and 1830, of which only about two thousand are extant. The work was revised in 1922. A third revised edition was printed by Bowker in 1934.

Johnson, Clifton. *"The New England primer,"* in his *Old-time schools and schoolbooks,* p. 69–99. New York: Macmillan, 1904; reprint: New York: Dover, 1963.
Outlines the history and contents of the *Primer* and discusses its use. Includes portions from different editions and reproductions of old woodcuts.

Livermore, George. The origin, history and character of the New England primer, being a series of articles contributed to the *Cambridge Chronicle.* New York: C. F. Heartman, 1915.
Reprinted from the edition of 1849. Contains three newspaper articles and a facsimile reprint of the only fragment extant of a *New England primer* reprinted in Germantown, Pa., 1764.

Meigs, Cornelia. "The New England primer," in Meigs et al., *A critical history of children's literature,* p. 110–19. Rev. ed. New York: Macmillan, 1969.
Although its information is not always entirely correct, this is an excellent introduction to *The New England primer* and other Puritan books. Compares the contents of the "Rhyming alphabets" from different periods.

Stone, Wilbur Macey. *"The New England primer* and Watts' *Divine songs,"* Horn book magazine 17:217–29 (May, 1941).
A description of a later *Primer* that has as part of its text Isaac Watts's famous poem beginning, "Hush, my dear, lie still and slumber. . . ." Discusses the research done by Livermore and Heartman.

Weigle, Luther Allan. *"The New England primer,"* in *The pageant of America,* edited by Ralph Henry Gabriel. v. 10, p. 265–66. New Haven, Conn.: Yale University Press, 1928.
Contains four illustrated pages reproduced from *The New England primers* of 1727 and 1800.

Winship, George P. Notes on a reprint of the New-England primer improved for the year 1777, for the more easy attaining the truth. . . . Cambridge in New England: printed by C. P. Andare to be had in Boston where the good monk speed up Beacon-Hill away from Brimstone Corner, 1922.

Other Early Schoolbooks

Carpenter, Charles. History of American schoolbooks. Philadelphia: University of Pennsylvania Press, 1963.
Mostly eighteenth-century texts, but some seventeenth-century material included.

Chargin, Madeleine. "The hornbook in America," *Horn book magazine* 16: 280–86, 357–66 (July-August, 1940; September-October, 1940).
Pt. 2 describes George Plimpton's hornbook collection (now at Columbia University), the collections at the New York Public Library, the Huntington Library, the Newberry Library, and the Wadsworth Atheneum at Hartford, Conn. Chargin concludes that today "the hornbook is rarer than a Caxton."

Earle, Alice Morse. "Hornbook and primer," "School-books," in her *Child life in colonial days,* p. 117–32, 133–50. New York: Macmillan, 1899; reprint: Folcroft, Pa.: Folcroft, 1974.
Describes three American hornbooks and their contents. The chapter on schoolbooks deals with advanced texts.

Freeman, Ruth S. Yesterday's school books. Watkins Glen, N.Y.: Century House, 1960.
Books for young children and textbooks used in pre-Revolutionary Massachussets and post-Revolutionary New York State. Facsimile illustrations.

Library for young schollers, compiled by an English scholar priest about 1655. (Illinois studies in language and literature, v. 48.) Edited with bibliographical index by Alma de Jordy and Harris Francis Fletcher. Urbana: University of Illinois Press, 1961.
Description and analytic study of this early manuscript catalog which displays "the scholarly interests of [the] time."

Littlefield, George Emery. Early schools and school-books of New England. Boston: Club of Odd Volumes, 1904; reprint: New York: Russell & Russell, 1965.
First edition limited to 167 copies.
Covers both seventeenth and eighteenth centuries. A long chapter, "Education in Massachusetts," covers the Massachusetts laws concerning educational policy, the first public schools in Boston, and other grammar schools in Massachusetts. Good descriptions of the schools, the teachers, etc.

Chapters on catechisms, hornbooks (including battledores and samplers), spelling books, readers, arithmetic books, bookkeeping texts, English grammars, Latin grammars, geographies, histories, and dictionaries. No bibliography.

Plimpton, George A. The marks of merit, together with an article by G. A. Plimpton on hornbooks and their use in America. Boston: Ginn, 1916.
Published also as *Proceedings* of the American Antiquarian Society in the same year. Discusses to what extent hornbooks were used in America and early mention of them here. Though hornbooks were used extensively in the colonies, with the criss-crosses methodically obliterated, few have been found. Plimpton himself owned one of the largest collections of hornbooks, including one from seventeenth-century Mexico, which is described and illustrated in detail.

Other Emblems and Primers

Choice emblems, natural, historical, fabulous, moral and divine. 11th ed. London: John Harris, 1812.
Subtitle: "for the improvement and pastime of youth, displaying the beauties and morals of the ancient fabulists; the whole calculated to convey the golden lessons of instruction under a new and more delightful dress; for the use of schools; written for the amusement of a young nobleman." A curious and quaint little book, first published in 1772. The young nobleman was Lord Newbattle, and the first dedication is to his sister, the Lady Elizabeth Kerr, daughter of Lord Ancram. On the title page is the quotation:

Say, should the philosophic mind disdain
That good which makes each humble bosom vain?
Let school-taught pride dissemble all it can,
These little things are great to little man.

The emblems and morals are in verse followed by prose comments and "applications." Each emblem is illustrated with a small picture, and there is an engraved frontispiece.

Emblems for the entertainment and improvement of youth: containing hieroglyphical and enigmatical devices, relating to all parts and stations of life. London: R. Ware, [1750?].
Nine hundred engraved emblems with accompanying mottoes. Owned by the Pierpont Morgan Library.

Emblems of mortality: representing, in upwards of fifty cuts, death seizing all ranks and degrees of people. London: T. Hodgson, 1789.
Subtitle: "intended as well for the information of the curious, as the instruction and entertainment of youth." Editions of the Holbein *Dance of death* were often produced for youth. The illustra-

tions in this edition, a copy of which is owned by the Pierpont Morgan Library, were done by John and Thomas Bewick.

Harris, Benjamin. Protestant tutor: instructing children to spel and read English and grounding them in the true Protestant religion and discovering the errors and deceits of the papists. London: published for Benjamin Harris, 1679.
The precursor of the *New England primer*, written by its alleged author.

"Miss Thoughtful." Instructive and entertaining emblems of various subjects, in prose and verse. Hartford, Conn.: J. Babcock, 1795.
An emblem book for children in chapbook form with woodcuts. In the Pierpont Morgan Library collection.

The royal primer, or, an easy and pleasant guide to the art of reading . . . adorn'd with cuts. London: printed for John Newbery, [1751?].
The author is said to have been Benjamin Collins. First American printing was in Boston in 1767.

The royal primer improved, being an easy and pleasant guide to the art of reading. Philadelphia: T. Chattin, 1753.

Wynne, John Huddlestone. Choice emblems, natural, historical, fabulous, moral and divine, for the improvement and pastime of youth. London: George Riley, 1772.
Gottlieb calls this "one of the most famous emblem books ever written for children." It later became known as *Riley's emblems* (for the publisher) and was printed throughout the eighteenth and nineteenth centuries.

The young scholar's pocket companion. Glasgow: J. & J. Robertson, 1779.
Subtitle: "being an early introduction to the art of reading, in three parts, containing the first principles of pronunciation; the Assembly's *Shorter catechism,* divided into lessons on a new and easy play; easy lessons in prose and verse." Interesting example of an attempt at a compendium for children. The last part is "adorned" with woodcuts. The binding is an example of wallpaper applied to book covers.

Heartman, Charles F. American primers, Indian primers, royal primers, and 37 other types of non–*New England primers* issued prior to 1830. Highland Park, N.J.: Harry B. Weiss, 1935.
A scholarly bibliography with an introduction.

Merritt, Percival. "The Royal primer," in *Bibliographical essays: a tribute to Wilberforce Eames.* p. 35–60. Cambridge, Mass.: Harvard University Press, 1924.

First printed in England by John Newbery about 1745, it was the first to include the famous lines:

> He who ne'er learns his A, B, C,
> Forever will a Blockhead be.
> But he who learns these letters fair,
> Shall have a Coach to take the air.

Merritt contrasts *The royal primer* with *The New England primer* by saying, "It [*The royal primer*] represents the more liberal Anglican standpoint as contrasted with the rigid Puritanical background of *The New England primer.*"

Divine and Moral Songs: Seventeenth and Eighteenth Centuries

The ancient Greeks used the word *hymn* to signify "a song or poem composed in honour of gods, heroes or famous men, to be recited on some joyful, mourning or solemn occasions."[1] Much has happened to the hymn form since it appeared in the time of the Greeks, but the definition has remained somewhat the same. Jeremiah Reeves wrote in 1924 in his *The hymn as literature:*

> The hymn itself may be defined as a lyrical composition expressive of religious aspiration, petition, confession, communion, or praise; a song devoted to the fellowship of souls and the worship of God . . . The good hymn combines in quite remarkable effect the straitest simplicity, clarity, dignity, and melody, rich ideas about the basic matters of life and death, with strong emotion under sure control. [p. 6–7]

In the twentieth century, the English hymns, Reeves went on to assert with absolute confidence, "of all forms of English poetry, stand first in popular favor." As a form of poetry in their own right, hymns, like other forms of poetry, must follow a special set of rules: a hymn must be singable, written in a simple measure; the imagery must be basic and clear; the poem must never be "a piece of private poetry," but must have a wide appeal to an audience that might include persons of widely varying educational, social, and religious backgrounds.

Even though today the hymn is considered something of an English institution, its acceptance in its present form is a relatively recent historical event. "Although," says Pollard, "the Christian Church has always sung," it was the Reformation in Germany and later in England that gave hymn writing and singing their impetus. The Reformation "cleansed" the Church, substituted the vernacular for Latin, and gave the congregation a more prominent part in the service.[2]

Martin Luther is known to have loved music. Realizing the potential of public singing for his new religion, Luther himself wrote and published a small volume of eight hymns in 1522, translated Latin hymns into the vernacular, and encouraged hymn writing and singing in his country. The Germans under Luther were the first to produce both a Bible and a hymnal in the native tongue, and for two hundred years after Luther, Germany stood practically alone as a source of Christian hymns.

Lutheran hymnody was innovative in its form because, although respectful of the Scripture, the Lutherans did not restrict themselves to literal paraphrases of the psalms as others before them had done. The English, however, got their hymns mostly from the Calvinists, who, unlike the Lutherans, restricted their hymns to metrical psalmody. In England in

1. *Encyclopaedia Britannica* 14th ed., s.v. "Hymns."

2. Arthur Pollard, *English hymns* (London: Longmans, Green, 1960), p. 1.

the sixteenth century, the metrical psalm was the only accepted, in fact, permitted, form of public religious singing. During Henry VIII's reign, the first book of Protestant metrical psalms was published by Thomas Sternhold in 1549. Since only psalm singing was permitted in English churches during the Tudor regime, it is not at all surprising that the very first book published in America by the Protestants was the *Bay psalm book*, printed in Cambridge in 1640.

Despite the prevailing popularity of this form of church singing, three seventeenth-century poets foreshadowed the coming of the true English hymn. George Wither, the first of these, was a prolific writer of religious materials. His *Hymns and songs of the Church* appeared in 1622–23, and his *Halelviah*, in 1641. The latter collection has 233 hymns written for all ages, some of which were simple enough to be read and understood by children. The most famous of these, "A rocking hymn," begins:

> Sleep baby sleep: what ails my dear?
> What ails my darling thus to cry?
> Be still, my child, and lend thine ear,
> To hear me sing thy lullaby.

Although Wither's hymns are considered to be quite beautiful, it is generally believed that they were more suited to family or private devotion than to the church.

Bishop Jeremy Taylor appended a group of twenty-one hymns to his *The golden grove, or, a manual of daily prayers and litanies*, 1655. Intended for "younger or pious persons," they are today considered erratic and disorganized.

Toward the end of the century (1675), Bishop Thomas Ken wrote *A manual of prayers for the boys at Winchester College*, where he had been a student. Later editions, beginning in either 1694 or 1695, had appended three hymns: for morning, evening, and midnight. Though slow in coming into general use, the morning and evening hymns are included in most contemporary hymnals. Beginning with the lines "Awake my soul, and with the sun" and "All praise to Thee, my God, this night," each hymn ends with a stanza that begins with the famous line "Praise God from whom all blessings flow"—perhaps the most often sung phrase in Christendom.

Although these men (and a few others) had written some very beautiful hymns when Isaac Watts began to write, the prevailing belief at the beginning of the eighteenth century was still that public singing in church ought to be confined to the psalms. At first Watts, a Nonconformist minister, began by "christianizing the psalms," and his two hymnals for adults, *Horae lyricae*, 1705, and *Hymns and spiritual songs*, 1715, contained both hymns and psalms. His great work for children, *Divine and moral songs attempted in easy language for the use of children*, to which he appended the lovely "A cradle hymn" in 1727, contained only hymns.

The *Divine and moral songs . . .* were given to little, eighteenth-century children to be memorized, which was how children were most efficiently given "a relish for virtue and religion," as Watts put it in his introduction. But these hymns were different from prevailing Puritan literature for reasons Watts stated in his introduction. He said, "I have endeavour'd to sink the language to the level of a child's understanding . . . [and] desinged [sic] to profit all (if possible) and offend none."

Most historians of children's literature today (William Sloane is an exception) deem Watts's efforts at writing uncondescendingly and simply for children a success. Harvey Darton says:

> In mere verse technique, they [the *Songs*] were unprecedented for children; they were not seriously rivalled in that respect till Ann and Jane Taylor appeared in 1804. And, being by a Puritan, they were yet the denial, and, in a social sense, the end of the Puritan aggressive, persecuting, frightened love of children. They made up a real child's book, even if they had a didactic aim. They must ever be a landmark, early but clear, in the intimate family history of the English child. . . .[3]

Altogether Watts wrote about seven hundred hymns, some of which—including "A cradle hymn," "When I survey the wondrous cross," and "O God, our help in ages past"—are unforgettable hymns. Historians of hymnody will always remember Watts as the man to whom is due the triumph of the hymn in the English language; but historians of children's literature will remember him because he was one of the

3. *Children's books in England* (New York: Cambridge University Press, 1932), p. 111.

earliest kind, serene, and understanding writers of books specifically intended for children.

Several distinguished hymnists were contemporaries of Watts. Christopher Smart, one of them, was influenced by Watts as well as by the earlier Puritan writers, Bunyan and Janeway. A religious fanatic, hospitalized for "insanity and jailed for drunkenness and poverty, Smart wrote his *Hymns for the aumsement of children* during the last years of his life while in prison. The poems summarize the religious themes he wrote about all his life: fearing God, being kind to the poor, shunning worldly temptation, loving and practicing prayer, and the joy of religion. Like Watts, Smart had some insight into the "psychology" of childhood, and his poems are clear and lucid and "Blake-like in their confirmation of vivid realism and childish sympathy."[4]

Another of Watts's contemporaries was Charles Wesley, who is estimated to have written between 6,500 and 9,000 poems. Wesley's *Hymns for children,* 1763 (later called *Hymns for children and others of riper years*), was written directly for children. Charles's brother, John, who produced in Georgia in 1737 the first Methodist hymnal, wrote the introduction to *Hymns for children,* in which he stated a difference with Watts's philosophy:

> There are two ways of writing and speaking [to children]: the one is, to let ourselves down to them; the other, to lift them up to us. Dr. Watts has wrote in the former way, and has succeeded admirably well, speaking to children as children, and leaving them as he found them. The following hymns are written on the other plan: they contain strong and manly sense, yet expressed in such plain and easy

language as even children may understand. But when they do understand them, they will be children no longer, only in years and in stature.

The nineteenth century, spurred on by the Sunday school movement (see p. 98), produced several great hymnists, though none of the stature of Watts or Wesley. Ann and Jane Taylor were perhaps the greatest, but other women writers produced increasing numbers of hymns for children, among them Mrs. Felicia Hemans, "one of the archetypal 'Gothic romantic' poetesses of the early nineteenth century,"[5] Mrs. Anna Laetitia Barbauld, and Mrs. Cecil Frances Alexander, "the queen of children's hymn writers."[6]

By the mid-nineteenth century, hymn writing moved into the hands of the Anglicans, who in the eighteenth century had scorned hymn singing in church as an undignified activity. When it became quite evident that the Anglicans must either adopt church singing or lose their hold, several Anglican hymnists appeared. Reginald Heber, one of the first, wrote fifty-seven hymns, including "Holy, holy, holy, Lord God almighty." John Keble, another Anglican, along with several of his contemporaries, compiled *The Christian year,* which was intended to be suitable for children.

The nineteenth century was a prolific time, with no fewer than 220 hymnbooks appearing in the Church of England between 1800 and 1880.[7] The predominating trends were an increase of women writers of hymns and increased attention given to hymns for children, both of which parallel the trends in nineteenth-century children's literature as a whole.

4. Sophia B. Blaydes, *Christopher Smart as a poet of his time* (The Hague: Mouton, 1966), p. 160.

5. Erik Routley, *Hymns and human life* (New York: Philosophical Library, 1952), p. 209.
6. Ibid., p. 254.
7. Pollard, *English hymns,* p. 1.

OUTLINE

GENERAL REFERENCES

Benson, Louis Fitzgerald. The English hymn: its development and use in worship. Richmond, Va.: John Knox Press, 1915; reprinted, 1962.
  A scholarly account of the history of hymns from 1530 through the nineteenth century. Details the struggle of the Dissenter hymnists to win a place for hymns in the service. Chap. 3, p. 108–60, deals with Watts, his hymns, and their place in England and America.

Bett, Henry. Hymns of Methodism. London: Epworth, 1945.
  This book is concerned primarily with the hymns of the Wesleys.

Brownlie, John. The hymns and hymn writers of the church hymnary. London: H. Frowde, 1899.
  Notes on hymns for children, p. 259–84, 312–16. Also brief accounts of Isaac Watts, p. 123–27; Charles Wesley, p. 131–37; and Mrs. Alexander, p. 240–41.

Duffield, Samuel Willoughby. English hymns: their authors and history. New York: Funk & Wagnalls, 1886.
  A long, often garbled, chronology of English hymnists. No table of contents.

England, Martha Winburn, and **John Sparrow.** Hymns unbidden: Donne, Herbert, Blake, Emily Dickinson, and the hymnographers. New York: New York Public Library, 1966.
Reprinted from the *Bulletin* of the New York Public Library. April, December, 1964; February, 1965; January–April, 1966. Compares Wesley to Blake and Dickinson to Watts.

Fox, Adam. English hymns and hymn writers. London: Collins, 1947.
This beautifully illustrated book traces the history of the hymn. There is a chapter on Isaac Watts and Charles Wesley.

Frost, Maurice, ed. Historical companion to hymns ancient and modern. London: William Clowes, 1962.
A very complete source of hymns. Includes a long introduction on hymnody in the early church, Latin hymnody, monastic and medieval hymnody, metrical psalms, and later hymns. Along with each hymn there are notes on the text, its author, and the composer. Includes also an index of first lines and an alphabetical listing of authors and composers, as well as an index of titles.

Gillman, Frederick. The evolution of the English hymn. London: Allen & Unwin, [1927].
A historical survey of the origins and development of the hymns of the Christian church. Includes a chapter on Watts and one on the Wesleys.

Horder, William Garrett. "Children's hymns," in his *The hymn lover: an account of the rise and growth of English hymnody*, p. 431–71. 2d ed. rev. London: Curwen, 1882.
General survey, including representative hymns of different writers.

Howson, Edmund W. "Hymns and hymn writers of the eighteenth century," in his *The Sunday magazine* 30; n.s., 23: 461–65, 550–54 (1894).
The hymns are classified in three different schools: literary, Anglican, and Evangelical; and the authors, the periods, and the circumstances under which they were written are considered. Includes brief mention of Bishop Ken, Isaac Watts, and Charles Wesley.

Ingram, Tom, and **Douglas Newton,** comps. Hymns as poetry: an anthology. London: Constable, [1956].
Arranges hymns chronologically from 1560 to 1953. Has excellent, brief introductions to each section. Very useful.

Julian, John, ed. A dictionary of hymnology, setting forth the origin and history of Christian hymns of all ages and nations. Rev. ed. with new supplement. London: John Murray, 1907.
Classic reference, still of great use. Contains many valuable articles on English and German hymnody, children's hymns, Bishop Ken, and other hymn writers.

Lawrence, Ralph. "The English hymn," in *Essays and studies* (English Association), n.s., 7:105–22 (1954).
Seventeenth- through nineteenth-century hymns seen solely as poetry.

Ninde, Edward S. Nineteen centuries of Christian song. New York: Revell, 1938.
An early, but adequate, history through the eighteenth century.

North, Louise McCoy. The psalms and hymns of Protestantism: from the sixteenth through the nineteenth centuries. Madison, N.J.: Drew University Press, 1936.
Good introduction.

Pollard, Arthur. English hymns. (Bibliographical series: Writers and their works, no. 123) London: Longmans, Green for the British Council and the National Book League, 1960.
Determines "to show the extent of this hymnody which has permeated so strongly the literary consciousness of the English nation," and "to indicate some of the intrinsic poetic value of the best hymns in the language."—preface. Includes excellent bibliographies of English hymnists, English hymnals, and works about English hymns and hymn writers.

Reeves, Jeremiah B. The hymn as literature. New York: Century, 1922.
A classic text on English hymnody. Calling the hymn "the most popular kind of English poetry," Reeves traces its history from the Middle Ages through the nineteenth century. Isaac Watts, Robert Herrick, the Wesleys, Bishop Ken are considered, among many others.

Routley, Erik. Hymns and human life. New York: Philosophical Library, 1952.
Up-to-date book of history and criticism of hymnody from the Middle Ages through the nineteenth century. The chapter "Youth and hymns," p. 243–62, discusses the subject fully.

Ryden, Ernest Edwin. The story of our hymns. Rock Island, Ill.: Augustana Book Concern, 1930.
Discusses Martin Luther, Bishop Ken, Isaac Watts, Charles Wesley, Mrs. Alexander, and several other women who wrote hymns for children.

Sampson, George. "The century of divine songs," in his *Seven essays*, p. 199–232. Cambridge: Cambridge University Press, 1947.
An excellent, well-written essay primarily about the eighteenth-century hymnists and their hymns, which he calls the "poor man's poetry" and the "ordinary man's theology."

Thompson, Ronald W. Who's who of hymn writers. London: Epworth, [1967].
A reference work listing alphabetically English and other hymn writers with a paragraph for each.

COLLECTIONS

■ The title of this chapter is taken from the famous little book by Isaac Watts (see p. 75) but the syllabus and bibliographies cover a broad span from the anonymous songs and carols of the Middle Ages to familiar verses of the nineteenth century.

Bacon, Mary Schell Hoke (*pseud.* Dolores Bacon), ed. Hymns that every child should know: a selection of the best hymns of all nations for young people. New York: Doubleday, 1907.
Includes hymns by Luther, Watts, Wesley, and others, with notes regarding words and music.

Chisholm, Louey, comp. "Carols, hymns, and sacred verse," in her *The golden staircase,* p. 313–56. New York: Putnam, 1907.
A handsome book with illustrations by M. Dibdin Spooner. Selections date from Martin Luther through the nineteenth-century poets.

Dearmer, Percy, et al. Prayers and hymns for little children. New York: Oxford University Press, 1932.

————. Songs of praise for boys and girls. London: Oxford University Press, 1929.
Includes music.

Graham, Eleanor. A thread of gold: an anthology of poetry. London: Bodley Head, 1964.
Attractively illustrated in black and white by Margery Gill and intended for children, this collection gives special attention to religious poetry by anonymous authors of early periods and by poets of the seventeenth and eighteenth centuries.

Hymnal of the Protestant Episcopal Church. New York: Church Pension Fund, 1916.
The original *Hymnal of the Protestant Episcopal Church* was published in Philadelphia in 1786 and included 51 hymns and "eight pages of tunes." The 1916 edition of over 200 hymns includes those of Mrs. Alexander, Mrs. Barbauld, Bishop Heber, Reverend John Keble, Rudyard Kipling, Cardinal Newman, Alfred Lord Tennyson, Isaac Watts, and John Wesley. A 1940 edition entitled *A new hymnal of the Protestant Episcopal Church* includes a section of hymns for children. An historical overview of hymns used in the American Episcopal Church was published as *The hymnal 1940 companion* (New York: Church Pension Fund, 1940).

Hymns ancient and modern: for use in the services of the Church, with accompanying tunes. Comp. and arranged by William Henry Monk. London: William Clowes, [1868].
Most popular nineteenth-century hymnal in England and America. By 1894, more than ten thousand churches in the United States were using it.

"Hymns for the nursery," and "Hymns for childhood," in Our children's songs, p. 181–203. New York: Harper, 1877.
Includes Isaac Watts, John Keble, Charles Wesley, Christina Rossetti, Nahum Tate, Bishop Ken, Bishop Heber, Joseph Addison.

Ingpen, Roger, ed. "Hymns," in his *One thousand poems for children,* p. 404–21. New York: Jacobs, 1903.

————. "Poems of praise," in his *One thousand poems for children,* p. 453–73. Rev. and enl. ed. New York: Macrae, 1923.
The selection of hymns differs from that in the edition of 1903.

Palgrave, *Sir* **Francis Turner,** comp. The treasury of sacred song, selected from the English lyrical poetry of four centuries. London: Clarendon Press, 1890.
Watts, Wesley, and other hymn writers are represented, and there are explanatory and biographical notes.

Wiseman, Herbert, and **W. E. Hamilton,** eds. Children praising. New York: Oxford University Press, 1937.
With words and music.

INDIVIDUAL WRITERS

Mrs. Alexander

Alexander, Cecil Frances Humphreys. Hymns for little children. London: Joseph Masters, 1858.
First published in 1848. Prefatory note by "J. K." (John Keble).

Mrs. Hemans

Hemans, Felicia Dorothea Browne. Complete works of Mrs. Hemans. Edited by her sister. 2v. New York: Appleton, 1847.
Vol. 1 includes her poems "Hymns for childhood."

———. Hymns on the works of nature for the use of children. Boston: Hilliard, Gray, Little, & Wilkins, 1827.
A separate publication of Mrs. Hemans's children's hymns. Originally written for her own children, this edition includes "Introductory verses" and poems entitled "To one of the author's children" and "To a younger child." These are not included in the *Complete works* listed above.

———. Poems. 6v. Edinburgh: W. Blackwood, 1859.
"Hymns for childhood" are in vol. 5 under the heading "Moral and religious poems."

———. Poems of Felicia Hemans: a new edition chronologically arranged, with illustrative notes, and a selection of contemporary criticisms. Edinburgh and London: W. Blackwood, 1852.
A section titled "Juvenile poems" includes the "Hymns for childhood," p. 528–34.

———. The poetical works of Felicia Hemans . . . with a memoir by Mrs. L. H. Sigourney. Philadelphia: Grigg & Elliot, 1839.
Lists the children's hymns as "Hymns on the works of nature, for the use of children."

———. ———. Boston: Phillips, Sampson, 1853.
Includes all but two of the poems in the Philadelphia edition listed above. "Hymns for childhood" are found on p. 589–94.

BIOGRAPHY

Courtney, Janet Elizabeth Hogarth. "The poets: Mrs. Hemans," in her *The adventurous thirties: a chapter in the women's movement*, p. 19–33. Oxford: Oxford University Press, 1933.
Portrait facing p. 21.

Hughes, Harriet. "Memoir," in *The works of Mrs. Hemans*. Edinburgh: W. Blackwood; London: Thomas Cadell, 1839.

Robert Herrick

Herrick, Robert. "Graces for children," in his *The Hesperides, or, the works both humane & divine (His noble numbers: or, his pious pieces, wherein [amongst the things] he sings the birth of his Christ . . .).* 2 pts. London: John Williams & Frances Egglesfield, 1648.

———. ———, in his *The Hesperides, and Noble numbers* (Muses' Library), edited by Alfred Pollard, v. 2, p. 202. London: Scribner, 1897. With a preface by A. C. Swinburne.

———. ———, in his *Hesperides, or the works both humane and divine of Robert Herrick*, v. 2, p. 220–21. London: Pickering, 1848.

———. ———, in his *Hesperides and His noble numbers*, p. 309. Menston, England: Scolar Press, 1969, 1973.
This is a facsimile edition of the original. This edition and the two listed above are representative of the many available editions of Herrick's poetry, all of which contain the three poems written for children, "What God gives, and what we take," "Here a little child I stand," and the two-line grace,

> Honor thy parents; but good manners call
> Thee to adore thy God the first of all.

■ There are several scholarly biographies of Herrick, but none consider his work for children, and so they are excluded from this study.

John Keble

Keble, John. The child's Christian year: hymns for every Sunday and holy-day, compiled for the use of parochial schools. Oxford: J. H. Parker, 1841.
Written for children by Keble and his Evangelical contemporaries.

Bishop Ken

Ken, Thomas, *bishop of Bath and Wells.* A manual of prayers for the use of scholars of Winchester College and all other devout Christians: to which is added, three hymns, for morning, evening, and midnight . . . not in the former editions. London: for C. Brome, 1697.
Includes the three hymns for the first time in this edition. The manual was published without the hymns in 1674. The hymns were also printed separately under the title: *Three hymns. By the author of *The Manual. London: C. Brome, 1694.

———. A manual of prayers for young persons, or, Bishop Ken's Winchester manual adapted to general use. London: F. C. & J. Rivington, 1826. Edition "undertaken in compliance with a wish . . . that the Manual of Prayers composed by Bishop Ken for the use of the Scholars of Winchester College, might be presented to the public freed from allusions to the customs of that School . . . . The alterations . . . consist, chiefly of omissions . . . . The directions which precede the Prayers have been generally abridged, and in the latter part of the Manual, a somewhat different arrangement has been adopted."—advertisement. The three hymns by Bishop Ken are included, p. 87–90, but in shortened form, and with variations in text from the earlier versions.

BIOGRAPHY

Hawkins, William. A short account of the life of the Right Reverend Father in God, Thomas Ken, D.D. London: John Wyat, 1713.
On the title page: "Sometime Lord Bishop of Bath and Wells, to which is added a small specimen in order to a publication of his works at large." This very early biography appends several hymns and odes other than the three poems in the *Manual.*

Plumptre, Edward Hayes. The life of Thomas Ken, D.D., bishop of Bath and Wells. 2v. New York: E. & J. B. Young, [1888]; London: William Isbister, 1888. 2d ed. rev. London: William Isbister, 1890.
For *The manual of prayers for Winchester scholars,* see 1:92, 96–104; for the morning, evening, and midnight hymns, 2:210–30. The text is given in full from the edition of the Winchester *Manual* of 1697, noting in italics the various readings of that of 1712. Discusses such matters as when and where Ken wrote the hymns, with what circumstances they were connected, and of what inner experiences they were the outcome.

Martin Luther

Luther, Martin. Luther as a hymnist. Compiled by Bernhard Pick. Philadelphia: Lutheran Book Store, 1875.
Translations of Luther's hymns, with a biographical sketch, p. 9–27, and explanatory notes. Includes "A child's song at Christmas concerning the little child Jesus," p. 36–39.

CRITICISM

Buszin, W. E. "Luther on music," *Music quarterly* 32:80–90 (January 1946).

Nettl, Paul. Luther and music. Translated by Frida Best and Ralph Wood. Philadelphia: Muhlenberg Press, 1948.

This book "attempts a survey of Luther's relation to music and gives a short outline of evangelical church music with a consideration of contemporary theological and religious movements."—introduction. Charts the impact of the Reformation on religious music.

Christopher Smart

Smart, Christopher. Collected poems, with an introduction and critical comments by Norman Callan. 2v. London: Routledge & Kegan Paul, 1949.
"The parable of our Lord," p. 851–963; "Hymns for the amusement of children" (1775 ed.), p. 963–1005. Illustrated.

———. Hymns for the amusement of children. Dublin: T. Walker, [1772?].
Sole copy of a hitherto unrecorded edition of a famous book of hymns. This copy is in the Pierpont Morgan Library. Another 1772 edition, published by W. Sleator and J. Williams (Dublin), is in the British Museum.

———. ———. Philadelphia: William Spotswood, 1791.
Subtitle: "to which are added, Watts's *Divine songs for children.*" Also in the Morgan collection.

———. ———. Oxford: Basil Blackwell for the Luttrell Society, 1947.
Introduction is by Edmund Blunden, a Smart scholar. A facsimile from the 1775 edition at the Bodleian Library.

———. ———. Menston, England: Scolar Press, 1973.
Facsimile edition of a 1772 edition (now in the British Museum) that was printed for W. Sleator and J. Williams in Dublin. The introduction is by Thomas Minnick. Includes the original illustrations.

———. Poems. Edited with an introduction and notes by Robert Brittain. Princeton, N.J.: Princeton University Press, 1950.
Brittain, a Smart scholar, says of the poet, "He is a religious lyricist whose talents may be enjoyed and studied in scores of poems, and whose works may be ranked with the best of its kind in English." Selections from *Hymns for the amusement of children,* p. 255–67. Notes on these hymns, p. 314–17.

BIOGRAPHY AND CRITICISM

Ainsworth, Edward G., and Charles E. Noyes. Christopher Smart: a biographical and critical study. (University of Missouri studies, v. 18, no. 4) Columbia: University of Missouri Press, 1943.

Chap. 7, p. 151–62, is a bibliographical study of *The parables* and *Hymns for the amusement of children*. The biography is sympathetic.

Anderson, Frances E. Christopher Smart. New York: Twayne, 1974.
Chapter 6, "Last works of Christopher Smart," p. 112–25, deals, in part, with the *Hymns for the amusement of children*.

Blaydes, Sophia B. Christopher Smart as a poet of his time: a re-appraisal. (Studies in English literature, v. 28) The Hague: Mouton, 1966.
Good biography that attempts to prove that Smart's genius was not dependent on his madness as Browning contends (see below). Complete bibliography.

Bottling, Roland B. "Christopher Smart and the *Lilliputian magazine*," *Journal of English literary history* 9:286–87 (1942).
Attributes the anonymous "Morning hymn" found in Newbery's *Lilliputian magazine* to Smart. The first stanza goes:

> O thou! who lately clos'd my eyes,
> And calm'd my soul to rest,
> Now the dull blank of darkness flies,
> Be thank'd, be prais'd, be blest.

Brittain, Robert E. "Christopher Smart's *Hymns for the amusement of children*," *The Papers of the Bibliographic Society of America* 35:61–65 (1941).
Brittain discovered the 1791 copy in the American Antiquarian Society library.

Browning, Robert. "Christopher Smart," in his *Parleying with certain people of importance in their day*, p. 179–95. London: Smith & Elder, 1887.
In this work, Browning set forth the theory that Smart's great poem, *Song of David*, could only have been written by a madman.

Dearnley, Moira. The poetry of Christopher Smart. London: Routledge & Kegan Paul, 1968.
In chap. 12, "*The parables* and the *Hymns for the amusement of children*," p. 282–303, the author shows how Smart was influenced by Bunyan, Watts, Keach, and Chear.

Devlin, Christopher. Poor Kit Smart. London: Rupert Hart-Davis, 1961.
Places Christopher Smart's hymns for children in historical context.

Feldmeier, Linda. "Where skipping lambkins feed: Christopher Smart's *Hymns for the amusement of children*," *Children's literature* 4:64–69 (1975).
Details how the *Hymns* were influenced by Locke's philosophy of education. The author concludes, "While as a model for children's poetry,

the *Hymns* can be faulted both in content and technique, they are still valuable because they show the passion and concern with which children's books can be written; and as such provide a welcome antidote to children's literature that is cute and condescending."

Grigson, Geoffrey. Christopher Smart. (Writers and their work series, no. 161) London: Longmans, Green for the British Book Council, 1961.
The author sees Smart as being mad with a "religious mania," and from this viewpoint speaks of the "somewhat exhausted simplicity of his last effort of praise [the *Hymns*]."

Sherbo, Arthur. Christopher Smart: scholar of the university. East Lansing: Michigan State University Press, 1967.
A well-written, up-to-date study of Smart. P. 260–65 cover the *Hymns*, about which Sherbo concludes, "At the heart of the hymns of 1770 is the trinity of virtues he [Smart] had celebrated in the greater part of the poetry he had written—praise, charity, and gratitude."

Williamson, Karina. "Another edition of Smart's *Hymns for the amusement of children*," *The library*, 5th ser., 10:280–82 (1955).
This newly found copy of the *Hymns*, published in Dublin, contains an appendix not in the other extant copies, comprising sixteen hymns and a paraphrase of the Lord's Prayer. The author believes only one of the hymns is by Smart.

Bishop Jeremy Taylor

Taylor, Jeremy, *bishop of Down and Connor.* "Festival hymns," in his *The whole works, with a life of the author, and a critical examination of his writings; by the Rev. R. Heber,* p. 76–91. London: Longmans, Green, 1854.

———. The golden grove, or, a manuall of daily prayers and letanies fitted to the dayes of the week: containing a short summary of what is to be believed, practised, desired. Also festival hymns according to the manner of the ancient Church. London, 1655.
The full title of these poems is "Hymns—Celebrating the mysteries and chief festivals of the years, according to the manner of the ancient Church; fitted to the fancy and devotion of the younger and pious persons; apt for memory, and to be joined to their prayers."

BIOGRAPHY AND CRITICISM

Dowden, Edward. "An Anglican and a Puritan Eirenicon: Jeremy Taylor: Baxter," in his *Puritan and Anglican: studies in literature,* p. 197–213. London: Kegan Paul, 1900.

Gosse, Edmund. Jeremy Taylor. (English men of letters series) London: Macmillan, 1904.
Gosse says, "the greater part of the *Festival Hymns* is a sort of cantata on the mysteries of religion, arranged in connected sections. It misses either perfection, and is merely a brilliant instance of the failure of a great genius to express itself in an unfamiliar medium."

Heber, Reginald. Life of the Right Rev. Jeremy Taylor, D.D., Lord Bishop of Down, Connor, and Dromore. 2v. London: James Duncan & Priestley, 1824.
In vol. 2, p. 169–72, there is a brief discussion of *The golden grove* and the appended poems.

Patterson, John Brown. "An essay on his life and writing," in *The beauties of Jeremy Taylor* by Jeremy Taylor, p. ix–xliii. London: Blackie, 1834.
Includes letters of condolence to John Evelyn on the death of his two sons, Richard and George, p. xxxvii. Mention of *The golden grove*, p. xxxiii.

Stranks, Charles James. The life and writing of Jeremy Taylor. London: S.P.C.K. for the Church Historical Society, 1952.
A later account of Taylor's life. In a chapter on *The golden grove*, in which Strank discusses the "Festival hymns," he concludes, "It is a pity he decided to make them known, for everybody who reads them must say the same thing; they are ingenious, they are full of fancy, they are written in a complicated metre; but they are not poetry or anything like it . . . . Taylor leaves us with the impression that he is struggling with a task which is too difficult for him." A select bibliography is appended.

Williamson, Hugh Ross. Jeremy Taylor. (A Pegasus biography) London: Dennis Dobson, [1952].
A scholarly biography. Does not deal with the hymns.

Isaac Watts

Watts, Isaac. The art of reading and writing English, or, the chief principles and rules of pronouncing our mother-tongue, both in prose and verse, with a variety of instructions for true spelling. London: John Clark, 1722.
"Written at first for Private Use and now published for the Benefit of all Persons who desire a better acquaintance with their Native Language." Dedicated to the daughters of Sir Thomas Abney.

———. Divine and moral songs for children. London: Mathews, [1896].
This edition should be supplemented if possible by some of the earlier editions (see below under *Divine songs . . . .*). Under the heading "Moral songs" are included only "The sluggard" and "Innocent play." "Good advice to children" and two prayers are added. Contains the author's preface "To all, who are concerned in the education of children." Includes color illustrations by Mrs. Arthur Gaskin.

———. Divine and moral songs for the use of children. London: John van Voorst, 1848.
With nineteenth-century illustrations.

———. "Divine songs," in his *Horae lyricae and divine songs*, p. 296–348. Boston: Little, 1954.
Includes "The moral songs" also. Book has a memoir by Robert Southey.

———. Divine songs attempted in easy language for the use of children. London: M. Laurence, 1715.
The Pierpont Morgan Library owns one of the only two known perfect copies of the first edition.

———. ———. London: Oxford University Press, 1971.
This is a facsimile of the first edition of the *Divine songs* published in 1715, with an introduction and bibliography by J. H. P. Pafford. Titled as above, it contained a dedication, a preface; twenty-eight Divine songs; the Ten Commandments; our Saviour's Golden Rule; duty to God and our neighbour; the Hosanna; and Glory be to the Father; with a prefatory note headed by "A slight specimen of moral songs," including, "The sluggard," and "Innocent play." The "Cradle song" was not added until the 8th edition in 1727, and by the 16th edition, five more "Moral songs" were added. Pafford's biographical and historical notes are scholarly, complete, and extremely valuable. His bibliographical account of the different editions of the work corrects and updates that of Wilbur Stone.

———. Dr. Watts's celebrated cradle hymn, illustrated with appropriate engravings. London: John Harris, 1812.
This volume contains only the single poem. Owned by the Pierpont Morgan Library.

———. Songs, divine and moral. London: Simpkin & Marshall, 1826.
Includes the "Divine songs"; "Slight specimen of moral songs"; an appendix, which includes "The cradle hymn," "The kite," "The fly," and "The beggar's petition"; and a memoir of the author. Woodcut illustrations.

———. Songs, divine and moral, attempted in easy language for the use of children. New ed. Stourport: G. Nicholson, n.d.
Does not include the original preface but contains the "Moral songs" and also an additional poem, "The beggar's petition." Frontispiece and title page in color; also small woodcuts.

BIOGRAPHY AND CRITICISM

Darton, Frederick Joseph Harvey. "Interim: between the old and the new," in his *Children's books in England*, p. 108–12. 2d ed. Cambridge: Cambridge University Press, 1958.
Includes extract from original preface of Watts's *Divine songs* . . . .

Davis, Arthur Paul. Isaac Watts: his life and works. London: Independent, [1948].
This classic text attempts to "paint Watts as a forgotten genius" in the fields of education, theology, philosophy, and poetry. The chapter about Watts as a religious and secular educator, p. 73–102, depicts him as a teacher from the infant through the university level and as a writer of children's poetry, textbooks, religious educational texts (including catechisms), and educational theory. Excellent bibliographies.

Escott, Harry. Isaac Watts, hymnographer: a study of the beginnings, development, and philosophy of the English hymn. London: Independent, [1962].
The chapter entitled, "Children's songs and praises," p. 190–216, discusses Watts as a follower of the seventeenth-century writers Janeway and Bunyan, analyses the contents of *Divine songs* in terms of the Puritan "good godly" books, and suggests, finally, where the hymn's originality and supremacy lie.

Field, Louise Frances Story (Mrs. E. M. Field). "Dr. Watts," in her *The child and his book*," p. 258–63. 2d ed. London: Wells Gardner, 1892; reprint: Detroit: Singing Tree, 1968.
Includes the beginning of Watts's *Young child's catechism*.

Gibbons, Thomas. Memoirs of the Rev. Isaac Watts. London: James Buckland, 1780.
The first full-length biography of Watts, allegedly based on a manuscript given the author by Watts and his immediate family. Davis calls it an ill-arranged, clumsy compilation that, though a fountainhead for subsequent works, is basically unsatisfactory. No index, no bibliography.

Hood, Edwin Paxton. Isaac Watts: his life and writings, his home and friends. London: Religious Tract Society, 1875.
A readable, popular version of the material found in prior biographies.

Hope, Evelyn P. "Isaac Watts," *Fortnightly* 170: 400–6 (December, 1948).
Excellent résumé of his life and works.

"Isaac Watts: an educational divine," *London Times educational supplement* 1752:671 (November 27, 1948).
Discusses his educational theories and writing for children.

Johnson, Samuel. "Isaac Watts," in his *Lives of the most eminent English poets*, v. 3, p. 238–48. New ed. London: Nichols, 1810.
A laudatory biographical sketch.

Manning, Bernard L. The hymns of Wesley and Watts. London: Epworth, [1942].
A comparison of Wesley's and Watts's hymns. Includes an excellent general discussion of nineteenth- and twentieth-century hymns.

Milner, Thomas. The life, times and correspondence of the Rev. Isaac Watts, D.D. London: Simpkin & Marshall, 1834.
The second full-length biography of Watts; includes his letters.

Moses, Montrose Jonas. "The poets," in his *Children's books and reading*, p. 119–24. New York: Kennerley, 1907.
Notes the educational ideas of Watts as expressed in his "Discourse on the education of children and youth."

Muir, Percy. "Getting under weigh," in his *English children's books, 1600–1900*, p. 55–58. New York: Praeger, [1954]; London: Batsford, [1969].
A section in this chapter deals with Watts and cites him as a sympathetic versifier of children's hymns, "closer to the Taylor sisters than to Bunyan."

Pinto, Vivian de Sola. "Isaac Watts and the adventurous muse," in his *Essays and studies by members of the English association*, v. 20, p. 86–107. Oxford: Oxford University Press, 1935.
Speaks of Watts the poet, calling his poetry, "a link between the Puritan movement of the 17th century and the Romantic movement of the 19th century."

———. "Isaac Watts and William Blake," *Review of English studies* 20: 214–23 (1944).
Compares the work of Watts and Blake.

Rogal, Samuel J. "A checklist of works by and about Isaac Watts (1674–1748)," *Bulletin*, (New York Public Library) 71:207–15 (April, 1967).
The fullest bibliography of works by and about Watts. Includes bibliographical information about editions.

———. "Isaac Watts' London printers, publishers and booksellers (1700–1748)," *Gazette* (Yale University Library) 46:167–75 (January, 1972).

Shepherd, T. B. "Children's verse of Dr. Watts and Charles Wesley," *London quarterly and Holborn review* 164:173–84 (April, 1939).
Compares the poetry for children of Watts and Wesley and concludes that Wesley is more joyful and his poems more lasting.

Sloane, William. Children's books in England and America in the seventeenth century. New York: King's Press, Columbia University Press, 1955.
Sloane speaks harshly of Watts and his hymns in the chapter "A sad tale's best for winter," which summarizes the attitudes toward children in the seventeenth century.

Stone, Wilbur Macey. A brief list of editions of Watt's [sic] *Divine songs* located since 1918. New York: Park Row, 1929.

————. The divine and moral songs of Isaac Watts: an essay thereon and a tentative list of editions. Sewanee, Tenn.: University Press of Sewanee for the Triptych, 1918.
Limited edition of 250 copies. This bibliography was the first attempt to list all British and American editions of the *Divine and moral songs* between 1715 and 1915. It has been superseded by the Pafford facsimile edition, and Pafford considers this to be "incorrect, suppositional, and now incomplete."

————. "The *New England primer* and Watts's *Divine songs*," *Horn book magazine* 17:217–29 (May, 1941).
Considers Watts's hymns as a companion to the *Primer*. A short biographical sketch of Watts is included.

Surman, C. E. "Isaac Watts, schoolmaster," *Transactions* (Unitarian Historical Society) 13:122–23 (1965).

Thwaite, Mary F. "The Christian tradition—from Isaac Watts to the Sunday schools," in her *From primer to pleasure in reading*, p. 53–65. 2d ed. London: Library Assn., 1972.
Discusses the place of both Watts and Smart in literary and historical perspective.

Watson, Foster. "Isaac Watts as an educationist," *Gentleman's magazine* 71:531–36 (1903).

Wright, Thomas. Isaac Watts and contemporary hymn writers. (*The lives of the British hymnwriters, being personal memoirs derived from unpublished materials*, v. 3) London: C. J. Farncombe, 1914.
Discusses the *Divine and moral songs* in the chapter titled "Humorist, logician, preacher," p. 143–70.

Charles Wesley

Wesley, Charles. Representative verse of Charles Wesley. Selected and edited with an introduction by Frank Baker. London: Epworth, [1962].

Baker has found and analyzed about 9,000 poems by Wesley. The introduction to this work is excellent. A selection from *Hymns for children*, with biographical notes, is included on p. 140–46.

CRITICISM

Baker, Frank. Charles Wesley's verse. London: Epworth, [1964].
The text is the same as that in *Representative verse* (above). A concise bibliography is appended.

Manning, Bernard L. The hymns of Wesley and Watts. London: Epworth, [1942].
Noted above in the section on Isaac Watts.

Routley, Erik. "Charles Wesley and Methodist music," in his *The musical Wesleys*, p. 28–42. New York: Oxford University Press, 1968.
A good summary of Wesley's hymns and his educational theories.

George Wither

Wither, George. Halelviah, or, Britans second remembrancer. London, 1641.
Subtitle: "bringing to remembrance (in three . . . hymns, spirituall songs, and morall-odes) meditations, advancing the glory of God; . . . and applied to easy tunes . . . ." There are 233 hymns in three groups: "Hymns occasional," "Hymns temporary," and "Hymns personall." A few of these were definitely intended for children and young people. Includes "A rocking hymn," of which Wither quaintly remarks: "Nurses usually sing their children asleep; and through want of pertinent matter, they oft make use of unprofitable (if not worse) Songs. This was therefore prepared, that it might help acquaint them, and their Nurse-Children, with loving Care and Kindnesse of their heavenly Father."

————. ————. London: J. R. Smith, 1857.
Title reads: Hallelujah; or Britain's second remembrancer; bringing to remembrance (in praiseful and penitential hymns, spiritual songs, and moral odes) meditation, advancing the glory of God, in the practise of piety and virtue; composed in a three-fold volume. Introduction by Edward Farr.

————. ————. (Spenser Society publications nos. 26–27) 3v. in 1. London: Charles E. Simms for the Spenser Society, 1879.
The title reads: *Halelviah; or Britans second remembrancer* (1641).
Reproduction of the 1641 edition including the original title page.

Instruction and Amusement:
The Eighteenth Century

John Newbery, a London bookseller whose shop, the Bible and Sun, was in St. Paul's Churchyard, published *A little pretty pocket-book* in 1744. It is a date of such importance for the history of children's literature that all books for children can be viewed as coming either before or after John Newbery. In *Children's books in England*, Harvey Darton devotes his introductory essay almost entirely to *A little pretty pocket-book*, which, as Newbery said, was "intended for the Instruction and Amusement of Little Master Tommy and Pretty Miss Polly." Elva Smith used Newbery's idea in her title for a chapter on the eighteenth century in the first edition of *History of children's literature*.

Yet children in the first half of the century, before Newbery, were not to be pitied for want of "instruction and amusement." As in earlier times, books appeared, written for adults but with such a strong appeal for children that they were quickly adopted by young readers. The late seventeenth century had given them *Pilgrim's progress*. Now they were to have *Robinson Crusoe* (1719) and *Gulliver's travels* (1726). In *A critical history of children's literature*, Cornelia Meigs has pointed out that all three of these adult classics are in one way or another "tales of travel," and certainly children have loved them, not for their spiritual, social, or satirical implications, but for the charm of the tales they tell. All three are still found on any list of the world's great literature, and since their first publication countless editions for children have appeared, illustrated by artists of the first rank, the texts adapted, retold, abridged, translated into many languages, modernized, or published as schoolbooks. Stories based on the themes of these three "adopted" children's books are legion. There is even a coined word, *Robinsonades*, for stories derived from the idea of *Robinson Crusoe*.

It remained for John Newbery to give children books of their own—and not only schoolbooks or moral treatises. John Locke had written *Some thoughts concerning education* (1690), laying down the rule that children "should be allowed their liberties and freedom suitable to their ages . . . . They must not be hindered from being children." His words had enormous influence on the rearing of English children. Newbery read Locke and quoted him at length in the note "to the parents, guardians and nurses in Great-Britain and Ireland" with which *A little pretty pocket-book* begins.

Newbery was himself a gentle and amiable man who clearly wanted children to be happy with this, his first publishing venture especially intended for them. In the facsimile edition of *A little pretty pocket-book*, M. F. Thwaite calls the book a landmark and notes, "To avow 'amusement' as a principal end in a book for boys and girls indicated that a revolution had taken place." The very look of the *Pocket-book* was revolutionary. As an invitation to amusement, the little volume was bound in blue, green, and red flowered and gilt Dutch paper.

Today's children have forgotten *A little pretty pocket-book*, but another of John Newbery's publications for children has become immortal. About 1760 he gave them *Mother Goose's melody*, a compilation of rhymes that were already part of their heritage through oral tradition. From that time onward, Mother Goose rhymes have continued to appear in a great variety of editions, calling forth an outpouring of talent from artists and of scholarly research.

Like the children of today, the young seem always to have liked small, cheap books with paper bindings—books that can be tucked into a pocket, torn up, or thrown away. The eighteenth century gave children a wealth of such publications in the chapbooks, which included titles for children as well as for adults. In price and popularity, chapbooks may be compared to the comic book of the twentieth century. The *Oxford English dictionary* says that chapbooks "formed the chief popular literature of Great

Britain and the American colonies. They consisted of lives of heroes, martyrs, and wonderful personages, stories of roguery and broad humor, of giants, ghosts, witches, and dreams, histories in verse, songs and ballads, theological tracts, etc. They emanated principally from the provincial press, and were hawked about the country by chapmen or peddlars."

With the passage of time, these cheap and humble little books have through their very nature moldered away or been destroyed. As a result they are prized by rare book specialists, and a sizable collection of chapbooks is highly valued in any library. The New York Public Library has a large collection. In 1905 the Harvard College Library published a catalog of its outstanding collection of chapbooks, compiled in large part by Charles Welsh, with the eminent scholar George Lyman Kittredge as consultant. The fascinating subject of chapbooks continues to attract serious interest on both sides of the Atlantic.

OUTLINE

I. Historical and literary background
  A. Children's books in the early eighteenth century; prevailing types and general character
  B. Rise of fiction for adults
    1. Use in family groups
    2. Abridgments for children
    3. *Robinson Crusoe* and *Gulliver's travels*
  C. John Locke's views on education and reading; their effects on the eighteenth century
II. The mid-eighteenth century and the new developments in children's books
  A. John Newbery (1713–67) and his publishing venture
    1. The personal side
      a) The life of Newbery
      b) His personal characteristics
      c) His business undertakings
    2. The children's books
      a) Their purpose and value
      b) Their writers
      c) Their format
      d) Their literary characteristics
      e) Ingenious methods of advertising
      f) Illustrative books
        (1) *Goody Two Shoes* (attributed to Goldsmith)
          (*a*) Evidence as to authorship
          (*b*) The story and the manner of writing
          (*c*) The character of Goody Two Shoes
          (*d*) The humor
          (*e*) The connection between pictures and text
          (*f*) Reflection of the educational and moral ideas of the period
          (*g*) Different editions
          (*h*) Comparison of original with modern abridged and adapted editions
          (*i*) Use with children of the present time
        (2) *Circle of the sciences* and other books
    3. Later history of the Newbery publications
  B. Other publishers and their children's books
  C. Nursery rhymes
    1. *Tommy Thumb's pretty song book*
    2. *The top book of all*
    3. *Mother Goose's melody, or, sonnets for the cradle* (John Newbery?)
      a) Probable derivation of title
      b) Hypothesis as to Goldsmith's editorship
      c) Preface
      d) The rhymes and the humorous "reflections"
      e) American edition of Isaiah Thomas
    4. *Gammer Gurton's garland, or, the Nursery Parnassus*
  D. Chapbooks
    1. The chapman and his wares
    2. Different types of chapbooks and the subjects with which they deal
    3. Chapbook publishers
    4. Banbury chapbooks and their illustrators
    5. Chapbooks of the nineteenth century compared with those of an earlier period
    6. What the chapbook meant to the English people in the eighteenth century
  E. Card battledores of the eighteenth century
    1. The inventor, Benjamin Collins
    2. Description and comparison with hornbooks
    3. Varieties
    4. Period of their use

LIFE AND LITERATURE

Ashton, John. Social life in the reign of Queen Anne, taken from original sources. New ed. London: Chatto & Windus, 1883; reprint: Detroit: Singing Tree, 1968.
Excellent general background for the period with illustrations taken from contemporary prints. Chapter 1, "Childhood and education (boys)" and chapter 2, "Childhood and education (girls)" are especially helpful.

Gottlieb, Gerald. Early children's books and their illustration. New York: Pierpont Morgan Library; Boston: Godine, 1975.
For descriptions of important early editions and commentary on the significance of the books, see chapters on *Robinson Crusoe* and Robinsonades, p. 147–59; *Gulliver's travels*, p. 160–63; Thomas Boreman, p. 191–93; Baron Munchausen, p. 205–7.

Hodges, Margaret. Lady Queen Anne: a biography of Queen Anne of England. New York: Farrar, 1969.
Intended for the general reader, placing the figures of the Augustan Age—including Defoe, Locke, Newton, Pope, Swift and others—against the political and social background of eighteenth-century England.

Stuart, Dorothy Margaret. "The eighteenth-century boy," in her *The boy through the ages*, p. 235–56. London: Harrap, 1926.

———. "In Augustan England," in her *The girl through the ages*, p. 198–218. London: Harrap, 1933; reprint: Detroit: Singing Tree, 1969.

The Educational Ideas of Locke

Bator, Robert. "Out of the ordinary road: John Locke and English juvenile fiction in the eighteenth century," *Children's literature, the great excluded* 1:46–54 (1972).
An essay emanating from the Modern Language Association seminar on children's literature. Shows how "largely because of Locke, the child in the eighteenth century was prodigally supplied with books designed for him."

Locke, John. Some thoughts concerning education, abridged and edited by F. W. Garforth. London: Heinemann; Woodbury, N.Y.: Barron's, 1964.
The editor's introduction covers Locke's life and character, his writings, Locke as philosopher, Locke's educational thought, his sources and later influence, his literary style. See especially the section entitled "Reading," p. 186–92. Bibliography.

Robinson Crusoe

Aikin, Lucy (*pseud.* Mary Godolphin). Robinson Crusoe in words of one syllable. London and New York: Routledge, 1868; New York: McLoughlin, 1869.
A popular retelling for young readers. One of several classics retold in this manner, using no word of more than one syllable except for *Xury, Friday*, and the captions under the illustrations, which are in color.

Defoe, Daniel. The adventures of Robinson Crusoe. Leeds: J. Roberts, n.d.
A nineteenth-century chapbook with woodcuts.

———. Life and adventures of Robinson Crusoe. Banbury: J. G. Rusher, n.d.
A nineteenth-century chapbook with woodcuts.

———. The life and strange surprising adventures of Robinson Crusoe of York, mariner. New York: Russell, 1900.
With nearly a hundred original drawings and decorations done from sketches made in the tropics specially for this work by the brothers Louis and Frederick Rhead.

———. The life and strange surprizing adventures of Robinson Crusoe, of York, mariner . . . . written by himself. 3d ed. London: W. Taylor, 1719.
One of four editions that appeared within four months during the year of first publication.

———. Robinson Crusoe. New York: Cosmopolitan Book Corp., 1920; reprint: New York: Scribner, 1957.
With an illustrator's preface and the famous illustrations by N. C. Wyeth.

———. Robinson Crusoe. New York and London: Macmillan, 1962.
With illustrations by Federico Castellon and a perceptive afterword by Clifton Fadiman on the appeal of *Robinson Crusoe* for children.

Politzer, Anie. Robinson Crusoe: my journals and sketchbooks. New York: Harcourt, 1974.
First American edition, translated from the French *Robinson Crusoe: mes carnets de croquis*. Many of Robinson Crusoe's adventures, told in his "own" words, illustrated with his "own" sketches as recorded in his journal and sketchbook, supposedly unearthed years later in an old Scottish manor house. Helpful as an introduction to Defoe's book.

Brigham, Clarence S. Bibliography of American editions of Robinson Crusoe to 1830. Worcester, Mass.: American Antiquarian Society, 1858; reprint: Charlottesville: University of Virginia Press, 1958.

de la Mare, Walter. Desert islands and Robinson Crusoe. New York: Farrar, 1930.
Quotations from literature with added discussion. A classic on the subject of Robinsonades.

Hardy, Barbara. "Robinson Crusoe," *Children's literature in education* 8, no. 1:3–11 (1977).
Examines the continuing appeal to children of Defoe's book.

Hoffman, Margit. "Robinsonades: the J. A. Ahlstrand collection," *Signal* 17:61–74 (May, 1975).
A useful account of the books published as "a form of imitation of the Robinson theme as developed by Defoe." Notes.

Watson, Francis. Daniel Defoe. (Men and books series) London and New York: Longmans, 1952; reprint: Port Washington, N.Y.: Kennikat Press, 1969.
Brief biography with chronology.

Gulliver's Travels

Swift, Jonathan. Gulliver's travels. New York: Heritage, 1940.
With engravings on wood by Fritz Eichenberg.

–––. –––. Retold by Padraic Colum. New York and London: Macmillan, 1917, 1962.
With illustrations by Willy Pogany. Padraic Colum's introduction gives an excellent biographical sketch of Swift and an approach to *Gulliver's travels* outstanding for its insight and literary distinction. Clifton Fadiman's afterword is equally to the point. Directed to young readers.

–––. –––. Adapted by Sarel Eimerl. New York: Golden Press, 1962.
Illustrations in full color by Maraja and a somewhat simplified abridgment do justice to the original text and make a good selection for young readers.

–––. –––. Retold by Elaine Moss. London: Constable, 1961.
This is an abridgment for children. (The first abridgement was published without authorization by J. Stone and R. King one year after the original publication of *Gulliver's travels* in 1726.) The large colorful illustrations by Hans Baltzer were originally published in a German edition.

–––. Gulliver's travels into several remote nations of the world. London: Dent; New York: Dutton, 1909.

Most of the designs, by Arthur Rackham, appeared as line drawings in an edition of 1899, now "worked over, revised and coloured by the artist while some entirely new designs have been added . . . designed *virginibus puerisque*." A new edition with Rackham illustrations in the Dent/Dutton Children's illustrated classics series appeared in 1952.

Rowse, Alfred Leslie. Jonathan Swift. New York: Scribner, 1976.
In this biography by a major historian, the circumstances surrounding the publication and success of *Gulliver's travels* are described, and the book itself is outlined in lively style, p. 141–85.

Ward, David. Jonathan Swift: an introductory essay. London: Methuen, 1973.
Gulliver's travels is discussed in a study that "aims to be stimulating rather than exhaustive," p. 121–83.

White, Terence Hanbury. Mistress Masham's repose. New York: Putnam, 1946; reprint: New York: Capricorn, 1960.
The first edition is illustrated by Fritz Eichenberg. A witty satire based on the Lilliputian adventures of Gulliver and intended for young readers.

John Newbery and Children's Books

Barry, Florence Valentine. "The Lilliputian library," in her *A century of children's books*, p. 58–84. New York: Doran, 1923; reprint: Detroit: Singing Tree, 1968.
Discusses typical books published by John Newbery; also some of the "late 'Lilliputians' that have the true Newbery touch, and even a fresh spice of satire."

Dalgliesh, Alice. "In Mr. Newbery's bookshop," *Horn book magazine*, 4:275–79 (July, 1940).
An imaginary visit to the shop in St. Paul's Churchyard and a description of Newbery's *Important pocket book, or, the valentine's diary*, used as background for the character of the child in Alice Dalgliesh's *Book for Jennifer*, which brings Newbery's shop to life.

Earle, Alice Morse. "Story and picture books," in her *Child life in colonial days*, p. 264–304. New York: Macmillan, 1899; reprint: Folcroft, Pa.: Folcroft, 1974.
Concerns the American printer Isaiah Thomas and his reprints of English books, chiefly those of John Newbery.

Field, Louise Frances Story (Mrs. E. M. Field). "From 1740 to about 1810," in her *The child* *and his book*, p. 273–79. 2d ed. London: Wells Gardner, 1892; reprint: Detroit: Singing Tree, 1968.

The first seven pages of this chapter comment on Oliver Goldsmith as a writer of children's books for John Newbery.

Fielding, Sarah. The governess, or, little female academy. London: printed for the author, 1749; facsimile reprint: London: Oxford University Press, 1968.

Stories thought suitable for children, told by a Mrs. Teachum to a group of children. Mrs. Teachum has a touch of humor like that of Henry Fielding, brother of the author. Some of the stories are fairy tales that were retold in a bowdlerized version by Mrs. Sherwood (1820). The editor of *The Osborne collection of early children's books* questions the 1749 date.

Goldsmith, Oliver. ["The philanthropic bookseller,"] p. 101 in his *The vicar of Wakefield*. New York: Dutton, 1965.

A description of John Newbery, whom the good Dr. Primrose encounters in his pursuit "to reclaim a lost child to virtue."

Grey, Jill E. "Mrs. Teach'em: children's authors and Sarah Fielding," *Junior bookshelf* 32:285–88 (October, 1968).

An enumeration of women writers of the eighteenth century, including less-known names.

——. "The *Lilliputian magazine;* a pioneering periodical," *Journal of librarianship* 2:107–15 (April, 1970).

A valuable article giving detail on a mid-eighteenth-century book as known from surviving copies and showing that John Newbery planned this title as a periodical.

Halsey, Rosalie Vrylina. "The playbook in England," "Newbery's books in America," and "Patriot printers and the American Newbery," in her *Forgotten books of the American nursery*, p. 31–118. Boston: Goodspeed, 1911.

The American Newbery is Isaiah Thomas of Worcester, Massachusetts, who published pirated editions of many of the Newbery books.

Lee, Emma. "At the sign of the Bible and Sun; a play for marionettes or people," *Wilson library bulletin* 9:120–29, 148 (1934).

"The play was created to honor John Newbery, that little London publisher, whose quaint little books for children did, indeed, prove the beginning of great things.'"—author's note.

Opie, Peter. "John Newbery and his successors," *Book collector* 24:259–69 (Summer 1975).

A scholarly bibliographical essay on the development of documentation of early children's books, especially on Sydney Roscoe's monumental work (see below).

Roscoe, Sydney. "A bibliographer's progress," *Top of the news* 24:276–81 (April, 1968).

Personal recollections of the author on his background and work up to the time of his landmark bibliography on John Newbery.

——. John Newbery and his successors, 1740–1814: a bibliography. Wormley, Hertfordshire: Five Owls, 1973.

The definitive work on this subject, with approaches through names of publishers, booksellers and printers, artists, woodcutters and engravers, titles and dates of publications in the second half of the eighteenth century, London.

Stone, Wilbur Macey. The *Gigantick histories* of Thomas Boreman. Portland, Me.: Southworth, 1933.

Traces and describes the publishing venture that produced a series of ten little volumes, 1740–43, popular in London for the instruction and amusement of children. Includes reproductions of frontispieces, titles, and other pages.

Thwaite, Mary F. "John Newbery: two centuries after," *Horn book magazine* 44:155–61 (April, 1968).

A biographical sketch with excellent coverage of Newbery's work and publications for children. Written to commemorate the 200th anniversary of his death.

Weedon, M. J. P. "Richard Johnson and his successors to John Newbery," *The library*, 5th ser., 4, no. 1:25–63 (June, 1949).

Detailed and descriptive account of Richard Johnson's daybook recording his commissioned writings for Newbery. Identifies ninety-one titles. A valuable source for studying early English juvenile books.

Welsh, Charles. A bookseller of the last century. London: Griffith, 1885; reprint: Clifton, N.J.: A. M. Kelley, 1972.

Subtitle: "being some account of the life of John Newbery and of the books he published, with a notice of the later Newberys." The author—a partner in the firm of Griffith, Farran, Okeden and Welsh—identified Newbery as "the first bookseller who made the issue of books, specially intended for children, a business of any importance." Welsh endeavored to bring together all the scattered information about John Newbery and produced a catalog of books published by the Newberys, an important piece of research on this subject. See especially chapter 6, which deals with the books for children; also the interesting descriptive list, p. 168–335. "List of Newbery's publications from 1740–1802," p. 337–47.

——. "Some notes on the history of books for children," *The Newbery House magazine* 3:468–71, 599–610 (1890).

In the main a reprint of the chapter on children's books in the author's *A bookseller of the last century.*

BOOKS ILLUSTRATING THE ADVERTISING METHODS OF NEWBERY AND HIS CONTEMPORARIES

Berquin, Arnaud. The looking-glass for the mind. London: Griffith, 1885.

Subtitle: "a reprint of the edition of 1792, with the original illustrations by Bewick, with an introduction by Charles Welsh." In the story "Anabella's journey to market," a good old woman inquires what books she reads. "But when Anabella told her that her books were all bought at the corner of St. Paul's church-yard, she seemed perfectly satisfied."

[Cooper, W. D., ed.] The blossoms of morality. London: E. Newbery, 1796. 2d ed.

Subtitle: "intended for the amusement and instruction of young ladies and gentlemen, by the editor of *The looking-glass for the mind,* with forty-seven cuts designed and engraved by J. Bewick." The young Theophilus, in one of the tales, remarks to his father: "I cannot help pitying those poor little boys, whose parents are not in a condition to purchase them such a nice gilded library, as that with which you have supplied me from my good friend's at the corner of St. Paul's church-yard. Surely such unhappy boys must be very ignorant all their lives; for what can they learn without books?"

Little King John of No-Land, *pseud.* The proverbs of little Solomon. (Youth's pocket library, v.1) London: John Fairburn, 1797.

Subtitle: "exemplified in pleasing stories, historic anecdotes, and entertaining tales, to which are added moral reflections and poetical applications to real life, illustrated with eight beautiful copper plate prints." The preface calls attention to the publisher's other entertaining books which have "very pleasing stories, and several pretty pictures." The publisher, John Fairburn, was an imitator of John Newbery.

A little pretty pocket-book. London: printed for J. Newbery, at the Bible and Sun in St. Paul's Church-yard, 1767.

Subtitle: "intended for the instruction and amusement of Little Master Tommy, and Pretty Miss Polly. With two letters from Jack the giant-killer; as also a ball and pincushion; the use of which will infallibly make Tommy a good boy, and Polly a good girl. To which is added, *A little song-book,* being a new attempt to teach children the use of the English alphabet, by way of diversion."

———. London: Oxford University Press, 1966.

A facsimile reproduction. With an introductory essay and bibliography by M. F. Thwaite. Other books printed for and sold by J. Newbery are listed at the end of the original text.

The oracles. London: E. Newbery, [1801?].

Subtitle: "containing some particulars of the history of Billy and Kitty Wilson, including anecdotes of their playfellows, &c., intended for the entertainment of the little world and illustrated by engravings." Chapter 3 (p. 23–24) not only contains a reference to Mrs. Newbery but also gives the full and very lengthy title and the price of a set of books describing the Tower of London. A list of the "books printed for E. Newbery . . . for the instruction and entertainment of all the good little masters and misses of Great-Britain, Ireland, and America" is appended. Reference is made to *The history of Tommy Playlove and Jacky Lovebook,* another Newbery publication, in the author's dedication.

The polite lady, or, a course of female education in a series of letters from a mother to her daughter. London: John Newbery, 1760.

In the letter entitled "Writing," the mother, who signs herself Portia, says, "I have sent you Newbery's dictionary, to assist you in spelling."

Tagg, Tommy, *pseud.* A collection of pretty poems for the amusement of children three foot high, adorned with above sixty cuts. 55th ed. London: [John Newbery], 1756.

On p. 7 (p. 11 in the edition of 1781) is a Bewick cut of a printer composing *The Lilliputian magazine.* On the next page is a four-line verse headed, "On a fine gilt library," with a picture to correspond. Following the preface in the earlier edition is an advertisement stating that "speedily will be published by the same Author, A Collection of Pretty Poems for the Amusement of Children six foot high."

———. ———. 16th ed. 1781.

This edition is presumably one of the publications of Carnan and Newbery. The numbering of the editions is probably arbitrary. See also the note for the facsimile edition of "Goody Two Shoes." p. 84.

BOOKS ILLUSTRATING TITLES AND INGENIOUS PSEUDONYMS

Circle of the sciences. 3d ed. v.1–6. London: Newbery & Carnan, 1769.

v.1. Grammar made familiar and easy to young gentlemen, ladies, and foreigners.

v.2. Arithmetic made familiar and easy to young gentlemen and ladies.

v.3. Rhetoric made familiar and easy to young gentlemen and ladies, and illustrated with several beautiful orations from Demosthenes, Cicero, Sallust, Homer, Shakespeare, Milton, &c.

v.4. Poetry made familiar and easy to young gentlemen and ladies, and embellished with a great variety of the most shining epigrams, epitaphs, songs, odes, pastorals, &c., from the best authors.

v.5. Logic made familiar and easy to young

gentlemen and ladies, to which is added a compendious system of metaphysics or ontology.

v.6. Geography made familiar and easy to young gentlemen and ladies.

This edition was published by Newbery & Carnan, but the books were first issued by John Newbery in ten small volumes, 1745–46. The little books, constructed on the question-and-answer principle, and less than four inches by three in size, were all "Published by the King's Authority" and were dedicated to children of the royal family or to some noble personage. The series was so popular that it was reprinted in part in various corrected and revised editions up to 1793. Some of the selections included in the volume on poetry indicate the free-spoken character of the times.

Comical, Christopher, *pseud.* A lecture upon games and toys for the amusement of good girls and boys by Christopher Comical, master of the revels to the king of Funnyland and poet laureat to the Lilliputians. 2 pts. in 2v. London: Francis Power, 1789.

The publisher was a grandson of John Newbery.

Ticklecheek, Timothy, *pseud.* The cries of London. (Youth's pocket library, v.3) London: John Fairburn, 1797.

Subtitle: "displaying the manners, customs & characters of various people who traverse London streets with articles to sell, to which is added some pretty poetry applicable to each character, intended to amuse and instruct all good children, with London and the country contrasted, embellished with thirteen elegant copper plate prints.

Goody Two Shoes

Goody Two Shoes, *pseud.* Goody Two-Shoes: a facsimile reproduction of the edition of 1766, with an introduction by Charles Welsh. London: Griffith, 1881.

According to the editor, this reprint of the third edition is a photographic facsimile of the earliest complete copy that it was possible to procure. The edition includes "The golden dream, or, the ingenuous confession," "An anecdote, respecting Tom Two-Shoes," and "A letter from the printer"; also a list of "The books usually read by the scholars of Mrs. Two-Shoes." There are several references in the text to other books published by John Newbery (see p. 33, 61, 67), and Dr. James's powder, of which Newbery had the sole sale, is referred to on p. 13. The original is bound in the once-familiar Dutch flowered and gilt pattern paper and is 4 inches by 2¾ in size. The reprint is somewhat larger in size. The introduction reproduces the advertisement which appeared in the *London Chronicle* for Dec. 19–Jan. 1, 1765, and also discusses the question of the authorship.

———. Goody Two Shoes, or, the history of little Margery Meanwell, in rhyme. London: J. Harris, 1825.

"The best motive that the Author . . . can offer for introducing this well-known history to the public in a new dress, is the excellence of the moral interwoven with its diversified incidents, and the admirable lessons it conveys under the form of amusement."—preface. Printed in clear, well-spaced type and illustrated with a small engraving at the beginning of each section. There is a title-page cut of Margery showing her new shoes. This copy is imperfect, the text beginning with chapter 7 on p. 17.

———. The history of Goody Two Shoes, with the adventures of her brother Tommy, embellish'd with elegant engravings. Glasgow: Lumsden, 1810.

The story is very much shortened in this "improved edition"; but the illustrations are better than those in the earlier issues. Instead of being scattered through the text they are printed on separate pages with two small pictures on a page. There is also a title-page design and a frontispiece of Tommy Two Shoes showing the Indians his watch.

———. The history of little Goody Two Shoes, otherwise called Mrs. Margery Two Shoes (The little library) New York: Macmillan, 1924, 1966. Reprinted with new pictures, by Alice Woodward.

———. ———. Edited by Charles Welsh. Boston: Heath, 1901.

This title and the one above are modern abridged editions used for comparison.

———. The history of little Goody Two-Shoes, otherwise called Mrs. Margery Two-Shoes, with the means by which she acquired her learning and wisdom, and in consequence thereof, her estate. Coventry: Luckman & Suffield, [17-?].

According to the title page, this story is "set forth at large for the benefit of those,

> Who from a State of Rags and Care,
> And having Shoes but Half a Pair,
> Their Fortune and their Fame would fix,
> And gallop in their Coach and Six.

This edition is somewhat abridged from the original, and the political preface is omitted. The "Anecdote respecting Tom Two-Shoes" is included, but in abridged form. Illustrated with woodcuts, similar in character, but differing from those in the Newbery edition. Cover of flowered gilt paper.

■*Goody Two Shoes* is also included in Scudder's *Children's book,* in Tappan's *Old fashioned stories and poems,* and in vol. 1 of Charlotte Yonge's *Storehouse of stories.*

Nursery Rhymes

Barchilon, Jacques, and **Henry Pettit,** eds. The authentic Mother Goose fairy tales and nursery rhymes. London: printed for E. Power, 1791; reprint: Denver: Swallow, 1960.
The facsimile reprint also includes *Mother Goose's melody.* The title page reads: "*Mother Goose's Melody, or, Sonnets for the Cradle . . .* Embellished with cuts, and illustrated with notes and maxims, historical, philosophical and critical." Includes a good introduction which discusses the rhymes as literature. Bibliography.

Baring-Gould, Sabine, ed. A book of nursery songs and rhymes. London: Methuen, 1895; Chicago: McClurg, 1907; reprint: Detroit: Singing Tree, 1969.
An important illustrated collection with an introduction in which the scholarly editor places the rhymes in social history. Notes.

Baring-Gould, William S., and **Cecil Baring-Gould.** The annotated Mother Goose: nursery rhymes old and new, arranged and explained. New York: Potter, 1962.
Brings together much valuable material otherwise hard to find. Each section has an introduction giving biographical, historical, and bibliographical detail. Illustrations include work by Walter Crane, Randolph Caldecott, Kate Greenaway, Arthur Rackham, Maxfield Parrish, and early historic woodcuts. Heavily annotated for the general reader.

Gammer Gurton's garland, or, the nursery Parnassus: a choice collection of pretty songs and verses for the amusement of all little good children who can neither read nor run. London: R. Triphook, 1810.
"Originally issued at Stockton, as a small twopenny *brochure,* in 32mo, without a date, 'printed by and for R. Christopher.' Sir Harris Nicholas says it appeared in the year 1783 'one of the most prolific of Ritson's pen.' . . . 'Gammer Gurton's Garland' was again printed, with additions, 1809, in 8vo."—publisher's note. This collection, attributed to Joseph Ritson, is divided into four parts and contains many rhymes not found in Newbery's Mother Goose rhymes.

Mother Goose melodies. New York: Putnam, 1919.
Subtitle: "the Boyd Smith Mother Goose, with numerous illustrations in color and in black and white from original drawings by E. B. Smith; the text carefully collated and verified by Lawrence Elmendorf." Includes a reprint of *The original Mother Goose's melody* as issued by John Newbery of London, 1760[?], and Isaiah Thomas of Worcester, Massachusetts, 1785[?]. There are, however, changes in arrangement and also occasionally in the text.

———. New York: Dodd, 1914.
Subtitle: "the Jessie Willcox Smith Mother Goose, a careful and full selection of the rhymes, with illustrations." The first fifty-one rhymes with their morals are taken from the facsimile reproduction of the Isaiah Thomas edition, but there are some variations in the text.

Mother Goose's melodies. Boston: C. S. Francis, [1842?].
Subtitle: "the only pure edition containing all that have ever come to light of her memorable writings, together with those which have been discovered among the MSS. of Herculaneum, likewise every one recently found in the same stone box which hold [sic] the golden plates of the book of Mormon." Copyrighted by Munroe & Francis in 1833. The imprint of Munroe & Francis appears on the wrapper.

Mother Goose's melodies, or, songs for the nursery. Edited by W. A. Wheeler. Boston: Hurd and Houghton, 1869.
The introduction, "The Goose or Vergoose family," presents the arguments for the claim that the association of Mother Goose with traditional rhymes is due to Thomas Fleet of Boston. The collection is based on Halliwell's *Nursery rhymes of England,* though with some variations, and historical or explanatory notes are appended. Illustrated.

The nursery rhyme book. Edited by Andrew Lang. London and New York: Warne, 1897; new ed., 1947.
The preface by Andrew Lang offers conjectures on the events and persons referred to in the nursery rhymes. The illustrations by L. Leslie Brooke are outstanding for humor and storytelling quality.

Opie, Iona, and **Peter Opie,** eds. The Oxford nursery rhyme book. New York: Oxford University Press, 1955.
A collection of 800 rhymes, often including variations. Illustrations from toy books and chapbooks of the latter half of the eighteenth century and the early nineteenth century. Appendix gives information on dates, places of publication, and publishers of toy books and chapbooks.

The original Mother Goose's melody. Albany, N.Y.: Munsell, 1889; reprint: Detroit: Singing Tree, 1969.
Subtitle: "as first issued by John Newbery of London, about A.D. 1760, reproduced in facsimile from the edition as reprinted by Isaiah Thomas, of Worcester, Mass., about A.D. 1785, with introductory notes by W. H. Whitmore." The introduction discusses the derivation of the title and gives a list of books published by Isaiah Thomas, bibliographical notes about different editions of the nursery rhymes, and a list of the rhymes included in the editions published by Munroe & Francis in 1824 and 1833. The compilation of the

Newbery edition is ascribed to Oliver Goldsmith. The first part includes fifty-one rhymes with humorous footnotes. The second part contains "the lullabies of Shakespear."

Rimbault, Edward F., ed. Nursery rhymes, with the tunes to which they are still sung in the nurseries of England. London: Cramer, Wood, [n.d.].
Obtained principally from oral tradition. The earliest attempt to preserve the notation for the nursery rhymes.

Wood, Ray, comp. The American Mother Goose. New York: F. A. Stokes, 1940.
Foreword by John A. Lomax. Alphabetically arranged collection of American folk rhymes from all parts of the United States. Illustrated.

CRITICISM

Nolen, Eleanor W. "Cock robin," *Horn book magazine* 15:101–8 (March–April, 1939).
" . . . one of the most persistent of the hundreds of nursery rhymes . . . the subject of many charming examples of the toy book" of the late eighteenth and early nineteenth centuries.

Opie, Iona, and **Peter Opie,** eds. "Nursery rhymes," in *Bibliophile in the nursery* edited by William Targ, p. 262–320. Cleveland: World, 1957.
Reprinted from *Oxford dictionary of nursery rhymes* described below.

———. The Oxford dictionary of nursery rhymes. Oxford: Clarendon, 1951.
A landmark in research on the subject, this gives notes on origins, first appearances, and historical associations for 550 nursery rhymes. The authors' introduction is a notable piece of writing.

Smith, Elva S. "Mother Goose yesterday and today," in *Children's library yearbook* (American Library Assn.) 4:27–39 (1932).
Written when Elva Smith was head of work with children, Carnegie Library of Pittsburgh. Discusses Perrault's *Contes* and Newbery's *Mother Goose's melody,* mentioning later editions, and attempts to reform the rhymes. Bibliography and lists of "Collections with historical interest for children," also collections with music.

Thomas, Della F. "Matriarch of the nursery: Mother Goose," *Library journal* 92:1300–2 (March 15, 1967); *School library journal* 14:110–12 (March, 1967).
Brief descriptions of many editions and a bibliography taken from *Books in print,* 1966, for use as a buying guide.

Thomas, Katherine E. The real personages of Mother Goose. Boston: Lothrop, 1930.
The author connects historical names with those in the rhymes. Although critical opinion is divided

about this work, it is full of interest. Index of references, p. 340–52.

Weedon, M. J. P. "Mother Goose's melody," *The library,* 5th ser. 6:216–18 (December, 1951).
This bibliographical note is "a discussion on the dating of Newbery's missing edition and on the claim that the woodcuts were engraved by Bewick."

Weiss, Harry Bischoff. "Something about Simple Simon," *Bulletin* (New York Public Library) 44:461–70 (June, 1940).
Discusses the origins of the rhyme, tracing it as far as a seventeenth-century prose history. Various chapbook editions are noted. Facsimiles and preliminary checklist.

Chapbooks and Primers

Ashton, John. Chap-books of the eighteenth century, with facsimiles, notes, and introduction. London: Chatto, 1882; reprint: New York: Kelley, 1970.
"List of chap-books published in Aldermary and Bow churchyards," p. 483–86. Some chapbooks are reproduced in full. Others are represented by extracts or by title pages only.

Darton, Frederick Joseph Harvey. "The pedlar's pack: The running stationers," in his *Children's books in England: five centuries of social life,* p. 70–84. 2d ed. Cambridge: Cambridge University Press, 1958.
Jonathan Cott calls this "still the wittiest, most informative, and most interesting book on the history of this literature."

Harvard University. Catalogue of English and American chap-books and broadside ballads in Harvard College Library. (Bibliographical contributions, v. 4, no. 56) Cambridge, Mass.: Library of Harvard University, 1905.
Gives 2,461 titles, arranged by subject. An index of subjects and titles and an index of publishers, printers, and booksellers.

Haviland, Virginia. "Who killed Cock Robin?" *Quarterly journal* (Library of Congress) 30:95–139 (April, 1973).
Describes Library of Congress holdings of chapbook editions of *Cock Robin* from 1780 to 1966.

Heartman, Charles F. American primers, Indian primers, royal primers, and thirty-seven other types of non–New England primers, issued prior to 1830. Highland Park, N.J.: Printed for Harry B. Weiss, 1935.
"A bibliographical checklist embellished with twenty-six cuts, with an index & indexes. . . ." Indicates thirty-six private and institutional holders. Each type of primer is discussed.

Hindley, Charles. A collection of the books and woodcuts of James Catnach, late of Seven Dials, printer. London: Reeves & Turner, 1869.
With an account of his life, compiled by Charles Hindley. Profusely illustrated with hundreds of woodcuts, including several by Thomas Bewick. Includes full reprints of many rare juvenile chapbooks issued by Jemmy Catnach.

———. The history of the Catnach Press at Berwick-upon-Tweed, Alnwick and Newcastle-upon-Tyne, in Northumberland, and Seven Dials, London. London: Charles Hindley, 1886; reprint: Detroit: Gale, 1969.
Reproduces text and illustrations of a number of children's chapbooks, including "The tragical death of an apple pie," "The butterfly's ball," "Jack Jingle," and "Cock Robin." "A collection of juvenile books printed and published by James Catnach," p. [95]–217.

John Cheap, the chapman's library: Scottish chap literature of the last century, classified. 3v. Glasgow: Robert Lindsay, 1877–78.
Includes biography of Dougal Graham. Profusely illustrated; printed from stereotyped plates used for producing the texts of many of these old chapbooks, making veritable facsimiles.

Merritt, Edward Percival. The royal primer. Cambridge, Mass.: Harvard University Press, 1925.
A historical survey of the primer that antedated and influenced the New England primer.

Neuburg, Victor E. Chapbooks: a bibliography of references to English and American chapbook literature of the eighteenth and nineteenth centuries. London: Vine Press, 1964.
Groups chapbooks under folk material, adaptations, and abridgments, and a "very few" pieces of original work.

———. Chapbooks: a guide to reference material on English, Scottish and American chapbook literature of the eighteenth and nineteenth centuries. London: Woburn, 1972.

———. The penny histories: a study of chapbooks for young readers over two centuries. London: Oxford, 1968; New York: Harcourt, 1969.
A commentary on the history of chapbooks from the late 1600s to the late 1800s. Illustrated, including reprints of seven early titles—from Aldermary Church Yard tracts to works published by Kendrew (of York) and Solomon King (New York).

———. "Three hundred years of Tom Thumb," *Scientific monthly* 34:157–66 (February, 1932).
Illustrated with reproductions of early editions, from 1630 to the 1840s.

———. comp. A catalogue of chapbooks in the New York Public Library. New York: New York Public Library, 1936.

The New-England primer. Edited by Paul Leicester Ford. New York: Teachers College, Columbia University, 1962.
Subtitle: "a history of its origin and development with a reprint of the unique copy of the earliest known edition and many facsimile illustrations and reproductions." Contains a famous alphabet published in many editions throughout the eighteenth century.

New York Public Library. A catalogue of the chapbooks in the New York Public Library. Compiled by Harry B. Weiss. New York: New York Public Library, 1936.
Reprinted from the *Bulletin* of the New York Public Library, vol. 39 (January–October, 1936). Covers 1,171 items from about 1510 to 1850 with an introduction on chapbooks of various countries. Bibliography.

Pearson, Edwin. Banbury chapbooks and nursery toy book literature. London: Arthur Reader, 1890.
Subtitle: "with impressions from several hundred original wood-cut blocks by T. & J. Bewick, Blake, Cruikshank, Craig, Lee, Austin, and others illustrating favourite nursery classics, with their antiquarian, historical, literary, and artistic associations, faithfully gleaned from the original works in the Bodleian library, Oxford, the British and South Kensington museums, &c.; with very much that is interesting and valuable appertaining to the early typography and topography of children's books relating to Great Britain and America, including Jack the Giant Killer, Cock Robin, Tom Thumb, Whittington, Goody Two Shoes, Philip Quarll, Tommy Trip, York and Banbury Cries, Children in the Wood, Dame Trot, horn books, battledores, primers, etc." Covers the eighteenth and early nineteenth centuries.

Pyle, Howard. "Chapbook heroes," "A famous chapbook villain," *Harper's monthly magazine* 81:123–38, 186–97 (1890).
The first article treats of the chapman and his books, Monsieur Claude Duval, Jack Sheppard, and Dick Turpin; the second article deals with Jonathan Wild. Illustrations by the author.

Thomsen, Frances M. Newcastle chapbooks in Newcastle upon Tyne University Library. Newcastle, England: Oriel Press, 1969.
Illustrated catalog.

Weiss, Harry Bischoff. American chapbooks. Trenton, N.J.: privately printed, 1938.
Discusses American originals and those reproduced from English titles, 1713 to about 1860.

————. American chapbooks, 1722–1842. New York: New York Public Library, 1945.
Reprinted from the *Bulletin* (New York Public Library) 49:491–98, 587–96 (July–August, 1945).

————. "American editions of Sir Richard Whittington and his cat," *Bulletin* (New York Public Library) 42:477–85 (June, 1938).

————. "The autochthonal tale of Jack the giant killer," *Scientific monthly* 28:126–33 (February, 1929.

————. A book about chapbooks: the people's literature of bygone times. Ann Arbor, Mich.: Edwards Bros. for Trenton, 1942.
Includes notes entitled "Some collectors and collections." Bibliography.

————. "Three hundred years of Tom Thumb," *Scientific monthly* 34:157–66 (February, 1932).
Illustrated with reproductions of early editions from 1630 to the 1840s.

———— comp. A catalogue of chapbooks in the New York Public Library. New York: New York Public Library, 1936.

Card Battledores and Other Alphabets

The New England primer A B C. New York: The Triptych, 1930.
According to the foreword by Wilbur M. Stone, this pictured and rhymed alphabet formed a part of a children's book entitled *The father's gift, or, the way to be wise and happy,* issued by Francis Newbery, nephew of John Newbery, in 1776. The book was reprinted many times, and this reprint was made from an edition of 1793 published by J. & M. Robertson in Glasgow. The cuts and couplets below them are to be found in the *New England primer* but the origin of the "over cut rhymes" has not been discovered.

Tuer, Andrew White. ["Cardboard battledores,"] in his *History of the horn-book,* p. 389–415. London: Leadenhall; New York: Scribner, 1897.
Contains cuts reproducing *The royal battledore* and other examples. Invaluable information on the development of the A B C book.

Whalley, Joyce Irene. Cobwebs to catch flies: illustrated books for the nursery and schoolroom 1700–1900. Berkeley and Los Angeles: University of California Press, 1975.
A survey of two centuries, including discussion of the battledore. Illustrated. See "Primers and ABC books," p. 48–49.

French Influence:
The Eighteenth Century

As the eighteenth century opened in England, the Puritan influence on children's books was waning, and the public was ready for fresh ideas, which were soon to come from France. Many of these ideas were not only fresh but extreme.

In France the century opened with the Sun King, Louis XIV, still enthroned, setting the scene for a brilliant court where it was all the rage to tell and listen to fairy tales. Charles Perrault had gathered a handful of French folktales and retold them to please the sophisticated ladies and gentlemen of Louis's court, but the name of his son appeared as author of the dedication, perhaps as an indication that the father saw the appeal the stories would have for the young also. However this may be, the title page of the first edition of *Histoires ou contes du temps passé* showed a grandmotherly figure sitting by a hearth with a group of children. She was Ma Mère l'Oye in France and became Mother Goose in England, where the stories were to be France's greatest gift to English children's literature. Several literary French ladies followed Perrault with original stories based on folklore. These too were translated for English children and eagerly adopted by them. It was not long before Antoine Galland's expurgated translation of the *Arabian nights* into French (1704–17) was in part re-translated for English children. A chapbook called *Arabian nights entertainments* appeared in 1708.

Halfway through the century came the controversial philosopher and theorist Jean Jacques Rousseau. His *Émile* laid out plans for the education of children, based on the theories of John Locke, but following new directions and going to extreme lengths. Locke had paved the way when he urged that virtue should be cultivated in the child "by Reasoning and mild Discipline," with only *Aesop* and *Reynard the fox* as recreational reading. Rousseau's *Émile* went further. It pictured a boy, living in the open country and brought up to develop his own innate powers, learning by direct observation and personal experience, under the guidance of a tutor. Not until his teenage years would Émile be exposed to literature, and then only to one book, *Robinson Crusoe*, in which the natural man triumphs where civilization fails. Translated into English in 1763, *Émile* immediately caught the imagination of the educated English public.

The influence of Rousseau on children's books was less direct than that of the fairy-tale tellers, but in the long run it was equally profound. Among his followers in France were idealists who cared deeply about education, and, paradoxically, although *Émile* was to read nothing but *Robinson Crusoe*, some of Rousseau's disciples wrote for children. They used a recognizable pattern. The text was simple, and much of it was in the form of a conversation between a child or children and an all-wise father, mother, or adult friend who pointed out lessons to be learned from nature, from common sense, and from the simple life.

Three names stand out among this group of writers. Mme. D'Épinay, friend and patron of Rousseau, won an award in 1783 from the Académie Française for *Conversations d'Émilie*, a feminine counterpart of *Émile*. That same year, Mme. de Genlis published *Adèle et Théodore*, which frowned on all the old fairy tales, including the *Arabian nights* and the stories of Mme. d'Aulnoy, because none of them had the "moral tendency" that reading for children should have. Little girls were to have no books until the age of seven, when they would be allowed *Conversations d'Émilie*. They could

then go on to *Veillées du château* ("Tales of the castle"), written by Mme. de Genlis herself. She was not an outstanding writer, but she was an extraordinary woman, who claimed that she knew enough of twenty different trades to earn her living at any of them. Among the twenty was teaching; she was governess to the daughters of the Duchess of Chartres and "governor" to the sons of the Duke of Orleans. Another of her trades may have been acting, since she used what is now called "creative dramatics" to make learning pleasant for her young charges.

Both Mme. d'Épinay and Mme. de Genlis soon found an English audience through translations of their works, but perhaps the most widely read, and translated, of all the French books for children in the latter half of the eighteenth century was *L'ami des enfans*, 1782–83, by Arnaud Berquin. While following Rousseau's principles closely, Berquin's short stories had an attractively gentle and playful style that appealed to young readers on both sides of the Atlantic. The author, like Mme. d'Épinay, was honored by the Académie Française. *L'ami des enfans* was first translated into English as *The children's friend* and later as *The looking glass for the mind, or, intellectual mirror*. Louis XVI even invited Berquin to come to court as tutor for his son. Berquin refused, and the turmoil of the Revolution closed in around him. He was sent into exile as a member of the moderate Gerondists and died in 1791.

During the eighteenth century, children's books in France had changed greatly. The century had begun with the fairy tales of Perrault, told for the splendid but decadent court of Louis XIV ("*Après moi le déluge*"). It ended with the earnest little stories of writers who followed Rousseau, sure that his theories, made into children's books, would develop good citizens for the Republic. It is ironic that Rousseau was himself a careless father and a faithless friend. It is even more ironic, that in the egalitarian twentieth century, the fairy tales are alive and the moral tales of the French reformers are forgotten, except by students of children's literature.

The last decade of the 1700s brought extremes of ferocity in the aftermath of the French Revolution. Children were protected, to a degree, but those who might once have grown up to be dukes and duchesses now became plain citizens, and their reading was inevitably laid out along the principles of *liberté*, *égalité*, and *fraternité*.

These French influences—the fairy tales, the

new educational theories, and the egalitarian spirit—made a strong impact on the reading of English and American children during and after the eighteenth century.

OUTLINE

I. Fairy tales
  A. Vogue in France in the latter part of the reign of Louis XIV
  B. Principal writers of fairy tales
    1. Charles Perrault (1628–1703)
      a) Brief account of his life
      b) Fairy tales
        (1) Bibliographical history
        (2) Uncertainty as to real authorship; opinions of Andrew Lang and others
        (3) Introduction of Mother Goose as the author of children's stories
        (4) General characteristics
    2. Madame d'Aulnoy (1650–1705)
      a) Comparison of fairy tales with those of Perrault
      b) Bibliographical history
    3. Other writers
  C. Introduction of French fairy tales into England and their popularity
  D. Beginnings of idealistic literature for children.
II. Rousseau's *Émile*
  A. Theory of education

  B. Influence upon the life and thought of the time
  C. Influence upon children's literature
III. General characteristics of children's stories written by "Rousseau-inspired writers."
IV. French writers for children in the later 18th century.
  A. Comtesse de Genlis (1746–1830)
    1. Life
    2. Educational theories and methods
      a) *Adèle et Théodore*
    3. Stories and plays for children
      a) *Théâtre d'éducation*
      b) *Les veillées du château*
      c) *Les petits émigrés*
  B. Madame d'Épinay (1726–83)
    1. Comparison of *Les conversations d'Émilie* with the work of Madame de Genlis
  C. Arnaud Berquin (1749–91)
    1. Character and style of his books for children
    2. *L'ami des enfans*
      a) Popularity in England
      b) English translations and editions
      c) Illustration of *The looking-glass for the mind*, edition of 1792

GENERAL REFERENCES

Barry, Florence Valentine. "Fairy tales and eastern stories," in her *A century of children's books*, p. 13–57. New York: Doran, 1923; reprint: Detroit: Singing Tree, 1968.
A valuable chapter covering the ground with considerable fullness and giving many illustrative examples.

Darton, Frederick Joseph Harvey. "Fairy-tale and nursery rhyme." in his *Children's books in England*, p. 85–105. 2d ed. Cambridge: Cambridge University Press, 1958.
An outstanding source from the point of view of style and of the author's judgment.

Field, Louise Frances Story (Mrs. E. M. Field). "Some nursery classics," in her *The child and his book*, p. 233–42. 2d ed. London: Wells Gardner, 1892; reprint: Detroit: Singing Tree, 1968.
Fairy tales of Perrault and Mme. d'Aulnoy compared with tales of other nations.

Mazon, Jeanne Roche. Autour des contes de fées, recueil d'études, accompagnées de pièces complémentaires. Paris: Didier, 1968.
Essays on the fairy tales by a French authority with additional material by other critics. Interesting sidelights on the lives of authors of fairy tales, especially Mme. d'Aulnoy, Perrault, and Mme. Leprince de Beaumont.

The old, old fairy tales. Collected and edited by Mrs. Valentine. London and New York: Warne, 1889.
The preface traces the origins of the French tales as far as versions in Italian by Straparola, published at Venice in *Notti piacevoli*, 1550. This collection includes thirty-nine stories, mostly by Mme. d'Aulnoy, Perrault, "La Princesse de Beaumont" [sic] and de Caylus.

Palmer, M. D. "*History of Adolphus* (1691); the first French conte de fée in English," *Philological quarterly* 49:565–67 (October, 1970).

Shows how social, erotic, and allegorical allusions were added in the English version of the tale by Mme. d'Aulnoy.

Palmer, N. B., and **M. D. Palmer.** "The French conte de fée in England," *Studies in short fiction* 11:35–44 (Winter, 1974).
Analyzes the influence of Mme. d'Aulnoy and her followers. The plots of several stories are given in brief.

Quiller-Couch, *Sir* **Arthur Thomas.** In powder and crinoline. London: Hodder, 1913.
Old fairy tales retold with illustrations by Kay Nielsen. Includes "Minon-Minette" (attributed to the Comte de Caylus) from *Bibliothèque des fées et des génies,* collected by the Abbé de la Porte and originally found in *Le potpourri: ouvrage de ces dames et de ces messieurs*; "Felicia," rendered from the *Fortunée* of Mme. d'Aulnoy; and "Rosanie" from de Caylus (*Féeries nouvelles*).

Storer, Mary E. La mode des contes de fées (1685–1700): un épisode littéraire de la fin du XVII siècle. Paris: E. Champion, 1928.
Covers the work of sixteen writers and includes discussion of sources for the stories. Extensive bibliography on works by and about each writer, with listings of editions chronologically arranged.

Taylor, Una Ashworth. "Fairy tales as literature," *Signal*, no. 21, 123–38 (September, 1976).
First published anonymously in *The Edinburgh review* 188 (July, 1898). Pt. 1 of this essay is edited with an introduction by Lance Salway and gives a survey of (predominantly) French writers of the fairy tale in the eighteenth century. Helpful biographical notes are appended.

Yonge, Charlotte. "Nursery books of the eighteenth century," *Signal* 2:50–58 (May, 1970).
Includes considerable discussion of the French fairy tales. Originally published as the first part of "Children's literature of the last century" in *Macmillan's magazine* 20 (July, 1869).

FAIRY TALES

Madame d'Aulnoy

FRENCH EDITIONS

Aulnoy, Marie Catherine Jumelle de Berneville, comtesse d'. "Belle-Belle, ou le chevalier Fortuné," in *Bibliothèque universelle des romans* 2:179–96 (July, 1775).
This entry follows the customary form, but some authorities contend that Madame d'Aulnoy's title should be baronne and not comtesse.

———. Le cabinet des fées et des génies. 14 v. Brussels: Le Francq, 1785.
Illustrated.

———. Contes de Saphir. Paris: Hatier, 1957.
Illustrated by Françoise Bertier. Contents: "Gracieuse et Percinet" and "Belle-Belle ou le chevalier Fortuné."

———. "Les contes des fées," "Les fées à la mode," in *Le cabinet des fées, ou, collection choisie des contes de fées et autres contes merveilleux.* v. 2–4. Geneva: Barde, 1785.
Illustrated. The fairy tales are:
v.2. Gracieuse et Percinet; La Belle aux cheveux d'or; L'oiseau bleu; Le prince Lutin; La princesse printanière; La princesse Rosette; Le rameau d'or; L'oranger et l'abeille; La bonne petite souris; Le mouton; Finette Crendon.
v.3. Fortunée; Babiole; Le nain jaune; Serpentin vert; La princesse Carpillon; La grenouille bienfaisante; La biche au bois; La chatte blanche.
v.4. Belle-Belle; ou, le chevalier Fortuné; Le

pigeon et la colombe; La princesse Belle-Étoile et le prince Chéri; Le prince Marcassin; Le dauphin.

———. Les contes des fées, ou, les fées à la mode: contes choisis publiés avec une préface par M. de Lescure. 2v. Paris: Librairie des Bibliophiles, 1881.
v.1. Gracieuse et Percinet; La belle aux cheveux d'or; L'oiseau bleu; Le prince Lutin; La princesse Rosette.
v.2. Finette Cendron; La biche au bois; La chatte blanche; Belle-Belle, ou, le chevalier Fortuné.
Gives a complete list of Mme. d'Aulnoy's fairy tales, indicating the novels in which a number of them first appeared, vol. 1, p. xxiv. The first volume also contains a valuable preface giving an account of the author's life and writings.

———. Les contes des fées par Madame D. . . . Auteur des memoires & voyages d'Espagne . . . à Amsterdam: Aux dépens d'Estienne Roger, 1708.
Two volumes in one. Contents:
v.1. Gracieuse et Percinet; La belle aux cheveux d'or; L'oiseau bleu; Le prince Lutin.
v.2. La princesse printanière; La princesse Rosette; La rameau d'or; L'oranger et l'abeille; La bonne petite souris.
This is the earliest edition in the Library of Congress.

———. L'oiseau bleu: gravures sur bois en couleurs de Théo Schmied. Montrouge, France: Théo et Florence Schmied, 1947.
Imaginative illustrations printed from colored wood blocks add freshness and charm to this old French fairy tale.

Aulnoy, Marie Catherine Jumelle de Berneville, *comtesse* d'. Children's fairyland, translated and adapted from the fairy tales of the Countess d'Aulnoy. New York: Holt, 1919.
With illustrations in silhouette by H. M. Olcott.

————. A collection of novels and tales, written by that celebrated wit of France, the Countess d'Anois, in two volumes . . . translated from the best edition of the original French, by several hands. London: printed for W. Taylor & W. Chetwood, 1721.
First edition of this important translation.

————. Fairy tales. Translated by J. R. Planché. Philadelphia: McKay, n.d.
Excellent translation, including twenty-two stories with the incidental verse and the "moralities." The preface traces the history of publication of Mme. d'Aulnoy's fairy tales. The introduction gives a biographical sketch of the author and a list of her fairy tales and other writings. Black-and-white illustrations by Gordon Browne.

————. ————. Philadelphia: McKay, 1923.
With additional illustrations in color by Gustaf Tenggren.

————. The hind in the forest (and other tales by the Countess d'Aulnoy). Retold by Hilda Mary McGill. New ed., rev. and reset. Manchester, England: Ingram, 1965.
Illustrated by Silvia Green. Tales selected from *Contes des fées* and *Fées à la mode.*

Works by this author printed in America before 1801 are available in the Readex Microprint edition of *Early American imprints* published by the American Antiquarian Society.

Madame de Beaumont

Le Prince de Beaumont, Marie. "La belle et la bête," in *Le cabinet des fées, ou, collection choisie des contes des fées et autres contes merveilleux.* Amsterdam, Paris, and Geneva: 1785–89.
Illustrated. *Le cabinet* appeared periodically, totaling forty-one vols. *Beauty and the beast* is the choice story in this collection. Mme. de Beaumont is credited as being the author of the first version for children.

Le Prince de Beaumont, Marie. Beauty and the beast. Translated from the French by P. H. Muir. New York: Limited Editions Club, 1949.
With illustrations by Edy Legrand.

————. ————. New York: Knopf, 1968.
Illustrations in black and white by Erica Ducornet. A note on the origin of the tale (p. 53) gives credit to Gabrielle-Suzanne Villeneuve as the original author of the French version, published in 1740 and later "shortened and polished by Mme. Leprince de Beaumont."

————. Beauty and the beast: a fairy tale. Translated by Richard Howard. New York: Macmillan, 1963.
With an afterword by Jean Cocteau and illustrations by Hilary Knight.

Charles Perrault

Perrault, Charles. Les contes. Paris: J. Hetzel, 1862.
Contains nine tales, including "Peau d'âne" in prose form, by Gustave Dóre. Preface by P.-J. Stahl. This famous edition was reprinted many times.

————. ————. Paris: Laurens, 1897.
Introduction by Gustave Larroumet. Contains the eight prose tales; also "Peau-d'âne." The illustrations are by ten famous French artists, including E. Courboin.

————. Les contes de Charles Perrault: contes en vers: histoires ou contes du temps passé (*Contes de ma mère Loye*). Paris: C. Marpon & E. Flammarion, 1875.
Subtitle: "avec deux essais sur la vie et les oevres de Perrault et sur la mythologie dans ses contes, des notes et variantes et une notice bibliographique, par André Lefèvre." With bibliography, p. 167–79.

————. "Les contes des fées," in *Le cabinet des fées, ou, collection choisie des contes des fées et autre contes merveilleux,* v. 1, p. 1–220. Geneva: Barde, 1785.
Illustrated. "Précis de la vie et des ouvrages de Charles Perrault, avec l'analyse de ses contes," p. 1–16. Contents: Le chaperon rouge; Les fées; La barbe bleue; La belle au bois dormant; Le chat botté; Cendrillon; Riquet à la houppe; Le petit poucet; L'adoite princesse; Griselidis; Peau d'âne; Les souhaits ridicules. This volume contains also "Les nouveaux contes des fées," by the Countess Murat. First published in *Recueil de pièces curieuses et nouvelles, tant en prose qu'en vers,* 1696–97.

————. Contes de fées, tiré de Claude [sic] Perrault, de Mme. d'Aulnoy et de Mme. Leprince de Beaumont. Paris: Librairie de L. Hachette, 1856.
An early example of the publication of these three writers as a group. Illustrated by Bertail, Beauce, and others.

————. Contes de ma mère l'oye; Mother Goose's tales. A la Haye: chez J. Neaulme, 1745.
French and English on opposite pages.

————. Griselidis nouvelle avec le conte de Peau d'-asne, et celui des souhaits ridicules: histoires ou contes du temps passé. 2v. Paris: Firmon-Didot, 1929.
Accurate facsimile reprints of the rare 1695 and 1697 editions of Perrault's fairy tales. Historically valuable.

————. Perrault's tales of Mother Goose: the dedication manuscript of 1695 reproduced in collotype facsimile with introduction and critical text by Jacques Barchilon. 2v. New York: Pierpont Morgan Library, 1956.
Vol. 1 gives the text. Vol. 2 is the facsimile.

————. Popular tales. Edited from the original editions, with introduction by Andrew Lang. Oxford: Clarendon Press, 1888.
In French. Contents: La belle au bois dormant; Le petit chaperon rouge; La barbe bleue; Le Maistre chat, ou, le chat botté; Les fées; Cendrillon, ou, la petite pantouffle de verre; Riquet à la houppe; Le petit poucet; Contes en vers: Peau d'-asne; Les souhaits ridicules; Griselidis. The introduction contains a brief sketch of Perrault and of the circumstances in which his tales were composed and published. Each prose study has also been made the subject of a special comparative research.

ENGLISH EDITIONS

Barchilon, Jacques, and Henry Pettit, eds. The authentic Mother Goose fairy tales and nursery rhymes. Denver: Swallow, 1960.
At head of title: Jacques Barchilon and Henry Pettit. A facsimile reproduced from a photostatic copy in the Houghton Library, Harvard University. The title page reads: "Histories or tales of past times . . . with morals. By M. Perrault. Translated into English. London: Printed for J. Pote and R. Montagu. MDCCXXIX."

Perrault, Charles. Bluebeard, and other fairy tales. Translated by Richard Howard. New York: Macmillan, 1964.
With an introduction by Simone de Beauvoir. A large and colorful edition illustrated by Saul Lambert. Translations are based on the first edition of Perrault's *Contes de ma mère l'oye*, 1697.

————. Cinderella. Retold by C. S. Evans. Philadelphia: Lippincott; London: Heinemann, 1919; reprint: New York: Viking, 1972.
With illustrations by Arthur Rackham.

————. Cinderella or the little glass slipper. New York: Walck, 1971.

Illustrated by Shirley Hughes in a style that accurately depicts the France of Louis XIV. Based on the translation by Robert Samber. A note by Kathleen Lines (p. 48) comments on the history of the story, its parallels, and the problems of translation.

————. French fairy tales, retold. New York: Didier, 1945.
With a foreword by Louis Untermeyer giving a biographical sketch of Perrault and an appreciation of the illustrations by Gustave Doré, reproduced here from the 1862 French edition. Contents: Puss in Boots; Sleeping Beauty; Little Red Riding Hood; Hop O'-My-Thumb; The fairy.

————. Histories or tales of past times told by Mother Goose, with morals; written in French by M. Perrault, and Englished by G. M. Gent. Newly edited by J. Saxon Childers. London: Nonesuch, 1925.
Elva Smith's note in the first edition of *History of children's literature* reads: "Until recently the first English edition was thought to have been issued in 1729, but the discovery of a copy of the 11th edition, 1719, has proved the assumption incorrect. The illustrations of this reprint have been recut on wood from photographs of those in the 1719 edition and are hand-colored."

————. ————. London: Fortune Press, 1930.
The text is that of the 12th edition dated 1802 and is taken from the copy in the British Museum. The woodcuts are reproduced from photographs and are probably the same as those used in the first English edition, published about 1700. These in turn had been copied from the illustrations to the 1697 edition published in Paris. It is believed that the initials G. M., with which the pictures are signed, are those of Guy Miege (condensed from "Note on the text," p. 106–8). Binder's title reads *Mother Goose*.

————. Old-time stories. Translated by A. E. Johnson. London: Constable, 1921.
With illustrations by W. Heath Robinson. Includes eleven tales by Perrault; Mme. Le Prince de Beaumont's "Beauty and the beast"; Mme. d'Aulnoy's "Princess Rosette," and "The friendly frog." The moralities" are given.

————. Perrault's complete fairy tales. New York: Dodd, 1961; London: Constable, 1962.
A new edition of *Old-time stories*.

————. Puss in Boots, the Sleeping Beauty and Cinderella: a retelling of three classic fairy tales based on the French of Charles Perrault [by] Marianne Moore. New York: Macmillan, 1963.
With illustrations by Eugene Karlin. The preface by the distinguished American poet analyzes the charm of Perrault's tales and describes the hand-

written copy belonging to Elizabeth Charlotte d'-Orleans, now in the Pierpont Morgan Library.

————. Sleeping Beauty, told by C. S. Evans. Philadelphia: Lippincott; London: Heinemann, 1920; reprint: New York: Viking, 1972.
With illustrations by Arthur Rackham.

————. The tales of Mother Goose as first collected by Charles Perrault in 1696: a new translation by Charles Welsh. Boston: Heath, 1901.
The work of an early researcher in children's literature. With illustrations by D. J. Munro after drawings by Gustave Doré.

Quiller-Couch, Sir Arthur Thomas, ed. The sleeping beauty, and other fairy tales from the old French. London: Hodder, 1910.
Retellings by a notable writer and scholar. Illustrations by Edmund Dulac. Other tales in this volume: Blue Beard; Cinderella; Beauty and the beast (originally by Madame de Villeneuve).

CRITICISM

Adams, Frederick B., Jr. "Family friend of all the world," *Wilson library bulletin* 41:573–75 (February, 1967).
The director of the Pierpont Morgan Library describes the original manuscript of Perrault's *Tales of Mother Goose*, dated 1695, and tells how it was acquired by the library.

Burns, Lee. "Red Riding Hood," in *Children's literature: the great excluded* 1:30–36 (1972).
A brief survey of some of the psychological and mythical interpretations that have been made of the old nursery tale.

Cox, Marian Roalfe. Cinderella: three hundred and forty-five variants of Cinderella, Catskin, and Cap o' rushes, abstracted and tabulated, with a discussion of medieval analogues, and notes. (Publications of the Folk Lore Society, no. 31). London: Folk Lore Society, 1893; reprint: Nendeln, Liechtenstein: Kraus, 1967.
The introduction by Andrew Lang and a preface by M. R. Cox are of value to students wishing to explore the parallels and variants of French and English versions. An exhaustive study.

Lang, Andrew. "Rich and poor," in his *Books and bookmen*, p. 21–28. New York: Longmans, 1899.
Notes on the early editions of Perrault's *Contes*.

Moore, Annie Egerton. "The contributions of Charles Perrault," in her *Literature old and new for children*, p. 82–87. Boston: Houghton, 1934.

Sainte-Beuve, Charles Augustin. "Charles Perrault," in his *Causeries du lundi*, v. 5, p. 255–74. 3d ed. Paris: Garnier Frères, [18-?].

————. ————. in his *Causeries du lundi*, translated by E. J. Trechmann, v. 8, p. 203–18. London: Routledge, 1909.

Soriano, Marc. Les contes de Perrault: culture savante et traditions populaires. Paris: Gallimard, 1968.
A study of "all the problems posed by the Contes" including their sources, their significance, and the point of view of their authors. "A work for both amateurs and specialists."

Whalley, Irene. "The Cinderella story, 1724–1919," *Signal*, no. 8, p. 49–62 (May, 1972).
A study of the illustrations and changes in text over a period of two hundred years.

■ An excellent portrait of Perrault will be found in the *Gazette des Beaux-Arts* 103:199 (1908).

ROUSSEAU AND HIS FOLLOWERS

Jean Jacques Rousseau

Rousseau, Jean Jacques. Émile. Translated by Barbara Foxley. London: Dent, 1963; New York: Dutton, 1911 (Everyman's library), 1963.
An introduction by André Boutet de Monvel gives a biographical sketch of Rousseau, places *Émile* in the framework of the philosopher's thought, assesses the originality of the book's educational theory, and sums up its influence today.

————. Émile, ou, de l'éducation. Paris, 1762.
First publication, four pts., in two vols.

————. Émile: selections. Translated and edited by William Boyd. New York: Columbia University Press, 1962.
"Published in London in 1956 under the title *Émile for today*."

BIOGRAPHY AND CRITICISM

Barry, Florence Valentine. "Rousseau and the moral tale," in her *A century of children's books*, p. 85–104. New York: Doran, 1923; reprint: Detroit: Singing Tree, 1968.
Discusses the new concept of childhood and the more important French books for children, including Berquin's *L'ami des enfans*, Mme. d'Épinay's *Les conversations d'Émilie*, and the work of Mme. de Genlis.

Boyd, William. The educational theory of Jean Jacques Rousseau. London and New York: Longmans, 1911; reprint: New York: Russell & Russell, 1963.
A thorough and authoritative study that focuses on the influences of Rousseau's life and work most pertinent to students of children's literature. Bibliography. Useful subject index.

Darton, Frederick Joseph Harvey. "The theorists: Thomas Day, the Edgeworths, and French influence," in his *Children's books in England*, p. 141–57. 2d ed. Cambridge: Cambridge University Press, 1958.
Includes discussion of the moral works of Mme. de Genlis and Berquin.

Davidson, Thomas. Rousseau and education according to nature. New York: Scribner, 1898; reprint: New York: AMS Press, 1971.
First published in the Great educators series edited by Nicholas Murray Butler. Rousseau's life; educational theories for infancy, childhood, boyhood, adolescence, youth, manhood; his influence.

Gardiner, Dorothy Kempe. "Rousseau and the education of girls," in her *English girlhood at school*, p. 442–48. London: Methuen, 1929.
Considers the failure of Rousseau to apply to girls the lofty principles advocated in the education of Émile.

Josephson, Matthew. Jean-Jacques Rousseau. New York: Harcourt, 1931.
Written in the light of new evidence and modern psychological views. See especially chapter 16, "Émile, or, the philosophy of Rousseau."

Patterson, Sylvia W. Rousseau's *Émile* and early children's literature. Metuchen, N.J.: Scarecrow, 1971.
Useful in this context for its introduction, which gives an estimate of *Émile* as a milestone in thought on education, and a summary of the five books into which *Émile* is divided.

Sainte-Beuve, Charles Augustin. Causeries du lundi. (New universal library) Translated by E. J. Trechmann. v. 2, 4. London: Routledge, 1909.
"Memoires of Madame d'Épinay," v. 2, p. 150–65; "Works of Madame de Genlis," v. 4, p. 16–30; "The confessions of Jean-Jacques Rousseau," v. 4, p. 63–78.

Arnaud Berquin

FRENCH EDITIONS

Berquin, Arnaud. Abrégé de *L'ami des enfants*, v. 1. Paris: De Pelafol, 1818.
Illustrated. "Notice sur Berquin," p. iii–iv. *L'ami des enfants* was first published in Paris, 1782–83, in twenty-four monthly parts.

————. L'ami des enfants. Paris: Laurens, [1898].
Illustrations by H. Gerbault; introduction by M. L. Tarsot. Contents: Un bon coeur fait pardonner bien des étourderies; Colin-Maillard; Le petit joueur de violon; La petite glaneuse; La levrette et la bagne; Les étrennes; La vanité punie; L'épée. Charming illustrations in black and white and in color show the characters as child actors.

ENGLISH EDITIONS

Berquin, Arnaud. The children's companion. Philadelphia: Crissy & Markley, 1840.
Stories in dialogue form, translated from the first part of the *Livre des familles*. Illustrations are copied from those in the French edition.

————. The children's friend. 2v. in 1. New York: C. S. Francis, 1857.
Thirty engravings from original designs. Most of the stories are in dialogue form.

————. An introduction to the study of nature, with other pieces from the French of M. Berquin. Philadelphia: Crissy & Markley, c1841.
In the form of little talks to children about such topics as the wheat field, domestic animals, insects, the ocean, the sun, planets, comets, and fixed stars. A large part of this work is a retranslation of Berquin's French version of Sarah Kirby Trimmer's *Easy introduction to the knowledge of nature* (p. 118).

————. The looking-glass for the mind. London: Griffith, 1885.
A reprint of the edition of 1792. Introduction by Charles Welsh. According to the original preface, *The looking-glass for the mind* is to "be considered rather as a Collection of the Beauties of M. Berquin, than as a literally abridged translation of that Work." The editor or translator was the Rev. W. D. Cooper and the first edition was published in 1787. A second edition was published in 1789. The 3d ed. of 1792, and its reprint, are noteworthy for their illustrations, seventy-four cuts, designed and engraved on wood by John Bewick.

————. The looking-glass for the mind, or intellectual mirror. 20th ed. London: Longmans, Orme, 1840.
Subtitle: "being an elegant collection of the most delightful little stories and interesting tales, chiefly translated from that much admired work, *L'ami des enfants;* illustrated with engravings on wood by George Baxter."

————. ————. (Early children's books) New York: Johnson, 1969.
A reprint of the 1794 edition.

Madame d'Épinay

Épinay, Louise Pétronille Tardieu d'Esclavelles, *marquise* d'. "Conversation between Rousseau and Madame d'Épinay on the subject of education," in *The memoirs and correspondence,* translated with introduction and brief notes by J. H. Freese, v. 3, p. 30–33. London: Nichols, 1899.
See also the edition translated by E. G. Allingham and published by Routledge in 1930, which contains comment on *Les conversations d'Émilie,* p. 16–18.

——. The conversations of Emily, abridged from the French. Philadelphia: M. Carey, 1817.
Short didactic stories in dialogue form.

Hall, Evelyn Beatrice (*pseud.* Stephen G. Tallentyre). "Madame d'Épinay," in her *The women of the salons,* p. 62–87. New York: Putnam, 1926.
Presents an unflattering portrait. Reference to *Les conversations d'Émilie,* p. 84.

Valentino, Henri. Madame d'Épinay, 1726–1783: une femme d'esprit sous Louis XV. Paris: Librairie academique Perrin, 1952.
See chapter 5 for "Rousseau à l'Ermitage" and chapter 7 for "Le drame de l'Ermitage."

Comtesse de Genlis

Genlis, Stéphanie Félicité Ducrest de Saint-Aubin, *comtesse de,* later *marquise de Sillery.* Adèle et Théodore, ou, lettres sur l'éducation. 4th ed. 3v. Paris: Maradan, 1804.
The fruit, according to the author, of fifteen years of reflections, observations, and study of the inclinations, the faults, and the "ruses" of children —preface.

——. Arabesques mythologiques, ou, les attributs de toutes les divinités de la fable, en 54 planches graveés d'après les dessins coloriés de Madame de Genlis; ouvrage fait pour servir à l'éducation de la jeunesse. 2v. Paris: Barrois, 1810–11.

——. Leçons d'une gouvernante à ses élèves, ou, fragmens d'un journal, qui a été fait pour l'éducation des enfans de Monsieur d'Orléans. 2v. Paris: Onfroy, 1791.

——. Théâtre d'éducation. 4v. in 2. Brussels: Meline, 1840.
Contains the sacred dramas; also other plays.

——. Les veillées du château, ou, cours de morale à l'usage des enfans. 3v. Paris: Libraires Associés, 1784.

——. ——. New ed., rev. and corrected. v. 1. Paris: Didier, 1844.
Contains original preface, p. v–xii; also a foreword to the new edition. Dedicated to the author's nephew.

Genlis, Stéphanie Félicité Ducrest de Saint-Aubin, *comtesse de,* later *marquise de Sillery.* Adelaide and Theodore, or, letters on education. 2d ed. 3v. London: Bathurst & Cadell, 1784.
Subtitle: "containing all the principles relative to three different plans of education, to that of princes, and to those of young persons of both sexes, translated from the French."

——. Alphonso and Dalinda, or, the magic of art and nature: a moral tale. Translated by Thomas Holcroft. New ed. Philadelphia: Thomas Dobson, 1787.

——. Sacred dramas, written in French. Translated by Thomas Holcroft. London: Robinson, 1786.
Contents: The death of Adam; Hagar in the wilderness; The sacrifice of Isaac; Joseph made known to his brethren; Ruth and Naomi; The widow of Sarepta; The return of Tobias. Dedicated to the author's daughters.

——. Tales of the castle, or, stories of instruction and delight, being *Les veillées du chateau,* written in French by Madame la comtesse de Genlis. Translated by Thomas Holcroft. 9th ed. 5v. in 2. Brattleboro Vt.: Fessenden, 1813.
The translator considered himself eminently fortunate to be able to bestow his labors upon a book "in which the powers of genius are ever ardent to inculcate the purest morality." *New tales of the castle, or, the noble emigrants* by Mary Hopkins Pilkington, English story writer, was probably inspired by the work of Mme. de Genlis and may be used for comparison with its French prototype.

——. The young exiles, or, correspondence of some juvenile emigrants: a work intended for the entertainment and instruction of youth, from the French of Madame de Genlis. 2v. London: V. Dowling & J. Stockdale, 1799.
In the "Epistle dedicatory" to her grandchildren, the author says, "I have copied from nature all the portraits of my virtuous characters."

Bearne, Catherine Mary Charlton. "Madame de Genlis," in her *Heroines of French society,* p. 349–485. New York: Dutton, 1907.
Useful as a shorter account of the life and strange career of Mme. de Genlis than that provided by her *Memoirs,* though quite detailed in its biographical information.

Dobson, Austin. "Madame de Genlis," in his *Four French women,* p. 105–207. New York: Dodd, 1890; reprint: London and New York: Oxford University Press, 1923.
Entertaining essay. The *Memoirs* of Mme. de Genlis are considered from the social point of view, chiefly as records of bygone manners. Includes portraits.

Mackay, Constance d'Arcy. "The development of child-drama," in her *How to produce children's plays*, p. 4–5, 11–14. New York: Holt, 1915.
References to the theater of education of Mme. de Genlis.

Wyndham, Violet. Madame de Genlis: a biography. New York: Roy, 1960.
A well-written account of the life of Mme. de Genlis, giving some first-hand descriptions of her school theories and practices. Portraits. Bibliography.

Yonge, Charlotte Mary. "Children's literature of the last century," *Macmillan's magazine* 20:234–36 (1869).
Compares *Les veillées du château* with its rival, *Les conversations d'Émilie*, by Mme. d'Épinay, and gives an outline of some of the stories contained in the former.

English Didactic Writers: The Late Eighteenth and Early Nineteenth Centuries

England in the late eighteenth and early nineteenth centuries was in a state of social and religious upheaval. It was an extraordinary period in history, influenced greatly by the American War of Independence and the French Revolution, the theories of Locke and Rousseau, church fragmentation—Protestant groups, papism, the Church of England—and the beginnings of industrialization. All these factors, says Margaret Gillespie, "were forces which propelled adults to cling to their mores in an attempt to keep the wobbling ship of state steady. The manner in which they sought to do this was by preaching and teaching to youth the morals and manners which they themselves held dear."[1]

It is probably not coincidental that the same period also saw the rise of children's-book publishing as a business venture. John Newbery, who laid the foundations of such publishing, was succeeded first by his wife and then by John Harris. Several other publishing houses began at this time. Furthermore, publishers began to commission authors to write expressly for children. These writers, mainly women, produced juvenile books in incredible numbers. They were, Percy Muir says in *English chil-*

1. *Literature for Children* (Dubuque, Iowa: William C. Brown, 1970), p. 84.

dren's books "a monstrous regiment," and "indefatigable."

The books that the women turned out were primarily didactic or moralistic, with intent clearly to educate and inculcate morality by example. These women were educators at heart —educational theorists whose own philosophies were derived from those of Jean Jacques Rousseau. The women theorists diverged from Rousseau in varying degrees. Those who remained closest to his philosophies omitted, as he had done, any reference to religion. Other women writers of the period, while adhering to Rousseau's basic tenets, continued to link morality with religion in their works for children.

Maria Edgeworth and Thomas Day are representative of the former, "nonreligious" school of thought. Of these two writers, Day was the closer disciple, Maria Edgeworth the better writer. Day's *Sandford and Merton* is a long and heavy-handed bit of didacticism (Muir called it "a feast of nausea"). Maria Edgeworth's numerous short stories for children were also moralistic, and her characters were priggish, unrealistically rational, and diligent (the late Georgian adult ideal of the child), but she possessed a great gift for narrative, and she was one of the best storytellers this period produced.

Other writers of the nonreligious strain were the Kilner sisters-in-law. Their stories for children were unique in that they employed slapstick, practical jokes, and farce to teach good manners. Although their *Adventures of a pincushion, Jemima Placid*, and *Memoirs of a peg-top* include advice on manners and social conduct, they are, at moments, full of fun. Dorothy Kilner's *Life and perambulations of a mouse* is considered the first full story for children to use an animal as the main character.

The writers of religious stories for children, particularly Sarah Kirby Trimmer, Mary Martha Sherwood, and Hannah More, were fighting their battles at the same time as the strict Rousseauists. For them, religion was the most important aspect of the educational process.

Education in England at the end of the eighteenth century was largely a philanthropic endeavor. The charity school movement of the eighteenth century gave way to the Sunday school movement, which got its impetus from Robert Raikes, with help from Hannah More and others. The Sunday school was the agency through which "gracious Providence dispensed relief" to those who through "the miserable condition of their parents must be daily exposed to perishing." Considered a part of the Evangelical revival that began in the 1780s and 1790s, the movement provided schooling on Sundays for thousands of working-class children. It is estimated that, by the late 1830s, every working-class child must have attended one of these schools, where the youngsters learned to read and write. Both the Sunday School Union in England and the American Sunday School Union pioneered in children's periodicals. Tracts, books, Testaments, and Bibles that they published were distributed in the tens of millions, telling children how to pray and how to behave.

Hannah More was one of the first of the religious writers. Very active in the Sunday school movement, she and her sisters and friends wrote the *Cheap repository tracts* to combat the atheistic and political pamphlets printed during the French Revolution and the chapbook romances that were then circulating among the lower classes. These simple stories about the plight (and ultimate spiritual rewards) of the rural English worker were intended to teach the poverty-stricken, suffering English workingman and farmer to be contented with his miserable lot because God wished it so. Because many of Hannah More's poor heroes and heroines were able to raise themselves up materially as well as spiritually, she was criticized during her own lifetime for attempting to "better" the lot of the poor "until they were no longer fit for servants." The understanding of economics then current saw upward mobility as damaging to industrial productivity.

Another notable writer of religious books for children was Anna Laetitia Barbauld. Her early works, *Hymns in prose for children* and *Lessons for children* (done in series for different age levels), were both written for her adopted nephew, Charles. They unite the philosophy of Rousseau and her own deeply felt religious beliefs by teaching that the contemplation of Nature will lead the child to God—a notion that would have revolted Rousseau. Mrs. Barbauld's later book, *Evenings at home*, in six volumes from 1792 to 1796, was written with her brother, John Aikin. It is a vast compilation of short stories, plays, and articles that were to be read by the entire (obviously middle-class) family for entertainment in the evenings. Although very literal and instructive, they are less dated than other works of this period.

Sarah Trimmer, another of the religious story writers, published her well-known *The history of the robins*, in 1786 (originally with the title *The fabulous histories: designed for the instruction of children respecting their treatment of animals*). Possessed of an educational philosophy considerably more conservative than Maria Edgeworth's or Day's, Sarah Trimmer wrote for and edited her own journal, *Guardian of education* (1802–6), sending forth attacks on fairy tales, the monitorial systems of Lancaster and Bell, and other educational theories. A deeply religious, well-meaning woman, she initiated several Sunday schools in her village of Brentford.

The last and perhaps the most fanatic of the religious story writers was Mary Sherwood, who has been characterized as a brilliant writer with an extreme Calvinistic point of view. Before going to India in 1802, she published *The history of Susan Grey*, a pious but popular book for children. In India, Mary Sherwood met the missionary Henry Martyns, who influenced her greatly, and it was there that the first part of *The Fairchild family* was written. Completed in 1848 and subtitled *The child's manual, being a collection of stories calculated to show the importance and effect of a religious education*, the book includes masterful descriptions of family life. It is, however, for contemporary tastes, marred by "Calvinistic thunderings" on religion and the sins of familial disobedience, and it contains some of the most brutally descriptive passages in children's literature. Mary Sherwood carried on the tract tradition and supplied children with her tales throughout the first half of the nineteenth century.

The literature of the late eighteenth and early nineteenth centuries was completely realistic. "Real" people and "real life" situations were used to show that the hand of God was at work for divine ends. Fairy tales and all fanciful literature—including, of course, chapbook romances—were abolished from the nursery and railed against by all the educational theorists. The literature was unremitting in its attempts to teach by example. The late Georgian child, characterized by Gillian Avery in her book *Nineteenth century children* as diligent rather than religious, was inundated no longer by warnings of "be good or you will go to Hell," but by examples of how the good child behaves.

OUTLINE

I. Influences affecting writers
  A. Educational ideas of Rousseau
  B. The Sunday school movement; Robert Raikes (1736–1811), Hannah More (1745–1833)
  C. Religious movements of the nineteenth century
  D. The movement toward popular education
II. Outstanding authors
  A. Thomas Day (1748–89)
    1. Character
    2. Association with Richard Lovell Edgeworth and influence of Rousseau
    3. *Sandford and Merton*
      a) Origin and purpose
      b) Main story
        (1) Outline
        (2) Characters
        (3) Literary method
        (4) Philosophical and radical bias
        (5) Character of incidents
        (6) "Improving dialogue"
        (7) Encyclopedic lore
        (8) Moralizing tendency
      c) Stories included within the main story
        (1) Character
        (2) Sources
        (3) Moral lessons
      d) Popularity
    4. *The history of Little Jack*
      a) Outline of story
      b) Underlying theme
      c) Moral
  B. Sarah Trimmer (1741–1810)
    1. Religious and educational interests
    2. Attitude toward fairy tales
    3. Books for children
      a) *Fabulous histories*

      (1) Aim
      (2) Two stories interwoven: general character
      (3) Story of the robin family
        (a) Analogy to family of children
        (b) Individuality of birds
        (c) Faults of birds, those of children
        (d) Training of birds and the lessons taught
      (4) Story of the Benson children
        (a) Contrast with "Master Jenkins"
        (b) Mrs. Addis and the lesson taught by her example
        (c) Lessons taught by comparison of children and birds
        (d) Examples of primness and correct manners
      (5) Style
      (6) Qualities that have made the book live
      (7) Contrast with abridged and simplified modern version
      (8) Use of modern edition with children
  C. John Aikin (1747–1822) and Anna Laetitia Barbauld (1743–1825)
    1. Education and general literary work
    2. Mrs. Barbauld's *Lessons for children*
      a) Origin
      b) Use
    3. Mrs. Barbauld's *Hymns in prose*
    4. Mrs. Barbauld and Aikin's *Evenings at home*
      a) Educational theories illustrated
      b) General plan of book

c) Types of material included
(1) Informational articles
(2) Moral stories
  (*a*) Realistic type
  (*b*) Fairy tale nature
  (*c*) Practical character of moral teaching
  (*d*) Religious tolerance and attitude toward war and slavery as shown in stories
(3) Poetry
d) Style
(1) Narrative
(2) Dialogue
D. Mary Wollstonecraft (1759–97)
  1. Life
  2. Probable motives for writing children's books
  3. *Original stories from real life*
    a) General plan and outline of main story
    b) Illustrative stories included
    c) Character of Mrs. Mason
    d) Illustrations by Blake for edition of 1791
  4. *Elements of morality;* translation of *Moralisches elementarbuch* by C. G. Salzmann
    a) Object
    b) Character of incidents
    c) Method of enforcing lessons taught
    d) Changes made by Mary Wollstonecraft
    e) Comparison with her original work
E. Maria Edgeworth (1767–1849)
  1. Life and literary association of father and daughter
  2. Methods of work
  3. *The parent's assistant*
    a) Origin
    b) Method of enforcing moral lessons
    c) Character of incidents
    d) Characterization
    e) Construction
    f) Style
    g) Illustration of English life and customs
    h) Editions
  4. *Early lessons*
    a) Origin and bibliographical history
    b) Rousseauistic principles
    c) Recognition of importance to be given study of science in future
    d) Value for its own period; opinions of Ruskin, Scott, and Edward Everett Hale
  5. *Moral tales* and *Popular tales*
    a) Comparison of characters and incidents with those of *The parent's assistant*
    b) Variety of scene
    c) Use with older boys and girls

6. *Rosamond*
  a) Theme
  b) Rosamond's position in her own family; contrast with modern children's books
  c) Comparison of construction, general character, and interest with those of *The parent's assistant*
  d) Use with older boys and girls
7. Value to children of Maria Edgeworth's stories
  a) Criticisms of her method
  b) Contrast with idealistic literature in lessons taught and effect upon children
  c) Emphasis upon relation of cause and effect
  d) Clear distinction of right and wrong. "A truth is not less true because it is in large print"
  e) Value in developing reasoning power, moral judgment, choice in right action
  f) Literary value
F. Mary Sherwood (1775–1851) and her writings
  1. Life: influence of Henry Martyn
  2. Literary ability and volume of work
    a) Character of books determined by religious beliefs
  3. Some representative books
    a) *The history of Susan Grey*
    b) *Little Henry and his bearer Boosy*
    c) *The history of Henry Milner*
    d) *The flowers of the forest*
    e) *The potters' common*
    f) *Stories explanatory of the church catechism*
    g) *The history of the Fairchild family*
      (1) Good features
        (*a*) Home atmosphere
        (*b*) Attractive descriptions of country life
        (*c*) Childlike characteristics
      (2) Theory of education upon which story is based
        (*a*) Contrast with the American belief in the value of responsibility and training in self-reliance
      (3) The dogmatic character of the religious instruction
      (4) The psychological effect upon children of constant analysis of religious feelings and experiences
      (5) The complacency and self-righteousness of the Fairchild family
      (6) The snobbishness of the Fairchilds
      (7) Unsuitability of some of the incidents for children

(8) The element of "pious slaughter"
(9) The "ministering child" as exemplified in the story of little Henry
(10) The "besetting sins" of the children and the disproportionate punishments
(11) Unevenness of literary merit
(12) The characterization
(13) The short stories included within the main story
    (a) Contrast of method, plot, construction, and characters with those of Maria Edgeworth
(14) The style
(15) Bibliographical history
(16) The popularity of the story in the nineteenth century and some reasons for it

4. In imitation of Bunyan
    a) *The infant's progress from the valley of destruction to everlasting glory*
    b) *The Indian pilgrim*
5. Mary Sherwood as editor
    a) *The governess, or, the little female academy* by Sarah Fielding
    b) Attitude toward fairy tales
III. Other representative writers of didactic stories for children
  A. Authors of books of information
    1. Lady Eleanor Fenn (1743–1813)
  B. Authors of stories
    1. Mary Elliott (1794?–1870)
    2. Sarah Fielding (1710–68)
    3. Dorothy (1755–1836) and Mary Jane Kilner (1753–1831)
    4. Alicia Catherine Mant (1788?–1869)
    5. Mary Pilkington (1766–1839)

THE EDUCATIONAL BACKGROUND

■ The references indicated below serve as an educational background, not only for this section, but also for the subsequent sections that deal with England in the late eighteenth and early nineteenth centuries.

Adamson, John William. English education, 1789–1902. Cambridge: Cambridge University Press, 1964.
This basic text on nineteenth-century education traces the move to state-controlled public education as influenced by Locke, Rousseau, the French Revolution, Bentham, Mills and the late-eighteenth-century move to industrialism. The chapter "Pre-Victorian education," p. 13–122, is an excellent summary of British educational theory up to 1839.

Altick, Richard R. "Elementary education and literacy," in his *The English common reader: a social history of the mass reading public, 1800–1900*, p. 141–72. Chicago: University of Chicago Press (Phoenix Books), 1957.
The movement to provide elementary education for the working classes is charted.

Armytage, W. H. G. Four hundred years of English education. Cambridge: Cambridge University Press, 1963.
Chapters 4, 5, and 6, deal with the periods from 1732 to 1839.

Barnard, Howard Clive. A short history of English education, from 1760. 2d ed. London: University of London Press, 1961.

Binns, Henry Bryan. A century of education, being the centenary history of the British and Foreign School Society, 1808–1908. London: Dent, 1908.
Deals with Joseph Lancaster and his educational theories.

Birchenough, Charles. History of elementary education in England and Wales from 1800 to the present day. London: W. B. Clive, 1914.

Cruse, Amy. "The school room," in her *The Englishman and his books in the early nineteenth century*, p. 78–92. London: Harrap, 1930.
Describes types of schools for children from 1800 to 1900, their textbooks, and books used for pleasure reading.

Curtis, Stanley James. History of education in Great Britain. London: London University Tutorial Press, 1948.
Traces the history of English education from the Reformation through 1940. The chapter "Elementary education in the age of philanthropy" covers dame schools, charity schools, the Sunday school movement, Hannah More, Sarah Trimmer, Bell and Lancaster, Robert Owens, and the Reform Law of 1832.

——— and **M. E. A. Boultwood.** An introductory history of the English education since 1800. London: London University Tutorial Press, 1960.
Chapter 1 deals with English schools in 1800: charity schools, children in the factory system, monitorial schools, private and public education, grammar schools, and education received at home. Chapter 2 covers Adam Smith's economic theories as applied to education, the Sunday school movement, and the impact on education of the political theories of Paine, Godwin, and Bentham. Chapter

6 incorporates Edgeworth's and Arnold's educational theories, as well as those of Pestalozzi, Herbart, and Froebel.

Darton, Frederick Joseph Harvey. "Bell and the dragon," *The fortnightly review* 91, n.s. 85: 896–909 (1909).
Discusses the circumstances in which the National Society had its origin and the part taken by Sarah Trimmer in the educational controversy of the time.

de Montmorency, James Edward Geoffrey. State intervention in English education: a short history from the earliest times down to 1833. Cambridge: Cambridge University Press, 1902.
Traces the relationship of education and the state from Saxon times through the nineteenth century.

Dobbs, Archibald Edward. Education and social movements, 1700–1850. London: Longmans, 1919.
Includes a discussion of all the philanthropic institutions of the eighteenth century. Chapter 6, "Libraries and literature," deals with the scarcity of public libraries, the endeavors of the tract societies, and the impact of the newspaper on education as well as politics.

Higham, Charles Strachan Sanders. "The three Rs," in his *Pioneers of progress,* p. 69–79. London: Longmans, 1929.
A short account of Joseph Lancaster, Andrew Bell, and their schools.

Jarman, Thomas Leckie. Landmarks in the history of education: English education as part of the European tradition. London: Cresset, 1951.
"The evolution of education in England is traced as part of the historical development of European education, from its origins in ancient Greece to the modern practice of education for all."—preface. Discusses the impact of the industrial revolution on a national system of education.

Jones, Mary G. The Charity School movement: a study of 18th century Puritanism in action. Cambridge: Cambridge University Press, 1938; reprint: Hamden, Conn.: Shoe String (Archon), 1964.
A scholarly work that views the charity school—the favorite form of benevolence of eighteenth-century men and women—as a neglected aspect of social history. Discusses "the literary curriculum," the Methodist schools, Sunday schools, the schools of industry, and the Lancastrian schools.

Lancaster, Joseph. The practical parts of Lancaster's improvements and Bell's experiment. Edited by David Salmon. Cambridge: Cambridge University Press, 1932.

Introduction, p. vii–li, gives an account of the lives of and the educational systems developed by Lancaster and Bell. In part reprinted from the British and Foreign School Society's *Educational record.*

Lawson, John. A social history of education in England. London: Methuen, 1973.

MacGregor, Geddes. "Public schools in the 18th century," *The quarterly review* 285:580–91 (1947).
Discusses the rise of the public schools—holdovers from the medieval grammar schools—as a place for the education of aristocrats.

Middleton, Nigel, and **Sophia Weitzman.** A place for everyone: a history of state and education from the end of the 18th century to the 1970's. London: Victor Gollancz, 1976.
Chapter 1 provides an "outline of educational development from the earliest times to the start of the first national schemes in the 19th century."

Midwinter, Eric. Nineteenth century education. (Seminar studies in history series) New York: Harper, 1970.
Begins with the premise that nineteenth-century education was influenced by eighteenth-century charity schools, which bequeathed a dogmatic style of religious instruction firmly centered on Bible study.

Neuberg, Victor E. Popular education in eighteenth century England. London: Woburn, [1971].
An excellent, concise summary of charity education in the eighteenth century and the use of chapbooks among the newly literate class. Neuberg establishes evidence for the existence of a mass reading public about 1800 created by the availability of chapbooks and other cheap reading material.

Salmon, David. Joseph Lancaster. London: Longmans, 1904.
Includes a discussion of the controversy between Lancaster and Sarah Trimmer. Illustrations of a monitorial school and monitors' badges.

Simon, Brian. Studies in the history of education, 1780–1870. London: Lawrence & Wishart, 1960.
A major work that attempts "to relate the ideas of reformers and the changes introduced to contemporary social and political conflicts."

Smith, Frank. "The eighteenth century," "The education of the poor in the eighteenth century," "Day schools for the poor," "Educational ideas to the time of the reform bill," in his *A history of English elementary education, 1760–1902,* p. 1–136. London: University of London Press, 1931.

For the development of Sunday schools, see p. 48–69; for the Bell and Lancaster schools, p. 70–84.

Smith, Sydney. "Trimmer versus Lancaster," in his *Essays, social and political*, p. 49–55. 1st and 2d series in 1v. London: Ward, Lock, [187?].
A review of Sarah Trimmer's book written in opposition to the Lancastrian plan of education for the laboring class. The article was published originally in *The Edinburgh review*.

Trapp, Asher. The school teachers: the growth of the teaching profession in England and Wales from 1800 to the present day. New York: Macmillan, 1957.
One chapter, "The birth of the profession," p. 5–25, relates the role of the charity school and discusses early-nineteenth-century teachers and their training.

Wardle, David. English popular education, 1780–1970. Cambridge: Cambridge University Press, 1970.
A concise, scholarly history that attempts (1) to show educational change in historical, political, social, and economic background and (2) "to make historical experience bear upon contemporary problems."—preface.

Robert Raikes, Hannah More, and the Sunday School

Altick, Richard. "The time of crisis, 1791–1800," in his *The English common reader: a social history of the mass reading public, 1800–1900*, p. 67–80. Chicago: Chicago University Press (Phoenix Books), [1957].
This covers the impact of the Sunday school movement on literacy.

Armytage, A. J. Green-. "Hannah More," in his *Maids of honour*, p. 1–40. London: W. Blackwood, 1906.
Mention of the Sunday school movement and the *Cheap repository tracts*, p. 23–27.

Cope, Henry Frederick. The evolution of the Sunday school. Boston: Pilgrim, 1911.
Includes chapters on the Sunday school movement, Robert Raikes, early schools in North America, and the adoption of the school by the church.

Courtney, Luther Weeks. Hannah More's interest in education and government. Waco, Tex.: Baylor University Press, 1929.
The purpose is "to show that the works of Hannah More . . . were in many respects an expression of the feeling of the period in which she lived."—preface.

Cropper, Margaret. "Hannah More, in her *Sparks among the stubble*, p. 145–81. New York: Longmans, Green, 1955.
Chiefly about Miss More's religious endeavors.

Green, Samuel G. The story of the Religious Tract Society for 100 years. London: Religious Tract Society, 1899.

Harris, J. Henry, ed. Robert Raikes: the man and his work. Bristol, England: J. W. Arrowsmith; New York: Dutton, 1899.
Includes biographical notes collected by Josiah Harris; unpublished letters by Robert Raikes; letters from the Raikes family; opinions on influence of Sunday schools. Valuable for its indications of the conditions that led to the Sunday school movement and that affected the character of many books written for children. Portrait of Raikes used as frontispiece.

———. Robert Raikes: the man who founded the Sunday schools. London: National Sunday School Union, n.d.
A priggish report intended for young people.

Hopkins, Mary Alden. Hannah More and her circle. New York: Longmans, 1947.
Includes chapters on the Sunday school movement, Hannah More's association with the Clapham sect, the educational works of the More sisters, and the tract writing.

Jones, Mary G. Hannah More. Cambridge: Cambridge University Press, 1952; reprint: New York: Greenwood, 1968.
A major biographical and critical work. Lists the tracts and other major writings.

———. "The Sunday school," in her *The charity school movement*, p. 142–54. Cambridge: Cambridge University Press, 1938; reprint: Hamden, Conn.: Shoe String (Archon), 1964.
Analyzes the Sunday school movement as a "revival and continuation of the earlier day charity schools."

Kendall, Guy. Robert Raikes: a critical study. London: Nicholson & Watson, 1939.
The object of this book is "to give an evaluation, from a modern standpoint, of the work of Robert Raikes of Gloucester, and his contribution to our national education of today."—preface.

Laguer, Thomas Walter. Religion and respectability: Sunday schools and working class culture, 1780–1850. New Haven, Conn.: Yale University Press, 1976.
A scholarly study of the Sunday school movement as "the central feature of working class community life."

More, Hannah. Cheap repository tracts, entertaining, moral and religious [By Hannah More and others]. 3v. London: F. & C. Rivington, 1798.
This is the first complete edition listed in the *British Museum catalogue.* Another edition, published in London by Marshall and in Bath by S. Hazard in 1797, is listed as incomplete. They were sold from 1795 on, and more than two million copies were sold. The originals are rare but are available on microfilm. (See Spinney below for complete bibliographical information.)

————. Domestic tales and allegories, illustrating human life. New York: Appleton, 1840.
Contents: The shepherd of Salisbury Plain; Mr. Fantom; The two shoemakers; Giles the poacher; The servant turned soldier; The general jail delivery.
The first of these stories is the most famous of the series of *Cheap repository tracts* and may be used to illustrate early Sunday school literature.

————. Essays on various subjects, principally designed for young ladies. London: J. Wilkie & T. Cadell, 1777.
Essays on dissipation, conversation, envy, "sentimental connexions," "true and false meekness," etc.

————. Letters of Hannah More. Selected by R. Brimley Johnson. London: John Lane, 1925.
A section of letters concerns the schools.

————. Sacred dramas. Newark, N.J.: W. Tuttle, 1806.
Subtitle: "chiefly intended for young persons: the subjects taken from the Bible. To which are added, 'Reflections of King Hezekiah,' 'Sensibility,' 'a poem,' and 'Search after happiness.' "

————. ————. Philadelphia: Thomas Dobson, 1787.
Subtitle: "principally designed for young ladies."

————. Sheperd [sic] of Salisbury Plain. Richmond: Baird, 1871.

————. Strictures on the modern system of female education, with a view of the principles and conduct prevalent among women of rank and fortune. New York: Printed for George Long, 1813.
The author expresses her not particularly liberal views on education for women.

Patterson, Sylvia. "Hannah More and Sarah Kirby," in her *Rousseau's Émile and early children's literature,* p. 143–58. Metuchen, N.J.: Scarecrow, 1971.
Patterson asserts that the tracts were written, not for children, but for semiliterate adults; however, as the children had nothing better to read, they turned to these tracts.

Raikes, Robert. "First institution of Sunday schools," *The gentleman's magazine* 54:410–12 (1784).
Letter written by Robert Raikes giving an account of his "new and excellent scheme."

Rice, Edwin Wilbur. "Origin of the modern Sunday school," in his *The Sunday school movement, 1780–1917,* p. 11–39. Philadelphia: American Sunday School Union, 1917.
Deals with Raikes, Hannah More and their schools. Another chapter, "Creating juvenile literature," p. 139–87, provides information on juvenile literature in 1800, libraries for schools, and various Sunday school movements' periodicals for children.

Roberts, William. The life of Hannah More, with selections from her correspondence. London: Seeley, Jackson & Halliday, 1856.
Includes several letters to her sisters about the tracts.

————. Memoirs of the life and correspondence of Mrs. Hannah More. 4v. London: R. B. Seeley & Burnside, 1834.
The standard biography of Hannah More; author is now criticized for his "ineptness, his emendations, corrections and distortions."

————. ————. 2v. New York: Harper, 1836.

Scott, Walter Sidney. "Hannah More," in his *Bluestocking ladies,* p. 122–40. London: John Green, 1947.
A biographical sketch with an account of Hannah More's philanthropic work.

Spinney, Gordon Harold. "Cheap repository tracts," *The library,* 4th ser., 20:295–340 (1939).
A complete bibliography of the first editions of the *Cheap repository tracts.* Based on the collection in the British Museum, the public libraries of Bath and Bristol, and the register of the Stationers' Company.

Thompson, Henry. The life of Hannah More. London: Thomas Cadell, 1838.
An admiring early biography.

Town, E. L. "Robert Raikes," in his *History of religious educators.* Grand Rapids, Mich.: Baker, 1975.
Although Raikes was not the first to start Sunday schools, his were unique and lasting because they stressed general education, not just religious indoctrination.

Trumbull, Henry Clay. "The Sunday-school: its modern revival and expansion," in his *The Sunday school: its origin, mission, methods, and auxiliaries,* p. 109–22. Philadelphia: Wattles, 1888.

Webster, G. Memoir of Robert Raikes, the founder of Sunday schools. Nottingham, England, 1873.
Gives details regarding the origin of the Sunday school and Raikes's work as a social reformer in establishing a systematic plan of instruction. Twenty-six-page pamphlet.

Weiss, Harry Bischoff. "Hannah More's *Cheap repository tracts,*" *Bulletin* (New York Public Library) 15:539–49, 634–41 (July–August, 1946).

Pt. 1 is a biographical account, pt. 2, "A preliminary checklist of the *Cheap repository tracts* published in America."

Yonge, Charlotte Mary. Hannah More. London: W. H. Allen, 1888.
Best nineteenth-century biography. Includes some analysis of the tracts and the times.

THE RELIGIOUS BACKGROUND

■ The references below serve as educational background through the Victorian period.

Baker, Joseph Ellis. The novel and the Oxford movement. Princeton, N.J.: Princeton University Press, 1932.
Gives an excellent summary of the movement. Analyzes the Evangelical novels of many writers, including Charlotte Yonge, Elizabeth Sewell, and others of the 1840s and 1850s.

Balleine, George Reginald. A history of the Evangelical party in the Church of England. New ed. London: Longmans, 1933.
Chapter 5 deals with the Clapham sect and chapter 8 with the Oxford movement.

Bowen, Desmond. The idea of the Victorian church: a study of the Church of England, 1833–1889. Montreal: McGill University Press, 1968.
Two sections, "The Church and the intellectual revolution," p. 139–84, and "The Church and education," p. 185–240, are pertinent.

Brilioth, Yngve T. The Anglican revival: studies in the Oxford movement. London: Longmans, 1925.
The chapter on the Romantics and neo-Anglicanism deals with the impact of the movement on English literature.

Chapman, Edward Mortimer. "Clapham and Oxford," in his *English literature in account with religion, 1800–1900,* p. 161–98. New York: Houghton, 1910.
The book as a whole aims "to set forth something of the debt which literature owes to religion;" also "to suggest the debt which religion as indisputably owes to literature for the extension of its influence and the humanizing of its ideals." This chapter deals with the evangelical and tractarian movements.

Chapman, Raymond. Faith and revolt: studies in the literary influence of the Oxford movement. London: Weidenfeld & Nicholson, 1970.
"The Oxford Movement impinged on society and was consequently noticed by many of the great Victorian writers."—introduction. Discussion of Dickens, Christina Rossetti, Charlotte Yonge, Kingsley, and others.

Church, R. W. The Oxford movement: twelve years, 1833–1845. London: Macmillan, 1909.
Written in the 1880s by the dean of St. Paul's, this is a classic analysis of the movement.

———. ———. Edited with an introduction by Geoffrey Best. (Classics of British historical literature series) Chicago: University of Chicago Press, [1970].

Cruse, Amy. "The Clapham sect," in her *The Englishman and his books in the early nineteenth century,* p. 58–77. London: Harrap, [1930].
Discusses this Evangelical sect and what its members read and wrote.

———. "The Tractarians and the Chapelfolk," in her *The Victorians and their reading,* p. 21–41. Boston: Houghton, 1935.
A short history.

Dawson, Christopher Henry. The spirit of the Oxford movement. New York: Sheed & Ward, 1933.
A historical interpretation bringing out "the intellectual traditions and the social environment from which the Oxford movement sprang."—preface.

Faber, Geoffrey. Oxford apostles: a character study of the Oxford movement. Harmondsworth, Eng.: Penguin, 1954.
A study primarily of Newman's life and mind to 1845, with minor portraits of Keble, Pusey, and Froude.

Froude, James Anthony. "The Oxford counter-reformation," in his *Short studies on great subjects,* p. 151–234. 4th series. New York: Scribner, 1893.
Appeared originally (1881) in an English monthly periodical, *Good words.* Presented in the form of letters.

Gaselee, Stephen. "The aesthetic side of the Oxford movement," in *Northern Catholicism: centenary*

studies in the Oxford and parallel movements, edited by N. P. Williams and Charles Harris, p. 424–45. London: S.P.C.K.; New York: Macmillan, [1933].
The author discusses ecclesiastical prose writing and the hymns of the period.

Gosse, Edmund William. Father and son: biographical recollections. London: Heinemann; New York: Scribner, 1907.
"Records of the author's childhood and youth in a home where the most austere Puritanism prevailed; of his father, a scientist of distinction, devoted first of all to the religious bringing up of his son. Tells of the development of the boy's individuality, and the final break between father and son, between the rigid religion of the past and the liberality of the present, which sacrificed neither the love of the father nor the respect of the son. Written with great charm, with delicacy of feeling, poetic insight, and not a little humor."—*Booklist* (1908). Valuable in this connection as showing the effects upon children of certain types of religious literature.

Leslie, Shane. The Oxford movement, 1833–1933. London: Burns, 1933.
"This sketch offers a skeleton-key to the Movement, which in turn is a pass-key to the Victorian era."

Ollard, S. L. A short history of the Oxford movement. London: A. R. Mowbray, [1915].
Chapter titled "Some results" reflects on the impact of the Oxford movement on poetry (primarily Keble's) and prose (primarily Charlotte Yonge's).

——. What England owes to the Oxford movement. London: Mowbray, [1923].
Speaks of the writing of Newman, Keble, Sewall, Charlotte Yonge ("the spiritual child of Mr. Keble"), and Christina Rossetti.

Peck, William George. The social implication of the Oxford movement. New York: Scribner, 1933.
The Hale lectures delivered in the Seabury-Western Theological Seminary in 1933.

Shafer, Robert. "Cardinal Newman," in his *Christianity and naturalism: essays in criticism*, p. 70–120. 2d ser. New Haven, Conn.: Yale University Press, 1926.
For the Oxford movement, see p. 96–109.

Stephen, Sir James. "The Clapham sect," in his *Essays in ecclesiastical biography*, v. 2, p. 289–385. 3d ed. London: Longman, Brown, 1853.
An account of the leaders in the Evangelical party. Useful for its indication of the influences that helped to determine Mary Sherwood's characteristics as a writer for children. For Henry Martyn, whom she knew in India, see p. 337–45.

CHILDREN'S BOOKS AND THEIR AUTHORS

Ainger, Alfred. "Mrs. Barbauld," "The children's books of a hundred years ago," in his *Lectures and essays*, v. 1, p. 367–93. London: Macmillan, 1905.
Appreciative and retrospective view of Mrs. Barbauld's life and literary achievement and of Maria Edgeworth's merits as a writer of children's stories. "I undertake to say that those who remember these stories, remember them not as names, but as pictures indelibly impressed upon their imaginations, and as lessons which have become part of their stock of moral wisdom."

——. "The children's books of a hundred years ago," in *A peculiar gift: nineteenth century writings on books for children*, edited by Lance Salway, p. 62–76. Harmondsworth, Eng.: Penguin, [1976].

Avery, Gillian. Childhood's pattern: a study of the heroes and heroines of children's fiction, 1770–1900. London: Hodder [1975].
Chapter 2 deals with the child of the period, and chapter 3, "The Sunday scholar," p. 54–70, covers moralistic fiction, didactic literature, and Sunday school literature.

——. Nineteenth century children: heroes and heroines in English children's stories, 1780–1900. [London]: Hodder, [1965].
In this book, Avery concentrates on the "changing nature of the fictitious child" in children's literature in the Georgian and Victorian periods. Chapter 1, "Facts and morals," p. 11–40, deals with the writings of the "dedicated hordes of female writers" (Barbauld, Pilkington, Trimmer, Edgeworth, the Kilners, Lady Fenn, Mant, Hack, and Hofland). Avery concludes that "in one or two of the hundreds of dry little books produced between 1782–1820 . . . can be detected the faint flickering of imagination, the pale shadow of a real child."

Barry, Florence Valentine. "The English school of Rousseau," "Devices of the moralist," "Some great writers of little books," "Miss Edgeworth's tales for children," in her *A century of children's books*, p. 105–52, 175–93. New York: Doran, [1923]; reprint: Detroit: Singing Tree, 1968.
The first chapter notes the effects of Rousseau's teaching in England with special reference to the work of Thomas Day and Mary Wollstonecraft. Sarah Trimmer's *Fabulous histories* is discussed in

chapter 2, with a number of other books less outstanding in character. The opening pages of the following chapter, p. 147–52, treat of Anna Barbauld's *Hymns in prose*, and *Evenings at home* by Aikin and Barbauld. The final chapter deals with the educational theories of the Edgeworths and the children's books of Maria Edgeworth.

Bedford, Jessie (*pseud.* Elizabeth Godfrey). "Reaction," "The little female academy," "The superior parent," in her *English children in the olden time*, p. 232–46, 247–67, 268–87. London: Methuen, 1907.
Covers the work of Hannah More and Sarah Fielding, the theories of Rousseau, and the writing of the Edgeworths, Thomas Day and Jane Marcet.

———. "Children yesterday and to-day," *The quarterly review* 183:374–96 (1896).
Points out the literary characteristics of the didactic story tellers and reviews *Evenings at home*, Day's *Sandford and Merton*, Sarah Trimmer's *Fabulous histories*, and Maria Edgeworth's *Parent's assistant*; also some of the later books for children.

———. ———, in *A peculiar gift*, edited by Lance Salway, p. 77–105. Harmondsworth, Eng.: Penguin, [1976].
The author, Alexander Innes Shand, is named.

Cone, Helen Gray, and **J. L. Gilder,** eds. Pen-portraits of literary women. v. 1. New York: Cassell, 1887.
Compilation of extracts from various sources. For Hannah More, see p. 11–41; Mary Wollstonecraft, p. 81–106; Maria Edgeworth, p. 161–92.

Cutt, Margaret N. "In their own time: footnotes to social history," *Horn book magazine* 49:617–23 (December, 1973); and 50:24–31 (February, 1974).
Discusses tract tales, especially those of Mary Sherwood. Pt. 2 deals with mid-nineteenth-century Sunday school literature of the Religious Tract Society, including that by such authors as Charlotte Maria Tucker (*pseud.* A.L.O.E. [A lady of England]) and Sarah Smith (*pseud.* Hesba Stretton). Through analysis of *Little Henry and his bearer*, this essay shows how, "although many of the tract tales are superficial and repetitive, the best of them are closely tied to the great social, economic, religious, and—sometimes—political issues of their day."

Darton, Frederick Joseph Harvey. "The theorists," "The moral tale: didactic," in his *Children's books in England*, p. 141–49, 154–81. 2d ed. Cambridge: Cambridge University Press, 1958.
Includes Day, the Edgeworths, Trimmer, Aikin and Barbauld, the Kilners, Lady Fenn, Wakefield, and Sherwood.

Ellis, Alec. "Light in the darkness, 1740–1830,"

in his *A history of children's reading and literature*, p. 1–13. London: Pergamon, [1968].
Deals primarily with eighteenth-century educational texts and the few children's books available at the time.

Elwood, Anne Katherine. Memoirs of the literary ladies of England. 2v. London: Colburn, 1843; reprint: New York: AMS Press, 1973.
For Trimmer, see v. 1, p. 202–23; Barbauld, v. 1, p. 224–40; More, v. 1, p. 259–83; Wollstonecraft, v. 2, p. 125–54.

Fawcett, Millicent Garnett. Some eminent women of our times. London: Macmillan, 1894.
For Maria Edgeworth, see p. 145–62; Anna Barbauld, p. 198–204; Hannah More, p. 211–22.

Field, Louise Frances Story (Mrs. E. M. Field). "To point a moral and adorn a tale," "From 1740 to about 1810," in her *The child and his book*, p. 243–57, 263–72, 282–86. 2d ed. London: Wells Gardner, 1892; reprint: Detroit: Singing Tree, 1968.
For Thomas Day, see p. 253–55; Barbauld, p. 263–64; Trimmer, p. 265–68; Edgeworth, p. 265–72; and Wollstonecraft, p. 282–85.

Gardiner, Dorothy Kempe. "Mrs. Trimmer and the More sisters," "Towards revolution, 1762–1800," in her *English girlhood at school*, p. 327–32, 439–42, 448–76. London: Oxford University Press, 1929.
The introductory section of the chapter entitled "Towards revolution" indicates the social backgrounds of the educational writers of the period. Other topics are: Rousseau and some English writers; Catherine Macaulay and Mary Wollstonecraft; The attack on accomplishments; Ladies' libraries and school books for girls. Includes references to Thomas Day's *Sandford and Merton*, Anna Barbauld's *Early lessons for children*, Maria Edgeworth's *Moral tales* and *Parent's assistant*.

Gillespie, Margaret. "The female admonishers plus male moralizers," in her *Literature for children: history and trends*, p. 84–91. Dubuque, Iowa: William C. Brown, 1970.
Includes Fielding, Barbauld, the Kilners, Trimmer, Sherwood, More, Day, and the Edgeworths.

Godley, Eveline C. "A century of children's books," *The national review* 47:437–49 (1906).
An unsympathetic view of the moralistic and didactic writings of Maria Edgeworth and of Mary Sherwood.

———. ———. in *A peculiar gift*, edited by Lance Salway, p. 92–105. Harmondsworth, Eng.: Penguin, [1976].

Hall, Evelyn Beatrice (*pseud.* Stephen G. Tallentyre). "The road to knowledge a hundred years ago," *The Cornhill magazine* 82, n.s., 9:815–27 (1900).

Humorous presentation of the moral tale, the "improving game," and the "properties" of the didactic era in children's literature.

Hamilton, Catharine Jane. "Mrs. Barbauld," in *A peculiar gift*, edited by Lance Salway, p. 450–62. Harmondsworth, Eng.: Penguin, [1976].

———. Women writers: their works and ways. 1st series. London: Ward, Lock, 1892.

Includes chapters on Anna Barbauld, p. 66–81; Hannah More, p. 82–95; Maria Edgeworth, p. 158–74.

Meigs, Cornelia. "The little female academy," "Launching a century," "Rousseau and his companions," in Meigs et al., *A critical history of children's literature*, p. 66–76, 77–87, 88–98. Rev. ed. New York: Macmillan, 1969.

Chapter 1 deals with Sarah Fielding, Sarah Trimmer, Hannah More, Mary Wollstonecraft, Anna Barbauld and Aikin; chapter 2 covers Mary Sherwood, Lady Fenn, and the Kilners; and chapter 3 is concerned with Thomas Day and the Edgeworths.

Morgan, F. C., ed. Children's books published before 1830, exhibited at Malvern Public library in 1911. Hereford, England: privately printed, 1976.

Moses, Montrose Jonas. "The old-fashioned library," in his *Children's books and reading*, p. 76–119. New York: Kennerly, 1907.

For the Edgeworths, see p. 76–86; Thomas Day, p. 86–93; Barbauld and Aikin, p. 93–100; Robert Raikes, p. 101–6; Sarah Trimmer, p. 106–11; Hannah More, p. 111–19.

Muir, Percy. "A monstrous regiment," in his *English children's books, 1600–1900*, p. 82–100. New York: Praeger, [1954]; London: Batsford, [1969].

Discusses the trade aspect of children's book publishing. Covers Mary Pilkington, the Kilners, Lady Fenn, Priscilla Wakefield, Sarah Trimmer, Mary Sherwood, Sarah Fielding, Maria Edgeworth, Anna Barbauld, and Hannah More.

Patterson, Sylvia W. Rousseau's *Émile* and early children's literature. Metuchen, N.J.: Scarecrow, 1971.

Originally a dissertation, this excellent work covers all the women writers of the period and their works, as well as Thomas Day.

Repplier, Agnes. A happy half-century, and other essays. Boston: Houghton, 1908.

The period illustrated extends approximately from 1775 to 1825. There are intimate details of the life of the time and many references to Anna

Barbauld, Hannah More, Maria Edgeworth, and other literary ladies. Some of the essays are reprinted from the magazines in which they first appeared. The treatment is humorous, but the comments are to the point. See particularly the sections entitled "The child," p. 138–54, and "The educator," p. 155–76.

Ritchie, Anne Isabella Thackeray. "Mrs. Barbauld," "Miss Edgeworth," in her *A book of sibyls*, p. 1–148. London: Smith & Elder, 1883.

According to the writer, she first learned to read from Mrs. Barbauld's little yellow books, and the cheerful presence of Miss Edgeworth's bright, busy clever children remained, she said, more vividly in her mind than that of the real little boys and girls who used to appear and disappear disconnectedly. The articles are reprinted from *The Cornhill magazine*.

Rosenthal, Lynne M. The child informed: attitudes towards the socialization of the child in nineteenth century English children's literature. Ph.D. dissertation, Columbia University, 1974.

A discussion of "various representations of the socialization of children in 19th century children's books in an attempt to deduce how attitudes towards children changed as society itself changed." Chapter 2 deals with the didactic books of Thomas Day, Maria Edgeworth, and Mary Sherwood.

Scott, Walter Sidney, ed. Letters of Maria Edgeworth and Anna Laetitia Barbauld, selected from the Lushington papers. London: Golden Cockerel Press, 1953.

Beautifully printed book includes "a brief memoir" of both Miss Edgeworth and Mrs. Barbauld along with their letters.

Stuart, Dorothy Margaret. "In Augustan England," "From the age of reason to the age of steam," in her *The girl through the ages*, p. 198–218, p. 219–38. London: Harrap, 1933; reprint: Detroit: Singing Tree, 1969.

Chapter 1 mentions Maria Edgeworth and the education of girls at that time; chapter 2 is concerned with the Sunday schools and the texts used in them, as well as home education received by girls.

Thwaite, Mary F. "Rousseau and the moral school," in her *From primer to pleasure in reading*, p. 65–80. 2d ed. London: Library Assn., 1972.

Discussion of the French and English followers of Rousseau.

Townsend, John Rowe. Written for children: an outline of English language children's books. Rev. ed. Philadelphia: Lippincott, 1975.

Pt. 1, "Before 1840," p. 17–55, discusses Rousseau and the lady writers.

Whalley, Joyce Irene. "Moral improvement," in her *Cobwebs to catch flies: illustrated books for the nursery and schoolroom, 1700–1900*, p. 65–

74. Berkeley and Los Angeles: University of California Press, 1975.
Includes a discussion of some of the less well-known moralistic books.

Woolf, Virginia. "The Taylors and the Edgeworths," in her *The Common reader*, 1st series, p. 110–20. New York: Harcourt, 1925; Harvest ed. (Paperbound), n.d.
A vivid appreciative essay in a section titled, "The lives of the obscure." Of Thomas Day she writes, "With a character like Thomas Day, in particular, whose history surpasses the bounds of the credible, we find ourselves oozing amazement, like a sponge which has absorbed so much that it can retain no more but fairly drips."

Yonge, Charlotte M. "Children's literature of the last century," *Living age* 102–3: 373–80, 612–18, 96–102 (August 7, September 4, October 9, 1869).

Short Stories

De Vries, Leonard. Flowers of delight. New York: Pantheon, [1963].
Excerpts of children's literature from 1765 to 1830, taken from the Osborne Collection. These selections are depicted as typical of this period. An excellent analysis. "The anthropologist's apology," is on p. 221–25.

Lucas, Edward Verrall, comp. Forgotten tales of long ago. London: Wells Gardner, [1906].
Comprises twenty stories from the period 1790–1830, including "The farm-yard journal" by John

Aikin and "Waste not, want not, or, two strings to your bow" by Maria Edgeworth. Illustrations by F. D. Bedford.

———. Old fashioned tales. London: Wells Gardner, [1905].
Illustrations by F. D. Bedford. Partial contents: The history of Little Jack, and The good-natured little boy and the ill-natured little boy, both by Thomas Day; The purple jar, and The basket-woman, both by Maria Edgeworth; Trial of a complaint made against sundry persons for breaking in the windows of Dorothy Careful, widow and dealer in gingerbread, by John Aikin; The misses, by A. L. Barbauld.

Scudder, Horace Elisha, ed. The children's book. Boston: Houghton, 1909.
Contains "Eyes and no eyes" and "The boy without a genius" by John Aikin and "Waste not, want not" by Maria Edgeworth.

Tappan, Eva March, comp. Old fashioned stories & poems. (The children's hour, v. 6) Boston: Houghton, 1907.
Includes seven selections by Maria Edgeworth, four by John Aikin and Anna Barbauld, two by Thomas Day, and one by Hannah More.

Tuer, A. W. Pages and pictures from forgotten books. London: Leadenhall, 1898–99.

Yonge, Charlotte Mary, ed. A storehouse of stories. New ed. 2v. London: Macmillan, 1885–91.
A selection from didactic writers.

INDIVIDUAL WRITERS

John Aikin and Mrs. Barbauld

Aikin, John. The arts of life: of providing food, of providing clothing, of providing shelter: described in a series of letters for the instruction of young persons, by the author of *Evenings at home*. 4th ed. London: Baldwin, Cradock & Joy, 1821.

———. The calendar of nature: designed for the instruction and entertainment of young persons. London: J. Johnson, 1822.
A charming little book in which Aikin describes nature during different months of the year.

———. The juvenile budget opened, being selections from the writings of Doctor John Aikin, with a sketch of his life by Mrs. Sarah Hale. Boston: Marsh, Capen, Lyon & Webb, 1839.
Selections from *Evenings at home*. Object, as set forth in the preface: to separate the productions of Dr. Aikin from those of his sister in order to bring him "familiarly as a friend before the minds of his readers."

———. Letters from a father to his son, or various topics . . . written in the years 1792 and 1793. London: J. Johnson, 1793.
A book of manners. Includes also Aikin's educational philosophy.

———. Letters from a father to his son, or, various topics relative to literature and the conduct of life. Philadelphia: Samuel Harrison Smith, 1794.
Same as above with a variation of title.

Aikin, John, and Anna Laetitia Aikin Barbauld. Evenings at home, or, the juvenile budget opened, consisting of a variety of miscellaneous pieces for the instruction and amusement of young persons. 6v. London: J. Johnson, 1792–96.
Chiefly by Aikin, but Anna Barbauld contributed fourteen selections to the first edition and one additional article in subsequent editions. The work was commenced in 1792 and completed in six volumes in 1796.

———. ———. Corrected and revised by Cecil Hartley. London: Routledge, 1851.

———. Evenings at home, or, the juvenile budget opened, consisting of a variety of miscellaneous pieces for the instruction and amusement of young people. New ed. rev. London: Ward, Lock, 1860.
A lovely Victorian edition illustrated with 100 engravings by the Brothers Dalziel.

———. Evenings at home [retold] in words of one syllable. By Mary Godolphin (*pseud.* Lucy Aikin). London: Cassell, Petter & Galpin, 1869.
Lucy Aikin was Anna Barbauld's niece and Aikin's daughter. She made one-syllable revisions of several other books for children.

Barbauld, Anna Laetitia Aikin. Hymns in prose for children. London: J. Johnson, 1781.
Subtitle: "by the author of *Lessons for children.*"

———. ———. Edinburgh: Oliver & Boyd, n.d.
Subtitle: "calculated to impress the infant mind with early devotion." This edition is "embellished with neat engravings on wood."

———. ———. (Classics of children's literature, 1621–1932) New York: Garland, 1977.
Facsimile of 1781 edition. Introduction by Miriam Kramnick.

———. A legacy for young ladies. Edited by Lucy Aikin. London: Reed, 1826.
Subtitle: "consisting of miscellaneous pieces, in prose and verse."

———. "A legacy for young ladies," in *A selection from the poems and prose writings of Mrs. Anna Laetitia Barbauld* by Grace Atkinson Little Oliver, p. 346–472. Boston: Osgood, 1874.

———. Lessons for children. London: Benjamin Warner, 1818.
Originally published in four parts in London, 1778, 1779, 1787, 1788. Pt. 1 is for children from two to three years old; pts. 2 and 3 for children three years old; and pt. 4 for children from three to four years old. The "particular child" for whom the lessons were written was "Little Charles," the adopted son of the Barbaulds.

———. ———. Philadelphia: Benjamin Warner, 1810.
Also on title page: "improved by cuts designed by S. Pike and engraved by Dr. Anderson."

———. "The misses," in *A selection from the poems and prose writings of Mrs. Anna Laetitia Barbauld* by Grace Atkinson Little Oliver, p. 374–80. Boston: Osgood, 1874.
Short story addressed "to a careless girl," interesting "for its ingenuity, and old-fashioned naivete." The story, according to Anna Barbauld's biographer, was first printed after the author's death, in one of the annuals for children, the *Forget-me-not* of 1830. Also in *Old fashioned tales*, compiled by E. V. Lucas.

——— ed. The female speaker, or, miscellaneous pieces, in prose and verse, selected from the best writers, and adapted to the use of young women. London: J. Johnson, 1811.
A selection of pieces by Barbauld, More, Watts, Samuel Johnson, Aikin, Addison, Cowper, Franklin, Goldsmith, and Edgeworth. The collection contains moral and didactic pieces, narratives, "Descriptive and pathetic" pieces, dialogues and epistles.

BIOGRAPHY AND CRITICISM

Aikin, Lucy. "Memoir," in *Works* by Anna Laetitia Barbauld, v. 1, p. v–lxxii. London: Longman, Hurst, 1825.
Notes the character of Mrs. Barbauld's education, her teaching experience, and the origin of the children's books.

———. Memoir of John Aikin, with a selection of his miscellaneous pieces, biographical, moral and critical. v. 1. London: Baldwin, Cradock & Joy, 1823.
A detailed account of the life and literary interests of Aikin by his daughter. Reference is made to *Evenings at home,* p. 156–59, 186, and to the *Lessons for children* of Mrs. Barbauld, p. 43. A list of Aikin's writings is given in the preface, and an engraved portrait serves as frontispiece.

"A forgotten children's book," *Hibbert journal* 63: 27–34 (Autumn, 1964).
An anonymous article about *Hymns in prose for children* by Anna Barbauld—a work that was first published in 1781 and was "endlessly reprinted until well on in the 19th century," but is now almost forgotten.

le Breton, Anna Letitia. Memoir of Mrs. Barbauld, including letters and notices of her family and friends. London: G. Bell, 1874; reprint: New York: AMS Press, 1974.
An early biography by a grandniece.

Moore, Catherine Elizabeth. "The literary career of Anna Laetitia Barbauld." Ph.D. diss., University of North Carolina, 1970.
An excellent study that includes a section on Mrs. Barbauld's writings for children, p. 207–62. Moore concludes: "The first in England to impose certain rationalistic theories upon children's literature, Mrs. Barbauld launched a new school of juvenile writing without meaning to do so."

Oliver, Grace Atkinson Little. A memoir of Mrs. Anna Laetitia Barbauld with many of her letters. 2v. Boston: Osgood, [1874].
Mention of *Lessons for children,* vol. 1, p. 85–88; *Hymns in prose,* p. 96–99; *Evenings at home,* p. 43, 201. Spine on both volumes reads *Life and works of Anna Laetitia Barbauld.* Vol. 1 is subtitled "Life and letters"; vol. 2 has the subtitle "A

selection from the poems and prose writings." Author's name varies as Grace A. Ellis.

Patterson, Sylvia W. "Anna Laetitia Barbauld," in her *Rousseau's Émile and early children's literature,* p. 40–61. Metuchen, N.J.: Scarecrow, 1971.
Shows how Mrs. Barbauld's books for children support and diverge from Rousseau's theories on education.

Rogers, Betsy Aikin-Sneath. Georgian chronicle: Mrs. Barbauld and her family. London: Methuen, 1958.
Three generations of the Jennings and Aikin families from whom Anna Barbauld was descended, with full treatment of the author herself.

Whiting, Mary Bradford. "A century-old friendship: unpublished letters from Mrs. Barbauld," *The London mercury* 26:434–45 (1932).
"To read through a packet of old letters is to don the galoshes of Fortune and to be transported into the past." These letters and comments give interesting sidelights on the life and character of Anna Barbauld.

Thomas Day

Day, Thomas. The history of Little Jack. London: Stockdale, 1788.
Subtitle: "embellished with twenty-two beautiful cuts." First published in Stockdale's *Children's miscellany,* 1788, and afterward published separately for those "whose circumstances do not permit them to become purchasers of expensive publications." The story was intended to show the superiority of natural good manners to artificial manners. The woodcuts are said to be by John Bewick, and the cover is of flowered Dutch paper.

———. ———. (Classics of children's literature 1621–1932) New York: Garland, 1977.
Facsimile of the 1788 edition with an introduction by Isaac Kramnick.

———. "The history of Little Jack," in *The story teller,* edited by Charles Eliot Norton, p. 108–34. Boston: Hall & Locke, 1910.

———. ———, in *A storehouse of stories,* edited by Charlotte Mary Yonge, v. 1, p. 412–37. New ed. London: Macmillan, 1891.
Also in *Old fashioned tales,* compiled by E. V. Lucas.

———. The history of Sandford and Merton: a work intended for the use of children. 3v. London: J. Stockdale, 1783, 1786, 1789.
The first abridged version appeared in 1790. The author's preface explains the book's origin and purpose.

———. ———. 3v. in 1. Baltimore: Warner & Hanna, 1809.
A very early American edition.

———. ———. Corrected and revised by Cecil Hartley. London: Routledge, [1874].

———. ———. (Classics of children's literature 1621–1932) New York: Garland, 1977.
Facsimile of the three-volume edition published in 1783–89. Introduction by Isaac Kramnick.

BIOGRAPHY AND CRITICISM

Blackman, John A. A memoir of the life and writings of Thomas Day. London: J. Leno, 1862.

Charnwood, Dorothea Mary Roby Thorpe. "A habitation's memories," *The Cornhill magazine* 136, n.s. 63:664–77 (1927).
The "habitation" is Stowe House, once the residence of Day. The article gives interesting anecdotes of his life.

Chase, Mary Ellen. "A goodly heritage," *Bulletin* (American Library Association) 27, no. 3:800–2 (1933).
Analyzes *Sandford and Merton* for the qualities that have made the book live.

Clyne, A. "Sandford and Merton," *Junior bookshelf* 12:103–6 (October, 1948).

Fyvie, John. "The author of *Sandford and Merton* (Thomas Day)," in his *Some literary eccentrics,* p. 35–64. London: Constable, 1906.
The essay seems to support the author's conclusions that Day was "an original."

Gignilliat, George Warren, Jr. The author of Sandford and Merton: a life of Thomas Day, Esq. New York: Columbia University Press, 1932.
A valuable study of an eccentric, but versatile and interesting, personality—an eighteenth-century idealist. The first chapters are descriptive of Day's boyhood and education, his travels with Maria Edgeworth, adventure in female education, and association with the Lichfield group. One of the later chapters, p. 234–308, is devoted to the children's books. Extracts from Day's letters and other writings are freely used, and there are numerous footnotes and a bibliography, p. 351–56.

Hitchman, Francis. "The author of *Sandford and Merton,*" in his *Eighteenth century studies,* p. 334–59. London: Low, 1881.
Good short account of Day's life and character. Reference to *Sandford and Merton,* p. 356–58.

Keir, James. Account of the life and writing of Thomas Day. London: J. Stockdale, 1862; reprint: New York: Garland, 1970.
This is the first biography of Day, by a man who knew him for twenty years.

Lucas, Edward Verrall. "Honora Sneyd's later lovers," in his *A swan and her friends*, p. 89–100. London: Methuen, 1907.
Brings out Day's connection with the Lichfield circle and his matrimonial experiments. Contains an interesting portrait.

Patterson, Sylvia W. "Thomas Day," in her *Rousseau's Émile and early children's literature*, p. 62–78. Metuchen, N.J.: Scarecrow, 1971.
Discusses the tremendous impact of Rousseau on Day's life and writing.

Sadler, *Sir* Michael Ernest. Thomas Day, an English disciple of Rousseau. Cambridge: Cambridge University Press, 1928.
The Rede lecture, 1928. P. 29–47 deal with *Sandford and Merton*.

Scott, *Sir* Samuel Haslam. The exemplary Mr. Day, 1748–1789, author of *Sandford and Merton*: a philosopher in search of the life of virtue and a paragon among women. London: Faber & Faber, 1935.
A biography written for the "ordinary reader," about Day, who was "an extraordinary and very entertaining character, besides being a very fine man and very nearly a great man."

Seward, Anna. "Thomas Day," in her *Memoirs of the life of Dr. Darwin, chiefly during his residence in Lichfield, with anecdotes of his friends and criticisms on his writings*, p. 12–55. Philadelphia: W. Poyntell, 1804.
The author digresses from the principal subject of the memoir to give some account of "the circumstances of Mr. Day's disposition, habits, and destiny"—he having been drawn for a time into the Lichfield circle through the fame of Darwin's various talents.

Maria Edgeworth

Edgeworth, Maria. Early lessons. 6v. London: J. Johnson, 1801.
Contents: Harry and Lucy pt. 1; Harry and Lucy pt. 2; Rosamond pt. 1 (including The Purple jar, The two plums, and The day of misfortunes); Rosamond pt. 2 (including Rivuletta, The thorn, and The hyacinths); Rosamond pt. 3 (The story of the rabbit); Frank pt. 1; Frank pt. 2; Frank pt. 3; Frank pt. 4, Little dog Trusty (including Little dog Trusty [a repeat], The orange man; The cherry orchard).

————. Continuation of *Early lessons*. 2v. London: J. Johnson, 1814.
Contents: Frank; Rosamond: the wager; The party of pleasure; The black bonnet; The India cabinet; The silver cup; Rosamond: the bee and the cow; The happy party; Wonders; The microscope; To parents; Harry and Lucy.

————. Frank: a sequel to Frank in *Early lessons*. 3v. London: R. Hunter, 1822.

————. Harry and Lucy concluded, being the last part of *Early lessons*. 4v. London: R. Hunter, 1825.

————. Letters for literary ladies. London: J. Johnson, 1795; reprint: New York: Garland, 1974.
With an introduction by Gina Luria. This was the author's first published book. Elizabeth Harden, in *Maria Edgeworth's art of prose fiction*, says of it, "the letters reflect the Edgeworth strong belief in the all-pervasive power of education as a guide to the growth and development of female character, to the adjustment of woman in society, and to her achievement of happiness in general."

————. Little plays. London: R. Hunter, 1827.
Contents: The grinding organ; Dumb Andy; The dame school holiday. Published as the seventh volume of the 1800 edition of *The parent's assistant*.

————. Moral tales for young people. 3v. London: J. Johnson, 1801.
Contents: Forester; The Prussian vase; The good aunt; Angelina, or l'amie inconnue; The good French governess; Mademoiselle Panache; The knapsack. Tales written to illustrate the opinions expressed in *Practical education*. The preface, by Richard Edgeworth, notes the particular purpose of each story.

————. The parent's assistant, or, stories for children. 3v. London: J. Johnson, 1796.

————. ————. 6v. London: J. Johnson, 1800.
For complete bibliographical information, see Pollard (below). The 1800 version is a complete revision of the 1796 collection, with three tales transferred to *Early lessons* and eight new ones added. Contents: Vol. 1: Lazy Lawrence; Tarlton; The false key. Vol. 2: The birth-day present; Simple Susan [not in first edition]. Vol. 3: The bracelets; The little merchants [not in first edition]. Vol. 4: Old Poz; The mimic; Mademoiselle Panache. Vol. 5: The basket-woman; The white pigeon [not in first edition]; The orphans [not in first edition]; Waste not, want not; Forgive and forget. Vol. 6: The barring out [not in first edition]; Eton Montem [not in first edition]; The little dog Trusty; The orange man; The purple jar [last three not in third edition].

————. ————. London: Routledge, Warne & Routledge, 1864.
With illustrations by Phiz.

————. ————. (Classics of children's literature 1621–1932) 6v. in 2. New York: Garland, 1977.
Introduction by Christina Edgeworth Colvin.

———. Popular tales. 3v. London: J. Johnson, 1804.
Contents: Lame Jervas; The will; The Limerick gloves; Out of debt, out of danger; The lottery; Rosanna; Murad the unlucky; The manufacturers; The contrast; The grateful negro; Tomorrow.

———. Rosamond: a sequel to *Early lessons*. 2v. London: R. Hunter, 1821.
Contains twelve stories.

———. Tales. London: Stokes, 1926.
Introduction by Austin Dobson and illustrations by Hugh Thomson. Twelve stories from *The parent's assistant*. First published in 1903.

———. Tales and novels of Maria Edgeworth. 10v. London: Longford, 1893; reprint: New York: AMS Press, 1967.
Vol. 1 contains the *Moral tales;* vol. 2, *Popular tales.*

———. ———. 18v. London: Cradock & Baldwin, 1832–33.

BIOGRAPHY AND CRITICISM

Butler, Harriet Jessie Edgeworth, and **H. E. Butler.** The black book of Edgeworthstown, and other Edgeworth memories. London: Faber, [1927].
"The memoirs . . . are drawn partly from material published more than a century ago, and partly from family letters and an unpublished manuscript, known to the family as the 'Black book of Edgeworthstown.' "—preface.

Butler, Marilyn. Maria Edgeworth: a literary biography. Oxford: Clarendon, 1972.

Clarke, Isabel Constance. Maria Edgeworth, her family and friends. London: Hutchinson, 1950; reprint: Folcroft, Pa.: Folcroft, 1972.
A detailed biography of Miss Edgeworth and her family. Includes several photographs of her home and several facsimiles of her writings.

Dobson, Austin. "The parent's assistant," in his *De libris: prose & verse,* p. 69–86. London: Macmillan, 1908; reprint: *Signal* 17:96–104 (May, 1975).
Bibliographic details of the first two editions. See Pollard article listed below for more up-to-date information.

Edgeworth, Maria. Chosen letters. Boston: Houghton; London: Jonathan Cape, 1931; reprint: AMS Press, 1976.
The editor, Florence Valentine Barry, had access to original letters previously unpublished and to the *Memoir of Maria Edgeworth,* by the fourth Mrs. Edgeworth. The introduction is on p. 7–39.

———. Letters from England, 1813–1844; ed. by Christina Colvin. Oxford: Clarendon, 1971.

———. The life and letters. Edited by A. J. C. Hare. 2v. Boston: Houghton; London: Edward Arnold, 1894.
"There is nothing more unlike the life of the typical literary lady than that of Maria Edgeworth as we see it in her letters. They are full of the happy cheerfulness of a lovable woman whose heart was in her home and her multifarious duties, and who took her writing mainly as one of the permissible healthy recreations. . . ."—*The Saturday review,* 1895. A reference to the first publication of *The parent's assistant,* indicating that the title was chosen by the publisher, will be found in vol. 1, p. 47–48. For other references to the children's books, see vol. 1, p. 49, 74–75, 145, 229; vol. 2, p. 432. On p. 69, vol. 1, there is an interesting glimpse of Mr. and Mrs. Barbauld, whom Mr. and Mrs. Edgeworth met at Clifton.

———. ———. New York: Books for Libraries, 1971.
Reprinted from the 1926 edition.

Edgeworth, Maria, and **Richard Lovell Edgeworth.** Practical education; 2v. London: J. Johnson, 1798. 2d. ed. 3v. London: J. Johnson, 1801.
Valuable for its indication of the motives or theories that determined the character of Miss Edgeworth's work and made her for more than a generation one of the most important writers for children. The chapter on books is interesting, not only because of the point of view presented, but also for its comments on the work of contemporary writers.

———. ———. (Classics of children's literature 1621–1932) New York: Garland, 1974.
Reprint of the 1798 edition.

Edgeworth, Richard Lovell. Memoirs, begun by himself and concluded by his daughter Maria Edgeworth. 2v. London: R. Hunter, 1820.

———. ———. 3d. ed. 1v. London: Bentley, 1844.
Revisions made by Maria Edgeworth.
There is a detailed account of the method followed in writing the moral tales, p. 442–46.

———. ———. Dublin: Shannon University Press, 1970.
Introduction by Desmond Clarke.

"Edgeworth family: anticipators of A. Froebel," *Time educational supplement* no. 1778, p. 355 (May 27, 1949).
Outlines the educational theories of the Edgeworths, especially the theory of learning as an active process. Claims that Maria wrote sixteen chapters of *Practical education.*

Flanagan, Thomas J. B. "Maria Edgeworth," in his *Irish novelists, 1800–1850,* p. 53–106. New York: Columbia University Press, 1959.
A major essay. The tales are discussed on p. 63–68.

Hall, Anna Maria Fielding (Mrs. S. C. Hall). "Edgeworthstown: memories of Maria Edgeworth," *The art journal* 11:225–29 (1849).
Pictures and descriptions of the Edgeworth home and library, p. 224. Vol. 11 is indexed in *Poole's index to periodical literature* as vol. 1.

————. ————. *Littell's living age* 22:320–29 (1849). Reprinted without illustrations.

Harden, Elizabeth McWhorter. Maria Edgeworth's art of prose fiction. The Hague: Mouton, 1970.
Detailed analysis of *The parent's assistant, Practical education,* and *Early lessons,* p. 16–42; *Moral tales* and *Popular tales,* p. 108–35.

Hawthorne, Mark D. Doubt and dogma in Maria Edgeworth. (University of Florida monographs, no. 25) Gainesville: University of Florida Press, 1967.
This scholarly work discusses the writings for children on p. 23–38.

Hill, Constance. Maria Edgeworth and her circle in the days of Buonaparte and Bourbon. London: John Lane, 1910.
Concerns Maria Edgeworth's journeys to France and England rather than her home life in Ireland or her literary work. Interesting for the background of the period—the first twenty years of the nineteenth century; the unusual viewpoint regarding Miss Edgeworth; and the references to Mme. de Genlis, Mrs. Barbauld and others. Numerous illustrations and reproductions of contemporary portraits.

Ingliss-Jones, Elizabeth. The Great Maria: a portrait of Maria Edgeworth. London: Faber & Faber, 1959.
Maria Edgeworth seen within the framework of her family and of contemporary society. Brief but revealing appraisals of her writings. No bibliography.

Lawless, Emily. Maria Edgeworth. (English men of letters) London: Macmillan, 1904.
Sympathetic and intimate account of Miss Edgeworth, her family and friends, and her literary work. "First books," p. 50–58.

Lazarus, Rachel Mordecai. The education of the heart: the correspondence of Rachel Mordecai Lazarus and Maria Edgeworth. Edited by Edgar E. McDonald. Chapel Hill: University of North Carolina Press, 1977.
A fascinating correspondence between Maria Edgeworth and Rachel Lazarus, a schoolmistress who lived in North Carolina.

Murray, Patrick. Maria Edgeworth: a study of the novelist. . . . Cork, Ireland: Mercier, [1971]. Paperbound.
Chapter 4, "English novels and miscellaneous writings," p. 58–73, deals, in part, with Maria Edgeworth's educational theories and moral tales.

Newby, Percy Howard. Maria Edgeworth. London: Barker; Denver: Swallow, 1950; reprint: Folcroft, Pa.: Folcroft, 1975.
Children's books discussed on p. 24–39. Includes a bibliography of her works.

Newcomer, James. Maria Edgeworth. (The Irish writers series) Lewisburg, Pa.: Bucknell University Press, 1973.
See in particular Chapter 2, p. 31–43, "Writings in the service of education," and chapter 3, p. 44–50, "Some moral fiction." A complete bibliography of Maria Edgeworth's books is included.

————. Maria Edgeworth, the novelist, 1767–1849: a bicentennial study. Fort Worth: Texas Christian University Press, 1967.
Critical analysis of Miss Edgeworth's life and writings.

Oliver, Grace Atkinson Little. A study of Maria Edgeworth, with notices of her father and friends. Boston: Williams, 1882.
Maria Edgeworth is allowed to tell her own story as much as possible. Includes a number of references to her children's books.

Paterson, Alice. The Edgeworths: a study of later eighteenth century education. London: W. B. Clive, 1914.

Patterson, Sylvia W. "Maria Edgeworth," in her *Rousseau's* Émile *and early children's literature,* p. 79–100. Metuchen, N.J.: Scarecrow, 1971.
Discusses Maria Edgeworth's educational theories as influenced by Rousseau.

Pollard, M. "Maria Edgeworth's *The parent's assistant,* first edition," *The book collector* 20:347–51 (Autumn, 1971).
Pollard found, recorded, and described a first edition that had previously been missing. Includes also a checklist of this and other early editions.

Slade, Bertha Coolidge. Maria Edgeworth, 1767–1849: a bibliographic tribute. Edition limited to 250 copies. London: Constable, [1937].
An annotated bibliography of early editions, with an introduction concerning the life of the author.

Vipont, Elfrida. "Old stories never die," *Junior bookshelf* 22:245–55 (November, 1958).
Discusses the "vitality"—as opposed to the morality and preaching—that has kept "Rosamond" and "The purple jar" alive.

Zimmern, Helen. Maria Edgeworth. London: W. H. Allen, 1883.
Chapter 5, p. 52–72, deals with *Essays on prac-*

tical education and Miss Edgeworth's children's books. *Moral tales,* published in 1801, is discussed.

Mary Belson Elliott

Jordan, Philip D., comp. "The juvenilia of Mary Belson Elliott: a list with notes," *Bulletin* (New York Public Library) 39 no. 11:869–81 (November, 1935).
A special bibliography for Mary Elliott.

———. ———. with additions and revisions by Daniel J. Haskell. New York: New York Public Library, 1936.

Lady Fenn

Fenn, Eleanor Frere. Cobwebs to catch flies: dialogues in short sentences, adapted for children from the age of three to eight years. 2v. London: Lockwood, [1783?].
One of the first books for children to attribute words to animals.

———. The fairy spectator, or, the invisible monitor, by Mrs. Teachwell [*pseud.*] and her family. London: John Marshall, 1789.
Although one character in the book is a Rousseauan governess, it conflicts with Rousseau's theories in that it is a collection of fairy tales, of which he heartily disapproved. In fact, it is the only book of its kind that uses magic.

———. The juvenile tatler, by a society of young ladies under the tuition of Mrs. Teachwell [*pseud.*]. London: John Marshall, 1789.
A collection of five moral dialogues and drama for use in educating girls.

———. Morals to a set of fables, by Mrs. Teachwell [*pseud.*]. London: John Marshall, 1783.

CRITICISM

Patterson, Sylvia. "Lady Eleanor Fenn, the Kilner sisters," in her *Rousseau's Émile and early children's literature,* p. 114–42. Metuchen, N.J.: Scarecrow, 1971.
Demonstrates that Lady Fenn's theories were closely allied with those of Rousseau.

Sarah Fielding

Fielding, Sarah. The adventures of David Simple. 3v. London: A Millar, 1744–53.
Subtitle: "containing an account of his travels through the cities of London and Westminster in the search of a real friend, by a lady."

———. ———. Edited with a preface by Henry Fielding. London: Routledge; New York: Dutton, 1904.
Introduction by E. A. Baker.

———. ———. London: Oxford University Press, 1967.
Introduction by Malcolm Kelsall.

———. The governess. 2d ed. London: A Millar, 1749.
Subtitle: "or, the little female academy calculated for the entertainment and instruction of young ladies in their education, by the author of David Simple." This tale, very popular in its time, has been called "the first full-length novel for children in which the plot has a contemporary setting and characters drawn from life. . . ."

———. ———. 7th ed. rev. and corrected. London: F. C. & J. Rivington, 1789.

———. ———. (Juvenile library series) London: Oxford University Press, 1968.
Facsimile of 1749 edition. Includes a bibliography of this and other school stories.

BIOGRAPHY AND CRITICISM

Werner, Herman Oscar. The life and works of Sarah Fielding. Cambridge, Mass.: Harvard University Press, 1937.
The governess is discussed in great detail on p. 240–65.

Dorothy and Mary Jane Kilner

Kilner, Dorothy (*pseud.* Mary Pelham). Anecdotes of a boarding-school, or, an antidote to the vices of those useful seminaries. 2v. London: John Marshall, [1790].
This book advances the theory that children should be educated at home. The work had a three-fold purpose: to protect young ladies from the evils of boarding schools, to amuse them, and to instruct them.

Kilner, Dorothy (*pseud.* M. P.). The life and perambulations of a mouse. London: John Marshall, 1783–84.
The woodcuts in this first edition are attributed to John Bewick. The author said she wrote it "no less to *instruct* and *improve,* than . . . to *amuse* and *divert* [the reader]."—preface.

———. ———. London: J. Harris, 1828.

———. "The life and perambulations of a mouse," in *A storehouse of stories,* edited by Charlotte Yonge, p. 262–334. 1st ser. London: Macmillan, 1872.

———. The rational brutes, or, talking animals. London: printed for Vernor & Hood by Tegg & Bewick, 1799.

———. "The village school," in *A storehouse of stories,* edited by Charlotte Yonge, p. 335–402. 1st ser. London: Macmillan, 1872.

————. The village school, or, a collection of entertaining histories for the instruction & amusement of all good children. 2v. London: John Marshall, [1785?].

Kilner, Mary Jane (*pseud.* S.S.). Adventures of a pincushion: designed chiefly for the use of young ladies. 2 vols. London: John Marshall, [1781?]; Worcester, Mass.: Isaiah Thomas, 1788.
A charming story in which a pincushion moves from person to person and overhears and witnesses incidents of each owner.

————. "Jemima Placid," in *A storehouse of stories,* edited by Charlotte Yonge, p. 223–62. 1st ser. London: Macmillan, 1872.

————. Jemima Placid, or, the advantages of good nature, exemplified in a variety of familiar incidents. London: John Marshall [1783?].
The experiences of a country clergyman's six-year-old child are charmingly recounted.

————. Memoirs of a peg-top. London: John Marshall [1783?]; reprint: (Classics of children's literature 1621–1932) New York: Garland, 1977.
Darton in *Children's books in England* calls it Miss Kilner's "most successful book."

————. ————. Worcester, Mass.: Isaiah Thomas, 1788.

CRITICISM

Patterson, Sylvia W. "Lady Eleanor Fenn, the Kilner sisters," in her *Rousseau's Émile and early children's literature,* p. 114–42. Metuchen, N.J.: Scarecrow, 1971.
Notes that little is known about the lives of the Kilner sisters.

■ Although Patterson, along with Darton (*Children's books in England*) and many others, refers to Mary Jane and Dorothy as sisters, both Thwaite (*From primer to pleasure in reading*) and Gottlieb (*Early children's books and their illustration*) have defined their relationship as sisters-in-law. Thwaite says Mary Jane was born Maze.

Alicia Catherine Mant

Mant, Alicia Catherine. The canary bird. London: J. Harris, 1817.
In autobiographical form: the bird gives an account of his life and adventures and especially of the children of different dispositions and various tempers with whom he has become acquainted during the course of his career.

————. The cottage in the chalk-pit. London: Harvey & Darton, 1822.
Story of some children who with their mother live for a year in a Surrey cottage where they have a happy time in spite of many lessons of self-denial and self-reliance.

————. Ellen, or, the young godmother: a tale for youth, by a young lady. Southampton, England.: T. Shelton, 1812.
A popular book that went into several printings.

————. Tales for Ellen. 2v. London, 1825.
A group of didactic short stories.

————. The young naturalist: a tale. London: H. Holloway, 1824.
The hero's taste for natural history is the source of much "rational and satisfactory amusement," but a series of delinquencies, due to his interest in the subject and his impetuosity, result in a sad accident.

Mary Pilkington

Pilkington, Mary. The Asiatic princess: a tale. 2v. London: Vernor & Hood, 1800.

————. Biography for boys, or, characteristic histories calculated to impress the . . . mind with an admiration for virtuous principles. London: Vernor & Hood, 1800.

————. Biography for girls, or, moral and instructive examples for young ladies. London: Vernor & Hood, 1799.
Harvey Darton in *Children's books in England* says of the author, "She was popular because of her moral sense. It is hard to find any individuality in her work, and she had none of the humour which one detects almost smothered in some of her contemporaries."

————. The calendar, or, monthly recreations: chiefly consisting of dialogues between an aunt and her nieces. London: J. Harris, 1807.

————. Marvellous adventures, or, the vicissitudes of a cat. London: J. Harris, and Vernor & Hood, 1802.
In *From primer to pleasure in reading* Thwaite wrote: "A serious tale by Mrs. Pilkington where the feline narrator shows up the weaknesses and virtues of the human beings she encounters, but is not permitted to sacrifice her life by springing into the grave of her mistress at the end."

————. Tales of the cottage, or, stories moral and amusing, for young persons. London: Vernor & Hood, 1798.
Subtitle: "written on the plan of the celebrated work *Les veillées du chateau* by Madame la Comptesse de Genlis." Mary Pilkington's most famous work.

Mrs. Sherwood

Sherwood, Mary Martha Butt. The Fairchild family. Edited with introduction by Mary E. Palgrave. New York: Stokes, 1902.
An abbreviated version of *The history of the Fairchild family* (below), omitting the prayers, hymns, and part of the text, notably the chapter in which the children's father takes them to visit a gallows. The introduction gives a biographical sketch of Mary Sherwood.

————. The flowers of the forest. London: Religious Tract Society, 1830.
Story of a French curé who is led to see the errors of his church through the conversation of a little Protestant girl.

————. The history of Henry Milner, a little boy who was not brought up according to the fashions of this world. 4 pts. London: Hatchard, 1822–37.
Later editions were revised and corrected by Mrs. Sherwood.

————. The history of little Henry and his bearer. 2d ed. Wellington, Salop, England: Houlston, 1815.
Written in India, 1809–10, and published in 1814. A slight story, but, as the first missionary story for children, it produced a great sensation when it first came out. Mrs. Sherwood said that her "lionship" commenced at this time.

————. The history of Susan Grey, as related by a clergyman, designed for the benefit of young women when going to service, etc. Wisbech, England: J. White, 1815.
First published anonymously in 1802 by Hazard of Bath. Written for the older girls in Sunday school and read to them chapter by chapter. A tale of youthful piety and early death.

————. The history of the Fairchild family. 3v. London: Hatchard, 1818–47.
Subtitle: "or, the child's manual, being a collection of stories calculated to show the importance and effects of a religious education." One of the first "family stories." *The history of the Fairchild family* was published in England as late as 1931.

————. The Indian pilgrim. Wellington, Salop, England: Houlston, 1818.
Subtitle: "or, the progress of the pilgrim Nazareenee . . . from the city of the Wrath of God to the city of Mount Zion, delivered under the similitude of a dream." Written in India in 1810 and first published in 1818. An imitation of *Pilgrim's progress*, containing many allusions to Indian customs and usages.

————. The infant's progress from the Valley of Destruction to Everlasting Glory. Wellington, Salop, England: Houlston, 1821.
"Story about some little children who . . . were born in a state of sin. . . . I have personified the Sin of our nature, and introduced it as the constant companion of these children. . . . Composed in the East Indies during the year 1814."

————. The potters' common. 4 pts. London: W. Whittemore; Wellington, Salop, England: Houlston, 1822–23.
A good example of the religious story for the poor. The London edition in the British Museum is dated 1822. Another edition has the title *The happy choice, or, the potters' common*.

————. Stories explanatory of the church catechism. Wellington, Salop, England: Houlston, 1817.
The stories were written about 1817 for the use of the children of the 53rd Regiment stationed at that time at Cawnpore, India, and the characters and scenes are those of the infantry barracks there. Written chiefly in dialogue form.

————. The works of Mrs. Sherwood, being the only uniform edition ever published in the United States. 15v. New York: Harper, 1834–58.
There were many American editions of individual stories by Mary Sherwood, often published by religious tract societies.

————. ed. The governess, or, the little female academy. Wellington, Salop, England: Houlston, 1820.
Originally written by Sarah Fielding, the sister of the novelist, and published about 1749. It was edited by Mrs. Sherwood at the suggestion of "a Parent, who is now no more."—introduction. Darton says, "Her labours probably constitute the most unconscionable abuse of editorial powers on record."—*The life and times of Mrs. Sherwood*, p. 35. Also included in *The works of Mrs. Sherwood*, vol. 6.

BIOGRAPHY AND CRITICISM

Cutt, Nancy N. Mrs. Sherwood and her books for children. London: Oxford University Press, 1974.
A thorough biography and critical analysis. Includes facsimiles of "The little woodman and his dog Caesar" and "Soffrona and her cat Muff." A bibliography of primary and secondary sources is given.

Darton, Frederick Joseph Harvey. "The moral tale: didactic," in his *Children's books in England*, 2d ed., p. 158–81. Cambridge: Cambridge University Press, 1958.
A succinct biographical sketch of Mrs. Sherwood and a perceptive discussion of the moralizing missionary in her writings. Special attention is given to *The Fairchild family*, including quotation of a long passage usually omitted "for moral reasons," explaining why this "was perhaps as widely read, as completely ridiculed, and as honestly condemned by child-lovers, as any English book ever written for children."

Guthrie, Thomas Anstey (*pseud.* F. Anstey). "On an old-fashioned children's book," "Mrs. Sherwood's notion of a model youth," in his *The last load*, p. 70–90, 101–24. London: Methuen, 1925.
The first of these essays may be found also in *The new review* 14:392–403, and in *Littell's living age* 209:436–43. The second essay is concerned with *The history of Henry Milner, a little boy who was not brought up according to the fashions of this world*.

Lang, Leonora Blanche. "The Fairchild family and their creator," *Longman's magazine* 21:579–94 (April, 1893); reprint in *A peculiar gift*, edited by Lance Salway, p. 463–78. Harmondsworth, Middlesex, England: Penguin, 1976.
A wry commentary with detailed "analysis of the teaching and tendency of the book."

Meigs, Cornelia. "Launching a century: Little Henry," in Meigs et al., *A critical history of children's literature*, p. 77–81. Rev. ed. New York and London: Macmillan, 1969.
A vivid, though brief, account of Mary Sherwood's life, and a sympathetic appraisal of her writing, focusing on *Little Henry and his bearer* and *The Fairchild family*.

St. John, Judith, ed. Osborne collection of early children's books, 1566–1910: a catalogue. Toronto: Public Library, 1958.
Includes bibliographic descriptions and synopses of thirty-five titles by Mary Sherwood.

Sherwood, Mary Martha Butt, and **Henry Sherwood.** The life and times of Mrs. Sherwood (1775–1851), from the diaries of Captain and Mrs. Sherwood. Edited by F. J. H. Darton. London: Wells Gardner, 1910.
Valuable work of over 500 pages, with introduction, footnotes, and appendixes. There are numerous references in the text to Mrs. Sherwood's books for children, and a portrait serves as frontispiece. Ten other illustrations.

Thwaite, Mary F. From primer to pleasure in reading, p. 60–63. 2d ed. London: Library Association, 1972.
A brief discussion of Mary Sherwood's life and writing, placing her with her sister, Lucy Cameron, and with Hannah More, as foreshadowing "the era of State Schools, compulsory education, and public libraries . . . ."

Mrs. Trimmer

Trimmer, Sarah Kirby. A description of a set of prints of ancient history, contained in a set of easy lessons, 3 pts. in 3v. London: John Marshall, 1795.
Justin Schiller says that other series were prepared including descriptions of Scripture history, 1786, and Roman history, 1789.

———. An easy introduction to the knowledge of nature, adapted to the capacities of children. London: printed for the author, 1780.
An American edition, published anonymously, but evidently Sarah Trimmer's work, was printed in Boston by the American Sunday School Union in 1846. See also entry for Berquin's *An introduction to the study of nature*, p. 95.

———. Fabulous histories, designed for the instruction of children, respecting their treatment of animals. London: Longman, G. G. J. & J. Robinson, and J. Johnson, 1786.
The author suggests in her introduction that, before reading these stories, children should be "taught to consider them, not as containing the real conversations of birds . . . . but as a series of Fables, intended to convey moral instruction applicable to themselves, at the same time that they excite compassion and tenderness for those interesting and delightful creatures, on which such wanton cruelties are frequently inflicted." The dedication to Her Royal Highness, Princess Sophia, is dated Nov. 3, 1785. Justin Schiller, in the Garland reprint of *Fabulous histories*, says the first illustrated edition was probably Whittingham and Arliss, 1815. The title was revised to read *Fabulous histories of the robins* in 1818 and shortened to *History of the robins* in 1819.

———. ———. (Classics of children's literature 1621–1932) New York: Garland, 1977.
Preface by Ruth Perry. This has a good bibliography of Sarah Trimmer's work by Justin Schiller.

———. Mrs. Trimmer's history of the robins in words of one syllable by Rev. Charles Swete. New York: Routledge, n.d.
Illustrations by Harrison Weir.

———. Oeconomy of charity. London: Longman, 1787.
Subtitle: "or, an address to ladies concerning Sunday schools; the establishment of schools of industry under female inspection; and the distribution of voluntary benefaction. To which is added an appendix containing an account of the Sunday schools in old Brentford." A later edition published by J. Johnson and F. & C. Rivington in 1801 had the title *Oeconomy of charity, or, an address to ladies adapted to the present state of charitable institutions in England: with a particular view to the cultivation of religious principles among lower orders*. Expresses Mrs. Trimmer's educational theories, and gives a history of religious education in England to that time and practical essays on what to teach, how to do it, etc.

———. Sacred history selected from the Scriptures, with annotations and reflections, suited to the comprehension of young minds. 6v. London: J. Dodsley, 1782–85.

———. Scripture lessons designed to accompany a series of prints from the Old Testament. London: John Marshall, [1787?].
A series of prints taken from the Old Testament designed to illustrate Sarah Trimmer's Scripture lessons from that portion of the Holy Scriptures.

BIOGRAPHY AND CRITICISM

Balfour, Clara Lucas. A sketch of Mrs. Trimmer. London: W. & F. G. Cash, 1854.
In *Children's books in England,* Darton gives the author's name as Bower, not Balfour.

Patterson, Sylvia W. "Hannah More, Sarah Trimmer," in her *Rousseau's Émile and early children's literature,* p. 143–55. Metuchen, N.J.: Scarecrow, 1971.
Deals essentially with the influence of Rousseau on Mrs. Trimmer's works.

St. John, Judith. "Mrs. Trimmer: guardian of education," *Horn book magazine* 46:20–25 (February, 1970).
An excellent summary of Sarah Trimmer's literary career.

Trimmer, Sarah Kirby. Some account of the life and writings of Mrs. Trimmer, with original letters and meditations and prayers selected from her journal. 2v. London: F. C. & J. Rivington, 1814.
See vol. 1, p. 49–67, for account of the children's books and *The guardian of education,* edited by Mrs. Trimmer.

———. Some account of the writings of Mrs. Trimmer," in *A peculiar gift,* edited by Lance Salway, p. 441–49. Harmondsworth, Eng.: Penguin, [1976].
This is a portion of the book listed above.

Williams, A. R. "Curiosities of the past: 1. the robins," in *Junior bookshelf* 17:61–62 (March, 1953).
Of the *Fabulous histories,* the author writes, "Beneath the sententiousness, complacency and gaucherie of this eighteenth century morality runs a vein of almost embarrassing sincerity."

Yarde, Doris M. Life and works of Sarah Trimmer, a lady of Brentford. Hounslow and District Historical Society, 1971.

Mary Wollstonecraft

Wollstonecraft, Mary. Original stories from real life, with conversations calculated to regulate the affections, and form the mind to truth and goodness. London: J. Johnson, 1788.
The first illustrated edition was published in 1791 by J. Johnson.

———. ———. London: H. Frowde, 1906.
Includes five illustrations by William Blake. Introduction by E. V. Lucas. Includes facsimile of 1791 title page.

———. ———. (Classics of children's literature 1621–1932) New York: Garland, 1977.
Introduction by Miriam Kramnick. Includes a bibliography of Mary Wollstonecraft's works.

———. Thoughts on the education of daughters, with reflections on female conduct in the more important duties of life. London: J. Johnson, 1787.
Valuable as background material to better understand Mary Wollstonecraft's educational theories as incorporated into *Original stories.* Edna Nixon says in *Mary Wollstonecraft,* "The author's intention was to awaken parents to the dangers of the low grade of education they were prepared to give their daughters and the consequences of such a skinflint policy."—p. 33.

———, trans. Elements of morality for the use of children, with an introductory address to parents, by Christian Gottlief Salzmann. 2v. London: J. Johnson, 1790.
The author (1744–1811) was a German educator. Mary Wollstonecraft discovered the book in her study of German and found it in accordance with her own ideas: it taught children by practical illustration why virtue is good and vice is evil. As a result, she made a free translation. Illustrated with fifty copper plates adapted and engraved by William Blake from the work of the German artist Chodowiecki.

———. ———, in *Storehouse of stories,* edited by Charlotte M. Yonge, v. 2, p. 148–345. London: Macmillan, 1885.
Footnotes indicate variations from the original German.

———. Wollstonecraft anthology. Edited with an introduction by Janet W. Todd. Bloomington: Indiana University Press, 1977.
Pt. 1, "Courtesy books," p. 25–62, includes selections from *Thoughts on the education of daughters* and *Original stories,* as well as "Letters on the management of infants."

BIOGRAPHY AND CRITICISM

"A female Sandford and Merton," *The Saturday review* 102:294 (1906).
Review of the reprint of *Original stories,* edited by E. V. Lucas.

Flexner, Eleanor. Mary Wollstonecraft: a biography. New York: Coward, 1972.
A detailed biography of Mary Wollstonecraft and her family. For *Original stories,* see p. 93–97.

George, Margaret. One woman's "situation": a study of Mary Wollstonecraft. Urbana: University of Illinois Press, 1970.
Using the life of Mary Wollstonecraft, the author contradicts the contemporary statement (1967) that "women have a situation, not a continuous history."

Godwin, William. Memoirs of Mary Wollstonecraft. London: Constable, 1927; reprints: New York: Haskell, 1969; New York: Garland, 1974.
With a preface, a supplement "chronologically arranged and containing hitherto unpublished or uncollected material, and a bibliographical note by W. C. Durant."
Originally published as *Memoirs of the author of "A vindication of the rights of women,"* 1798. Portrait and twelve illustrations, ten of these being reproductions of original drawings by Blake, including five engraved for *Original stories.* The picture of the angelic harper in his hut is also reproduced.

James, Henry Rosher. Mary Wollstonecraft: a sketch. London: Oxford University Press, 1932.
Presents the personal aspect. Portraits of Mary Wollstonecraft; Joseph Johnson, the publisher; William Godwin; and Mary Shelley. "Books written by Mary Wollstonecraft," p. 153–64; "Books about Mary Wollstonecraft," p. 165–71.

Linford, Madeline. Mary Wollstonecraft (1759–1797). London: L. Parsons; Boston: Small, Maynard, 1924; reprint: Folcroft, Pa.: Folcroft, 1973.
Calls *Original stories* a failure because the author "pours down instruction in thick and nauseating draughts."

Nixon, Edna. Mary Wollstonecraft: her life and times. London: Dent, 1971.
A scholarly work. The author says of *Original stories* that, though it was popular, it "was not yet imbued with Mary's mature spirit."

Patterson, Sylvia W. "Mary Wollstonecraft," in her *Rousseau's Émile and early children's literature,* p. 101–13. Metuchen, N. J.: Scarecrow, 1971.

Although Rousseau influenced Mary Wollstonecraft as much as he influenced Maria Edgeworth, the latter, according to Patterson, had a "natural talent for telling stories, whereas Mary Wollstonecraft allowed her desire to teach to overpower her desire to entertain. The result was that her characters are less human—her stories more didactic."

Pennell, Elizabeth Robins. Mary Wollstonecraft Godwin. London: W. H. Allen, 1885; reprint: Folcroft, Pa.: Folcroft, 1974.
For *Original stories,* see p. 120–26; *Elements of morality,* p. 127–28.

Rauschenbusch-Clough, E. A study of Mary Wollstonecraft and the rights of woman. London: Longmans, Green, 1896.

Sunstein, Emily W. A different face: the life of Mary Wollstonecraft. New York: Harper, 1975.
A new, scholarly biography of Mary Wollstonecraft and critical study of her works. For *Original stories,* see p. 161–64.

Tomalin, Clare. The life and death of Mary Wollstonecraft. New York: Harcourt, [1974].
An extremely detailed biography. Compares Mary Wollstonecraft to Hannah More and Maria Edgeworth. Good bibliographies of Wollstonecraft's works.

Wardle, Ralph Martin. Mary Wollstonecraft: a critical biography. Lincoln: University of Nebraska Press, 1951.
The author agrees with many critics of Mary Wollstonecraft that, although *Original stories* was one of her most popular works, it was probably her worst.

Woolf, Virginia. "Mary Wollstonecraft," in her *Second common reader,* p. 141–48. New York: Harcourt, (Harvest Books), [1932].
An exquisitely written little essay in which the author concludes that Mary Wollstonecraft was a product of "sordid misery," in which the only thing that mattered to her was independence.

———. ———. in her *Collected essays,* v. 3, p. 193–98. New York: Harcourt, 1953.

Poetry: The Late Eighteenth and Early Nineteenth Centuries

The eighteenth century ended with two wars that influenced the mood of major poets in England. The revolutions in America and in France molded in part the thought of both William Blake (1757–1827) and William Wordsworth (1770–1850), who, like many others, saw the wars as violent expressions of old ways ending and new worlds coming to birth. With the new freedoms, children were seen in a different, more kindly and gentle light, not as limbs of Satan, born in sin, but as bright angelic spirits. As such they appear in Blake's *Songs of innocence*:

O what a multitude they seem'd,
  these flowers of London town!
Seated in companies, they sit with
  radiance all their own.
The hum of multitudes was there,
  but multitudes of lambs,
Thousands of little boys and girls
  raising their innocent hands.

Wordsworth's "Ode on intimations of immortality from recollections of earliest childhood" reached a peak of emotion in the same vein:

Not in entire forgetfulness,
And not in utter nakedness,
But trailing clouds of glory do we come
From God, who is our home.

Although neither Blake nor Wordsworth specifically intended his poetry to be read by children, any discussion of poetry for children of this period must take note that the educated young were not limited to poetry written for them. In the journals of the Scottish Marjorie Fleming (1803–11), we have a unique self-portrait of a child at the opening of the nineteenth century and of the poetry she loved and learned by heart. Needless to say, she was encouraged to do this, but she wrote with obvious pleasure of lines she had learned from

Shakespeare, Scott, James Thomson, Swift, and Pope.

From the beginning of the Romantic period, ushered in by Blake, Wordsworth, and their contemporaries, it becomes increasingly difficult to separate poetry written for children from poetry appealing to children or written about them. The latter types appeared more and more often in anthologies of poetry for children throughout the nineteenth century. For example, Coleridge's "Rime of the ancient mariner" was favorite juvenile reading for generations and, as recently as 1969, was issued in an illustrated edition for young readers.

Blake's place as a children's poet is hard to assess; he wrote for himself more than for any other reader. However, Walter de la Mare's *Come hither*, addressed to "the young of all ages," includes more than a dozen poems by Blake, chosen not from *Songs of innocence* alone. *Songs of experience* gave children "Tiger, tiger, burning bright," and many schools today still sing Blake's gloriously apocryphal hymn from *Milton*, ending with:

Bring me my bow of burning gold!
Bring me my arrows of desire!
Bring me my spear! O clouds, unfold!
Bring me my chariot of fire!
I shall not cease from mental strife
Nor shall my sword rest in my hand
Till we have built Jerusalem
In England's green and pleasant land.

While the major poets were striking the grandest chords, and some children were listening, a few publishers were beginning to think that children would welcome poetry written especially for them. Coleridge and Charles Lamb were advocating the return of fancy and imagination for the young. Lamb and his sister Mary set about writing verses that appealed directly to children and in the sprightly

"Prince Dorus" and "The king and queen of hearts" introduced humor. (Publications of the Lambs' single poems with comical illustrations in color are listed with toy books in this volume's bibliographies for "Evolution from didacticism: the early nineteenth century," which necessarily blends with poetry in the late eighteenth and early nineteenth centuries. Many subjects, even religion and morality, were presented to children in verse at this time.)

M. F. Thwaite's *From primer to pleasure* has paid tribute to Ann and Jane Taylor as the first makers of rhymes who "really entered into the child's world, and interpreted it in easy, entertaining fashion." They entertained and instructed with "cautionary verses" and gave children the never-to-be-forgotten "Twinkle, twinkle, little star."

In the United States, one bit of verse achieved fame during the same period. Clement Clarke Moore wrote for his own children "A visit from Saint Nicholas" (1823) and thereby gave children everywhere an authentic little classic, the essence of fanciful delight and infectious good humor, the very spirit of childhood. We today cannot imagine the world of children's literature without the all-time American favorite now called "The night before Christmas," which quickly became the possession of English children, too.

The period that had begun with two wars ended with the growth of more settled relationships within the English-speaking world and the resulting exchange of children's poetry back and forth across the Atlantic.

OUTLINE

I. The moral tale in verse
  A. Ann (1782–1866) and Jane
    Taylor (1783–1824)
    1. The literary gift of the Taylor family
    2. Character of the father and his
      ingenious methods of education
    3. *The minor's pocket book* and the
      first poems of Ann and Jane
    4. *Original poems* and *Rhymes for
      the nursery*
      a) Bibliographical history
      b) Individual characteristics of
        the collaborators
      c) Jane's method of composition
      d) Characteristics of the poems
        (1) Comparison with the moral
          verses of Watts
        (2) Choice of subjects
        (3) Lessons in manners and morals
        (4) Simplicity of expression
        (5) Playful humor
        (6) Feeling for nature
        (7) Metrical skill
      e) Popularity
      f) Editions
    5. *Hymns for infant minds*
    6. The prose tales of Jane Taylor
  B. The imitators of the Taylors
    1. Elizabeth Turner (d.1846): *The daisy,
      The cowslip, The crocus,*
      and *The pink.*
      a) Character of the verses
      b) Comparison with the verses of
        Ann and Jane Taylor
      c) Format and illustrations
      d) Success

    2. Other imitators.
II. The poetry of Charles and Mary Lamb
  May be discussed in this connection if
  desired (see p. 132–35 for references), or
  allusion may be made to the poems at this
  point and the work of Charles and
  Mary Lamb considered as a whole later.
III. The poetry of William Blake (1757–1827)
  A. Life and visionary character
  B. Unique quality of Blake's genius
    1. Dissimilarity to other writers of
      the period
    2. Lack of knowledge on the part of
      his contemporaries
    3. Influence upon such later writers as
      Bulwer-Lytton, Coleridge, and Poe
    4. No real part in the development of
      children's literature in his own time
  C. *Songs of innocence* and *Songs of
    experience*
    1. Peculiar method of first issue:
      illuminated printing
    2. Artistic merit of illustrations
    3. Scarcity of early copies and value
      to modern collectors
    4. Character of poems
      a) Attitude toward childhood
      b) Recurrence of a few types
      c) Symbolism
      d) Lyric quality
      e) Other qualities: spontaneity,
        joyousness, delicate fancy,
        tenderness
      f) Literary value for children
      g) Comparison in use and popularity
        with verses of the Taylors

GENERAL REFERENCES

Barnes, Walter. "Ann and Jane Taylor," "William Blake," in his *The children's poets: analyses and appraisals of the greatest English and American poets for children*, p. 49–67, 86–102. Yonkers, N.Y.: World, 1924.
The book as a whole "is an attempt to analyze the qualities and to appraise the contributions of the most important of the children's poets." Selections are included.

Barry, Florence V. A century of children's books. London: Methuen, 1922; reprint: Detroit: Singing Tree, 1968.
Chapter 9, "The old-fashioned garden of verses," describes the work of Ann and Jane Taylor, Charles and Mary Lamb, and Elizabeth Turner; also *The butterfly's ball* "and other festivals," for which see "Evolution from didacticism: the early nineteenth century" in this volume.

Darton, Frederick Joseph Harvey. "The moral tale: persuasive, chiefly in verse," in his *Children's books in England*, p. 182–204. 2d ed. Cambridge: Cambridge University Press, 1958.
A highly readable and perceptive discussion of Blake, the Lambs, and the Taylors, with briefer treatment of John Marchant, Nathaniel Cotton, Sara Coleridge. The "brief book list" gives information important to the researcher on this period.

Field, Louise Frances Story (Mrs. E. M. Field). "William Blake," "The Taylors," in her *The child and his book*, p. 307–10, 318–25. 2d ed. London: Wells Gardner, 1892; reprint: Detroit: Singing Tree, 1968.
Brief biographical sketches of these poets and appraisals of their work, with useful detail about early editions.

Muir, Percy. English children's books 1600–1900. New York: Praeger, [1954]; London: Batsford, 1969.
Includes detailed bibliographical information on books of poetry in this period, especially those by the Lambs and the Taylors. See index for references.

Opie, Iona, and **Peter Opie,** eds. The Oxford book of children's verse. New York and Oxford: Oxford University Press, 1973.
This book's chronological arrangements and fine selectivity bring together a unique grouping of poems by Blake, the Lambs, the Taylors, Elizabeth Turner, and Clement Clarke Moore. There are important additions of poems intended for children by poets who might be overlooked, including Burns, Southey, Coleridge, Wordsworth, Scott, Keats, and others.

INDIVIDUAL WRITERS

William Blake

Blake, William. Complete writings of William Blake, with variant readings. Edited by Sir Geoffrey Keynes. London: Oxford University Press, 1966.

———. The lyrical poems. Oxford: Clarendon, 1905.
Textual notes by John Sampson; introduction by Walter Raleigh. "Professor Raleigh's essay is an intensely sympathetic reading of the mind and art of Blake . . . a little masterpiece in criticism"—*The outlook* (London) 1906.

———. The poetical works of William Blake. Edited by John Sampson. London: Oxford University Press, 1928.
With a bibliographical introduction and textual notes. Adheres scrupulously to the actual text of Blake.

FACSIMILE EDITIONS

Blake, William. Songs of experience. Edmonton: William Muir, 1885.
Includes some poems previously counted as *Songs of innocence*. Reproduced from original belonging (1885) to the nineteenth-century bibliophile and scholar Bernard Quaritch. The illustrations are hand colored.

———. ———. New York: Minton, Balch, 1927.
Reproduced from a copy in the British Museum.

———. Songs of innocence. London: J. Pearson, 1884.
Reproduced "from the volume that Blake gave to Flaxman."

———. ———. New York: Minton, Balch, 1926.
Reproduced from a copy in the British Museum.

Facsimile edition "in the size and colors of the original."

——. ——. London: Trianon Press, 1954.
A facsimile in color, published for the William Blake Trust.

——. ——. London: Quaritch, 1927.
Facsimile reproduction of the Beaconsfield original in the British Museum. Twenty-eight plates.

——. ——. New York: Dover, 1971.
Facsimile of the 1789 edition, made from the copy in the Rosenwald collection in the Library of Congress with an added introduction, table of contents, and text of the poems in letterpress.

EDITIONS FOR CHILDREN

Blake, William. The land of dreams: twenty poems by William Blake. Selected and illustrated by Pamela Bianco. New York: Macmillan, 1928.
Each poem is illustrated in black and white. The preface is addressed to "Dear mr Blake" and explains in childlike fashion how the artist did her work and made the selection of poems, most of which are from *Songs of innocence.*

——. Songs of innocence. London: Dent, 1912; New York: Dutton, 1912.
"Decorated" by Charles Robinson and M. H. Robinson. Contains eleven additional poems.

——. ——. Boston and New York: Medici Society, 1927.
Illustrated by Jacynth Parsons, with a prefatory letter by W. B. Yeats.

——. ——. (A Wonderful world book) New York: Barnes, 1961.
"Decorations" by Harold Jones. Illustrations in black and white or in color on every page.

BIOGRAPHY AND CRITICISM

Ainger, Alfred. ["William Blake,"] in his *Lectures and essays,* v. 2, p. 30–32. London and New York: Macmillan, 1905.
Notes the contribution of Blake's lines on the chimney sweeper to the *Chimney-sweeper's friend and climbing-boys' album,* and Charles Lamb's appreciation of him as "one of the most extraordinary persons of the age."

Daugherty, James. William Blake. New York: Viking, 1960.
A biography that makes a good introduction to Blake for young readers. Includes reproductions of drawings by Blake and a list, "Important collections of Blake's pictures, prints, and books in the United States."

de Selincourt, Basil. William Blake. (Studies in Blake, no. 3)London: Duckworth; New York:

Scribner, 1909; reprint: Brooklyn: Haskell, 1971.
Considered an important contribution to criticism of Blake as mystic and artist.

Gillham, D. G. Blake's contrary states: the *Songs of innocence and of experience* as dramatic poems. Cambridge: Cambridge University Press, 1966.
This scholarly study suggests that *Songs of innocence and of experience* may explore "possible states of being and feeling in which spiritual energy expresses itself."

Hirsch, Eric Donald. Innocence and experience: an introduction to Blake. New Haven, Conn.: Yale University Press, 1964.
Blake's works arranged by period. See commentaries on individual poems, p. 169–294.

Keynes, Geoffrey, and Edwin Wolf 2d. William Blake's illuminated books: a census. New York: Grolier Club, 1953.
Includes the provenance of twenty-three copies of *Songs of innocence* and a note about Blake's work on this masterpiece from its inception, p. 9–18. Further notes on *Songs of innocence and experience,* p. 50–69. Plates.

Lister, Raymond. William Blake: an introduction to the man and to his work. New York: Ungar, 1969.
Chapters entitled "Childhood and youth" and "Dawning vision" are of special interest to students of children's literature. For *Songs of innocence,* see p. 28–35. Illustrations from numerous works by Blake. Bibliography. Index.

Primeau, Ronald. "Blake's chimney sweeper as Afro-American minstrel," *Bulletin* (New York Public Library) 78, no. 4: 418–30 (Summer, 1975).
Describes "Blake's ways of dealing with oppression primarily as they are depicted in his characterization of the "sweep" and suggests "some tentative connections between Blake's theme of overcoming servitude and similar themes in the long tradition of Afro-American literature."

Wicksteed, Joseph H. Blake's innocence & experience: a study of the songs & manuscripts. New York: Dutton, 1928.
A beautiful volume providing commentary in minute detail on each poem, with reproductions of the pages engraved by Blake.

Clement Clarke Moore

Moore, Clement Clarke. The night before Christmas. Chicago: Reilly & Britton, 1905.
A miniature book with fourteen color lithographs. Introduction by L. Frank Baum.

———. ———. London: Harrap, 1931; Philadelphia: Lippincott, 1931.
Includes four plates in color by Arthur Rackham.

———. 'Twas the night before Christmas: a visit from St. Nicholas. Boston and New York: Houghton, 1912.
With twelve full-page colored lithographs by Jessie Willcox Smith and fourteen decorative initials.

———. A visit from St. Nicholas. New York: Henry M. Onderdonck, 1848.
The first independent publication of the poem. The woodcuts were executed by Theodore C. Boyd, and the little book was conceived as "a present for good little boys and girls." Saint Nicholas is shown as a recognizable Santa Claus.

———. ———. New York: Spalding & Shepard, 1849.
Another publication of the Onderdonck edition (above), reset with different type and borders but with the Boyd woodcuts of the 1848 edition.

FACSIMILE EDITIONS

Moore, Clement Clarke. A visit from St. Nicholas. New York: Spalding & Shepard, 1849; reprint: New York: Young & Rubicam, 1963.
The 1963 edition is a facsimile from the original at the New York Public Library. The facsimile has "faded red and blue for cover, black for text, and a brownish tint to simulate marginal soilings on the pages of the original."—Lawrence (see below).

———. A visit from St. Nicholas with original cuts designed and engraved by Boyd. New York: H. M. Onderdonck, 1848; reprint: New York: Simon & Schuster, 1971.
The facsimile of the 1848 edition is made from the copy in the Columbia University library. Includes reproductions of the black-and-white engravings by T. C. Boyd. An afterword by Kenneth A. Lohf, librarian for rare books and manuscripts at Columbia University, gives a short biographical sketch of Moore and tells how he came to write the poem.

BIOGRAPHY AND CRITICISM

Lawrence, George Hill Mathewson, comp. "The night before Christmas": an exhibition catalogue. Pittsburgh: Pittsburgh Bibliophiles, 1964.
Detailed bibliographic description of 148 American editions, 1823–1963. The foreword, by Anne Lyon Haight, gives a brief biography of Moore and traces the history of his poem. Includes a reproduction in facsimile of a holograph copy of the poem written by Moore in 1862.

Patterson, Samuel W. The poet of Christmas Eve; a life of Clement Clarke Moore, 1779–1863. New York: Morehouse-Gorham, 1956.

A satisfactorily complete biographical study. Includes full-color reproduction of the Robert W. Weir painting inspired by the poem. Three appendixes cover: the writing of Clement Clarke Moore; various editions of A visit from St. Nicholas; the claims of Henry Livingston, Jr., as the author of the poem.

Ann and Jane Taylor

Taylor, Ann (later Mrs. Gilbert). The wedding among the flowers, by one of the authors of Original poems, rhymes for the nursery, etc. London: Darton & Harvey, 1808.
A successful little poem written in imitation of The butterfly's ball.

——— and Jane Taylor. Hymns for infant minds. London: Printed for T. Conder, 1810.
The first work published by the two sisters entirely alone.

———. Limed twigs to catch young birds. London: Darton & Harvey, 1808.
Easy reading dialogue, beginning with words of three letters and ending with words of three or four syllables.

———. The Original poems and others by Ann and Jane Taylor and Adelaide O'Keefe. Edited by E. V. Lucas. London: Wells Gardner, Darton; New York: Stokes, 1903.
A centenary edition commemorating first publication of Original poems for infant minds, 1804–5. Includes "Rhymes for the nursery." Illustrations by F. D. Bedford. The appendixes give poems omitted from the later editions, Ann Taylor's "The wedding among the flowers," 20 pieces from Adelaide O'Keefe's Original poems and Poems for young children, and four original fables by Jefferys Taylor. The notes and introduction add to the value for study and reference.

Taylor, Jane. "A curious instrument," in Eyes and no eyes, and other stories by John Aikin et al.; edited with introduction and notes by M. V. O'Shea, p. 58–63. Boston: Heath, 1900.

———. "The discontented pendulum," in The children's book, edited by Horace Elisha Scudder, p. 360–61. Boston: Houghton, 1907.

———. Prose and poetry. London: Milford, 1925.
Introduction by F. V. Barry. Contents: Introduction; Some letters; Original poems and Rhymes for the nursery; Pages from Display; From Essays in rhyme; From The contributions of Q. Q.

———. "The sore tongue," "Busy idleness," in Old fashioned stories and poems, compiled by Eva March Tappan, p. 39–45, 191–200. Boston: Houghton, 1907.

—— and **Ann Taylor** (*later* Mrs. Gilbert). Little Ann, and other poems. London and New York: Routledge, 1883.

Illustrated by Kate Greenaway. Printed in colors by Edmund Evans. Forty-two poems from *Original poems for infant minds.* Dedicated to four children whose portraits appear above the dedication.

——. Meddlesome Matty, and other poems for infant minds. New York: Viking, 1926.

Introduction by Edith Sitwell; illustrated by Wyndham Payne. Includes twenty-three poems.

——. Original poems for infant minds, by several young persons. 2v. London: Darton & Harvey, 1804–5.

Contains pieces by the Taylors, Adelaide O'Keefe, and others. The publisher requested the Taylor sisters to write "specimens of easy poetry for young children . . . moral songs or short tales in verse." Considered a landmark in children's literature. Many editions appeared in both England and America.

——. Rhymes for the nursery. London: Darton, Harvey & Darton, 1806.

Contains "Twinkle, twinkle, little star" by Jane. Credited: "by the authors of *Original poems.*"

BIOGRAPHY AND CRITICISM

Armitage, Doris Mary. The Taylors of Ongar. Cambridge: Heffer, 1939.

Subtitle: "portrait of an English family of the eighteenth and nineteenth centuries; drawn from family records by the great-great niece of Ann and Jane Taylor." Illustrations.

Harris, G. Edward. Contributions towards a bibliography of the Taylors of Ongar and Stanford Rivers: the Rev. Isaac Taylor, Mrs. Ann Taylor, Ann Taylor Gilbert, Jane Taylor, Jefferys Taylor, &c. Hamden, Conn.: Shoe String (Archon), 1965.

Complete bibliographical detail is given, when known, for the writings of this family, especially for Ann and Jane, who "definitely inaugurated a new style of writing for children." Folding genealogical chart, four additional plates.

Lucas, Edward Verrall. "Ann and Jane Taylor," in *A peculiar gift,* edited by Lance Salway, p. 216–27. Harmondsworth, Eng.: Penguin, [1976].

From the introduction to *The original poems.* Gives a good picture in brief of the family life of the Taylors, with special sections on their poetry.

Stewart, Christina Duff. The Taylors of Ongar: an analytical bio-bibliography. 2v. New York: Garland, 1974.

"A definitive and documented study with descriptions and collations of all first editions (1804–1853) besides bibliographic and textual changes in later printings, listing of contributions to books and periodicals, translations into foreign languages, indexes of published drawings and engravings, and cumulative indexes for all printers and publishers of every title."—Justin Schiller, *Catalogue 31.*

Elizabeth Turner

Turner, Elizabeth. The cowslip, or, more cautionary stories, in verse. London: B. Crosby, 1811.

Written at the request of Crosby. Some of the poems were written by the author's brother, Thomas Turner.

——. The crocus: another series of cautionary stories in verse. London: Harvey & Darton, 1844; Whitchurch, Salop, England: R. B. Jones, 1844.

The author lived at Whitchurch, Shropshire.

——. The daisy, or cautionary stories, in verse, adapted to the ideas of children, from four to eight years old. London: Griffith, Farran, Okeden and Welsh, 1885.

A facsimile edition of the first publication, 1807. The introduction, signed C. W. (Charles Welsh), gives information about Elizabeth Turner and Samuel Williams, the artist who drew and engraved the illustrations.

——. Mrs. Turner's cautionary stories. (The Dumpy books for children, no. 2.) London: Grant Richards, 1897.

The introduction by E. V. Lucas states that the sixty-nine stories in verse are taken from five books by Elizabeth Turner: *The daisy, The cowslip, The crocus, The pink,* and *Short poems.*

CRITICISM

Darton, Frederick Joseph Harvey. "The moral tale: (ii) persuasive; chiefly in verse," in his *Children's books in England,* p. 193–95. 2d ed. Cambridge: Cambridge University Press, 1958.

A witty commentary on the verses of Elizabeth Turner, suggesting that she may have written tongue-in-cheek. Examples are included.

Evolution from Didacticism:
The Early Nineteenth Century

In 1802, Charles Lamb complained to his friend Coleridge in an oft-quoted letter:

> Goody Two-Shoes is almost out of print. Mrs. Barbauld's stuff has banished all the old classics of the nursery; and the shopman at Newbery's hardly deigned to reach them off an old exploded corner of the shelf, when Mary asked for them. Mrs. B's and Mrs. Trimmer's nonsense lay in piles about . . . Damn them!—I mean the cursed Barbauld Crew, those Blight and Blasts of all that is Human in man and child.—*Letters*

However, by 1810, the moral tale, as Darton put it, "was beginning to change its soul. It was becoming the Matter-of-Fact tale with a strong sound unquestioned foundation of English (or, now British) morality."[1]

By this time, juvenile literature was, in Darton's words, "in a flourishing state." At the turn of the century, many publishing houses for the sole purpose of producing children's books had not only been founded but had succeeded. They produced many small-size, relatively inexpensive books called toy books, which might very well be called the modern picture book's predecessors. By 1830, children's book publishing was a reputable business, a money-making venture, and most children were able to read.

Toy books were radical, not only because of their enchanting new format, but because of their content. In 1807, John Harris published in toy book form a poem that began:

Come, take up your Hats, and away let us haste,
To the Butterfly's Ball and the Grasshopper's Feast.

The unlikely author of the poem was William Roscoe, an English politician and scientist of

some note, who had written *The butterfly's ball* for his son's seventh birthday. It was and still is a charming work, very fresh and spritely, and totally unlike the typical dreary fare of the period. So successful was it that Harris published a series of sequels, some of which—*The peacock at home*, for example—were written by one Mrs. Dorset.

Other publishing houses followed suit, and toy books began to be produced in droves. Dean and Munday, competitor of Harris, produced an equally charming poem called *Dame Wiggins of Lee and her seven wonderful cats: a humorous tale written principally by a woman of ninety*. Published first in 1823, the verses were accompanied by sixteen woodcut illustrations. Later, in 1885, the poem was edited and added to by no less a luminary than John Ruskin, whose friend Kate Greenaway added some of her illustrations to the originals.

Charles Lamb and his sister, Mary, themselves contributed greatly to the change that was occurring in children's literature. In 1807, five years after Charles Lamb's lament to Coleridge and the same year as the publication of *The butterfly's ball*, the Lambs' *Tales from Shakespear* was printed. Nothing else like it had ever been attempted for children. Their aim was to reveal to children the grandeur of the classics that had heretofore not been rewritten for them. Charles was responsible for rewriting six of the plays, all tragedies, while Mary rewrote the major portion of the text. Charles wrote *Prince Dorus* and *The adventures of Ulysses*, both of which, like the *Tales from Shakespear*, are distinguished by their relative lack of the moralism that so drenched some of the earlier works of the century. *Mrs. Leicester's school*, one of the earliest collections of school stories, is mostly the work of Mary Lamb. Mary F. Thwaite feels that the reason children no longer read this book, despite its "delicate charm," is that it lacks action. The Lambs also wrote *Poetry for children*, gentle

1. *Children's books in England*, 2d ed. (Cambridge: Cambridge University Press, 1958), p. 218.

verses with rhythmic swing. All the Lambs' books were published by William Godwin, then considered a radical thinker and writer, and his second wife. (Godwin's first wife was the writer Mary Wollstonecraft.)

Two others who contributed to the return of the imagination in children's literature were the Grimm brothers, Jacob and Wilhelm, who collected and wrote down traditional tales in Germany between 1812 and 1818. It is indicative of this new trend that these stories were published in England very soon after their original appearance. Edgar Taylor was their first English translator, and they were published between 1823 and 1826 under the title *German popular tales*. Although the "lady writers" of the late eighteenth century had tried to abolish a fairy tale from the nursery, a collection of tales had been printed in England in 1818. In that year, Sir Richard Phillips had compiled *Popular fairy tales, or, a Liliputian [sic] library, now first collected and revised by Benjamin Tabart*, a collection of all the Perrault tales, some tales indigenous to England, and others.

The Grimm brothers, however, produced a fresh, new collection. Scholars, primarily philologists, they worked in a period of great German nationalism, collecting stories from countrywomen in Kassel and Hesse, writing down versions close to what they were told. (How much they diverged from the originals is disputed.) Although the original collection was intended by the Grimms for "adults and serious people," they did expect the stories to be read to children by parents. The 1823–26 English translation, however, is clearly meant for children and contains illustrations by the leading English illustrator of the period, George Cruikshank. Needless to say, the tales were immediately taken up by the fantasy-starved children of the early nineteenth century. Nevertheless, no other major works of fantasy were produced until 1839.

The butterfly's ball, the "classic" stories of the Lambs, and the Grimms' tales mark the first true relief from religion, morality, and didacticism to which the young had been subjected for many years. The toy books and the fairy tales foreshadowed a new era in children's literature.

OUTLINE

I. Nursery toy books of the early nineteenth century
  A. The new idea in children's literature
    1. Indication of change in public opinion concerning children's books
    2. Importance of the toy books and other nursery literature considered collectively
    3. Method used for the early color book
  B. Examples of toy books
    1. Publications of John Harris
      a) *The butterfly's ball* by William Roscoe (1753–1831)
        (1) Origin of the poem
        (2) First appearance in *The gentleman's magazine* (November, 1806)
        (3) Subsequent editions and changes in form
        (4) Illustrations by William Mulready
        (5) Quality of the verse
        (6) Popularity
      b) Imitations of *The butterfly's ball*
        (1) Number and titles
        (2) *The peacock "at home"* and *The lion's masquerade*

      (a) The author, how discovered
        (3) The evolution of the color book as shown in *The peacock and the parrot*
      c) Other toy books published by Harris
        (1) Variations in format
    2. Publications of Dean & Munday
      a) General character of books and illustrations
      b) *Dame Wiggins of Lee*
      c) *Deborah Dent and her donkey*
    3. Publications of the Godwins
II. The children's books of Charles (1775–1834) and Mary Lamb (1764–1847)
  A. Attitudes of the Lambs toward children's literature
    1. Charles Lamb's dislike of the work of the didactic school
    2. Recognition of value to children of great idealistic literature
    3. Relation of children's books to period
      a) Moralistic elements
  B. Association of the Lambs with the Godwins
    1. First meeting with William Godwin

GENERAL REFERENCES

Allen, Mary E. "Picture-books of olden days," *The cosmopolitan* 26:337–44 (1899).
Describes four of the little volumes belonging to Isaac Taylor's Little tarry-at-home travellers series, "scientific" geographical studies of America, Europe, Asia, and Africa. Quotes from the volumes and reproduces a number of the woodcuts.

Bedford, Jessie (*pseud.* Elizabeth Godfrey). "The superior parent," "Children in the country," "Transition," in her *English children in the olden time*, p. 260–87, 288–306, 307–23. London: Methuen, 1907.
About life in the early nineteenth century and the return of romance, with special emphasis on Sir Walter Scott and the Lambs.

"Children's books," *The quarterly review* 74:1–26 (1844).

Argues against didacticism and notes the Lambs' *Tales* as an exception to what is in evidence. Also includes a bibliography of "Good books."

———. in *Children and literature: views and reviews,* edited by Virginia Haviland, p. 8–18. Glenview, Ill.: Scott, Foresman, [1973]. Paperbound.

Cruse Amy. "The schoolroom," in her *The Englishman and his books in the early nineteenth century,* p. 78–90. London: Harrap, [1930].
References to some early texts and informational books.

Darton, Frederick Joseph Harvey. "Children's books," in *The Cambridge history of English literature,* v. 11, p. 418–20, 426–29. New York: Putnam, 1914.

———. "The moral tale: persuasive," "Interim again: the dawn of levity," in his *Children's books in England,* p. 196–203, 205–23. 2d ed. Cambridge: Cambridge University Press, [1958].
Describes the Lambs and the Godwins, the toy book publishers and some of their productions, and some of the representative writers of the period. Mentions the Grimm brothers and the translations of their fairy tales into English.

Barry, Florence Valentine. "Some great writers of little books," "The old-fashioned garden of verses," in her *A century of children's books,* p. 152–61, 208–23. New York: Doran, 1923; reprint: Detroit: Singing Tree, 1968.
Good analysis of *Mrs. Leicester's school* and the poetry of Charles and Mary Lamb. Discusses also *The butterfly's ball* and its sequels.

De Vries, Leonard. Flowers of delight. New York: Pantheon, 1965.
A selection of chapbooks, rhymes, and stories from the Osborne collection, representing the period 1765–1830. Chosen because they were "so different from those published in the next half-century and in their get-up so superior." Lavishly illustrated. Bibliographies.

Ellis, Alec. "Light in the darkness," in his *A history of children's reading and literature,* p. 1–13. London: Pergamon, [1966].
Includes a discussion of the publications of John Harris, John Marshall, Darton & Harvey, J. Johnson, Dean & Munday, and Baldwin, Cradock & Joy; also discusses the toy book trade, William Roscoe's *The butterfly's ball,* the Lambs' works, and the Grimms' fairy tales.

Field, Louise Frances Story (Mrs. E. M. Field). "From 1740 to about 1810," "Modern developments," in her *The child and his book,* p. 283–89, 325–47. 2d ed. London: Wells Gardner, 1892; reprint: Detroit: Singing Tree, 1968.
Includes the Lambs, the Godwins, and the Taylor family, as well as the work of Barbara Hofland, Maria Hack, and Jane Marcet.

Fish, Helen Dean. "The charm of the old-fashioned story: about some books written for our grandparents," *Horn book magazine* 2:27–34 (March, 1926).

Hosmer, Herbert H. A brief history of toy books, exemplified in a series of characters with figures to dress and undress, 1810–1830. South Lancaster, Mass.: John Greene Chandler Museum, 1954.
Covers toy books published by S. & J. Fuller of London during the nineteenth century and their later imitations in France, Holland, and the United States. Bibliography.

Moon, Marjorie. John Harris's books for youth, 1801–1843. Cambridge: Cambridge University Press, 1976.
A checklist.

Moses, Montrose Jonas. "Concerning now and then," in his *Children's books and reading,* p. 143–50. Boston: Kennerley, 1907.
Brief introduction, with list of English writers of minor importance but "foreshadowers of the new era."

Muir, Percy. "From Harris to 'Alice'," in his *English children's books, 1600–1900,* p. 100–34. New York: Praeger, [1954]; London: Batsford, [1969].
Notes the revival of the fairy tale and the work of the new publishing firms of John Harris (successor to E. Newbery) and the Godwins.

Stone, Wilbur Macey. "The butterfly's ball," *Horn book magazine* 18:44–53 (January, 1942).
Tells how the poem was written by Roscoe for his son's seventh birthday. Gives its bibliographic record as well as those of the books by Catherine Ann Dorset. Names other important Harris imprints.

Thwaite, Mary F. "The dawn of imagination," in her *From primer to pleasure in reading,* p. 79–92. 2d ed. London: Library Assn., 1972.
"From Blake to Grimm" includes a discussion of toy books, the Godwins, and the Lambs. Thwaite says of this period, "The heady waters of imagination were breaking through the firm ramparts of reason slowly but surely."

Tuer, Andrew White, comp. Old London street cries and the cries of to-day with heaps of quaint cuts including hand-coloured frontispiece. London: Field & Tuer, 1885.
Bibliographical notes are given for the "cries," and there are reproductions of early illustrations. Ten of these, by Thomas Rowlandson, "are copied *in facsimile* from a scarce set . . . published in 1820."

———. Stories from old-fashioned children's books. London: Leadenhall, 1899–1900.
A companion volume to *Pages and pictures from forgotten children's books.* Contains many reproductions of old woodcuts. Good introduction.

———. Pages and pictures from forgotten children's books. London: Leadenhall, 1898–99.
Collection of facsimile pages from children's books published between 1788 and 1830.

Whalley, Joyce Irene. Cobwebs to catch flies: illustrated books for the nursery and schoolroom 1700–1900. Berkeley and Los Angeles: University of California Press, 1975.
Useful especially for the "Index of publishers," p. 153–56, which lists the books by various publishing firms that the author has discussed in the text.

TOY BOOKS PUBLISHED BY DEAN & MUNDAY

Dame Wiggins of Lee and her seven wonderful cats: a humorous tale written principally by a lady of ninety. London: Dean & Munday, 1823. Sixteen colored engravings by R. Stennett.

———. (Leadenhall Press series of forgotten picture books for children) London: Field & Tuer, 1887.
A reprint of the 1823 edition, illustrated from the original blocks. Contains an introduction by A. W. Tuer. The authorship of *Dame Wiggins* is uncertain. It has been attributed to the joint authorship of R. S. Sharpe and Mrs. Pearson.

———. Edited, with additional verses, by John Ruskin. London: G. Allen, 1885.
The woodcuts are facsimiles, by W. H. Hooper, of those in the edition of 1823, but they are not colored. There are additional illustrations by Kate Greenaway.

———. ———. New York: McGraw-Hill, 1963.
Original and Ruskin text with colorful, modern illustrations by Robert Bromfield.

———. New York: Dutton, 1928.
Has twenty-two woodcuts.

Deborah Dent and her donkey: a humorous tale. London: Dean & Munday, 1823.
Text is "embellished with ten beautifully-coloured engravings."

———. (Leadenhall Press series of forgotten picture books for children) London: Field & Tuer, 1887.
The author of the amusing rhymes is not known, but the name of R. Stennett appears in an advertisement of the period as the illustrator. The original blocks have been used for this facsimile reprint. The introduction is by A. W. Tuer.

TOY BOOKS PUBLISHED BY JOHN HARRIS

[B., W.] The elephant's ball and grande fête champêtre. (Harris's cabinet) London: John Harris, 1807.

———. ———. London: Griffith, 1883.
Facsimile reproduction of the edition of 1807, with an introduction by Charles Welsh. "Besides the interest and merit of . . . [the Harris's cabinet series] on literary grounds these earlier editions are especially noteworthy because they were illustrated by the painter William Mulready, and the drawings he made for them are amongst the earliest efforts of his genius."—introduction.

[Dorset, Catherine Ann.] The lion's masquerade: a sequel to *The peacock "at home"*; written by a lady. (Harris's cabinet) London: John Harris, 1807.

———. ———. London: Griffith, 1883.
Facsimile reproduction of the edition of 1807, with an introduction by Charles Welsh.

———. The peacock "at home": a sequel to *The butterfly's ball;* written by a lady. (Harris's cabinet) London: John Harris, 1807.

———. ———. London: Griffith, 1883.
Facsimile reproduction of the edition of 1807, with an introduction by Charles Welsh.

Marmaduke Multiply. (Harris's cabinet) Pts. 1, 2. London: John Harris, 1816.
This was first printed in 1816 as part of the Harris's cabinet series and was issued in four small volumes in 1816–17. The full title, as given on the title page of the edition reproduced by Andrew Tuer in his *Stories from old-fashioned children's books* (see above), is *Marmaduke Multiply's merry method of making minor mathematicians, or, the multiplication table illustrated by sixty-nine appropriate engravings.*

The New Year's feast on his coming of age. London: John Harris, 1824.
A versification of the prose article by Charles Lamb entitled "Rejoicings upon the New Year's coming of age," which appeared in the *London magazine* for January, 1823. The poem has twelve illustrations colored by hand and notes taken mainly from *Clavis calendaria* by Brady.

The peacock and parrot on their tour to discover the author of *The peacock "at home."* (Harris's cabinet) London: John Harris, 1816.
Illustrated with engravings. On p. 31, a footnote indicates that Catherine Ann Dorset was the author of *The peacock "at home." The peacock and parrot* was intended for publication immediately after the book to which its title refers, but it was not actually printed until several years later. The illustrations are excellent and represent an important stage in the evolution of the color book.

Peter Prim's pride, or, proverbs that will suit the young or the old. (Harris's cabinet) London: John Harris, 1810.
Contains outline illustrations colored by hand.

Pug's visit, or, the disasters of Mr. Punch. (Harris's cabinet) London: John Harris, 1806.

This is in verse. There are sixteen leaves without pagination, and the pictures are in color. An interesting reference to a companion volume will be found in George Eliot's *Mill on the Floss*, chapter 4. "Harris's cabinet" appears on the paper wrapper; the date, 1806, on the first page. Probably not originally one of this series, as *The butterfly's ball* (1807) is believed to be the first one published.

The remarkable adventures of an old woman and her pig: an ancient tale in modern dress. London: John Harris, [18–?].
Told in rhyme and illustrated with pictures colored by hand. The title on the cover reads *Old woman & her pig*.

Roscoe, William. The butterfly's ball and the grasshopper's feast. (Harris's cabinet) London: John Harris, 1807.
The poem first appeared in *The gentleman's magazine*, November, 1806 and the following year became first in the Harris's cabinet series.

———. ———. London: Griffith, 1883.
Facsimile reproduction of the edition of 1808, with an introduction by Charles Welsh. In the 1807 edition, "the text and pictures were engraved together on copperplates. An edition, with the pictures on separate pages appeared early in the next year, which is the one here reproduced."—introduction.

———. ———. New York: McGraw-Hill, 1967.
Illustrated by Don Bolognese.

———. ———. New York: Grossman, 1975.
Illustrated by Alan Aldridge.

Whittington and his cat. (Harris's cabinet) London: John Harris, [1825?].
The story is told in verse, and the hand-colored pictures are particularly interesting. On p. 17 is an advertisement for *Margery Meanwell*, newly published, and on the inside cover a list of books in the series.

BIOGRAPHY AND CRITICISM

Chandler, George. William Roscoe of Liverpool. London: Batsford, [1953].
A biographical essay and selections from Roscoe's poetry. *The butterfly's ball* is reprinted on p. 410–11, and a poem called *The butterfly's birthday* is reprinted on p. 412–13. A selection of Roscoe's verses from *Poems for youth by a family circle* (1821) and *Poems by William Roscoe and his children* (ms.) is also included.

Charles and Mary Lamb

Lamb, Charles. The adventures of Ulysses. London. M. J. Godwin, 1808.
The suggestion for this book seems to have come from William Godwin and was probably due to the success of *Tales from Shakespear.* "Lamb based his retelling from Homer upon George Chapman's excellent, though not entirely faithful, translation entitled *Odysseys* (London 1614–1615)."—David Greene, in introduction to facsimile edition listed below.

———. ———. London: Ştokes, [1926].
Illustrations by Doris Pailthorpe and T. H. Robinson.

———. ———. (Classics of children's literature 1621–1932) New York: Garland, 1977.
Facsimile of the 1808 edition. Excellent introduction by David L. Greene. Includes a bibliography of biographical works and works written by the Lambs.

———(?). Beauty and the beast. London: M. J. Godwin, 1811; reprint: London: Rodale Press, 1955.
The authorship of this little book is hotly debated, and Greene feels there is little reason to ascribe it to Lamb. The Pierpont Morgan Library owns an "extremely rare first issue of the first edition," with two fold-out sheets of music for "Beauty's song." The reprint includes plates from the original edition.

———(?). The book of the ranks and dignities of British society. London: Tabart, 1805.
This book is attributed to Lamb, although most Lamb scholars have found little evidence to prove he did write it.

———. ———. London: Jonathan Cape; Cambridge: Cambridge University Press, 1924.
Subtitle: "lately attributed in the press and elsewhere to Charles Lamb; including an introductory note by Clement Shorter, with eight coloured plates and sixteen in monochrome." This is a reprint of the above edition. According to the title page, which is reproduced, the book was chiefly intended for young persons and was illustrated with twenty-four colored engravings. It was dedicated by permission to Her Royal Highness the Princess Elizabeth.

———. The king and queen of hearts. London: Thomas Hodgkins, 1805.
Probably the first children's book written by Charles Lamb. It was published in 1805 by the Godwins, who at that time were publishing under cover of Hodgkins's name in Hanway Street.

———. ———. London: Methuen; New York: Mc-Clure, Phillips, 1902.
Subtitle: "an 1805 book for children, illustrated by William Mulready; now reissued with an introduction by E. V. Lucas." The introduction outlines the bibliographical history of the book and the contemporary evidence on which the authorship is attributed to Lamb.

———. A masque of days, from the last essays of Elia. London: Cassell, 1901.
Subtitle: "newly dressed and decorated by Walter Crane." Tells how the New Year, coming of age, gave a dinner party, to which all the days in the year were invited. Magnificently illustrated by Crane, with hand-lettered text.

———. Prince Dorus, or, flattery put out of countenance: a poetical version of an ancient tale. London: M. J. Godwin, 1811.
A fairy tale in rhyme founded on the French.

———. ———. London: Leadenhall, 1890–91.
Includes nine colored illustrations in facsimile. Introduction by A. W. Tuer. In this reprint, the woodcut of the long-nosed king and the aged fairy that adorned the paper cover of the original edition is reproduced in facsimile in the introduction.

——— and **Mary Lamb.** Mrs. Leicester's school, or, the history of several young ladies, related by themselves. London: M. J. Godwin, 1809.
Published at the end of 1808, but dated 1809 on the title page. Of the ten stories, three are by Charles Lamb and seven by Mary Lamb. They are of special interest because the authors drew largely on their own childhood experiences.

———. ———. London: Dent, [1904].
Drawings by G. E. Brock.

———. ———. New York: Three Sirens Press, 1934.

———. ———. London: Dent, 1899.
Illustrated by Winifred Green.

———. Mrs. Leicester's school, and other writings in prose and verse. London: Dent, 1885.
Introduction and notes by Alfred Ainger. Includes *The adventures of Ulysses.*

———. Poetry for children. 2v. London: M. J. Godwin, 1809.
Described as: "entirely original. By the author of *Mrs. Leicester's school.*"

———. ———. Edited and prefaced by Richard Herne Shepherd. London: Basil Montagu Pickering, 1872; New York: Scribner, 1889.
There is a short introduction relating the singular history of the book and giving an estimate of the poems.

———. ———. v. 8, *The Works,* edited by E. V. Lucas. London: Dent, 1903–5; reprint: New York: AMS Press, 1968.
Both original and reprint have the same introduction by William MacDonald. They contain, in addition to the shorter poems, *The king and queen of hearts, Prince Dorus,* and *Beauty and the beast.*

———. Tales from Shakespear, 2v. London: T. Hodgkins, 1807.
Subtitle: "designed for the use of young persons." The first edition contained twenty copperplate illustrations, "engraved by Blake from Mulready's drawings."—A. W. Tuer, in *Prince Dorus,* p. xi. Charles Lamb's name appeared alone on the title page; however, he is responsible for only seven of the tales, principally the tragedies.

———. Tales from Shakespeare. New York: Scribner, 1894. Illustrated by N. M. Price.
Contains the preface written in part by William Godwin, in part by Lamb.

———. ———. (Golden treasury series). London and New York: Macmillan, 1899.
Introduction by Alfred Ainger.

———. ———. London: Dent; New York: Dutton [1906]; reprint: New York: Dutton, 1960.
Noteworthy for illustrations by Arthur Rackham. The earlier editions had only line drawings. The later ones have an additional eight color plates.

———. ———. New York: Harper, [1918].
Numerous illustrations by Louis Rhead. Includes an "artist's preface." Line drawings only.

———. ———. New York: Macmillan, 1923.
Illustrated by Maud and Miska Petersham.

———. Ten tales from Shakespeare. New York: Watts, 1969.
Full-color edition strikingly illustrated by Grabianski.

———. The works. Edited by E. V. Lucas. v. 2, 3, 6, 7. London: Methuen, 1903–5; reprint: New York: AMS Press, 1968.
Vol. 2 of this set contains the essays of Elia, several of which are of particular interest in connection with *Mrs. Leicester's school.* Among the illustrations reproduced is the one of *Saul consulting a witch at Endor,* referred to in the story of "The witch aunt." Vol. 3 comprises all the stories and verses known to have been written by Charles and Mary Lamb, and also *Beauty and the beast,* which has been attributed to Charles Lamb. The text is that of the first or second edition. There are reproductions and also valuable bibliographical notes. Vol. 6 and 7 are made up of letters, some of which contain allusions to the children's books. Several other editions of the *Complete works* which

contain the children's books and poems are available. Vols. 6–8 of the *Works*, edited by William MacDonald; vols. 4 and 7 of *The life and works of Charles Lamb*, edited by Alfred Ainger.

Mylius, W. F. The first book of poetry for the use of schools, intended as reading lessons for the younger classes. London: M. J. Godwin, 1811.
Contains twenty-two poems of Charles and Mary Lamb that were first published in *Poetry for children*, 1809. In addition, there is a 24-line poem, p. 19–20, signed "M.L." which was changed in later editions to "C.L."

BIOGRAPHY AND CRITICISM

Ainger, Alfred. Charles Lamb. London: Macmillan, 1882.
A short biographical and critical study, the author being one of the chief authorities on the subject of Charles and Mary Lamb's literary work.

———. "Introduction," in *Tales from Shakespeare* by Charles and Mary Lamb, p. iii–xvi. New York: Crowell, [1918].
Traces the early history of the book and gives an appreciation of its literary merits. The introduction is dated 1878.

———. ed. The life and works of Charles Lamb. 12v. London: Macmillan, 1899–1900.

Anthony, Katherine. The Lambs: a study of pre-Victorian England. New York: Knopf, 1945.
The household of an odd pair of literary personalities, seen in the light of modern psychology. The relations between Charles and other writers like Coleridge, Hazlitt, and their circle, are discussed. Bibliography.

Barnett, George L. Charles Lamb. Boston: Twayne, 1976.
The children's books are touched on in the chapter titled, "Author in search of a form," p. 49–57. Includes a complete bibliography of books by and about Lamb.

Blunden, Edmund Charles. Charles Lamb. London: Longmans for the British Council, 1954.
A short biographical work with critical analyses of Lamb's writing.

———. Charles Lamb and his contemporaries. Cambridge: Cambridge University Press, 1937.
The chapter "Charles and Mary," p. 64–93, describes their literary accomplishments and their friendships.

———. comp. Charles Lamb: his life recorded by his contemporaries. London: Hogarth, 1934; reprint: Norwood, Pa.: Norwood, 1977.
Contains criticisms of the children's books of the Lambs.

Foxon, David. "The chapbook editions of the Lambs' *Tales from Shakespear*." in *The book collector* 6:41–53 (1957).
Bibliographical essay on the chapbook editions of the *Tales*.

Gilchrist, Anne Burrows. Mary Lamb. London: Roberts, 1883.
For the *Tales from Shakespear*, see p. 154–67; for *Mrs. Leicester's school* and *Poetry for children*, p. 207–22.

Hazlitt, William Carew. The Lambs: their lives, their friends, and their correspondence; new particulars and new material. London: Elkin Matthews; New York: Scribner, 1897.
Attributes three "new books" to the Lambs: *Poetry for children, Beauty and the beast,* and *Prince Dorus*.

———. Mary and Charles Lamb: poems, letters, and remains now first collected with reminiscences and notes. London: Chatto & Windus, 1874.
The letters and poems of Mary are separated from those of Charles.

Howe, Will. Charles Lamb and his friends. Indianapolis: Bobbs-Merrill, [1944].
Chapter 2 gives a biographical account of Charles's life and his relationship with his sister. Chapter 3, "And Mary," p. 44–62, considers Mary's mental disturbances and her writing.

Jerrold, Walter. Charles Lamb. (Miniature series of great writers) London: George Ball, 1905.
The section on Lamb's writings covers his works for children.

Lamb, Charles. The letters, newly arranged with additions. Edited with introduction and notes by Alfred Ainger. 2v. London and New York: Macmillan, 1888.

———. Letters of Charles and Mary Lamb. Edited by Edwin W. Marrs, Jr. 2v. to date. Ithaca, N.Y.: Cornell University Press, 1975–76.

———. Letters of Charles Lamb. Boston: Bibliophile Society, 1905.
Subtitle: "in which many mutilated words and passages have been restored to their original form; with letters never before published and facsimiles of original ms. letters and poems." Introduction by Henry W. Harper. An elegant, limited edition on Dutch handmade paper. Includes facsimiles of the handwritten letters. Vol. 1 is a folio.

———. The letters of Charles Lamb to which are added those of his sister, Mary Lamb. 3v. Edited by E. V. Lucas. New Haven, Conn.: Yale University Press, 1935; reprint: New York: AMS Press, 1968.

———. The letters of Charles Lamb, with a sketch of his life. 2v. Edited by Thomas Noon Talfourd. London: Moxon, 1837.

The Talfourd letters, published only three years after Charles Lamb's death while Mary was still alive, are very incomplete. Approximately two hundred more letters have been found and printed since then. The *Letters* edited by Edwin Marrs, Jr. (see above) will be the most complete when finished.

———. The life and letters of Charles Lamb. Philadelphia: W. P. Hazard, 1837.

A reprint of the 1837 Moxon edition of *The letters of Charles Lamb* listed above.

———. The life and letters, and writings of Charles Lamb. Edited by Percy Fitzgerald. 6v. London: Constable, [1875].

Known as the Enfield edition.

Livingston, Luther S. A bibliography of the first editions . . . of Charles and Mary Lamb, published prior to . . . 1834. New York: De Vinne, 1903.

———. "Some notes of three of Lamb's juveniles," *Bibliographer* 1, no. 6:215–30 (June, 1902).

Lucas, Edward Verrall. The life of Charles Lamb. 2v. New York: Putnam, 1903–5.

"Enables the reader to obtain a completer picture of Charles Lamb than he can gain from any other source. Apart from its value as literature the book is a Lamb encyclopedia which with its carefully compiled and accurate index and appendices forms a complete mine of information of every kind about the author."—*The Saturday review*, 1905.

McCusker, Honor. "Charles Lamb and his friends," *More books* (Boston Public Library) 16:459–68 (December, 1943).

Reference to *Mrs. Leicester's school.* Includes description of the second edition.

Moore, Anne Carroll. "Mrs. Leicester's school," in her *The three owls, third book*, p. 297–302. New York: Coward, 1931.

Appreciative review.

Moses, Montrose Jonas. "Charles and Mary Lamb; the Godwins," in his *Children's books and reading*, p. 130–40. New York: Kennerley, 1907.

In connection with Lamb's *Ulysses*, Moses discusses how much of the brute element in early literature should be included in literature for children.

Procter, Bryan Waller (*pseud.* Barry Cornwall). Charles Lamb: a memoir by Barry Cornwall. Boston: Roberts, 1866.

A very early biography.

Ross, Ernest Carson. The ordeal of Bridget Elia: a chronicle of the Lambs. Norman: University of Oklahoma Press, 1941.

Considered the best analysis of the life and writings of Mary Lamb.

Taylor, Sue. "M. J. Godwin & Co.," *Horn book magazine* 20:79–87 (March–April, 1944).

An account of the Godwins' business relations with the Lambs.

Thomson, Joseph Charles. Bibliography of the writings of Charles and Mary Lamb: a literary history. Hull, England: J. R. Tutin, 1908.

Ward, Alfred Charles. The frolic and the gentle: a centenary study of Charles Lamb. London: Methuen, 1934; reprint: Folcroft, Pa.: Folcroft, 1973.

See p. 164–71 for a valuable chapter that discusses the children's books of the Lambs.

Woodring, Carl R. "Charles Lamb in the Harvard Library," *Bulletin* (Harvard University Library) 10:208–39, 367–401 (1956).

Questions the attributions of *Book of the ranks* . . . and *Beauty and the beast* to Charles Lamb.

Representative Books by English Writers

Hack, Maria Barton. Grecian stories. London: Darton, Harvey & Darton, 1819.

———. Lectures at home. London: Darton & Harvey, 1834.

Contents: Discovery and manufacture of glass; Refractions, lenses, mirrors; Spectacles and telescopes; Microscopes and camera-obscura; The eye.

———. Winter evenings, or, tales of travellers. London: Darton, Harvey & Darton, 1819–20.

Hofland, Barbara Wreaks Hoole. The daughter of a genius: a tale for youth. London: John Harris, 1823.

The heroine has the misfortune to be "portionless, fatherless, and the Daughter of a Genius"; but she overcomes the deficiencies of her early education and meets successfully all the trials that come to her. An example of the novelette.

———. Matilda, or, the Barbadoes girl: a tale for young people. London: A. K. Newman, 1816.

———. The son of a genius: a tale for the use of youth. London: John Harris, 1812.

The "short and simple annals" of Ludovico, who has many sorrows and difficulties in his early life, due to the improvidence of his father, a painter of talent. The lesson that genius should become a stimulus to industry is concretely brought out, and the book is dedicated to the author's own son to show him that "boys who *have* fathers may, in some cases, suffer many privations and afflictions."

———. Tales of the priory. 4v. London: Longmans, Hurst, Rees, Orme & Brown, 1820.

———. The young Crusoe, or, the shipwrecked boy. London: A. K. Newman, 1828.

Marcet, Jane Haldimand. Conversations on natural philosophy, in which the elements of that science are familiarly explained, and adapted to the comprehension of young pupils. London: Longman, Hurst, Rees, Orme & Brown, 1819.
A typical text by this author. She also prepared "conversations" on chemistry, political economy, vegetable physiology (botany), and language.

———. Stories for young children. London: Longman, Rees, Orme, Brown & Green, 1831.
Afterwards printed under the title *Willy's stories* (London: Longman, Brown, Green & Longmans).

Scott, *Sir* Walter. Tales of a grandfather, being stories taken from Scottish history. Edinburgh: Cadell, 1828.
The author dedicated the tales to Hugh Little-john.

Taylor, Isaac. Advice to the teens, or, practical helps toward the formation of one's own character. 2d. ed. London: R. Fenner, 1818.

———. Scenes in America, for the amusement and instruction of little tarry-at-home travellers. London: John Harris, 1821.
Verse and prose alternate in the text, and the sections are numbered to correspond with the pictures they explain. The book is one of a series, including volumes on Europe, Asia, and Africa, published in England from 1818 to 1830.

———. ———. New York: Johnson, 1968.
Facsimile of the London edition of 1821. With a preface by Christiana Duff Stewart of the Toronto Public Library.

———. The ship. (Little library, v. 2) London: John Harris, 1830.
Includes sixteen engravings on steel.

Taylor, Jefferys. The farm: a new account of rural toils and produce. (Little library, v. 8) London: John Harris, 1832.
Includes eight engravings on steel and twenty-six on wood.

Wakefield, Priscilla Bell. Domestic recreation, or, dialogues illustrative of natural and scientific subjects. London: Darton & Harvey, 1805.
Conversations between a well-informed mother and her daughters on such topics as insects, instinct, meteors, light, the progress of civilization.

———. Excursions in North America, described in letters from a gentleman and his younger companion, to their friends in England. London: Darton & Harvey, 1806.

———. A family tour through the British empire. London: Darton & Harvey, 1804.
Subtitle: "containing some account of its natural and artificial curiosities, history and antiquities, interspersed with biographical anecdotes, particularly adapted to the amusement and instruction of youth." Semieducational in character and written partly in narrative form, partly in letters.

———. Instinct displayed, in a collection of well-authenticated facts, exemplifying the extraordinary sagacity of various species of the animal creation. London: Darton, Harvey & Darton, 1811.
Letters narrating stories of animals.

———. Juvenile anecdotes, founded on facts. 2v. London: Darton & Harvey, 1795–98.

———. Leisure hours, or, entertaining dialogues. 2v. London: Darton & Harvey, 1794–96.

———. Sketches of human manners. 1st American ed. Philadelphia: Johnson & Warner, 1811.
Subtitle: "delineated in stories intended to illustrate the character, religion, and singular customs, of the inhabitants of different parts of the world."

THE BROTHERS GRIMM

■ The editions below, all of which are collections of tales, are listed alphabetically by title. *Kinder- und Hausmärchen* was published in Berlin between 1812 and 1818. The first translation into English appeared between 1823 and 1826 under the title *German popular stories*, translated by Edgar Taylor. See entry below for full bibliographical details.

Grimm, Jakob Ludwig Karl, and Wilhelm Karl Grimm. About wise men and simpletons: twelve tales from Grimm. Translated by Elizabeth Shub. New York: Macmillan, [1970].
Illustrated with exquisite etchings by Nonny Hogrogian. A good introduction.

———. The complete Grimm's fairy tales. New York: Pantheon, 1944.
Two hundred and ten stories. Introduction by Padraic Colum; folkloristic commentary by Joseph Campbell. Two hundred and twelve illustrations by Josef Scharl.

———. Fairy tales. Chicago: Follett, 1948.
Based on the Frances Jenkins Olcott edition of the English translation of Margaret Hunt. Includes an introduction by Frances Clarke Sayers and paintings in full color by children of fifteen nations. A beautiful edition.

———. ———. New York: Viking, Studio Book, [1973].
Includes twelve full-color illustrations by Arthur Rackham. Twenty stories.

———. ———. Offenbach A/M.: Limited Editions Club, 1931.
A limited edition of 1,500 copies. Illustrated with woodcuts by Fritz Kredel; introduction by Harry Hansen. Eleven tales, including "King Thrushbeard," "Little Snow White," "Rapunzel," "Hansel and Grethel."

———. German popular stories. Translated from the *Kinder- und Hausmärchen* by Edgar Taylor. 2v. London: C. Baldwyn, 1823–26.
Includes Cruikshank illustrations.

———. ———. London: J. C. Hotten, [1869].
Includes ten additional etchings by George Cruikshank. Introduction by John Ruskin.

———. Grimms' fairy tales: a new translation. Translated by Mrs. H. B. Paull. London: Guildford, [1872].

———. ———. New York: Scribner, 1920.
Selected and illustrated by Elenore Abbott.

———. The house in the wood and other fairy stories. London: Warne, [1944].
Ten stories from Grimm with lively illustrations by L. Leslie Brooke, several in color.

———. Household stories, from the collection of the Brothers Grimm. Translated by Lucy Crane. London: Macmillan, 1923, 1927, 1953.
Thirty-two stories. Nine full-color illustrations by Walter Crane.

———. Household tales, with the author's notes. Translated by Margaret Hunt. 2v. London: G. Bell, 1884.
There is a long, scholarly introduction by Andrew Lang titled, "Household tales: their origin, diffusion, relations to the higher myths," p. xi–ixxv.

———. The juniper tree, and other tales from Grimm. Selected by Lore Segal and Maurice Sendak. Translated by Lore Segal and Randall Jarrell. 2v. New York: Farrar, 1973.
This new collection of little-known fairy tales has caused some controversy. Illustrations, by Maurice Sendak, are haunting.

———. Other tales: a new selection by Wilhelm Hansen. Translated and edited by Ruth Michaelis-Jena and Arthur Ratcliffe. London: Golden Cockerel Press, 1956.
Illustrated with ten wood engravings by Gwenda Morgan. A collection of some less-famous tales from the 1812 edition of *Kinder- und Hausmärchen* that Taylor omitted from his edition (above). A splendidly printed and illustrated book.

———. Popular stories. Edited by Edgar Taylor. London: Chatto & Windus, 1920.
Introduction by John Ruskin. The first edition of *Popular stories* appeared in England in 1823 with twelve etchings by Cruikshank; in the second series, he added ten more etchings. This is a reprint of both series.

———. Tales. New York: Oxford University Press, 1954.
Sixteen tales are illustrated by Helen Sewell and Madeleine Gekiere in very different styles.

———. Tales for young and old: the complete stories. Translated by Ralph Manheim. Garden City, N.Y.: Doubleday, 1977.
Translated from the complete *Kinder- und Hausmärchen* (Munich: Winkler-Verlag, 1819).

———. Tales from Grimm. Freely translated and illustrated by Wanda Gág. New York: Coward, [1936].
The translator/illustrator avowedly "simplified" the stories for the four-to-twelve age group. Includes sixteen of the best-loved stories. Seven full-page illustrations with one color frontispiece.

BIOGRAPHY AND CRITICISM

Campbell, Joseph. "The work of the Brothers Grimm," in *Bibliophile in the nursery*, edited by William Targ, p. 371–78. Cleveland: World, [1957].
This is from the introduction to the Pantheon edition of the folktales (listed above).

Crouch, Marcus S. "Illustrators of Grimm," *Junior bookshelf* 14: 237–43 (December, 1950).

Eaton, Anne Thaxter. "The Brothers Grimm," in *A critical history of children's literature*, edited by Cornelia Meigs et al., p. 184–86. Rev. ed. New York: Macmillan, 1969.
Analyzes the tales as part of the nineteenth-century Romantic movement.

Hansen, Harry. "The Brothers Grimm," *Horn book magazine* 15:113–20 (March, 1939).
Explains how the brothers' collecting coincided with a deep-seated patriotic purpose that grew out of the rise of nationalism in middle Europe in the latter half of the eighteenth century. This essay is the introduction to the limited edition *Fairy tales* with illustrations by Fritz Kredel (listed above).

Hazard, Paul. "The Brothers Grimm," in his *Books, children, & men,* translated by Marguerite Mitchell, p. 152–57. 4th ed. Boston: Horn Book, 1960.
An outstanding essay about Jacob and William Grimm, who "collected tales, much as though they were running after butterflies." To Hazard, the triumph of the Grimms heralded the child's commonsense triumph over didacticism.

Hürlimann, Bettina. "The Brothers Grimm and their times," in *Three centuries of children's books in Europe,* translated and edited by Brian W. Alderson, p. 31–38. Cleveland: World, [1968].
Defines the value of the original versions in German for the adult scholar and the alterations that were made to accommodate the tales to children.

Ker, W. P. Jacob Grimm. London and New York: Oxford University Press, 1915.
An address delivered at the annual meeting of the Philological Society on Friday, May 7, 1915.

———. ———. in *Collected essays*, v. 2, p. 222–33. London: Macmillan, 1925.

Michaelis-Jena, Ruth. The Brothers Grimm. New York: Praeger, 1970.

———. "Oral tradition and the Brothers Grimm," *Folklore* 82:265–75 (Winter, 1971).
Describes how the Grimms collected the tales, their changes, and the nineteenth-century translations. Michaelis-Jena concludes that the Grimms' vitality changed the approach to oral literature and, in particular, gave a new status to the folktale.

Peppard, Murray B. Paths through the forest: a biography of the Brothers Grimm. New York: Holt, 1971.
A thorough, scholarly treatise on the life of the Grimm brothers and their effect on folklore. Peppard says that they were typical of their time and representative of important aspects of nineteenth-century Germany. Chapters 4 and 5, p. 39–74, deal with the fairy tales, and chapter 7, p. 93–101, with fairy tale or *sage*.

Roscoe, Theodora. "Home of the Grimms' fairy tales," *Contemporary review* 174:231–33 (October, 1948).
Concerns mainly the Grimms' informant Frau Katherina Dorothea Viehmann.

Ussher, Arland. Enter these enchanted woods. Dublin: Dolmen, in association with the Sandymount Press, [1957]; Chester Springs, Pa.: Dufour Editions, 1966.
These essays deal with the folktales as illustrative of archetypal ideas.

American Literature: From the Revolution to the Mid-Nineteenth Century

During the colonial period, there were few books of American origin for children. The religious literature of the seventeenth century —John Cotton's *Milk for babes*, Cotton Mather's *Token for the children of New England,* and the widely used *New England primer*—did not differ in character from their English prototypes. The books of amusement and instruction printed by Isaiah Thomas in the eighteenth century were chiefly reprints of English publications. It was not until the period following the Revolution that the American development of children's literature may be said to have begun, and there were no individual authors of importance before the second quarter of the nineteenth century. The group of writers that emerged at this time was in the direct line of succession from Hannah More and Maria Edgeworth, so that it seems logical at this point to direct attention to the influences contributing to the American evolution and work of the more prominent authors.

Of those who wrote specifically for children, even the names of authors well known in their day are now largely forgotten, but their influence was far from negligible. In America as in England at this period, women led the field in writing for children. On both sides of the Atlantic, female writers produced books "with a moral and educational tendency." In America they also aimed at improving social manners and the household arts. More important, they eloquently espoused high causes such as the antislavery movement and the movement for women's rights. Clearly, these were women of brains and courage, not mere hack writers or dilettantes, and their books for children were published in numerous editions over a span of many years. We are indebted to Sarah Josepha Hale for her "Mary's lamb" and for her successful campaign to make Thanksgiving Day a national holiday. Lydia Maria Child gave us "Over the river and through the woods." She stands out as worthy of remembrance today because of her antislavery booklets, her appeal on behalf of the American Indians, and her *Brief history of the condition of women, in various ages and nations.* Lydia H. Sigourney is surprisingly prominent among writers represented in American collections of rare books. All five of the women writers listed in this chapter can be remembered as editors of and prolific contributors to children's magazines of the period.

Before 1850, Nathaniel Hawthorne had begun to do some writing specifically for children, and the work of other major American writers was being adopted by children for their own. Through the widely practiced custom of family reading, James Fenimore Cooper and Washington Irving quickly became favorites of the young. Both authors are still published in annotated editions for scholars but reach their largest American audience through the beautifully illustrated editions produced as "children's classics." Ironically, although Cooper has lost his appeal to the adult "general reader" in his own country, he has an enormous following through foreign-language editions abroad. His books describe the pioneer and Indian life that foreign readers find the most fascinating aspect of the American ethos. In Germany, *Lederstrumpf* is a more familiar catchword than *Leatherstocking* is in the United States. The listings of editions of Cooper and Irving in the present chapter focus on a number intended for the general reader, especially the young, and, outstanding for fine illustrations.

Although this *History of children's literature* does not attempt to include the history of school textbooks, William Holmes McGuffey and his *Eclectic reader*s must be an exception to the rule. Lifelong memories of the McGuffey readers pervaded the lives of those who grew up in nineteenth-century America, and the subject has a place in any study of children's literature covering the period. The prose and poetry in the McGuffey readers were drawn from classic sources in both English and American literature and helped to form the taste of generations of American children. The McGuffey *Fifth Eclectic reader*, first published in 1844, is noteworthy in this respect. The table of contents includes pieces by Goldsmith, Patrick Henry, Sir Walter Scott, Washington Irving, Shakespeare, Charles Lamb, Pope, Longfellow, Cowper, Cooper, and Coleridge. This was indeed teaching the young how to shoot. In theory, and in the practical experience of many young Americans, a taste of "high literature" through exposure to the McGuffey readers whetted an appetite for serious reading in adult life.

OUTLINE

I. Historical and literary background
  A. Conditions retarding literary development
  B. Reading of American children previous to 1825
    1. General use of English books or American reprints
    2. Scarcity of literature of distinctively American origin
      a) Lack of American nature descriptions, American scenes, and local color
  C. Motives contributing to the development of American books for children in the late eighteenth and early nineteenth centuries
    1. Patriotic
    2. Local interest
      a) *Cries of New York*
    3. Religious

II. Some special developments
  A. Sunday school literature
    1. The sponsors
    2. The formula
    3. The writers
    4. Effect of the American Sunday School Union
  B. Children's magazines
    1. *The children's magazine* (1789)
    2. Johnson's *Juvenile magazine* (1802)
    3. *Juvenile olio* (1802)
    4. *Juvenile magazine* (1811)
    5. *The juvenile miscellany for the instruction and amusement of youth* (1826)
    6. *The youth's companion* (1827)
    7. *Parley's magazine* (1833)
    8. *Merry's museum* (1841)
  C. Literary annuals
    1. Character and use
    2. Illustrations: the steel engraving
    3. Importance of *The token*
    4. Special annuals for children
    5. Period of popularity

III. American writers for children in the second quarter of the century
  A. Sarah J. Hale (1788–1879)
    1. *Poems for our children*
    2. *The school song book*
  B. Eliza Leslie (1787–1858)
    1. *The American girl's book*
    2. Stories
  C. Catharine Maria Sedgwick (1789–1867)
    1. *A love token for children*
    2. *Stories for young persons*
  D. Lydia H. Sigourney (1791–1865)
    1. *Poetry for children*
    2. *Tales and essays for children*
    3. *Olive buds*
    4. *Olive leaves*
  E. Lydia Maria Child (1802–80)
    1. *Hobomok*
      a) Its origin

    2. *The rebels*
      a) Imaginary speech by James Otis
    3. Literary activities and popularity
    4. Work as a social reformer and effect of the "Appeal in behalf of that class of Americans called Africans"
    5. Children's books
      a) *The girls' own book*
      b) *Flowers for children*
        (1) Comparison with *Evenings at home*
  F. Samuel G. Goodrich, or Peter Parley (1793–1860)
    1. Early life and struggle for an education
    2. Reading tastes of his childhood
    3. Business and literary undertakings
    4. Versatility of Goodrich and diversity of subjects treated in his books
    5. Origin of the Peter Parley books
    6. Method used and character of style
    7. Popularity of books in America and England
    8. The spurious Peter Parley books
    9. Importance of Goodrich in the history of American literature
  G. Jacob Abbott (1803–79)
    1. Long period of authorship
    2. Educational work and theories
    3. Character of *The young Christian*
    4. Origin of the Rollo books
    5. Number of books; grouped according to subject: religion, education, science, travel, history and biography, children's story books
    6. Purpose in writing
    7. The story books
      a) Educational character
      b) Knowledge of children's interests
      c) Representative child and representative mentor
      d) Relations of children to each other and to their elders
      e) Incidents based upon facts
      f) Realistic treatment
      g) Accurate representation of country life in the nineteenth century
      h) New England atmosphere
      i) Lack of imaginative power and dramatic sense
      j) The Franconia stories
    8. Books of travel
      a) Based upon observation and experience
    9. Historical biographies
      a) Character and style
      b) Value to children of the nineteenth century
      c) Modern criticism
    10. Abbott's attention to detail
      a) Choice of titles, indications of scenes, characters, etc.

     b) Footnotes
     c) Suggestions for original drawings
    11. Influence upon children's literature
      in America
   H. Nathaniel Hawthorne (1804–64)
     1. First American writer to show
       appreciation of idealistic literature for
       children
     2. Association with Samuel G. Goodrich
       a) *The token*
       b) *Peter Parley's universal history on
         the basis of geography*
     3. *Grandfather's chair* and *Biographical
       stories*
       a) Equipment for writing stories of
         this type
       b) Distinctive style
     4. *A wonder-book* and *Tanglewood tales*
       a) Origin
       b) Spirit
       c) Style
  IV. The McGuffey readers
    A. Comparison with earlier primers and
      readers
    B. Background of the McGuffey family
    C. Purpose of the readers
    D. Their format and type of selections
    E. Their wide publication and influence

  V. Major American writers whose work was
    adopted by children
    A. James Fenimore Cooper (1789–1851)
     1. Influence of the Romantic movement in
       American literature
     2. Cooper's life experience as a background for his writing
     3. The Leatherstocking series
       a) Various names for Natty Bumppo
       b) His character
       c) The settings as essential parts of the plots
       d) Attitude toward the Indians
       e) Style
       f) Influence of Cooper's writing abroad
    B. Washington Irving (1783–1859)
     1. Youthful travels from New York to the British Isles
       a) Efforts to promote international understanding
       b) Friendship with Sir Walter Scott
     2. *The sketch book*
       a) *Rip Van Winkle*
       b) *The legend of Sleepy Hollow*
     3. Irving as secretary of legation at Madrid
       a) *Legends of the Alhambra*
     4. Irving as folklorist

GENERAL REFERENCES

American Antiquarian Society. Exhibit of American children's books printed before 1800. Worcester, Mass.: American Antiquarian Society, 1928.
List of books, with a foreword.

Cushman, Alice B. "A nineteenth century plan for reading: the American Sunday school movement," *Horn book magazine* 33:61–71 (February, 1957); 33:159–66 (April, 1957).
The 1956 Caroline M. Hewins lecture. Describes the publications of the American Sunday School Union of Philadelphia, organized in 1824. Pt. 2 gives the names of editors and writers for the literature of the Sunday school movement.

Dickinson, Thomas Herbert. "The romantic period (1789–1855)," in his *The making of American literature,* p. 255–498. New York: Century, 1932.
For the historical and social background, see p. 269–83; literary conditions, p. 284–92; Noah Webster, p. 368–69; references to magazines and annuals, p. 386–89; Hawthorne as a writer, p. 418–23.

Halsey, Rosalie Vrylina. "The child and his book at the end of the eighteenth century," "Toy-books in the early nineteenth century," "American writers and English critics," in her *Forgotten books of the American nursery,* p. 121–229. Boston: Goodspeed, 1911; reprint: Detroit: Gale, 1969.
The most complete study of American children's books of the period 1790–1840.

Haviland, Virginia. The travelogue storybook of the nineteenth century. (A Caroline Hewins lecture, 1949) Boston: Horn Book, 1950.
The fictionalized travel book for children as exemplified by Samuel Griswold Goodrich's Peter Parley books, Jacob Abbott's Rollo series, and other series by Horace Scudder, Hezekiah Butterworth, Charles Asbury Stephens, Frederick Albion Ober, Elizabeth Williams Champney, and others.

———, and **Margaret N. Coughlan.** Yankee Doodle's literary sampler of prose, poetry and pictures. New York: Crowell, [1974].
Subtitle: "being an anthology of diverse works published for the edification and/or entertainment of young readers in America before 1900."

Hopkins, Frederick M. "Early American juveniles," *Publishers weekly* 116:2359–98 (1929).
Notes the "crystalization of interest in this by-path of book collecting" and describes briefly five exhibitions held during the winter of 1927–1928.

Johnson, Clifton. Old-time schools and school-books. New York: Macmillan, 1904; reprint: New York: Dover, 1963.

Partial contents: Noah Webster and his spelling-book; Primary readers; Arithmetics; The first American geography; Grammars, histories, and minor textbooks. Includes extracts from some of the books described, reproductions of title pages, and cuts. For the geographies of Peter Parley, see bibliography on Samuel G. Goodrich (p. 149).

———. "One hundred years of textbook making," *Publishers Weekly* 108:217–21 (1925).
Illustrations from *Old-time schools and school-books.*

Jordan, Alice M. "Children's books in America: the first two hundred years," *Horn book magazine* 10:9–19 (January, 1934).
Review of *Early American children's books* by A. S. W. Rosenbach and *Children's books of yesterday* by Philip James. Useful also as a general survey.

———. "The dawn of imagination in American books for children," *Horn book magazine* 20:168–75 (May, 1944).
Pictures the emergence of romance and fancy, as in Hawthorne and Christopher Cranch, after the "matter-of-fact world set by Peter Parley and Jacob Abbott."

———. From Rollo to Tom Sawyer and other papers. Boston: Horn Book, 1948.
A survey of the nineteenth century in children's books, with chapters on Peter Parley, Jacob Abbott, Susan Warner, Nathaniel Hawthorne, Elijah Kellogg, Horace Scudder, and the best of the nineteenth-century magazines for children.

Kiefer, Monica. American children through their books, 1700–1835. Philadelphia: University of Pennsylvania Press, 1948.
A social history that shows how books were used to influence the manners and morals of children in the early days of the colonies and the young republic. Extensive footnotes and bibliography.

Livengood, William W., comp. Americana, as taught to the tune of a hickory stick. New York: Women's National Book Assn., 1954.
Introduction by Mary Ellen Chase. An anthology of original extracts from American textbooks. Illustrated.

Peabody, Elizabeth P. Record of a school. Boston: Munroe, 1835; reprint: New York: Arno, 1969.
An account of the remarkable and controversial school that Bronson Alcott (Louisa's father) developed on the educational principles of Pestalozzi.

Roller, Bert. "Early American writers for children," *The elementary English review* 8:213–17, 224, 241–42, 250 (1931); 9:233–34, 244, 248 (1932).
The subject of the first two articles is Eliza Lee Follen; and of the third, Lydia H. Sigourney.

Rosenbach, Abraham S. Wolf. "American children's books," in his *Books and bidders, the adventures of a bibliophile,* p. 179–209. Boston: Little, 1927.
Written from the standpoint of a collector, but gives descriptions of a number of interesting volumes and also includes illustrations.

———. Early American children's books. Portland, Me.: Southworth, 1933; reprint: New York: Kraus, 1966.
Includes bibliographical descriptions of the books in his private collection; foreword by A. E. Newton.
For annotation, see "General bibliography" under "Catalogs and bibliographies."

Shaffer, Ellen. "The children's books of the American Sunday-School Union," *American book collector* 17, no. 2:21–28 (October, 1966).
An important article by the former rare books librarian at the Free Library of Philadelphia, tracing the history of the American Sunday School Union and describing the types of books edited by this most prolific of all nineteenth-century American publishers for children. Numerous illustrations and facsimiles.

Shipton, Clifford K. Isaiah Thomas, printer, patriot and philanthropist, 1749–1831. Rochester, N.Y.: Leo Hart, 1948.
Chapter 4 covers books for children published by this early American printer.

Tassin, Algernon. "Books for children," in *The Cambridge history of American literature,* edited by William P. Trent et al., v.2, p. 396–409. New York: Putnam, 1918.
A general survey. Bibliography, p. 631–38.

Thompson, Lawrence R. "The printing and publishing activities of the American Tract Society from 1825 to 1850," *Papers* (Bibliographical Society of America) 35:81–114 (2d quarter, 1941).
See especially "Publications for children," p. 92–97.

Train, Arthur. "A grandfather discovered," in his *Puritan's progress,* p. 84–94. New York: Scribner, 1931.
Pictures the district school in the time of the author's grandfather, with mention of the books commonly used or read by children.

University of Chicago. Science in nineteenth century children's books. Edited by Patricia B. Pond. Chicago: University of Chicago Press, n.d.
Subtitle: "an exhibition based on the Encyclopaedia Britannica Historical Collection of books for children in The University of Chicago Library, held during the celebration of the University's seventy-fifth anniversary year, August through October, 1966, Harper Memorial Library." In-

cludes numerous titles published in America before 1850. Arranged in categories to show: The beginnings of science books for children; Science as a source of salvation and moral behavior; Science as a source of knowledge about the world; Science as a source of progress; Science as a source of conflict.

Walter, Frank Keller. "A poor but respectable relation: the Sunday school library," *Library quarterly* 12:731–39 (July, 1942).
Traces the development, assesses the importance, and describes the characteristics of the Sunday school library from the late eighteenth to the early twentieth century.

Weiss, Harry Bischoff. "Mahlon Day, early New York printer, bookseller and publisher of children's books," *Bulletin* (New York Public Library) 45:1007–21 (December, 1941).
Classifies publications by type, sources of themes; describes illustrations; and gives prices.

————. The printers and publishers of children's books in New York City, 1698–1830. New York: New York Public Library, 1948.
Reprinted from the *Bulletin* of the New York Public Library, 52:383–400 (August, 1948). An essay giving the history of publishing trends, important printing and publishing houses, and their characteristic publications. Includes a list of about one hundred printers and publishers with dates, addresses, lists of publications. The Rosenbach, Evans, and Gumuchian catalogs are cited.

————. "Samuel Wood & sons, early New York publishers of children's books," *Bulletin* (New York Public Library) 46:755–71 (September, 1942).
Identifies this publisher of cautionary verses and other pieces in which a strong element of religion was almost always present. Includes a checklist of publications, 1806–61.

————. William Charles, early caricaturist, engraver and publisher of children's book. New York: New York Public Library, 1932.
Includes a list of works by Charles in the New York Public Library and certain other collections, as well as six reproductions from children's books. Reprinted from the *Bulletin* of the New York Public Library, December, 1931.

Welch, d'Alté A. A bibliography of American children's books printed prior to 1821. Worcester, Mass.: American Antiquarian Society, 1972.
A landmark publication in the study of children's literature, collating and locating books in alphabetical arrangement. Index of printers, publishers, and imprints.

Welsh, Charles. "The early history of children's books in New England," *New England magazine* 26, n.s., 20:147–60 (1899).
Good résumé.

Wishy, Bernard. The child and the republic: the dawn of modern American child nurture. Philadelphia: University of Pennsylvania Press, 1967.
A study of the period from 1830 to 1900, showing how American parents "tried to instill the highest moral virtues in their children and at the same time prepare them for the hustling world of commerce."

BIOGRAPHICAL SKETCHES

Gaine, Hugh. The journals of Hugh Gaine, printer. Edited by Paul Leicester Ford. 2v. New York: Dodd, 1902; reprint: New York: Arno, 1970.
Like John Newbery, Hugh Gaine, a pioneer printer of colonial New York, sold patent medicines. His attractive toy books antedate those of Isaiah Thomas.

Jordan, Alice M. "Susan Warner and her *Wide, wide world*," in her *From Rollo to Tom Sawyer*, p. 82–92. Boston: Horn Book, 1948.
The author calls Susan Warner "the first writer to combine for girls in their teens American characters with the national background."

MacLeod, Anne Scott. A moral tale: children's fiction and American culture 1820–1860. Hamden, Conn.: Shoe String Press, 1975.
Contains extensive analysis of work by most of the writers listed in this chapter, and some useful references to less-known authors.

Marble, Annie Russell. From 'prentice to patron: the life story of Isaiah Thomas. New York: Appleton, 1935.
An account of the early printer of Worcester, Massachusetts, famous for his publication of children's books.

Meigs, Cornelia. "Printer's ink," in Meigs et al., *A critical history of children's literature*, p. 120–25. Rev. ed. New York: Macmillan, 1969.
Gives detail on publications for children by Isaiah Thomas of Worcester, Hugh Gaine of New York City, and other early American printers. Also assesses the role played by Sunday school tracts.

————. "Two indefatigable Americans," in Meigs et al., *A critical history of children's literature*, p. 131–40. Rev. ed. New York: Macmillan, 1969.
Good coverage of the work of Samuel Goodrich and Jacob Abbott.

SOME REPRESENTATIVE BOOKS

Bunyan, John. The Christian pilgrim. . . . 2v. Worcester, Mass.: Isaiah Thomas, 1798.
An abridgment of *Pilgrim's progress*, stressing the "wonderful adventures and miraculous escapes" most enjoyed by children.

Dodsley, Robert. Select fables of Aesop and other fabulists. Philadelphia: Robert Bell, 1777.

The famous and remarkable history of Sir Richard Whittington. Boston: T. and J. Fleet, 177–?.

Fielding, Sarah. The governess, or, little female academy. Philadelphia: Thomas Dobson, 1791.

The history of little King Pippin. Philadelphia: Young, Stewart, & M'Culloch, 1786.

John-the-Giant Killer, *esq.*, *pseud.* Food for the mind, or a new riddle-book, compiled for the use of the great and the little good boys and girls, in the United States. Boston: S. Hall, 1798.
Taken from a book of the same title "compiled for . . . England, Scotland and Ireland, originally published in London, 1778."

A little pretty pocket-book. Worcester, Mass.: Isaiah Thomas, 1787.
One of many titles pirated from the publications of John Newbery.

Nurse Truelove's New Year's gift, or, the book of books for children. Worcester, Mass.: Isaiah Thomas, 1786.
Advertised other books published by Thomas, following Newbery's example. Slightly retold for American children with appropriate American references.

Perrault, Charles. Fairy tales, or, histories of past times. Haverhill, Mass.: Peter Edes, 1794.

The prodigal daughter, or, a strange and wonderful relation. Danvers, Mass.: E. Russell, 1776?.
Harvard College has English chapbooks with this title. The story is a long moral tale, with a trance and a vision.

The renowned history of Valentine and Orson. Haverhill, Mass.: Peter Edes, 1794.
In Irish edition of 1734 describes this story as having been "translated out of French into English, above two hundred years ago, by one Henry Watson."

Swift, Jonathan. The adventures of Captain Gulliver, in a voyage to the islands of Lilliput and Brobdingnag. Philadelphia: Young & M'Culloch, 1787.

Telescope, Tom, *pseud.* The Newtonian system of philosophy. London: John Newbery, 1761; reprint: Philadelphia: Jacob Johnson, 1803.
Subtitle: ". . . adapted to the capacities of young gentlemen and ladies, and familiarized and made entertaining by objects with which they are intimately acquainted: being the substance of six lectures read to the Lilliputian society, by Tom Telescope, A.M." Charles Welsh supposes that this was written by Oliver Goldsmith.

Wiseman, Billy, *pseud.* The puzzling cap: a choice collection of riddles, in familiar verse. New York: William Durell for Thomas B. Jansen, 1800.

The world turned upside down. Boston: John D. M'Dougall, 1780?.
Nonsense rhymes.

Zeisberger, David. Essay of a Delaware-Indian and English spelling-book. Philadelphia: Henry Miller, 1776.

LITERARY ANNUALS

■ A few representative annuals are listed, but many others of interest may be added or substituted. Annuals available should be studied for the authors whose work is included and for the "embellishments." The following entries are based in part upon data in Faxon's *Literary annuals and gift-books*. See also the work by Thompson listed below.

The American juvenile keepsake. Edited by Mrs. Barbara Hoole Hofland. New York: C. Wells, 1834.
Interesting because of its international character.

The child's gem. 1833–45.
Issues for 1833, 1838, 1842, 1844–45 are noted in *Literary annuals and gift-books*. Some of the volumes were published by Samuel Colman of New York; the one for 1845 was a publication of T. H. Carter of Boston.

The gift: a Christmas and New Year's present. Edited by Eliza Leslie. Philadelphia: Carey & Hart, 1836–40.
No volume was issued in 1838. Earlier volumes of this annual and those published later than 1840 do not indicate Eliza Leslie as editor.

The pearl, or, affection's gift: a Christmas and New Year's present. Philadelphia: various publishers, 1829–49.
Issues for 1829–1834, 1836–1837, 1840 and 1849 are noted in *Literary annuals and gift-books*.

The talisman. New York: Elam Bliss, 1828–30.
Volumes for 1828 and 1829 were edited by Wil-

liam Cullen Bryant under the name Francis Herbert.

The token: a Christmas and New Year's present. Edited by S. G. Goodrich. Boston: various publishers, 1828–42.
Issued first in 1828, it continued yearly until 1842. All of the volumes were edited by Goodrich with the exception of the second, edited by N. P. Willis. Some of Hawthorne's *Twice-told tales* first appeared in *The token*.

Youth's keep-sake: a New Year, Christmas, and birthday present, for both sexes. New York: J. C. Ricker, 1834.

BIBLIOGRAPHY AND CRITICISM

Cairns, William B. "Annuals and gift-books," in *The Cambridge history of American literature,* edited by William P. Trent, et al. v. 2, p. 170–75. New York: Macmillan, 1965.

Faxon, Frederick Winthrop, comp. Literary annuals and gift-books: a bibliography with a descriptive introduction. (Useful reference series, no. 6) Boston: Boston Book Co., 1912; reprint: Pinner, Middlesex, England: Private Libraries Association, 1973.
An alphabetical listing, by title. Also a chronological index of English and American publica-

tions. Reprint includes supplementary essays by Eleanore Jamieson and Iain Bain.

Kirkham, Edwin Bruce, and John W. Fink, comps. Indices to American literary annuals and gift books 1825–65. New Haven, Conn.: Research Publishers, 1975.
To be used with Thompson's *American literary annuals and gift books 1825–1865* (below).

"Old annuals," *The Atlantic monthly,* 71:138–41 (1893).
A reminiscent article in which the (anonymous) author records his delight as a boy in these old volumes from which he "won a love of letters of high-bred style and finished surroundings which did him good in after years."

Repplier, Agnes. "The accursed annual," in her *A happy half-century, and other essays,* p. 196–216. Boston: Houghton, 1908.
A notable satirist writes of a period "when literary reputations were . . . cheaply gained."

Thompson, Ralph. American literary annuals and gift books, 1825–1865. New York: Wilson, 1936; reprint: Hamden, Conn.: Shoe String Press, 1967.
Includes an extensive catalog.

PERIODICALS

■ The sets of these periodicals that have been available for examination are incomplete. It has seemed advisable, therefore, not to attempt full entries, but to give titles and inclusive dates when known. Whatever examples of early magazines are at hand may be used for illustration.

The juvenile magazine, or, miscellaneous repository of useful information. 1802–3(?).
There were four volumes in 1802. The contents "were so largely drawn from English sources that it was probably, like the toy-books, pirated from an English publisher."—Halsey's *Forgotten books of the American nursery.*

The juvenile miscellany. Edited by Mrs. D. L. Child. 1826–34.
Established in September, 1826. Three numbers were issued in that year and "thereafter it appeared every other month until Aug. 1834, when it was succeeded by a magazine of the same name conducted by Sarah J. Hale."—Halsey's *Forgotten books of the American nursery.* Lydia Child's name appears on the title page of some of the volumes, but not on all. A new series was commenced in September, 1828, and a third series in September, 1832.

The juvenile miscellany. Edited by Mrs. S. J. Hale. 1834–?.

"This periodical is a landmark in the history of story-writing for the American child. . . . For its pages Mrs. Sigourney, Miss Eliza Leslie, Mrs. Wells, Miss Sedgwick . . . gladly sent stories of American scenes and incidents."—Halsey's *Forgotten books of the American nursery.*

The juvenile repository. Edited by a lady. 1833–35(?).
This was published in Boston.

Merry's museum. 1841–72?
Commenced in 1841 by S. G. Goodrich. After the discontinuance of *Parley's magazine* the latter title was added. Continued under the exclusive editorship of Goodrich until he went to Europe in 1850, when the Rev. S. T. Allen became home editor. At the close of the fourteenth year (the twenty-eighth semiannual volume, 1854) Goodrich's connection with the work ceased.—Adapted from Goodrich's *Recollections of a lifetime.* There were several variations in title during the period of publication. Beginning in 1842, there were regular semiannual volumes. A new series numbering begins with 1868.

Parley's magazine. 1833–44.
Commenced by S. G. Goodrich. He gave up the editorship after the first year, but "the popularity of the name of Peter Parley insured a goodly num-

ber of subscriptions from the beginning, and the life of 'Parley's Magazine' was somewhat longer than any of its predecessors."—Halsey's *Forgotten books of the American nursery*. After this magazine ceased publication the name was added to *Merry's museum*.

The youth's companion: an illustrated weekly paper for young people and the family. 1827–29.
Established in Boston in 1827 by Nathaniel Willis, joint owner with Asa Rand of the *Boston recorder*. In 1857 Willis sold *The youth's companion* to Daniel S. Ford and John W. Olmstead, who continued it together until 1867. Ford, however, devoted his energies to the development of the magazine until 1899. In the nineties, the circulation was more than half a million. The *Companion* was merged with *The American boy* in September, 1929.

Youth's penny gazette. 1843–?.
Published by the American Sunday School Union. A list of the publications of the American Sunday School Union is given in the second volume, in an insert between p. 74 and 75.

CRITICISM

Altstetter, M. F. "Early American magazines for children," *Peabody journal of education* 19:131–36 (November, 1941).
Includes brief discussion of some little-known titles, with dates of publication.

Magoun, F. Alexander. "In the *Companion's* youth," *The youth's companion* 100:856 (November 11, 1926).
Appreciative sketch of Daniel Ford, who succeeded Nathaniel Willis as owner and editor of *The youth's companion*, derived from an interview with a former reader for *The youth's companion* staff and a niece of Ford.

Mott, Frank Luther. A history of American magazines, 1741–1850. New York: Appleton, 1930.
Does not deal to any extent with magazines for children, but there are general references, p. 29, 144–45, 492–93; also brief references for a few individual magazines, such as *Parley's magazine,*

p. 622–23 and *Merry's museum*, p. 713–15. "Chronological list of magazines," p. 785–809.

Nolen, Eleanor Weakley. "Nineteenth century children's magazines," *Horn book magazine* 15:55–60 (January–February, 1939).
An excellent discussion that covers numerous magazines of the first half of the century.

Richardson, Lyon Norman. "The children's magazine," in his *A history of early American magazines, 1741–1789*, p. 334–37. New York: Nelson, 1931; reprint: New York: Octagon, 1966.
Account of the first American magazine for children. It was published in Hartford, Connecticut, in 1789, but only four numbers were issued.

Smith, Janie M. "*Rose bud*, a magazine for children," *Horn book magazine* 19:15–20 (January–February, 1943).
Describes a magazine of high quality, but little known, published during the 1830s in Charleston, South Carolina.

Stephens, Charles Asbury. "How I came to write for *The youth's companion*," *The youth's companion* 100:891 (November 18, 1926).
Author was one of the periodical's mainstays for a number of years.

Trowbridge, John Townsend. ["*The youth's companion*,"] in his *My own story*, p. 326–31. Boston: Houghton, 1903.
Supplements the accounts of the origin of *The youth's companion* by telling something of the magazine's later history and especially of Daniel Ford, to whom, as editor, the success of the magazine was largely due. Trowbridge's autobiography appeared in a condensed form in *The Atlantic monthly*, January–May, 1903.

Youth's Companion. Edited by Lovell Thompson, with three former *Companion* editors, M. A. De Wolfe Howe, Arthur Stanwood Pier, and Harford Powel. Boston: Houghton, 1954.
An anthology with many selections, divided chronologically into four sections. The editor's foreword gives a brief history of the magazine. Index of authors' names.

INDIVIDUAL WRITERS

Jacob Abbott

Abbott, Jacob. Aunt Margaret, or, how John True kept his resolutions. (Harper's story books) New York: Harper, c1856.

———. The Franconia stories. 10v. New York: Harper, 1878–81.
The volumes are: Malleville, Wallace, Mary Erskine, Mary Bell, Beechnut, Rodolphus, Ellen Linn, Stuyvesant, Caroline, Agnes. This series represents Abbott at his best. The volumes were first published between 1851 and 1854, when he gave

up teaching to devote himself to writing, and at the beginning of his twenty years of greatest literary activity.

———. History of King Alfred of England. New York: Harper, c1849.
Includes engravings.

———. History of Nero. New York: Harper, c1853.
Includes engravings. Of the long list of historical biographies, twenty-two were written by Jacob Abbott; the others by his brother, John Stevens Cabot Abbott.

————. Jasper, or, the spoiled child recovered. (Harper's story books) New York: Harper, c1857.
This series numbered thirty-six volumes, published 1852–57.

————. John True, or, the Christian experience of an honest boy. (Harper's story books) New York: Harper, c1856.

————. Learning to talk, or, entertaining and instructive lessons in the use of language. (Harper's picture books for the nursery) New York: Harper, c1855.
Includes engravings.

————. Rambles among the Alps. (Harper's story books) New York: Harper, c1856.

————. Rollo on the Rhine. (Rollo's tour in Europe) Boston: De Wolfe, c1858.
There were ten volumes of Rollo's tour in Europe.

————. Rollo's museum. New ed. rev. Boston: Phillips, c1855.
The well-known Rollo series comprised fourteen volumes. The first of these, *Rollo learning to talk*, was published in 1834.

■ Only a few of Abbott's many books are suggested here. These are representative, but others may be added or substituted.

BIOGRAPHY AND CRITICISM

Abbott, Jacob. The Harper establishment, or, how the story books are made. New York: Harper, 1855; reprint: Hamden, Conn.: Shoe String Press, 1956.
Reprint includes an epistle dedicatory by Jacob Blanck. Reprint half title: "his Harper's story books: a series of narratives, dialogues, biographies, and tales, for the instruction and entertainment of the young. A reproduction of Jacob Blanck's copy of the original edition published in 1855.

Abbott, Lyman. "My father," in his *Reminiscences*, p. 141–58. Boston: Houghton, 1923.
The incidents related illustrate the character of Jacob Abbott and his methods of dealing with children. Numerous other references are scattered throughout the book.

————. ————, *The outlook* 107:718–29 (1914).
Reproductions of a daguerrotype picture and a silhouette of Jacob Abbott.

————. "My father, the friend of children," *The outlook* 129:55–58 (1921).
Indicates the philosophical principles of family and school government which were inculcated and illustrated in Jacob Abbott's books for children.

Abbott, Willis John. ["Jacob and John S. C. Abbott,"] in his *Watching the world go by*, p. 34–36. Boston: Little, 1933; reprint, Brooklyn: Beekman, 1974.
Reference to the connection of the Abbotts with

the house of Harper. The writer was the grandson of J. S. C. Abbott.

Jordan, Alice M. "The children of Jacob Abbott," *Horn book magazine* 10:221–27 (1934).
How the educational principles of Jacob Abbott were exemplified in his Rollo and Jonas, Beechnut, and other characters.

Osgood, Fletcher. "Jacob Abbott: a neglected New England author," *New England magazine* 36, new ser. 30:471–79 (1904).
"To help restrain our literary straining . . . to make our writing genuine to the core and very limpid, to aid our characterizations to be strong and true . . . we need today . . . a Jacob Abbott literary cult."

Titcomb, Mary. "A delightful grandfather: Jacob Abbott among children," *Wide awake* 14:85–92 (1882).
Though written for young people, this article is of value in showing how the principles underlying Abbott's stories for children were exemplified in practice. Brings out his humanness, his real interest in children, and his novel methods of dealing with them, emphasizing especially his wonderful faculty of combining amusement and instruction.

Weber, Carl J. A bibliography of Jacob Abbott. Waterville, Me.: Colby College, 1948.
Subtitle: "based primarily upon the Abbott collection in the Colby College Library and supplemented by the Jacob Abbott books in a score of other libraries." A checklist of books by the author of the Rollo series, the Franconia stories, Harper story books, and others. Index of titles.

Lydia Maria Child

Child, Lydia Maria Francis. Flowers for children. 3v. New York: C. S. Francis; Boston: J. H. Francis, 1844–46.
Arranged in three parts "for children eight or nine years old; for children from four to six years old; for children of eleven and twelve years of age."

————. The girl's own book. Boston: Clark Austin, 1833.
The illustrations for the games are by Francis Graeter, and there is a frontispiece in color. Includes two songs with music.

————. Hobomok: a tale of early times. Boston: Cummings & Hilliard, 1824.
Massachusetts in the colonial period. The author's first book.

————. Philothea: a romance. Boston: Otis, Broaders, 1836.
"The delight of girls. The young Alcotts made a dramatic version . . . which they acted under the

trees. Louisa made a magnificent Aspasia, which was a part much to her fancy."—Ednah Dow Cheney, *Louisa May Alcott*.

———. The rebels, or, Boston before the Revolution. Boston: Cummings & Hilliard, 1836.
Subtitle: "by the author of Hobomok . . . ."

———. Biographical sketches of great and good men, designed for the amusement and instruction of young persons. Boston: Putnam & Hunt; Philadelphia: Thomas T. Ash, 1828.
"These biographical 'Sketches' were prepared by the editor of the *Juvenile miscellany*."—Advertisement. Contents: Benjamin Franklin; Captain John Smith; General Israel Putnam; Christopher Columbus; John Ledyard; Sir Benjamin West; William Penn; Baron De Steuben; Rev. John Elliot; Baron De Kalb.

BIOGRAPHY AND CRITICISM

Child, Lydia Maria Francis. Letters, with a biographical introduction by J. G. Whittier and an appendix by Wendell Phillips. Boston: Houghton, 1883; reprint: New York: Arno, 1969.
"Introduction," p. v–xxv. "List of Mrs. Child's works; with the date of their first publication as far as ascertained," p. 272–74.

Higginson, Thomas Wentworth. "Lydia Maria Child," in James Parton et al., *Eminent women of the age*, p. 108–41. Hartford, Conn.: S. M. Betts, 1868.
An appreciative account of her life and work.

Jordan, Alice M. "*The juvenile miscellany* and its literary ladies," in her *From Rollo to Tom Sawyer*, p. 46–60. Boston: Horn Book, 1948.
America's "first real magazine for children," its editor, Lydia Maria Child, and some of the best-known women who contributed to *The juvenile miscellany*.

Lowell, James Russell. "A fable for critics," in his *The poetical works*, p. 142–44. Household ed. Boston: Houghton, 1917.
A poetical sketch, ending with the lines,

> What a wealth would it bring
> to the narrow and sour
> Could they be as a Child but
> for one little hour!

McDonald, Gerald D. "A portrait from letters: Lydia Maria Child 1802–1880," *Bulletin* (New York Public Library) 36:617–22 (September, 1932).
An excellent biographical sketch, identifying Lydia Child as the author of her verses for Thanksgiving Day, "Over the river and through the wood."

Whittier, John Greenleaf. "Lydia Maria Child," in his *Old portraits and modern sketches*, p. 286–308. Boston: Houghton, 1889.
A biographical sketch written as an introduction to a collection of the *Letters of Lydia Maria Child* published in 1883 (see above).

James Fenimore Cooper

Cooper, James Fenimore. The deerslayer, or, the first war-path. London: Richard Bentley, 1841; Philadelphia: Lea & Blanchard, 1841.

———. ———. New York: Scribner, 1925.
This is the beautiful edition with pictures by N. C. Wyeth. In his "Preface to the Leather-stocking tales," the author makes an interesting comment on the character of Natty Bumppo and gives the order of publication of the famous series. *The deerslayer* is the first in order of reading and the last of publication.

———. The last of the Mohicans: a narrative of 1757. New York: Scribner, 1919.
Second in the Leather-stocking series, showing Natty Bumppo as "middle-aged and in the fullest vigor of manhood."

———. ———. Edited, abridged, and annotated by Robin S. Wright. Twickenham, England: Felix Gluck Press, 1973; New York: McKay, 1976.
Copiously illustrated to show wildlife, Indian tools, and military equipment of the period in America.

BIOGRAPHY AND CRITICISM

Cruse, Amy. "Books from America," in her *The Victorians and their reading*, p. 236–39. Boston: Houghton, 1935.
This chapter begins with a description of the impact made by The Leather-stocking tales on English readers of the period.

Grossman, James. James Fenimore Cooper. London: Methuen, 1950.
A portrait of Cooper and his family, with a discussion by a literary critic of Cooper's adventure tales, among other types of writing.

House, Kay S. Cooper's Americans. Columbus: Ohio State University Press, 1966.
In a series of connected essays, the author shows how Cooper explored America's links with, and separation from, both aboriginal and European cultures.

Meigs, Cornelia. "War paint and the glimmerglass," in Meigs et al., *A critical history of children's literature*, p. 128–30. Rev. ed. New York: Macmillan, 1969.
A succinct assessment of Cooper's place in children's literature and of his stature as a writer.

Samuel Griswold Goodrich

Goodrich, Samuel Griswold (*pseud.* Peter Parley).
The balloon travels of Robert Merry and his
young friends over various countries in Europe,
edited by Peter Parley. New York: J. C. Derby,
1859.
Written in dialogue form. Illustrated by engravings from original designs.

————. The first book of history, for children and
youth, by the author of Peter Parley's tales.
Boston: Richardson, Lord & Holbrook, 1831.
A history of America. Engravings and maps.

————. Parley's present for all seasons. New York:
Appleton, 1854.
Short stories and dialogues.

————. Peter Parley's tales about Asia. Boston: Gray
& Bowen, 1830.
With a map and numerous engravings.

————. Tales about the sea and the islands in the
Pacific ocean, by Peter Parley. London: Richards, 1902.
Originally published in 1831 in two volumes,
Peter Parley's tales of the sea and *Peter Parley's
tales about the islands in the Pacific ocean*. Engravings.

————. The tales of Peter Parley about Africa. Boston: Gray & Bowen, 1830.
Engravings.

————. The tales of Peter Parley about America.
Boston: S. G. Goodrich, 1827.
With this book, Goodrich began his adventures
in authorship for children. It was designed to give
the first ideas of geography and history. Engravings.

BIOGRAPHY AND CRITICISM

Darton, Frederick Joseph Harvey. "Peter Parley
and the battle of the children's books," *The
Cornhill magazine* 73:542–58 (November, 1932).
Chiefly an account of the spurious Parley books
and of Goodrich's relations with English publishers. Also notes the conflict of educational ideas as
represented in the matter-of-fact Peter Parley books
and the imaginative literature presented in Felix
Summerly's *Home treasury*.

————. "Two New Englands: 'Peter Parley' and
'Felix Summerly'," in his *Children's books in En-
gland*, p. 227–43. 2d ed. Cambridge: Cambridge
University Press, 1958.

Goodrich, Samuel Griswold (*pseud.* Peter Parley).
Peter Parley's own story. New York: Sheldon,
1864.
An abridgment of Goodrich's *Recollections of a
lifetime* (listed below). Does not include the appendix.

————. Recollections of a lifetime, or, men and
things I have seen, in a series of familiar letters
to a friend, historical, biographical, anecdotical,
and descriptive. 2v. New York: Miller, Orton &
Mulligan, 1857; reprint: Detroit: Gale, 1967.
For an account of the books Goodrich read as a
child, see vol. 1, p. 164–74; self-education, vol. 1,
p. 417–22; visit to Hannah More, vol. 2, p. 163–
68; the Peter Parley books, vol. 2, p. 279–323. The
appendix, vol. 2, p. 537–52, includes notes about
Goodrich's various literary undertakings, a list of
works written or edited by him, and a list of spurious Parley books.

Jordan, Alice M. "Peter Parley," in her *From Rollo
to Tom Sawyer*, p. 61–71. Boston: Horn Book,
1948.
A short biographical sketch of Samuel Griswold
Goodrich with a critical estimate of his influence
in America and abroad.

Roselle, Daniel. Samuel Griswold Goodrich, creator of Peter Parley: a study of his life and work.
Albany: State University of New York Press,
1968.
Goodrich as publisher, writer, social reformer,
and civil servant. There are three chapters on
"Peter Parley."

Stevens, William Oliver. " 'Uncle' Peter Parley,"
St. Nicholas 53:78–81 (1925).
Written for children, emphasizing the contrasts
between the Peter Parley books and those available in 1925. Reproduces the cover for *Parley's
magazine* and one of the pages; also other cuts.

Sarah Josepha Hale

Hale, Sarah Josepha Buell. "Mary's lamb by S. J.
H.," *The juvenile miscellany* n.s. 5:64 (Septem-
ber, October, 1830).
The first appearance of this poem.

————. Poems for our children. Pt. 1. Boston: Marsh,
Capen & Lyon, 1830.
Subtitle: "designed for families, Sabbath schools,
and infant schools, written to inculcate moral truths
and virtuous sentiments." Slim paper-bound volume containing fifteen poems, of which "Mary's
lamb" is the second (p. 6). The dedication is "To
all Good Children in the United States," and the
author states that she hopes that the pretty songs
and poems will induce them "to love truth and
goodness." The first book appearance of "Mary's
lamb."

————. The school song book. Boston: Allen & Ticknor, 1834.
Subtitle: "adapted to the scenes of the school
room; written for American children and youth."
An 1841 edition, without music, has title *My little
song book*.

——. ed. Aunt Mary's new stories for young people. Boston: J. Munroe, 1849.

——. Gift to young friends, or, the guide to good. New York: E. Dunigan, [1842?].
Eight elegant engravings. Contents: The good man of the mill; From whom all things come; The lost purse; The great dunce; Self-will; The careless boy; Good boys; The way to save.
Typical of numerous other collections edited by Sarah Hale for juvenile readers.

BIOGRAPHY AND CRITICISM

Finley, Ruth Ebright. The lady of Godey's: Sarah Josepha Hale. Philadelphia: Lippincott, 1931; reprint: New York: Arno, 1974.
Valuable as a full-length portrait of Sarah Hale and for the habits, customs, and viewpoints of her era. See particularly the chapters "A female writer" and "Mary's lamb and Mr. Ford," p. 263–305. See also p. 310–11. Nine plates in color and other illustrations in half-tone, including a reproduction of the well-known poem as it appeared in *The juvenile miscellany* in 1830. For a note on *The juvenile miscellany* see "Periodicals" in this chapter.

Griffith, George Bancroft. "Author of 'Mary's little lamb,'" *Granite state magazine* 1:210–14 (1906).
The author claims that Sarah Hale was the author and that Newport in Sullivan county was the scene of the nursery rhyme. Mrs. Hale was born on a farm in the hamlet of Guild, about two miles from the center of Newport village, and it is said that one of her pet lambs frequently followed her to school.

Hale, Richard Walden. "'Mary had a little lamb,' and its author," *The century magazine* 67, n.s. 45:738–42 (1904).
An account of the controversy regarding the authorship of the poem, incidentally giving an outline of Sarah Hale's life. Reproduces the title page of *Poems for our children* and the page on which "Mary's lamb" appears. There is also a portrait of Sarah Hale. Richard Hale refutes the claim that the poem was written by John Roulstone as indicated in a publication of the Merrymount Press, which issued in 1920 a facsimile of the poem as copied and signed by Mary E. Tyler of Somerville, Massachusetts.

Mutch, Verna Eugenia. "Let us give thanks," *National historical magazine* 72:2–7 (1938).
The story of Sarah Josepha Hale and of her successful campaign for the national celebration of Thanksgiving Day.

Nathaniel Hawthorne

Hawthorne, Nathaniel. The complete Greek stories of Nathaniel Hawthorne from *The wonder book* and *Tanglewood tales.* New York: Watts, 1963.

In this edition, the original framework for each story is omitted. A foreword by Kathleen Lines gives a biographical sketch of Hawthorne and analyzes the style and method he used in retelling Greek myths for children. A postscript by Roger Lancelyn Green traces the sources of the myths. Illustrations by Harold Jones.

——. Grandfather's chair: a history for youth. Boston: E. P. Peabody; New York: Wiley & Putnam, 1841.
This was continued by his *Famous old people* and *Liberty tree*, 1841. The three were later issued together as *The whole history of grandfather's chair.*

——. Peter Parley's common school history. 4th ed. Philadelphia: Marshall, 1838.
Illustrated with engravings. Advertisement: "A few copies of this work, with considerable additions, will be published in 2 vols. under the title of Peter Parley's Universal History."

——. Peter Parley's universal history on the basis of geography. 2v. in 1. New York: Newman & Ivison, 1853.
The *Universal history*, first published in 1837, is the one written by Nathaniel Hawthorne with the assistance of his sister. Referring to this, Mr. G. P. Lathrop says, "There are various little particulars in this ingenious abridgment which recall Hawthorne . . . though the book has probably undergone some changes in successive editions." The *Universal history* should be used if available but the *Common school history* listed here would seem to be a shortened version. See, for example, the description of George the Fourth, p. 307. Hawthorne's name does not appear on the title pages and the books are usually listed under the name of Mr. Goodrich or Peter Parley. Maps and engravings.

——. Tanglewood tales for girls and boys; being a second Wonder-book. Boston: Ticknor, 1853.
Contents: The wayside [introductory]; The minotaur; The pygmies; The dragon's teeth; Circe's palace; The pomegranate seeds; The golden fleece. Illustrations.

——. A wonder-book for girls and boys. London: Henry G. Bohn, 1852; Boston: Ticknor, 1852.
Engravings by Baker from designs by Billings. Contents: The Gorgon's head; The golden touch; The paradise of children; The three golden apples; The miraculous pitcher; The Chimera.

■ Among illustrators of later editions of Hawthorne are Walter Crane, Maxfield Parrish, Arthur Rackham, and Fritz Eichenberg.

BIOGRAPHY AND CRITICISM

Van Doren, Mark. Nathaniel Hawthorne. New York: W. Sloane, 1949; reprint: Westport, Conn.: Greenwood, 1973.

Includes some pages of discussion on Hawthorne's books for children, valuable because of Van Doren's prestige as a critic. A long bibliographical note is appended.

Woodberry, George Edward. Nathaniel Hawthorne. Boston: Houghton, 1902; reprint: Detroit, Gale, 1967.
A biography chiefly valuable as an appreciative criticism of Hawthorne's writings. Discussion of *A wonder-book* and *Tanglewood tales,* noting the period at which they were written and their character, p. 220–24.

Washington Irving

Irving, Washington. The Alhambra, palace of mystery and splendor. (New children's classics) Selected and arranged by Mabel Williams. New York: Macmillan, 1953.
An edition for young readers, illustrated by Louis Slobodkin.

———. The bold dragoon and other ghostly tales. Selected and edited by Anne Carroll Moore. New York: Knopf, 1930, 1967.
Includes five of Irving's best mystery stories. Anne Carroll Moore gives an appreciation of Irving in an introduction.

———. The legend of Sleepy Hollow. Drexel Hill, Pa.: Bell Publishing Co., [n.d.]; Philadelphia: McKay, [1928?].
With illustrations by Arthur Rackham.

———. ———. New York: Watts, 1966.
With illustrations by Leonard Everett Fisher.

———. Rip Van Winkle. London: Heinemann; New York: Doubleday, Page, 1905.
With illustrations by Arthur Rackham.

———. ———. New York: McKay, 1921.
With illustrations by N. C. Wyeth.

———. Rip Van Winkle as played by Joseph Jefferson. New York: Dodd, 1895; reprint: New York: AMS Press, 1969.
A play that enjoyed a long run in American cities and introduced Washington Irving's folktale to generations of children. Generously illustrated.

BIOGRAPHY AND CRITICISM

Adams, Charles. Memoir of Washington Irving. New York: Carlton & Lanahan; San Francisco: E. Thomas, 1870; reprint: (Select bibliographies reprint series) Freeport, N.Y.: Books for Libraries, 1971.
The table of contents serves as an index.

Bruce, Wallace. Along the Hudson with Washington Irving. Poughkeepsie, N.Y.: A. V. Haight,

1913; reprint: Folcroft, Pa.: Folcroft, 1970.
Includes *Legend of Sleepy Hollow, Rip Van Winkle,* and other sketches by Irving. Also a biographical sketch: Washington Irving at home and abroad; his writings, journeys, associations; and his life.

Hellman, George Sidney. Washington Irving, esquire: ambassador at large from the new world to the old. New York: Knopf, 1925.
". . . why his own day regarded him as the most distinguished citizen of the United States." Illustrated with portraits and scenes. Index.

Meigs, Cornelia, "A somnolent Dutchman and a headless Hessian," in Meigs et al., *A critical history of children's literature,* p. 126–28. Rev. ed. New York: Macmillan, 1969.
A perceptive discussion of Irving's place in the estimation of his contemporaries and in children's literature.

Eliza Leslie

Leslie, Eliza. Althea Vernon, or, the embroidered handkerchief, to which is added, Henrietta Harrison, or, the blue cotton umbrella. Philadelphia: Lea & Blanchard, 1838.

———. The American girl's book, or, occupations for play hours. Boston: Munroe & Francis, 1831.

———. Atlantic tales, or, pictures of youth. New York: C. S. Francis, 1833.
Woodcuts by Alexander Anderson from original designs. Contents: The boarding-school feast; The tell-tale; The week of idleness; Madeline Malcolm; Russel and Sidney, or, the young revolutionists, a tale of 1777.

———. Wonderful travels, being the narratives of Munchausen, Gulliver, and Sinbad abridged from the original works with numerous alterations and original designs. Boston: Munroe & Francis, 1832.

[**Leslie, Eliza.**] Stories for Adelaide, being a second series of easy reading lessons, with divided syllables, by the author of "Stories for Emma," "Young Americans," "Mirror," etc. Philadelphia: Thomas T. Ash, [n.d.].
Six plates.

BIOGRAPHY AND CRITICISM

Haven, Alice Bradley. "Personal reminiscences of Miss Eliza Leslie," *Godey's lady's book* 56:344–50 (1858).
Includes an autobiographical sketch written by Eliza Leslie in 1851.

McCauley, Helen A. "Eliza Leslie," *The magazine of history* 16:161–64 (1913).

Notes that Leslie, a little station on the Baltimore and Ohio line between Baltimore and Philadelphia, perpetuates the name of the old and distinguished Maryland family and the lady who in her day was one of the best-known writers. The *Woman's home companion* for February, 1911, contains a reproduction of the portrait by Thomas Sully in the Pennsylvania Academy of Fine Arts, Philadelphia. The portrait represents Eliza Leslie carrying a red leather portfolio marked "pencil sketches."

William Holmes McGuffey

McGuffey, William Holmes. The annotated McGuffey: selections from the McGuffey eclectic readers, 1836–1920. Edited by Stanley W. Lindberg. New York: Van Nostrand, 1976.
Selections chosen to show the method by which McGuffey readers introduced young Americans to literature of high quality.

———. McGuffey's fifth eclectic reader. New York: New American Library, 1962.
A reprint of the 1879 edition. The foreword, by Henry Steele Commager, is an excellent critical essay on the significance of the readers, which have been described as more widely read and more influential in American life during the nineteenth century than any other book except the Bible.

———. Old favorites from the McGuffey readers, 1836–1936. Edited by Harvey C. Minnich; associate editors, Henry Ford [et al.]. New York: American Book, [1936]; reprint: Detroit: Singing Tree, 1969.
Published for the 100th anniversary of the first reader. Includes selections from the first through the sixth reader as originally printed.

BIOGRAPHY AND CRITICISM

Carpenter, Charles. History of American schoolbooks. Philadelphia: University of Pennsylvania Press, 1963.
Brief but significant coverage of the publications of McGuffey readers, p. 79–86.

Ford, Henry, and D. Kenneth Laub. "The McGuffey readers," in *Bibliophile in the nursery*, edited by William Targ, p. 417–26. Cleveland: World, 1957.
A brief account by Henry Ford of his restoration of the McGuffey log cabin at Greenfield Village, Dearborn, Michigan, and a description of problems and pleasures encountered in collecting McGuffey readers.

Mosier, Richard David. Making the American mind: social and moral issues in McGuffey readers. New York: King's Crown Press, 1947; New York: Russell & Russell, 1965.
Deals at length with the influence of the readers.

Ruggles, Alice McGuffey Morrill. The story of the McGuffeys. New York: American Book, 1950.
Written by a descendant of the "Reader branch" of the family, this account is based on the available facts and on family tradition, showing the human side of the McGuffeys and giving a picture of their times. Generously illustrated.

Catharine Maria Sedgwick

Sedgwick, Catharine Maria. A love token for children, designed for Sunday school libraries. New York: Harper, 1837.
Contents: The widow Ellis and her son Willie; The magic lamp; Our robins; Old Rover; The chain of love; Mill-hill; The bantem [sic].

———. Stories for young persons. New York: Harper, 1840.
Twelve short stories, including "Eighteen hundred thirty-eight's farewell." The first story is an example of gratitude. "Marietza" is a story of the Greek war for independence, 1821. The dedication is to "The girls of the L . . . School as a memorial of many happy hours spent in the society of her dear young friends."
Catharine Sedgwick's books for children were written over a period of fourteen years. *Home* was published in 1836. Some of the other books are: *The poor rich man and the rich poor man, Live and let live, Means and ends.*

BIOGRAPHY AND CRITICISM

"Lenox in literature," *The critic* (July, 1902), p. 38–39.
Includes a portrait of Catharine Sedgwick and a picture of her home at Stockbridge.

Mallary, Raymond De Witt. "Catharine Maria Sedgwick: her message and her work," in his *Lenox and the Berkshire highlands*, p. 108–35. New York: Putnam, 1902.
The author refers to Catharine Sedgwick as one of the "foundation writers [who] deserve to be recalled for what they did." Reference to her children's books written between 1836 and 1850, p. 123–25.

Sedgwick, Catharine Maria. Life and letters. Edited by Mary E. Dewey. New York: Harper, 1871.
The author's recollections of her childhood, p. 43–49, 67–68, are of special interest, and in the letters there are various references to her books.
Contains a short account of her literary work by William Cullen Bryant, p. 437–46.

Lydia Howard Sigourney

Sigourney, Lydia Howard Huntley. The book for girls, consisting of original articles in prose and poetry. New York: Turner & Hayden, 1844.

Running title: *The girl's reading-book*. The engravings are by Alexander Anderson.

———. The boy's reading-book, in prose and poetry, for schools. New York: J. O. Taylor, 1839.

———. Olive buds. Hartford, Conn.: W. Watson, 1836.
Contents: Frank Ludlow; Victory; The farmer and soldier; France in old times; War; Walks in childhood; Christmas hymn; A short sermon; Agriculture; Peace.

———. Olive leaves. New York: Carter & Bros., 1851.
Short stories, poems, and miscellaneous articles. Contents include such titles as, Entertaining books; Rome and its rulers; The good and bad emperor; The dying Sunday school boy; The precocious infant.

———. Tales and essays for children. Hartford, Conn.: F. Canfield for F. J. Huntington, 1835.
Eleven stories, mostly connected with New England; also, a hymn.

BIOGRAPHY AND CRITICISM

Collin, Grace Lathrop. "Lydia Huntley Sigourney," *New England magazine* 33, new ser. 27:15–30 (1902).
Discusses Lydia Sigourney's literary work, chiefly her poetry, and gives an interesting picture of the period. The illustrations are from originals in the Connecticut Historical Society rooms, Hartford, and a portrait of Mrs. Sigourney serves as a frontispiece for the volume.

Haight, Gordon Sherman. Mrs. Sigourney, the sweet singer of Hartford. New Haven, Conn.: Yale University Press, 1930.
Full-length study based upon original correspondence and manuscript material. Eight illustrations. "Bibliography," p. 175–78.

"Lydia Huntley Sigourney," *American literary magazine* 4:387–400 (1849).
A contemporary sketch with portrait.
Portraits of Mrs. Sigourney will also be found in *The book buyer* for March, 1901, p. 100, and in *The delineator*, September, 1905, p. 403.

Sigourney, Lydia Howard Huntley. Letters of life. New York: Appleton, 1866.
An autobiography with descriptive list of works, p. 324–80.

Early Victorian Literature

By 1837, when Victoria came to the throne, children's literature had reached what Darton calls in *Children's books in England* "a solemn pause." The period from 1800 to 1820, called the "Dawn of Levity" by Darton and by Roger Lancelyn Green (in *Tellers of tales*), had come and gone, leaving behind such nondidactic, atypical works as *The butterfly's ball* and *The peacock "at home,"* Lambs' *Tales from Shakespear*, the poems of Ann and Jane Taylor, and *Dame Wiggins of Lee*. By 1830 or 1840, Darton says, "We have reached a period of apparent lack of central impulse." Fantasy had flamed up and died down; the moral tale had subsided in its anger and obsession. The literature can be compared to an England at peace at last.

The first twenty-five years of Victoria's reign, though peaceful, were enlivened by industrialism and reform. Reflecting the impact of these contemporary trends, children's literature began to smolder with energy and to reactivate itself to continue the revolt in children's stories begun at the turn of the century.

This period of growing energy is marked by many "firsts." Catherine Sinclair, born in 1800 in Scotland, wrote several novels, now forgotten, before she produced *Holiday house* in 1839. It is a work rife with new departures. She is considered the first writer to revolt actively, and in novel form, against the old kind of children's literature. Roger Lancelyn Green has said that in *Holiday house* she wrote the "first real story of happy childlife and the first real bit of nonsense literature." Furthermore, says Darton, "It [*Holiday house*] is the first example of real laughter and a full conscience." Catherine Sinclair was, he goes on, "the first to rollick."

Another first is Harriet Martineau's Playfellow series, including *The settlers at home, The peasant and the prince, Feats on the fiord,* and *The Crofton boys.* Published in 1841 by this social reformer and political economist, the books in the series are today considered to be among the first real adventure stories written for children.

Captain Frederick Marryat's *Masterman Ready, or, the wreck of the pacific,* also published in 1841, is considered a double first. Not only is it one of the first adventure stories written for young people; it is thought to be one of the first written specifically for boys.

The greatest first of this period, however, was not native to England. Hans Christian Andersen, born in 1805 in Odense, Denmark, published his first fairy stories and tales in Danish in 1835. They were translated into English by Mary Howitt and others, and in 1846 no fewer than four volumes of Andersen's tales appeared in England at once. Andersen's originality and his genius are unquestioned. He was undisputedly the first to create the fairy tale from within his own imagination rather than to collect and rewrite stories from traditional sources.

Darton characterizes Andersen, in part, as a symptom of the upheaval that had been brewing since 1800. Perhaps it is fair to say that he represented the climax of that revolt. By 1850, when several of Andersen's collections had become a part of nursery literature in both England and America, the victory of fantasy, as Darton terms it, was indeed in sight.

Though it produced few books for children that are read today (other than those by Andersen), the period from 1835 to 1850 can be thought of almost as a pioneering period, a time of growing energies, a ground-laying period that would lead the way for the glorious sixties and the Golden Age of children's literature that followed.

OUTLINE

I. Catherine Sinclair (1800–64)
  A. *Holiday house*
    1. Protest against prevailing type of informational book
    2. Realism of story
    3. Naturalness of characters and incidents
    4. Comparison of "Uncle David's nonsensical story" in manner and method with earlier didactic stories
    5. Modern spirit
  B. Other books
II. Mary Howitt (1799–1888)
  A. Restricted character of her early life and reading
  B. Interest in traditional tales and ballads
  C. Association of William and Mary Howitt in literary work
  D. Poetry for children
    1. Character of subjects
    2. Ballad simplicity
    3. Poems typical of her work
  E. Stories
    1. General character
    2. Literary qualities, as shown in *Strive and thrive*
    3. Popularity
    4. Character and purpose of *The children's year*
  F. Translations
    1. Andersen's *Wonderful stories for children*
    2. Otto Speckter's *Fable book*

III. Hans Christian Andersen (1805–75)
  A. Life
    1. Childhood in Odense
    2. Father's death
    3. Move to Copenhagen at age fourteen
    4. Interest and work in the theater
    5. Jonas Collins becomes Andersen's patron
    6. Andersen's late schooling
    7. Travels
    8. Popularity and fame in Denmark, Europe, and America
    9. Relationship with Jenny Lind and other women
    10. Complex personality
  B. Books and plays for adults
    1. *Improvisatore, or, life in Italy*
      a) Translated by Mary Howitt, London, 1845
    2. *Only a fiddler!* and *O.T., or life in Denmark*
      a) Translated by Mary Howitt, London, 1845
    3. *To be or not to be?*
      a) Translated by Anne S. Bushby, London, 1850
    4. *Lucky Peer*
      a) Translated by Horace E. Scudder in *Scribner's monthly*, January–April, 1871
    5. Travel books
  C. Books enjoyed by children
    1. *Eventyr og historier* (Fairy tales)

a) First published in 1835
b) Translated in four separate volumes, into English in 1846 by Mary Howitt, Caroline Peachey, and Charles Boner.
c) Problems of translation
d) Types and wide range of tales
e) Aspects of style
f) Tales of great literary accomplishment
g) Tales as miniature autobiographies
h) Modern, definitive, complete editions

D. Autobiographies
1. *Das Märchen meines Lebens ohne Dichtung*, 2v. Leipzig, 1847
   a) Translated by Mary Howitt as *The true story of my life* from the German edition, (1847)
2. *Mit livs eventyr*, Copenhagen, 1855
   a) Andersen's definitive autobiography
   b) Translated by Horace E. Scudder, New York, 1871, with an additional chapter covering the years 1855–67

IV. Harriet Martineau (1802–76)
A. Life
1. Unhappy childhood
2. First literary efforts; difficulties and successes
3. Literary industry and methods of literary work
4. Interest in social and political movements and value of work from this standpoint
5. Origin of The playfellow series
B. Children's books
1. *The settlers at home*
   a) Type of story and elements of interest
   b) Scene and period
   c) The children of the story
   d) Realistic detail
2. *The peasant and the prince*
   a) Suggestion for subject
   b) Construction of story
   c) Divided interest
   d) Effect of contrast between life of peasants and luxury of nobles
   e) Author's ability to vivify the past
   f) Use of book
3. *Feats on the fiord*
   a) Origin of book
   b) Theme and treatment
   c) Descriptions of home life and customs
   d) Characterization
   e) Style
   f) Elements of interest to boys; to girls
   g) Various ways in which book may be used
4. *The Crofton boys*
   a) Personal nature of book
   b) The heroic quality and ethical teaching

c) The character of Mrs. Proctor and the development of Hugh
d) The school spirit
e) Illustration of customs of the period
f) Comparison in interest with modern school stories

V. Captain Frederick Marryat (1792–1848)
A. His early life and naval experiences
B. His first books
1. Character and construction
2. Literary use of professional knowledge
3. Merits
4. Popularity among boys as well as with grown people
C. Books for young people
1. *Masterman Ready*
   a) How it came to be written
   b) Theories regarding books for young people
   c) Qualifications for writing this type of story
   d) Fidelity to truth and realistic detail
   e) Characters
      (1) Method of depicting
      (2) The central figure and the subordinate characters
      (3) Lack of complexity and of development
      (4) Use of contrast
         (a) The practical sailor with the theoretical Mr. Seagrave
         (b) The naughty boy with the steady and capable one
   f) Comparison with modern adventure story in part played by children
   g) Didactic quality: "One should never lose an opportunity for teaching the young"
   h) The ideals that are emphasized
   i) Comparison in literary character with *Robinson Crusoe* and *The Swiss Family Robinson*
2. *The settlers in Canada*
   a) Outline of story
   b) Salient characteristics
3. *The mission*
   a) Marryat's own description
   b) Good qualities
   c) Defects
4. *The children of the New Forest*
   a) Scene and period
   b) Elements of interest
      (1) Historical background; fairness in viewpoint
      (2) Practical interest
         (a) Resourcefulness of characters in the overcoming of difficulties
         (b) Realistic detail
      (3) Romantic interest
      (4) Spirit of adventure
   c) Use of modern illustrated edition

GENERAL REFERENCES

Cruse, Amy. The Victorians and their books. London: G. Allen & Unwin, 1935.
Attempts to show what books, good and bad, were actually read by the Victorians during the first fifty years of Victoria's reign, what they thought about them, and how their reactions influenced later books.

———. The Victorians and their reading. Boston: Houghton, 1935.
U.S. edition of *The Victorians and their books*.

Darton, Frederick Joseph Harvey. "Two New Englands," in his *Children's books in England*, p. 224–26, 243–58. 2d ed. Cambridge: Cambridge University Press, 1958.
Includes material on Catherine Sinclair, the Howitts, Marryat, and Harriet Martineau.

Eaton, Anne Thaxter. "The field of adventure in England and America," in *A critical history of children's literature*, edited by Cornelia Meigs et al., p. 214–24. Rev. ed. New York: Macmillan, 1969. Includes Marryat.

———. "The return of the fairy tale," in *A critical history of children's literature*, edited by Cornelia Meigs et al., p. 184–93. Rev. ed. New York: Macmillan, 1969.
Includes Andersen.

Ellis, Alec. Books in Victorian elementary schools. London: Library Assn., 1971.
Surveys "the availability of books in elementary schools in England and Wales during the Victorian period" and "attempts to isolate some of the conditions which were favourable or unfavourable to their use." First part covers 1830–70.

———. A history of children's reading and literature. New York: Pergamon, 1963.
Traces the development of working-class education in Britain, "relating the pattern of educational activity and the extent to which books have been used to further literacy."—preface. Chapter 2, "The dawn of literacy, 1830–1850," p. 14–29; chapter 3, "Reading for pleasure, 1830–1860," p. 30–37.

Field, Louise Frances Story (Mrs. E. M. Field). "Modern developments," in her *The child and

his book*, p. 329–31. 2d ed. London: Wells Gardner, 1892; reprint: Detroit: Singing Tree, 1968.
Discusses briefly Harriet Martineau, Mary Howitt, and Catherine Sinclair.

Green, Roger Lancelyn. "The dawn of levity," in his *Tellers of tales: British authors of books from 1800 to 1964*, p. 12–22. Rewritten and rev. ed., New York: Franklin Watts, 1965.
Includes Catherine Sinclair and Harriet Martineau.

Reinstein, Phyllis Gila. "Alice in context: a study of children's literature and the dominant culture in the eighteenth and nineteenth centuries." Ph.D. diss., Yale University, 1973.
An important study that shows how Carroll's *Alice* books depend on previous children's literature, especially the literature and cultural and social environment of the Victorian period. The author examines three classic novels, Thomas Day's *History of Sandford and Merton*, Catherine Sinclair's *Holiday house*, and Marryat's *Masterman Ready*, that represent "major subdivisions of children's literature and contain themes and techniques significant in the evolution of writing for children and relevant to the Alice books."

Stuart, Dorothy Margaret. "The early nineteenth-century boy," in her *The boy through the ages*, p. 259–81. London: Harrap, 1926.

———."In the nineteenth century," in her *The girl through the ages*, p. 299–58. London: Harrap, 1933; reprint: Detroit: Singing Tree, 1969.

Thackeray, William Makepeace. "On some illustrated children's books," *Fraser's magazine* 33:- 495–502 (1846).
Reviews Felix Summerly's *Home treasury*, Gammer Gurton's story books, Harriet Myrtle's stories for the seasons, and *The good-natured bear*, by R. H. Horne. Of interest also for its general observations on children's literature.

Thwaite, Mary F. "Flood tide: the Victorian age and Edwardian aftermath," in her *From primer to pleasure in reading*, p. 93–213. 2d ed. London: Library Assn., 1972.
Includes information about Andersen, Catherine Sinclair, Marryat, and Harriet Martineau.

INDIVIDUAL WRITERS

Hans Christian Andersen

COLLECTED TALES

■ Andersen wrote a total of 156 fairy tales and stories, a distinction he himself made. Of their crea-

tion, he said, "They lay in my thoughts like a seed-corn, requiring only a flowing stream, a ray of sunshine, a drop of wormwood, for them to spring forth and burst into bloom"—Bredsdorff, *Hans Christian Andersen*, p. 328. Although the first of his stories was published in Denmark in 1835, they were not translated into English until 1846. In that year, four separate volumes appeared in English. Since then, many people have attempted to translate Andersen. Several outstanding editions are still available.

Boner, Charles, trans. A Danish story book. London: Cundall, 1846.

———. The nightingale and other stories. London: Cundall, 1846.
Both of Boner's books were translated from German editions.

Haugaard, Erik, trans. The complete fairy tales and stories. New York: Doubleday, 1974.
Foreword by Virginia Haviland. Bredsdorff considers this latest complete translation a "failure" in terms of loyalty to the original and readability.—review in *Times literary supplement,* December 6, 1974.

Hersholt, Jean, trans. The complete Andersen. New York: Heritage, 1942.
The first complete edition by this collector of Andersenania.

Howitt, Mary, trans. Wonderful stories for children. London: Chapman & Hall, 1846.
The "most felicitous translation"—Bettina Hürlimann.

James, Montague Rhodes, trans. Hans Andersen: 42 stories. London: Faber & Faber, 1930.
Includes an important preface on translating Andersen. Considered by Bettina Hürlimann to be the "classical edition."

Keigwin, R. P., trans. Hans Christian Andersen's fairy tales. Edited by Svend Larsen. Odense, Denmark: World Editions, 1950.
"Too restrained and elegant an edition to appeal to children."—Bettina Hürlimann.

Kingsland, L. W., trans. Hans Andersen's fairy tales. London: Oxford, 1961.
Illustrated by Ernest Shepard. A good translation for young children.

Le Gallienne, Eva, trans. Seven tales. New York: Harper, 1959.
An exquisite edition, beautifully decorated and illustrated by Maurice Sendak. A simplified translation suitable for young children.

Leyssac, Paul, trans. It's perfectly true and other stories. New York: Harcourt, 1938.

Lucas, Mrs. E. V., trans. Fairy tales from Hans Christian Andersen. London: Dent, 1899; reprint: New York: Grossett, 1945.

Peachey, Caroline, trans. Danish fairy-legends and tales. Glasgow: Pickering, 1846.

Spink, Reginald, trans. Hans Christian Andersen's fairy tales. New York: Dutton, 1953.
There are many collected editions of Andersen's tales based on the above translations. They have been enlivened by the work of such famous illustrators as Edmund Dulac (1976), Elizabeth MacKinstry (1933), Kay Nielsen (1924), and Tasha Tudor (1945).

ILLUSTRATED SINGLE-STORY EDITIONS

■ There are also many single-story editions in print—too numerous to begin to list. However, several are noteworthy for their design and illustrations.

Blegvad, Erik, trans. and illus. The emperor's new clothes. New York: Harcourt, 1959.

———. The swineherd. New York, Harcourt, 1958.

Burton, Virginia. The emperor's new clothes. Boston: Houghton, 1949.

James, M. R., trans. The steadfast tin soldier. New York: Scribner, 1953.
Illustrated by Marcia Brown.

———. The wild swans. New York: Scribner, 1963.
Illustrated by Marcia Brown.

Keigwin, R. P., trans. The snow queen. New York: Atheneum, 1968.
Illustrated by June Atkin Corwin.

———. Thumbelina. New York: Scribner, 1961.
Illustrated by Adrienne Adams.

———. The ugly duckling. New York: Scribner, 1965.
Illustrated by Adrienne Adams.

Le Gallienne, Eva, trans. The little match girl. Boston: Houghton, 1968.
Illustrated by Blair Lent.

———. The nightingale. New York: Harper, 1965.
Illustrated by Nancy Ekholm Burkert.

AUTOBIOGRAPHY

■ "He was obsessed with writing about himself and his own life and he left a whole series of autobiographies and autobiographical sketches."—Bredsdorff, *Hans Christian Andersen,* p. 6.

Howitt, Mary, trans. The true story of my life. London: Longmans, 1847; reprint: (Scandinavian classics, v. 26) New York: Scandinavian Foundation, 1926.
The first autobiographical sketch of Andersen.

Jones, J. Glyn, trans. The fairy tale of my life. Copenhagen: Arnold Busch, 1954.
This edition of Andersen's autobiography is based on his revised 1859 text, generally considered to be the most authoritative. Andersen wrote the original version in 1855. With 50 full-page color illustrations by Niels Larsen Steuns.

Michael, Maurice, trans. The mermaid man: the autobiography of Hans Christian Andersen. London: Barker, 1955.
An abridged translation of *Mit livs eventyr.*

Scudder, Horace, trans. The story of my life. Boston: Houghton, 1871; reprint: London: Paddington, 1975.
This autobiography has an added section spanning the years 1855–67.

BIOGRAPHY AND CRITICISM

Andersen, Hans Christian. Andersen–Scudder letters: Hans Christian Andersen's correspondence with Horace Elisha Scudder. Edited and translated by Waldemar Westergaard. Berkeley: University of California Press, 1949.
A fascinating exchange of letters between the then famous author Andersen and the young Scudder. Scudder eventually published many of Andersen's stories in his *Riverside magazine* before they were published in Denmark. Introduction by Jean Hersholt.

Bain, Robert Nisbet. Hans Christian Andersen. New York: Dodd, 1895.
Bain was the first English biographer of Andersen.

Böök, Fredrik. Hans Christian Andersen: a biography. Translated by C. Schoolfield. Norman: University of Oklahoma Press, 1962.
A reliable, though laudatory, biography. Two chapters deal specifically with the tales: chapter 13, "The fairy tales," p. 193–207, and chapter 14, "The philosophy of the fairy tales," p. 208–23.

Bredsdorff, Elias. Hans Andersen and Charles Dickens: a friendship and its dissolution. (Anglistica, v. 7) Cambridge: Heffer, 1956.

–––. Hans Christian Andersen: the story of his life and work, 1805–1875. London: Phaidon, 1975; New York: Scribner, 1975.
"The most accurately detailed biography yet to appear in English. Discussion of the stories is perfunctory."–*Phaedrus* (Spring 1976). This Cambridge professor demonstrates that the fairy tales were the "off-hand productions of a vast and thwarted literary ambition." In two parts, the first deals with the life of Andersen and attempts to characterize his complex personality; the second is a discussion and critical appraisal of some of the tales.

Danish journal. Special issue commemorating the 100th anniversary of the Danish writer Hans Christian Andersen's death on August 4, 1875.
Includes articles by Andersen scholars and translators on all aspects of his life and work.

Dreslov, Aksel. A river—a town—a poet: a walk together with Hans Christian Andersen. Copenhagen: Skandinavisisk Bogforlag, n.d.
Beautiful color illustrations detail the town of Odense where Andersen lived from his birth in 1805 to 1819. The text is slight.

Godden, Rumer. Hans Christian Andersen: a great life in brief. New York: Knopf, 1955.
A well-written account that tries to show how Andersen's stories emanated from his life experience.

"Hans Christian Andersen: a bibliographical guide to his work," *Scandinavica* 6:26–42 (1967).

Hans Christian Andersen anniversary number. *The American-Scandinavian review* 18:203–34 (April, 1930).
Articles written to honor Andersen's 125th birthday.

Haugaard, Erik. Portrait of a poet: Hans Christian Andersen and his fairy tales. Washington, D.C.: Library of Congress, 1973.
Lecture delivered March 5, 1973, as part of the tenth anniversary program of the Children's Section of the Library of Congress. Using three lesser-known stories, "She was no good," "The bell," and "The philosopher's stone," Haugaard speaks of the difficulties of the translator.

Hazard, Paul. "Hans Christian Andersen," *Horn book magazine* 19:141–48 (May-June, 1943); in his *Books, Children and Men,* translated by Marguerite Mitchell. p. 92–105. 4th ed. Boston: Horn Book, 1960.
A fine essay on Andersen, whom Hazard calls "the very prince of all story writers for children."

Hürlimann, Bettina. "The ugly duckling," in her *Three centuries of children's books in Europe,* translated and edited by Brian W. Alderson, p. 42–52. Cleveland: World, 1968.
Stresses how Andersen's tales are unique in three aspects: (1) Everything in Andersen has a soul of its own; (2) for the first time in the fairy tale, Andersen admits the tragic ending; and (3) there is tremendous fantasy in association with nature and the cosmos.

Larsen, Svend. Hans Christian Andersen. Translated by Mabel Dyrup. Odense, Denmark: Flensted, 1967.

Manning-Sanders, Ruth. Swan of Denmark: the story of Hans Christian Andersen. New York: McBride, 1950; reprint: New York: Dutton, 1966.
For young people.

Meynell, Esther. The story of Hans Andersen. New York: Henry Schuman, 1950.
A competent biography intended for young people.

Moore, Annie E. "Hans Christian Andersen," in her *Literature old and new for children*, p. 216–56. Boston: Houghton, 1934.
Shows how the tales serve as transition from the pure folktale to the modern fairy tale.

Reumert, Elith. Hans Andersen the man. Translated by Jessie Bröchner. London: Methuen, 1927; reprint: Detroit: Book Tower, 1971.
An early biography that attempts to deal honestly with this complex figure.

Scudder, Horace. "Hans Christian Andersen," in his *Childhood in literature and art*, p. 201–16. Boston: Houghton, 1894; *Atlantic monthly* 36: 203–34 (November, 1975); in *Children and literature*, edited by Virginia Haviland, p. 50–56. Glenview, Ill.: Scott, Foresman, 1973.
Scudder, who clearly idolized Andersen, saw him "not only as an interpreter of childhood," but as "the first child who made a contribution to literature."

Spink, Reginald. Hans Christian Andersen and his world. London: Thames & Hudson, 1972.
A lovely picture book with an adequate but brief text. Many photographs and drawings of and by Andersen.

———. Hans Christian Andersen: the man and his work. Copenhagen: Host, 1972.
A short biographical sketch by this English translator of Andersen.

———. Young Hans Christian Andersen. London: Roy, 1963.
A book on Andersen's childhood written as part of a British biographical series for children.

Stirling, Monica. Wild swan: the life and times of Hans Christian Andersen. New York: Harcourt, 1965.
This long biography places Andersen literarily, socially, and politically in the nineteenth century.

Toksvig, Signe. The life of Hans Christian Andersen. New York: Harcourt, 1934; reprint: New York: Kraus, 1969.
A lengthy, complete biography that leans heavily on the autobiography.

Wheeler, Opal. Hans Andersen: son of Denmark. New York: Dutton, 1951.
A good, fictionalized biography for children that contains several of the tales, greatly abbreviated.

Mary Howitt

Howitt, Mary Botham. Ballads, and other poems. London: Longman, Brown, [1847].

———. The childhood of Mary Leeson. (The juvenile library) Boston: Crosby, Nichols, [1848].
Embodies Mary Howitt's "idea of the spirit which ought to direct the education of a child."—preface.

———. The children's year. London: Longman, Brown, 1847.
Includes four illustrations by John Absolon from original designs by Anna Mary Howitt. The author kept a chronicle for one year of the voluntary occupations, plays, and pleasures of her two youngest children. The little story of Herbert and Meggy was the result. Its merit lies in the kindly home atmosphere, the naturalness of the children, and the simple manner in which the incidents are told.

———. Lillieslea, or, lost and found: a story for the young. London: Routledge, [1861].
Elva Smith dated this 1860, but the *Dictionary of national biography* dates it 1861. Illustrated by John Absolon.

———. Love and money; an every-day tale. London: Tegg, 1843.

———. Midsummer flowers, for the young. Philadelphia: Lindsay & Blakiston, 1854.
Short stories and poems. Illustrated.

———. My juvenile days, and other tales. New York: Appleton, 1850.

———. Our cousins in Ohio. London: Darton, 1849.

———. Sketches of natural history. London: Darton, 1834; reprint: New York: Johnson, 1970.
Poems about flowers, insects, animals, etc. Includes "The spider and the fly." Reprint of 1851 edition.

———. Sowing and reaping, or, what will come of it. London: Tegg, 1841; reprint, New York: Johnson, 1970.
Reprint of 1851 edition.

———. Stories in rhyme. Boston: Brown, Bazin & Co., 1855.
Illustrated with woodcuts.

———. Strive and thrive: a tale. London: Tegg, 1840.
Elva Smith dated this 1839, but the *Dictionary of national biography* dates it 1840.

———. Tales in verse. (Moral library for the young) London: Darton, 1836.

———. Tales of English life, including Middleton and the Middletons. London: Warne, [1881].
Contents: Sowing and reaping; My uncle the clockmaker; Strive and thrive; All is not gold that glitters; Love and money; Middleton and the Middletons. Elva Smith says, "My uncle the clockmaker" was written by William Howitt; however,

the *Dictionary of national biography* lists a separate book, *My uncle the clockmaker: a tale.* (London: William Tegg, 1844), s.v. Howitt, Mary.

———. Which is the wiser? or, people abroad: a tale for youth. London: Tegg, 1842.

TRANSLATIONS

Andersen, Hans Christian. Wonderful stories for children. Translated from the Danish by Mary Howitt. London: Chapman & Hall, 1846.
Contents: Ole Luckoie; The daisy; The naughty boy; Tommelise; The rose-elf; The garden of paradise; A night in the kitchen; Little Ida's flowers; The constant tin soldier; The storks. "Nobody ever caught the spirit of Andersen as she [Mrs. Howitt] has done, and she is loyally literal or fearlessly free as the occasion demands it."—R. N. Bain.

Speckter, Otto. The child's picture and verse book, commonly called Otto Spekter's fable book. Translated from the German by Mary Howitt. London: Tegg, 1844.
One hundred illustrations.

Stober, Karl. The curate's favorite pupil. Translated from the German by Mary Howitt. London: Orr, 1844.
The running title is *The favorite scholar.* Illustrated by John Absolon.

BIOGRAPHY AND CRITICISM

Howitt, Mary Botham. Mary Howitt: an autobiography. Edited by Margaret Howitt. 2v. London: Isbister, 1889; reprint: New York: AMS Press, 1973.
Edited by the writer's daughter. Includes sections from family letters; also portraits and other illustrations. Reprint is a facsimile, also two volumes.

———. "Reminiscences of my later life," *Good words* 27:52–59, 172–79, 330–37, 394–401, 592–601 (1886).

Lee, Amice Macdonell. Laurels and rosemary: the life of William and Mary Howitt. London and New York: Oxford University Press, 1955.
Written by a grandniece, this biography does not touch on Mary Howitt's books for children.

Parkes, Bessie Rayner. "Mary Howitt," in her *In a walled garden,* p. 78–99. London: Ward & Downey, 1895.
By a personal friend. Relates especially to Mary Howitt's conversion to the Roman Catholic faith.

Rowton, Frederic. "Mrs. Mary Howitt," in his *The female poets of Great Britain,* p. 350–73. Philadelphia: Baird, 1854.

Subtitle: "chronologically arranged, with copious selections and critical remarks, with additions by an American editor."

Symonds, Emily Morse (*pseud.* George Paston). "William and Mary Howitt," in her *Little memoirs of the nineteenth century,* p. 325–76. New York: Dutton, 1902.

Woodring, Carl Ray. Victorian samplers: William and Mary Howitt. Lawrence: University of Kansas Press, 1952.
Traces the writers' lives, characterizing simultaneously "their creative leadership and critical sensitivity." The chapter, "International relations," p. 82–114, discusses Mary Howitt's relationship with Andersen. Contains a chronological table.

———. "William and Mary Howitt: bibliographical notes," *Bulletin* (Harvard University Library) 5:251–54 (Spring, 1951).
This supplements the bibliography in the *Dictionary of national biography.*

———. "William and Mary Howitt and their circle." Ph.D. diss., Harvard University, 1951.
Contains a complete bibliography of works by and about the Howitts.

Captain Frederick Marryat

Marryat, *Capt.* Frederick. The children of the New Forest. (The Juvenile library) 2v. London: H. Hurst, 1847.
Story of the English civil war period. Part of the interest is due to the resourcefulness of the characters, but adventure and romance also abound.

———. Masterman Ready, or, the wreck of the Pacific, written for young people. 3v. London: Longman, Orme, 1841–43.

———. ———. London: Macmillan, 1928.
Illustrations by Fred Pegram and an introduction by David Hannay. "When the book was still new, John Forster said that it was the best liked and the most often re-read of children's books."—from the introduction, p. vii–xv, which gives an account of the origin of the story and analyzes its literary qualities.

———. ———. New York: Harper, 1928.
Illustrations by John Rae. Gives Marryat's own account of the writing of the story; also a prefatory note about the family of the Mastermans, shipowners and builders, whose name, residence, and occupation Marryat had by a strange coincidence assumed for the godfather of "Masterman Ready."

———. ———. (Classics in children's literature, 1621–1932) New York: Garland, 1976.
Introduction by John Seelye.

———. The mission, or, scenes in Africa. 2v. London: Longman, Brown, 1845.

This is Marryat's own account: "It is composed of scenes and descriptions of Africa in a journey to the northward from the Cape of Good Hope—full of lions, rhinoceroses, and all manner of adventures, interspersed with a little common sense here and there, and interwoven with the history of the settlement of the Cape up to 1828—written for young people, of course, and, therefore trifling, but amusing."—prefatory note, p. vii–viii.

———. The novels of Captain Marryat. Edited by R. Brimley Johnson. 26v. London: Phoenix, 1929–30.

The standard edition of the complete works.

———. The settlers in Canada. 2v. London: Longman, Brown, 1844.

Story of an English family who emigrate to Canada in 1794. Marryat excelled in his delineation of eccentric types of human nature, and this book is interesting not only for its details of pioneer life but for three of its characters: Martin Super, the trapper; Malachi Bone, the hunter; and the boy, John, who is a backwoodsman born.

BIOGRAPHY AND CRITICISM

Biron, H. C. "Captain Marryat," *National review* 68:392–401 (1916).

Deals chiefly with the sea novels.

Conrad, Joseph. "Tales of the sea," in his *Notes on life and letters*, p. 53–57. London: Dent, 1949.

First published in 1921. "Conrad's invaluable assessment of his precursor in fiction relating to the sea."—Warner. Conrad says of Marryat, "He wrote before the great American language was born, and he wrote as well as any novelist of his time."

Hannay, David. Life of Frederick Marryat. London: Scott, 1889; reprint: New York: Haskell House, 1973.

Bibliography by John P. Anderson. A standard biography. "An admirable little book so far as the main text is concerned. Its bibliography, however . . . is very unreliable as an authority on first editions."—Sadleir.

———. Life and writing of Frederick Marryat. London: W. Scott, 1920.

A reprint of the 1889 *Life of Frederick Marryat*.

Iddesleigh, *Sir S. H. Northcote, earl of.* "Captain Marryat as a novelist," *The monthly review* 16: 121–34 (September, 1904); *Littell's living age* 243:212–20 (1904).

Discusses the books that best illustrate Marryat's merits and powers, including the children's books.

Lean, Florence Marryat Church. Life and letters of Captain Marryat. 2v. London: Bentley, 1872.

Written by Marryat's daughter. ". . . a rather shapeless work, . . . it succeeds, for it was written with affection, and contains information not to be found elsewhere."—Warner (below).

Lloyd, Christopher. Captain Marryat and the old navy. New York: Longmans, 1939.

"Based on research, this is a full account of the naval side of Marryat's life."—Warner (below).

McGrath, M. "Centenary of Marryat," *Nineteenth century* 106:545–55 (1929).

Tersely describes Marryat's literary career and calls him "one of the best, perhaps the best of all writers of boys' tales."

Philip, M. "Cultural myth in Victorian boys' books by Marryat, Hughes, Stevenson, and Kipling." Ph.D. diss., Indiana University, 1975.

Sadleir, Michael. "Captain Marryat: a portrait," *The London mercury* 10:495–510 (1924).

Study of Marryat's personal characteristics and of the qualities that give permanent value to his best works. Notes "the fine, elastic English of a most English author."

———. ———. *Yale review* 32, new ser. 13:774–89 (1924).

An abridged version.

———. "Frederick Marryat: essay and bibliography," in his *Excursions in Victorian bibliography*, p. 75–103. London: Chaundy, 1922; reprint: Folcroft, Pa.: Folcroft, 1969.

This scholar and bibliographer feels that "Marryat's fame as a novelist of naval escapades, of risk and makeshift among pirates and barbarians, is fame deserved."

———. XIXth century fiction. 2v. London: Constable, 1951.

Contains "the fullest bibliography [of Marryat's work] which is likely to appear."—Warner (below).

Warner, Oliver. Captain Marryat: a rediscovery. New York: Macmillan, 1953.

A fascinating, readable account of Marryat's life as a naval serviceman and writer. Beautifully illustrated with photographs and drawings of and by Marryat. Bibliography.

———. "Marryat," *Junior bookshelf* 17:91–94 (July, 1953).

A short biography of his adventuresome life and a critical evaluation of his career as a writer for adults and children.

Woolf, Virginia. "The captain's death bed," in her *The captain's death bed, and other essays*, p.

37–47. New York: Harcourt, 1950; in *Collected essays*, v. 1, p. 173–80. New York: Harcourt, 1967.
"A collection of posthumous essays, the title piece being concerned with Marryat. It is a lovely miniature and may stand as representative of all fugitive pieces on Marryat."—Warner (above).

Harriet Martineau

Martineau, Harriet. The Crofton boys. (The playfellow. v. 4) London: Charles Knight, 1841.
Presents school life in the second quarter of the nineteenth century. Interesting as a forerunner of the modern school story and also because of its personal character, having been written by Harriet Martineau in the belief that it was the last time she would ever express herself in writing.

———. Feats on the fiord: a tale of Norway. (The playfellow. v. 3) London: Charles Knight, 1841.
Story of country life in Norway, the special theme being the influence upon people of national customs and the effect of superstitions upon the peasant mind. Because of the elements of romance and adventure, this is more generally read at the present time than Harriet Martineau's other stories.

———. Five years of youth, or, sense and sentiment. London: Harvey & Darton, 1831.
The author's first book for children. It belongs to the period of her early literary efforts. Contains an engraved frontispiece and other plates. The story is indicative of the author's developing interests in economic and political reform, and it also serves as a contrast to the more modern characteristics of her later work with its elements of adventure and romance.

———. The peasant and the prince: a story of the French revolution. (The playfellow. v. 2) London: Charles Knight, 1841.
The prince is the unfortunate dauphin, son of Louis XVI of France, and the story follows the fortunes of the royal family during the stormy scenes of the French Revolution. The suggestion for the subject came from a friend. The author considered this the least successful of her children's books except among poor people. They read it eagerly, and they called it the "French revelation."

———. The settlers at home. (The playfellow. v. 1) London: Charles Knight, 1841.
Regarding the origin of this book, the author said, "An article of DeQuincey's . . . made me think of snow-storms for a story:—then it occurred to me that floods were less hackneyed . . . . Floods suggested Lincolnshire for the scene."—*Autobiography*, v. 1, p. 448.

BIOGRAPHY AND CRITICISM

Adams, William Henry Davenport. "Harriet Martineau," in his *Child-life and girlhood of remarkable women*, p. 7–27, New York: Dutton, 1895.

———. "Miss Harriet Martineau," in his *Celebrated women travellers of the nineteenth century*, p. 404–17. London: Sonnenschein, 1883.

Bosanquet, Theodora. Harriet Martineau: an essay in comprehension. London: Etchells, 1927.
Aims "to relate Miss Martineau's life and opinions, and her continual, if sometimes eccentric, progress towards the final phase of her remarkable career, to the personal influences which so clearly and powerfully affected her. The memories of the *Autobiography* have been supplemented as much as possible by reference to the contemporary records of the men and women who knew her."—preface.

Cone, Helen Gray, and **J. L. Gilder,** eds. "Harriet Martineau," in their *Pen-portraits of literary women*, v. 2. p. 9–56. New York: Cassell, 1887.
Biographical sketch, followed by extracts from the *Autobiography* and other sources.

Hamilton, Catherine Jane. "Harriet Martineau," in her *Women writers: their works and ways*, p. 72–95. 2d ser. London: Ward, Lock, 1893.
Chiefly biographical.

Martineau, Harriet. Autobiography. Edited by Maria Weston Chapman. 2v. Boston: Osgood, 1877.
Memorials of Harriet Martineau, by Maria Chapman, vol. 2, p. 131–596. "This is doubtless one of the very honestest autobiographies ever written; and in respect to careful self-analysis, it probably stands at the head of its whole class."—*The nation*, 1877. An invaluable source, but should be supplemented by other references.

———. ———. 2d ed. 3v. London: Smith & Elder, 1877.
Memorials, vol. 3.

Miller, Florence Fenwick. Harriet Martineau. (Famous women series) Boston: Roberts, 1884; reprint: Port Washington, N.Y.: Kennikat Press, 1972.
"Good, compact, unambitious summary of the career of a remarkable woman."—*The nation*, 1885.

Morley, John Morley, *viscount*. "Harriet Martineau," in his *Critical miscellanies*, v. 3, p. 175–211. London: Macmillan, 1904.
Excellent short account of Harriet Martineau's characteristics, her social interests, and her literary work. Does not discuss her children's books.

Nevill, John Cranstoun. Harriet Martineau. London: Muller, 1943.
A classic biography of Harriet Martineau and an account of her work.

Pope-Hennesy, *Dame* **Una Birch.** "Harriet Martineau," in her *Three English women in America* [Fanny Trollope, Fanny Kemble, Harriet Martineau], p. 211–304. London: Benn, 1929.
Chiefly an account of Harriet Martineau's experiences in America and her contacts with anti-slavery advocates.

Rivlin, Joseph B., comp. Harriet Martineau: a bibliography of her separately printed books. New York: New York Public Library, 1937.
A comprehensive list of writings with location key. List is alphabetical by title.

———. "Harriet Martineau: a bibliography of her separately printed books," *Bulletin* (New York Public Library) 50:387–408, 476–98, 550–72, 789–808, 838–56, 888–908; 51:26–48 (May, July, October, 1946; January, 1947).

Webb, Robert Kiefer. Harriet Martineau: radical Victorian. New York: Columbia University Press, 1960.
Webb, a historian, devotes a great deal of space to "unidolizing" Miss Martineau and proving the former biographies dishonest in their adulatory stances. Deals with the children's books in a chapter, "Tynemouth: The uses of suffering," p. 204–65. He concludes, "The Playfellow tales for children are a startlingly morbid collection, likely, one would guess, to produce trauma in any child who read them." They are meant, he goes on, "to teach children fortitude, endurance, self-control and energy, those Victorian traits that Miss Martineau possessed and she believed all children should possess."

Wheatley, Vera. Life and work of Harriet Martineau. New York: Essential, 1957.
An extensive biography with a lengthy list of her writings. "Based on quite wide reading in England . . . it is nearly as adulatory as Mrs. Chapman would have wanted, and both as biography and history it is thoroughly amateur."—Webb (above).

Catherine Sinclair

Sinclair, Catherine. Holiday house: a book for the young. Edinburgh: W. Whyte, 1839; reprint: (Classics in children's literature 1621–1932) New York: Garland, 1976.
The introduction humorously protests against the prevailing type of informational books for children. "The first children's book . . . in which the modern spirit manifests itself."—E. V. Lucas. Reprint has preface by Alison Lurie.

———. "Uncle David's nonsensical story about giants and fairies," in *Old fashioned tales*, compiled by Edward Verrall Lucas, p. 378–90. London: Wells Gardner, 1905.
Taken from *Holiday house.* For comment on Catherine Sinclair and her nursery scepticism, see "Introduction," p. xv–xxi.

BIOGRAPHY AND CRITICISM

A brief tribute to the memory of the late lamented Catherine Sinclair who died at Kensington, August 6, 1864. London: Gilbert & Rivington, 1864.
A twenty-three-page account of her life and literary work, with anecdotes to show her wit and ready conversation. For references to *Holiday house,* see p. 6–7, 15.

Doyle, Brian, ed. "Catherine Sinclair," in his *Who's who of children's literature,* p. 246–47. New York: Schocken, 1968.
A concise biographical sketch, including information regarding the writing of her children's books.

Green, Roger Lancelyn. "The dawn of levity," in his *Tellers of tales,* p. 15–21. Rewritten and rev. ed. New York: Watts, 1965.
Green believes that Catherine Sinclair's work led the way toward less-didactic books. "It is like coming out into the clear, bright sunshine to take up *Holiday house* . . . . It is not quite the end of the wood, of course, but it is the first sure sign that the trees are thinning and that the pleasant meadowland of fancy and amusement is not far ahead."

Mid-Victorian Literature in England and America

The mid-Victorian period is referred to as the Golden Age of children's literature. In terms of both quantity and quality, this chapter can only touch briefly on some of the major trends that occurred roughly between 1850 and 1875.

Undoubtedly the most significant and far-reaching happening was what Mary F. Thwaite, in *From primer to pleasure in reading*, has called "the ascendancy of the imagination," for with it came "freedom, originality, and above all, ever widening horizons."

Although Lewis Carroll's *Alice's adventures in Wonderland* (1865) is often considered the first book written purely to give pleasure to children, Edward Lear's *A book of nonsense* (1846) preceded and anticipated *Alice* in this respect. Like the Lear book, *Alice* is considered "revolutionary" because it was written without any trace of a moral, because it was designed purely and simply to amuse the child, and because it is directly written. Its humor is universal and its message is honest and ageless. It gave pleasure to children and adults of the nineteenth century just as it continues to give pleasure to children and adults today. Its implications—in an age in which children's books were still highly moralistic (for example, Kingsley's *Water babies* [1863])—were enormous. As a stepping-off place for books published during the last thirty-five years of the nineteenth century, *Alice* pointed the way to complete freedom of the imagination in children's books and to ultimate banishment of the moralistic story. For the first time, entertainment—pure fun—was legitimized as a proper aim for children's books.

In the field of nonsense, which is indigenous to the English, Lewis Carroll and Edward Lear were supreme. Lewis Carroll wrote only a few other books for children, none as good as the *Alice* books, but Edward Lear continued to write wonderfully imaginative verse into the 1870s.

Other pieces of imaginative writing also flowered in the 1860s and 1870s. The fictional fairy tale had survived Puritan and eighteenth-century disapproval and could be found in the chapbook. Hans Christian Andersen's stories were translated and published in England in 1846. In 1844, Francis Edward Paget wrote *The hope of the Katzekopfs, or, the sorrows of selfishness*, with a less-than-subtle moral but a playful spirit. Using the Grimms' stories as inspiration, the great English critic John Ruskin wrote *The king of the Golden river* in 1841; it was finally published in 1851 with illustrations by Richard Doyle. This tale also emphasizes that kindness leads to success and selfishness to disaster—a common theme of the Victorian writers.

Some great English writers found a vehicle for their talents in the literary fairy tale. In 1855, William Makepeace Thackeray wrote for his daughters and their friends *The rose and the ring*, a satire that is devoid of sentimentality or morality and is still funny today. *Water-babies* by Charles Kingsley appeared in book form in 1863, having been serialized in *Macmillan's magazine* in 1862 and 1863. It is a difficult book, written by a man of great religious belief, idealism, enthusiasm, as well as prejudice—a man who was obviously sympathetic to the human condition of Victorian England. Not unlike *Water babies*, but much lighter, is Jean Ingelow's *Mopsa the fairy*, which appeared in 1869.

George MacDonald's fantasy is unique. In 1867, his book *Dealings with the fairies* was published, containing the stories "The light princess" and "The golden key." His most famous book, *At the back of the north wind*, appeared in 1871; *The princess and the goblin* in 1872; and *The princess and Curdie* in 1883. A contemporary and friend of Lewis Carroll, he was, like Kingsley, a deeply religious man. MacDonald's books, which are now enjoying a revival, are sometimes sentimental, often symbolic, and always moralistic. They are difficult for the average child of today.

Another development in children's literature at this time was the creation of realistic books for older boys and girls. For the first time, authors (and publishers) began to realize that these readers needed books different from those written for their younger brothers and sisters; and that boys needed different types of books than girls.

Boys' fiction had begun with the writing of James Fenimore Cooper in America and Capt. Frederick Marryat in England. Their work was carried on by W. H. C. Kingston and Capt. Thomas Mayne Reid, both of whom, through the 1870s, wrote many adventure stories especially for boys. R. M. Ballantyne was a contemporary of Kingston and Reid, but his books were based almost entirely on life experience, and he invented heroes and heroines more believable than those of the other adventure writers. Ballantyne's books, still quite readable today, reflect imperial England and its aim to bring Christianity to the "untamed" parts of the world. As the century progressed and became "more warlike," Gillian Avery suggests, in *Childhood's pattern*, the adventures became more far-flung and extravagant. In the United States, stories for boys—exemplified by those of Horatio Alger and "Oliver Optic" (W. T. Adams)—appear to be less concerned with adventure and more with the principal character's trials and tribulations. These two men wrote series of books that were widely read into the twentieth century.

Both boys and girls read what we now call the school story. The mid-nineteenth-century school story had several precedents, one of which—Sarah Fielding's *The governess, or, the little female academy*—was published as early as 1749. In it, Mrs. Teachum, a governess, with typically eighteenth-century didactic techniques, has to inculcate proper learning in her nine young students. Other writers of this type of didactic school story were Dorothy Kilner and Maria Edgeworth. Mary Lamb's *Mrs. Leicester's school* (1809) merely uses a school setting as a framework for her didactic tales. Harriet Martineau's *The Crofton boys* (1841), about a young lad who goes off to Crofton and has an unhappy accident, is considered the first real school story. This led the way for the most famous of the genre, Thomas Hughes's *Tom Brown's school days* (1857), based on Hughes's experiences at Rugby while Thomas Arnold was headmaster. *Tom Brown's school days* inspired F. W. Farrar's *Eric, or, little by little*, another English public school story, but morbidly sentimental. In *Childhood's pattern* Gillian Avery suggests that these books are not so much about public school reform as they are about manliness, patriotism, and authority—traits held dear by mid-Victorian Englishmen.

The domestic tale, written especially for girls, is the most historically significant of all the mid-Victorian books, because it is such an obvious mirror of the age. The religious feelings (which ran high at the time), social habits, and attitudes of the mid-Victorians are clearly seen in these books for young ladies.

Charlotte Mary Yonge has been called "the historian and interpreter of the Oxford Movement." She was also a great storyteller. Charlotte Yonge was typical of the highly educated, middle-class, unmarried women of this period, extremely intelligent, inordinately religious, and very parochial in outlook. She wrote more than 120 books and edited *The monthly packet* from 1851 to 1890. Her most famous book, *The heir of Redclyffe*, published in 1853, was an English best-seller and was read widely in the United States. She was a skilled writer of family chronicles, the first of which, *The daisy chain* (1856), is about the motherless May family of eleven children and how they occupied their time in Victorian England. It is a well-written, energetic book, with memorable, believable characters. The fact that it can be enjoyed today is a credit to its good writing. Charlotte Yonge also wrote historical fiction and books for younger children. She continued to write into the twentieth century.

She had several followers in the 1860s and 1870s. The best of these were Margaret Scott Gatty and her daughter, Juliana Horatia Ewing, both of whom wrote charming domestic tales as well as fantasy. Mrs. Ewing, the better and more prolific of the two, is famous for *Jackanapes* (1879), the story of the brief life and sacrificial death of a soldier's son.

Interestingly enough, the domestic novel reached its peak of excellence not in England but in America. Louisa May Alcott, daughter of an educational theorist and teacher, wrote

Little women in 1868. It was widely read in England and America on its publication and is still loved today.

The influence of all these writers was incalculable. Imitators abounded in America and England, and thousands of such books were printed. Furthermore, the beginnings of a public library system at the end of this period made it possible for more people to read the books that were being turned out. It is noteworthy that, with some exceptions, the books that are still read are the nonsense books and some of the fantasies, particularly those with little religious or moralistic overcast. The books that best mirror the period are so foreign to our contemporary sensibilities that they are no longer read by anyone but social historians. To them, they are invaluable.

OUTLINE

I. The Victorian scene
II. Varied developments in children's literature
  A. Advance in realism in stories of boy and girl life
  B. The evolution of imaginative writing
    1. Fictional fairy tales: moral, symbolistic, satirical, and humorous
    2. The novel for older girls
  C. The discovery of nonsense
  D. The importance of children's magazines
III. Representative authors and their books
  A. Legend and history
    1. Grace Greenwood (1823–1904)
      a) *The little pilgrim*
      b) *Merrie England, Bonnie Scotland,* and other books
        (1) Value of semihistorical romance for young girls
        (2) Emphasis on picturesque incidents
        (3) Spirit and atmosphere of early times
        (4) Use in awakening interest in famous people and places
    2. Charles Dickens (1812–70)
      a) *A child's history of England*
        (1) Narrative form
        (2) Picturesqueness of scenes
        (3) Interpretation of historical characters
        (4) Personal viewpoint
      b) The Christmas books
      c) Holiday romance
  B. Poetry
    1. Alice (1820–71) and Phoebe Cary (1824–62)
      a) Early life and lack of educational opportunity
      b) Love of nature
      c) *Ballads for children*
        (1) Choice of subjects
        (2) Directness and simplicity of treatment
        (3) Moral lessons
    2. William Brighty Rands (1823–82)
      a) *Lilliput levee* and other books

    3. Edward Lear (1812–88)
      a) The children for whom Lear wrote
      b) The author's description of himself: "How pleasant to know Mr. Lear"
      c) The Lear limerick and the nursery songs
      d) Original conceptions and odd names, absurdities, and exaggerations
      e) Appeal of grotesque drawings
    4. Christina Rossetti (1830–94)
      a) *Sing-song*
        (1) Literary values: lyrical quality, simplicity, spontaneity, fancifulness, playful humor
        (2) Technical workmanship
        (3) Use with children
      b) "The goblin market" and other selected poems
  C. Story literature
    1. John Ruskin (1819–1900)
      a) *The king of the Golden river*
        (1) Genesis
        (2) Structure and setting
        (3) Value as literature
    2. Charles Kingsley (1819–75)
      a) *The heroes*
        (1) Comparison with Hawthorne's *Wonder-book* and *Tanglewood tales*
      b) *The water-babies*
        (1) Moral purpose
        (2) Literary evaluation
        (3) Poems
      c) *Glaucus* and *Madam How and Lady Why*
    3. Mrs. Gatty (Margaret Scott) (1809–73)
      a) Personal characteristics; effect in determining character of books
      b) Literary and scientific tastes
      c) *The fairy godmothers* and other stories
      d) *Parables from nature*
        (1) Method of developing spiritual truths
        (2) Literary style
        (3) Usefulness in the twentieth century

e) *Aunt Judy's magazine*
   (1) Reflection of editor's interests in contents
   (2) Interest due to first publication of Mrs. Ewing's stories
   (3) Social and humanitarian projects
4. Jean Ingelow (1820–97)
   a) Early life and religious training
   b) *Stories told to a child*
      (1) Origin and first publication
      (2) Representative stories: "Anselmo," "The prince's dream"
   c) *Mopsa the fairy*
      (1) Plot; element of suspense
      (2) Childlike simplicity and spontaneity
      (3) Lyrics
5. George MacDonald (1824–1905)
   a) Personal and literary aptitudes
   b) Spiritual insight
   c) Fairy tales
      (1) Feeling for nature
      (2) Homeliness
      (3) Poetic imagination
      (4) Symbolism
6. Mrs. Craik (Dinah Maria Mulock) (1826–87)
   a) Place as a novelist
   b) Children's books
      (1) Elements of interest
      (2) Literary and ethical values
7. William Makepeace Thackeray (1811–63)
   a) *The rose and the ring*
      (1) Origin
      (2) Humor contrasted with that of Lear and Lewis Carroll
      (3) Mock heroic style
      (4) Illustrations by the author
8. Lewis Carroll (1832–98)
   a) As boy and man
   b) Wonderland stories and nonsense poetry
      (1) Accounts of their origin
      (2) Imaginative reality
      (3) Logical reasoning
      (4) Dream psychology
      (5) Craftsmanship
      (6) Illustrations
9. Mrs. Ewing (Juliana Gatty) (1841–85)
   a) Contrast with Mrs. Gatty in variety and character of work
   b) Beginning of career as home storyteller
   c) Personal qualities and self-revelation in "Madam Liberality"
   d) Early stories and their publication in *Monthly packet* and *Aunt Judy's magazine*
   e) Reflection in stories of author's own interests

f) Literary style; comparison with that of Charlotte Yonge
   (1) Use of autobiographical form
   (2) Types of characters and skill in delineation
   (3) Humor and pathos
   (4) Vivid description
   (5) Truth to nature
g) Value of Mrs. Ewing's books
   (1) Cultural and spiritual qualities; high ideals
   (2) Suggestions that arouse and develop new interest and sympathies
   (3) Varied character and use for children of different ages
      (a) Old-fashioned fairy tales
      (b) Moral stories of semi-fairy tale nature
      (c) Short stories, simple in plot, centralized in interest, and with few characters
      (d) Stories of home and school life for older boys and girls
      (e) Hero stories of different types
      (f) Flower stories, animal stories, ghost stories, Christmas and Easter stories, stories of poor boys who made their own way, etc.
      (g) Stories that may be dramatized
h) Analysis of selected stories
i) Rank as a writer for children
j) Use of Mrs. Ewing's books with twentieth-century children
   (1) Reasons why the stories are not more popular
   (2) Methods of interesting children in these stories
10. Charlotte Yonge (1823–1901)
    a) Personal characteristics
       (1) Influence of race and place
       (2) Home training and education
       (3) Spiritual influence of Keble
       (4) Church, missionary, and literary interests
       (5) Attitude of family toward literary pursuits and use of money received for books
    b) Editorial work
       (1) *Monthly paper of Sunday teaching*
       (2) *The monthly packet*
       (3) *Mothers in council*
    c) Books
       (1) Religious home stories for girls

(*a*) Most characteristic work
of Charlotte Yonge
(*b*) Method contrasted with
that of other religious
stories
(*c*) Emphasis in application
of Christian ideals to
everyday trials and
problems
(2) Historical stories
(*a*) Romantic character
(*b*) Value for girls
(3) Other books
(*a*) Histories
(*b*) Biographical books
(*c*) Geographical books
(*d*) Religious books
d) *The heir of Redclyffe*
(1) Reasons for choice of this
book for special study
(2) Difficulties of publication and
phenomenal success of book
(3) Reflection of religious and
social enthusiasms of period
(4) Influence in the nineteenth
century, especially upon the
pre-Raphaelite group and in
particular upon William
Morris
(5) Literary analysis
(*a*) Novel type of story and
new type of hero
(*b*) Combination of detailed
realistic treatment with
romantic spirit and
idealistic hero
(*c*) Characters
i) Indication of intellectual tastes and inter-
ests of the period
(*d*) Incidents: pathetic,
dramatic
(*e*) Defects of construction
and style
(6) Allusions in other books to
The heir of Redclyffe
(7) Historical value
(8) To what extent and with
what girls is the book
still useful?
e) Choice of books for library
collections of today
(1) Books best from a
literary standpoint
(2) Books not too much colored
by High Church sympathy
(3) Books most likely to interest
boys and girls of the
present time
11. Thomas Hughes (1822–96) and
Dean Farrar (1831–1903)
a) First full-length school stories

b) Comparison with *The
Crofton boys*
c) *Tom Brown's school days*
versus *Eric.*
12. Thomas Bailey Aldrich (1836–1907)
and Louisa May Alcott (1832–88)
a) *Story of a bad boy*
(1) Origin and first publication
(2) Biographical, psychological,
and historical interest
(3) Literary qualities
(*a*) Contrast with *Little
women*
b) Merits of *Little women* and
other stories of Louisa May Alcott
c) Influence of Louisa May Alcott's
life and work upon girls
d) Comparison of American realistic
stories with those representing
contemporary English life
13. Susan Warner (1819–85)
a) As a writer for girls
b) *Wide, wide world* today seen as
an old-fashioned, lachrymose,
sentimental work with a heavy
religious tone
c) *Queechy*
14. Harriet Beecher Stowe (1811–96)
a) Her family background
and early writings
b) Her marriage and children
c) *Uncle Tom's cabin*
(1) Its place in history
(2) Its place today
d) Stories written for children
15. Writers of adventure stories
a) Extension and popularization
of the adventure tale
b) Travel interests
c) Literary methods
d) Mayne Reid (1818–83)
(1) Antecedents and temperament
(2) Adventurous life
(3) Popularity and reputation
as a storyteller
(4) Books
(*a*) Picturesque and
extravagant episodes
(*b*) Imperturbable character
of heroes and invariable
success
(*c*) Method of imparting
information
(*d*) Rhetorical expression
e) Robert Michael Ballantyne
(1825–94)
(1) Personal experience as
a basis for writing
(2) *Young fur traders, Coral
island,* and other books
f) William Henry Giles Kingston
(1814–80)

(1) Business and journalistic
   experience
(2) Character of stories and
   comparison with those of
   Reid and Ballantyne
g) "Oliver 'Optic" (W. T. Adams)
   (1822–97) and Horatio Alger
   (1832–99)

(1) Their similar backgrounds
(2) Prolific writers of series
   books for boys
(3) Comparison of style and
   content of writing
(4) Alger's life in reality and as
   revealed in his biography

GENERAL REFERENCES

Abbott, Jacob. The Harper establishment, or, how the story books are made. New York: Harper, 1855.
Illustrated account of the printing of books in mid-nineteenth-century America.

Altick, Richard. "The nineteenth century," in his *The English common reader*, p. 81–378. Chicago: University of Chicago Press (Phoenix Books), 1957.
Discusses the influence of religion, society, education, the public library concept, the book trade, and periodicals and newspapers on the mass reading public from 1800 to 1900.

Andrews, Siri, ed. The Hewins lectures, 1947–1962. Boston: Horn Book, 1963.
The introduction, by Frederic Melcher, describes this as "a series of annual papers on the writing and publishing of children's books in New England's fertile years."

Avery, Gillian. Childhood's pattern: a study of the heroes and heroines of children's fiction, 1770–1950. London: Hodder, [1975].
A scholarly study of children's books that views them as "literature," in the sense that they mirror a "constantly shifting moral pattern." Of particular interest are the chapters, "The cottage child and his Sunday school prize, 1800–80," p. 71–91; "The evangelical child, 1818–80," p. 92–120; "The happy family, 1830–80," p. 121–42.

———. Nineteenth century children: heroes and heroines in English children's stories, 1780 to 1900. [London]: Hodder, [1965].
In this excellent book, the author traces the image of the child in children's literature through the period and concludes that, in these twelve decades, "the world of the juvenile novel changed from a place where all childishness was exorcised, to one where the child was supreme and the adults only shadows."

———. "The parting of the ways," *Children's literature*, 4:153–61 (1975).
A reprint from *Childhood's pattern* (above).

———. Victorian people, in life and in literature. New York: Holt, [1970].
The author contrasts the real people with literary characters in all classes of Victorian life—the aristocracy, upper middle class, squirearchy, the lower middle class, the clergy, the industrial workers and the poverty stricken.

Barnes, Walter. The children's poets: analyses and appraisals of the greatest English and American poets for children. Cleveland: World, 1924.
Partial contents: Christina Rossetti; Edward Lear; Lewis Carroll.

Blanck, Jacob. A twentieth century look at nineteenth century children's books. (Books and publishing lecture series. v. 1) Boston: Simmons College School of Library Science, 1954.
The 19th-century juvenile book in America "evolved not as a result of adult celebration but by the will, by the unspoiled instinct, if you please, of the juvenile reader himself."

———. "A twentieth-century look at nineteenth century children's books," in *Bibliophile in the nursery*, edited by William Targ, p. 427–51. Cleveland: World, [1957].

Cammaerts, Émile. The poetry of nonsense. New York: Dutton, 1926.
Notes the important part played by nonsense in the history of English literature, with special emphasis on the work of Edward Lear and Lewis Carroll.

Caroline M. Hewins: her book; containing *A mid-century child and her books* by Caroline Hewins and *Caroline M. Hewins and books for children* by Jennie Lindquist. Boston: Horn Book, 1954.
In *A mid-century child and her books*, Caroline Hewins "gives us a charming picture of the reading open to a child in a cultivated home in New England during the 1850s and sixties, when she herself was between the ages of five and fifteen." —Alice Jordan, *From Rollo to Tom Sawyer*. Jennie Lindquist has written an appreciation of the early children's librarian.

"**Children's books of the year,**" *The North American review* 102:236–49 (1866).
Reviews children's books of 1865 and 1866, "Oliver Optic," Kingston, Trowbridge, Sophie May, and Jane Andrews being among the authors mentioned.

"**Children's literature,**" *The London quarterly review* 13:469–500 (1860).
The value of imaginative literature is discussed in this general review, which covers, among others, Mary Howitt's *Children's year*, Ruskin's *King of the Golden river*, Kingsley's *Heroes*, and Thackeray's *Rose and the ring*.

Cott, Jonathan, ed. Beyond the looking glass: extraordinary works of fantasy and fairy tales. New York: Stonehill, [1973].
Introduction by Leslie Fiedler, p. xi–xx, and "Notes on fairy truth and the idea of childhood," p. xxi–1. Partial contents: King of the Golden river (Ruskin); Petsilla's posy (Hood); The golden key (MacDonald); Goblin market (Christina Rossetti).

Cruse, Amy. The Victorians and their books. London: G. Allen & Unwin, 1935.
The chapters of special interest are: "The world of Miss Charlotte Yonge," "The Browns of England," "A young Victorian's library," and "Books from America," which shows how American writers such as James Fenimore Cooper and Harriet Beecher Stowe became popular in England. Other chapters may also be useful for background. The material has been drawn from autobiographies, correspondence, and other contemporary sources.

———. The Victorians and their reading. Boston: Houghton, 1935.
Same as *The Victorians and their books* (listed above).

Darton, Frederick Joseph Harvey. "The 'sixties: Alice and after," in his *Children's books in England*, p. 259–97. 2d ed. Cambridge: Cambridge University Press, 1958.
This eminent critic says that in a period without "violent revolutionaries" Lewis Carroll "changed the whole cast of children's literature, although he founded, not followed, a gracious type."

Delafield, E. M. Ladies and gentlemen in Victorian fiction. New York: Harper, 1937.
Amusing sidelights on family and social ideals as they appear in the works of Charlotte Yonge and other popular writers, including Susan Warner.

De Vries, Leonard, comp. Little wide-awake: an anthology from Victorian children's books and periodicals in the collection of Anne and Fernand G. Renier. Cleveland: World, 1967.
Selections "taken almost entirely from the secondary and ephemeral literature of the period." Generously illustrated in black and white and in color. The introduction is by M. F. Thwaite.

Eaton, Anne Thaxter. "Widening horizons: 1840–1890," in *A critical history of children's literature*, edited by Cornelia Meigs et al., p. 155–263. Rev. ed. New York: Macmillan, 1969.
Includes chapters on Yonge, Gatty and Ewing; Kingsley, Hughes, Thackeray and Dickens; the nonsense writing of Lear, Carroll and Craik; *Little women;* and the adventure stories of Marryat and "Oliver Optic."

Ellis, Alec. The history of children's reading and literature. New York: Pergamon, [1968].
This book traces the development of working-class education in England and Wales through the nineteenth century. Relevant chapters include: "Books in schools, 1850–1870"; "School and public libraries, 1850–1870"; "The golden years of children's literature, Part 1: 1860–1890"; "School books and literacy, 1870–1902"; "Public libraries for children, 1870–1902."

Eminent women of the age, by James Parton [and others]. Hartford, Conn.: S. M. Betts, 1868.
Includes articles on Grace Greenwood, by J. B. Lyman, p. 147–63; and Alice and Phoebe Cary, by Horace Greely, p. 164–72.

Fox, Claire Gilbride. "Merits and morals," *Horn book magazine* 45:80–84 (February, 1969).
An explanation of the certificates, awarded to children in the nineteenth century, that carried verses with character-shaping themes.

Gottlieb, Gerald, ed. and comp. Early children's books and their illustrations. New York: Pierpont Morgan Library; Boston: Godine, 1975.
Many first editions of the books from this period are excerpted here, with excellent information by Gottlieb.

Green, Roger Lancelyn. Tellers of tales: British authors of books from 1800–1964. Rewritten and rev. ed. New York: Franklin Watts, 1965.
Chapters or partial chapters on George MacDonald, Charlotte M. Yonge, Dinah M. M. Craik, Jean Ingelow, Dickens, Juliana Ewing and Margaret Gatty.

Haviland, Virginia. The travelogue storybook of the nineteenth century. (A Caroline Hewins lecture, 1949.) Boston: Horn Book, 1950.
Fictionalized travel books for the young, with an introduction by Frederic G. Melcher. Bibliography.

———, ed. Children and literature: views and reviews. Glenview, Ill.: Scott, Foresman, [1973].
Reprints of nineteenth-century writings on and reviews of children's books from this period.

—— and **Margaret N. Coughlan.** "Stories after 1850," in their *Yankee Doodle's literary sampler of prose, poetry, and pictures,* p. 190–318. New York: Crowell, [1974].
Selections from *Pictures and stories from Uncle Tom's cabin* (1853), in which Harriet Beecher Stowe herself adapted her great work "to the understanding of the youngest readers . . . to foster in their hearts a generous sympathy for the wronged Negro Race in America." Included also is a selection from Alger's *Ragged Dick* (1868).

Helson, Ravenna. "The psychological origins of fantasy for children in mid-Victorian England," *Children's literature: the great excluded* 3:66–76 (1974).
This essay propounds the thesis "that works of fantasy for children reflect experiences of inner conflict, growth and renewal of the sort Jung described as accompanying the individuation process and that the intensity of these experiences, and also their themes and characters, may be understood in relation to the particular social conditions of mid-Victorian England."

——. "Through the pages of children's books," *Psychology today* 7:107–12 (November, 1973).
Analyzes the literature of the Victorian and Edwardian periods and contemporary books to test the hypothesis that "characters in fantasy for children differ significantly from one historical period to another, and the fantasy itself holds up a curious kind of mirror to the culture."

Hürlimann, Bettina. "Jabberwocky," in her *Three centuries of children's books in Europe,* translated and edited by Brian W. Alderson, p. 64–75. Cleveland: World, 1968.
The writer calls nonsense "the great contribution of the British to children's literature." She compares the *Alice* books to Hans Hoffman's *Struwwelpeter.*

Jones, Helen L. "The part played by Boston publishers of 1860–1900 in the field of children's books," *Horn book magazine* 45:20–28, 153–59, 329–36 (February, April, June, 1963).

Jordan, Alice. "From Rollo to Tom Sawyer," in her *From Rollo to Tom Sawyer, and other papers,* p. 14–45. Boston: Horn Book, 1948.
A survey of American literature from about 1830 to about 1870.

"Juvenile literature," *The British quarterly review* 47:128–49 (1868).
Ostensibly a review of Margaret Gatty's *Parables from nature,* Juliana Ewing's *Melchior's dream,* and other books of the 1860s, but also discusses methods of moral and religious teaching through stories, requisite qualities of writers, and other general topics.

Knickerbocker, Frances Wentworth. "Those nonsensical Victorians," *The bookman* 75:465–71, 584–89 (1932).
Discusses Lear, Thackeray, and Lewis Carroll. Illustrated with drawings and sketches.

Muir, Percy. "The triumph of nonsense," "After Carroll," in his *English children's books 1600–1900,* p. 134–71. New York: Praeger, [1954] reprint: London: Batsford, [1969].
Chapter 5 covers primarily Lear and Carroll. Chapter 6 extends to 1900 but includes Mayne Reid, Hesba Stretton (*Jessica's first prayer,* [1867?]), George MacDonald, Jean Ingelow, and Christina Rossetti.

Nesbitt, Elizabeth. "The early record," *Horn book magazine* 47:268–74 (June, 1971).
Sums up the Golden Age of children's literature, starting with the *Alice* books.

O'Gara, Florence. "A group of English favorites," *Publisher's weekly* 116:2055–60 (1929).
Discusses briefly some of the books of Juliana Ewing, Charlotte Yonge, George MacDonald, and other writers, from the standpoint of reading for the twentieth-century boy and girl.

Our famous women, by Elizabeth Stuart Phelps et al. Hartford, Conn.: Worthington, 1883.
Includes articles on Louisa May Alcott, by Louise Chandler Moulton, p. 29–52; Mary Mapes Dodge, by Lucia Gilbert Runkle, p. 276–94; Mrs. A. D. T. Whitney, by Harriet Beecher Stowe, p. 652–67; Harriet Beecher Stowe, by Rose Terry Cooke, p. 581–601.

Page, H. A. "Children and children's books," *The contemporary review* 11:7–26 (1869).
A general book review, covering, among others, *Stories told to a child* by Jean Ingelow, and Juliana Ewing's *Mrs. Overtheway's remembrances,* with reflections on the qualities required for writing children's books.

Pauly, T. "*Ragged Dick* and *Little women*: idealized homes and unwanted marriages," *Journal of popular culture* 9:583+ (Winter, 1975).
A fascinating analysis of both books, published within a year of each other, from a social point of view.

Priestley, John Boynton. ["Edward Lear and Lewis Carroll,"] in his *English humour,* p. 97–102. London: Longmans, Green, 1929.
A perceptive philosophical essay.

Rosenthal, Lynn Meryl. "The child informed: attitudes towards the socialization of the child in nineteenth century English literature." Ph.D. diss., Columbia University, 1974.
The author "undertakes to examine the changing image of the child in a representative group

of children's books and to consider ways in which attitudes towards the child changed as society itself changed." Chapter 3 deals with books in which the child appears within the context of the school, especially Hughes's *Tom Brown's schooldays*, Farrar's *Eric*, and Kipling's *Stalky & Co*.

Sadleir, Michael. XIX century fiction, a bibliographical record based on his own collection. 2v. London: Constable, [1951]; Berkeley and Los Angeles, University of California Press, 1951.
A bibliography of the author's first editions. Includes bibliographies for Ballantyne, Dickens, Maria Edgeworth, Henty, Kingsley, MacDonald, Marryat, Harriet Martineau, Ouida (de la Ramée), Mayne Reid, Catherine Sinclair, Hesba Stretton, and Thackeray.

St. John, Judith. "Second thoughts about Victorian children's fare," *Wilson library bulletin* 41:590–92 (February, 1967).
A comparison of the work of Hesba Stretton and Amelia Frances Howard Gibbon, creator of "the earliest Canadian picture book for children."

Salmon, Edward. Juvenile literature as it is. London: Henry J. Drane, 1888.
A contemporary account.

Salway, Lance, ed. A peculiar gift: nineteenth century writing on books for children. Harmondsworth, Eng.: Penguin, [1976].
Contemporary writings on children's books, fairy tales, poetry, illustration, what boys and girls should read, boys' stories, and some biographical sketches. Excellent bibliography.

Sewell, Elizabeth. The field of nonsense. London: Chatto & Windus, 1952.
A study, not only of Edward Lear and Lewis Carroll, but also of the philosophical concepts involved in the art of writing nonsense. Bibliography.

Stuart, Dorothy Margaret. "In the 19th century," in her *The girl through the ages*, p. 239–58.

London: Harrap, 1933; reprint: Detroit: Singing Tree, 1969.
Tells what the mid-Victorian child, characterized as "the quintessence of primness," read.

Tassin, Algernon. "Books for children," in *The Cambridge history of American literature*, edited by W. P. Trent et al. v. 2, p. 396–409. New York: Putnam, 1918.
A survey.

Thwaite, Mary F. "Flood-tide: the Victorian age and Edwardian aftermath," in her *From primer to pleasure in reading*, p. 93–224. 2d ed. London: Library Assn., 1972.
Includes a discussion of the innovations in fairy lore and fantasy, nonsense writing, the story of home and school, the adventure story, the animal story, picture books for young children, books of knowledge and periodicals.

Townsend, John Rowe. Written for children: an outline of English language children's literature. Rev. ed. Philadelphia: Lippincott, 1975.
Written in 1965, Pt. 2, "1840–1915," covers adventure stories for boys, "domestic dramas," fantasy, the school story, animal stories, poetry, and illustration.

Turner, Ernest S. Boys will be boys. Rev. ed. London: Michael Joseph, 1974; Harmondsworth, Middlesex, England: Penguin, 1976.

Wood, Michael. "Valley of the dolls," *New society* 34:95–96 (October, 1975).
Examines the plots of Castle Smith, Margaret Gatty, and Frances Hodgson Burnett and concludes that they reflect Victorian middle-class social and moral attitudes toward the poor.

Yonge, Charlotte Mary. What books to lend and what books to give. London: National Society's Repository, 1887.
A contemporary judgment.

EDUCATIONAL BACKGROUND

■ This section covers educational thought and theory through 1900.

Adamson, John William. English education, 1789–1902. Cambridge: Cambridge University Press, 1964.
This fine text on nineteenth-century education traces the movement from religious education to state-controlled public education as influenced by Locke, Rousseau, the French Revolution, Bentham, Mills, and others. Pts. 2 and 3, on the early and late Victorian eras, cover the educational laws and how they affected elementary education.

Altick, Richard R. "Elementary education and literacy," in his *The English common reader: a social history of the mass reading public, 1800–1900*, p. 141–72. Chicago: University of Chicago Press, Phoenix Books, 1957.
The movement to provide public elementary education for the working classes is charted.

Armytage, W. H. G. Four hundred years of English education. Cambridge: Cambridge University Press, 1963.
Chapters 7, 8, and 9 cover the period of educational reform from 1851 to 1900.

Arnold, Matthew. Reports on elementary schools, 1852–1882. London: Macmillan, 1889.
Matthew Arnold was a school inspector from 1851 to 1856. This book contains annual reports made by him and presents a clear picture of elementary education during this period.

Barnard, Howard Clive. A history of English education, from 1760. 2d ed. rev. London: University of London Press, 1961.
This was first printed in 1947 under the title, *A short history of English education, 1760–1944.* There is a section on the mid-Victorian period, which covers state action and state supervision in elementary education, the Education Act of 1870, and the education of girls and women. A bibliography is appended.

Binns, Henry Bryan. A century of education, being the centenary history of the British and Foreign School Society. 1808–1908. London: Dent, 1908.

Craik, Henry. The state in its relation to education. London: Macmillan, 1884.
A fascinating contemporary plea for a more reformed education bill than the Act of 1870.

Curtis, Stanley James. History of education in Great Britain. London: University Tutorial Press, 1948.
Chapters 6, 7, and 8 cover the period from the beginning of state intervention to the founding of a national system.

———, and **M. E. A. Boultwood.** An introductory history of English education since 1800. London: University Tutorial Press, 1960.
Chapter 8, "English thought on education, 1850–1900," discusses the influence of Newman, Matthew Arnold, Mill, Huxley, Spencer, Kingsley, and Ruskin.

Dent, Harold Collett. 1870–1970: century of growth in English education. London: Harlow, Longmans, 1970.
Pt. 1, "Building a national system," covers this period.

Ellis, Alec. Books in Victorian elementary schools. London: Library Association, 1971.
Describes the schoolbooks available from 1830 to 1901. The author concludes that, although books were available, their contents were "irrelevant to the experience of the majority," and they did not attempt "to arouse the interest of those for whom they were ostensibly written."

———. "Elementary education for all, 1870–1902," "School books and literacy, 1870–1902," in his *A history of children's reading and literature,* p. 82–88, 89–99. London: Pergamon, [1968].
Chapter 1 concerns the Education Act of 1870. It provided for the formation of school boards in every school district that did not possess adequate facilities and empowered them to formulate by-laws that would render compulsory the attendance at school of children ages five to thirteen. Chapter 2 discusses the literacy standards effected in codes of 1871, 1881, and 1882.

Lawrence, Evelyn Mary, ed. Frederich Froebel and English education. New York: Philosophical Library, 1953.
Traces the founding of the kindergarten and its history in England from 1852 to 1952.

Lawson, John. A social history of education in England. London: Methuen, 1973.
Includes a discussion of the Education Act of 1870, literacy and school attendance, school codes and subjects, grammar schools, the education of girls, and public schools.

Maclure, J. Stuart. One hundred years of London education, 1870–1970. London: Allen Lane, 1970.
P. 13–76 cover this period.

Manning, John. Dickens on education. Toronto: University of Toronto Press, [1959].
Dickens gave impetus to the move for state-supported education. He provided an exposé of the callous exploitation of certain children and demanded that cruelty to them be stopped. His contribution, says the author, was "emotional rather than intellectual."

Medlin, William K. The history of educational ideas in the West. New York: Center for Applied Research, [1964].
The last part of the book deals with national systems of education in several countries. The section on the American decentralized system is especially good.

Middleton, Nigel, and **Sophia Weitzman.** A place for everyone: a history of state education from the end of the 18th century to the 1970's. London: Gollancz, 1976.

Midwinter, Eric. Nineteenth century education. (Seminar studies in history) New York: Harper, 1970.
Pt. 2, "The growth of public education," covers the monitorial system, state intervention in education, collectivism and education, the school boards, local educational authorities, and secondary education.

Newsome, David. Godliness and good learning: four studies in a Victorian ideal. London: Murray, [1966].
Analyzes the relationship between education and religion in nineteenth-century public schools.

Reisner, Edward H. Nationalism and education since 1789. New York: Macmillan, 1922.

Selleck, Richard Joseph Wheeler. The new education 1870–1914. London: Pitman, 1968.
Discusses the social and political background behind the educational reforms of the mid-nineteenth century.

Shuttleworth, *Sir* **James Kay.** Memorandum on popular education. London: Ridgway, 1868; reprint: (The social history of education series) Fairfield, N.J. Augustus M. Kelley, 1969.
This important document was written by the man most influential in effecting school reform in the nineteenth century.

———. Sir James Kay Shuttleworth on popular education. (Classics in education) Edited with an introduction by Trygve R. Tholfsen. New York: Teachers College Press, [1974].

Some important papers by the English educational reformer.

Simon, Brian. Studies in the history of education, 1780–1870. London: Wishart, 1960.
Relates the social and political reforms of this period to educational reform. Chapter 6 deals with the establishment of a state-supported educational system; chapter 7, with the relationship between the state and education; and chapter 8, with elementary schooling for the working class.

——— and **Ian Bradley,** eds. The Victorian public school: studies in the development of an educational institution. [Dublin]: Gill & Macmillan, [1975].
Advances the theory that the Victorian age and the public school system matured together in the second half of the nineteenth century. Includes many excellent essays, including "The school and the novel: *Tom Brown's school days*," by Patrick Scott, p. 34–57.

INDIVIDUAL WRITERS

Louisa May Alcott

■ Only first editions are listed here. For later editions, consult Madeleine Stern's *Louisa May Alcott* (1950), p. 343–60, or Judith Ullom's *Louisa May Alcott: a centennial for Little women: an annotated, selected bibliography* (1969).

Alcott, Louisa May. Aunt Jo's scrap-bag. Boston: Roberts, 1872–82.
Contents: Vol. 1: My boys, etc., 1872; vol. 2: Shawlstraps, etc., 1872; vol. 3: Cupid and Chowchow, etc., 1874; vol. 4: My girls, etc., 1878; vol. 5: Jimmy's cruise in the *Pinafore*, 1879; vol. 6: An old-fashioned Thanksgiving, 1882.

———. Comic tragedies, written by "Jo" and "Meg" and acted by the "little women." Boston: Roberts, 1893.
"Six elaborate plays, with production notes, that are of the same type as the 'Operatic Tragedy' performed in chapter two of Little Women . . . written and acted by the Alcott sisters around 1848."–Ullom.

———. Eight cousins, or, the aunt-hill. Boston: Roberts, 1875.

———. Flower-fables. Boston: Briggs, 1855.

———. Jack and Jill: a village story. Boston: Roberts, 1880.
Serialized in St. Nicholas, December, 1879–October, 1880.

———. Jo's boys and how they turned out: a sequel to *Little men*. Boston: Roberts, 1886.
The author did not consider this a children's book, as the main characters are all grown men.

———. Little men: life at Plumfield with Jo's boys. Boston: Roberts, 1871.
Sequel to *Little women*.

———. Little women, or, Meg, Jo, Beth, and Amy. 2v. Boston: Roberts, 1868–69.
Illustrated by Louisa May Alcott. Published in two volumes in two years.

———. Lulu's library. 3v. Boston: Roberts, 1886, 1887, 1889.
Vol. 3 has a story titled, "Recollections of my childhood," which is an autobiographical account.

———. Morning-glories, and other stories. Boston. H. B. Fuller, 1868.

———. An old-fashioned girl. Boston: Roberts, 1870.
Serialized in *Merry's museum*, 1869.

———. Proverb stories. Boston: Roberts, 1882.

———. The rose family: a fairy tale. Boston: Redpath, 1864.

———. Rose in bloom: a sequel to *Eight cousins*. Boston: Roberts, 1876.

———. Silver pitchers; and Independence: a centennial love story. Boston: Roberts, 1876.

———. Spinning-wheel stories. Boston: Roberts, 1884.
Serialized in *St. Nicholas,* 1884–85.

———. Under the lilacs. Boston: Roberts, 1878.
Serialized in *St. Nicholas,* 1877–78.

———. Will's wonder book. Boston: H. B. Fuller, [1870]. (The Dirigo series) Serialized in *Merry's museum,* 1868. Discovered by Madeleine Stern.
The original publication of what was later called *Louisa's wonder book* (see below).

BIOGRAPHY AND CRITICISM

Anthony, Katherine Susan. Louisa May Alcott. New York: Knopf, 1938.
"A psychoanalytic study of Louisa May Alcott." —Ullom. An early biography, considered inaccurate.

Barrett, C. Waller. "*Little women* forever," in *Bibliophile in the nursery,* edited by William Targ, p. 379–86. Cleveland: World, 1957.
Presents some "little known facts of interest to all students and collectors."

Blanck, Jacob N. "Louisa May Alcott," in his *Bibliography of American literature,* v. 1, p. 27–35. New Haven, Conn.: Yale University Press for the Bibliographical Society of America, 1955.
A bibliographic essay of first editions, chronologically arranged. Other bibliographies included.

Bradford, Gamaliel. "Louisa May Alcott," in his *Portraits of American women,* p. 165–94. Boston: Houghton, 1919.
"Every creative author builds his books out of his own experience . . . . But few have drawn upon the fund more extensively and constantly than Miss Alcott."

Brophy, Brigid. "A masterpiece and dreadful," *New York Times book review,* January 17, 1965, p. 2; in *Children and literature: views and reviews,* edited by Virginia Haviland, p. 66–70. Glenview, Ill.: Scott, Foresman, 1973.
A beautifully written essay, which concludes that *Little women* is a gently sentimental masterpiece.

"**Centenary of *Little women,* 1868–1968,**" *Horn book magazine,* v. 45. October, 1968.
An entire issue of *Horn book magazine* devoted to Louisa May Alcott's perennially popular story of American family life. Includes articles by Cornelia Meigs, Lavinia Russ, Aileen Fisher, and Olive Rabe.

Cheney, Ednah Dow Littlehale. Louisa May Alcott: the children's friend. Boston: Prang, [1888].

———. The story of the Alcotts. Boston: Little, n.d.
A short biographical sketch, condensed from her longer work. Includes several portraits of Louisa and her family.

———, ed. Louisa May Alcott: her life, letters, and journals. Boston: Roberts, 1889; reprint: Boston: Little, 1928.
The extracts from journals and letters are characteristic in feeling and expression, and the book as a whole is indispensable for reference.

Crompton, M. "*Little women:* the making of a classic," *Contemporary review* 218:99–104 (February, 1971).
A concise biography.

Fisher, Aileen, and **Olive Rabe.** We Alcotts: the story of Louisa May Alcott's family as seen through the eyes of Marmee, mother of *Little women.* New York: Atheneum, 1968.
This is an informal biography for children "of a happy and loving family, holding to high principles and natural gaiety in the face of uncommon privations . . . ."—Publisher's note. Decorations by Ellen Raskin.

Gulliver, Lucile, comp. Louisa May Alcott: a bibliography, with an appreciation by Cornelia Meigs. Boston: Little, 1932.
Includes a chronologically arranged checklist of Louisa May Alcott's books for children.

Janeway, E. "Meg, Jo, Beth, Amy, and Louisa," *New York Times book review,* September 29, 1968, p. 42+.

Meigs, Cornelia. Invincible Louisa: the story of the author of *Little women.* Boston: Little, 1968.
At the head of title: Alcott Centennial Edition. A reprint of *The story of the author of* Little women (listed below). This edition has been reset in smaller format and includes a new introduction by the author.

———. Louisa M. Alcott and the American family story. (Walck and Bodley Head monographs) New York: Walck; London: Bodley Head, 1971.
The author says that, for the first time, Louisa Alcott offered a completely true chronicle of an American family exactly as it was. Pt. 1 is a biography of Louisa May Alcott; pt. 2 is a study of the American family story.

———. The story of the author of *Little women:* invincible Louisa. Boston: Little, 1933.
Little women, the book that first brought fame to its author, is still one of the most popular girls' stories. The incidents were drawn from the real life of the four sisters, one of whom was the "invincible Louisa." This interesting account of her battle for achievement is written by one whose own life and books owe much to the inspiration of Louisa May Alcott. Includes illustrations. This book was awarded the Newbery medal for 1934.

Moses, Belle. Louisa May Alcott, dreamer and worker: a story of enchantment. New York: Appleton, 1909.
Introduces Louisa May Alcott "to her girl friends as a girl like themselves who worked, who struggled, and who conquered by sheer force of energy and perseverance."—introduction.

Pearce, Catherine Owens. Louisa May Alcott: her life. New York: Holt, 1954.
A fictionalized account intended for young people. Uses quotations from Louisa Alcott's journal.

Rosenberg, Leona. "Some anonymous or pseudonymous thrillers of Louisa M. Alcott," *The papers of the Bibliographical Society of America,* 37: 131–40 (1943).
Records the "sensational fiction" written anonymously and under the name of A. M. Barnard.

Saxton, Martha. Louisa May: a modern biography of Louisa May Alcott. Boston: Houghton, 1977.
A psychoanalytic study of the woman and her art. Analyzes Louisa May Alcott as a part of a domineering family and concludes that *Little women,* which has a place in American culture along with taffy pulling and Flag Day, "is the story of the childhood Louisa would have had if her parents had described it." There is one chapter on *Little women.*

Stearns, Frank Preston. "Louisa M. Alcott," in his *Sketches from Concord and Appledore,* p. 69–88. New York: Putnam, 1895.
In commenting upon *Little women,* the author notes that the book, though the style is not classic, "filled a vacant place in American and perhaps also in English literature, and must continue to fill it."

Stern, Madeleine B. Louisa May Alcott. Norman: University of Oklahoma Press, 1950; London: Peter Nevill, 1952.
The standard and complete biography, which brings out the connections between the writing of *Little women* and the author's family. Bibliography and notes on sources.

———. "Louisa M. Alcott: an appraisal," *New England quarterly* 22:475–98 (December, 1949).
A scholarly work about Louisa May Alcott's technique, her "composite" method style of writing, her characters, and those who influenced her work: Bunyan, Dickens, Carlyle, Thoreau, Emerson, and Hawthorne.

———. "Louisa M. Alcott's contribution to periodicals, 1868–1888," *More books* (Boston Public Library) 18:411–20 (1943).

———. Louisa's wonder book: an unknown Alcott juvenile. Mount Pleasant: Central Michigan University Press, 1975.

Along with a reprint of an 1870 edition of *Will's wonder book,* this includes an introduction and a chronological bibliography of Alcott's writings.

———. "The witch's cauldron to the family hearth: Louisa M. Alcott's literary development, 1848–1868 . . . including full notes and a selective bibliography of the works of Louisa May Alcott, 1848–1868," *More books* (Boston Public Library) 18:363–80 (1943).
An interpretation of the early writing that led up to the author's *Little women.*

———, ed. Behind a mask: the unknown thrillers of Louisa May Alcott. New York: Morrow, 1975.
Four "blood-and-thunder" thrillers written anonymously or pseudonymously. Edited and introduced by this Alcott scholar.

———. Plots and counterplots: more unknown thrillers of Louisa May Alcott. New York: Morrow, 1976.
A continuation of the above work.

Ticknor, Caroline. May Alcott: a memoir. Boston: Little, 1928.
Intimate picture of the Alcott family.

Ullom, Judith C. Louisa May Alcott: a centennial for *Little women*: an annotated, selected bibliography. Washington, D.C.: Library of Congress, 1969.
A bibliography prepared for use as a catalog of the exhibit of Louisa May Alcott items at the Library of Congress in 1968 to celebrate the centennial of the publication of *Little women.* Includes sections entitled "Early writings," "Novels," "*Little women* series," "Multi-volume collections," "Single-volume collections," "Separate editions of stories," "Collections with contributions by Miss Alcott," "Modern anthologies," and "Bio-critical studies."

Winterich, John Tracy. "Little women," *Publishers weekly* 120:607–11 (1931).
One of a series entitled Romantic stories of books. Reproduces title page of first edition.

Worthington, Marjorie. Miss Alcott of Concord. Garden City, N.Y.: Doubleday, 1958.
Includes many excerpts from Louisa May Alcott's journals.

Thomas Bailey Aldrich

Aldrich, Thomas Bailey. A midnight fantasy *and* The little violinist. Boston: Osgood, 1877.

———. Pansy's wish: a Christmas fantasy with a moral. Boston: Marion, 1870.

————. The story of a bad boy. Boston: Fields, Osgood, 1870.
When he reviewed the book, William Dean Howells wrote that it was "an absolute novelty" in its creation of a real boy. It was originally published in twelve installments in *Our young folks*, January to December, 1869.

————. ————. Boston: Houghton, 1894.
Illustrated by A. B. Frost. "A preface, in which the author declines to write one," p. iii–viii.

————. ————. (Classics of children's literature 1621–1932) New York: Garland, 1976.
The preface is by Ann Beattie.

————, tr. The story of a cat. From the French of Émile de la Bedollierre. Boston: Houghton, 1879.

BIOGRAPHY AND CRITICISM

Aldrich, *Mrs.* Thomas Bailey. Crowding memories. Boston: Houghton, 1920.
Pleasantly written reminiscences giving intimate glimpses of the home life of Mrs. Aldrich and her husband.

Beattie, Ann. "The story of a bad boy," *Children's literature* 5:63–65 (1976).
Compares Aldrich's book with Twain's *Tom Sawyer*.

Cosgrove, Mary S. "The life and times of Thomas Bailey Aldrich," *Horn book magazine* 42:223–32, 350–55, 464–73 (April, June, August, 1966).
Aldrich's New England and the writing of *The story of a bad boy*, concluding with a critical judgment of Aldrich as a writer.

Geller, Evelyn. "Tom Sawyer, Tom Bailey, and the bad-boy genre," *Wilson library bulletin* 50: 245–50 (November, 1976).
Shows how Twain's classic is based on *The story of a bad boy*, the original of the "bad boy" genre, a term coined by Richard Darling.

Greenslet, Ferris. The life of Thomas Bailey Aldrich. Boston: Houghton, 1908.
"Mr. Greenslet has brought to his work delicacy and reticence, together with a skill in words that reproduces something of the charm of one who made refinement the end of all his labor. It is a happy life gracefully told."—condensed from *The nation*, 1908. The first chapter, entitled "Tom Bailey," p. 1–17, describes Aldrich's boyhood in Portsmouth. The publication and historical importance of *The story of a bad boy* are noted, p. 91–93. There are numerous illustrations; also a bibliography, p. 261–92.

Howells, William Dean. "Review and literary notices," *Atlantic* 25:124 (January, 1879).
Howell's positive review of *The story of a bad boy*.

Perry, Bliss. "Thomas Bailey Aldrich," in his *Park-street papers*, p. 141–70. Boston: Houghton, 1908.
Written after the death of Aldrich in 1907.

Samuels, Charles S. Thomas Bailey Aldrich. (Twayne's U.S. authors series) New York: Twayne, 1965.
A section on *The story of a bad boy*, p. 82–92, deals with the novel as a realistic portrait of a young boy and boyhood. Includes a bibliography of primary, secondary, and background sources.

Winter, William. "Thomas Bailey Aldrich," in his *Old friends: literary recollections of other days*, p. 132–52. New York: Moffat, 1909.
Intimate personal glimpses.

Horatio Alger

■ Over 120 books bear Horatio Alger's name. Listed below are a few of his series. For a complete bibliography, see Ralph Gardner's *Horatio Alger, or the American hero era*, which includes a listing of 123 books (by title), poems, short stories, and articles.

Alger, Horatio. Atlantic series. Philadelphia: Porter & Coates.
v. 1. The young circus rider; or, The mystery of Robert Rudd. 1883.
v.2. Do and dare; or, A brave boy's fight for fortune. 1884.
v. 3. Helping himself; or, Giant Thornton's ambition. 1886.

————. Brave and Bold series. Boston: Loring.
v. 1. Brave and bold; or, The fortunes of a factory boy. 1874.
v. 2. Jack's ward; or, The boy guardian. 1875.
v. 3. Shifting for himself; or, Gilbert Greyson's fortunes. 1876.
v. 4. Wait and hope; or, Ben Bradford's motto. 1877.

————. Campaign series. Boston: Loring.
v. 1. Frank's campaign; or, What boys can do on the farm for the camp. 1864.
v. 2. Paul Prescott's charge. 1865.
v. 3. Charlie Codman's cruise. 1866.

————. Luck and pluck series. Boston: Loring.
v. 1. Luck and pluck; or, John Oakley's inheritance. 1869.
v. 2. Sink or swim; or, Harry Raymond's resolve. 1870.
v. 3. Strong and steady; or, Paddle your own canoe. 1871.

v. 4. Strive and succeed; or, The progress of Walter Conrad. 1872.

v. 5. Try and trust; or, The story of a bound boy. 1873.

v. 6. Bound to rise; or, Harry Walton's motto. 1873.

v. 7. Risen from the ranks; or, Harry Walton's success. 1874.

———. Pacific series. Boston: Loring.

v. 1. The young adventurer; or, Tom's trip across the plain. 1878.

v. 2. The young miner; or, Tom Nelson in California. 1879.

v. 3. The young explorer; or, Among the Sierras. 1880.

v. 4. Ben's nugget; or, A boy's search for fortune. Philadelphia: Porter & Coates, 1882.

———. Ragged Dick series. Boston: Loring.

v. 1. Ragged Dick; or, Street life in New York. 1868.

v. 2. Fame and fortune; or, The progress of Richard Hunter. 1868.

v. 3. Mark, the match boy; or, Richard Hunter's ward. 1869.

v. 4. Rough and ready; or, Life among the New York newsboys. 1869.

v. 5. Rufus and Rose; or, The fortunes of rough and ready. 1870.

v. 6. Ben, the luggage boy; or, Among the wharves. 1870.

———. Way to Success series. Philadelphia. Porter & Coates.

v. 1. The store boy; or, The fortunes of Ben Barclay, 1887.

v. 2. Bob Burton; or, The young ranchman of Missouri. 1888.

v. 3. Luke Walton; or, The Chicago newsboy. 1889.

BIOGRAPHY AND CRITICISM

Alger, Horatio. "Writing stories for boys," *The writer* 9:36–37 (March, 1896).

Allen, Frederick L. "Horatio Alger, Jr.," *The Saturday review of literature* 18:3–4, 16–17 (September 17, 1938).
Discusses Horatio Alger's "far-reaching influence upon the economic and social thought of America —an influence all the greater . . . because it was innocently and naively and undogmatically exerted."

Bales, J. "Herbert R. Mayes and Horatio Alger, Jr., or the story of a unique literary hoax," *Journal of popular culture* 8:317–19 (Fall, 1974).

Gardner, Ralph. Horatio Alger, or the American hero. Mendota, Ill.: Wayside Press, 1964.

Gardner, "an Alger collector, is an amateur scholar, and allowed himself the creative licence which a more academic mind would have avoided." —John Seelye. Includes a long bibliography of Alger's prose and poetry, p. 394–497.

———. Road to success: a bibliography of Horatio Alger. Mendota, Ill.: Wayside Press, 1971.

Gruber, Frank. Horatio Alger, Jr.: a biography and bibliography of the best-selling author of all times. Los Angeles: Grover Jones Press, 1961.
Privately printed, 700 copies. Gruber was the first to realize that the Mayes biography was "inaccurate," probably because Alger had indeed led a rather dull life.

Hoyt, Edwin P. Horatio's boys: the life and works of Horatio Alger, Jr. Radnor, Pa.: Chilton, 1974.
A complete, unflinching biography that details Alger's relationship with W. T. Adams and his personal crusade against the plight of poor waifs in the city.

Mayes, Herbert R. Alger: a biography without a hero. New York: Macy-Masius, 1928.
This biography, allegedly based on a diary kept by Alger during his lifetime, is now considered one of the greatest literary hoaxes. When pressed, Mayes finally admitted the book was a fraud, saying, "Not merely was my Alger biography partly fictional, it was practically all fictional."

Seelye, John. "Who was Horatio Alger? the Alger myth and American scholarship," *American quarterly* 17:749–56 (Winter, 1965).
A critical evaluation of the biographical works about Alger.

Tebbel, John W. From rags to riches: Horatio Alger, Jr., and the American dream. New York: Macmillan, 1963.
Analyzes the reasons for the popularity of Alger as a writer. As biography, this almost duplicates the material in Herbert Mayes's biography.

Zuckerman, Michael. "Nursery tales of Horatio Alger," *American quarterly* 24:191–209 (May, 1972).
A long, analytical study of the Ragged Dick series.

Robert M. Ballantyne

■ R. M. Ballantyne published well over 100 books in his lifetime. Eric Quayle's book *R. M. Ballantyne: a bibliography of first editions* (listed below) is an excellent chronological bibliography of Ballantyne's complete published works. Only the best known are listed below.

Ballantyne, Robert Michael. The coral island: a tale of the Pacific Ocean. London: Nelson, 1858.
Ralph Rover, who thirsts for adventure in foreign lands, relates his story for boys "in the earnest hope that they may derive valuable information, much pleasure, great profit, and unbounded amusement."—preface.

————. The dog Crusoe: a tale of western prairies. London: Nelson, 1861.

————. The gorilla hunters; a tale of the wilds of Africa. London: Nelson, 1861.
Quayle says this book was based on a book by Paul du Chaillu, *Explorations in equatorial Africa,* published in spring, 1861, one of the earliest accounts of the "ferocious wild men of the forest," as he termed the apes.

————. Martin Rattler, or, a boy's adventures in the forests of Brazil. London: Nelson, 1858.

————. Ungava: a tale of Esquimaux-land. London: Nelson, 1858.
According to Quayle, Ballantyne based this book largely on his own experiences when he worked as a clerk for the Hudson's Bay Company in the 1840s.

BIOGRAPHY AND CRITICISM

Atherton, Stan. "Escape to the Arctic: R. M. Ballantyne's Canadian stories," *Canadian children's literature* 1:29–34 (Spring, 1975).

Ballantyne, R. M. "Personal reminiscences," edited with an introduction by Lance Salway. *Signal* 15:141–53 (September, 1974).
This is a reprint of the introduction to *Personal reminiscences* (listed below), in which Ballantyne discusses his research techniques.

————. Personal reminiscences in book-making. London: J. Nisbet, [1893].
This autobiography was written only a year before Ballantyne died.

Butts, D. R. M. "Ballantyne," *School librarian* 14:268–72 (December, 1966).
Discusses *Coral island, Young fur trader, Ungava, Dog Crusoe,* and *Martin Rattler* as examples of late-nineteenth-century romantic adventure stories, written from personal experience.

Collingwood, Frances. "The boys' friend," *Library review* 25:63–64 (Summer, 1975).
To boys, "Ballantyne was that admirable man who had provided them with the sort of adventure stories for which they craved."

Green, Roger Lancelyn. "Stories of adventure," in his *Tellers of tales,* p. 74–84. Rewritten and rev. ed. New York: Watts, 1965.

Green says that now Ballantyne's books are even more popular than Marryat's, because he "wrote more simply, and with a great attention to the exciting nature of his stories. He had an easy racy style, and an excellent first-hand knowledge of nearly every scene of which he chose to write."

Osborne, Edgar. "Ballantyne, the pioneer," *Junior bookshelf* 8:6–11 (March, 1944).

Quayle, Eric. Ballantyne the brave: a Victorian writer and his family. London: Hart-Davis, 1967.
An excellent study in which Quayle, a Ballantyne bibliographer and collector, relates the adventure books to Ballantyne's life and work. He concludes, "Not only was Ballantyne one of the romantic figures of literature in the later Victorian era, he was also a pioneer of the straightforward adventure story set in a factual background."

————. R. M. Ballantyne: a bibliography of first editions. London: Dawsons, 1968.
A chronological listing of Ballantyne's stories for young people, a selected bibliography of his works that appeared in newspapers, magazines, and periodicals, and a list of his unpublished works.

"Robert Michael Ballantyne," *The chimney corner* (Leeds, England, Public Libraries) 24:185–87 (March, 1935).
Short biographical account with notes for four of Ballantyne's most popular stories.

Rodd, Lewis Charles. Young fur trader: the story of R. M. Ballantyne. (Know your authors series) Melbourne: Cheshire, 1966.
A biography intended for young people.

Lewis Carroll

THE ALICE BOOKS

Dodgson, Charles Lutwidge (*pseud.* Lewis Carroll). Alice's adventures in Wonderland. London: Macmillan, 1865.
Forty-two illustrations by John Tenniel. This is the first issue of the first printing. Carroll was displeased with the printing and he recalled it. The second issue has a 1866 date.

————. Alice's adventures in Wonderland *and* Through the looking-glass and what Alice found there. London: Oxford University Press, 1971.
Illustrated by John Tenniel. Introduction by Roger Lancelyn Green.

————. Alice's adventures underground, being a facsimile of the MS. book. London: Macmillian, 1876; reprint: 1932.
The 1932 edition honored the Lewis Carroll centenary.

———. ———. Ann Arbor, Mich.: University Micro-
films, 1964.
A facsimile of the original Lewis Carroll manuscript.

———. ———. New York: McGraw-Hill and Dover,
1965.
A facsimile of the original Carroll manuscript,
with additional material from the facsimile edition
of 1886, and an introduction by Martin Gardner.
Prepared with the cooperation of the British Museum. The introduction gives the history of the
facsimile editions. Also contains Carroll's preface,
his "Easter greeting," and his poem "Christmas
greetings."

———. The annotated Alice: *Alice's adventures in
Wonderland* and *Through the looking-glass.*
New York: Potter, 1960.
Illustrated by John Tenniel. With an introduction and notes by Martin Gardner. Reproduces the
text of both *Alice* books with Tenniel illustrations.
Explains in marginal notes most of the parodies
and allusions to contemporary sayings and events,
as well as the references to the card game in *Alice*
and the chess game in *Through the looking-glass.*
Bibliography covers several aspects of Carrolliana.

———. Nursery "Alice" containing twenty coloured
enlargements from Tenniel's illustrations to
Alice's adventures in Wonderland, with text
adapted to nursery readers by Lewis Carroll.
London: Macmillan, 1890.
An 1889 edition was suppressed.

———. ———. New York: McGraw-Hill, 1966.
With a new introduction by Martin Gardner.
This facsimile of the second edition of the *Nursery
"Alice"* also includes "A nursery darling," "Christ-
mas greetings," and "Cautions to readers."

———. Through the looking-glass, and what Alice
found there. London: Macmillan, 1872 [1871].
With fifty illustrations by John Tenniel.

HUNTING OF THE SNARK

Dodgson, Charles Lutwidge (*pseud.* Lewis Carroll). The annotated snark: the full text of
Lewis Carroll's great nonsense epic, *The hunting
of the snark*, and the original illustrations by
Henry Holiday. New York: Simon & Schuster,
1962.
Introduction and notes by Martin Gardner.

———. The hunting of the snark. Nine illustrations by Henry Holiday. London: Macmillan,
1876.

———. ———. New Rochelle, N.Y.: Peter Pauper,
1932.
Illustrated by Edward Wilson. Other editions
of *The hunting of the snark* have been illustrated

by Kelly Oechsli (1966) and Helen Oxenbury
(1971).

———. The snark puzzle book. New York: Simon &
Schuster, 1973.
Introduction by Martin Gardner. Includes the
original illustrations by Harry Furniss for *The
hunting of the snark* and those by Henry Holiday
for *Jabberwocky.*

SYLVIE AND BRUNO

Dodgson, Charles Lutwidge (*pseud.* Lewis Carroll).
Sylvie and Bruno. 2v. London: Macmillan,
1889 and 1893.
Illustrations by Harry Furniss. The preface to
vol. 1 indicates the genesis of the book, and the
preface to vol. 2, the theory on which the story
is constructed. Title of vol. 2 reads *Sylvie and
Bruno concluded.*

———. ———. (Classics of children's literature 1621–
1932) New York: Garland, 1976.
Vol. 1 only. Introduction by Edwin J. Kenney,
Jr.

OTHER WORKS

Dodgson, Charles Lutwidge (*pseud.* Lewis Carroll).
The collected verse of Lewis Carroll. New
York: Dutton, 1929.
Introduction by J. F. McDermott.

———. The collected verse of Lewis Carroll (the
Rev. Charles Lutwidge Dodgson). New York:
Macmillan, 1933.
Illustrations by John Tenniel, A. B. Frost, Harry
Furniss, Henry Holiday, and the author.

———. The complete works of Lewis Carroll. New
York: Random, Modern Library, 1936; reprint:
New York: Vintage, 1976.
Introduced by Alexander Woolcott and illus-
trated by John Tenniel.

———. Doublets: a word puzzle. London: Macmillan, 1879.

———. "Feeding the mind," *Harper's monthly
magazine* 112:937–39 (1906).
First publication of a humorous essay regarding the proper kind, amount, and variety of our
mental food.

———. The humorous verse of Lewis Carroll. New
York: Dover, 1933; reprint, 1960.
Illustrated by John Tenniel and others.

———. The Lewis Carroll book. Edited by Rich-
ard Herrick. New York: Dial, 1931.
Illustrated by John Tenniel and Henry Holiday.
Contents: Alice in Wonderland; Phantasmagoria;
Through the looking-glass; A tangled tale; The
hunting of the snark; Nonsense from letters.

———. The Lewis Carroll picture book: a selection from [his] writings and drawings . . . together with reprints from scarce and unacknowledged work. Edited by Stuart Dodgson Collingwood. London: T. Fisher Unwin, 1899.
Profusely illustrated.

———. Logical nonsense: the works of Lewis Carroll. Edited by Philip C. Blackburn and Lionel White. New York: Putnam, 1934.

———. The mad gardener's song. Indianapolis, Ind.: Bobbs-Merrill, 1967.
Illustrated by Sean Morrison.

———. The pig-tale. Boston: Little, 1975.
Illustrated by Leonard B. Lubin.

———. The rectory umbrella *and* Mischmasch. London: Cassell, 1932.
Foreword by Florence Milner of the Harvard College Library. *Rectory umbrella* and *Mischmasch* were two of the eight manuscript magazines that Dodgson began as a child. They are included in the Harcourt Amory collection of Lewis Carroll in the Harvard University Library.

———. Rhyme? and Reason? London: Macmillan, 1883.
A collection of seventeen of Carroll's long and short poems, including *The hunting of the snark*. Sixty-five illustrations by Arthur B. Frost and by Henry Holiday.

———. ———. (Classics in children's literature 1621–1932) New York: Garland, 1976.
Includes a preface by K. Naryan Kutty and a biographical note by Susan M. Kenney.

———. A selection from the letters of Lewis Carroll (the Rev. Charles Lutwidge Dodgson) to his child-friends, together with "Eight or nine words about letter-writing." Edited with an introduction and notes by Evelyn M. Hatch. London: Macmillan, 1933; reprint: Folcroft, Pa.: Folcroft, 1973.

———. Six letters by Lewis Carroll. London: printed for private distribution, 1924.
Six letters not included in Collingwood.

———. A tangled tale. London: Macmillan, 1885.
Six illustrations by Arthur B. Frost.

———. Three sunsets, and other poems, with 12 fairy fancies. London: Macmillan, 1898.

———. Useful and instructive poetry. New York: Macmillan, 1954.
Introduction by Derek Hudson.
This is Carroll's first work, written when he was thirteen years old for his younger brother and sister. Includes his own drawings.

BIOGRAPHY AND CRITICISM

Allen, Philip Loring. "The sketch-books of Wonderland," *The bookman* 26:648–51 (1908).
Compares the illustrations of Peter Newell and Arthur Rackham for *Alice's adventures in Wonderland* with those of Sir John Tenniel.

Ayres, Harry Morgan. Carroll's *Alice*. New York: Columbia University Press, 1936.
A lecture delivered at Columbia University, commemorating the 100th anniversary of the birth of Lewis Carroll.

Bowman, Isa. Lewis Carroll as I knew him. New York: Dover, 1972.
A reprint of *The story of Lewis Carroll* (see below).

———. The story of Lewis Carroll. New York: Dutton; London: Dent, 1899.
Subtitle: "told for young people by the real Alice in Wonderland, Miss Isa Bowman, with a diary and numerous facsimile letters written to Miss Isa Bowman and others; also many sketches and photos by Lewis Carroll and other illustrations." Isa Bowman was the first to portray Alice on the stage.

Bowman, Kathleen. Play, games and sport: the literary works of Lewis Carroll. Ithaca, N.Y.: Cornell University Press, 1974.
A study of the theme of play in Carroll's works, because "play of all sorts infuses Carroll's imaginative literature, infuses meaning and structure, and the author's attitude toward his work and his reader."—introduction.

Collingwood, Stuart Dodgson. "Before *Alice*: the boyhood of Lewis Carroll," *The Strand magazine* 16:616–27 (1898).

———. The life and letters of Lewis Carroll. London: T. Fisher Unwin, 1898.
Quotes entertaining letters to and from children and gives interesting details about his books. Numerous illustrations, including sketches and photographs by Lewis Carroll. Includes a bibliography.

de la Mare, Walter John. Lewis Carroll. London: Faber & Faber, [1932]; reprint: Detroit: Gale, 1967.
This version has a few omissions and occasional changes in wording from the essay published in *The eighteen-eighties*, noted below. The excellent introduction traces the advent of humor in literature of the nineteenth century.

———. "Lewis Carroll," in *The eighteen-eighties*, edited by Walter de la Mare, p. 218–55. Cambridge: Cambridge University Press, 1930.
An appreciative and discriminating essay. Shorter articles by de la Mare will be found in *The fort-*

nightly review for September, 1931 (134, new ser. 128:319–31) and in _The Saturday review of literature_ for October 11, 1930 (7:202–3).

Dodgson, Charles Lutwidge. The diaries of Lewis Carroll. Edited and supplemented by Roger Lancelyn Green. New York: Oxford University Press, 1954; reprint: Westport, Conn.: Greenwood, 1971.
Aside from Stuart Collingwood, nephew of Dodgson, no one was given access to the diaries until 1950, when they were given to Green to edit. There is a biographical introduction. Chapter 5, p. 168–208, concerns "The making of _Alice_, 1860–1863."

Empson, William. "Alice in Wonderland," in his _Some versions of pastoral_, p. 251–94. London: Chatto & Windus, 1935.
A well-known scholar theorizes that "both _Alice_ books are so frankly about growing up that there is no great discovery in translating them into Freudian terms."

Fadiman, Clifton. "The maze in the snow," in his _Party of one_, p. 404–10. Cleveland: World, 1955.
Discusses "the whole phenomenon of Carrollatry" and concludes that "what gives the _Alice_ books their varying but permanent appeal is the strange mixture in them of this deep passion for children and the child's world with an equally deep and less conscious passion for exploring the dream world, even the nightmare world, filled with guilts and fears, which is a major part of the child's life, and therefore a major part of our grown-up life."

Fisher, John. The magic of Lewis Carroll. New York: Simon & Schuster, [1973].
About Carroll's interest in magic—games, puzzles, riddles, charades, mazes, labyrinths, etc.

Gattégno, Jean. Lewis Carroll: fragments of a looking-glass. Translated by Rosemary Sheed. New York: Crowell, 1976.
A deliberately episodic biography/interpretation of Carroll and his writings, intended to fall together (in puzzle form) at the conclusion.

Gernsheim, Helmut. Lewis Carroll, photographer. New York: Chanticleer, 1949; Rev. ed. (paperback): New York: Dover, 1969.
Dodgson was one of the nineteenth century's outstanding photographers. The book, which includes a chapter on the state of nineteenth-century photography, also includes many of Carroll's photographs of such famous people as the Rossettis, the MacDonalds, Arthur Hughes, Tennyson, and Charlotte Yonge.

Green, Roger Lancelyn. Lewis Carroll. London: Bodley Head, 1960; New York: Walck, 1962.
Brief biographical material as the background for a critical comment on the development of the _Alice_ books. Also contains a twentieth-century appraisal of _Alice_ as children's literature. Bibliography.

———. "Lewis Carroll," in his _Tellers of tales_, p. 49–62. Rewritten and rev. ed. New York: Watts, 1965.

Greenacre, Phyllis. Swift and Carroll: a psychoanalytic study of two lives. New York: International Universities, 1955.
The standard psychoanalytic study of Lewis Carroll. The section on Carroll is on p. 117–246, and there is a chapter called "Notes on nonsense," p. 263–77.

Guiliano, Edward, ed. Lewis Carroll observed: a collection of unpublished photographs, drawings, poetry, and new essays. New York: Potter, [1976].
Contents: Laughing and grief: what's so funny? by Donald Rackin; Speak roughly, by Martin Gardner; Arthur Rackham's adventures in Wonderland, by Michael Hearn; Lewis Carroll as photographer: a series of photographs of young girls, by Edward Guiliano; The nonsense system in Lewis Carroll's work and in today's world, by Elizabeth Sewell; High art and low amusement, by Roger B. Henkle; Assessing Lewis Carroll, by Jean Gattégno; Carroll's "The Ligniad": an early mock epic in facsimile, by R. L. Green; Hark the snark, by Morton Cohen; Whale or Boojum: an agony, by Harold Beaver; The _Sylvie and Bruno_ books as Victorian novel, by Edmund Muller; Lewis Carroll as artist, by Edward Guiliano; Lewis Carroll the Pre-Raphaelite, by Jeffrey Stein; The game of logic: a game of universe, by Ernest Coumet; The film collector's _Alice_, by David Schaefer.

Hatch, Beatrice. "'Lewis Carroll' (Charles Lutwidge Dodgson)," _The Strand magazine_ 15:413–23 (1898); in _A Peculiar gift_, edited by Lance Salway, p. 492–502. Harmondsworth, Eng.: Penguin, 1976.
A personal reminiscence written at the time of Carroll's death by a "child-friend" of his. Illustrations from photographs, facsimiles, and drawings. A silhouette and three reproductions from photographs will be found on p. 412 of _The Strand magazine_.

Heath, Peter Lauchlon. The philosopher's Alice: _Alice's adventures in Wonderland_ and _Through the looking-glass_. New York: St. Martin's, 1974.
Provides for adults "accessible guidance to its [the _Alice_ books'] logico-philosophical content."

Hellems, Fred Curton Ranney. "Alice and education," _The Atlantic monthly_ 111:256–65 (1913).
Argues that

> The dream-child moving through a land
> Of wonders wild and new,

"is simply the human race in its search . . . for education and educational methods."

Hudson, Derek. Lewis Carroll. (Writers and their work series) London: Longmans for the British Council and the National Book League, [1958].
A separate, shortened work derived from the work listed below. Analyzing prevailing myths about Carroll, Hudson says, "Never perhaps has a writer turned his repressions to such healthy uses as Lewis Carroll. He triumphed over his dilemma, and though his own life was not entirely happy, he has given pleasure to millions. He belongs neither to the 'highbrow' nor to the psychoanalyst; he belongs to the children and to all who have the gift of laughter, anywhere in the world." Includes good select bibliography.

―――. Lewis Carroll. London: Constable, 1954.
This well-known biography is influenced by the publication of Carroll's diaries and the overwhelming Freudian analysis of Carroll's personality.

Huxley, Francis. The raven and the writing desk. New York: Harper, [1976].
A scholarly look at nonsense.

"Immortal Alice," *Littell's living age* 342:53–59 (1932).
Same as "Lewis Carroll" article listed below.

Jabberwocky (Lewis Carroll Society of England).
This journal is intended to publish and assist "in the publication of material dealing with aspects of the life, work, time and influence of Lewis Carroll." Published quarterly. (Note: There is also a Lewis Carroll Society of North America.)

Jorgens, Jack J. "Alice our contemporary," *Children's literature: the great excluded* 1:152–61 (1972).
Discussion of the limitations of the stereotypes in *Alice*.

Kirk, Daniel F. Charles Dodgson, semeiotician. (University of Florida monographs. Humanities, no. 11) Gainesville: University of Florida Press, 1962.
Discussion of Dodgson's semeiotic interest, or his concern for literary, as well as mathematical, symbols.

Lehmann, John F. Lewis Carroll and the spirit of nonsense. (Nottingham Byron lecture, 1972) Nottingham, [England]: University of Nottingham Press, 1974.

Lennon, Florence Becker. The life of Lewis Carroll. New rev. ed. New York: Collier, 1962; reprint (paperback): New York: Dover, 1972.
Originally appeared under the title: *Victoria through the looking-glass* in 1945. Views Carroll's writing for children as his reaction against the repressive influence of the Victorian nursery.

"Lewis Carroll," in *The London Times literary supplement* 31:49–50 (1932).

Essay "showing in what respects the author and his work were products of their time."

Moses, Belle. Lewis Carroll in Wonderland and at home: the story of his life. New York: Appleton, 1910.
Written for young people.

Ovenden, Graham, ed. The illustrations of *Alice in Wonderland* and *Through the looking-glass*. London: Academy; New York: St. Martin's, 1972.
More than 100 artists have illustrated the two books. This study shows the approaches of several different artists to each of various episodes.

Parry, *Sir* Edward Abbott. "The early writings of Lewis Carroll," *The Cornhill magazine* 129, n.s. 56:455–68 (1924); *Littell's living age* 322:465–72 (1924).

Phillips, Robert, ed. Aspects of Alice: Lewis Carroll's dream-child seen through the critics' looking-glass 1865–1971. New York: Vanguard, 1971; reprint: Random, Vintage, 1977.
Several outstanding critics look at Alice from the following points of view: (1) personal and biographical, (2) as Victorian and children's literature, (3) in comparison with other writers, (4) philosophical and others, (5) chess, (6) language, parody, and satire, (7) Freudian interpretation, (8) Jungian and mythic, and (9) psychedelic.

Potter, G. L. "Millions in Wonderland," *Horn book magazine* 41:593–97 (December, 1965).
Traces the sale of first edition Carrolls and discusses the manuscript of the original sold to A. S. W. Rosenbach in 1928 for $75,000.

Pratt, Helen Marshall. "How *Alice in Wonderland* came to be written," *St. Nicholas* 35:1012–16 (1908).

Pudney, John. Lewis Carroll and his world. London: Thames & Hudson, [1976].
A beautiful book, lavishly illustrated with Tenniel, Holiday, and Furniss drawings and Dodgson photographs.

Reed, Langford. The life of Lewis Carroll. London: Foyle, 1932.
Attempts to reveal "the personality, characteristics, sayings and doings of Lewis Carroll."

Taylor, Alexander L. The white knight: a study of C. L. Dodgson. Edinburgh: Boyd, 1952; reprint: Philadelphia: Dufour, 1963.
Views Carroll's life and art as dominated by Alice Liddell.

Weaver, Warren. Alice in many tongues. Madison: University of Wisconsin Press, 1964.

An examination of the translations of *Alice in Wonderland* into forty languages. Includes letters between Dodgson and his publisher about early French and German translations and the author's comments on the problems of translating parodies, puns, invented words, and twists of language. "Checklist of editions of translations."

Wilson, Edmund. "The poet-logician," *The new republic* 71:19–21 (1932).
Notes the piquancy of the *Alice* books, their symbolic logic, and their value as studies in dream psychology.

Wood, James Playsted. The snark was a boojum: a life of Lewis Carroll. New York: Pantheon, 1966.
In this biography, the author urges against the split-personality theory, saying, "In actuality, Charles Dodgson was a closely integrated man of many talents who sought to express all that he was through many means: through his sketching pencil, his pen and typewriter, the theater, his religiousness, his delight in words, and above all, his love."

BIBLIOGRAPHY

Columbia University. Catalogue of an exhibition at Columbia University to commemorate the one hundredth anniversary of the birth of Lewis Carroll (Charles Lutwidge Dodgson), 1832–1898. New York: Columbia University Press, 1932.
More than 400 items are listed, many with annotations. Includes games, puzzles, and realia, besides numerous editions and special copies of the *Alice* books and other writing for children by Lewis Carroll.

Green, Roger Lancelyn. The Lewis Carroll handbook. Rev. ed. London and Folkestone: Dawson, 1970.
This revision brings the Williams et al. work (below) up to 1970. Guiliano's work (below) updates this.

Guiliano, Edward. Lewis Carroll: an annotated bibliography for 1974. (Carroll Studies 1) New York: The Lewis Carroll Society of North America, 1975.
This is the first annual bibliography intended to update Green's handbook (above).

Harvard University Library. The Harcourt Amory Collection of Lewis Carroll in the Harvard College Library. Compiled by Flora V. Livingston. Cambridge, Mass.: Harvard University Press, 1932.

The Lewis Carroll Centenary in London, including a catalogue of the exhibition (with notes); an essay on Dodgson's illustrations by Harold Hartley; and additional literary pieces (chiefly unpublished). Edited by Falconer Madan. London: Bumpus, 1932.
Edition limited to 400 copies.

Smith, Robert Dennis Hilton, comp. Alice one hundred, being a catalogue in celebration of the 100th birthday of Alice's adventures in Wonderland. Victoria, B.C.: Adelphi Book Shop, 1966.
Checklist for a collection now in the library of the University of British Columbia. Includes other books by Carroll, dramatizations, parodies, books about Carroll and his illustrators. Indexes.

Williams, Sidney. A bibliography of the writings of Lewis Carroll. London: Bookman's journal, 1924.

————, and Falconer Madan. A handbook of the literature of the Rev. C. L. Dodgson (Lewis Carroll) with supplements and illustrations: London: Oxford University Press, 1931.
Represents "the evolution and development of [the] former book," listed above.

————, ————, and Roger Lancelyn Green. The Lewis Carroll handbook. London: Oxford University Press, 1962.
A revised, augmented edition of the 1931 handbook (listed above), brought up to 1960. The edition revised by Green (above) brings the bibliography up to 1970.

Alice and Phoebe Cary

Cary, Alice. Ballads, lyrics and hymns. New York: Hurd & Houghton, 1866.

————. Clovernook children. Boston: Ticknor & Fields, 1855.
Stories about the "West" (near Cincinnati) where the Cary sisters grew up. A sequel to *Clovernook, or, recollections of our neighborhood in the West,* written for adults.

Cary, Alice, and **Phoebe Cary.** Ballads for little folk. Edited by Mary Clemmer. Boston: Houghton, 1873.
Published as a joint collection under this title after the death of the sisters.

————. Poetical works of Alice and Phoebe Cary, with a memorial of their lives by Mary Clemmer. Boston and New York: Hurd & Houghton, 1878.
"Biographical sketch," p. 1–90; "Poems for children," p. 254–80, 405–26.

BIOGRAPHY

Hudson, Mary Clemmer Ames. A memorial of Alice and Phoebe Cary, with some of their later poems. Boston: Houghton, 1872.
Familiar, personal account by an intimate friend.

Mrs. Craik

Craik, Dinah Maria Mulock. The adventures of a brownie, as told to my child. London: S. Low, Marston, Low & Searle; New York: Harper, 1872.
"Recounts the mischievous pranks of a brownie who lives in a coal cellar in Devonshire and the everyday life of the children whose playmate he becomes." Green, *Tellers of tales*.

———. The adventures of a brownie *and* The little lame prince. New York: Garland, 1977.
Preface by Madeleine Cohen Oakley.

———. Alice Learmont: a fairy tale. London: Chapman & Hall, 1852.
Green, in *Tellers of tales*, calls this "a fairy tale of a most unusual sort," because it "harks back to a primitive fairy land."

———. Avillion and other tales. London: Smith & Elder, 1853.

———. Children's poetry. London: Macmillan, 1881.

———. The fairy book: the best popular fairy stories selected and rendered anew. London: Macmillan, 1863.
A collection and retelling of Grimm, Mme. d'Aulnoy, and Perrault fairy tales.

———. A hero: Philip's book. London: Addey, 1853.
Green, in *Tellers of tales*, calls it a "real life story."

———. His little mother and other tales. London: Hurst & Blackett, 1881.

———. How to win love, or, Rhoda's lesson: a story for the young. London: Arthur Hall, 1848.

———. Is it true? tales curious and wonderful. New York: Harper, 1872.

———. John Halifax, gentleman. 3v. London: Hurst & Blackett; New York: Harper, 1856.

———. The little lame prince and his travelling cloak: a parable for young and old. London: Daldy, Isbister, 1875.
Prince Dolor, imprisoned in a tower and unable to use his legs, escapes with the help of his magic travelling cloak. Also published in *Adventures of a brownie* and *The little lame prince*, listed above.

———. Little Lizzie and the fairies, *and* Sunny Hair's dream, with other tales. Boston: Crosby, Nichols, [1852].
Contains six tales.

———. The Little Lychetts. London: Sampson, Low, 1855.

———. Little Sunshine's holiday: a picture from life. New York: Harper, 1871.

———. A new year's gift to sick children. Edinburgh: Hamilton, 1865.

———. Our year: a child's book in prose and verse. Cambridge: Macmillan, 1840.
Illustrated by Clarence Dobell.

———. The unkind word and other stories. London: Hurst & Blackett, 1870.

BIOGRAPHY AND CRITICISM

Martin, Frances. "Mrs. Craik," *The Atheneum* 90: 539 (1887).
Written at the time of Mrs. Craik's death. Notes personal and literary qualities and gives a list of her books.

Parr, Louisa Taylor. The author of *John Halifax, gentleman*: a memoir. London: Hurst & Blackett, 1898.

———. "Dinah Mulock (Mrs. Craik)," in *Women novelists of Queen Victoria's reign* by Mrs. M. O. Wilson Oliphant and others, p. 217–48. London: Hurst & Blackett, 1897.
Chiefly concerned with Mrs. Craik as a novelist, with "the merits and weaknesses of her style, her treatment of her subjects, and her delineation of character."

Reade, Aleyn L. The Mellards and their descendants, including the Bibbys of Liverpool, with memoirs of Dinah Maria Mulock and Thomas Mellard Reade. London: Arden Press for the author, 1915.
Contains a genealogical table and a substantial biographical sketch of the author of *The little lame prince* and *The adventures of a brownie*.

Charles Dickens

Dickens, Charles. A child's dream of a star. Boston: Fields, Osgood, 1871.
Originally published in *Household words*, April 6, 1850.

———. A child's history of England. 3v. London: Bradbury & Evans, 1852–54; reprint: New York, Dutton, 1970.
Serialized in *Household words*, January, 1851 to December, 1853.

———. "A child's history of England," in *Master Humphrey's clock* and *A child's history of England*. London: Oxford University Press, 1958.
Introduction is by Derek Hudson.

THE CHRISTMAS BOOKS

Dickens, Charles. A Charles Dickens Christmas: A *Christmas carol, The chimes, The cricket on the hearth.* New York: Oxford University Press, 1976. Charmingly illustrated by Warren Chappell.

———. Charles Dickens' stories from the Christmas numbers of *Household words* and *All year round,* 1852–1867. Edited with an introduction and notes by Charles Dickens the younger. New York and London: Macmillan, [1896].

———. Christmas books. 5v. London: Chapman & Hall, 1843–48.
They include: *A Christmas carol, in prose, being a ghost story of Christmas* (1843); *The chimes: a goblin story of some bells that rang an old year out and a new year in* (1845); *The cricket on the hearth: a fairy tale of home* (1846); *The battle of life: a love story* (1846); *The haunted man and the ghost's bargain: a fancy for Christmas time* (1848).

———. Christmas stories, and sketches by Boz illustrative of every-day people . . . . Boston: Ticknor & Fields, 1867.
With original illustrations by S. Eytinge, Jr.

Single Editions

Dickens, Charles. The annotated Christmas carol. New York: Potter, 1976.
Introduction and bibliography by Michael Patrick Hearn.

———. The chimes: a goblin story of some bells that rang an old year out and a new year in. London: Chapman & Hall, 1845.

———. ———. London: Dent; New York: Dutton, 1905.
Illustrated by E. E. Brock.

———. ———. London: G. W. Jones for the members of the Limited Editions Club, 1931.
Illustrated by Arthur Rackham. Introduction by Edward Wagenknecht.

———. ———. 2v. Harmondsworth, Middlesex, England: Penguin, 1971.

———. ———. London: Oxford University Press, 1954.
With sixty-five illustrations by Landseer, Maclise, Tenniel, and Stanfield, and an introduction by Eleanor Farjeon.

———. A Christmas carol, in prose, being a ghost story of Christmas. London: Chapman & Hall, 1843.
With illustrations by John Leech.

———. ———. London: Heinemann, 1915.
Illustrated by Arthur Rackham.

———. ———. Boston: Merrymount Press for the Limited Editions Club, 1934.
Illustrated by Gordon Ross and introduced by Stephen Leacock.

———. ———. Chicago: Holiday, 1940; reprint: New York: Atheneum, 1960.
Illustrated by Philip Reed.

———. ———. London: Macmillan, 1923.
Illustrated by F. D. Bedford.

———. ———. New York: Columbia University Press, 1956.
A facsimile of the first edition. Introduction and bibliographical note by Edgar Johnson.

———. ———. London: Heinemann, 1967; New York: Dover, 1971.
The original manuscript by Charles Dickens. A facsimile of the manuscript in the Pierpont Morgan Library. With illustrations by John Leech and the text from the first edition.

———. Cricket on the hearth: a fairy tale of home. London: Bradbury & Evans, 1846 [1845].
With illustrations by D. Maclise, R.A., R. Doyle, S. Stanfield, J. Leech, and E. Landseer.

———. ———. London: Dent; New York: Dutton, 1905.
Illustrations by C. E. Brock.

———. ———. Waltham, St. Lawrence, England: Golden Cockerel Press, printed for the members of the Limited Editions Club, 1933.
With seven posthumously published illustrations by Hugh Thomson.

HOLIDAY ROMANCE

Dickens, Charles. A holiday romance. Boston: Ticknor & Fields, 1868; reprint: London: Cecil Palmer, 1920.
Serialized in four parts in *Our young folks* 4, nos. 1, 3, 4, 5 (January, March, April, May, 1868).

———. "A holiday romance," in *The king of the golden river* [Ruskin], *A holiday romance, Petsetilla's posy* [Hood]. (Classics of children's literature, 1621–1932) New York: Garland, 1976.
Preface by Diane Johnson.

Single Editions

Dickens, Charles. Captain Boldheart and the Latin-grammar master: a holiday romance from the pen of Lieut-Col. Robin Redforth, aged 9. (The Orange tree series of children's books, no. 4) London: Constable, [1912].

————. The magic fishbone: a holiday romance from the pen of Miss Alice Rainbird, aged 7. London: James Nisbet, [1911].

————. ————. London: Warne, 1921.
Illustrated by F. D. Bedford.

————. ————. New York: Vanguard, 1953.
Illustrated by Louis Slobodkin.

————. Mrs. Orange. London: Herbert Jenkins, 1948.
Illustrated by Robert Stewart Sherriffs.

————. Trial of William Tinkling, written by himself at the age of 8. (Orange Tree series of children's books, no. 3) London: Constable, [1912].

BIOGRAPHY AND CRITICISM

Dickens, Charles. The letters of Charles Dickens. Edited by Mamie Dickens and Georgina Hogarth. London: Macmillan, 1893.

Donovan, Frank Robert. The children of Charles Dickens. London: Frewin, 1969.
Same as *Dickens and youth* (see below).

————. Dickens and youth. New York: Dodd, Mead, 1968.
A discussion of Dickens's fictional children.

Forster, John. The life of Charles Dickens. 2v. London: Chapman & Hall, 1911.
With 500 portraits, facsimiles, and other illustrations collected, arranged, and annotated by B. W. Matz.

House, Arthur Humphry. The Dickens world. London: Oxford University Press, 1941.
"The most important contribution to Dickensian scholarship for at least a decade."—*Books*.

Hughes, James Laughlin. Dickens as an educator. New York: Appleton, 1901.
Written "to prove that Dickens was the great apostle of the 'new education' to the English-speaking world, and to bring into connected form, under appropriate headings, the educational principles of one of the world's greatest educators."

Johnson, Edgar. Charles Dickens: his tragedy and triumphs. New York: Simon & Schuster, 1952.
Widely acclaimed as the definitive biography of Dickens.

Kitton, Frederick George. Dickens: his life, writings and personality. London: T. C. & E. C. Jack, 1902.
Reference to *A child's history of England*, p. 199, and to *A holiday romance*, p. 345–46. Numerous illustrations.

Kotzin, Michael C. Dickens and the fairy tale. Bowling Green, Ohio: Bowling Green University Popular Press, 1972.
Considers the fairy tales of Dickens's youth as the inspiration for his fiction. The author talks about Dickens's use of the fairy tale in his stories for *Household words* and his relationship with Andersen, George MacDonald, and Cruikshank.

Stone, Harry. "Dark corners of the mind: Dickens' childhood reading," *Horn book magazine* 39:306–21 (June, 1963).
Dickens was "profoundly affected by his childhood reading," i.e., Watts, romances, chapbook tales, *Sandford and Merton, Gulliver's travels*, etc.

Szladits, L. L. "Dickens and his illustrators," *Bulletin* (New York Public Library) 74:351–53 (June, 1970).
A Dickens scholar and curator of the Berg collection, New York Public Library, discusses Dickens's illustrators: Cruikshank, Robert Seymour, John Leech, and H. R. Browne (Phiz).

Whitaker, Muriel. "The proper bringing up of young Pip," *Children's literature: the great excluded* 2:152–58 (1973).
Expounds the theory that, in *Great expectations*, Dickens attacks both the brutal Puritan and the Georgian methods of child rearing as well as the genre of the cautionary tale.

Mrs. Ewing

Ewing, Juliana Horatia Gatty. Brothers of pity, and other tales of beasts and men. London: S.P.C.K., 1882.

————. The brownies and other tales. London: Bell & Daldy, 1870.
Illustrated by G. Cruikshank.

————. Daddy Darwin's dovecot. London: S.P.C.K., [1884]; reprint: New York: Garland, 1977.

————. Daddy Darwin's dovecot, Melchior's dream, and other tales. Boston: Little, [1909].
Illustrated by Randolph Caldecott, Gordon Browne, and other artists.

————. A flat iron for a farthing, or, some passages in the life of an only son. London: Bell & Daldy, 1873.

————. A great emergency, and other tales. London: G. Bell, 1877.
Other tales: A very ill-tempered family; Our field; Madame Liberality.

————. A great emergency *and* A very ill-tempered family. New York: Schocken, 1969.
With an introduction by Gillian Avery.

————. Jackanapes. London: S.P.C.K., 1884 [1883]; reprint: (Classics of children's literature 1621–1932) New York: Garland, 1977.
Illustrations by Randolph Caldecott. Reprint has preface by Alison Lurie.

————. Jan of the windmill: a story of the plains. London: Bell & Daldy, 1876.
Published in *Aunt Judy's magazine*, November, 1872 to October, 1873, under the title *The miller's thumb*.

————. Lob Lie-by-the-fire. London: Bell & Daldy, 1874; reprint: (Classics of children's literature 1621–1932) New York: Garland, 1977.

————. Mary's meadow *and* Letters from a little garden. London: S.P.C.K., [1886].
Illustrated by Gordon Browne. *Mary's meadow* appeared in *Aunt Judy's magazine* from November, 1883, to March, 1884, and the *Letters* in the same magazine from November, 1884 to February, 1885.

————. Mary's meadow, and other tales of fields and flowers. Edited by Horatia K. F. Eden. London: Bell & Daldy, 1915.

————. Mother's birthday review, & seven other tales in verse. London: S.P.C.K., [1885].
Illustrative of the picture books of the period as well as of a special phase of the author's work. The illustrations, by R. Andre, are lithographs. *The blue bells on the lea* is a companion volume.

————. Mrs. Overtheway's remembrances. London: Bell and Daldy, 1869; reprint: (Classics of children's literature 1621–1932) New York: Garland, 1977.
Contents: Ida; Mrs. Moss; The snoring ghost; Reka Dom; Kerguelen's land. Reprint has preface by Susan Kenney.

————. Old-fashioned fairy tales. London: S.P.C.K., [1882].
Includes twelve original designs by A. W. Bayes and Gordon Browne, and other illustrations.

————. Six to sixteen: a story for girls. London: G. Bell, 1876; reprint: (Classics of children's literature 1621–1932) New York: Garland, 1976.
First appeared in *Aunt Judy's magazine* in 1872. This work is best known for its account of mid-Victorian family life. It illustrates "a belief in the joys and benefits of intellectual hobbies." Reprint has preface by Gillian Avery.

————. The story of a short life. London: S.P.C.K., [1885].
Printed in *Aunt Judy's magazine* from May to October, 1882, under the title *Laetus sorte mea, or, the story of a short life*.

————. We and the world: a book for boys. London: G. Bell, 1881 [1880].
First published in *Aunt Judy's magazine* from 1877 to 1879.

BIOGRAPHY AND CRITICISM

Avery, Gillian. Mrs. Ewing. (Bodley Head and Walck monographs) London: Bodley Head, 1961; New York: Walck, 1964.
Includes a discussion of Margaret Gatty, Juliana Ewing's mother, from whose work as a writer she developed her own style. Portrays Mrs. Ewing as a person, as a writer, and as the editor of *Aunt Judy's magazine*. Bibliography.

Eden, Horatia K. F. Gatty. Juliana Horatia Ewing and her books. London: Hurst & Blackett, 1887; reprint: Folcroft, Pa.: Folcroft, 1969.
A memoir by Juliana Ewing's sister, who discusses the writings in chronological order as they relate to Mrs. Ewing's own life. Contains selections from letters and a full bibliography, p. 138–43.

Green, Roger Lancelyn. "Juliana Horatia Ewing," in his *Tellers of tales*, p. 97–103. Rewritten and rev. ed. New York: Watts, 1965.
Green concludes that Juliana Ewing was a far "cleverer and greater writer than her mother, and [that she] seldom allowed any kind of a 'purpose' to become visible in her stories."

Hazeltine, Alice Isabel. "Aunt Judy: Mrs. Gatty and Mrs. Ewing," *Horn book magazine* 16:323–30, 457–66 (1940).
Discusses the lives and writings of mother and daughter; Mrs. Gatty in the September-October issue, Mrs. Ewing in the November-December issue.

"Juliana Horatia Ewing," *London Times literary supplement*, January 26, 1911, p. 27; *Littell's living age* 268:622–25 (1911).
Singles out the qualities of Mrs. Ewing's work that run the risk of being overlooked when she is considered a writer for children only.

Kent, Muriel. "Juliana Horatia Ewing," *The junior bookshelf* 5:123–28 (1941).

Laski, Marghanita. Mrs. Ewing, Mrs. Molesworth, and Mrs. Hodgson Burnett. London: Barker, 1950; Oxford: Oxford University Press, 1951.
Three typical "lady writers" of the nineteenth century who produced "a literature wholesome, witty, immensely readable, extremely well-constructed, and essentially middle-class."—introduction. Includes bibliography.

Marshall, Emma Martin. "Mrs. Ewing," in *Women novelists of Queen Victoria's reign* by Mrs. M. O. (Wilson) Oliphant et al., p. 298–312. London: Hurst & Blackett, 1897.
An appreciation of the stories for children.

Maxwell, Christabel Ward. Mrs. Gatty and Mrs. Ewing. London: Constable, 1949.
Written by a granddaughter of Margaret Gatty and niece of Juliana Ewing. A lively and personal view of both writers. Bibliographies. Reviewed by Marcia Dalphin in *Horn book magazine* 26:174–86 (May, 1950).

Molesworth, Mary Louise. "Mrs. Ewing's less well-known books," in her *Studies and stories*, p. 31–62. London: Innes, 1893; *The contemporary Review* 49:675–86 (1886); in *A peculiar gift*, edited by Lance Salway, p. 503–16. Harmondsworth, Eng.: Penguin, 1976.
Discusses *Mrs. Overtheway's remembrances, A flat-iron for a farthing, Six to sixteen, Jan of the windmill, We and the world,* and *A great emergency.*

Seymour, Helen Minturn. "An almost forgotten English writer." *The dial* 60:324–25 (1916).
"Testimony in favor of an old friend."

Whitney, Elinor. "Country tales of Juliana Horatia Ewing," *Horn book magazine* 2:12–16 (1926).
Discusses the country village settings of *Daddy Darwin's dovecot* and other stories.

Dean Farrar

Farrar, Frederic William. Christmas carols. New York: Thomas Whittaker, n.d.
A charming little book of Farrar's own hymns. Illustrated.

———. Eric, or, little by little: a tale of Roslyn School. Edinburgh: Adam & Charles Black, 1858; reprint: London: Hamish Hamilton, 1971.
"Written with but one single object—the vivid inculcation of inward purity and moral purpose, by the history of a boy who, in spite of the inherent nobleness of his disposition, falls into all folly and wickedness."—preface to the fourth edition. Reprint introduced by John Rowe Townsend.

———. ———. Edinburgh: A. & C. Black, 1892; reprint: (Classics of children's literature 1621–1932) New York: Garland, 1977.
Reprint introduced by Gillian Avery.

———. Julian Home: a tale of college life. Edinburgh: Adam & Charles Black, 1859.

———. St. Winifred's, or, the world of school. Edinburgh: Adam & Charles Black, [1862].

———. The three homes: a tale for fathers and sons. By F. T. L. Hope [*pseud.*]. London: Cassell, Peter, & Galpin, 1873.

BIOGRAPHY AND CRITICISM

Farrar, Reginald. The life of Frederic William Farrar, sometime dean of Canterbury. London: J. Nisbet, 1904.
Estimate of Dean Farrar's work as a writer of schoolboy fiction, p. 71–82. By the author's son.

Jamieson, A. F. W. "Farrar and novels of public schools," *The British journal of educational studies* 16:271–78 (1968).
Although Farrar's novels are "too prolix and effusive for our more laconic taste, and overly sentimental, [they] are important social documents."

R., J. D. "Dean Farrar as headmaster, by his old pupil, J.D.R.," *The Cornhill magazine* 87, 14:597–608 (1903); *Littell's living age* 237: 577–85 (1903).
Recollections of Dean Farrar as headmaster of Marlborough College, presenting his virtues and his frailties as they appeared "a generation ago."

Raven, Simon. "Eric and St. Dominic's," *The spectator* 227:245–46 (1971).
Eric, or, little by little is seen as a "morality, a fierce, uncompromising, blood-and-thunderous, lightning literature—tempest tossed, doom-dealing morality."

Scott, P. J. "School novels of Dean Farrar," *The British journal of educational studies* 19:163–82 (1971).
Compares Farrar's fictional school with factual accounts of Victorian public schools and concludes that Farrar's novels are a remarkably accurate reflection of life in particular schools in the late 1850s.

Mrs. Gatty

Gatty, Margaret Scott. Aunt Judy's letters. London: Bell & Daldy, 1862.
Contents: The goose; Aunt Sally's life; The Flatland's Fun Gazette; Grandmamma's throat; The black bag; The gossip of a blotting-book.

———. Aunt Judy's tales. London: Bell & Daldy, 1859.
Contents: The little victims; Vegetables out of place; Cook stories; Rabbits' tails; Out of the way; Nothing to do.

———. The circle of blessings, and other parables from nature. New York: General Protestant Episcopal Sunday School Union and Church Book Society, 1861.

———. Domestic pictures and tales. London: Bell & Daldy, 1866.

———. The fairy godmothers, and other tales. London: G. Bell, 1851.

Other tales: Joachim, the mimic; Darkness and light; The love of God.

———. The human face divine, and other tales. London: Bell & Daldy, 1860.
Other tales: My childhood in art; The dull watering place.

———. The hundredth birthday, and other tales. Rev. ed. London: Bell & Daldy, 1868.

———. Legendary tales. London: Bell & Daldy, 1858.
With illustrations by Phiz [*pseud.*] Contents: A legend of Sologne; The hundredth birthday; The treasure seeker.

———. Parables from nature. Ser. 1–4. 5 v. London: G. Bell, 1871–74.

———. ———. (Classics of children's literature 1621–1932) New York: Garland, 1976.
Reprint of 1880 edition by G. Bell, London.

———. Parables from nature . . . with notes on natural history. Ser. 1 and 2. London: Bell & Daldy, 1861.
Illustrated by C. W. Cope, H. Calderon, W. Holman Hunt, W. Millais, Otto Specktor, G. Thomas, and E. Warren. Contents: A lesson of faith; The laws of authority and obedience; The unknown land; Knowledge not the limit of belief; Training and restraining; The light of truth; Waiting; A lesson of hope; The circle of blessing; The law of the wood; Active and passive; Daily bread; Not lost, but gone forever; Motes in the sunbeam; Notes.

———. ———. Ser. 3 and 4. London: Bell & Daldy, 1865.
Illustrations by Lorenz Frolich, W. B. Scott, M. E. Edwards, Harrison Weir, John Tenniel, E. B. Jones, G. H. Thomas, W. P. Burton, J. Wolff, and Charles Keene. Contents: Red snow; Whereunto; Purring when you're pleased; The voices of the earth; The wastes of the harvest; The deliverer; Inferior animals; The general thaw; The light of life; Gifts; Night and day; Kicking; Imperfect instruments; Cobwebs; Birds in the nest; Notes.

———. Parables from nature . . . with notes on natural history, with a memoir by her daughter, Juliana Horatia Ewing. London: G. Bell, 1885.
Especially valuable for the memoir, p. ix–xxi. The mental characteristics and tastes of Margaret Gatty are noted, and there is a personal account of her literary work. Seventeen stories.

———, ed. Aunt Judy's magazine for young people. 1866–1885.
Established by Mrs. Gatty in 1866 and named after her *Aunt Judy's tales.* It was continued until October, 1885, having been edited after Mrs. Gatty's death in 1873 by her daughter H. F. K. Gatty. The magazine is important in the history of children's literature from the fact that nearly all of Mrs. Ewing's stories for children first appeared in its pages.

BIOGRAPHY AND CRITICISM

Ewing, Juliana Horatia Gatty. "In memoriam: Margaret Gatty," in her *Miscellanea,* p. 179–87. London: Society for Promoting Christian Knowledge, [1896]; in *A peculiar gift,* edited by Lance Salway, p. 479–83. Harmondsworth, Eng.: Penguin, [1976].
Speaks of her mother's life and loves, her literary influences, her artistic and literary talent, and her scientific interest. First published in *Aunt Judy's magazine,* November, 1873.

Hazeltine, Alice Isabel. "Aunt Judy: Mrs. Gatty and Mrs. Ewing," *Horn book magazine* 16:323–30, 457–66 (1940).
Noted in the section on Juliana Ewing.

Maxwell, Christabel Ward. Mrs. Gatty and Mrs. Ewing. London: Constable, 1949.
Listed under Juliana Ewing.

Grace Greenwood

Lippincott, Sara Jane Clarke (*pseud.* Grace Greenwood). Bonnie Scotland: tales of her history, heroes, and poets. Boston: Ticknor, Reed, & Fields, 1860.
Stories associated with Glasgow, Edinburgh, and other places.

———. History of my pets. Boston: Ticknor, Reed, & Fields, 1851.

———. Merrie England: travels, descriptions, tales, and historical sketches. Boston: Ticknor, Reed, & Fields, 1855.
Contents: Sherwood forest: Robin Hood; Nottingham castle: Alice Vane; Warwick castle: Guy of Warwick; Yorkminster: Queen Philippa; London and the Tower: Sir Walter Raleigh; Ladies Jane and Catharine Grey; Arabella Stuart; Westminster Abbey: the two wills; The new palace of Westminster: The prorogation; Kenilworth castle: Little Rosamond; Stratford-upon-Avon: Shakespeare.

———. Recollections of my childhood, and other stories. Boston: Ticknor, Reed, & Fields, 1852.
With engravings from designs by Billings. Dedication to Una and Julian Hawthorne, Horace and George Mann. Short stories based on childhood memories.

———. Stories and sights of France and Italy. Boston: Ticknor, Reed, & Fields, 1867.

————. Stories from famous ballads. Boston: Ticknor & Fields, 1860.
Contents: Patient Griselda; The King of France's daughter; Chevy Chase; The king and the miller of Mansfield; The England merchant and the Saracen lady; The beggar's daughter, or, Bednall-Green; The heir of Linne: Sir Patrick Spens; Auld Robin Gray; Fridolin, or, the message to the forge.

————, ed., with Leander Lippincott. The little pilgrim. 1853–66.
A monthly for children.

BIOGRAPHY

Ross, Ishbel. "Sara Jane Clarke," in her *Ladies of the press,* p. 327–39. New York: Harper, 1936.
A short biographical sketch of this busy woman as a journalist.

————. Sara Jane Clarke. New York: Arno, 1974.
A reprint of the above.

Thorp, Margaret Farrand. "Greenwood leaves: 'Grace Greenwood' (Sara J. C. Lippincott)," in her *Female persuasion,* p. 143–78. New Haven, Conn.: Yale University Press, 1949.
A long biographical sketch. Includes an engraving and a photograph of Sara Lippincott.

Thomas Hughes

Hughes, Thomas. Brown and Arthur: an episode from *Tom Brown's school days.* Richmond, Va.: West & Johnston, 1861.

————. Tom Brown at Oxford. 3v. Cambridge: Macmillan, 1861.
A sequel to *Tom Brown's school days.* Printed in Boston (Ticknor & Fields, 1857) under the title *Tom Brown at Oxford: a sequel to School-days at Rugby.*

————. Tom Brown's school days, by an old boy. Cambridge: Macmillan, 1857.
The first illustrated edition, with drawings by Arthur Hughes and Sydney Prior Hall, appeared in 1869, published by Macmillan. Published in Boston under the title *School days at Rugby, by an old boy* (Ticknor & Fields, 1859). All editions from the sixth (1858) on include the author's preface.

————. ————. Edited by F. Sidgwick. London: Sidgwick & Jackson, 1913.
With a preface by Lord Kilbracken, an introduction, notes, and illustrations. The introduction covers the life of Thomas Hughes, the history of the book, identification of the characters, and notes on some of the incidents. The prefatory matter also includes a memorial poem by Arthur Gray

Butler. The text is supplemented by thirty plates, some of them reproduced from contemporary sources, and text illustrations by W. F. Loveday.

————. ————. (The Riverdale school library) Boston: Houghton, 1895.
With an introductory sketch and portraits. Also includes "A glance at English public schools," p. xv–xix, and "A suggestion of books to be read in illustration of *Tom Brown's school days,*" p. xx–xxi.

————. ————. New York: Harper, 1911.
Introduction by W. D. Howells. With numerous illustrations made at Rugby school by Louis Rhead. "Remarks of the illustrator on present aspects of Rugby school," p. xiii–xv.

BIOGRAPHY AND CRITICISM

Beith, John Hay (*pseud.* Ian Hay). "School stories," in his *The lighter side of school life,* p. 123–43. Boston: Houghton, 1920.
Tom Brown's school days and *Eric* are contrasted with each other and with newer types of school stories.

Briggs, Asa. "Thomas Hughes and the public schools," in his *Victorian people: a reassessment of persons and themes, 1851–67,* p. 140–67. Chicago: University of Chicago Press, 1955, 1973.
Discusses the influence of the public school system on mid-Victorian thought. Defines *Tom Brown's school days* as "a jolly book," intended "to popularize the public school with the middle-class and later on with the working-class reading public. . . ."

Hibberd, Dominic. "Where there are no spectators: a rereading of *Tom Brown's school days,*" *Children's literature in education* 21:64–73 (Summer, 1976).
Analyzes the response of today's reader, due to Hughes's "irrepressible gusto, the pleasure he takes in writing, and his artless style."

Hughes, Thomas. "Fragments of autobiography," *The Cornhill magazine* 586:280–89, 472–78, 663–72 (1925).
This excerpt was found by Mr. Hughes's daughter, May Hughes, and was edited by Henry Shelley. Pt. 1, "Early memories," is a "delightful recollection" of Uffington, where part of *Tom Brown's school days* takes place. Pt. 2, "Secret adventures," starts at Hughes's twenty-third year, when he had finished at Oxford and had come to London. Pts. 3 and 4 are entitled "The working men's college" and "Dreaming."

Little, John. Thomas Hughes, 1822–1896. Uffington, England: [J. E. Little], 1972.

Mack, Edward Clarence, and **W. H. G. Armytage.**
Thomas Hughes: the life of the author of *Tom Brown's school days.* London: Benn, [1952].
Discusses the social philosophy of Hughes and its influence on the writing of his school stories for boys. The authors conclude, "His was literally the first book of fiction to present a real world of boys in the setting of a real English public school. And it is still, despite the many recent novels on the subject, the most vigorous, the most convincing, and the most deeply moving of all."

Philip, M. "Cultural myths in Victorian boys' books by Marryat, Hughes, Stevenson, and Kipling." Ph.D. diss., Indiana University, 1975.

Shelley, Henry Charles. "The centenary of Thomas Hughes," *The outlook* 133:275–76 (1923).
Account of the genesis of *Tom Brown's school days* and its associations.

Stanley, Arthur Penrhyn. The life and correspondence of Thomas Arnold. 2v. in 1. New York: Scribner, 1892.
"School life at Rugby," p. 96–173.

Williams, Stanley Thomas. "The parent of schoolboy novels," *The English journal* 10:241–46 (1921).
Of all stories of English school life, "*Tom Brown's school days* is first, and the rest are nowhere." The article indicates some of the reasons.

Jean Ingelow

Ingelow, Jean. The fairy who judged her neighbours, and other stories. London: Griffith, Farran, Okeden, & Welsh, 1887.

———. "The fairy who judged her neighbours," "The prince's dream," "Anselmo," in *Good old stories for boys and girls,* compiled by Elva S. Smith, p. 23–34, 82–96, 155–64. Boston: Lothrop, 1919.

———. The Jean Ingelow birthday book. Boston: Roberts, 1883.

———. The little wonder-box. 6v. London: Griffith, Farran, Okeden & Welsh, 1887.
Contents: Vol. 1. The ouphe of the woods; The Middle Ages. Vol. 2. The fairy who judged her neighbours; As the crow flies. Vol. 3. The prince's dream; Night's divining-glass. Vol. 4. The snowflake; The water-lily; 1972. Vol. 5. A lost wand. Vol. 6. Rocking cradle; Muschachito mio.

———. The little wonder-horn: a new series of *Stories told to a child.* London: Henry S. King, 1872.

———. Mopsa the fairy. London: Longmans, Green, 1869.

"The adventures of a mortal boy and the fairy child, Mopsa, as they journey through Fairyland."

———. ———. Boston: Roberts, 1869.
First American edition.

———. ———. New York: Harper, 1927.
Illustrated by Dorothy P. Lathrop.

———. ———. (Classics of children's literature 1621–1932) New York: Garland, 1977.
Preface by John Hollander. A reprint of the 1869 Longmans edition. Other editions have been illustrated by Maria L. Kirk (1910) and Dugald Stewart Walker (1947).

———. A sister's bye-hours. London: Strahan, 1868.

———. The snowflake, The water-lily, *and* 1972. London: Griffith, Farrar, Okeden & Welsh, 1887.

———. Stories told to a child. 2v. London: Strahan, 1865.
Contents: The grandmother's shoe; Little Rie and the rosebuds; Two ways of telling a story; The one-eyed servant; The lonely rock; The minnows with silver tails; The golden opportunity; The wild-duck shooter; I have a right; Can and could; Deborah's book; The suspicious jackdaw; The life of Mr. John Smith; The Moorish gold. These short stories were first contributed to *The youth's magazine.*

———. Studies for stories. 2v. London: Strahan, 1864.
Contents: Vol. 1. The cucumbers; My great-aunt's picture; Dr. Deane's governess. Vol. 2. The stolen treasure; Emily's ambition.

———. Studies for stories from girls' lives. London: Strahan, 1865.
Same as *Studies for stories.*

———. Three fairy tales. Edited by C. F. Dole. Boston: Heath, 1901.
Contents: The ouphe of the wood; The fairy who judged her neighbours; The prince's dream.

———. The very young *and* Quite another story. London: Longmans, Green, 1890.

BIOGRAPHY AND CRITICISM

Bell, Henry Thomas Mackenzie. "Jean Ingelow," in *The poets and the poetry of the century,* compiled by Alfred Henry Miles, v. 7, p. 385–92. London: Hutchinson, [1892].
Selected poems, p. 393–416.

Black, Helen C. "Jean Ingelow," in her *Notable women authors of the day,* p. 299–312. Glasgow: Bryce, 1893.
Biographical sketch with portrait.

Hall, W. C. J. "Jean Ingelow," *Papers* (Manchester Literary Club) 57:145–65 (1931).

Peters, Maureen. Jean Ingelow: Victorian poetess. Totowa, N.J.: Rowman & Littlefield, 1972.
A scholarly full-length biography of Jean Ingelow. See p. 78–81 for *Mopsa*, about which the author writes, "The whole of the book is a vivid tapestry of colour and movement and excitement, with a tender quality too delicate to analyse."

Some recollections of Jean Ingelow and her early friends. London: Wells Gardner, [1901]; reprint: Port Washington, N.Y.: Kennikat Press, 1972.
"Unassuming little memoir."—*The Athenaeum*, 1901. Origin of *Stories told to a child*, p. 63–67. See also p. 101–2.

Stuart, G. B. "Personal recollections of Jean Ingelow, the home-poet," *Lippincott's monthly magazine* 77:306–13 (1906).
Jean Ingelow was, for twelve or fourteen years, a familiar figure in the writer's home circle.

Charles Kingsley

Kingsley, Charles. The heroes, or, Greek fairy tales for my children. Cambridge: Macmillan, 1856.
Illustrated by the author. The preface is addressed to the author's children.

———. ———. (New children's classics) New York: Macmillan, 1954.
Illustrated by Vera Bock.

———. Madame How and Lady Why, or, first lessons in earth lore for children. London: Bell & Daldy, 1869.
Serialized, November, 1868–October, 1869, in *Good words for the young.* Dedicated to the author's son, Grenville Arthur, and his schoolfellows. In the preface, p. vii–xv, Kingsley expresses his indebtedness to the story "Eyes and no eyes" by John Aikin.

———. The water-babies: a fairy tale for a landbaby. London and Cambridge: Macmillan, 1863.
The original edition contained only one illustration, by J. Noel Paton.

———. ———. London: Macmillan, 1886; reprint: (Classics of children's literature 1621–1932) New York: Garland, 1976.
One hundred illustrations by Linley Sambourne. This is the first edition that was lavishly illustrated. Sambourne was a cartoonist for *Punch* magazine. The reprint is a facsimile.

———. ———. New York: Dodd, 1916.
Illustrated by Jessie Willcox Smith. Illustrators of other editions include Warwick Goble and W. Heath Robinson.

———. Westward ho! or, the voyages and adventures of Sir Amyas Leigh . . . . Cambridge: Macmillan, 1855.

BIOGRAPHY AND CRITICISM

Baldwin, Stanley E. Charles Kingsley. Ithaca, N.Y.: Cornell University Press; London: Milford, 1934.
Some discussion of *The Heroes* and *Waterbabies* in the conclusion, p. 190–93. Good bibliography.

Chitty, Susan. The beast and the monk: a life of Charles Kingsley. London: Hodder, [1974].
A new biography that contains a chapter on *Water-babies*, p. 211–23.

Colloms, Brenda. Charles Kingsley: the lion of Eversley. London: Constable, 1975.
A hundred years after Kingsley's death, the author wrote "to appraise the man . . . to clarify and assess the influence of his ideas, actions, and writings upon the social and political movements of his day and to pay tribute to what we also owe to him."

Kendall, Guy. Charles Kingsley and his ideas. London: Hutchinson, 1947.

Kingsley, Frances Grenfell, ed. Charles Kingsley: his letters and memories of his life. 2v. London: Henry S. King, 1877.
The editor was Kingsley's wife.

———. Charles Kingsley: letters and memories. 2v. in 1.
Reference to *The heroes, The water-babies,* and *Madame How and Lady Why.*

Leavis, Q. D. "The water-babies," *Children's literature in education* 23:155–63 (Winter, 1976).
Suggests some uses for modern children's education in "an excitingly written and splendidly imaginative Victorian classic."

Martin, Robert Bernard. The dust of combat: a life of Charles Kingsley. London: Faber & Faber, 1959.
Not about the children's works, but *Waterbabies* is considered on p. 235–36.

Pope-Hennessy, *Dame* Una Birch. Canon Charles Kingsley: a biography. London: Chatto & Windus, 1948.
Includes a chapter, "The professor and the water babies," that describes the genesis of the story.

Thorp, Margaret Farrand. Charles Kingsley, 1819–1875. Princeton, N.J.: Princeton University Press, 1937.
For *Water-babies,* see p. 17–72. The author analyzes Kingsley as a typical Victorian. She says, "Born in the same year as the Queen, Kingsley typifies the Victorian man as closely as she presents the Victorian woman." Includes a bibliography of his writings.

William Henry Giles Kingston

Kingston, William Henry Giles. Afar in the forest: a tale of adventure in North America. London: T. Nelson, 1884.

———. Great African travellers from Bruce and Mungo Park to Livingstone and Stanley. London: Routledge, 1890.

———. My first voyage to southern seas. London: T. Nelson, 1860.

———. Old Jack: a man-of-war's man and south-sea whaler. London: T. Nelson, 1859.

———. Round the world: a tale for boys. London: T. Nelson, 1861.

———. Virginia: a centennial story. Boston: D. Lothrop, 1876.

———, ed. The Swiss family Robinson by Johann David Wyss. London: Routledge, 1889.
Translated from the German and revised by Kingston in 1879.

BIOGRAPHY AND CRITICISM

Kingsford, Maurice Rooke. Life, work and influence of William Henry Giles Kingston. Toronto: Ryerson Press, 1948.

Edward Lear

■ Edward Lear wrote five nonsense books for children, which are listed below. All first editions are very rare. The British Museum, for example, has no *Book of nonsense* earlier than a third edition, dated 1861.

Lear, Edward. The book of nonsense, by Derry Down Derry. London: McLean, 1846.
Another edition, published by Routledge in 1862, was enlarged by Lear.

———. Laughable lyrics: a fresh book of nonsense poems, songs, botany, music, etc. London: Robert John Bush, 1877.

———. More nonsense, pictures, rhymes, botany, etc. London: Robert John Bush, 1872.

———. Nonsense songs, stories, botany and alphabet. London: Robert John Bush, 1871.

———. Nonsense songs and stories, with additional songs. London: Warne, 1895.
The introduction, dated 1894, is by Sir E. Strachey and contains Lear's "By way of preface."

■ Most of the following books are either compilations of the above five books or excerpts from them.

Lear, Edward. A B C. New York: McGraw-Hill, 1965.
The material from this book is not included in any of the above books, but was discovered and bought by Theodore Besterman, who says it is "quite unlike the other A B C's." In this facsimile the alphabet was penned and illustrated by Lear himself.

———. The complete nonsense book. Edited by Lady Strachey. London: Mills & Boon, 1912; reprint: New York: Dodd, 1961.
Introduced by the Earl of Cromer. This includes the first four books above.

———. The complete nonsense of Edward Lear. Edited and introduced by Holbrook Jackson. London: Faber & Faber, 1947; reprint (paperback): New York: Dover, 1951.
Contains all five books. The standard complete Lear.

———. The dong with a luminous nose. New York: Scott, 1969.
Illustrated by Edward Gorey. In an edition intended for children.

———. Four little children who went around the world. New York: Macmillan, 1968.
Illustrated by Arnold Lobel.

———. The jumblies. New York: Scott, 1968.
Black-and-white line drawings by Edward Gorey.

———. The jumblies and other nonsense verses. London: Warne, 1910.
Other nonsense verses: The owl and the pussy cat; The duck and the kangaroo; The dong with a luminous nose; The courtship of the yonghy-bong-hy-bo.
The illustrations are by L. Leslie Brooke.

———. The Lear coloured bird book for children. London: Mills & Boon, 1912.
Foreword by J. St. Loe Strachey.

———. Lear in the original. New York: Kraus, 1975.
On the title page: "drawings and limericks by Edward Lear for his *Book of Nonsense.* Now first printed in facsimile, together with other unpub-

lished Nonsense Drawings." Introduction and notes by Herbert W. Liebert. This folio volume includes several pieces not previously published, from the collection of Mr. and Mrs. Hans P. Kraus of New York. It includes a scholarly biographical introduction with critical analyses of Lear's works. A lavish production.

———. The Lear omnibus. (Hutchinson's books for young people) London: Hutchinson, n.d.
Contains an "Introduction (skipable): the genius of Edward Lear," p. 7–22, by R. L. Mégroz.

———. Nonsense drolleries: The owl and the pussycat; The duck and the kangaroo. London: Warne, 1889.

———. Nonsense songs. London: Warne, 1917.
Drawings by L. Leslie Brooke.

———. Nonsense songs and laughable lyrics. Mount Vernon, N.Y.: Peter Pauper, 1936.
All the lyrics, two unfinished and hitherto unpublished poems with Lear's diverting illustrations. Foreword by Philip Hofer gives a lively and sympathetic characterization of the artist who taught drawing to Queen Victoria.

———. The owl and the pussy-cat. London: Warne, 1975.
Illustrated by Harold Kind.

———. ———.   New York: Atheneum, 1977.
Illustrated by Gwen Fulton.

———. Pelican chorus. London: Warne, 1907.
With drawings by L. Leslie Brooke.

———. The Quangle Wangle's hat. New York: Watts, 1969.
Full-color, large-scale illustrations by Helen Oxenbury.

———. Queery Leary nonsense: a Lear nonsense book. Edited by Lady Strachey. London: Mills & Boon, [1911].
Introduction by the Earl of Cromer. Letters, verses, and drawings hitherto unpublished. The most important part of the book is the reproduction of the *Bird book,* a delightful volume of nonsense birds that Lear prepared for Lord Cromer's eldest son when the latter was about three years old.

———. The Scroobious Pip. New York: Harper, 1968.
The book was completed by Ogden Nash, and the illustrations were done by Nancy Ekholm Burkert. The story relates in verse how "all the animals in the world gather around a strange inscrutable creature—part bird, beast, insect, and fish"—who looks like Lear.

———. Teapots and quails, and other new nonsenses. Edited and introduced by Philip Hofer and Angus Davidson. Cambridge, Mass.: Harvard University Press, 1953.
Edited by two Lear scholars. Presents the author's own poems written out with the text printed beneath. Contains short poems, limericks, "The adventures of Mr. Lear," "The Polly and the pussybite," "Flora Nonsensica," "The Scroobious Pip," and "Cold are the crabs."

———. The two old bachelors. New York: McGraw-Hill, 1962.
A nonsense verse that begins, "Two old bachelors/Were living in one house;/One caught a Muffin./The other caught a Mouse."

———. Whizz: six limericks. New York: Macmillan, 1975.
Illustrated by Janina Domanska.

BIOGRAPHY AND CRITICISM

Davidson, Angus. Edward Lear: landscape painter and nonsense poet (1812–1888). London: John Murray, 1938; reprint: New York: Barnes & Noble, 1968.
A biography with many facsimiles of Lear's paintings and drawings. "The children of the owl and the pussy-cat," an unfinished sequel to "The owl and the pussy-cat," is included. A list of Lear's illustrations is added.

Fadiman, Clifton. "How pleasant to know Mr. Lear!" in his *Party of one,* p. 411–20. Cleveland: World, [1955].
Characterizes Lear as "one of those unquiet souls the Victorian era produced in wholesale quantities, his inner turmoil and desperation overlaid by an outer orthodoxy of conduct imposed upon him by the conventions of his time."

Field, William B. Osgood. Edward Lear on my shelves. New York: privately printed, 1933.
A biographical sketch with a bibliography of original drawings, watercolors, engravings, and woodcuts owned by this Leariana collector.

Hofer, Philip. Edward Lear. (Grolier Club monograph, no. 71) New York: Oxford University Press, 1962.
Appreciative comment on the nonsense rhymes and the drawings.

Kelen, Emery. Mr. Nonsense: a life of Edward Lear. London: MacDonald & Jones, 1974.
A short, sometimes dull, biography.

Lear, Edward. Later letters of Edward Lear to Chichester Fortescue (Lord Carlingford), Lady Waldegrave and others. Edited by Lady Stra-

chey. London: Duffield, 1911; reprint: Plainview, N.Y.: Books for Libraries, 1971.
The preface, p. 11–27, by Herbert Congreve, a friend of Lear's from San Remo days, gives a vivid personal remembrance. There are several references to the nonsense books; also numerous reproductions of paintings and sketches.

———. Letters of Edward Lear to Chichester Fortescue, Lord Carlingford, and Frances, countess Waldegrave. Edited by Lady Strachey. London: T. F. Unwin, 1907.
Letters written between 1847 and 1864. There are many interesting anecdotes, such as that of the seafaring man who took a kind of monomaniac fancy to the *Book of nonsense*. The introduction, p. xiii–xxxv, includes Lear's own account of his work. Illustrated with reproductions in color and black and white of Lear's paintings and a number of humorous sketches.

———. A literary centenary: a short review of his life and works. London: Warne, [1932].

"Lear's nonsense books," *The spectator* 60:1251–52 (1887).
Interesting article, pointing out the "ludicrous appropriateness" of Lear's original wording, the melodiousness of his rhymes, and his happy gift of pictorial expression. Ends with an amusing set of examination questions, drawn up, the writer says, by a friend, "deeply versed in Mr. Lear's books."

Malcolm, *Sir* Ian Zackary. "Edward Lear," *The Cornhill magazine* 97, n.s. 24:25–36 (1908); *Littell's living age* 256:467–75 (1908).
"No subsequent writer has quite taken his place, though many have written brilliant nonsense since the Learics were published."

Noakes, Vivien. Edward Lear: the life of a wanderer. London: Collins; Boston: Houghton, 1968.
Clarifies some Lear "myths." Discusses the nonsense books and the songs, p. 222–27. A selected bibliography is appended.

Richardson, Joanna. Edward Lear. (Writers and their works, no. 184) London: published for the British Council and the National Book League by Longmans, [1965].
Brief but perceptive analysis of Lear as artist and nonsense poet. A selected bibliography is appended. There is a section entitled "The nonsense poet."

Smith, William Jay. " 'So they smashed that old man . . . ': a note on Edward Lear," *Horn book magazine* 35:323–26 (August, 1959).
Good article that analyzes Lear's art and his versatility.

West, Katherine. "Nonsense and wit," *The spectator* (London) 176:321 (March 29, 1946).

Discusses the essentially English quality of the nonsense of Lear and Carroll.

Williams, Orlo. "Edward Lear's nonsense," *The national review* 129:159–66 (August, 1947).
A review of *The complete nonsense of Edward Lear*, edited by H. Jackson (listed above). Of the nonsense songs, Williams writes, "There is a delicate sense of romance, of dream-journey into the realm of fancy, with an exoticism which, being purely childlike, fascinates a child."

George MacDonald

MacDonald, George. At the back of the north wind. London: Strahan, 1871.
Seventy-six illustrations by Arthur Hughes. Other illustrators of *At the back of the north wind* are Maria Kirk (1909), Jessie Willcox Smith (1919), George and Doris Hauman (1950), and Charles Mozley (1964).

———. ———. (Classics in children's literature 1621–1932) New York: Garland, 1976.
Reprint of 1871 edition published by G. Routledge. With a preface by Glenn E. Sadler.

———. Dealings with the fairies. London: Strahan, 1867.
Illustrated by Arthur Hughes. Contents: The light princess; The giant's heart; The shadows; Cross-purposes; The golden key.

———. The gifts of the child Christ, and other tales. 2v. London: Sampson, Low, 1882.

———. The gifts of the child Christ: fairytales and stories for all ages. Edited by Glenn Edward Sadler. 2v. Grand Rapids, Mich.: Eerdmans, 1973.
A centennial edition commemorating MacDonald's first visit to the United States.

———. The golden key. New York: Farrar, 1967.
Pictures by Maurice Sendak. Afterword by W. H. Auden.
Originally included in *Dealings with the fairies* (1867).

———. The light princess. New York: Macmillan, 1926.
Illustrated by Dorothy Lathrop.

———. ———. New York: Farrar, 1969.
Pictures by Maurice Sendak.

———. The light princess, and other fairy tales. London: Blackie, [1890].
Reprinted from *Dealings with the fairies*. Other tales: The giant's heart; The shadows; Cross-purposes; The golden key; The carasoyn; Little Daylight.

———. "Poems for children," v.3, *Works of George MacDonald*. London: Strahan, 1871.

———. The princess and Curdie. London: Chatto & Windus, 1883.
The original edition was illustrated by James Allen. Subsequent editions were illustrated by Maria Kirk (1908), Dorothy Lathrop (1927), Charles Folkard (1951), and Nora Unwin (1954).

———. The princess and the goblin. London: Chatto & Windus, 1883 [1872].
The original had thirty illustrations by Arthur Hughes; a 1900 edition added a frontispiece by Laurence Housman. Later editions were illustrated by Maria Kirk (1907), F. D. Bedford (1926), Jessie Willcox Smith (1934), Elizabeth Mackinstry (1937), and Nora Unwin (1957).

———. The wise woman: a parable. (Classics of children's literature 1621–1932) New York: Garland, 1977.
Preface by Mark Zaitchick. This was printed under the title "A double story" in *Good things*, December, 1874, through July, 1875. It was later published under both these titles and also as *The Princess Rosamund* and *The lost princess*.

BIOGRAPHY AND CRITICISM

Auden, W. H. "Introduction," in *Visionary novels of George MacDonald*, edited by Anne Freemantle. New York: Noonday, 1954.
Auden calls *The Princess and the goblin* "the only English children's book in the same class as the *Alice* books."

Blishen, Edward. "Maker of fairy tales," *Books and bookmen* 19:92–95 (May, 1974).
"As a maker of fairy tales, he stands easily alongside Hans Andersen."

Bulloch, John Malcolm. A centennial bibliography of George MacDonald. Aberdeen, Scotland: Aberdeen University Press, 1925.
Reissued from the Aberdeen University Library *Bulletin* of February, 1925. The introductory pages give an account of MacDonald's literary work, and there are full notes for the separate stories.

Douglass, Jane. "Dealings with the fairies: an appreciation of George MacDonald," *Horn book magazine* 37:327–35 (August, 1961).
Chiefly a discussion of *Phantastes, Dealings with the fairies*, and *At the back of the north wind*.

Hutton, M. "Writers for children: George MacDonald," *School librarian* [England] 12:244, 246–50 (December, 1964).
An excellent analysis of the criticism of MacDonald, of his writings, and of how and why they appeal to contemporary children.

Johnson, Joseph. George MacDonald: a biography and critical appreciation. London: Pitman, 1906.
Reis (below) calls it "largely a worthless book, deficient in understanding and full of factual errors; but it accurately reflects the adulation which MacDonald received from his contemporaries."

Lewis, C. S. "Introduction," in his *George MacDonald: an anthology*. New York: Macmillan, 1947.
An important essay on MacDonald.

MacDonald, George. "The fantastic imagination," in his *A dish of orts: chiefly papers on the imagination and on Shakespere*, p. 313–22. London: Sampson Low Marston, 1895 [1893?]; in *A peculiar gift*, edited by Lance Salway, p. 162–67. Harmondsworth, Eng.: Penguin, [1976].
In this important essay, MacDonald defines what he means by the fairy tale (or *mährchen*, as he prefers to call it) and compares it to music.

MacDonald, Greville. George MacDonald and his wife. London: Allen & Unwin; New York: Dial, 1924.
Introduction by G. K. Chesterton. Authoritative biography of George MacDonald written by his son. Includes a generous selection of the author's letters. Bibliography, p. 563–65.

Manlove, C. N. "George MacDonald's fairy tales: their roots in MacDonald's thought," *Studies in Scottish literature* 8:97–108 (October, 1970).
Deals with adult as well as children's fairy tales in an attempt to differentiate fairy tale from allegory.

Moffatt, James. "George MacDonald *and* A brief sketch of the life of George MacDonald by Mary Gray," *The bookman* (London) 29:59–67 (1905).
This issue of *The bookman* contains twenty-one illustrations of, or relating to, MacDonald, including a large-size photograph used as a supplement.

Reis, Richard H. George MacDonald. (Twayne's English authors series) New York: Twayne, 1972.
A "critical-analytical" study of George MacDonald. Chapter 4, "Imaginative fiction," p. 75–105, deals with shorter works for children, and full-length children's stories.

Sadler, Glenn Edward. "An unpublished children's story by George MacDonald," *Children's literature: the great excluded* 2:18–34 (1973).
An analysis of this previously unpublished short story, the manuscript of which is in the Houghton Library, Harvard University. The story, "The little girl that had no tongue," is printed in full.

Wolff, Robert L. The golden key: a study of the fiction of George MacDonald. New Haven, Conn.: Yale University Press, 1961.

A scholarly study of MacDonald's writing, with special attention given to *At the back of the north wind* and *The princess and the goblin.*

Yates, Elizabeth. "George MacDonald," *Horn book magazine* 14:23–30 (January–February, 1938).
An appreciative biographical sketch and survey of MacDonald's works for children. Includes a bibliography of his works in print in 1938.

Oliver Optic

■ From about 1850 to 1890, William Taylor Adams, under the pseudonym Oliver Optic, published about 1,000 stories in magazines and papers as well as 116 full-length books. Listed below are some of the most popular series titles and the books found in each series.

Adams, William Taylor (*pseud.* Oliver Optic). Army and navy stories series. Boston: Lee & Shepard.
v.1. The soldier boy, or, Tom Somers in the army: a story of a great rebellion. [1863]
v.2. The sailor boy, or, Jack Somers in the navy: a story of a great rebellion. [1863]
v.3. The young lieutenant, or, the adventures of an army officer: a story of a great rebellion. 1865.
v.4. The Yankee middy, or, the adventures of a naval officer: a story of a great rebellion. 1866.
v.5. Fighting Joe, or, the fortunes of a staff officer: a story of a great rebellion. 1866.
v.6. Brave Old Salt: a story of a great rebellion. 1865.

———. Boat club series. Boston: Lee & Shepard.
v.1. Boat club, or, the bunkers of Rippleton. [1855].
v.2. All aboard, or, life on the lake. [1856].
v.3. Now or never, or, the adventures of Bobby Bright. [1857].
v.4. Try again, or, the trials and triumphs of Harry West. [1858].
v.5. Poor and proud, or, the fortunes of Katy Redburn. [1858].
v.6. Little by little, or, the cruise of the Fly-away. [1861].

———. Great western series. Boston: Lee & Shepard.
v.1. Going west, or, the perils of a poor boy. 1876.
v.2. Out west, or, roughing it on the Great Lakes. 1878.
v.3. Lake breezes, or, the cruise of the Sylvania. 1879.
v.4. Going south, or, yachting on the Atlantic coast. 1879.
v.5. Down south, or, yacht adventures in Florida. 1880.

———. Lake shore series. Boston: Lee & Shepard.
v.1. Through by daylight, or, the young engineer of the Lake Shore Railroad. [1869].
v.2. Lightning Express, or, the rival academies. 1870.
v.3. On time, or, the young captain of the Ucayga steamer. 1870.
v.4. Switch off, or, the way of the students. 1870.
v.5. Brake up, or, the young peacemakers. [1869].
v.6. Bear and forbear, or, the young skipper of Lake Ucayga. 1871.

———. The Riverdale series. Boston: Lee & Shepard.
v.1. The little merchant: a story for little folks. 1863.
v.2. The young voyagers: a story of little folks. 1863.
v.3. The Christmas gift: a story for little folks. 1863.
v.4. Dolly and I: a story for little folks. 1863.
v.5. Uncle Ben: a story for little folks. 1865.
v.6. The birthday party: a story for little folks. 1863.
v.7. Proud and lazy: a story for little folks. 1862.
v.8. Careless Kate: a story for little folks. 1863.
v.9. Robinson Crusoe, Jr.: a story for little folks. 1863.
v.10 The picnic party: a story for little folks. 1863.
v.11 The gold thimble: a story for little folks. 1863.
v.12 Do-Somethings: a story for little folks. 1863.

———. The starry flag series. Boston: Lee & Shepard.
v.1. The starry flag, or, the young fisherman. 1867.
v.2. Breaking away, or, the fortunes of a student. 1867.
v.3. Seek and find, or, the adventures of a smart boy. 1868.
v.3. Make or break, or, the rich man's daughter. 1868.
v.4. Freaks of fortune, or, half around the world. 1868.
v.5. Down the river, or, Buck Bradford and his tyrants. 1869.

———. Upward and onward series. Boston: Lee & Shepard.
v.1. Field and forest, or, the fortunes of a farmer. 1871.
v.2. Plane and plank, or, the mishaps of a mechanic. 1871.
v.3. Desk and debit, or, the catastrophes of a clerk. 1871.
v.4. Cringle and cross-fire, or, the sea swashes of a sailor. 1870.
v.5. Bivouac and battle, or, the struggle of a soldier. 1871.
v.6. Sea and shore, or, the tramps of a traveller. 1872.

———. The Woodville series. Boston: Lee & Shepard.
v.1. Rich and humble, or, the mission of Bertha Grant: a story for young people. 1864.
v.2. In school and out, or, the conquest of Richard Grant: a story for young people. 1864.
v.3. Watch and wait: a story for young people. 1864.
v.4. Work and win, or, Noddy Newman on a cruise: a story for young people. 1864.
v.5. Hope and have, or, Fanny Grant among the Indians: a story for young people. 1866.
v.6. Haste and waste, or, the young pilot of Lake Champlain: a story for young people. 1866.

———. The yacht club series. Boston: Lee & Shepard.
v.1 Little Bobtail, or, the wreck of the Penobscot clubs. 1874.
v.2. Yacht club, or, the young boat builder. 1874.
v.3. Money-maker, or, the victory of the Basilisk. 1874.
v.4. Coming wave, or, the hidden treasure of High Road. 1875.
v.5. Dorcas Club, or, girls afloat. 1875.
v.6. Ocean born, or, the cruise of the clubs. 1875.

———. Young Americans abroad series. Boston: Lee & Shepard.
v.1. Outward bound, or, young America afloat. 1867.
v.2. Shamrock and thistle, or, young Americans in Ireland and Scotland. 1868.
v.3. Red Cross, or, young Americans in England and Wales. 1868.
v.4. Dikes and ditches, or, young Americans in Holland and Belgium. 1868.
v.5. Palace and cottage, or, young Americans in France and Switzerland. 1868.
v.6. Down the Rhine, or, young Americans in Germany. 1869.
v.7. Up the Baltic, or, young Americans in Norway, Sweden, and Denmark. 1871.
v.8. Northern lands, or, young Americans in Russia and Prussia. 1872.
v.9. Cross and crescent, or, young Americans in Turkey and Greece. 1872.
v.10. Sunny shores, or, young Americans in Italy and Austria. 1875.
v.11. Vine and olive, or, young Americans in Spain and Portugal. 1876.
v.12. Isles of the sea, or, young Americans homeward bound. 1877.

MAGAZINES

Adams, William Taylor, ed. Oliver Optic's magazine for boys and girls. v. 1–18. January, 1867–December, 1875.

———, ed. Student and schoolmate, 1855–72.

BIOGRAPHY AND CRITICISM

Gleason, Gene. "Whatever happened to Oliver Optic?" *Wilson library bulletin* 49:647–50 (May, 1975).
The article covers Adams, Alger, and Alcott.

William Brighty Rands

Rands, William Brighty. Lazy lessons and essays on conduct. London: James Bowden, 1897.
"Designed to interest children in facts and ideas, to welcome them to the school room, and to illustrate the relations of 'lessons' to 'life.' "

———. Lilliput lectures. London: Strahan, 1871.
Talks on various subjects such as art, the family, government, and character, each ending with a poem. Includes "Great, wide, beautiful, wonderful world," p. 22–23.

———. Lilliput legends. London: Strahan, 1872.
"The preface . . . tells how he went to a country full of story-book folk. . . . He came back full of stories about the place, but found he could not write them. Then he told the stories to write themselves: 'So they did. And the telling of them is true.' "—F. J. H. Harvey Darton, in *Children's books in England*, p. 281.

———. Lilliput levee: poems of childhood, child-fancy, and child-like moods. London: Strahan, 1864.
Illustrated by Millais and Pinwell.

———. Lilliput revels [*and*] Innocents' island. Edited by R. B. Johnson. London: John Lane, [1905].
Illustrated by Griselda Wedderburn. "The 'Revels' was first published in *Good words for the young*, 1870–1872. . . . 'Innocents' Island' appeared in the same magazine, 1872."—editor's note.

Capt. Mayne Reid

■ Capt. Mayne Reid was a prolific writer of tales of adventure and romance for children and adults of the Victorian period. A complete bibliography of his writings can be found in *The Bulletin of bibliography* 29:95–97 (July–September, 1972). Listed below are some of his most popular books for children.

Reid, *Capt.* Thomas Mayne. Afloat in the forest, or a voyage among the treetops. Boston: Ticknor & Fields, 1867.
Adventures of a party of English people lost in the flooded forest of the Amazon. Appeared in *Boys' journal* (1865) and *Our young folks* (1866).

———. The boy hunters, or, adventures in search of a white buffalo. London: D. Bogue, 1853. Illustrated by William Harvey.

———. The boy slaves. London: C. H. Clarke, 1865. Appeared in *Boys' journal* (1865).

———. Bruin: the grand bear hunt. London: Routledge, 1861.

——— The bush boys, or, the history and adventures of a Cape farmer and his family in the wild karoos of southern Africa. London: D. Bogue, 1856.

———. The desert home, or, the adventures of a lost family in the wilderness. London: D. Bogue, 1852.
Also published under the title, *The English family Robinson.*

———. The forest exiles, or, the period of a Peruvian family amid the wilds of the Amazon. London: D. Bogue, 1855 [1854].

———. The plant hunters, or, adventures among the Himalaya mountains. London: Ward, Lock, 1857.
Has Edmund Evans engravings.

———. The young voyageurs, or, the boy hunters in the North. London: D. Bogue, 1854.
Adventures of four boys while endeavouring to reach one of the remote posts of the Hudson's Bay fur company.

BIOGRAPHY AND CRITICISM

Holyoake, Maltus Questell. "Captain Mayne Reid: soldier and novelist," *The Strand magazine* 2:93–102 (July, 1891); in *A peculiar gift*, edited by Lance Salway, p. 404–11. Harmondsworth, Eng.: Penguin, [1976].
A fascinating account of the life and writing of this multifaceted man. The author characterizes his work as "thoroughly manly, healthy in tone, and good in purpose."

Reid, Elizabeth Hyde, and C. H. Coe. Captain Mayne Reid: his life and adventures. London: Greening, 1900.
"This biography, although often inaccurate, in some instances offers the only substantiation of publication possible."—Joan Steele.

Starrett, Vincent. "Mustache and saber," in his *Bookman's holiday*, p. 167–82. New York: Random, 1942.
A popularized account of the "novelist, daredevil, controversialist; and soldier of fortune."

Steele, Joan. "Mayne Reid: a revised bibliography," *The bulletin of bibliography* 29:95–110 (July, 1972).
This is an excellent bibliography. In her introduction, the author characterizes Reid as somewhere "between a 'British Cooper' and an 'American Defoe.'"

Christina Rossetti

Rossetti, Christina Georgina. Goblin market and other poems. Cambridge and London: Macmillan, 1862.
With two designs by Dante Gabriel Rossetti. Completed in 1859, this is Christina Rossetti's most popular poem. Not written or intended for children, "it was apparently Victorian culture rather than the author's intention which identified the work as children's verse."—R. Loring Taylor.

———. ———. London: Macmillan, 1893. Illustrated by Laurence Housman.

———. ———. Philadelphia: Lippincott, n.d. Illustrated by Arthur Rackham.

———. Maude: prose and verse. Edited with an introduction by R. W. Crump. Hamden, Conn.: Archon, 1976.

———. Maude: a story for girls. Edited by William Michael Rossetti. London: James Bowden, 1897.
Written in 1850, this story about fifteen-year-old Maude Foster, who writes "broken-hearted poetry," is said to be autobiographical. This edition, published posthumously, was edited by her brother.

———. The poetical works. London: Macmillan, 1906.
Memoir, notes, etc. by William Michael Rossetti.

———. Sing-song: a nursery rhyme book. London: Routledge, 1872.
Illustrations by Arthur Hughes. "The book appeared at the height of the vogue for nonsense verse and was an immediate success."—R. Loring Taylor.

———. Sing-song, Speaking likenesses, [and] Goblin market. (Classics of children's literature 1621–1932) New York: Garland, 1976.
Includes an excellent preface by R. Loring Taylor.

———. Speaking likenesses. London: Macmillan, 1874.
"*Speaking Likenesses*, written expressly for children, is, on a crucial level, neither for nor about children. It is a sad and sometimes bitter parable of a lonely lady. The child who manages to read

it will be burdened with an awkward and painful understanding."—R. Loring Taylor.

BIOGRAPHY AND CRITICISM

Bald, Marjory Amelia. "Christina Rossetti," in her *Women writers of the nineteenth century*, p. 233–74. Cambridge: Cambridge University Press, 1923.

Battiscombe, Georgina. Christina Rossetti. (Writers and their work) London: published for the British Book Council by Longmans, 1965.
This short biography and critical study is concerned chiefly with the influence of the Pre-Raphaelites and the Oxford movement on the author's work.

Bell, Henry Thomas MacKenzie. Christina Rossetti: a biographical and critical study. London: T. Burleigh, 1898; reprint: Brooklyn: Haskell House, 1971.
For *Sing-song*, see p. 290–300; *Speaking likenesses*, p. 300–301, "Bibliography," p. 377–90.

Bellac, Ralph A. Christina Rossetti. (Twayne's English authors series) Boston: Twayne, 1977.
Chapter 7 deals with the children's verse. *Sing-song*, though influenced by Mother Goose rhymes, is characterized as continuing the didactic and moral tradition. Includes an excellent annotated bibliography.

Birkhead, Edith. Christina Rossetti and her poetry. London: Harrap, 1930; reprint: New York: AMS Press, 1972.
A capable biographical study.

Bowra, C. M. "Christina Rossetti" in his *The romantic imagination*, p. 245–70. Cambridge, Mass.: Harvard University Press, 1949.
Defines the basic conflict of her life, that between "the woman and the saint."

Cary, Elizabeth Luther. "Christina Rossetti," "Christina Rossetti, her poetry," in her *The Rossettis*, p: 228–75. New York: Putnam, 1900.
Includes portraits. Bibliography of Christina Rossetti's poems, p. 282–87.

Crump, Rebecca N. Christina Rossetti: a reference guide. Boston: G. K. Hall, 1976.
Annotated bibliographies of her books and shorter writings, and of books and articles written about her, arranged chronologically.

de la Mare, Walter John. "Christina Rossetti," *Transactions* (Royal Society of Literature in the United Kingdom) n.s. 6:79–116 (1926).
Brings out the qualities of Christina Rossetti's poetic style as well as her personal characteristics. Refers to *Sing-song* "as the simplest, quietest poems for childlike children in the language."

de Wilde, Justine Fredrika. Christina Rossetti, poet and woman. Amsterdam: C. C. Callenbach, 1923.
In a chapter titled "Poetry," p. 84–146, the author speaks of the poet as influenced by two principal motives: love and religion.

Ehrsam, Theodore, and R. H. Deiley. Bibliography of twelve Victorian authors. New York: Wilson, 1936.
Complete bibliography of her writings and writings about her. This bibliography is updated by one by J. C. Fucilla, in *Modern philology* 37 (1939).

Garlitz, Barbara. "Christina Rossetti's *Sing-song* and 19th century children's poetry," *PMLA* 70: 539–43 (1955).
Relates the poems to the moral and sentimental nineteenth-century universe of the child.

Gosse, Edmund William. "Christina Rossetti," in his *Critical kit-kats*, p. 133–62. New York: Dodd, 1897.
A little biography, a little criticism, a little gossip, always friendly.

Hueffer, Ford Madox (*pseud.* Ford Madox Ford). "Christina Rossetti," *The fortnightly review* 95, n.s. 89:422–49 (1911).
Chiefly a discussion of personal qualities.

Lowther, George. "Christina Rossetti," *Contemporary review* 104:681–89 (1913).
Does not attempt to consider in detail the varied range of Christina's genius, but rather "to show its unity by reason of the golden thread which runs through all."

Mary Joan, Sister. "Christina Rossetti: Victorian child's poet," *Elementary English* 44:24–28+ (January, 1967).
Puts forth the theory that, since Rossetti was not fond of children, her verse was her way of making contact with the little ones.

Mason, Eugene. "Christina G. Rossetti," in his *A book of preferences in literature*, p. 115–26. New York: Wilson, 1915.
"Poetess and saint—these are the two keynotes of Christina Rossetti's character."

More, Paul Elmer. "Christina Rossetti," in his *Shelburne essays*, v.3, p. 124–42. New York: Putnam, 1905; *The Atlantic monthly* 94:815–21 (1904).
The writer considers Rossetti's work as "the purest expression in English of the feminine genius."

Packer, Lona Mosk. Christina Rossetti. Berkeley and Los Angeles: University of California Press, 1963.

The most scholarly of all studies on Christina Rossetti; the author hopes it will fill a need for a biography with "more rigorous standards, one based upon original research, which utilizes modern scholarly techniques and insights but which at the same time aims at readability and sustained narrative interest." Many illustrations, with a long bibliography. For *Sing-song*, see p. 265–68; *Speaking likenesses*, p. 305–7:

Proctor, Ellen A. A brief memoir of Christina G. Rossetti. London: S.P.C.K., 1895.
Written by a friend soon after the poet's death. Contains some of her childhood poems.

Rossetti, William Michael, ed. The family letters of Christina Georgina Rossetti, with some supplementary letters and appendices. London: Brown, Langham, 1908; reprint: Brooklyn: Haskell House, 1968.
The preface includes a chronology of her life.

———. Rossetti papers, 1862 to 1870. London: Sands, 1903; reprint: New York: AMS Press, 1970.
Letters of the whole family, written mostly to each other.

Sandars, Mary Frances. The life of Christina Rossetti. London: Hutchinson, [1930].
Mention of *Sing-song*, p. 197–99.

Sawtell, Margaret. Christina Rossetti: her life and religion. London: Mowbray; Brooklyn: Haskell House, [1955]; reprint: Folcroft, Pa.: Folcroft, 1973.

Shove, Fredegond. Christina Rossetti: a study. Cambridge: Cambridge University Press, 1931; reprint: New York: Octagon, 1969.
Goblin market, The prince's progress, and *Sing-song* are discussed in a section titled "Her poems," p. 36–90.

Stuart, Dorothy Margaret. Christina Rossetti. London: Macmillan, 1930; reprints: Brooklyn: Haskell House, 1970; Folcroft, Pa.: Folcroft, 1973.
Reference to *Sing-song*, p. 84–87; *Speaking likenesses*, p. 151–52.

Swann, Thomas Burnett. Wonder and whimsy: the fantastic world of Christina Rossetti. Francestown, N.H.: M. Jones, 1960.
A discussion of Christina Rossetti's "fantastic poems" and fairy tales. There is a chapter entitled "*Goblin market*: fantastic masterpiece."

Thomas, Eleanor Walter. Christina Georgina Rossetti: New York: Columbia University Press, 1931.
There are sections on the tales and poems for children, and on the short stories.

Watts-Dunton, Theodore. "Christina Georgina Rossetti," in his *Old familiar faces,* p. 177–206. New York: Jenkins, 1916.

Woolf, Virginia. "I am Christina Rossetti," in her *Second common reader,* p. 257–65. New York: Harcourt, 1932.
As an "instinctive poet, her poetry must speak for her rather than her life."

Zaturenska, Marya. Christina Rossetti: a portrait with background. New York: Macmillan, 1949.
This detailed biography deals at length with family and friends. For *Sing-song*, see p. 94–96.

John Ruskin

Ruskin, John. The king of the Golden river, or, the black brothers: a legend of Stiria. London: Smith & Elder, 1851.
Written in 1841, but not published until 1851. The first illustrator was Richard Doyle.

———. ———. East Aurora, N.Y.: The Roycrofters, 1900.
Subtitle: "a legend of Stiria written in 1841 by John Ruskin, being a tale for young folks and their elders."

———. ———. Philadelphia: Lippincott, 1932.
Illustrated by Arthur Rackham.

———. ———. (Rainbow classics) Cleveland: World, 1946.
Illustrated by Fritz Kredel, with an introduction by May Lamberton Becker.

———. ———. London: Hamlyn, 1973.
Illustrated by Josef Vyetal.

———. ———. in *The king of the Golden river, A holiday romance* [Dickens], and *Petsetilla's posy* [Hood]. New York: Garland, 1976.
Introduction by Diane Johnson.

BIOGRAPHY AND CRITICISM

Beetz, Kirk H. John Ruskin: A bibliography, 1900–1974. Metuchen, N.J.: Scarecrow, 1976.
Complete bibliography of works by and about Ruskin.

Butler, Francelia. "From fantasy to reality: Ruskin's *King of the Golden river*, St. George's Guild, and Ruskin, Tennessee," *Children's literature: the great excluded* 1:62–73 (1972).
Points out the influence of Grimm on the writings of Ruskin and shows how the educational theories of John Ruskin are exemplified in the *King of the Golden river* and in the Ruskin Commonwealth, founded at Yellow Creek, Tennessee, in 1893.

Evans, Joan. John Ruskin. London: Oxford University Press, 1954.
A standard Ruskin biography.

James, *Sir* William Milburne, ed. John Ruskin and Effie Gray. New York: Scribner, 1947.
Subtitle: "the story of John Ruskin, Effie Gray and John Everett Millais in their unpublished letters." The grandson of Effie Gray tells of her marriage in 1848 to Ruskin, its annulment six years later, and her subsequent marriage to J. E. Millais, the painter. The book mentions that Ruskin wrote *King of the Golden river* for Effie Gray when she was only twelve years old—seven years before their marriage.

Leon, Derrick. Ruskin: the great Victorian. London: Routledge & Kegan Paul, [1949].
Chapter 3 deals with Ruskin's writing of *The king of the Golden river.*

Rosenberg, John D. The darkening glass: a portrait of Ruskin's genius. New York: Columbia University Press, 1961.

Ruskin, John. "Præterita": outlines of scenes and thoughts, perhaps worthy of memory, in my past life. 3v in 1. London: Bryan, Taylor & Co., 1912.
Chapters 1 through 4 give a record of Ruskin's childhood, his reading, and his attempts at writing. Reproduces a part of his conclusions to the *Early lessons* of the Edgeworths, written when he seven years old.

Wise, Thomas James, and James Smart. A complete bibliography of the writings in prose and verse of John Ruskin. With a list of the more important Ruskiniana. London: privately printed, 1893; reprint: London: Dawson, 1964.

Harriet Beecher Stowe

Stowe, Harriet Beecher. The annotated *Uncle Tom's cabin.* Edited with an introduction by Philip Van Doren Stern. New York: Paul Erikkson, [1969].

——. Pictures and stories from Uncle Tom's cabin. Boston, J. P. Jewett, [1853].
There is a dedicatory message that reads, "This little work is designed to adapt Mrs. Stowe's touching narrative to the understanding of the youngest readers and to foster in their hearts a generous sympathy for the wronged Negro race of America."

——. Stories and sketches for young people, v.16, *The writings of Harriet Beecher Stowe.* Boston: Houghton, n.d.; reprint: New York: AMS Press, 1967.
Contents: Queer little people; Little Captain Trott; Little pussy willow; The minister's watermelon; A dog's mission; Lulu's pupil; The daisy's first winter; Our Charley and the stories told him; Christmas, or, the good fairy; Little Fred, the canal boy.

——. Uncle Tom's cabin, or, life among the lowly. Boston: J. P. Jewett, 1852.
The 1878 edition contained an author's introduction.

——. ——. New York: Oxford University Press, 1965.
This edition has an introduction by John A. Woods and is based on the first American edition. The author's introduction is included, with a biographical sketch and a critical analysis of the book and its influence on history.

BIOGRAPHY AND CRITICISM

Adams, John A. Harriet Beecher Stowe. New York: Twayne, 1963.
The author feels that Stowe's writing abilities have been maligned. Includes a chapter on *Uncle Tom's cabin*, mentions *Queer little people*, p. 83, and *Pussy willow*, p. 84. Chronology.

Fields, Annie Adams, ed. Life and letters of Harriet Beecher Stowe. Boston: Houghton, 1898.
Includes liberal samplings of letters interspersed with biographical material.

Foster, Charles Howell. The rungless ladder: Harriet Beecher Stowe and New England Puritanism. Durham, N.C.: Duke University Press, 1954.
Written to clarify the "distorted image of an important American author" and her writings. Includes a chronological outline.

Gerson, Noel B. Harriet Beecher Stowe: a biography. New York: Praeger, 1976.
Tells of the writing of *Uncle Tom's cabin*, p. 64–75. Includes a bibliography of secondary sources.

Gilbertson, Catherine Peebles. Harriet Beecher Stowe. New York: Appleton, 1937.
An early appreciative biography.

Johnston, Johanna. Runaway to heaven: the story of Harriet Beecher Stowe. Garden City, N.Y.: Doubleday, [1963].
Sees Harriet Beecher Stowe as "a compound of contradiction—deep feeling and sentimentality, laughter and melancholy, self-righteousness and humility, dark fears and clear visions—all fused at one time in one person to produce a book that shook the world."—prologue.

Rourke, Constance M. Trumpet in Jubilee. New York: Harcourt; London: Jonathan Cape, 1927.

Stowe, Charles Edward. The life of Harriet Beecher Stowe, compiled from her letters and journals. Boston: Houghton, 1889.
  This is the biography by her son. Includes a "list
of novels, stories, sketches, and poems, by Harriet Beecher Stowe."

—— and **Lyman Beecher Stowe.** Harriet Beecher
Stowe: the story of her life. Boston: Houghton,
1911.
  The son and grandson of Harriet Beecher Stowe
intended this work, "not as a biography in the
ordinary sense. It is rather the story of a real
character; telling not so much what she did as
what she was, and how she became what she
was."—preface.

Stowe, Lyman Beecher. Saints, sinners and Beech-
ers. Indianapolis: Bobbs-Merrill, [1934].
  A biography of the whole family. Harriet Beecher Stowe, p. 154–235.

Wagenknecht, Edward Charles. Harriet Beecher
Stowe: the known and the unknown. New York:
Oxford University Press, 1965.
  The author calls this a "psychograph," or portrait, or character story of Harriet Beecher Stowe.
Includes scholarly chapter notes but no bibliography. Of special interest is a chapter titled "The
mother," p. 61–71, which outlines the writer's relationship to children, especially her own.

Wilson, Forrest. Crusader in crinoline: the life of
Harriet Beecher Stowe. Philadelphia: Lippincott,
1941.
  A lengthy biography. Mentions her juvenile writings for *Our young folks,* p. 504.

William Makepeace Thackeray

Thackeray, William Makepeace. The Christmas
books of Mr. M. A. Titmarsh. London: Chapman
& Hall, 1857.
  Illustrations by the author. Contents: Mrs. Per-
kins' ball; Our street; Dr. Birch; The Kickleburys
on the Rhine; The rose and the ring; The book of
snobs; Ballads.

————. Dr. Birch and his young friends, by M. A.
Titmarsh. London: Chapman & Hall, 1849.
  Also included in *The Christmas books* (see
above). Appeared in America as one of the volumes of a New York edition of Thackeray's minor
works published by Appleton in 1853. The story is
slight, consisting of little sketches of life at Dr.
Birch's academy, but it contains some happy
touches and is illustrated by the author. In the
English edition, the illustrations are colored.

————. The rose and the ring, or, the history of
Prince Giglio and Prince Bulbo: a fire-side pan-
tomime for great and small children, by Mr.
M. A. Titmarsh. London: Smith & Elder, 1855.

Illustrated by the author. "Prelude," dated 1854,
explains the origin of the story.

————. ————. London: Stokes, 1909.
  Illustrated by Gordon Browne.

————. ————. London: Kegan Paul, 1911.
  Illustrated by J. R. Monsell.

————. ————. New York: Pierpont Morgan Library,
1947.
  Reproduced in facsimile from the author's orig-
inal illustrated manuscript in the Pierpont Morgan
Library. With an introduction by Gordon N.
Ray.

————. The Thackeray alphabet, written and illustrated by William Makepeace Thackeray. London: Murray, 1929.
  A reproduction of the original manuscript still
in the possession of the family of Edward Frederick Chadwick, for whom it was written, probably about 1833. Introductory note signed, "One
of Eddy's seven children."

BIOGRAPHY AND CRITICISM

Benet, Laura. Thackeray, of the great heart and
humorous pen. New York: Dodd, 1947.
  Intended for young readers.

Benjamin, Lewis S. (*pseud.* Lewis Melville). William Makepeace Thackeray. New York: Doubleday, 1928.
  Bibliography, p. viii–xi.

Brander, Laurence. Thackeray. (Writers and their
work) London: Longmans for the British Council and the National Book League, [1959].
  Thackeray, the author says, "provides the best
portrait we have of the class that was ruling England one hundred years ago."

Ray, Gordon Norton. Thackeray. 2v. v.1. The uses
of adversity (1811–1846). v.2. The age of wisdom (1847–1863). New York: McGraw-Hill,
[1955, 1958].
  The origin of *The rose and the ring,* found in
vol. 2, p. 229–33; for *The Christmas books,* see p.
98–101.

Shepherd, Richard Herne. The bibliography of
Thackeray: a bibliographical list, arranged in
chronological order, of the published writings in
prose and verses and the sketches and drawings
of W. M. Thackeray (from 1829 to 1880). London: Elliot Stock, 1880.

Susan Warner

Warner, Susan (*pseud.* Elizabeth Wetherell). The
Christmas stocking. London: Stephenson &
Spence, 1855 [1854].

———. Queechy. 2v. New York: Putnam, 1852.
Susan Warner's second book for children.

———. Wide, wide world. 2v. New York: Putnam, 1850; reprint: St. Claire Shores, Mich.: Somerset, 1972.
Susan Warner's first and most famous book for children; Alice Jordan calls it "the first important example of Sunday-school book types," characteristic of which is "an atmosphere of fervent evangelism, overlaid with sentimentality, both religious and secular."—*From Rollo to Tom Sawyer.*

BIOGRAPHY AND CRITICISM

Jordan, Alice M. "Susan Warner and her *Wide, wide world*," in her *From Rollo to Tom Sawyer and other papers*, p. 82–91. Boston: Horn Book, 1948.
A critical analysis of Susan Warner's two most famous books with a biographical sketch.

Stokes, Olivia Egleston Phelps. Letters and memoirs of Susan and Anna Bartlett Warner. New York: Putnam, 1925.
A biography by a close friend of Susan and Anna Warner.

Warner, Anna B. Susan Warner ("Elizabeth Wetherell"). New York: Putnam, 1909.
A sister's biography, which excerpts freely from letters and diary entries. Includes many photographs, but no index and no bibliography.

Charlotte Yonge

■ A complete bibliography, arranged chronologically, can be found in Christabel Coleridge's *Charlotte Mary Yonge*, p. 355–68. Listed below are several of her most popular works.

Yonge, Charlotte Mary. A book of golden deeds of all times and all lands, gathered and narrated by the author of the *Heir of Redclyffe*. London: Macmillan, 1864.
Stories of heroism from the days of ancient Greece and Rome to 1864.

———. The chaplet of pearls, or, the white and black Ribaumont. London: Macmillan, 1868.
An historical romance, its scene laid in France in the sixteenth century. The sequel to this is *Stray pearls*. The preface, a plea for historical novels, is dated 1868.

———. Countess Kate. London: Mozley, 1862.
A charming story written for younger readers.

———. The daisy chain, or, aspirations: a family chronicle. 2v. London: J. W. Parker, 1856.
"A domestic record of home events, large and small, during those years of early life when the character is chiefly formed."—preface.

———. ———. London: Macmillan, 1860; reprint: (Classics of children's literature 1621–1932) New York: Garland, 1977.
The reprint has an introduction by Susan M. Kenney.

———. The dove in the eagle's nest. 2v. London: Macmillan, 1866.

———. ———. (Children's classics) New York: Macmillan, 1926.
Illustrated by Marguerite de Angeli. The author's introduction to the first edition is included.

———. The heir of Redclyffe. 2v. London: J. W. Parker, 1853.
A "classic of a period."—Arnold Bennett.

———. ———. London: Macmillan, 1914.
Illustrated by Kate Greenaway.

———. ———. London: Duckworth, 1964.

———. The lances of Lynwood. London: Macmillan, 1855.

———. The little duke, or, Richard the fearless. London: J. W. Parker, 1854.
Charlotte Yonge's most famous book of historical fiction.

———. The trial: more links of the daisy chain. 2v. London: Macmillan, 1864.
A sequel to *The daisy chain.*

———. Unknown to history: a story of the captivity of Mary of Scotland. London: Macmillan, 1882.

———. ed. The monthly packet. 1851–90.
From 1890 to 1899, Charlotte Yonge coedited the magazine with Christabel R. Coleridge.

BIOGRAPHY AND CRITICISM

Battiscombe, Georgina. Charlotte Mary Yonge: the story of an uneventful life. London: Constable, 1943.
Introduction by E. M. Delafield. A biography based on Charlotte Yonge's autobiography, which gives a picture of Victorian youth in a devoutly religious family. With illustrations and genealogies.

Bennett, Arnold. "Charlotte M. Yonge," in his *Fame and fiction*, p. 49–57. London: Richards, 1901; *The academy* 57:87–89 (1899).
The author considers *The heir of Redclyffe* to be the classic of a period and as such "a document of marvellous interest."

"Charlotte Mary Yonge," *The quarterly review* 194:520–38 (1901).
Reviews several of Charlotte Yonge's books and points out their outstanding characteristics.

Charlotte Yonge Society. A chaplet for Charlotte Yonge: papers by Georgina Battiscombe et al. London: Cresset, 1965.

Includes some chapters especially of interest to students of children's literature, notably one by Kathleen Tillotson, "Children and Charlotte Yonge."

Coleridge, Christabel Rose. Charlotte Mary Yonge: her life and letters. London: Macmillan, 1903.

Full-length biography, giving interesting details and valuable data concerning Charlotte Yonge's literary work. Full bibliography of her works.

——. "Charlotte Yonge," *Literature* 8:250–51 (1901).

An obituary, noting particularly the influence of Charlotte Yonge's books on the girls of the nineteenth century. A full-page reproduction of a portrait photograph is inserted.

Foster, S. "Unpublished letters of C. M. Yonge," *Notes and queries* 17:339–41 (September, 1970).

Godley, Eveline Charlotte. "A century of children's books," *The national review* 47:444–47 (1906).

Discusses the realistic character of Charlotte Yonge's books, especially as shown in *The little duke, The Stokesley secret,* and *Countess Kate.*

Green, Roger Lancelyn. "Charlotte Yonge and others," in his *Tellers of tales,* p. 85–96. Rewritten and rev. ed. New York: Watts, 1965.

Green discusses the popularity of the novels of Charlotte Yonge and despairs that her works today are read only by adults.

Mare, Margaret L., and **Alicia C. Percival.** Victorian best-seller: the world of Charlotte M. Yonge. London: Harrap, 1947.

Yonge is seen here as the chronicler of nineteenth-century English life. Emphasis focuses on the influence of the eminent clergyman John Keble. Frontispiece in color and sixteen plates in half-tone.

"The novels of Miss Yonge," *The Edinburgh review* 202:357–77 (1905).

Reviews *The heir of Redclyffe* and other books of Charlotte Yonge, suggesting her characteristic methods and emphasizing "her talent for interesting herself in the whole personality of a number of persons not obviously interesting and living most ordinary lives."

Owen, C. A. "Charlotte Mary Yonge," *Church quarterly review* 92:295–304 (1921).

A review of Charlotte Yonge's literary work, written twenty years after her death. The book chosen to illustrate her peculiar gifts and her characteristic defects is *Hopes and fears,* published in 1860. Notes especially the influence of Keble.

Romanes, Ethel Duncan. Charlotte Mary Yonge: an appreciation. London: A. R. Mowbray, 1908.

The writer set out "to show that Miss Yonge was indeed a leader of religion, and that she had a very great share in that movement which we know as the Oxford Movement."—preface. There is a chapter on her editorship of *The monthly packet* and another on books for children. Includes many photographs.

Saintsbury, George Edward Bateman. "The mid-Victorian novel," in his *The English novel,* p. 261–62. London: Dent, 1913.

Estimate of Charlotte Yonge's work from the standpoint of literature.

Sichel, Edith. "Charlotte Yonge as a chronicler," *The monthly review* 3:88–97 (May, 1901).

The author considers the "domestic chronicles" to be Charlotte Yonge's most original work and most representative of her personality. She calls *The daisy chain* "an epic—the Iliad of the schoolroom—" and "a moral classic."

The Late Nineteenth Century

Mark Twain called the last quarter of the nineteenth century "The Gilded Age." He was thinking of the vast increase in commercialism and industrialism that was fast spreading its wealth over the simpler, homespun America he had loved. The period was also one of outpouring energy and growing national confidence. There was a new sense of unity after the Civil War and a new world view of America's place among the nations, which found expression in the Philadelphia Exposition of 1876. (Lucretia P. Hale's Peterkin family visited the Exposition.)

Under the gilt, all was not dross. The old American virtues were still revered, and for reading children this was truly a Golden Age. In the pages of children's books and magazines the American dream shone. Writers for children looked forward with hope to a society that with the help of the rising generation would indeed be "one nation, indivisible, with liberty and justice for all." Perhaps it is symptomatic that the Pledge of Allegiance to the Flag was composed to celebrate in 1892 the 400th anniversary of the discovery of America. Highmindedness, moral earnestness, and the will to win set the tone for children's books. Individual initiative could make a difference, the children were told, and this was more to be valued than ancient tradition.

It was an age of simple emotions. Side-splitting laughter and pleasurable tears were given free rein in the pages of children's books. There was healing there too. Though wounds of the Civil War were still raw and sore for adults, the younger generation was encouraged to understand the past in stories written for that purpose. There was now a national audience for stories showing tolerance and brotherhood between North and South. With the goal of universal education in view and the principles of John Dewey just over the horizon, the need and demand for books were insistent. Children's periodicals flourished, and some authors, writing to order for the market, produced children's books in interminable series of varying quality. Myths and legends were splendidly retold for young Americans.

Across the Atlantic children's literature was enjoying a similar "golden age." In England Victoria was queen and empress, moving into the final years of her reign on a wave of national devotion to her. After the irresponsibility and licentiousness of her predecessors, her conscientiousness as a sovereign and the impeccable morality of her private life were sources of gratitude among her people.

All was not "sweetness and light," in the phrase resurrected from Swift by Matthew Arnold, at this time. It was a time of vested property and of spreading slums, of smugness as well as reform. But for children's literature, the attendant rise of the middle class meant enormous growth of a reading public and the spread of learning. Major authors could be enjoyed by a wide audience of young readers, and many of the best writers published one or more novels that were to become "children's classics."

The queen's example as devoted wife, and mother of nine, was reflected in stories of "happy families," while the widening world of empire building beckoned young readers in stories of adventure and romance with faraway, exotic settings. In England as in America, laughter and tears infused the pages of children's books, many of which were shared in family reading. Kipling followed Dickens and Thackeray with stories ageless in their appeal.

The rhymes and rhythms of Tennyson, Browning, and Matthew Arnold were familiar to children. Their schooling saw to it that "The lady of Shalott," "The pied piper of Hamelin" and "The forsaken merman" were coin of the realm. And now some verses of pure gold were being written specifically for children, notably by Robert Louis Stevenson. Hilaire Belloc's spoofs on the old alphabet rhymes, bestiaries, and moral tales in verse brought peals of laughter from young and old alike.

By the last decade of the century, a lucky English child could have received for Christmas Belloc's *Bad child's book of beasts*, Oscar

Wilde's *Happy prince* and a new edition of *Treasure island* to replace the one he had read to pieces. Such a feast of laughter, of tears, and suspense would have been almost too rich to digest.

A firsthand look at reading recommended for children of this period can be found in Caroline M. Hewins's *Books for the young*, published in 1882. This list, however, was too early to include most of the contemporary writing, and any period in children's literature must be seen in context with the future as well as with the past. "Dates can be used as sign-posts," says Harvey Darton, "but like good sign-posts they point both back and forth." Many authors thought of as mid-Victorians were still writing. Some whose main contributions would be in the early twentieth century had barely begun to appear in print. It is only by recognizing Beatrix Potter as an artist that her work can be included in bibliographies of the late nineteenth century. By 1893 she was drawing rabbits in costume for a little book of limericks, *A happy pair*, by Frederic E. Weatherley. In 1896 she brought her genius to bear on Clifton Bingham's "A frog he would a-fishing go," where the future Jeremy Fisher could be foreseen. In 1893 Peter Rabbit himself appeared in a letter to a child friend of Beatrix Potter, but he would not reach the printed page until 1901 (in a privately printed edition). Kenneth Grahame can legitimately belong within the confines of the late nineteenth century only because his *Reluctant dragon* comes from the pages of *Dream days*, 1898. Grahame's *The golden age* is about, but not for, children.

In the final chapter of *From Rollo to Tom Sawyer*, Alice M. Jordan writes of "The Golden Age" in children's literature that came at the end of the nineteenth century: "There was to be a full quarter of a century of marking time, but in this Golden Age were the seeds of the new flowering of children's books which opened in 1920." Harvey Darton, looking forward at the end of his *Children's books in England*, calls his last chapter "The Eighties and to-day: freedom." (To-day was 1932.) He

wrote, "It was left for the most serious of all grown-up epochs, the Victorian, to break down for good and all, in poetry as well as in prose, the high fence that for centuries shut in the imagination of mankind at the very stage of its periodic growth [childhood] when it is most naturally fitted to be free."

Flowering and freedom. Teachers, bibliographers, and students will be lured on to explore the work of writers who contributed to children's literature during the twentieth century. But there was to be a veritable flood of books for children during the twentieth century, and the flood is still rising. With the books has come recognition of their significance, often of their beauty, and always of the need to distinguish gold from dross. Book reviews, retrospective articles, critical biographies of authors pour from presses on both sides of the Atlantic. Many more books in foreign languages have become available through translation into English. Books for English-speaking children have become "a world of children's books," and "a syllabus with selected bibliographies" such as the present expanded and revised edition of Elva Smith's work, would be welcomed, covering at least the first half of the twentieth century. Elva Smith's introduction to the first edition of this *History of children's literature* states the problem and the need in these words:

"The changes in the social and economic life of the people, the international contacts resulting from the European war [World War I], studies in child psychology, new educational theories and methods, more critical reviewing of children's books, new processes in printing and illustration, the establishment of children's rooms in public libraries and special departments in publishing houses—these and other causes have resulted not only in a greatly accelerated production but in a new literature for children differing from the old in subject, literary method, format, and illustration. These books . . . will constitute the next important chapter in the history of children's literature when time shall have given perspective."

OUTLINE

I. Child life in the last quarter of the century
II. The continuing influence of Lewis Carroll, Mrs. Ewing, and other writers upon their successors
  A. Imitations of the *Alice* books
III. American writers
  A. Humor and fancy
    1. Lucretia Peabody Hale (1820–1900)
      a) *The Peterkin papers*
        (1) The foolishness of characters; resemblance to the "drolls" of folklore
        (2) The resourcefulness of "the lady from Philadelphia," which has passed into a proverb
        (3) Absurdities of situation
        (4) Plays upon words
        (5) Lesson: necessity of thinking problems through
        (6) Reaction of children
    2. Frank R. Stockton (1834–1902)
      a) Personality
      b) Connection with *St. Nicholas*
      c) Fairy tales and fanciful stories
        (1) Reality of fairy tale characters
        (2) Ingenuous fancy and rich imagination
        (3) Whimsical humor
      d) Other books
        (1) Inventive facility
        (2) Quotable expressions
      e) Stevenson's verdict
    3. Samuel Clemens (*pseud.* Mark Twain) (1835–1910)
      a) *Adventures of Tom Sawyer* and *Huckleberry Finn*
        (1) Naturalness and force
        (2) Lifelike characters
        (3) Human sympathy and psychological truth
        (4) Typically American humor
        (5) Use of dialect
        (6) Historical value
        (7) Interest for children and popularity
      b) *Tom Sawyer abroad* and *Tom Sawyer, detective*
        (1) The demand for sequels
      c) *A Connecticut Yankee in King Arthur's court*
        (1) Satirical romance
        (2) American ingenuity confronts medieval chivalry
      d) *The prince and the pauper*
        (1) Historical romance with a vein of satire
  B. Regional stories
    1. New England
      a) Kate Douglas Wiggin (1856–1923)
        (1) *Rebecca of Sunnybrook farm*
        (2) *The Birds' Christmas carol*

    2. The Midwest
      a) Edward Eggleston (1837–1902)
        (1) *The Hoosier schoolmaster*
        (2) *The Hoosier schoolboy*
    3. The South
      a) Joel Chandler Harris (1848–1908)
        (1) *Daddy Jake the runaway*
        (2) *Plantation pageants*
        (3) *The story of Aaron*
  C. Romantic realism
    1. Frances Hodgson Burnett (1849–1924)
      a) *Little Lord Fauntleroy*
      b) *Editha's burglar*
      c) *Sara Crewe*
      d) Stories published after 1900
  D. Mary Mapes Dodge (1838–1905) and *St. Nicholas*
    1. Natural gifts and literary interests
    2. Books for children
      a) *Hans Brinker*: origin and popularity
    3. Lifework as editor
      a) Contributors to *St. Nicholas*
      b) Well-known stories first published in its pages
      c) Literary influence
    4. Other magazines
      a) *Harper's young people*
      b) *Riverside magazine*
      c) *Wide awake*
  E. Writers of series
    1. Martha (Farquharson) Finley (1828–1909)
      a) The Elsie Dinsmore series
    2. Charles Austin Fosdick (*pseud.* Harry Castlemon) (1842–1915)
      a) "Boy thrillers"
    3. Harriet Mulford Lothrop (*pseud.* Margaret Sidney) (1844–1924)
      a) The Five Little Peppers series
    4. Elijah Kellogg (1813–1901)
      a) The Elm Island books, and other series
    5. L. Frank Baum (1856–1919)
      a) The Oz books
      b) Continuation of the series under other authors
    6. Annie Fellows Johnston (1863–1931)
      a) The Little Colonel series
  F. Howard Pyle (1853–1911) and other notable writers of the late nineteenth century in America
IV. English writers
  A. Helen Bannerman (1862 or 3–1946)
    1. *Little black Sambo*
      a) The continuing controversy
      b) Sequels
  B. Hilaire Belloc (1870–1953)
    1. The alphabets
    2. The bestiaries
    3. The cautionary tales
  C. Sir Arthur Conan Doyle (1859–1930)

1. *The sign of four*
2. *The memoirs of Sherlock Holmes*
3. Sherlock Holmes and Dr. Watson as characters
4. The Holmes cult; the Baker Street Irregulars

D. Kenneth Grahame (1859–1931)
   1. The author's childhood
      a) *The golden age*
      b) *Dream days*
   2. His business career
   3. Family life
   4. Work published after 1900
      a) *The wind in the willows*
      b) *Bertie's escapade*

E. H. Rider Haggard (1856–1925)
   1. Early life and reading
   2. *King Solomon's mines* and sequels
   3. Success, acclaim, and criticism

F. George Alfred Henty (1832–1902)
   1. Habits as a writer
   2. Life experience as a background for writing
   3. Adventure and history combined in his books
   4. The response of Henty's readers
   5. Some typical titles

G. Rudyard Kipling (1865–1936)
   1. Education and experience
   2. Connection with *St. Nicholas*
   3. *The jungle books*
      a) The East Indian background
      b) Kipling's attitude toward animals
      c) The law of the jungle
      d) Imaginative reality and vivid description
      e) Originality
   4. *Just so stories*
      a) Fantastic humor
      b) Elements of surprise
      c) Repetitive quality
      d) Appeal to sense of sound
      e) Effect of unusual wording
      f) Illustrations
   5. *Kim*
      a) Authenticity of the Indian background
      b) Kim and the English Secret Service
      c) The lama and his mystic quest
   6. *Puck of Pook's hill*
      a) Kipling at Batemans
      b) Folklore in *Puck*
      c) The ancient history of England
   7. *Stalky & Co.*
      a) Kipling at Westward Ho!
      b) The "school story" before *Stalky & Co.*
      c) Admirers and critics of *Stalky & Co.*

H. Andrew Lang (1844–1912)
   1. Legends and lore of Tweedside
   2. Education for a scholarly career
   3. Original fairy tales
      a) *The gold of Fairnilee*

      b) *Prince Prigio*
      c) *The princess Nobody*
   4. Color fairy books
      a) Collecting as research
      b) Retelling as art
   5. Translations of Homer

I. Mrs. Molesworth (1842–1921)
   1. Different types of books
   2. Realism; sympathy with the child's point of view
   3. Stories of home life
      a) Characteristic faults and virtues of the children
      b) Use of the autobiographical form
      c) Underlying moral lesson
   4. Semi-fairy tales
      a) Combination of realistic and fanciful qualities
   5. Books for older girls

J. Edith Nesbit Bland (*pseud.* E. Nesbit) (1858–1924)
   1. *The treasure seekers* and its sequels
      a) Contrast of the Bastable children with those in Catherine Sinclair's *Holiday house*
      b) Humorous incidents
      c) Appearance of the author's ideals and theories in the stories
   2. *The enchanted castle* and other stories of magic
      a) Their influence on Kipling and C. S. Lewis

K. Anna Sewell (1820–78)
   1. *Black beauty*
      a) Qualities making it "the most successful animal story ever written"
      b) Influence on the Society for the Prevention of Cruelty to Animals

L. Robert Louis Stevenson (1850–94)
   1. Personal charm
   2. *A child's garden of verses*
      a) Reminiscent of the author's own childhood
      b) Themes
      c) Simplicity of style and musical rhythm
      d) Psychological truth
      e) Satirical touches
      f) Influence upon later writers of verse for children
   3. *Treasure island*
      a) Literary skill and artistry
      b) Vital and human characters
      c) First publication and lack of success
      d) Later and lasting popularity in book form
   4. *Kidnapped* and *Catriona*
      a) Two novels about "David Balfour"
      b) Treatment of the period and setting
      c) Contrast between David Balfour and Alan Breck Stewart
   5. *The strange case of Dr. Jekyll and Mr. Hyde*

GENERAL REFERENCES

Avery, Gillian. Nineteenth century children, heroes and heroines in English children's stories, 1780–1900. [London]: Hodder, [1965].
Examples from children's literature under headings: The child improved; The child amused; Adult attitudes.

Bragin, Charles. Bibliography of dime novels, 1860–1928. Brooklyn: Bragin, 1938.

———. Dime novels, 1860–1964: a bibliography. Brooklyn: Bragin, 1964.
Includes a brief history of this type of publishing and a chronological listing of publishers and of various series.

Darling, Richard L. The rise of children's book reviewing in America, 1865–1881. New York: Bowker, 1968.
Includes a bibliography of reviews.

Darton, Frederick Joseph Harvey. "The eighties and to-day: freedom," in his *Children's books in England,* p. 299–317. 2d ed. Cambridge: Cambridge University Press, 1958.
Outstanding analysis of Stevenson's *Treasure island,* H. Rider Haggard's *King Solomon's mines,* the novels of Jules Verne, and the place of these writers in the evolution of adventure stories for boys. Also includes excellent coverage of books for girls, Kipling's role in the change that came about in the school story, and a succinct discussion of the influence of magazines.

Davidson, Gustav. "Little-known pseudonyms of 19th century American juvenile authors," *Publishers weekly* 137:2292–95 (1940).
Brief but useful coverage of writers mostly in the latter half of the century.

De Vries, Leonard. Little Wide Awake: an anthology of Victorian children's books and periodicals. Cleveland and New York: World, 1967.

Contains about 60 stories, 150 poems, and about 350 illustrations in black and white or in color from one of the largest private collections of Victorian books and periodicals. The late nineteenth century is generously represented. A valuable introduction by M. F. Thwaite sets the social scene for books written for children.

Farjeon, Eleanor. A nursery in the nineties. London: Victor Gollancz, 1935; reprint: London: Oxford University Press, 1960.
Reminiscent detail based on documents, letters, journals, and memoirs showing "the inner lives and the outer circumstances of children of the '90s."

———. *Portrait of a family.* New York: Stokes, 1936.
Same as A nursery in the nineties.

Green, Roger Lancelyn. Tellers of tales: British authors of children's books from 1800–1964. Rewritten and rev. ed. New York: Watts, 1965.
The text covering the late nineteenth century is outstanding. Includes a chronological table of famous children's books and lists of titles by each author.

Jones, Helen L. "The part played by Boston publishers of 1860–1900 in the field of children's books," *Horn book magazine* 45:20–28; 153–59; 329–36 (February, April, June, 1969).
A careful and useful tracing of the changes undergone by Boston firms and of the titles that they published.

King, Arthur, and **Albert F. Stuart.** The house of Warne: one hundred years of publishing. London and New York: Warne, 1965.
Contains chapters on Kate Greenaway, Randolph Caldecott, L. Leslie Brooke, Beatrix Potter, and less-known authors and artists. Illustrations, some in full color.

Kunitz, Stanley J., and **Howard Haycraft,** eds. The junior book of authors. New York: Wilson, 1934.
Subtitle: "an introduction to the lives of writers and illustrators for younger readers from Lewis Carroll and Louisa Alcott to the present day."

Manthorne, Jane. "The lachrymose ladies," *Horn book magazine* 43:375–84, 501–13, 622–31 (June, August, October, 1967).
A humorous analysis of Susan Bogert Warner, Maria Susanna Cummins, and Martha Farquharson Finley as writers of popular "tear-jerkers" for girls.

Nesbitt, Elizabeth. "A rightful heritage" in *A critical history of children's literature,* edited by Cornelia Meigs et al. Rev. ed. New York: Macmillan, 1969.
Excellent coverage of this period with references to little-known authors found through the index. See especially "A new era" (Howard Pyle), p. 275–87; "A new impulse in romance" (R. L. Stevenson), p. 302–9; and "The great originator" (Rudyard Kipling), p. 310–17.

Raverat, Gwen Darwin. Period piece: a Cambridge childhood. London: Faber & Faber, 1952; New York: Norton, 1953.
The American edition does not have the subtitle. Entertaining recollections of a member of the Darwin family who grew up in Cambridge during the late nineteenth century. See especially chapters entitled "Theories," "Education," "Propriety," "Religion," "Sport," "Clothes," "Society."

Strahan, Alexander. "Bad literature for the young," *The contemporary review,* v. 26 (November, 1875); reprint: *Signal* 20:83–95 (May, 1976).
This essay represents "the many outbursts against the penny dreadful which were published in the last decades of the nineteenth century." Reprint edited with an introduction by Lance Salway.

Turner, Ernest S. Boys will be boys: the story of Sweeney Todd, Deadwood Dick, Sexton Blake, Billy Bunter, Dick Barton, et al. London: Michael Joseph, 1948.
A survey of the penny dreadful, which followed the chapbook as popular reading for boys in the late nineteenth and early twentieth centuries. With an introduction by C. B. Fry.

INDIVIDUAL AMERICAN WRITERS

L. Frank Baum

Baum, Lyman Frank. Father Goose: his book. Chicago: G. M. Hill, 1899.
Illustrated by William W. Denslow. Bright pictures and jingles.

———. Mother Goose in prose. Chicago: Way & Williams, 1897.
Illustrated by Maxfield Parrish. The last story in the book introduces a little farm girl named Dorothy.

———. A new Wonderland, being the first account ever printed of the beautiful valley, and the wonderful adventures of its inhabitants. New York: Russell, 1900.
With pictures by F. Verbeck. An example of the continuing Wonderland theme.

———. The wonderful wizard of Oz. Chicago: Hill, 1900.
With pictures by W. W. Denslow. The series was continued by Baum and by others writing under his name.

BIOGRAPHY AND CRITICISM

Baum, Frank Joslyn, and **Russell P. MacFall.** To please a child: a biography of L. Frank Baum, royal historian of Oz. Chicago: Reilly & Lee, 1961.
Written by Baum's son, with help from many who knew and worked with Baum. Numerous photographs.

Gardner, Martin, and **Russel B. Nye.** The wizard of Oz and who he was. East Lansing: Michigan State University Press, 1957.
An appreciation by Russell B. Nye analyzes Baum's accomplishment as a writer of fantasy and the reasons for his success. In an essay, "The royal historian of Oz," Martin Gardner gives a biographical sketch of Baum and traces the history of the Oz series in print, on the stage, and as film. Bibliography.

Hearn, Michael Patrick. The annotated wizard of Oz. New York: Potter, 1973.
The introduction brings together much valuable material with photographs, facsimiles. A facsimile of the first edition of *The wonderful wizard of Oz* follows, with many annotations in the margins. Bibliography and checklist of Baum's writings.

John Bennett

Bennett, John. Barnaby Lee. New York: Century, 1900.
With illustrations by Clyde O. Deland. A story of Maryland in the colonial period. First appeared in *St. Nicholas.*

———. Master Skylark: a story of Shakespere's time. New York: Century, 1897.

Most of the later editions were published with the illustrations of Reginald Birch. This novel remains outstanding as an example of historical fiction set in the Elizabethan period. Written for *St. Nicholas.*

———. The pigtail of Ah Lee Ben Loo, with seventeen other laughable tales & 200 comical silhouettes. New York and London: Longmans, 1928.

Illustrations by the author. Most of the stories appeared in *St. Nicholas.*

BIOGRAPHY

Bennett, Martha Trimble. "Youth in pleasant places," *Horn book magazine* 36:243–45 (June, 1960).

By Bennett's sister, recalling childhood in Chillicothe, Ohio. A note mentions the John Bennett Room for children, honoring him in the library at Charleston, South Carolina.

Smith, Janie M. "An author and children in the South," *Horn book magazine* 18:83–87 (March–April, 1942).

Describes an occasion during World War II (1941) when John Bennett spoke to children at the library in Charleston, South Carolina, and told of his childhood as a reader.

Charles Edward Carryl

Carryl, Charles Edward. The admiral's caravan. New York: Century, 1892.

Illustrated by Reginald B. Birch. Contains some brilliant nonsense verse.

———. Davy and the goblin, or, what followed reading *Alice's adventures in Wonderland.* Boston and New York: Houghton, 1885.

Illustrated by E. B. Bensell. This is Carryl's best-known book for children. It is the source of "A nautical ballad," beginning:

A capital ship for an ocean trip
Was the *Walloping Window Blind* . . .

BIOGRAPHY AND CRITICISM

Kunitz, Stanley J., and Howard Haycraft. "Charles E. Carryl," in their *Junior book of authors,* p. 81–83. New York: Wilson, 1934.

Harry Castlemon

Fosdick, Charles Austin (*pseud.* Harry Castlemon). The boy traders, or, the sportsman's club among the Boers. Philadelphia: Porter & Coates; Cincinnati: R. W. Carroll, 1877.

Under his pseudonym, this author wrote many stories for boys from the post–Civil War period until the first decade of the twentieth century. Typical titles during the late nineteenth century were: *The boy trapper; Don Gordon's shooting-box; Frank Nelson in the forecastle; George at the fort, or, life among the soldiers; The mail carrier; A sailor in spite of himself.*

BIOGRAPHY AND CRITICISM

Blanck, Jacob Nathaniel, comp. Harry Castlemon, boys' own author: appreciation and bibliography. Limited ed. of 750. New York: Bowker, 1941.

Includes an account of an interview with Charles Austin Fosdick; an article by him, "How to write stories for boys"; and a bibliography, annotated.

"Inventor of the boy-thriller," *Literary digest* 50:558–60 (September 11, 1915).

An editorial written at the time of Fosdick's death. Explains the great enthusiasm for "Harry Castlemon" as "one of the first writers to deliver the youth of America from the Rollo books," appealing to American love of sports.

Susan Coolidge

Woolsey, Sarah Chauncey (*pseud.* Susan Coolidge). What Katy did: a story. Boston: Roberts, 1872.

The first of a series of stories about family and school life in New England.

BIOGRAPHY AND CRITICISM

Darling, Frances C. "Susan Coolidge 1835–1905," *Horn book magazine* 35:232–46 (June, 1959).

A shortened version of the eleventh Caroline M. Hewins lecture. Traces the life story of Sarah Chauncey Woolsey (*pseud.* Susan Coolidge) and describes the background of her most popular writings, especially *What Katy did.* Bibliography.

Mary Mapes Dodge and Children's Magazines

Dodge, Mary Elizabeth Mapes. Donald and Dorothy. Boston: Roberts; London: Warne, 1883.

———. Hans Brinker, or, the silver skates: a story of life in Holland. New York: James O'Kane, 1866.

Inspired by early reading of Motley's *Rise of the Dutch republic.*

———. The land of pluck: stories and sketches for young folk. New York: Century, 1894.

———. Rhymes and jingles. New York: Scribner, Armstrong, 1874.

BIOGRAPHY AND CRITICISM

Clarke, William F. "In memory of Mary Mapes Dodge," *St. Nicholas* 32:1059–71 (October, 1905).

The man who followed Mary Mapes Dodge as editor of *St. Nicholas* writes an appreciation of her as a person and as editor of the magazine. A portrait of her appears on page 1058. Tributes in verse by R. W. Gilder and Josephine Daskam Bacon at end of article.

Commager, Henry Steele, ed. The St. Nicholas anthology. New York: Random, 1948.
Includes selections from *St. Nicholas* from 1891 onward. Among writers of the late nineteenth century are Lucretia P. Hale, Howard Pyle, Frank R. Stockton, Joel Chandler Harris, Alfred Tennyson, Henry W. Longfellow, Rudyard Kipling, Palmer Cox and James Whitcomb Riley, Frances Hodgson Burnett, and Louisa May Alcott. Contributions to "St. Nicholas League" are by teen-agers who became notable writers. Introduction by May Lamberton Becker.

Eakin, Mary K., and **Alice Brooks McGuire.** "Children's magazines yesterday and today," *Elementary school journal* 49:257–60 (January, 1949).
A tribute to the high quality of *St. Nicholas.*

Egoff, Sheila A. Children's periodicals of the 19th century: a survey and bibliography. London: Library Assn., 1951.
Traces the development of magazines published for the Sunday school movement and those published as boys' "blood and thunders" in England, 1752–1900.

Erisman, Fred. "The Utopia of *St. Nicholas*: the present as prologue," *Children's literature* 5:66–73 (1976).
Gives numerous examples to show how both fiction and nonfiction in *St. Nicholas* equipped young readers "to reconcile an increasingly impersonal, mechanized society with a system of values based upon individuality and open, decent personal relations."

Frye, Burton C., ed. A St. Nicholas anthology: the early years. New York: Meredith, 1969.
Selections chosen as representative of the best in stories, songs, and poems, with the original illustrations. Also includes selections from famous contributors to "St. Nicholas League."

Harris, Louise. None but the best, or, the story of three pioneers: *The youth's companion,* Daniel Sharp Ford, C. A. Stephens. Providence, R. I.: Brown University Press, 1966.
A history of the magazine and the collaboration between two men whose work made the publication outstanding.

Howard, Alice B. Mary Mapes Dodge of *St. Nicholas.* New York: Messner, 1943.
A biography for young readers. Bibliography.

Jordan, Alice M. "Good old *St. Nicholas,*" *Horn book magazine* 19:56–62 (January–February, 1943).

————. "Good old *St. Nicholas* and its contemporaries," in her *From Rollo to Tom Sawyer,* p. 131–43. Boston: Horn Book, 1948.
Includes brief but good comment on *Riverside magazine, Harper's young people,* and *Wide awake.*

————. "Horace E. Scudder," *Horn book magazine,* 5, no. 2:37–42 (May, 1929).
A discriminating essay on the man who edited *Riverside magazine* and assisted with *St. Nicholas.*

————. "Horace E. Scudder, critic and editor," in her *From Rollo to Tom Sawyer,* p. 113–22. Boston: Horn Book, 1948.

Kelly, Robert Gordon. Mother was a lady: self and society in selected American children's periodicals 1865–1890. Westport, Conn.: Greenwood, 1974.
The history of magazine publications, editorial requirements, and personal backgrounds of the editors. Analyzes the standards of conduct implicit in magazine stories of the period.

Kennedy, Regina Dolan. "*St. Nicholas*: a literary heritage," *Catholic library world* 37:239–41 (December, 1965).
Special mention of *St. Nicholas*'s unique departments, including the "Agassiz association," through which readers could exchange specimens of mineral, plant, and animal life.

Mott, Frank L. A history of American magazines, 1865–1885. Cambridge, Mass.: Harvard University Press, 1935.
The section on juvenile periodicals (p. 174–80) gives detail on numerous magazines of the time. See p. 500–505 for *St. Nicholas.*

Ranlett, L. Felix. "*Youth's Companion* as recalled by a staff member," *Horn book magazine* 28: 128–33 (April, 1952).
Condensation of part of the fourth Caroline M. Hewins Lecture, 1951. An inside view on editors, authors, and artists who frequented the Boston office of *Youth's companion.*

Schiller, Justin. "Magazines for young America: the first 100 years of juvenile periodicals," *Columns* (Columbia University Library) 23:24–39 (May, 1974).
By a bibliophile and rare-book dealer with detailed knowledge of the periodicals. Emphasizes magazines in the latter half of the nineteenth century.

St. John, Judith, ed. The Osborne collection of early children's books: a catalogue. Toronto: Toronto Public Library, 1958.

See the section "Periodicals and annuals," p. 398–408, for excellent detail on English magazines.

Sturges, Florence M. "The *St. Nicholas* bequest," *Horn book magazine,* 36:365–77 (October, 1960).
Excerpts from the Caroline M. Hewins Lecture, 1959. Focuses on notable authors who began by writing for *St. Nicholas,* and on many who paid tribute to its influence on them. Gives a résumé of the magazine's history.

Thompson, Lovell, et al., eds. *Youth's companion.* Boston: Houghton, 1954.
Selections from the magazine arranged backward in time from 1927 to 1827. The late nineteenth century is represented by contributions by Bret Harte, Mark Twain, Rudyard Kipling, Emily Dickinson, Lucy Larcom, Sarah Orne Jewett, Hamlin Garland, P. T. Barnum, Francis Parkman, Oliver Wendell Holmes, Jr., Thomas Wentworth Higginson, Louisa May Alcott, J. T. Trowbridge, W. D. Howells, Wilkie Collins, Joel Chandler Harris, and poems by Thomas Carlyle, John G. Whittier, and William Cullen Bryant.

White, Elwyn Brooks (*pseud.* E.B.W.). "The St. Nicholas league," *The New Yorker* 10, no. 43:38–52. (December 8, 1934).
An entertaining and nostalgic essay by one of the most distinguished writers ever to graduate from the "St. Nicholas League."

Edward Eggleston

Eggleston, Edward. The Hoosier school-boy. New York: Orange Judd, 1883; Magnolia, Mass.: Peter Smith, 1966.
A sequel to *The Hoosier school-master,* the author's best known book.

———. The Hoosier school-master. New York: Orange Judd, 1871.

———. The Hoosier schoolmaster: a story of backwoods life in Indiana. Revised with an introduction and notes on the dialect by the author Edward Eggleston. New York: Grosset, 1892.
With character sketches by F. Opper and other illustrations by W. E. B. Starkweather.

BIOGRAPHY AND CRITICISM

Eggleston, George Cary. The first of the Hoosiers. Philadelphia: Biddle, 1903.
Subtitle: "reminiscences of Edward Eggleston and of that western life which he, first of all men, celebrated in literature and made famous." The author was the brother of Edward Eggleston.

Randel, William Peirce. Edward Eggleston, author of The Hoosier schoolmaster. New York: King's

Crown Press, 1946; reprint: (Twayne's United States authors series) New York: Twayne, 1963.
See especially p. 91–97 for *The Hoosier school-master,* its popularity and its "historical significance as the pioneer of western dialect novels." *The Hoosier school-boy,* discussed on p. 115–17, was viewed as a potboiler by Eggleston. Bibliography, p. 263–313.

Martha Finley

Farquharson, Martha (*pseud.* Martha Finley). Elsie at home. New York: Dodd, 1897.
Farquharson is the Gaelic form of *Finley.*

———. Elsie at the world's fair. New York: Dodd, 1894.

———. Elsie Dinsmore. New York: Dodd, 1867.

———. Elsie's children: a sequel to Elsie's motherhood. New York: Dodd, 1877.

———. Mildred Keith. New York: Dodd, 1876.
An admittedly autobiographical novel.

BIOGRAPHY AND CRITICISM

Brown, Janet E. The saga of Elsie Dinsmore: a study in 19th century sensibility. Buffalo, N.Y.: University of Buffalo Press, 1945.
A brief biographical sketch and a humorous, perceptive analysis of "Martha Finley's" point of view and technique as a writer. Chronology of the Elsie and the Mildred books.

Morrow, Honoré Willsie. "My favorite character in fiction: Elsie Dinsmore," *The bookman* 62: 546 (January, 1926).
A vivid picture of the author's overwhelming response at the age of eight to her first reading of *Elsie Dinsmore.*

Stern, Gladys Bronwyn. "Onward and upward with the arts: Elsie reread," *The New Yorker* 4:52–55 (March 14, 1936).
A witty, tongue-in-cheek analysis of the psychological oddities of the Elsie Dinsmore series.

Suckow, Ruth. "*Elsie Dinsmore*: a study in perfection, or, how Fundamentalism came to the South," *The bookman* 66:126–33 (October, 1927).

Lucretia Peabody Hale

Hale, Lucretia Peabody. The complete Peterkin papers. Boston: Houghton, 1960.
With the original illustrations and an introduction giving a sketch of the author's family life, by Nancy Hale. Includes *The Peterkin papers* and *The last of the Peterkins.*

———. The last of the Peterkins, with others of their kin. Boston: Roberts, 1886.

———. The last of the Peterkins, with others of their kin, *and* The queen of the red chessmen. New York: Dover, 1965.

———. The Peterkin papers. Boston: Osgood, 1880; New York: Random, Looking Glass Library, 1959.
With the original illustrations.

———. ———. New York: Parents' magazine, 1966.
With illustrations by Harold M. Brett.

BIOGRAPHY AND CRITICISM

Wankmiller, Madelyn C. "Lucretia P. Hale and the Peterkin papers," *Horn book magazine* 34: 95–103, 137–47 (April, 1958); in *The Hewins lectures, 1947–1962,* edited by Siri Andrews, p. 235–51. Boston: Horn Book, 1963.
Shows how the Hale family of Boston can be compared or contrasted with the absurd Peterkins.

White, Eliza Orne. "Lucretia P. Hale," *Horn book magazine* 16:317–22 (September–October, 1940).
The author's mother was an intimate friend of Lucretia P. Hale. This article gives reminiscences told at greater length in *A little girl of long ago,* in which Lucretia Hale is called Leonora Heath.

Joel Chandler Harris

Harris, Joel Chandler. Daddy Jake the runaway, and short stories told after dark by "Uncle Remus." New York: Century, 1889.
Illustrated by E. W. Kemble. The title story first appeared in *St. Nicholas,* 1889. It concerns white children who go in search of their friend, Daddy Jake. Incorporates the story of a cruel overseer. There is also a folk tale within the story. The other stories in the book are mostly folk tales.

———. Little Mr. Thimblefinger and his queer country: what the children saw and heard there. New York and Boston: Houghton; London: Osgood, McIlvaine, 1894.
Author's note on the stories: "Some of them were gathered from the negroes, but were not embodied in the tales of Uncle Remus, because I was not sure they were negroe [sic] stories; some are Middle Georgia folklore stories, and no doubt belong to England; and some are merely inventions."

———. Mr. Rabbit at home. Boston and New York: Houghton, 1895.
Illustrated by Oliver Herford. A sequel to *Little Mr. Thimblefinger.*

———. Nights with Uncle Remus: myths and leg-

ends of the old plantation. Boston: Houghton, 1881.
The collection of tales on which Harris's fame chiefly rests. Later editions had varying titles. A. B. Frost was the best illustrator of the Uncle Remus stories.

———. Plantation pageants. Boston and New York: Houghton, 1899.
Illustrated by E. Boyd Smith. Elements of folklore are worked into connected pictures of plantation life.

———. The story of Aaron (so named) the son of Ben Ali, told by his friends and acquaintances. Boston and New York: Houghton, 1896.
Illustrated by Oliver Herford. An Arab slave is the central figure in this collection of stories, but the tales are told by talking animals.

BIOGRAPHY AND CRITICISM

Brookes, Stella Brewer. Joel Chandler Harris, folklorist. Athens: University of Georgia Press, 1950.
An attempt to classify and summarize the folklore elements in Harris's writings. Some study of background influences on his books. Bibliography.

Cousins, Paul M. Joel Chandler Harris: a biography. Baton Rouge: Louisiana State University Press, 1968.
A valuable study of the author, his period, and influences upon his work. Includes previously unpublished material taken from the Memorial Collection at Emory University. There are three chapters dealing with the stories of Uncle Remus. Bibliography.

Flusche, Michael. "Joel Chandler Harris and the folklore of slavery," *Journal of American studies* 9:347–63 (December, 1975).
Urges a closer look at tales in the Uncle Remus books as "eloquent statements of how [slaves] viewed the world and how they coped with life."

Harris, Julia Collier. The life and letters of Joel Chandler Harris. Boston: Houghton, 1918.
With portraits and other illustrations. Harris's daughter-in-law writes of him as a person of extreme modesty who did not recognize his own talent and originality. Documented with correspondence. Bibliography.

Reed, Henry M. The A. B. Frost book. Rutland, Vt.: Tuttle, 1967.
About the premier illustrator of Harris's work. With a foreword by Eugene V. Connett. Many full-page reproductions of Frost's illustrations and a chapter, "Brer Rabbit and Uncle Remus," containing letters from Harris to the artist. Includes quotations from reviews. Bibliography.

Wiggins, Robert L. The life of Joel Chandler Harris, from obscurity in boyhood to fame in early

manhood. Nashville: Publishing House, Methodist Episcopal Church, South, Smith & Lamar, 1918.
A biography with examples of Harris's early writing, published in *The countryman* and the *Atlanta constitution*. Bibliography.

Bret Harte

Harte, Francis Bret. The queen of the pirate isle. London and New York: Warne, [1886?]; Boston and New York: Houghton, 1887.
Illustrated by Kate Greenaway. An interesting book because of the contrast with Harte's better-known tales and because of the Greenaway illustrations.

BIOGRAPHY AND CRITICISM

Boynton, Henry W. Bret Harte. New York: McClure, Philips, 1903; reprint: New York: Arno, 1972.
A brief, well-written account of Harte's life, personality, and work.

Stewart, George R. Bret Harte, argonaut and exile. . . . Boston and New York: Houghton, 1931; reprint: New York: AMS Press, 1977.
The author has "paid much attention to . . . the biographical aspect of [Bret Harte's] writings" but "not in general attempted to expound their value as literature."

Sarah Orne Jewett

Jewett, Sarah Orne. Betty Leicester: a story for girls. Boston: Houghton, 1889.
Maine is the setting for this teenage novel.

————. Betty Leicester's English Xmas: a new chapter of an old story. Privately printed for the Bryn Mawr school, 1894; Boston and New York: Houghton, 1899.

————. The country of the pointed firs. Boston and New York: Houghton, 1896.
A simple and moving story of plain people and of Maine life. Highly praised.

————. A white heron, and other stories. Boston and New York: Houghton, 1886.
The title piece is about the conflicting feelings of a little girl devoted to a young ornithologist and also to the bird he wants to catch.

BIOGRAPHY AND CRITICISM

Cary, Richard. Sarah Orne Jewett. (Twayne's United States authors series) New York: Twayne, 1962.
An analysis of the author's materials, methods, and forms. Chronology and selected bibliography.

————. ed. Appreciation of Sarah Orne Jewett: 29 interpretive essays. Waterville, Me.: Colby University Press, 1973.

Frost, John Eldridge. Sarah Orne Jewett. Kittery Point, Me.: Gundalow Club, 1960.
An account of the author's life in Maine, of the authors and editors she knew, and of her "writing days." Assesses her talent as a "literary craftsman."

Matthiessen, Francis Otto. Sarah Orne Jewett. Boston and New York: Houghton, 1929.
Written with help and information from the author's sister. Numerous illustrations.

Annie Fellows Johnston

Johnston, Annie Fellows. The gate of the giant scissors. Boston: L. C. Page, 1898.
Illustrated by Etheldred B. Barry. One of the author's allegorical stories.

————. The little Colonel. Boston: L. C. Page, 1895.
Illustrated by Etheldred B. Barry. The first of a successful series of stories for girls. The setting is Pewee Valley, near Louisville, Kentucky.

————. The little Colonel stories. Boston: L. C. Page, 1899.
Illustrated by Etheldred B. Barry. Contents: The little Colonel; The giant scissors; Two little knights of Kentucky.

AUTOBIOGRAPHY

Johnston, Annie Fellows. The land of the little Colonel: reminiscence and autobiography. Boston: L. C. Page, 1929.
Illustrated from original photographs of the author, her friends, family, and houses in Pewee Valley that appear in the Little Colonel series.

Elijah Kellogg

Kellogg, Elijah. The ark of Elm Island. Boston: Lee & Shepard, 1875.
This is vol. 3 of the Elm Island stories.

————. The boy farmers of Elm Island. Boston: Lee & Shepard, 1869.

————. Burying the hatchet, or, the young brave of the Delawares. Boston: Lee & Shepard, 1879.

BIOGRAPHY

Jordan, Alice M. "Elijah Kellogg and the Elm island boys," in her *From Rollo to Tom Sawyer and other papers*, p. 102–12. Boston: Horn Book, 1948.
Describes the background, period, and point of view in Kellogg's work.

James Otis

Kaler, James Otis (*pseud.* James Otis). Mr. Stubb's brother: a sequel to *Toby Tyler*. New York: Harper, 1883.
Illustrated by W. A. Rogers.

————. Toby Tyler, or, ten weeks with a circus. New York: Harper, 1881.
The story of a runaway. His friendship with Mr. Stubb, a circus monkey, is the central, and touching, theme of the book.

BIOGRAPHY

Kunitz, Stanley J., and **Howard Haycraft,** eds. "James Otis," in their *Junior book of authors*, p. 281–82. New York: Wilson, 1934.

Thomas Nelson Page

Page, Thomas Nelson. Among the camps, or, young people's stories of the war. New York: Scribner, 1891.
Contents: A captured Santa Claus; Kittykin, and the part she played in the war; "Nancy Pansy"; Jack and Jake.

————. Two little Confederates. New York: Scribner, 1898.
The author's best-known book for children, written to broaden sympathy and understanding.

————. Two prisoners. New York: Russell, 1898.
This story in condensed form first appeared in *Harper's young people*.

BIOGRAPHY

Page, Rosewell. Thomas N. Page: a memoir of a Virginia gentleman. New York: Scribner, 1923; reprint: Port Washington, N.Y.: Kennikat Press, 1969.
Written by the brother of Thomas Nelson Page.

Howard Pyle
(See p. 251–52.)

Laura E. Richards

Richards, Laura Elizabeth Howe. Captain January. Boston: Estes & Lauriat, 1891.
The story of a storm, a lighthouse, an old seaman, and a rescued child. The author's most successful book.

————. Five mice in a mousetrap, by the man in the moon: done in the vernacular, from the lunacular. Boston: Estes, 1880.
Verses, illustrated by Kate Greenaway, Addie Ledyard, and others.

————. The golden windows: a book of fables for young & old. Boston: Little, 1903.

————. The Merryweathers. Boston: Estes, 1904.
The Richards' Camp Merryweather for boys was named for this book.

————. Queen Hildegarde: a story for girls. Boston: Estes, 1889.
The first of a popular series.

————. Tirra lirra: rhymes old and new. Boston: Little, 1932.
With a foreword by May Lamberton Becker and illustrations by Marguerite Davis. A runnerup for the Newbery Award, the only book of poetry ever honored by such recognition.

BIOGRAPHY AND CRITICISM

Eaton, Anne T. "Laura E. Richards," *Horn book magazine* 17:247–55 (July, 1941).
An appreciative essay focusing on two families, the Howes and the Richardses.

Richards, Laura Elizabeth Howe. Stepping westward. New York: Appleton, 1931.
An autobiography.

————. When I was your age. Boston: Estes & Lauriat, 1894.
Reminiscences of the author's childhood.

Viguers, Ruth Hill. "Laura E. Richards, joyous companion," *Horn book magazine* 32:87–97, 163–77, 376–88, 467–76 (April–December, 1956).
Laura Richards as wife, mother, and neighbor, mostly seen against the background of Gardiner, Maine. Bibliography and chronological list of books by Laura E. Richards.

Wood, Jessica. "Unafraid of greatness," *Horn book magazine* 32:127–36, 212–18, 222 (April, June, 1956).
An appreciation of Laura E. Richards as a woman and as a writer.

Margaret Sidney

Lothrop, Harriet Mulford Stone (*pseud.* Margaret Sidney). Dilly and the Captain. Boston: D. Lothrop, 1887.
Interesting for its illustrations by F. Childe Hassam.

————. Five little Peppers and how they grew. Boston: Lothrop, 1880.
First appeared in *Wide awake*.

BIOGRAPHY AND CRITICISM

Kunitz, Stanley J., and **Howard Haycraft.** "Margaret Sidney," in their *Junior book of authors*, p. 335–36. New York: Wilson, 1934.

Frank R. Stockton

Stockton, Frank Richard. The bee-man of Orn and other fanciful tales. New York: Scribner, 1887.
These stories appeared in *St. Nicholas*, 1882–85.

———. The casting away of Mrs. Lecks and Mrs. Aleshine. New York: Century, 1886.
Two middle-aged female Robinson Crusoes make their way to a desert island.

———. The clocks of Rondaine and other stories. New York: Scribner, 1892.

———. The floating prince and other tales. New York: Scribner, 1881.
Stories collected from *St. Nicholas*, 1878–81. This is one of Stockton's finest collections.

———. The queen's museum. New York: Scribner, 1887.

———. A storyteller's pack. New York: Scribner, 1897; new ed. 1968.
New edition has an introduction by the editors (not named) which gives a biographical sketch and a critique of Stockton's work, including quotations from contemporaries such as William Dean Howells.

BIOGRAPHY AND CRITICISM

Griffin, Martin Ignatius Joseph. Frank R. Stockton: a critical biography. London: Oxford University Press, 1939; Philadelphia: University of Pennsylvania Press, 1939; reprint: Port Washington, N.Y.: Kennikat Press, 1965.
Places Stockton among the outstanding American writers of his day, traces his contributions to *St. Nicholas*, and gives individual analyses of his stories for children. See bibliography, p. 149–73.

Harkins, Edward Francis. "Francis Richard Stockton," in his *Little pilgrimages among the men who have written famous books*, 1st ser., p. 107–22. Boston: L. C. Page, 1901.
Anecdotal, ending with Stedman's lines that begin, "I have stayed at the Rudder Grange" (referring to a novel by Stockton). "There is a Stocktonian touch in the familiar story that the Christian name of Francis Richard was imposed upon Mr. Stockton by one of his half-sisters, who borrowed half of it from Francis I of France and half from Richard Coeur de Lion." It is, however, as Frank R. Stockton that the author is generally known.

Stockton, Marian E. "A memorial sketch," in *The captain's toll-gate* by Frank Richard Stockton, p. ix–xxxii. New York: Appleton, 1903.
This book was the last of Stockton's work to be published. It contains a portrait and views of his homes; also a bibliographical list of his writings, p. 353–59.

Mark Twain

Clemens, Samuel Langhorne (*pseud.* Mark Twain). The adventures of Huckleberry Finn, Tom Sawyer's comrade. New York: C. L. Webster, 1885.
This sequel to *Tom Sawyer* is considered to be one of the most important American novels.

———. The adventures of Tom Sawyer. Hartford, Conn.: American Publishing Co.; San Francisco: A. Roman, 1876.
The author recalls his past as the "bad boy" of a small Missouri town in pre–Civil War days.

———. A Connecticut Yankee in King Arthur's court. New York: C. L. Webster, 1889.
Modern American inventions and ingenuity confronted by ancient ways and days.

———. The prince and the pauper: a tale for young people of all ages. New York: Harper, 1881.
A historical romance in satiric vein.

———. Tom Sawyer abroad, by Huck Finn [*pseud.*]. Edited by Mark Twain. London: Chatto & Windus; New York: C. L. Webster, 1894.
First appeared in *St. Nicholas*, November, 1893–April, 1894.

———. Tom Sawyer: detective, as told by Huck Finn, and other tales. London: Chatto & Windus, 1897.
Contents: Tom Sawyer, detective; The Californian's tale; Adam's diary; How to tell a story; Mental telegraphy again; What Paul Bourget thinks of us; A little note to M. Paul Bourget.

———. Tom Sawyer, detective, and other stories. New York: Grosset, [1878–1924].
Contents: Tom Sawyer, detective; The stolen white elephant; Some rambling notes on an idle excursion; The facts concerning the recent carnival of crime in Connecticut; About magnanimous-incident literature; Punch, brothers, punch.

BIOGRAPHY AND CRITICISM

Adams, Lucille, comp. Huckleberry Finn: a descriptive bibliography of the Huckleberry Finn collection at the Buffalo Public Library. Buffalo, N.Y.: Buffalo Public Library, 1900.

Allen, Jerry. The adventures of Mark Twain. Boston: Little, 1954.
For the general reader, a biography that incorporates in the text well-chosen selections from Mark Twain's own writing.

Chambers, Aidan. "Letter from England: a tale of two Toms," *Horn book magazine* 52:187–90 (April, 1976).
Written for the centenary of the publication of *The adventures of Tom Sawyer* in 1876, this ar-

ticle compares Mark Twain's hero with Thomas Hughes's hero of *Tom Brown's school days.*

Clemens, Samuel Langhorne. [Mark Twain issue] *The American book collector* 10, no. 10 (June, 1960).
Illustrated articles on the suppressed plate in the first edition of *Huck Finn,* Mark Twain and his Canadian publishers, etc.

David, Beverly R. "Pictorial Huck Finn: Mark Twain and his illustrator, E. W. Kemble," *American quarterly* 26:331–51 (October, 1974).
Shows through correspondence between Twain and Kemble how the illustrations for *Huckleberry Finn* converted the cruelty of the story into an adventure for boys.

De Voto, Bernard Augustine. Mark Twain at work. Cambridge, Mass.: Harvard University Press, 1942.
A literary critic shows how *Tom Sawyer* developed from a sketch by Mark Twain, "Boy's manuscript." Illuminating comment on the writing of *Huckleberry Finn* and on the author's methods of work.

———. Mark Twain's America. Boston: Little, 1932.
An essay in the correction of ideas, the effort being to perceive where and how the books of Mark Twain issue from American life. He "was a frontier humorist. His literary intelligence was shaped by the life of the frontier and found expression in the themes and forms developed by the humor of the frontier. . . . In [his books] an American civilization sums up its experience; they are the climax of a literary tradition."

Fadiman, Clifton. "A second look: a centennial for Tom," *Horn book magazine* 52:139–44 (April, 1976).
A notable critic points out the flaws in *Tom Sawyer* but concludes that the book is "alive and well" 100 years after its first publication.

Howells, William Dean. My Mark Twain: reminiscences and criticisms: New York: Harper, 1910; reprint: Brooklyn: Haskell House, 1977.
The reminiscences appeared in *Harper's monthly magazine* 121 (July–September, 1910), under the title "My memories of Mark Twain." The criticisms are reprinted from the reviews in which they were first published. For *The adventures of Tom Sawyer,* see p. 125–28.

Paine, Albert Bigelow. The boys' life of Mark Twain: the story of a man who made the world laugh and love him. New York: Harper, 1916.
For *Tom Sawyer* and *Huckleberry Finn,* see p. 24–35, 198–201, 207–8, 236–38. Reproduction of the first manuscript page of *Tom Sawyer,* p. 199.

———. Mark Twain, a biography: the personal and literary life of Samuel Langhorne Clemens. 4v. New York: Harper, 1912.
Authorized life, with letters, comments, and incidental writings. Illustrated with pictures, portraits, facsimiles, and reproductions. References to *Tom Sawyer* and *Huckleberry Finn* may be traced through the index. A number of references will also be found in *Mark Twain's letters,* arranged with comment by Paine. Chronological list of Mark Twain's work, vol. 4, p. 1674–84.

Phelps, William Lyon. "The American humorist: Mark Twain," in his *Some makers of American literature,* p. 163–87. Boston: Marshall Jones, 1923; reprint: Freeport, N.Y.: Books for Libraries, 1970.
"Only a literary genius could have created Huck."

Wecter, Dixon. Sam Clemens of Hannibal. Boston: Houghton, 1952.
Part of a biography planned to be definitive, this covers Clemens's life to the age of eighteen, when he left Hannibal, and makes connections between his later writing and the people and places he knew in his boyhood home.

Kate Douglas Wiggin

Wiggin, Kate Douglas Smith. The Birds' Christmas Carol. San Francisco: C. A. Murdock, 1887.
A touching story of a sick child and her friendship with a family of poor neighbors.

———. Children's rights: a book of nursery logic. Boston and New York: Houghton, 1892.
Includes Children's stories; How shall we govern our children? and The magic of "together," which were written by the author's sister, Nora A. Smith.

———. Rebecca of Sunnybrook Farm. Boston and New York: Houghton, 1903.
The author's best-known book, frequently dramatized for stage and screen.

———. The story of Patsy: a reminiscence. Boston and New York: Houghton, 1889.
"Originally written for the benefit of the Silver Street Free Kindergartens in San Francisco . . . the present story is more than double the length of the original brief sketch." Concerns the early death of a little boy. The scene is a kindergarten.

BIOGRAPHY AND CRITICISM

Benner, Helen F. Kate Douglas Wiggin's country of childhood. Orono, Me.: printed at the University Press, 1956.
A study of the work of an author who "was the first to portray realistically, yet with sympathetic humor, Maine inland village character." Bibliography.

Smith, Nora A. Kate Douglas Wiggin as her sister knew her. Boston: Houghton, 1925.
Based on a girlhood diary, letters, and notes on the writing of her books, especially *Rebecca of Sunnybrook Farm*.

Stebbins, Lucy Ward. "Kate Douglas Wiggin as a child knew her," *Horn book magazine* 26:447–54 (November–December, 1950).

Recollections of the Silver Street Kindergarten and of Kate Douglas Wiggin as teacher.

Wiggin, Kate Douglas. My garden of memory: an autobiography. Boston: Houghton, 1923.
Tells of the author's childhood in Maine, of the kindergarten in California, of home in New York, travels abroad, and friendship with many celebrated men and women.

INDIVIDUAL ENGLISH WRITERS

Helen Bannerman

Bannerman, Helen. The adventures of little black Mingo. London: Nisbet, 1901.
The first of several sequels to *The story of little black Sambo*.

———. The story of little black Sambo. London: Grant Richards, 1899.
The pictures are by the author. Published as the fourth title in the series Dumpy books for children, edited by E. V. Lucas.

BIOGRAPHY AND CRITICISM

Schiller, Justin G. "The story of little black Sambo," *Book collector* 23, no. 3:381–86 (Autumn, 1974).
A dealer in rare books describes the first edition of *Little black Sambo*, which was in 1899 "a revolutionary-style picture book" whose format probably influenced the overall design for *Peter Rabbit*. Traces publication of editions through 1904.

Stokes, Horace W. "Sambo and the twins," *Horn book magazine* 12:372–74 (November–December, 1936).
A member of the firm of Frederick A. Stokes writes of Helen Bannerman's reluctance to produce another sequel to *Little black Sambo*.

Yuill, Phyllis. "Little black Sambo: the continuing controversy," *School library journal* 22:71–75 (March, 1976).
Describes the history of the book's publication, its long and continuing popularity, and the reasons for protest and controversy that arose concerning the story and its illustrations.

Hilaire Belloc

Belloc, Hilaire. The bad child's book of beasts. Oxford: Alden; London: Simpkin, 1896.
With illustrations by Lord Basil Temple Blackwood (known as B.B. and B. T. B.).

———. Cautionary tales for children, designed for the admonition of children between the ages of eight and fourteen years. London: E. Nash, 1907.

———. Hilaire Belloc's cautionary verses. New York: Knopf, 1941.
Illustrated album edition with the original pictures by B. T. B. and Nicholas Bentley. Includes: Cautionary tales for children; New cautionary tales; The bad child's book of beasts; More beasts for worse children; More peers; A moral alphabet; Ladies and gentlemen.

———. A moral alphabet in words of from one to seven syllables. London: Arnold, 1899.
Illustrated by B. B.

———. More beasts (for worse children). London: Duckworth, n.d.; New York, Arnold, 1897.
Pictures by B. T. B.

BIOGRAPHY AND CRITICISM

Haynes, Renée. Hilaire Belloc. London and New York: Longmans, for the British Council, 1953.
For a critique of Belloc's satirical verses, see p. 5–12.

Lowndes, Marie Belloc. The young Hilaire Belloc. New York: Kenedy, 1956.
The childhood, youth, and early manhood of the author, by his sister, showing "the early influences which contributed to the making of the man and the poet."

Morton, John Bingham. Hilaire Belloc: a memoir. London: Hollis & Carter; New York: Sheed & Ward, 1955.
For students of children's literature, chapter 1, "Portrait of Hilaire Belloc," is the most helpful part of this book, written by an intimate friend.

Frances Hodgson Burnett

Burnett, Frances Hodgson. Editha's burglar: a story for children. Boston: Jordan, Marsh, 1888.
The innocence of a little girl touches the heart of a burglar.

———. Little Lord Fauntleroy. London: Warne, 1885–86; New York: Scribner, 1886.
First published in *St. Nicholas* 13 (1885–86). The author's best-known story, frequently dramatized. Many editions were illustrated by Reginald Birch.

———. ———. Garden City, N.Y.: Junior Deluxe editions, 1954.
Illustrated by Peter Spier.

———. A little princess: being the whole story of Sara Crewe now told for the first time. London: Warne; New York: Scribner, 1905.
The English edition was illustrated by Harold Piffard, the American edition by Ethel Franklin Betts.

———. Racketty-Packetty house. New York: Century, 1906.
Friendship and romance between a poor family of dolls and the rich dolls of Tidy Castle. Later editions were illustrated by Harrison Cady.

———. Sara Crewe, or, what happened at Miss Minchin's. New York: Scribner, 1888.

———. Sara Crewe, or, what happened at Miss Minchin's, *and* Editha's burglar. London: Warne, 1888.

———. The secret garden. New York: Phillips, 1910–11.
First appeared in *American magazine* 71–72 (1910–11).

———. Two little pilgrims' progress: a story of the City Beautiful. London: Warne, [1895?]; New York: Scribner, 1895.
With illustrations by Reginald B. Birch. Twins, a boy and girl, are inspired by Bunyan's allegory and run away to visit the Chicago World's Fair.

BIOGRAPHY AND CRITICISM

Baker, Margaret J. "Mrs. Burnett of Maytham Hall," *Junior bookshelf* 13, no. 3:126–36 (October, 1949).
A biographical sketch with commendation of *The secret garden* as a true picture of England. "In it was the best of herself."

Burnett, Constance Buel. Happily ever after. New York: Vanguard, 1965.
Written from source material in Frances Hodgson Burnett's own recollections of her childhood and youth, *The one I knew the best of all;* and *The romantick lady* by Vivian Burnett. An abridgment of two chapters, "Frances Hodgson Burnett: episodes in her life," appeared in *Horn book magazine* 41:86–94 (February, 1965).

Burnett, Frances Hodgson. The one I knew the best of all. London: Warne, 1893; facsimile ed.: London: Warne, 1974.
The author writes of herself as "the Small Person," a child with a strong imagination. The story ends as she sells her first manuscript.

Burnett, Vivian. The romantick lady: the life story of an imagination. New York: Scribner, 1927.

Frances Hodgson Burnett's son, the original Little Lord Fauntleroy, tells the life story of his mother.

Thwaite, Ann. "The fashion for Fauntleroy," *The times* (London), June 1, 1974, p. 9.
Why *Little Lord Fauntleroy* perfectly suited readers of all ages in "the age of escapism."

———. Waiting for the party: the life of Frances Hodgson Burnett 1849–1924. New York: Scribner, 1974.
A well-documented biography with numerous portraits, reproductions of photographs, a list of dates and places in the life of Mrs. Burnett. Also a list of plays with dates of first nights of production in London and New York. Bibliography attempts "to include every first publication of a book by Frances Hodgson Burnett both in America and England" but omits stories published only in magazines.

Sir Arthur Conan Doyle

Doyle, *Sir* Arthur Conan. The adventures of Sherlock Holmes. London: George Newnes; New York: A. L. Burt, 1892.
Grosset and Harper also published editions in 1892. Many stories by Doyle appeared in the *Strand magazine* 1891–93.

———. The hound of the Baskervilles. New York: Collier, 1901.
Appeared in the *Strand magazine,* 1901.

———. The sign of four. London: Spencer Blackett, 1890.
First appeared in *Lippincott's monthly magazine* as "The sign of the four," February, 1890.

———. A study in scarlet. London and New York: Ward, Lock, 1887.

———. The white company. London: Smith, Elder, 1896.
An adventure story of freebooters in the Middle Ages. Doyle's favorite among his own writings.

BIOGRAPHY AND CRITICISM

Carr, John Dickson. The life of Sir Arthur Conan Doyle. New York: Harper, 1949; London: Murray, 1954.
A full-length biography written by an Anglo-American detective-story writer. Based on family letters and other papers. Bibliography.

Doyle, *Sir* Arthur Conan. Memories and adventures. Boston: Little; London: Hodder, 1924.
An autobiography giving an excellent picture of the life of the author's time as well as "the simple, modest story of his own life."

Starrett, Vincent. The private life of Sherlock Holmes. New York: Macmillan, 1933. Rev. and enl. ed.: Chicago: University of Chicago Press, 1960; reprint: New York: AMS Press, 1971.
For the pleasure of Sherlock Holmes addicts.

Kenneth Grahame

Grahame, Kenneth. Bertie's escapade. Philadelphia: Lippincott, 1949.
First published in *First whisper of "The wind in the willows"* (see below).

————. Dream days. New York: J. Lane, 1898.
Includes "The reluctant dragon."

————. First whisper of "The wind in the willows." Edited, with an introduction by Elspeth Grahame (Mrs. Kenneth Grahame). London: Methuen, 1944.

————. The golden age. Chicago: Stone & Kimball, 1895.

————. The reluctant dragon. [New York]: Holiday, 1938.
Illustrations by E. H. Shepard.

————. The wind in the willows. London: Methuen; New York: Scribner, 1908.

BIOGRAPHY AND CRITICISM

Chalmers, Patrick R. Kenneth Grahame: life, letters and unpublished work. London: Methuen, 1933; Port Washington, N.Y.: Kennikat Press, 1971.
Pleasurable reading. Not a source for quick information. Chapter 8, *"The wind in the willows,"* p. 120–48, contains letters by the author on the book.

Graham, Eleanor. Kenneth Grahame. (A Bodley Head monograph) London: Bodley Head, 1963.
A record of the magazines where some of Grahame's short pieces appeared, and an account of how he wrote *Pagan papers, The golden age, Dream days,* and *The wind in the willows.* There are chapters on Grahame's illustrators and on reviews of his work. Bibliography.

Green, Roger Lancelyn. "Kenneth Grahame and A. A. Milne," in his *Tellers of tales,* p. 249–53. Rewritten and rev. ed. New York: Watts, 1965.
A brief biographical sketch, some detail about Grahame's earlier writing, and a moving description of how he began and wrote *The wind in the willows.*

H. Rider Haggard

Haggard, Sir Henry Rider. Allan Quatermain, being an account of his further adventures and discoveries in company with Sir Henry Curtis, Bart., Commander John Good, R. N., and one Umslopogaas. London: Longmans, 1887.
First published in *Longman's magazine.* A sequel to *King Solomon's mines.*

————. King Solomon's mines. London and New York: Cassell, 1885.
"Respectfully dedicated by the narrator . . . to all the big and little boys who read it."

————. She, a history of adventure. New York: Grosset, 1886.
A romance concerning an African sorceress whom death seems not to touch.

BIOGRAPHY AND CRITICISM

Cohen, Morton. Rider Haggard: his life and works. London: Hutchinson, 1960; New York: Walker, 1961.
A definitive study of this minor writer who was enormously popular with boys. Comprehensive documentation and an extensive bibliography.

Green, Roger Lancelyn. "Rider Haggard," in his *Tellers of tales,* p. 156–67. Rewritten and rev. ed. New York: Watts, 1965.
A biographical sketch and an enthusiastic appraisal of Rider Haggard's talent, quoting other admirers such as Andrew Lang and C. S. Lewis.

Haggard, Sir Henry Rider. The days of my life, an autobiography. Edited by C. J. Longman. London and New York: Longmans, 1926.

George Alfred Henty

Henty, George Alfred. Beric the Briton: a story of the Roman invasion. London: Blackie, 1893.
Among the best of Henty's books for boys.

————. Condemned as a nihilist: a story of escape from Siberia. London: Blackie, 1893.
Illustrated by Walter Paget.

————. Out on the pampas, or, the young settlers. London: Griffith, Farran, 1871.
Henty's first book for boys.

————. With Clive in India, or, the beginnings of an empire. London: Blackie, 1884.
With twelve full-page illustrations by Gordon Browne.

————. With Lee in Virginia: a story of the American Civil War. London: Blackie, 1890.
Illustrated by Gordon Browne.

■ The titles listed above are only a few of many that might be cited. Written in the period of Great Britain's expansion as an empire, Henty's military histories spanned many centuries.

BIOGRAPHY AND CRITICISM

Allen, William. "G. A. Henty," *The Cornhill magazine* 1082:71–100 (Winter, 1974–75).
Describes the author's early life, his career as a war correspondent, and how these influences shaped his writing.

Fenn, G. Manville. George Alfred Henty: the story of an active life. Glasgow: Blackie, 1907.

————. "Henty and his books," in *A peculiar gift: 19th century writings on books for children*, edited by Lance Salway, p. 424–36. Harmondsworth, Middlesex, England: Penguin, [1976].
Reprinted from *George Alfred Henty* (above). Henty's habits as a writer, his life experience as background for his stories, and the response from young readers..

Ford, Harvey S. "G. A. Henty," *Saturday review of literature* 21:3–4, 16–17 (March 2, 1940).
An appreciation and appraisal of Henty as "part of an expanding Britain; he was not suited to an empire on the defensive."

Kennedy, Roderick Stuart, and **B. J. Farmer.** Bibliography of G. A. Henty & Hentyana. London: Farmer, 1955.
An annotated list with detailed bibliographic data.

Trease, Geoffrey. "G. A. Henty: fifty years after," *Junior bookshelf* 16:149–55 (October, 1952).
Written for the fiftieth anniversary of Henty's death, this article gives a biographical sketch and pays tribute to him as a writer of adventure stories who "taught more lasting history to boys than all the schoolmasters of his generation."

Rudyard Kipling

Kipling, Rudyard. Captains courageous: a story of the Grand Banks. New York: Century, 1897.
Appeared in *McClure's magazine*, December, 1896–May, 1897.

————. The jungle book. London and New York: Macmillan, 1894.
With illustrations by John Lockwood Kipling, W. H. Drake, and P. Frenzeny.

————. Just so stories for little children. London: Macmillan; New York: Doubleday, 1902.
With illustrations by the author. The first three stories were published in *St. Nicholas*, December, 1897–February, 1898; others in the *Ladies home journal*, beginning April, 1900.

————. Kim. London: Macmillan; New York: Doubleday, 1901.
One of the best stories ever written about India.

————. Puck of Pook's Hill. London: Macmillan; New York: Doubleday, 1906.
The American edition was illustrated by Arthur Rackham.

————. Rewards and fairies. London: Macmillan; New York: Doubleday, 1910.
A sequel to *Puck of Pook's Hill*.

————. The second jungle book. London: Macmillan; New York: Doubleday, 1895.
With decorations by John Lockwood Kipling.

————. Stalky & Co. London: Macmillan; New York: Doubleday, 1899.
A school story with strong autobiographical elements.

————. Wee Willie Winkie, and other stories. New York: F. F. Lovell [189?].
An early edition with contents including "Baa baa, black sheep," which reveals Kipling's tortured memories of his early childhood school days. Also includes "His Majesty the king," a story of early childhood in India.

BIOGRAPHY AND CRITICISM

Amis, Kingsley. Rudyard Kipling and his world. New York: Scribner, 1975.
A new look at Kipling, written during a strong revival of interest in him. Generously illustrated.

Beresford, George Charles. Schooldays with Kipling. London: Victor Gollancz; New York: Putnam, 1936.
Illustrated by the author, who was McTurk in *Stalky & Co.*; with a preface by Maj. Gen. Lionel Charles Dunsterville (Stalky).

Brown, Hilton. Rudyard Kipling: a new appreciation. London: H. Hamilton; New York: Harper, 1945.
An authoritative account of Kipling's life and critical appraisal of his work, by an admirer. Foreword by Frank Swinnerton.

Carrington, Charles E. The life of Rudyard Kipling. Garden City, N.Y.: Doubleday, 1955.
"The first definitive biography" connects Kipling's writings for children with aspects of his own life. Chronology of Kipling's life and work, p. xiii–xiv.

Crouch, Marcus. "Puck country," *Junior bookshelf* 24:61–69 (March, 1960).
Describes features of the Sussex landscape that appear in *Puck of Pook's Hill*.

Green, Roger Lancelyn. Kipling and the children. London: Elek Books, 1965.

Relates Kipling's writing to his life and to other children's books of the period. Kipling's childhood is treated with special fullness. The background and production of his writings for children receive detailed consideration.

————. "Rudyard Kipling," *Junior bookshelf* 20: 312–19 (December, 1956).
Focuses on Kipling's stories for children, tracing sources. Connects the Mowgli stories with the Boy Scout movement.

Haines, Helen E. "The wisdom of Baloo: Kipling and childhood," *Horn book magazine* 12:135–43 (May–June, 1936).
Analyzes the moral of Kipling's stories for children: "individuality is brought to integration and harmony by the discipline enforced by experience."

Hart, Walter Morris. Kipling the story-writer. Berkeley: University of California Press, 1928; reprint: Folcroft, Pa.: Folcroft, 1969.
Examines the technique of the writing in Kipling's short stories.

Hindle, Alan. "Rudyard Kipling's *Rewards and fairies*," *School librarian* 21, no. 4:295–300 (December, 1973).
The author considers *Rewards and fairies* superior to *Puck of Pook's Hill* and calls Kipling, after Scott, "the first to make a significant advance in form of writing and approach to history."

Kipling, Rudyard. Something of myself for my friends known and unknown. New York: Doubleday, 1937.
A revealing autobiography filled with insights concerning people, places, and experiences that influenced the author's writing.

Nesbitt, Elizabeth. "The great originator," *Horn book magazine* 29:106–14 (April, 1953); in *A critical history of children's literature*, edited by Cornelia Meigs et al., p. 310–17. Rev. ed. New York: Macmillan, 1969.

Stewart, John M. Rudyard Kipling. New York: Dodd, 1966.
A biographical and critical analysis in which chapters 8 and 9 are of special help to students of children's literature.

————. Rudyard Kipling: a bibliographical catalogue. Edited by A. W. Yeats. Toronto: Dalhousie, 1959.

Sutcliff, Rosemary. Rudyard Kipling. (Bodley Head monograph) London: Bodley Head, 1960; (Walck monograph) New York: Walck, 1961.
Focuses on Kipling as an author of juvenile books and identifies some of his sources. Includes a list of his books for children.

Tompkins, Joyce Marjorie Sanxter. "Kipling and Nordic myths and saga," *English studies* 52: 147–57 (April, 1971).
Part of this article concerns the reflections of Kipling's interest in Nordic myths to be found in *Puck of Pook's Hill* and *Rewards and fairies*.

Andrew Lang

Lang, Andrew. The gold of Fairnilee. Bristol, England: J. W. Arrowsmith, 1888.
Illustrated by T. Scott and E. A. Lemann. A story of Tweedside and of a boy, born before the Battle of Flodden, who uses fairy magic water to discover Roman treasure near the old house of Fairnilee.

————. Prince Prigio. Bristol, England: J. W. Arrowsmith, 1889.
Illustrated by Gordon Browne. The story of a prince who does not believe in magic and fairy tales until he falls in love. (Lang pronounced the name to rhyme with Bridge-ee-o.)

————. The princess Nobody: a tale of fairy land. London: Longmans, 1884.
Written at the suggestion of Charles Longman to fit Richard Doyle's pictures for *In fairyland: pictures from the elf world*, 1869.

————, ed. The blue fairy book. London: Longmans, 1889.
An outstanding collection from all over the world, followed by a long series of similar collections known as The fairy book series or The color fairy books.

————, tr. The *Iliad* of Homer. London: Macmillan, 1883.
With W. Leaf and E. Myers as collaborators. Widely used in schools.

————, tr. The *Odyssey* of Homer. London: Macmillan, 1879.
With S. H. Butcher as collaborator. Among the finest of all prose translations.

BIOGRAPHY AND CRITICISM

Bookman (Indiana University Library). [An Andrew Lang issue.] No. 7 (April, 1965).
A Lilly Library publication based on the Falconer Collection, which was regarded as "a probably complete collection of the writings," later increased by Frank G. Darlington.

Green, Roger Lancelyn. Andrew Lang. (A Walck monograph) New York: Walck, 1962.
A critical study of Lang and of The color fairy books. Bibliography covers Lang's original writ-

ing for children as well as his retellings and collections, his writing about fairy tales, and writings by others about Lang and his work.

———. Andrew Lang: a critical biography with a short-title bibliography of the works of Andrew Lang. Leicester, England: Ward, 1946.
The first biography of Lang, based on his writing of more than 200 books.

Lang, Andrew. "Modern fairy tales," *Illustrated London news*, p. 714 (December 3, 1892); reprint: in *A peculiar gift: 19th century writings on books for children*, edited by Lance Salway, p. 133–36. Harmondsworth, Middlesex, England: Penguin, [1976].
The author criticizes literary fairy tales of the period as having "no human interest . . . no adventures where courage, loyalty and adroitness are indispensable."

Mrs. Molesworth

Molesworth, Mary Louisa Stewart. (*pseud.* Ennis Graham). "Carrots," just a little boy; by Ennis Graham. London: Macmillan, 1876.

———. The cuckoo clock, by Ennis Graham. London: Macmillan, 1877.
Illustrated by Walter Crane.

———. Four winds farm. London: Macmillan, 1887.
Illustrated by Walter Crane. The dedication to the author's youngest daughter is dated 1886.

———. The tapestry room: a child's romance. London: Macmillan, 1879.
Illustrated by Walter Crane.

———. "Us": an old-fashioned story. London: Macmillan, 1885.
With illustrations by Walter Crane.

BIOGRAPHY AND CRITICISM

Green, Roger Lancelyn. "Mrs. Molesworth," *Junior bookshelf* 21:101–8 (July, 1957).
Comments on renewed interest in Mrs. Molesworth and "her ability to enter into the personalities of her children."

———. Mrs. Molesworth. (A Bodley Head monograph) London: Bodley Head, 1961; (A Walck monograph) New York: Walck, 1964.
A biographical sketch that shows how the life of Mrs. Molesworth, "one of the most autobiographical of writers," was reflected in her stories. Includes a portrait and a Molesworth book list, giving names of illustrators.

Laski, Marghanita. Mrs. Ewing, Mrs. Molesworth, and Mrs. Hodgson Burnett. London: Barker, 1950.

The author is not an admirer of Mrs. Molesworth except as "a story-teller for very young children."

Molesworth, Mary Louisa Stewart. "On the art of writing fiction for children," *Atalanta* 6:583–86 (May, 1893); reprint: in *A peculiar gift: 19th century writings on books for children*, edited by Lance Salway, p. 340–46. Harmondsworth, Middlesex, England: Penguin, [1976].
The author gives advice to young would-be writers.

E. Nesbit

Bland, Edith Nesbit (*pseud.* E. Nesbit). The book of dragons. London and New York: Harper, 1901.
With illustrations by H. R. Millar and decorations by H. Granville Fell. A collection of short stories.

———. The children's Shakespeare. Edited by Edric Vredenburg. London: R. Tuck, 1895.
Illustrated by Frances Brundage et al. Simple retellings of selected tales.

———. The enchanted castle. London: T. Fisher Unwin, 1907.
Illustrated by H. R. Millar. One of the "magic" stories.

———. The new treasure seekers. London: T. Fisher Unwin, 1904.
Illustrated by Gordon Browne and Lewis Baumer. A sequel to *The story of the treasure seekers,* in which the Bastable children were introduced.

———. The railway children. London: Wells Gardner, Darton, 1906.
First appeared in the *London magazine*, 1904.

———. The story of the treasure seekers. London: T. Fisher Unwin, 1899.
Illustrated by Gordon Browne and Lewis Baumer. The first of the author's books about the Bastables.

———. The Wouldbegoods. London: T. Fisher Unwin, 1901.
Illustrated by Arthur H. Buckland et al. This was the first sequel to *The story of the treasure seekers.*

BIOGRAPHY AND CRITICISM

Bell, Anthea. E. Nesbit. (A Bodley Head monograph) London: Bodley Head, 1960); (A Walck monograph) New York: Walck, 1964.
A brief biography of Edith Nesbit Bland, the child, the woman, the writer; an account of her books; and an appraisal of her place in children's literature. Includes a portrait; summaries of plots, p. 76–79. Bibliography.

Bland, Edith Nesbit. Long ago when I was young. London: Whiting & Wheaton, 1966; New York: Watts, 1966.
Illustrated by Edward Ardizzone. Introduction by Noel Streatfeild. Reveals the connection between E. Nesbit's "storm-tossed" childhood and the contrastingly strong sense of home life in her books.

Cameron, Eleanor. The green and burning tree: on the writing and enjoyment of children's books. Boston: Little, 1969.
The author makes appreciative comments on E. Nesbit and Beatrix Potter, among other famous writers of fantasy.

Crouch, Marcus S. "E. Nesbit's Kent," *Junior bookshelf* 19:11–21 (January, 1955).
How Kent, especially at Well Hall, Eltham, was modified by imagination in E. Nesbit's stories.

Croxson, Mary. "The emancipated child in the novels of E. Nesbit," *Signal* 14:51–64 (May, 1974).
Shows parallels between other educational theorists and E. Nesbit's *Wings and the child*. Includes a list of her children's books.

de Alonso, Joan Evans. "E. Nesbit's Well Hall, 1915–1921: a memoir," *Children's literature: the great excluded* 3:147–52 (1973).
Reminiscences of school holidays spent at Well Hall where the author's mother lived after the death of Hubert Bland. An intimate glimpse of E. Nesbit's eccentricities.

Ellis, Alec. "E. Nesbit and the poor," *Junior bookshelf* 38:73–78 (April, 1974).
The socialistic ideals of E. Nesbit as they appear in her books for children.

Horn book magazine v. 34 (October, 1958).
In this issue, *Horn book magazine* paid tribute to E. Nesbit on the centenary of her birth. Includes "Daily magic" by Edward Eager, p. 348–58; "Places of enchantment" by Eleanor Graham, p. 364–65; "E. Nesbit as I knew her" by Mavis Strange, p. 359–63; "Oswald Bastable" by Noel Streatfeild, p. 366–73; "Out of the abundance" by Ruth Viguers, p. 341.

Green, Roger Lancelyn. "A further note on the illustrators of E. Nesbit," *Junior bookshelf* 22:321–22 (December, 1958).
Answers an anonymous article "Illustrators of E. Nesbit" in the October issue, 1958, p. 199–201. Traces illustrations by H. R. Millar, Gordon Browne, and others.

Lynch, Patricia. "Remembering E. Nesbit," *Horn book magazine* 29:342–43 (October, 1953).
A brief but vivid description of a visit with E. Nesbit at Well Hall, Kent.

Moore, Doris Langley-Levy. E. Nesbit, a biography. London: Benn, 1933. Rev. with new material: Philadelphia: Chilton, 1966.
The 1966 edition includes much detail concerning the author's unhappy marriage, which the earlier edition omitted. Bibliography.

Streatfeild, Noel. Magic and the magician: E. Nesbit and her children's books. London: Benn, 1958.
A biography with special relevance for those interested in the author's childhood and in her books for children. Illustrations and a bibliography.

Walbridge, Earle F. "E. Nesbit," *Horn book magazine* 29:335–41 (October, 1953).
An editor and bibliographer tells why he considers E. Nesbit's tales of magic her best work.

Anna Sewell

Sewell, Anna. Black Beauty, his grooms and companions: the "Uncle Tom's cabin" of the horse. Boston: Lothrop, [1890?].
Originally published in 1877. This edition has an alphabetical index of information on the care of horses, with page references to Anna Sewell's text. An "Introductory Chapter" by George T. Angell, president of the American Humane Education Society and the Massachusetts Society for the Prevention of Cruelty to Animals, is dated "Boston, 1890."

BIOGRAPHY AND CRITICISM

Baker, Margaret J. Anna Sewell and *Black Beauty*. London: Harrap, 1956.
A well-written book giving briefly the historical background of the author and her famous story. Bibliography.

Kunitz, Stanley J., and **Howard Haycraft,** "Anna Sewell," in their *Junior book of authors*, p. 330–32. New York: Wilson, 1934.

Starrett, Vincent. "Memoir of Anna Sewell," in *Black Beauty: the autobiography of a horse* by Anna Sewell, p. vii–xiv. London: Dent; New York: Dutton, 1921.

Robert Louis Stevenson

Stevenson, Robert Louis. The black arrow: a tale of the two roses. London: Cassell, 1888.
A story of the Wars of the Roses. First appeared as a serial in *Young folks*, 1883, published as "by "Captain George North."

———. Catriona: a sequel to *Kidnapped*, being the memoirs of the further adventures of David Balfour at home and abroad, &c. London: Cassell, 1893.

Originally published as "David Balfour" in *Atalanta, the magazine for girls*. The American edition used the title *David Balfour*.

———. A child's garden of verses. London: Longmans, 1885.
Inspired by Kate Greenaway's *Birthday book for children* and originally entitled *Penny whistles*. Many of the poems are based on Stevenson's own childhood memories.

———. David Balfour. New York: Scribner, 1893.
See *Catriona* above.

———. Kidnapped. London: Cassell, 1886.
Set in post-Jacobite Scotland, this is the first of two novels about David Balfour. Originally published in *Young folks*.

———. The strange case of Dr. Jekyll and Mr. Hyde. London: Longmans, 1886.
Stevenson's first great popular success.

———. Treasure island. London: Cassell, 1883.
Originally published as "by Captain George North" in *Young folks*, 1881–82.

———. ———, vol. 2, *Writings*. New York: Scribner, 1894.
See "My first book—'Treasure island,' " p. ix–xx.

BIOGRAPHY AND CRITICISM

Aldington, Richard. Portrait of a rebel: the life and work of Robert Louis Stevenson. London: Evans, 1957.
Shows how Stevenson's break with the traditional values of his family led to the flowering of his temperament as a writer. Selected bibliography.

Balfour, Graham. The life of Robert Louis Stevenson. 2v. London: Methuen, 1901; New York: Scribner, 1901. Abridged ed., rev. and illus. New York: Scribner, 1823; reprint: St. Clair Shores, Mich.: Scholarly, 1968.
Prepared with the assistance of Stevenson's family. Brief references to his books. Earliest edition has portraits, a map, and chronological list of Stevenson's writings, vol. 2, p. 248–61.

Butts, Dennis. "The child's voice," *Junior bookshelf* 29:331–37 (December, 1965).
For the eightieth anniversary of *A child's garden of verses*, this article describes the sources of numerous poems and gives a perceptive analysis of Stevenson as poet.

———. R. L. Stevenson. (A Bodley Head monograph) London: Bodley Head, 1966; (A Walck monograph) New York: Walck, 1966.
Especially intended for children's librarians and students of children's literature, this brief study is divided into chapters that focus on the books intended for a juvenile audience. Includes a portrait and bibliography.

Cohen, Morton N. "A voyage back to *Treasure island*," *Junior bookshelf* 23:122–29 (March, 1959).
Written for the seventy-fifth anniversary of *Treasure island*, recounting the circumstances under which Stevenson began the tale.

Cooper, Lettice U. Robert Louis Stevenson. Denver: Swallow, 1948. 2d ed.: London: Barker, 1967.
A brief and simple biography. Includes a bibliography and "Some books of reference."

Daiches, David. Robert Louis Stevenson. Norfolk, Conn.: New Directions, 1947.
Among the many biographies of Stevenson, this is recommended by Dennis Butts in his Walck monograph on Stevenson.

———. Robert Louis Stevenson and his world. London: Thames & Hudson, 1973.
Especially helpful for teachers who want to communicate the exciting quality of Stevenson's life. More than 100 illustrations.

Doyle, *Sir* Arthur Conan. "Mr. Stevenson's methods in fiction," *The national review* 14:646–57 (January, 1890); reprint: in *A peculiar gift: 19th century writings on books for children*, edited by Lance Salway, p. 391–403. Harmondsworth, Middlesex, England: Penguin, [1976].
The author discusses some of the short stories and novels (including *Treasure island* and *Kidnapped*) that he believes give Stevenson the right to "the contemporary popularity which he enjoys [and] lasting fame which springs from thorough work thoroughly done."

Edinburgh Public Libraries. Robert Louis Stevenson, 1850–1894: catalogue of the Stevenson collection in the Edinburgh Room. Edinburgh: Edinburgh Public Library, 1950.

Furnas, Joseph C. Voyage to windward: the life of Robert Louis Stevenson. New York: Sloane, 1951.
One of the most useful biographies of Stevenson, complete in its coverage of the author's life and sensitive to his artistic achievements. Bibliography and indexes.

Grover, Eulalie Osgood. Robert Louis Stevenson: teller of tales. New York: Dodd, 1940; reprint: Detroit: Gale, 1975.
For junior and senior high school readers, with emphasis on Stevenson's younger years. Bibliography.

Shaffer, Ellen. "Robert Louis Stevenson and the Silverado museum," *Top of the News* 30:169–75 (January, 1974).

A description of the books and memorabilia at St. Helena, California, in the largest private collection of Stevensoniana.

Slater, John Herbert. Robert Louis Stevenson: a bibliography of his complete works. London: G. Bell, 1914; Brooklyn: Haskell House, 1974.

Smith, Janet A. R. L. Stevenson. London: Duckworth, 1937.

Of special interest in this biography is an account of the writing of *Treasure island* and of its first appearance in *Young folks*. Bibliography.

Stern, Gladys Bronwyn. He wrote *Treasure island:* the story of Robert Louis Stevenson. London: Heinemann, 1954.

A brief biography stressing Stevenson's romantic appeal as storyteller and poet.

———. Robert Louis Stevenson. (Writers and their work series) London: Longmans for the British Council, 1952.

———. Robert Louis Stevenson, the man who wrote *Treasure island:* a biography. New York: Macmillan, 1954.

Same as *He wrote Treasure island*, listed above.

Steuart, John Alexander. Robert Louis Stevenson: a critical biography. Boston: Little, 1924.

A biography written with a "candor and absence of restraint not found in Balfour's earlier work."—*Book review digest* (1924).

———. Robert Louis Stevenson, man and writer: a critical biography. 2v. London: Sampson, Low, 1924.

Same as above listing.

Stevenson, Robert Louis. A Stevenson library: catalogue of a collection of writings by and about Robert Louis Stevenson formed by Edwin J. Beinecke. 2v. New Haven, Conn.: Yale University Press, 1951–52.

The definitive Stevenson bibliography.

Swinnerton, Frank A. R. L. Stevenson: a critical study. New York: Kennerley, 1915.

Chapter 1 brings out in detail the influence of Alison Cunningham, Stevenson's nurse, who told him stories and read aloud, thus developing his later sense of style.

Watson, Harold Francis. Coasts of *Treasure island*: a study of the backgrounds and sources for Robert Louis Stevenson's romance of the sea. San Antonio, Tex.: Naylor, 1969.

Winterich, John Tracy. "Treasure island," *Publishers weekly* 118:613–16 (1930).

Account of its origin and first publication. The article is one of a series, Romantic stories of books.

Oscar Wilde

Wilde, Oscar. The happy prince and other tales. London: D. Nutt, 1888.

Illustrated by Walter Crane and Jacomb Hood. Contents: The happy prince; The nightingale and the rose; The selfish giant; The devoted friend; The remarkable rocket.

———. A house of pomegranates. London: Osgood, McIlvaine, 1891; reprint: Portland, Me.: T. B. Mosher, 1906.

Contents: The young king; The birthday of the Infanta; The fisherman and his soul; The starchild.

BIOGRAPHY AND CRITICISM

Braybrooke, Patrick. Oscar Wilde: a study. London: Braithwaite & Millar, 1930; reprint: Folcroft, Pa.: Folcroft, 1970.

For a discussion of "The happy prince" and "The nightingale and the rose," see pt. 4, "The fairy-tale teller," p. 87–97.

Fido, Martin. Oscar Wilde. New York: Viking, 1973.

Illustrated with drawings, photographs, etc. of and by Wilde's brilliant circle. An absorbing account of the end of an era.

Jackson, Holbrook. The eighteen-nineties: a review of art and ideas at the close of the 19th century. London: Richards, 1913; reprint: Harmondsworth, Middlesex, England: Penguin, 1950.

Ransome, Arthur. Oscar Wilde: a critical study. London: Secker, 1912; reprint: Brooklyn: Haskell House, 1971.

Gives a biographical summary and discussion of various types of Wilde's writing.

INDIVIDUAL CONTINENTAL WRITERS

Carlo Collodi

Lorenzini, Carlo (*pseud*. Carlo Collodi). The story of a puppet, or, the adventures of Pinocchio. Translated from the Italian by M. A. Murray. London: T. Fisher Unwin, 1892.
Illustrated by E. Mazzanti. First written in serial form for the *Giornale dei bambini*, 1880. First appearance as a book, 1883. A beautiful edition appeared in 1925 with illustrations by Attilio Mussino and translation by Carol della Chiesa.

BIOGRAPHY AND CRITICISM

Bacon, Martha "Puppet's progress," *Atlantic monthly* 225:88–92 (April, 1970).
A short biographical sketch of Carlo Lorenzini, an assessment of his place among writers for children, and a judgment that "as a children's story *Pinocchio* is quite matchless."

Marchetti, Italiano. Carlo Collodi. Florence, Italy: Le Monnier, 1959.

Santucchi, Luigi. Collodi. Bresica, Italy: La Scuola, 1961.

Johanna Spyri

Spyri, Johanna Heusser. Gritli's children: a story for children and for those who love children. Translated from the German by Louise Brooks. Boston: Cupples & Hurd, 1887.
One of several less-known books by this author on child life in Switzerland.

————. Heidi: her years of wandering and learning: a story for children and those who love children. Translated from the German by Louise Brooks. 2v. Boston: De Wolfe, Fiske, 1884.
One of the translators of *Heidi*, Charles Tritten, wrote two sequels, *Heidi grows up* and *Heidi's children*.

BIOGRAPHY AND CRITICISM

Doyle, Brian. "Johanna Spyri," in his *Who's who of children's literature*, p. 249. New York: Schocken, 1968.

Paur-Ulrich, Marguerite. Johanna Spyri. Zurich, Switzerland: Waldmann, n.d.

Ulrich, Anna. Recollections of Johanna Spyri's childhood. Translated by Helen B. Dole. New York: Crowell, 1925.

A childhood friend describes the sources of Johanna Spyri's stories. There is a supplemental chapter on Johanna Spyri, the author.

Jules Verne

Verne, Jules. From the earth to the moon: passage direct in 97 hours and 20 minutes. Translated by J. K. Hoyt. Newark, N.J.: Newark Printing and Publishing Co., 1869.

————. A journey to the center of the earth. New York: Scribner, Armstrong, 1874.

————. Michael Strogoff, the courier of the czar. . . . New York: G. Munro, 1877.

————. The mysterious island. New York: J. W. Lovell, 1883.

————. The tour of the world in eighty days. Boston: Osgood, 1873.
Better known as *Around the world in eighty days*.

————. Twenty thousand leagues under the seas. . . . Boston: G. M. Smith; New York: Douglass & Myers, 1874.

BIOGRAPHY AND CRITICISM

Allott, Kenneth. Jules Verne. London: Cresset, 1940; New York: Macmillan, 1941.
Tells the story of Verne's career as a writer and paints a picture of the life and ideas of the nineteenth century that influenced him.

Allotte de la Fuye, Marguerite Pichelin. Jules Verne. Translated by Erik de Mauny. New York: Coward, 1956.
A carefully documented biography with critical comment on Verne's writing.

Stevenson, Robert Louis. "Jules Verne's stories," *The academy* n.s. 9:213 (June 3, 1876); reprint: in *A peculiar gift: 19th century writings on books for children*, edited by Lance Salway, p. 387–90. Harmondsworth, Middlesex, England: Penguin, [1976].
Stevenson writes admiringly of Verne's ability to construct a plot and sustain interest but sees the novels as particularly suitable for juvenile readers and "the dormitory storyteller."

Illustrators of Books for Children

The combining of text with illustrations in books for children is said to have begun with Comenius's *Orbis pictus* in 1657. There were, however, predecessors. For example, Caxton's *Aesop's fables* was adorned with 186 wood cuts, and many of the medieval bestiaries were illustrated by hand. The first illustrated alphabet appeared as early as 1570 in a work by John Hart titled *A methode or comfortable beginning for all unlearned* . . . and, in 1578, a book appeared in Germany, *Kunst und Lehrbuchlein*, with woodcut illustrations by Jost Amman.

If he was not the first person to illustrate a book for children, Comenius was probably the first to theorize about the effect of pictures on children, saying that, "for children, pictures are the most easily assimilated form they can look forward to." Comenius was followed by the philosopher and educational theorist John Locke, who wrote in 1693 in *Some thoughts concerning education*, "As soon as he [the child] begins to spell, as many pictures of animals should be got him as can be found, with the printed names to them, which at the same time will invite him to read, and afford him matters of enquiry and knowledge."

Although the literary works of the seventeenth century are considered on the whole a grim lot, the Puritans were not against pictures and allowed them so long as they were used for teaching purposes. The most widely read Puritan work in America, *The New England primer*, had many woodcut illustrations throughout, including an illustrated alphabet. The same type of crude woodcut was to be found in the chapbooks and broadsides of the late seventeenth and the eighteenth centuries, as well as in many of John Newbery's books of the eighteenth century.

The eighteenth century is considered by historians of children's literature to be the time when children's literature really began. It is also the century in which great children's book illustration began, although it was not until the end of the eighteenth century that John and

Thomas Bewick began illustrating children's books. Thomas Bewick not only produced some beautiful books for children, notably *A new lottery book of birds and beasts* (1771), *A pretty book of pictures for little masters and misses* . . . (1779), *Select fables* (1784), and *Fables of Aesop* (1818), but he also refined and perfected the technique of wood engraving, a method of illustration that was used in England for one hundred years.

Another rare light of the late-eighteenth century was *Songs of innocence* (1789), which was written, designed, copper-engraved, hand printed, and illustrated by William Blake. Blake also did drawings for *Pilgrim's progress* and for Mary Wollstonecraft's *Original stories from real life* (1791).

At the beginning of the nineteenth century, several innovative illustrators were in evidence. William Mulready's charming illustrations for Roscoe's *Butterfly's ball* (1807) and George Cruikshank's illustrations for Grimms' *Fairy tales* set trends by exhibiting humor in the illustrations and by showing a deep relationship with the text. Mulready and Cruikshank were both great illustrators of the time who also chose to illustrate children's books. This trend persisted throughout the century particularly with illustrators who worked in black-and-white. Richard Doyle, for example, was a cartoonist for *Punch*, yet some of his greatest illustrations are those he did for John Ruskin's *King of the Golden river* (1851). Arthur Hughes, another eminent artist, created many haunting and memorable illustrations for George MacDonald's fantasies as well as the exquisitely delicate and sentimental drawings for Christina Rossetti's *Sing-song*. A famous English caricaturist who also did children's work (though only rarely) was John Tenniel. His illustrations for the *Alice* books are even today inextricably woven with Carroll's texts. Edward Lear was a fine landscapist and naturalist whom we remember for giving English children their first taste of nonsense as early as 1846. Beatrix Potter, too, was a notable artist before she became an illustrator for children's books.

Although color printing was known and practiced—though crudely—from about 1840, it took a great engraver and printer, Edmund Evans, to "perfect" the technique and bring the art to maturity. Evans was not only the first to print picture books of high quality, he was responsible for hiring three great children's book illustrators to produce pictures for these books.

Walter Crane was Evans's first find. From 1865, Crane illustrated Evans's toy books, with their small-size format and their texts and illustrations geared to the young child, in a flat but bold style that encompassed the whole page and often the double page. Crane, who was greatly influenced by William Morris and the Arts and Crafts Movement, designed, illustrated, and often hand-penned the text for two series of nursery toy books for Warne and Routledge. He illustrated many of Mrs. Molesworth's books for young people, as well as *The baby's opera* (1877), *The baby's bouquet* (1879), *The baby's own Aesop* (1886), the Grimms' *Household stories* (1882) (for which his sister, Lucy, did the translation), and Hawthorne's *Wonder book for girls and boys* (1892).

Randolph Caldecott was the second of the Evans triumvirate. Already an established artist, Caldecott began to work for Evans in the 1870s when he illustrated a series of picture books for which he is justly remembered. Caldecott, for whom the Caldecott medal is named, provides a great contrast to Crane, excelling in scenes of British country life and scenes of action. His illustrations are full of broad humor and fun. His death at the age of forty cut short a career of one of the most innovative nineteenth-century illustrators for children's books.

The third of Evans's trio was Kate Greenaway. Beginning in 1878 with *Under the window*, Kate Greenaway provided many best-sellers for Evans. She often illustrated her own eminently forgettable verse with her staid, delicately costumed children "playing" primly in beautifully laid out English gardens. More static and decorative than Caldecott's drawings, lighter and more romantic than Crane's, Kate Greenaway's finely detailed work graced such

books as *Marigold garden* (1885), *Kate Greenaway's birthday book for children* (1880), *Mother Goose* (1881), *A apple pie* (1886), and her *Almanacs* (beginning with 1883).

In England, this great trio of artists was succeeded by another threesome of equally fine illustrators—L. Leslie Brooke, Arthur Rackham, and Beatrix Potter—all of whom worked on into the twentieth century.

L. Leslie Brooke illustrated his first book, *The nursery rhyme book,* in 1897, and this was followed by his *Johnny Crow* books, beginning with *Johnny Crow's garden* in 1903. His style—robust, humorous, and kinetic—is most like Caldecott's. Arthur Rackham, however, is better known. A prolific illustrator with a distinctive style, Rackham began his work with the Lambs' *Tales from Shakespear* (1899) and followed with books still popular, such as *Rip Van Winkle* (1905), *Peter Pan in Kensington Gardens* (1906), *Alice's adventure in Wonderland* (1907), *A midsummer night's dream* (1908), *The legend of Sleepy Hollow* (1928), and *The night before Christmas* (1931), to name just a few. Beatrix Potter wrote for a much younger audience. In 1893 she wrote "The tale of Peter Rabbit," in a letter to Noel Moore, a sick child of a friend. Privately printed in 1901 and published in 1902 by Warne, *The tale of Peter Rabbit* was followed during the next ten years by fifteen more exquisitely illustrated and charmingly written books.

In America, the first notable illustrator of children's books was Alexander Anderson, called the American Bewick, who used Bewick's white-line engraving technique with some success from 1775 on. It was not until 1840 that true American illustration was developed in children's books. The first of the great American illustrators, after Anderson, was F. O. C. Darley, whose *Peter Ploddy and other oddities*, illustrated with wood engravings, appeared in 1844. Darley also illustrated Washington Irving's *Sketch book* and *Rip Van Winkle*, both in 1848.

It was in the pages of the American magazines for young people—notably *Our young folks, The Riverside magazine for young people, St. Nicholas,* and *Harper's young people*—that many American artists began drawing pictures for stories written by American writers about America. Howard Pyle, Reginald Birch, and Thomas Nast all produced pictures in American magazines. Toward the end of the century, several notable American illustrators emerged, particularly E. W. Kemble, best known for his illustrations of *The adventures of Huckleberry Finn* (1885), and A. B. Frost, famed for his illustrations of Joel Harris's Uncle Remus books.

Howard Pyle is probably America's most famous illustrator of the period. Influenced by the late-nineteenth-century interest in the Middle Ages, Pyle wrote and illustrated *Men of iron* (1891) and *Otto of the silver hand* (1888); he also reworked for children the Arthurian legends and *The merry adventures of Robin Hood* (1883). Pyle, like Kemble and Frost, worked primarily in black and white. Pyle was not only a great illustrator and writer of chil-

dren's books, he was fortunately a great teacher, and he handed down a rich tradition of excellence in children's book illustration to some of his pupils, such as Maxfield Parrish, Jessie Willcox Smith, N. C. Wyeth, and Frank Schoonover, all colorists.

From our twentieth-century vantage point, it is difficult to look back on the engravings of Comenius or even the woodcut illustrations in the eighteenth-century chapbooks and imagine that such crude works could have given delight to a child. But we know they did, if only because they were all that children had at that time. Children's book illustration, like writing for children, has been an evolutionary process from simple beginnings to the present, when the range of medium and style is incredibly varied, encompassing all children's ages, interests and needs.

OUTLINE

I. Early illustrators of books for children
  A. Johan Amos Comenius (1592–1670)
    1. Philosopher of educational theory as it affected the illustration of children's books
    2. The pictures drawn by Comenius for The *Orbis sensualium pictus*
  B. The work of Thomas (1753–1828) and John (1760–95) Bewick
    1. Development of the white-line, wood engraving technique
    2. The smallness of the illustrations necessitated by the use of the end of the block
    3. The diversity of work for children by both Bewicks
  C. Alexander Anderson (1775–1870)
    1. Called the American Bewick
    2. Early book illustration in America
  D. William Blake (1757–1827)
    1. As artist, writer, engraver, and printer of *Songs of innocence* and *Songs of experience*
    2. Illustrator of the stories of Mary Wollstonecraft
  E. George Cruikshank (1792–1878)
    1. Great English illustrator of Dickens and London city scenes
    2. His humorous, exaggerated drawings for:
      a) Grimms' *Fairy tales*
      b) *The tragical comedy, or, comical tragedy of Punch and Judy*

      c) *The comic alphabet*
    3. Cruikshank's controversial rewritings of the Grimms' fairy tales and the retort by Charles Dickens in *Household words*
II. Nineteenth-century English and American illustrators in black and white
  A. William Mulready (1786–1863)
    1. Illustrator of Roscoe's *Butterfly's ball* and *The grasshopper's feast* and their sequels, all published by John Harris
  B. John Tenniel (1820–1914)
    1. His drawings for Carroll's *Alice's adventure in Wonderland* and *Through the looking-glass*
    2. The working relationship between Carroll and Tenniel
  C. Richard Doyle (1824–83)
    1. *Punch* illustrator
    2. Illustrator of Dickens's books
    3. The robust illustrations for John Ruskin's *King of the Golden river*
    4. His delicate illustrations for *In fairyland,* with the poem of William Allingham
  D. Arthur Hughes (1832–1915)
    1. Hughes's association with George MacDonald and his son, Greville
    2. First illustrator of *Tom Brown's school days*
    3. The delicate, sentimental illustrations for Rossetti's *Sing-song* and *Speaking likenesses.*

E. F. O. C. Darley (1822–88)
   1. Influenced by Cruikshank
   2. His wood engraving illustrations for
      Peter Ploddy and other oddities
   3. His drawings for Irving's *Sketch*
      book and *Rip Van Winkle*
F. American magazine illustrators
   1. Winslow Homer (1836–1910)
   2. Reginald Birch (1856–1943)
   3. Thomas Nast (1840–1902)
   4. E. W. Kimble (1861–1933)
   5. A. B. Frost (1851–1928)
G. E. W. Kemble (1861–1933)
   1. Illustrator of Mark Twain's
      Adventures of Huckleberry Finn
H. A. B. Frost (1851–1928)
   1. Illustrator of Joel Chandler Harris's
      Uncle Remus stories
I. Howard Pyle, author-illustrator
   (1853–1911)
   1. Life and character
   2. Illustrations for his fairy tales
      and medieval stories
      a) Individuality
      b) Versatility
      c) Harmony of theme and style
      d) Technique
      e) Influence upon illustrative art
         in America
   3. Pyle's teaching and influence on
      American graphic arts through
      his famous pupils
III. Nineteenth-century English and American
    illustrators in color
   A. Advance in illustration from the toy
      books of the early nineteenth century
      to the picture books of the 1870s.
   B. Illustration in books and magazines in
      the late nineteenth century
      1. Edmund Evans (1826–1905); his
         skill in color printing
      2. The English trio of Evans:

a) Walter Crane (1845–1915)
   (1) Preeminence as decorative
      artist
   (2) Japanese and Italian influences
   (3) Choice of subjects
   (4) Richness of coloring
   (5) Detail of costume and
      architecture
b) Randolph Caldecott (1846–86)
   (1) English scenes
   (2) Story-telling quality
   (3) Outdoor atmosphere
   (4) Irresistible humor, action
      and vigor
   (5) Contrast with Crane in
      drawing and color
c) Kate Greenaway (1846–1901)
   (1) Sympathy with children
   (2) Pictorial quality
   (3) Settings and costume
   (4) Daintiness and refinement,
      joyousness of spirit
   (5) Character of original verse
IV. Early-twentieth-century illustrators
   A. The second English trio:
      1. Beatrix Potter (1866–1943)
      a) Life
      b) Peter Rabbit picture books
         (1) Their small scale
         (2) Their use with small children
         (3) The originality of the texts
      c) Other drawings from nature
      2. Arthur Rackham (1867–1939)
      a) Distinctive style
      b) Work in color
      c) Work in black and white and
         silhouette
      3. L. Leslie Brooke (1862–1940)
      a) Comparison with Caldecott
      b) Illustrator of nursery rhymes
      c) Humor in his illustrations
      d) *Johnny Crow* books

GENERAL REFERENCES

Allen, Grace. "Color printing in books for children," *Horn book magazine* 12:7–15 (January–February, 1936).
Contrasts the printing techniques of the color books of the 1930s with those of Kate Greenaway, Caldecott, Crane, and Rackham.

"Art in the nursery," *The magazine of art* 6:127–32 (1883); in *A peculiar gift*, edited by Lance Salway, p. 248–59. Harmondsworth, Eng.: Penguin, [1976].
Discusses the greatness of late-nineteenth-century children's book illustration, with special emphasis on Tenniel, Cruikshank, Crane, Caldecott, and Greenaway.

Bader, Barbara. American picturebooks from Noah's ark to the beast within. New York: Macmillan, [1976].
Although the bulk of this book is concerned with the twentieth century, the chapters titled "Starting point," p. 2–12, and "E. Boyd Smith," p. 13–22, cover the period up to the twentieth century.

Blackburn, Henry. The art of illustration. Edinburgh: John Grant, 1901.
A classic text.

Bland, David. A history of book illustration: the illuminated manuscript and the printed book. Cleveland: World, 1958.
A definitive work that includes comment on Crane, Caldecott, and Greenaway as well as the important illustrators of children's books in the

twentieth century. Chapter 7 is about William Blake and Thomas Bewick, chapter 9 is on Victorian book illustration, and chapter 10 is concerned with lithography in the nineteenth century. Drawings and color reproductions. Bibliography.

———. ———. 2d rev. ed. Berkeley: University of California Press, 1969.

———. The illustration of books. New York: Pantheon, 1952.
. Pt. 1, dealing with the history of illustration, includes a full chapter on children's books. Pt. 2 is on the processes and their applications.

Bliss, Douglas Percy. A history of wood-engraving. London: Dent, 1928.
With 120 illustrations. Includes a very clear explanation of the techniques of wood engraving and traces its history and use to the twentieth century. Includes a chapter on Thomas Bewick, p. 179–93, and one on Blake and modern English wood engraving, p. 203–26.

Chappell, Warren. "Bench marks for illustrators of children's books," *Horn book magazine* 33: 413–20 (October, 1957).
A "bench mark" article in the history of illustration, in which Chappell discusses the craftsmanship of Blake, Hogarth, Rembrandt, Goya, Daumier, Delacroix, and others.

Cleaver, James. A history of graphic art. New York: Philosophical Library, 1963; reprint: New York: Greenwood, 1967.
An excellent overview of book illustration that covers technique and style.

Crane, Walter. Of the decorative illustration of books old and new. London: G. Bell, 1896.
In this book, which distinguishes between book illustration and decorative treatment, Crane sets forth general principles for both. Richly illustrated.

———. ———. Detroit: Singing Tree, 1968.
A reprint of the 1905 edition.

Cundall, Joseph. A brief history of wood-engraving from its invention. London: Sampson Low, Marston, 1895.
Cundall was the publisher of *The home treasury* books for children. This history of the wood engraving technique includes a chapter on Thomas Bewick and one on his successors.

Dalziel, George, and **Edward Dalziel.** The brothers Dalziel: a record of fifty years' work in conjunction with many of the most distinguished artists of the period 1840–1890. London: Methuen, 1901.
An autobiographical account of the relationship between the Dalziel brothers and their artists, some of whom were William Mulready, George Cruikshank, John Tenniel, Richard Doyle, Arthur Hughes, A. B. Houghton, and Edward Lear.

Darton, Frederick Joseph Harvey. Modern book illustration in Great Britain and America. London: The Studio, 1931.
Although it begins with a discussion of nineteenth-century illustration techniques, this book deals mainly with the late nineteenth and early twentieth centuries.

———. "The 'sixties: Alice and after," in his *Children's books in England*, p. 283–88. 2d ed. Cambridge: Cambridge University Press, 1958.
Darton says, "The illustrators of this period, indeed, are more truly characteristic, very often, than all but the best of the written works which they adorned." Includes a discussion of the Dalziel brothers, and Crane, Caldecott, and Greenaway.

Eaton, Anne Thaxter. "Illustrators who were more than illustrators," in *A critical history of children's literature*, edited by Cornelia Meigs et al., p. 225–37. Rev. ed. New York: Macmillan, 1969.
Includes a discussion of Cruikshank, Tenniel, Crane, Caldecott, and Greenaway.

Evans, Edmund. The reminiscences of Edmund Evans. Edited and introduced by Ruari McLean. Oxford: Oxford University Press, 1967.
A brief autobiography that includes description of Evans's work with Caldecott and Greenaway. A selected bibliography of Evans's books is appended. Illustrations and facsimiles, some in color.

Feaver, William. When we were young: two centuries of children's book illustration. New York: Holt, [1977].
Shows the influence of nineteenth-century illustration on twentieth-century illustration. Includes an annotated list of illustrations.

Field, Louise Frances Story (Mrs. E. M. Field). "Some illustrators of children's books," in her *The child and his book*, p. 293–315. London: Wells Gardner, 1892; reprint: Detroit: Singing Tree, 1968.
Covers illustrated broadsides, chapbooks, ballads, etc. and then progresses from Bewick to Thomas Stothard and William Blake, Thackeray, Mulready, Crane, Caldecott, and Kate Greenaway.

Freeman, G. La Verne, and **Ruth Freeman.** The child and his picture book. Chicago: University of Chicago Press, 1933.
Although a short history of picture book illustration is given, this is mainly "a discussion of the preferences of the [contemporary] nursery child."

Gillespie, Margaret. "Memorable moments in illustrating," in her *Literature for children: history and trends*, p. 107–14. Dubuque, Iowa: William C. Brown, [1970].
Traces the "gradual evolution" of illustration from the illuminated drawings of the medieval bestiaries through Kate Greenaway.

Hamilton, Sinclair, ed. "Early American book illustration," *Chronicle* (Princeton University Library) 6:101–26 (April, 1945).

Traces the history and development of American illustration as "a part of the cultural development of this country." Discusses American wood engraving, Alexander Anderson and his pupils, and illustration in America from 1840 to 1860.

Hardie, Martin. English coloured books. London: Methuen, 1906.

This classic source in the field of book illustration covers the period from the Middle Ages through the nineteenth century, discusses techniques, and gives examples of each. Chapter 8 is on William Blake: chapter 16 on George and Robert Cruikshank; chapter 17 on Leech, Thackeray, and Phiz; chapter 21 on the Chiswick Press and children's books; and chapter 22 on Edmund Evans and Crane, Greenaway, and Caldecott.

Hind, Arthur Mayger. A history of engraving and etching from the 15th century to the year 1914. London: Constable, 1923.

This is a revision of *Short history of engraving and etching,* 1908. This history discusses both techniques and masters of the art. Contains a classified list of engravers (by country), a general bibliography, an index of engravers, and individual bibliographies.

A history of children's books and juvenile graphic art. Lewiston, N.Y.: McIntyre, 1976.

Six silent filmstrips cover children's illustrated books from the end of the seventeenth century to the beginning of the twentieth. Includes reproductions of over 200 woodcut engravings, etchings, color prints, and water colors from the entire period.

Hunt, Mary Alice. "Trends in illustrations for children as seen in selected juvenile periodicals, 1875–1900." Ph.D. diss., Indiana University, 1973.

James, Philip. Children's books of yesterday. Edited by C. G. Holme. *The studio* (Autumn, 1933).

"The illustrations in this book were selected in great part from the Exhibition of Illustrated Books for Children held at the Victoria and Albert Museum in 1932. The arrangement follows the chronological history of children's books, beginning with a reproduced page from *Visible world* by Comenius, and closing with a cut from Kipling's *Just so stories.* The illustrations, in both color and black and white, are well reproduced and are accompanied by explanatory captions. The introduction by Philip James serves as a brief survey of children's books in England. An alphabetical list of illustrations and one of authors, illustrators, and publishers are included."—*Booklist,* 1934.

———. English book illustration, 1800–1900. London and New York: Penguin, 1947.

A generously illustrated history of artists who illustrated children's books, including the Bewicks, Blake, Cruikshank, Doyle, Tenniel, Lear, and numerous others.

Jussim, Estelle. "Photographic technology and visual communication in the 19th century American book." Ph.D. diss., Columbia University, 1970.

"To discover in what ways the introduction of photographic technologies altered the capabilities of the graphic arts for artistic expression and information transfer," the author studied three illustrators (Howard Pyle, William Hamilton Gibson, and Frederic Remington) and one subject area (art history).

King, Arthur, and **Albert F. Stuart.** The house of Warne: one hundred years of publishing. London and New York: Warne, [1965].

A "biography" of this great publishing house. Chapter 4 is about Kate Greenaway and Randolph Caldecott (excerpted from *A century of Kate Greenaway* by Anne Carroll Moore); chapter 6, L. Leslie Brooke; and chapter 7, Beatrix Potter (by Leslie Linder).

Lang, Andrew. "Illustrated books," in his *The library,* p. 122–78. London: Macmillan, 1881.

An excellent summary of illustrated books up to the 1880s. Includes a section on children's illustrated books and discusses Blake, Bewick, Stothard, and Mulready as well.

McLean, Ruari. Victorian book design and colour printing. Berkeley and Los Angeles: University of California Press, [1971].

Covers the period between 1837 and 1890, in which "more exciting things happened in book design . . . than in any other comparable period in the history of the world's printing, and most of them happened in London." Chapter 6, "Children's books up to 1850," p. 47–64.

Miller, Bertha Mahony, and **Elinor Whitney,** comps. Contemporary illustrators of children's books. Boston: Bookshop for Boys and Girls, 1930.

Includes the following articles on significant past influences: The Bewicks, by W. M. Stone; The fairies come into their own: George Cruikshank, Richard Doyle, John Tenniel and Arthur Hughes, by Jacqueline Overton; "Tuppence colored": Walter Crane, Randolph Caldecott and Kate Greenaway, by Jacqueline Overton; The Brandywine tradition: Howard Pyle and N. C. Wyeth, by D. C. Lunt.

———, et al., comps. Illustrators of children's books 1774–1945. Boston: Horn Book, 1947.

Reprinted by demand in 1961, this includes

ten essays by distinguished artists, critics, and editors. Brief biographies of more than 800 artists. Bibliographies list examples from the work of each artist and give much other useful information on the artists.

Morris, Charles H. The illustration of children's books. (Library Association pamphlet no. 16) London: Library Assn., 1957.
There is one section entitled "Early picture books from Comenius to Bewick" and another on the nineteenth century that covers Cruikshank, Mulready, Lear, Crane, Greenaway, and Caldecott.

Muir, Percy. "The importance of pictures," in his *English children's books 1600–1900*, p. 172–203. New York: Praeger, [1954]; reprint: London: Batsford, [1969].
Beginning with Bewick and Cruikshank, Muir traces the development of illustration in children's books to the twentieth century. Includes selected lists of the work of several British illustrators.

———. Victorian illustrated books. New York: Praeger, [1971].
Muir begins with a discussion entitled "Catnachery, chapbooks, and children's books" and traces the achievements of the Victorian illustrators, printers, and publishers. There is also a chapter on nineteenth-century American illustration. Selected bibliographies are appended to each chapter.

Nesbitt, Elizabeth. "A new era," "Classics in miniature," and "The march of picture books," in *A critical history of children's literature*, edited by Cornelia Meigs et al., p. 275–87, 318–27, 369–76. Rev. ed. New York: Macmillan, 1969.
Chapter 1 is about Howard Pyle and his pupils; 2, the work of Beatrix Potter; and 3, E. Boyd Smith, Boutet de Monvel, Gelett Burgess, Leslie Brooke, and Willebeek Le Mair.

Overton, Jacqueline. "Edmund Evans: color printer extraordinary,' *Horn book magazine* 22:109–18 (March, 1946).
Speaks of Evans as a businessman, artist, craftsman, and visionary.

Pennell, Joseph. Graphic arts. Chicago: University of Chicago Press, 1921.
Separate chapters on wood cutting, wood engraving, etching, and lithography. Gives for each a history of the method, as well as examples of old and new illustrators who use that method.

Peppin, Brigid. Fantasy: the golden age of fantastic illustration. New York: Watson-Guptill, [1975].
Contents include chapters on methods of reproduction; precursors (Rowlandson, Cruikshank, Doyle, Lear, and Tenniel); the period from 1860 to 1890 (Rossetti, Millais, Burne-Jones, Crane, A. B. Houghton, and Arthur Hughes); the period after

1890 (Beardsley, Charles Ricketts, Laurence Housman, W. Heath Robinson); fairy illustration (Rackham and Dulac); and the final phase (Kay Nielsen and Harry Clarke). Includes a bibliography of primary and secondary sources and many pages of reproductions.

Pittsburgh. Carnegie Library. Illustrated editions of children's books: a selected list. Pittsburgh: Carnegie Library, 1915.
Intended as a guide to the "selection of beautiful editions of children's classic and standard stories," this list provides a note commenting on the design and illustration of each title. Compiled by Elva S. Smith.

Pitz, Henry C. Illustrating children's books: history, technique, production. New York: Watson-Guptill, 1963.
Pt. 1, p. 13–104, covers the history of children's book illustration. Pt. 2 deals with techniques and production; pt. 3 with professional practice.

———, ed. A treasury of American book illustration. New York: American Studio Books & Watson-Guptill, 1947.
Includes chapters entitled "Pictures for childhood," "The growth of book illustration," and "Book jackets," illustrating the work of approximately 150 artists, with 100 pages of reproductions.

Pollard, Alfred W. Early illustrated books. London: Kegan Paul, Trench, Trübner, 1893.
Subtitle: "a history of the decoration and illustration of books in the 15th and 16th centuries." The chapter on illustration in England was written by E. Gordon Duff. A second edition was published in 1917 by Kegan Paul and by Dutton in the United States.

Poltarnees, Welleran. All mirrors are magic mirrors: reflections on pictures found in children's books. [La Jolla, Calif.]: Green Tiger Press, [1972].
Using nineteenth- and twentieth-century illustration, the author looks at "pictures of the realm of faërie," "the various relations of pictures to words within children's books," "pictures of domestic happiness," "the importance of stylistic and temperamental affinity between the author and illustrator," and "pictures of animals."

Reid, Forrest. Illustrations of the 'sixties. London: Faber & Groyer, 1928.
A classic text on English illustration.

Salaman, Malcolm Charles. British book illustrators, yesterday and today. London: The Studio, 1923; reprint: Detroit: Gale, 1974.

———. Modern book illustration. London: The Studio, 1914.

———. Modern woodcuts and lithographs by British and French artists. London: The Studio, 1919.

Includes chapters entitled "The woodcut in England," p. 3–52, and "Artists' lithography in England," p. 119–86.

Schiller, Justin G. "Artistic awareness in early children's books," *Children's literature: the great excluded* 3:177–85 (1974).

A paper read at the second Children's Book Showcase, Drexel University, Philadelphia, 1973, giving a survey of forms of design in children's books up to the late nineteenth century, "when specific improvements crystalized in the artistry of Walter Crane."

Sketchley, R. E. D. "Some children's books illustrators," *The library,* 2d ser. 3:358–59 (October, 1902); in *A peculiar gift,* edited by Lance Salway, p. 260–80. Harmondsworth, Eng.: Penguin, [1976].

This article is about some less-known illustrators of the nineteenth century: Robert Barnes, Mrs. Allingham, Miss M. E. Edward, Gordon Browne (son of "Phiz"), Lewis Baumer, Mrs. Arthur Gaskin, Miss Calvert, Charles Robinson, Alice Woodward, F. D. Bedford, Archie MacGregor, Alan Wright, J. D. Batten, H. J. Ford, H. R. Millar, Emily J. Harding, T. H. Robinson, Helen Stratton, R. M. M. Pitman, Percy Billinghurst, Carton More Park, Louis Wain, and J. A. Shepherd.

———. ———. in her *English book illustration of today: appreciations of their books,* p. 94–120. London: Kegan Paul, Trench, Trübner, 1903.

This is one of four essays. A corresponding bibliography of children's book illustrators is on p. 158–73. With an introduction by Alfred W. Pollard.

Smith, Janet A. Children's illustrated books. London: Collins, 1948.

The history of illustration in English books for children from the hornbook to the twentieth century. Illustrated in black and white and color.

Sparrow, Walter Shaw. Book of British etching. New York: Dodd, 1926.

Sullivan, Edmund Joseph. Art of illustration. London: Chapman and Hall, 1921.

Taylor, John Russell. The art nouveau book in Britain. London: Methuen for M.I.T. Press, [1966].

"Profusely illustrated study on late Victorian book production, the arts and crafts movement in Britain, with particular focus on Charles Ricketts, Aubrey Beardsley, and Laurence Housman."—Justin Schiller.

Thackeray, William Makepeace. "On some illustrated children's books," *Fraser's magazine* 33: 495–502 (1846); in *A peculiar gift,* edited by Lance Salway, p. 285–98. Harmondsworth, Eng.: Penguin, [1976].

A review of some illustrated books, including those of Cruikshank, Leech, and Doyle, and the works published by Joseph Cundall.

Thorpe, James. English illustration: the nineties. London: Faber & Faber, 1935; reprint: New York: Hacker Art Books, 1975.

The bulk of this book is concerned with the illustrated weeklies, daily newspapers, and some monthly and quarterly magazines and annuals. The chapter "Some illustrated books," p. 207–44, mentions E. A. Abbey; A. S. Boyd; H. M. Brock; L. Leslie Brooke; Walter Crane; Mrs. Gaskin; Laurence Housman; Charles Keene; H. R. Millar; William Nicholson; H. M. Paget; Arthur Rackham; Charles, T. H., and W. Heath Robinson (all brothers); Linley Sambourne; and Hugh Thomson.

Thwaite, Mary F. "Picture-books and books for young children," in her *From primer to pleasure in reading,* p. 188–200. 2d ed. London: Library Assn., 1972.

A concise survey of illustrated children's books from Comenius to the twentieth century.

Tooley, R. V. English books with coloured plates, 1790 to 1860. London: Batsford, [1954].

This is a revised and enlarged edition of *Some English books with coloured plates,* 1935. A bibliography of 517 titles illustrated by English artists in color aquatint and color lithography.

Townsend, John Rowe. "Pictures that tell a story," in his *Written for children: an outline of English language children's literature,* p. 142–59. Rev. ed. Philadelphia: Lippincott, 1975.

A good, concise survey of children's book illustration from Bewick and Blake to the twentieth century.

Vautier, Gerda, comp. A child's bouquet of yesterday. New York: American Studio Books, 1946.

Literary selections and illustrations from children's books of the eighteenth and nineteenth centuries. Identification list for illustrations.

Wakeman, Geoffrey. Victorian book illustration: the technical revolution. Detroit: Gale, 1973.

On the great improvements in illustration in the nineteenth century.

Watt, H. D., and **K. J. Holzknecht.** Children's books of long ago: a garland of pages and pictures. New York: Dryden, 1941.

Weitenkampf, Frank. American graphic art. New ed. rev. and enl. New York: Macmillan, 1924.

"A clear review of the whole field of American graphic art."—introduction.

———. The illustrated book. Cambridge, Mass.: Harvard University Press, 1938.

A definitive study. Chapter 10, p. 213–24, entitled "Color works and children's books," deals with the color processes in children's-book illustration.

Welsh, Charles. On coloured books for children. (Privately printed *opuscula* issued to the members of the Sette of Odd Volumes, no. 13) London: C. W. H. Wyman, 1887.
In this lecture, Welsh classifies the colored picture book into three types by period: (1) early (the hand-colored books of Griffith & Farran, Harris, etc.—to 1830); (2) middle (toy books, printed by lithographic processes by such firms as Dean, Routledge, Warne, etc.); (3) modern period (including the books by Crane, Caldecott, and Geenaway). A list of these books is appended.

Whalley, Joyce Irene. Cobwebs to catch flies: illustrated books for the nursery and schoolroom 1700–1900. Berkeley and Los Angeles: University of California Press, 1975.
Traces illustrated texts to the twentieth century and gives many examples of each type of book.

White, Gleeson. Children's books and their illustrators. *International studio* (Winter, 1897–98).

This special number of *International Studio* includes a survey of illustrated books from the eighteenth century to the late nineteenth century. Contains many black-and-white illustrations by well-known and less-known English illustrators.

———. Christmas cards and their chief designers. *The studio* (Winter, 1894).
This special issue is "profusely illustrated and authoritative, with lengthy discussions on Kate Greenaway, Walter Crane, Louis Prang, etc. . . . One of the very best references in this important field."—Justin Schiller.

———. English illustration: "the sixties": 1865–1870. London: Constable, 1897; reprint: Bath, England: Kingsmead, 1970.
This authoritative text on English book illustration deals only peripherally with children's book illustrations. Magazine illustration is discussed.

Woodberry, George E. History of wood-engraving. New York: Harper, 1888.

BIOGRAPHICAL SKETCHES

Bolton, Theodore. American book illustrators. New York: Bowker, 1938.
Includes a bibliographical checklist of 123 artists, including some nineteenth-century children's book illustrators. Lists works illustrated by each artist.

Clement, Clara Erskine, and **Laurence Hutton.** Artists of the nineteenth century. Boston: Houghton, 1884; reprint: St. Louis: North Point, 1969.
Encyclopedic listing gives nationality, date of birth, short biography.

Fielding, Martha. Dictionary of American painters, sculptors, and engravers. Philadelphia: printed for the subscribers, n.d.

Low, David. British cartoonists, caricaturists, and comic artists. London: Collins, 1942.

Latimer, Louise Payson, comp. Illustrators: a finding list. Bulletin of Bibliography pamphlet, no. 27, 1927; Boston: Faxon, 1929.
"The list includes American and foreign illustrators whose work seems of sufficient merit to warrant inclusion and is confined to books in English and in print." Unfortunately, the books listed are not dated.

Mallitt, Daniel Trowbridge. Mallitt's index of artists. New York: Bowker, 1935. Supplemented, 1940.

Smaridge, Norah. Famous author-illustrators for young people. New York: Dodd, 1973.
A reference source intended for use by young people. Covers several nineteenth-century illustrators.

Smith, Ralph Clifton. Biographical index of American artists. Baltimore: William & Wilkins, 1930.
Lists the names of "4,700 artists, arranged in alphabetical order, each followed by a brief statement of the place and date of birth and death, [and] the mediums in which the individual worked."

Ward, Martha E., and **Dorothy A. Marquardt.** Illustrators of books for young people. 2d ed. Metuchen, N. J.: Scarecrow, [1970].
Seven hundred and fifty biographies of artists, a few of whom are nineteenth-century English and American.

CATALOGS AND BIBLIOGRAPHIES

Brooklyn Museum. A century of American illustration. [Brooklyn]: Brooklyn Museum, March 22 to May 14, 1972.

"Lavishly illustrated exhibition catalogue, valuable for its biographies of artists and introductory essay on American illustration, 1850–1920."—Justin Schiller.

Gottlieb, Gerald, comp. Early children's books and their illustration. New York: Pierpont Morgan Library; Boston: Godine, 1975.

This exhibition catalog has examples of many of the famous nineteenth-century illustrators.

Gumuchian & Cie. Les livres de l'enfance du xve au xixe siecle. 2v. Paris: Gumuchian, [1931?].

Preface by Paul Gavault. Contents: vol. 1. Texte; vol. 2. Planches.

Descriptions of more than 600 items covering a wide range of children's reading. The publisher's introduction is in English, the notes are in French or English. The reproductions in vol. 2. are "hand-coloured plates . . . in the original colouring of the period unless otherwise stated."

Puttick & Simpson. An extensive collection of attractive old engraved copperplates and a quantity of old wooden blocks, collected with a view to replication by the late Mr. H. G. Bohn. London: Puttick & Simpson, 1891.

"Auction catalogue of 275 items, illustrated with six inserted engravings; including nearly two hundred woodcuts by and after George Cruikshank, including his 'Punch and Judy' series."—Justin Schiller.

Victoria and Albert Museum, South Kensington. Exhibition of illustrated books for children. London: Victoria and Albert Museum, Historical Section, 1932.

A catalog of this important exhibit.

INDIVIDUAL ILLUSTRATORS

■ In this section, only secondary sources are listed. Works illustrated by the different illustrators are listed alphabetically by illustrator in "A bibliography of illustrators and their works," in *Illustrators of children's books 1744–1945,* compiled by Bertha Mahony Miller, Louise P. Latimer, and Beulah Folmsbee, p. 383–448. (Boston: Horn Book, 1947). Since only those illustrators are listed here who are the subjects of monographic imprints, this list is by no means complete.

Alexander Anderson

Burr, Frederic Martin. Life and work of Alexander Anderson, M.D., the first American wood engraver. New York: Burr, 1893.

A concise, admiring biography. Appendix A includes "A brief sketch of Dr. Anderson's life (Written by himself in 1848)," p. 77–90; Appendix B includes "Extracts from the diary of Alexander Anderson for 1795–1798,"p. 91–210. Three portraits of Anderson and over thirty engravings by himself.

[Duyckinck, Evert Augustus]. Brief catalogue of books illustrated with engravings by Dr. Alexander Anderson. New York: Thompson Moreau, 1888.

Includes a "Biographical Sketch of Dr. Alexander Anderson," p. iii–vii.

––––. ed. and comp. Early American wood engravings by Dr. Alexander Anderson and others. New York: Burr & Boyd, 1877.

Contains "impressions from a series of Wood Blocks engraved for tracts and juvenile books published in the early part of the present century by the eminent Quaker publisher in New York, Samuel Wood." It is believed Anderson did most of these engravings.

Francis Donkin Bedford

"Francis D. Bedford, English illustrator," *Horn book magazine* 2:7+ (November, 1926).

The anonymous author sees F. D. Bedford as an artistic successor to Hugh Thomson and Kate Greenaway. Includes the text of a letter sent to the editor of *Horn book magazine* (Bertha E. Mahony) by F. D. Bedford which includes a short autobiographical sketch.

Thomas Bewick

Anderton, Basil. "Thomas Bewick: the Tyneside engraver," *The library* 26, ser. 3, 6:365–84; 27, ser. 3, 7:1–17 (1915–16).

Account of Bewick's life, more particularly his early years, with reproductions "to illustrate the countryside memories and scenes in which he took such delight."

Bain, Iain. "Thomas Bewick: engraver, of New Castle, 1753–1828: a checklist of his correspondence and other papers," *Private library,* 2d ser. 3:57–77, 124–40 (Summer and Fall, 1970).

A list of original sources, prepared as a preliminary step toward the annotated editions of Bewick's *Memoir* and a projected edition of Bewick correspondence.

Bewick, Thomas. A memoir of Thomas Bewick, written by himself. Newcastle-upon-Tyne: Robert Ward for Jane Bewick, 1862; reprint: Newcastle-upon-Tyne: Graham, 1974.
"Thomas Bewick's autobiographical *Memoir*, written at the end of his life and published posthumously in 1862, thirty-four years after his death, owes its reputation as a minor classic to two principal facts: first, that as a record of north country childhood and of a craftsman's life and work in the latter half of the eighteenth century, it is unique and secondly, that the achievement of its author as an artist-engraver on wood had no precedent and remains unequalled."—Bain (above).

———. ———. London: MacVeagh, 1925.
Introduction by Selwyn Image. Contains a portrait of Bewick and sixty other illustrations.

———. ———. Edited with an introduction by Iain Bain. London: Oxford University Press, 1975.
Excellent introduction.

Boyd, Julia, ed. Bewick gleanings. Newcastle-upon-Tyne: Andrew Reid, 1886.
Subtitle: "being impressions from copperplates and wood blocks, engraved in the Bewick workshop, remaining in the possession of the family until the death of the last Miss Bewick and sold afterwards by order of her executor. . . . To which are added, lives of Thomas Bewick and his pupils." A magnificently printed book, now rare. Biography p. 1–108. Notes accompany the drawings.

Cirker, Blanche. 1800 woodcuts by Thomas Bewick and his school. New York: Dover, 1962.

Cundall, Joseph. A brief history of wood-engraving from its invention. London: Low, 1895.
Excellent condensed account with well-chosen illustrations. "Thomas Bewick and his pupils," p. 108–15; "Thomas Bewick's successors," p. 116–28.

Dobson, Austin. "Bewick's tailpieces," in his *Eighteenth century vignettes*, 1st ser., p. 200–210. New York: Dodd, 1892.

———. Thomas Bewick and his pupils. London: Chatto & Windus, 1884.
A reprint, with some additions, of two articles that appeared in *The century magazine* (24:643–66 [1882]; 26:876–88 [1883]). Numerous illustrations reproducing the work of Bewick and his pupils, including two by John Bewick from *The looking-glass for the mind,* and one from *The blossoms of morality.* "Among writers of today probably none so well as Mr. Dobson would have blended the happy faculty of a narrator with the caution of a historian who is one of many. He is

scrupulously careful but never dull."—Ernest Radford, in *The academy.*

Garrison, W. P. "Thomas Bewick," *Harper's monthly magazine* 57:514–23 (1878).
Portrait and other illustrations.

Howitt, William. "Thomas Bewick, the reviver of wood engraving," *Howitt's journal of literature and popular progress* 2:178–80 (1847).
Describes a visit to the birthplace of John and Thomas Bewick. Portrait, p. 177.

Hugo, Thomas. The Bewick collector. London: L. Reeve, 1866; reprint: Detroit: Singing Tree, 1968.
A descriptive catalog for the work of Thomas and John Bewick "from the originals contained in the largest and most perfect collection ever formed, and illustrated with a hundred and twelve cuts."

———. Bewick's woodcuts. London: L. Reeve, 1870.
A folio volume with more than 2,000 cuts "engraved, for the most part, by Thomas and John Bewick" and arranged by source. The book illustrations are of special interest in the history of children's literature.

———. Catalogue of the choice and valuable collection of books, wood engravings, and engraved woodcut blocks, manuscripts, autograph letters and proof impressions, by or relating to Thomas & John Bewick, and their pupils. London: Sotheby, Wilkinson & Hodge, 1877.

———. A supplement [to The Bewick collector] . . . consisting of additions to the various divisions of cuts, wood blocks, etc. . . . . illustrated with a hundred and eighty cuts. . . . London: L. Reeve, 1868.

McPharlin, Paul. "Bewick's birds 1797–1804," *Publishers weekly* 145:47–54 (January 1, 1944).
The article concerns the illustrations for the two volumes of *The history of British birds.*

Powys, Llewelyn. "Thomas Bewick," in his *Thirteen worthies,* p. 181–92. New York: American Library Service, 1923.
Appreciative sketch.

Ritchie, Anne Isabella Thackeray. "Concerning Thomas Bewick," in her *Blackstick papers,* p. 260–75. London: Smith & Elder, 1908.
Impression of the English countryside that Bewick knew, with an account of a visit to the natural history museum in Newcastle where many of his engravings are to be seen.

Robinson, Robert. Thomas Bewick: his life and times. Newcastle-upon-Tyne: printed for the author, 1887.
Illustrated with engraved portraits, woodcuts by Bewick and his pupils.

Roscoe, Sydney. Thomas Bewick: a bibliography raisonné of editions of the *General history of the quadrupeds,* the *History of British birds,* and the *Fables of Aesop,* issued in his lifetime. London: Oxford University Press, 1953.
Includes facsimiles of many title pages of Bewick's books.

Ruzicka, Rudolph. Thomas Bewick, engraver. New York: The Typophiles, 1943.
The text is taken largely from *A memoir of Thomas Bewick, written by himself.* Illustrated with Bewick woodcuts accompanied by detailed notes.

Stone, Reynolds, ed. Wood engravings of Thomas Bewick. London: Hart-Davis, 1953.
Biographical introduction by Stone is on p. 7–47. "Bewick's best engravings" are beautifully and carefully printed.

Thomas Bewick: a checklist of his books and illustrations in the Olin Library. Middletown, Conn.: Wesleyan University Press, 1964.
A limited edition.

Thomson, David Croal. The life and works of Thomas Bewick. London: The Art Journal Office, 1882.
Subtitle: "being an account of his career and achievements in art, with a notice of John Bewick, with one hundred illustrations."

————. "The works of Thomas and John Bewick," "Thomas Bewick: a tribute on the 150th anniversary of his birth," *The art journal* 43:245–49 (1881); 65:366–70 (1903).
Good reproductions. Vol. 43 is indexed in *Poole's index to periodical literature* as vol. 33.

Walker, Robert. "Thomas Bewick," *Good words* 24:492–98, 667–74 (1883).
Illustrated.

Weekley, Montague. Thomas Bewick. London: Oxford University Press, 1953.
This account of Bewick's life, works, and times has two principal aims: "to re-introduce this remarkable Englishman to his own countrymen and others, largely through his own autobiography . . . and to describe his achievements and influence in relation to the history of his craft."

Williams, Gordon, ed. Bewick to Dovaston: letters 1824–1828. London: Nattali & Maurice, [1968].
Introduction by Montague Weekley. Letters between these two friends written during the last five years of Bewick's life.

Woodberry, George Edward. "Modern wood-engraving," in his *A history of wood-engraving,* p. 151–209. New York: Harper, 1882.

Begins with an account of the work of Thomas Bewick, indicating the changes he made in the method of wood engraving. Includes also mention of his pupils and brief record of the history of wood engraving in America.

Reginald Birch

Hamilton, Elizabeth Bevier. "Reginald Birch: gallant gentleman and distinguished illustrator," *Horn book magazine* 20:25–28 (January–February, 1944).
Written at Birch's death by a friend and publisher, who concludes, "He will be remembered even by those who never knew him, for his youthful spirit, his wit and intelligence are plain for anyone to see in the pages of hundreds of books he illustrated." Includes a select list of books illustrated by Birch.

————. ed. Reginald Birch: his book. New York: Harcourt, 1939.
Reginald Birch made every book he illustrated "his book." This collection of selections from books illustrated by Birch is an affectionate tribute to the artist.

William Blake

Baker, C. H. Collins. Catalogue of William Blake's drawings and paintings in the Huntington Library. San Marino, Calif.: Huntington Library, 1969.
Includes a Blake chronology, an introduction, and many reproductions.

Binyon, Laurence. The drawings and engravings of William Blake. London: The Studio, 1922.

————. The engraved designs of William Blake. London: Ernest Benn, 1926; reprint: New York: Da Capo Press, 1967.
Discusses Blake's line engravings, his invention of "illuminated printing," and his use of wood engraving and relief etching. The bulk of the book is a "Catalogue of Blake's engraved designs," divided by method, i.e. line engravings, lithographs, wood engravings, and relief etchings.

Blunt, Sir Anthony. The art of William Blake. New York: Columbia University Press, 1959.
These lectures are "meant to provide a general introduction to his art." Bibliography.

Butlin, Martin. William Blake. A complete catalogue of the works in the Tate Gallery. London: Tate Gallery, [1957].
There is an introduction by Anthony Blunt and a foreword by J. Rothenstein. Eighty-seven items are shown, each with notes.

Easson, Roger R., and **Robert N. Essick.** William Blake: book illustrator; a bibliography and catalogue of the commercial engravings. 2v. Normal: American Blake Foundation at Illinois State University, 1972.
The two volumes present "in one chronological sequence, all those book illustrations either engraved or designed by Blake." Divided into plates and notes.

Figgis, Darrell. The paintings of William Blake. London: Ernest Benn, 1925.
A catalog.

Garnett, Richard. William Blake, painter and poet. London: Seeley, 1895; reprint: Folcroft, Pa.: Folcroft, 1973.
Contains many reproductions.

Keynes, *Sir* **Geoffrey,** comp. and ed. Drawings of William Blake; ninety-two pencil studies. New York: Dover, 1970.
Includes an excellent introduction to the man and his art. Each drawing has ample notes by Keynes, who is chairman of the William Blake Trust of London.

———. Engravings by William Blake; the separate plates. A catalogue raisonné. Dublin: Emery Walker, 1956.
Forty-five plates are shown in this beautifully printed book.

———. Pencil drawings. London: Nonesuch, 1927.
Eighty-two drawings are reproduced with notes.

———. ———. Second series. London: Nonesuch, 1956.
Fifty-six drawings in the same format as the book above.

———. William Blake's engravings. London: Faber & Faber [1950].
This work is "intended to illustrate fully his career as an original engraver." Plates are divided by line engravings, relief etchings, and wood engravings.

Lister, Raymond. Infernal methods: a study of William Blake's art techniques. London: G. Bell, [1975].

Mongan, Elizabeth, comp. The art of William Blake. Bi-centennial exhibition October 18–December 1, 1957. Washington, D.C.: Smithsonian Institution, National Gallery of Art, [1957].
Includes an essay on the art of William Blake by Elizabeth Mongan, curator of graphic arts. The catalog includes 95 items.

Scott, William Bell. William Blake: etchings from his works. With descriptive text. London: Chatto & Windus, 1878.

Todd, Ruthven. William Blake, the artist. London: Studio Vista, 1971.
Intended to be "a handbook for those who would like to know something about the manner in which Blake lived as an artist until his death . . . ."—introduction. The bulk of the book is "a chronological survey of Blake's life as an artist."

Louis Maurice Boutet de Monvel

Bidou, Henry. "Boutet de Monvel," *Art et décoration* 33:137–48 (May, 1913).
An excellent study of his chief works. *Jeanne d'Arc* is the subject of five out of the ten black-and-white illustrations.

Kahn, Gustave. "Boutet de Monvel," *Art et décoration* 11:36–50 (February, 1902).
A study of the artist's work in line drawing and watercolor with emphasis on pictures of and for children. Reproductions in black and white and in color.

L. Leslie Brooke

Crouch, Marcus S. "Homage to Leslie Brooke," *Junior bookshelf* 16:86–93 (1952).

Horn book magazine [The Leslie Brooke number] 17 (May–June, 1941).
Contents: Editorial: to honor L. Leslie Brooke, by B. E. M.; L. Leslie Brooke, by Anne Carroll Moore; Creating a bookplate; In homage (poem), by Elizabeth Mackinstry; Johnny Crow's creator, by Reginald Birch; Expressing our gratitude, by Gladys English; Out of the Orient, by Leonore St. John Mendelson; The little child's artist, by Louis Latimer; All children invited, by Grace Allen Hogarth; From Westbury to Amnor, by Jacqueline Overton; A hearty vote of praise, by Edna Doughty Knox, Anne Thaxter Eaton, and Josephine White; A Canadian tribute to Leslie Brooke, by Lillian H. Smith; A letter to Leslie Brooke, by James Daugherty.

Moore, Anne Carroll. "Leslie Brooke: pied piper of picture books," *Horn book magazine* 1:10–13 (November, 1924).
An admiring essay. Includes a select list of books illustrated by Brooke.

Randolph Caldecott

Blackburn, Henry. Randolph Caldecott: a personal memoir of his early art career. London: Low; New York: Routledge, 1886.
"Written by a friend and fellow-labourer, one who knew the artist well, written most sympathetically, and adorned with a copious and representative series of drawings."—*Spectator*, 1886.

Chapman, Margaret. "St. Augustine [Florida] and Randolph Caldecott," *Florida libraries* 21:18–21 (March, 1970).
Caldecott went to Florida in 1886 for his health and "to sketch from life the American countryside and the manners and customs of Americans themselves." He died there and is buried in Evergreen Cemetery in St. Augustine, Florida.

Davis, Mary C. Randolph Caldecott, 1846–1886: an appreciation. Philadelphia and New York: Lippincott, 1946.
A critic eminent in the field of children's literature writes of Caldecott's picture books and of the man as an artist. Facsimile illustrations. Bibliography.

Engen, Rodney K. Randolph Caldecott: "Lord of the nursery." London: Oresko, [1976].
Appraisal of Caldecott as an illustrator of rural England. Black-and-white and colored plates. The appendixes include a list of books illustrated by Caldecott, periodical articles illustrated by Caldecott, paintings in oil, exhibitions, and secondary sources.

Gail Klemm Books. Original woodblocks drawn by Randolph Caldecott & engraved by Edmund Evans. Yucaipa, Calif.: Gail Klemm Books, 1972.
Sale catalog of sixty-nine carved woodblocks used for the illustrations of *The diverting history of John Gilpin* (1882), *Baby bunting* (1882), *Sing a song for sixpence* (1880), and *The babes in the wood* (1879).

Henley, William Ernest. "Randolph Caldecott," *The art journal* 43:208–12 (1881).
"Mr. Caldecott . . . is a kind of Good Genius of the Nursery, and—in the way of pictures—the most beneficent and delightful it ever had." Volumes of *The art journal* are variously numbered as there have been several different series.

Hutchins, Michael, ed. Yours pictorially: illustrated letters of Randolph Caldecott. London: Warne, 1976.
Letters written to friends arranged in alphabetical order according to the recipient. A chronological list of the letters is included in the back.

Miller, Bertha Mahony. "Randolph Caldecott," *Horn book magazine* 14:218–23 (July, 1938).
Speaks of Caldecott's love of children and his love for rural England. Includes a list of Caldecott's *Picture books.*

Stockum, Hilda van. "Caldecott's pictures in motion," *Horn book magazine* 22:119–25 (March, 1946).
A review of Caldecott's *Picture books* and the "ebb and flow of perpetual motion" that the author remembers particularly in Caldecott's work.

Palmer Cox

Cummins, R. W. Humorous but wholesome: a history of Palmer Cox and the brownies. Watkins Glen, N.Y.: Century, 1973.
Compares Cox with Lewis Carroll, Kenneth Grahame, A. A. Milne, Hugh Lofting, and Frank Baum and concludes that, like these humorists, "Cox achieved that unusual feat of filling a landscape with rare beings of his own creation, endowing them with distinguishing characteristics, and showing that a lot of the imagination can exist in its own right." Includes many illustrations and a bibliography of books by Palmer Cox, as well as a list of his contributions to *St. Nicholas* and *Harper's young people*. Bibliography of secondary sources.

Walter Crane

Bromhead, Cutts and Co. Catalogue of a memorial exhibition of paintings and water colour drawings by Walter Crane. London: Bromhead Cutts, 1920.

Crane, Walter. An artist's reminiscences, with one hundred and twenty-three illustrations by the author, and others from photographs. London: Methuen; New York: Macmillan, 1907; reprint: Detroit: Singing Tree, 1968.
Straightforward account of the author's life and work.

————. Ideals in art: papers theoretical, practical, critical. London: Bell, 1905.
The artist's own declarations on art.

————. "Notes on my own books for children," *Imprint* 1:81–87 (February 17, 1913); reprint: *Signal* 13:10–15 (January, 1974).
A charming essay in which the artist discusses his own art training, the state of children's book illustration, and his relationships with Edmund Evans, Randolph Caldecott, and Kate Greenaway.

————. The work of Walter Crane. London: The Art Journal Office, 1898.
The Easter art annual for 1898, extra number of *The Art Journal.* The artist's commentary upon his own life work, including accounts of the origin and success of his children's books. Profusely illustrated and especially valuable for reference.

Engen, Rodney K. Walter Crane as a book illustrator. London: Academy; New York: St. Martin's, 1975.
A short text includes a biographical sketch and places Crane historically as an important nineteenth-century illustrator. Analyzes Crane's book illustrations chronologically in three categories: (1) early work, 1867–76; (2) mature work, 1877–86; and (3) work predominantly for the adult, 1887–

1915. Includes many pages of illustrations in black and white and color and "A catalogue of books illustrated or written by Crane," chronologically given. Also includes a select bibliography of secondary sources.

Konody, Paul George. The art of Walter Crane. London: Bell, 1902.
"Gives a full opportunity for studying Mr. Crane's art in all its aspects. It is first and foremost an exhibition of his designs. These are excellently reproduced, many of them in colour, and include examples of the children's books."—*The Saturday review of literature*, 1902. "List of books illustrated or written by Walter Crane," p. 141–44.

Massé, Gertrude C. E. A bibliography of first editions of books illustrated by Walter Crane. London: Chelsea, 1923.
A bibliographical listing of books illustrated by Crane, arranged chronologically and with a special list of his picture books.

Pitz, Henry C. "The magic world of Walter Crane," *New York Herald Tribune Books* 5:8 (May 19, 1929).
Evaluation of Walter Crane's illustrations for children's books, noting the influences that affected his work and his continuing influence upon artists of the present day.

Soulier, Gustave. "Walter Crane," *Art de décoration* 4:165–79 (1898).
Adapted by Gleeson White. Designs illustrating Crane's many-sided work.

Spencer, Isobel. Walter Crane. London: Studio Vista, 1975.
"Examines many facets of Crane's talent as artist and craftsman from a foundation of careful research."

Vaughan, J. E. "Walter Crane: first, second or third?" *Junior bookshelf* 32:87–92 (April, 1968).
In a discussion of who was the best nineteenth-century color illustrator, Crane, Greenaway, or Caldecott, the author concludes, "Crane was a many-sided character of wide ranging talent and experience, a pioneering artist and craftsman respected by his contemporaries but not so overwhelmed by this as to find the illustrating of children's books beneath his nature."

Weinstein, Frederic Daniel. "Walter Crane and the American book arts, 1880–1915." Ph.D. diss., Columbia University, 1970.
The author attempts "to document the influences these [Crane's] works had upon the visual atmosphere of the late 19th century and early 20th century American book arts."

Wilkens, Lea-Ruth. "Walter Crane and the reform of the German picture book, 1865–1914." Ph.D. diss., University of Pittsburgh, 1973.

The author's hypothesis is that "the reform of the German colored picture book during the period 1865–1914 was largely and directly influenced by the work of Walter Crane."

George Cruikshank

Bates, William. George Cruikshank: the artist, the humorist, and the man, with some account of his brother Robert: a critico-bibliographic essay. 2d rev. ed. London: Houlston, 1879; Amsterdam: Emmering; New York: Schram, 1972.
Has numerous illustrations by George Cruikshank, including several from original drawings in the possession of the author. Bibliography of Crane's works, p. 77–94.

Borowitz, David. "George Cruikshank: mirror of an age," in *Charles Dickens and George Cruikshank: papers read at a Clark Library seminar on May 9, 1970*, p. 73–95. Edited by Joseph Hillis Miller and David Borowitz. [Los Angeles]: University of California, William Andrew Clark Memorial Library, 1971.
Cruikshank was Dickens's most famous illustrator, although they had a great falling-out over Cruikshank's rewriting of the Grimms' fairy tales.

Chesson, Wilfred Hugh. George Cruikshank. London: Duckworth; New York: Dutton, [1908].
The children's books are discussed on p. 155–61.

Cohn, Albert M. George Cruikshank: a catalogue raisonné. London: The Bookman's Journal, 1924.
Gives bibliographical descriptions for books illustrated by George Cruikshank and a bibliography arranged chronologically.

Davenport, Cyril James Humphries. "Illustrated books," in his *Byways among English books*, p. 103–5, 170–75. London: Stokes, 1927.
Estimate of George Cruikshank's work from the standpoint of a collector, supplemented by a list of books illustrated by him.

Douglas, Richard John Hardy. The works of George Cruikshank, classified and arranged with references to Reid's catalogue and their approximate values. . . . London: Davy, 1903.
Divided into two parts: (1) books with illustrations by George Cruikshank (including books, pamphlets, and tracts), and (2) separate prints. Frontispiece is a facsimile of the frontispiece to the rare *Holiday grammar*.

Feaver, William. George Cruikshank: [Exhibition held in] London, Victoria and Alfred Museum, 28 February–28 April 1974. London: Arts Council of Great Britain, 1974.
A catalog of this exhibition. Included are an introduction by William Feaver, a biographical outline of Cruikshank's life, and a select bibliography of secondary sources.

Hamilton, Walter. A memoir of George Cruikshank, artist and humourist. London: Elliot Stock, 1878.
Lecture on the life and works of Cruikshank.

Jerrold, William Blanchard. The life of George Cruikshank, in two epochs. 2v. London: Chatto & Windus, 1882.
A friend's memoirs. The second epoch refers to Cruikshank's life as a teetotaler. The controversy between Cruikshank and Dickens is told in the chapter titled, " 'Frauds on the fairies' and 'Whole hogs.' " Includes a bibliography.

Maurice, Arthur Bartlett. "Cruikshank in America," *The bookman* 44:288–98 (1916).
Chiefly about the Meirs collection at Princeton. Nine illustrations.

McLean, Ruari. George Cruikshank: his life and work as a book illustrator. London: Art & Technics; New York: Pellegrini & Cudahy, 1948.
Cruikshank as an artist reflecting a long span of Victorian English life. This biographical sketch describes his collaboration with Dickens and other writers. More than fifty pages of plates include most of Cruikshank's etchings for *Jack and the beanstalk.* "Select list of books illustrated by Cruikshank," p. 97–100.

Patten, R. L., ed. "George Cruikshank: a reevaluation, *Chronicle* (Princeton University Library) 35:1–257 (Autumn–Winter, 1973–74).
Includes articles by John Fowles, Richard Vogler, Harry Stone, and William Feaver.

Reid, George William, comp. A descriptive catalogue of the works of George Cruikshank. 3v. London: Bell & Daldy, 1871.
The first bibliography of Cruikshank's works.

Sitwell, Sacheverell. "George Cruikshank," in *Trio: dissertations on some aspects of national genius,* by Osbert Sitwell, Edith Sitwell, and Sacheverell Sitwell, p. 221–48. London: Macmillan, 1938.
Identifies George Cruikshank as a national genius in the realm of "pictorial comment" for, "in his works we find the entire picture of the first half of the 19th century."

Stephens, Frederic George. A memoir of George Cruikshank. (Illustrated biographies of great artists) New York: Scribner, 1891.
Many reproductions of Cruikshank's etchings and engravings. "List of the principal books illustrated by Cruikshank," p. 132–42.

Thackeray, William Makepeace. "An essay on the genius of George Cruikshank," *The Westminster review* 46:4–59 (June, 1840); reprint: in his *Essays on art,* p. 31–88. London: Kelmscott Society, [1904].

An appreciative essay on Cruikshank. All the illustrations are not included in the reprint. *Essays on art* includes a prefatory note on Thackeray as artist and art critic by W. E. Church.

Wedmore, Sir Frederick R. "George Cruikshank," in his *Studies in English art,* 2d ser., p. 101–52. London: Bentley, 1880.
Mention of the Grimms' *German popular stories,* p. 130–31.

William W. Denslow

Hearn, Michael Patrick. "W. W. Denslow: the forgotten illustrator," *American artist* 37:40–45, 71–73 (May, 1973).
The author contends that W. W. Denslow (1856–1915) was a dramatic figure in the field of American children's book illustration; he is virtually unknown today except for his illustrations for *The wonderful wizard of Oz.*

Gustave Doré

Gosling, Nigel. Gustave Doré. New York: Praeger, [1974].
A biographical sketch and a section on his work. Includes several reproductions of the Perrault *Contes* and a chronologically arranged list of books illustrated by Doré, p. 105–7.

Jerrold, William Blanchard. The life of Gustave Doré. London: W. H. Allen, 1891; reprint: Detroit: Singing Tree, 1969.
Written by his "oldest and closest friend," this is "a chronicle of the struggle between the blithe and free-minded Doré of early manhood, and the morbidly sensitive and staid painter of the great pictures which are to be found chiefly in the Doré gallery in Bond Street."—preface. Includes a list of his illustrated works, arranged chronologically, p. 411–15.

Leblanc, Henri. Catalogue de l'oeuvre complet de Gustave Doré: illustrations—peintures—dessins—sculptures—eaux-fortes—lithographies, avec un portrait et 29 illustrations documentaires. Paris: Bosse, 1931.

Lehmann-Haupt, Hellmut. The terrible Gustave Doré. New York: Marchbanks, 1943.
A concise, well-written biography with several full-page reproductions of pages from Perrault's *Contes.*

[Macchetta], Blanche Roosevelt Tucker. Life and reminiscences of Gustave Doré. New York: Cassell, 1885.
Subtitle: "compiled from material supplied by Doré's relatives and friends and from personal recollections. With many original unpublished

sketches, and selections from Doré's best published illustrations. A very long biography by a friend of Doré. No bibliography.

Valmy-Baysse, Jean. Gustave Doré. 2v. Paris: Marcel Seheur, 1930.
Vol. 2, by Louis Dézé, is titled *'Bibliographie et catalogue complet de l'oeuvre.'*

Richard Doyle

Hambourg, Daria. Richard Doyle: his life and work. London: Art & Technics, 1948.
A biographical sketch with a list of Doyle's work, which included the Grimms' fairy tales, Lang's *Princess Nobody,* and Ruskin's *King of the Golden river.* More than sixty pages of reproductions of drawings.

Morley, Alan. "Remembering Richard Doyle," *Signal* 5:78–84 (May, 1971).
Argues that Doyle was the equal of Caldecott, Crane, and Greenaway. Discusses especially Doyle's *Journal,* which he kept during his fifteenth year, and *Jack and the giants,* written in manuscript and illustrated in color when Doyle was seventeen.

Edmund Dulac

Larkin, David, ed. Dulac. London: Coronet, [1975].
Forty color plates from the work of Edmund Dulac. Includes an introduction by Brian Sanders.

Rutter, Frank. "The drawings of Edmund Dulac," *International studio* 36:103–13 (December, 1908).
Speaks of the great imaginative variety in Dulac's drawings for children's books.

Claud Lovat Fraser

Drinkwater, John, and **Albert Rutherston.** Claud Lovat Fraser. London: Heinemann, 1923.
"Claud Lovat Fraser: a memoir" is written by John Drinkwater; "The art of Claud Lovat Fraser," by Albert Rutherston. Includes excerpts from letters. Profusely illustrated.

Driver, Clive E. The art of Claud Lovat Fraser: an exhibition to commemorate the 50th anniversary of his death. . . . Philadelphia: Rosenbach Foundation, 1971.
Introduction by Seymour Adelman; tribute by Maurice Sendak. Illustrated with two color plates.

MacFall, Haldane. The book of Claud Lovat Fraser. London: Dent, 1923.
Written by "his most intimate friend," this beautifully printed and lavishly illustrated book covers: Lovat: the man; Lovat as artist; and Lovat: as dec-

orator, maker of books, trade tracts, posters, and cards.

Millard, Christopher, ed. The printed work of Claud Lovat Fraser. London: Danielson, 1923.
The bibliography is not comprehensive but is based on the "fairly comprehensive" collections of the compiler and of Fraser's family.

Arthur Burdett Frost

A book of drawings by A. B. Frost. New York: Collier, 1904.
In his introduction, Joel Chandler Harris writes about humor, the "negro's spirit and imagination," and Frost as "essentially and peculiarly American." There are many black-and-white and colored plates.

Reed, Henry M. The A. B. Frost book. Rutland, Vt.: Tuttle, 1967.
Foreword by Eugene V. Connett. A chapter on "'Brer Rabbit and 'Uncle Remus'" contains part of the correspondence between A. B. Frost and Joel Chandler Harris. Bibliography of books by A. B. Frost.

Harry Furniss

Furniss, Harry. Confessions of a caricaturist. London: Unwin, [1902].

———. "Confessions of an illustrator," *Jabberwocky* 2:11–12 (Autumn, 1973).

———. Harry Furniss at home. London: Unwin, 1904.
Illustrated by the author. Includes a charming satire on *Alice in Wonderland,* p. 68–76.

Kate Greenaway

Clark, Keith. "Bookplate designs of Kate Greenaway," *Private library,* 2d ser. 8:100–14 (Autumn, 1975).

———. "Kate Greenaway collection," *Books* 14:32 (Spring, 1974).

The complete Kate Greenaway, featuring *Language of flowers,* and listing all her illustrated books with value guide. Watkins Glen, N.Y.: Century, [1967].
Reproduced in the original 4½-by-6-inch format with ninety-one illustrations and vignettes.

Detroit Public Library. The John S. Newberry gift collection of Kate Greenaway presented to the Detroit Public Library. Compiled by Frances J. Brewer. Detroit: Friends of the Detroit Public Library, 1959.

A listing of (1) original watercolor drawings, letters, sketches, etc., (2) books written and illustrated by Kate Greenaway, (3) illustrations for works of others, (4) calendars, greeting and Christmas cards, etc., and (5) miscellanea.

Dobson, Austin. "Household art," in his *Collected poems*, p. 279. 2d ed. London: Kegan Paul, 1897.

———. "Kate Greenaway," "A song of the Greenaway child," in his *De libris: prose & verse*, p. 91–107. London: Macmillan, 1908.
Compares Kate Greenaway to Caldecott and Thomas Stothard. Dobson considers the illustrations for *Mother Goose* and *Marigold garden*, Kate Greenaway's most important efforts.

Doheny, Estelle Betzold. A collection of Kate Greenaway belonging to Mrs. Edward Doheny, originally assembled by Louise Ward Atkins. Los Angeles: Dawson's Book Shop, 1942.
Checklist compiled by Ellen Shaffer.

Doin, Jeanne. "Kate Greenaway et ses livres illustrés," *Gazette des beaux-arts* 106:5–22 (1910). Good reproductions.

Engen, Rodney K. Kate Greenaway. London: Academy; New York: Harmony, [1976].
The author says, "she was a shrewd escapist who created a universal, sugar-coated world of sexless, middle-class children, dressed in derivative costumes, romping blissfully in idyllic pastel-coloured landscapes." Includes a bibliography.

Ernest, Edward, and Patricia Tracy Lowe, eds. The Kate Greenaway treasury: an anthology of the illustrations and writings of Kate Greenaway. Cleveland: World, [1967].
Includes an introduction by Ruth Hill Viguers, a biographical sketch from the biography of Spielmann and Layard (listed below), selections from the artist's letters to and from John Ruskin, an essay by Anne Carroll Moore, and selections from many of Kate Greenaway's illustrated works. Includes a bibliography.

Hampstead Public Libraries. Handbook to the Kate Greenaway collection at the Central Public Library, Hampstead. Hampstead [England]: Central Library, [19–?].
Subtitle: "with some account of the life and work of Kate Greenaway, with coloured & other illustrations including drawings hitherto unpublished." This library in Hampstead, where Kate Greenaway lived, has the largest extant collection of her original pencil sketches and drawings, and many of her proofs (some with notes). Included also are several photographs of the artist.

Holme, Bryan. The Kate Greenaway book. New York: Viking, [1976].

Gives a short biographical sketch, analyzes some of Kate Greenaway's books, and reproduces many of her illustrations. Includes "A list of her books," p. 104–42.

Kate Greenaway the artist: a review and an estimate," *The critic* 47, n.s. 44:498–506 (1905).
Extract from *Kate Greenaway* by M. H. Spielmann and G. S. Layard (listed below).

Knaufft, Ernest. "Kate Greenaway: the illustrator of childhood," *The American monthly review of reviewers* 24:679–81 (1901).

Locker-Lampson, Oliver. "Kate Greenaway: friend of children," *The century magazine* 75:183–94 (1907).
By one who knew Kate Greenaway intimately and who says her childlike spirit "dominated every other attribute of her nature." A number of letters and drawings are included.

Lucas, Edward Verrall. "Kate Greenaway," *The academy* 61:466 (1901); *Littell's living age* 231:724–25 (1901).

Moore, Anne Carroll. A century of Kate Greenaway. London: Warne, 1946.
Booklet with an appreciative essay and illustrations.

Parrish, Anne. "Flowers for a birthday: Kate Greenaway, March 17, 1846," *Horn book magazine* 22:96–108 (March, 1946).
This chiefly biographical sketch speaks of the artist's relationships with Edmund Evans and John Ruskin. Analyzes some drawings and verse.

Ruskin, John. "Fairy land: Mrs. Allingham and Kate Greenaway," in his *The art of England*, p. 117–57. 3d ed. London: G. Allen, 1893.
An Oxford lecture.

Sargent, Irene. "Art in the home and in the school: a selection from the child-types of Kate Greenaway," *The craftsman* 7:519–29 (1905).

Spielmann, Marion Harry. "Kate Greenaway: in memoriam," *The magazine of art* 26:118–22 (1902).

——— and G. S. Layard. Kate Greenaway. London: Black, 1905.
"The life of the artist [1846–1901] whose delightful illustrations of children's books endeared her to two hemispheres is here admirably told. Innumerable pen-and-ink illustrations intersperse the text, many of them from Miss Greenaway's letters to John Ruskin, her friendship with whom was one of the important features of her life. The full-page illustrations have been done with particular care by the three-color process. . . . They have been

especially well chosen and give a very adequate idea of her art, which she devoted to the graces of childhood and all the incidents that make the joys and interests of child life."—*The Nation*, 1906. "List of books, etc., illustrated wholly or in part by Kate Greenaway," p. 285–89.

Under the window. (Kate Greenaway Society, Folsom, Pa.)
This is the journal of the Kate Greenaway Society.

Arthur Boyd Houghton

Arthur Boyd Houghton: a selection from his work in black and white, printed for the most part from the original wood-blocks. London: Kegan Paul, Trench, Trübner, 1896.
Introductory essay by Laurence Housman, p. 11–29, in which he praises the craft of A. B. Houghton and relates him to the Pre-Raphaelite movement. A list of works illustrated by A. B. Houghton, arranged chronologically, is appended.

Ford, Michael. "Arthur Boyd Houghton," *Arts review* 27:25 (December 12, 1975).

Arthur Hughes

Douglass, Jane. "The gentle gift: an appreciation of Arthur Hughes," *Horn book magazine* 36: 530–33 (December, 1960).
Deals chiefly with Hughes's illustrations for MacDonald's books, with some mention of Hughes's illustrations for *Tom Brown's school days* and *Speaking likenesses*.

Edward Windsor Kemble

Kinghorn, Norton D. "E. W. Kemble's misplaced modifier: a note on the illustrations for *Huckleberry Finn*," *The Mark Twain journal* 16:9–11 (Summer, 1973).
The essay discusses the relationship between the author and the illustrator and the integration of the text and the drawings.

Edward Lear

Henry E. Huntington Library and Art Gallery. Drawings by Edward Lear: an exhibition at the Henry E. Huntington Library and Art Gallery, November–December, 1962. San Marino, Calif.: Huntington Library, 1962.
The introduction to the exhibition catalog is by Robert R. Wark. The exhibit included zoological drawings, landscapes, and nonsense drawings—fifty-three items.

Liverpool. Public Libraries. Museums and Art Gallery. Walker Art Gallery. Edward Lear and Knowsley. Liverpool: Walker Art Gallery, 1975.
Catalog for an exhibition of bird and landscape watercolor drawings done by Lear at Knowsley.

Worcester, Mass., Art Museum. Edward Lear, painter, poet and draughtsman: an exhibition. Worcester, Mass.: The Art Museum, 1968.
An exhibition of 106 items, including some nonsense drawings. The notes are by Philip Hofer.

John Leech

Field, William B. Osgood. John Leech on my shelves. Munich: privately printed, 1930; reprint: [New York]: Collectors Editions, [1970].
155 copies were printed in 1930. Includes "A list of reference books for John Leech," p. 296. The bibliography is annotated.

Frith, William Powell. John Leech: his life and work. 2v. London: Richard Bentley, 1891.

Grolier Club. Catalogue of an exhibition of works by John Leech (1817–1864), held at the Grolier Club from January 22 until March 8, 1914. New York: Grolier Club, 1914.

Tidy, Gordon. A little about Leech. London: Constable, 1931.

William Mulready

Stephens, Frederic George. Memorials of William Mulready. (Great artist series) New York: Scribner, 1890.
Mulready's illustrations for the children's books published by William Godwin are discussed on p. 24–26.

Kay Nielsen

Britton, Jasmine. "Kay Nielsen: Danish artist," *Horn book magazine* 21: 168–75 (May, 1945).
Includes a short autobiographical sketch and a list of books illustrated by Nielsen.

Larkin, David, ed. Kay Nielsen. New York: Peacock, Bantam, 1975.
Forty color plates from works of the Danish artist.

———. The unknown paintings of Kay Nielsen, with an elegy by Hildegarde Flanner. Toronto and New York: Peacock, Bantam, 1977.

Maxfield Parrish

Ludwig, Coy. Maxfield Parrish: a critical biography and bibliography. New York: Watson-Guptill, 1973.

Profusely illustrated in color and black and white. Includes "A catalogue of selected works," p. 205–19, and a bibliography, p. 220.

Skeeters, Paul W. Maxfield Parrish: the early years, 1893–1930. Los Angeles: Nash Publishing, [1973].
Contains fine full-page color illustrations from *Dream days, The golden age, Arabian nights, Poems for childhood, Wonder book,* and *Tanglewood tales,* and commercial art.

Sweeney, M. S. Maxfield Parrish prints: a collector's guide. Dublin, N.H.: William L. Bauhan, 1974.

Beatrix Potter

Clark, Keith. "Beatrix Potter (1866–1943): the Linder collection," *Books* 7:7–9 (Spring, 1972).
Clark was a curator of the Linder collection.

Crouch, Marcus. Beatrix Potter. (Walck and Bodley Head monographs) London: Bodley Head, 1960; New York: Walck, 1961.
This is an attempt "to set down . . . a little of what her books have meant to children who in her company have learnt to laugh, to observe, to share vicariously in the creation of character and the shaping of words."—introduction. Includes a "Beatrix Potter check-list."

Godden, Rumer. "Beatrix Potter," *Horn book magazine* 42:390–400 (August, 1966); *The New York Times book review* 71:4–5, 45 (May 8, 1966).
This article marking the centenary of Beatrix Potter's birth speaks of the qualities—artistic and literary—that make her work popular with today's children.

Lane, Margaret. The tale of Beatrix Potter: a biography. London and New York: Warne, 1946.
The first full-length biography of Beatrix Potter. Includes a list of books, p. 161–62, several photographs, and a facsimile of the letter that became *The tale of Peter Rabbit.* In *Horn book magazine* (22:431–38 [November, 1946]), Marcia Dalphin credits Margaret Lane with two qualities indispensable to any biographer: imagination and understanding, and "a love for the subject great enough to overcome the difficulties of the search for material in a singularly elusive and retiring personality."

Linder, Leslie. "Beatrix Potter's code writing," *Horn book magazine* 39:141–56 (April, 1963).
Tells how Linder found the journals in code and transcribed them, as well as what the journals were about.

———. A history of the writings of Beatrix Potter, including an unpublished work. London: Warne, 1971.
A companion piece to *The art of Beatrix Potter* (below), intended "as a history of her published works," with some unpublished essays. Includes an introduction as well as a bibliography of her published works.

———, ed. Beatrix Potter, 1866–1943: centenary catalogue. London: National Book League, 1966.
A catalog of 365 items showing all the *Peter Rabbit* books.

The Linder collection of the works and drawings of Beatrix Potter. London: National Book League, 1971.

Miller, Bertha Mahony. "Beatrix Potter and her nursery classics," *Horn book magazine* 17:230–38 (May, 1941).
Shows why Beatrix Potter's books delight children all over the world.

———. "Beatrix Potter in letters," *Horn book magazine* 20:214–24 (May, 1944).
Letters written to Bertha Miller who was then editor of *Horn book magazine.* With photos.

Potter, Beatrix. The art of Beatrix Potter. London and New York: Warne, 1955. Rev. ed., 1972.
With an appreciation by Anne Carroll Moore. "Makes available 240 drawings and paintings from picture letters, sketch books, trial manuscripts and other sources." Janice Dohm reviewed the book in *Junior bookshelf* 19:199–206 (October, 1955). The notes to each section of the book are written by Enid and Leslie Linder. Pt. 1 is titled "Beatrix Potter—her work as an artist," and pt. 2, "Beatrix Potter; her art in relationship to her books." Includes a list of Beatrix Potter's books, p. 334–35.

———. The journal of Beatrix Potter from 1881–1897. Transcribed from her code writing by Leslie Linder. London and New York: Warne, [1966].
With an appreciation by H. L. Cox. Beatrix Potter wrote the journal in code between the age of seventeen and thirty. There is a short biographical sketch and a note by Leslie Linder on the code writings. Lavishly illustrated with many of her paintings and illustrations as well as several photos of Beatrix Potter and of places where she lived. A review of the book by Marcus Crouch, "A long apprenticeship," is available in *Junior bookshelf* 30:227–31 (August, 1966).

———. Letters to children. New York: Walker, 1966.
Letters owned by the Department of Print and Graphic Arts, Harvard University College Library. Book includes facsimiles of nine letters (1896–1902) owned by Philip Hofer.

———. "Letters to two children," *Signal* 8:74–80 (May, 1972).
Beatrix Potter's letters are noteworthy for the charming drawings sprinkled throughout.

———. "Roots of the Peter Rabbit tales," *Horn book magazine* 5:69–72 (May, 1929).
An important essay in which the author writes of the roots from which her work sprang.

Quinby, Jane. Beatrix Potter: a bibliographical check list. New York: privately printed, 1954.
A checklist of first editions mainly based on the Potter collection of Urling Iselin.

Sendak, Maurice. "Aliveness of Peter Rabbit," *Wilson library bulletin* 40:345–48 (December, 1965).
Sendak pays tribute to Beatrix Potter's Peter Rabbit books by saying, "The art of imaginatively writing and illustrating picture books is, at its best, a subtle art, exemplified with rare excellence and understatement in Beatrix Potter's work."

Shaffer, Ellen. "Beatrix Potter lives in the Philadelphia Free Library," *Horn book magazine* 42:401–5 (August, 1966).
Narrates how a fine collection of stories, manuscripts and drawings came to the Free Library of Philadelphia.

Howard Pyle

Abbott, Charles D. Howard Pyle: a chronicle. New York: Harper, 1925.
With an introduction by N. C. Wyeth and many illustrations from Howard Pyle's works. Account of Pyle's life, his work as an illustrator and as a writer, with many quotations from his letters. The chapters "Magic casements" and "The Middle Ages" deal particularly with his children's books. No bibliography.

Alden, Henry Mills. "Howard Pyle," *Harper's weekly* 55:8 (November 18, 1911).
An appreciation with examples of Pyle's work.

Carrington, J. B. "A tribute to Howard Pyle," *The studio* 54:sup.:lxxxv–lxxxvi (January, 1915).

Hilton, M. R. "The shining knight of the golden age: Howard Pyle," *Ontario library review* 48: 93–94 (May, 1964).

Hoeber, Arthur. "Howard Pyle: illustrator-painter," *The studio* 45:sup.:lxxi–lxxiv (January, 1912).
Six illustrations.

Howard Pyle. New York: Peacock, Bantam, 1975.
Beautiful plates, most in color. An introduction by Rowland Elzea.

"Howard Pyle: illustrator," *Harper's monthly magazine* 124:255–63 (1912).
One page of text and seven full-page illustrations.

Kirkus, Virginia. "Howard Pyle: a backward glance," *Horn book magazine* 5:37–39 (November, 1929).
Virginia Kirkus lived in Delaware and went to school with Howard Pyle's children.

Lawson, Robert. "Howard Pyle and his times," in *Illustrators of children's books: 1744–1945*, compiled by Bertha E. Mahony et al., p. 105–22. Boston: Horn book, 1947.
Lawson writes, "Howard Pyle was to become more than a great illustrator; he was to become an American institution. He was to stand as a symbol of all that is fine and honest and good in the art of illustration. He was a one-man movement which would exert an incalculable influence on the whole course of illustration in this country."

Marke, G. Mortimer. "Howard Pyle: author-illustrator, 1853–1911," *Arts and decoration* 2:136–39 (1912).
"A retrospect of his varied work." Illustrated.

Maxim, David. "Medieval children's books of Howard Pyle," *The California librarian* 32:121–26 (April–July, 1971).
Speaks of Pyle's work in the context of the late-nineteenth-century interest in medievalism, as exemplified by the Pre-Raphaelite Brotherhood and William Morris and the Arts and Crafts Movement.

McClanathan, Richard, ed. The Brandywine tradition: Howard Pyle, N. C. Wyeth, Andrew Wyeth, James Wyeth. Chadds Ford, Pa.: Brandywine River Museum, 1971. Distributed by the New York Graphic Society, Greenwich, Conn.
An exhibition catalog.

Morse, Willard S., and Gertrude Brincklé, comps. Howard Pyle: a record of his illustrations and writings. Wilmington, Del.: Wilmington Society of the Fine Arts, 1921; reprint: Detroit: Singing Tree, 1969.
The bibliography is divided as follows: (1) illustrations and writings of Howard Pyle published in periodicals (listed alphabetically by journal title); (2) books by Howard Pyle with his own illustrations; (3) books by others with Pyle's illustrations: (4) a subject index of illustrations, such as pirates; colonial and revolutionary subjects; medieval, mystical and allegorical subjects; fables and fairy tales; frontiers and Indian subjects. Also included is "A tribute," by Henry Mills Alden, excerpted from *Harper's weekly* (listed above).

Nesbitt, Elizabeth. Howard Pyle. London: Bodley Head; New York: Walck, 1966.
An authority in children's literature focuses on the work and influence of "the first truly great

American author and illustrator of children's books." Includes a full bibliography of writing by and about Pyle.

Oakley, Thornton. "Howard Pyle," *Horn book magazine* 7:91–97 (May, 1931).
An appreciation by one of Pyle's former pupils.

Pitz, Henry C. The Brandywine tradition. Boston: Houghton, 1969.
Includes nine chapters on Howard Pyle and one on N. C. Wyeth. Bibliography.

————. Howard Pyle: writer, illustrator, founder of the Brandywine school. New York: Potter, 1975.
A major work by a great Pyle admirer.

Trimble, Jessie. "The founder of an American school of art," *The outlook* 85:453–60 (1907).
Emphasizes the typically American traits of Howard Pyle and his fundamental belief that "character is the basis of art."

Vandercook, John Womack. "Howard Pyle," *The mentor* 15:1–10 (June, 1927).
Many illustrations, some of them full page.

Wyeth, N. C. "Howard Pyle as I knew him," *The mentor* 15:15–17 (June, 1927).
An admiring essay.

Arthur Rackham

Arthur Rackham issue. *Horn book magazine* 16 (May–June, 1940).
Contents: Arthur Rackham and Selma Lagerlöf, by Bertha Mahony Miller; The genius of Arthur Rackham, by Robert Lawson; Arthur Rackham and *The wind in the willows*, by George Macy; The home of the wee folk, by P. G. Konody; Bibliography of children's books illustrated by Arthur Rackham, by Sarah Briggs Latimore and Grace Clark Haskell.

Baldry, A. L. "Arthur Rackham: a painter of fantasies," *International studio* 25:189–200 (May, 1905).

Baughman, Roland, ed. The centenary of Arthur Rackham's birth, September 19, 1867: an appreciation of his genius and a catalogue of his original sketches, drawings, and paintings in the Berol Collection. New York: Columbia University Library, 1967.
An appreciation and an exhibition catalog of 400 items. Beautifully printed.

Craig, L. "The fairy world of Arthur Rackham," *Antique dealer and collector's guide* (Britain), December, 1974, p. 88, 90.

Crouch, Marcus. "Arthur Rackham, 1867–1939," *Junior bookshelf* 31:297–300 (October, 1967).

An astute analysis of the man and artist. Crouch concludes that, although Rackham was "one of the finest draughtsmen who devoted himself to illustration" and "had a most rare insight into the spirit of the books on which he worked," his art "falls short of highest excellence" and his books "lack the timeliness and the universality of Beatrix Potter's and Leslie Brookes's," because "he lacked tenderness, the wealth of understanding and love for his subject which awakens an equal love and understanding in the reader."

Edwards, Barbara. "Try to look like a witch," *Columns* (Columbia University Library) 17:3–7 (May, 1968).
A memoir written by his daughter.

Hudson, Derek. Arthur Rackham: his life and work. New York: Scribner, 1960; reprint: London: Heinemann, 1974.
The definitive biography of Arthur Rackham. Contains a bibliography of secondary sources, a list of drawings and paintings by Arthur Rackham in public and semipublic collections, a checklist of books illustrated wholly or partially by Arthur Rackham arranged separately and chronologically. Reprint has a revised bibliography by Anthony Rota. In a review of this work in *Horn book magazine* 37:32–33 (February, 1961), Ruth Hill Viguers says, "In this splendid book Derek Hudson presents Arthur Rackham, the man and the artist, who knew so completely the world he interpreted that whenever the curtain rose his scene was whole."

Larkin, David, ed. Arthur Rackham. New York: Bantam, 1975.
Forty color plates selected from a variety of Rackham's work.

Latimore, Sarah Briggs, and **Grace Clark Haskell.** Arthur Rackham: a bibliography. Los Angeles: Suttonhouse, 1936; reprint: New York: Burt Franklin, 1970.
Includes a brief sketch of Arthur Rackham and a special section on Rackham's children's books. This section was also reprinted in *Horn book magazine* 16:197–213 (May–June, 1940).

McWhorter, George T. "Arthur Rackham: the search goes on," *Horn book magazine* 8:82–87 (February, 1972).
About collecting rare and not-so-rare Rackham-illustrated books.

Rackham, Arthur. Arthur Rackham's book of pictures. London: Heinemann, 1913.
With an introduction by Sir Arthur Quiller-Couch.

Shaffer, Ellen. "Arthur Rackham, 1867–1939," *Horn book magazine* 43:617–21 (October, 1967).
Relates how two of the greatest Rackham collections in the United States (owned by his bib-

liographers, Haskell and Latimore) came to the Philadelphia Free Library, and gives an analysis of several of Rackham's works.

Charles Robinson

De Freitas, Leo J. Charles Robinson. London: Academy, 1976.
"The text traces the strong influence of Dürer and of Japanese prints in Robinson's graphics."—Marshall Hall, in a review of Charles Robinson, in *Junior bookshelf*, October, 1976, p. 256.
Includes many illustrations and a bibliography.

William Heath Robinson

Day, Langston. The life and art of W. Heath Robinson. London: Herbert Joseph, 1947; reprint: London: The British Book Centre, 1977.
"There is more about the 'life' than the 'art' in this study."—John Lewis, *Heath Robinson*.

Johnson, A. E. The book of W. Heath Robinson. London: Black, 1913.
Johnson was Robinson's agent.

Jordan, R. Furneaux, ed. The Penguin Heath Robinson. Harmondsworth, Middlesex, England: Penguin, 1966.
Includes many illustrations.

Lewis, John. Heath Robinson: artist and comic genius. New York: Barnes & Noble, 1973.
Includes a section on Robinson's illustrations for Andersen's *Fairy tales,* a section on *Water-babies,* as well as reproductions of several other illustrations for children's books. The author compares the work of Rackham with that of Heath Robinson. A bibliography of books illustrated by Robinson and secondary sources.

E. Boyd Smith

Bader, Barbara. "E. Boyd Smith," in her *From Noah's ark to the beast within,* p. 13–22. New York: Macmillan, [1976].
Uses the pictures of E. Boyd Smith as a starting point in her history of contemporary book illustration for children.

Eaton, Anne Thaxter. "E. Boyd Smith," *Horn book magazine* 20:94–96 (March, 1944).
Includes a list of books illustrated by E. Boyd Smith.

Jessie Willcox Smith

Freeman, Ruth S. Jessie Willcox Smith (1863–1935): childhood's great illustrator. Watkins Glen, N.Y.: Century, 1977.

John Tenniel

Crouch, Marcus. "Must it be Tenniel?" *Junior bookshelf* 17:172 (October, 1953).
Raises the question of whether Tenniel's shadow should lie fixed over the *Alice* books. Reply to this appeared in *Junior bookshelf* 19:207–8 (October, 1955). The article, written anonymously, said, "Alice is like a literary Mt. Everest—other illustrators may attempt it, but they must remember that Sir John's flag was there first, and his name enduringly linked with her creator's."

Mespoulet, M. Creators of Wonderland. New York: Arrow, [1934].
Discussion of Carroll and Tenniel and other writers and illustrators of Victorian nonsense and fantasy.

Sarzano, Frances. Sir John Tenniel. London: Art & Technics; New York: Pellegrini & Cudahy, 1948.
The standard work on the famous English caricaturist and illustrator of Carroll's *Alice* books. Includes a list of "Books illustrated solely by Tenniel," "Books containing illustrations by Tenniel," and "Periodicals containing illustrations by Tenniel."

Hugh Thomson

Dobson, Austin. "Mr. Hugh Thomson," in his *De libris: prose and verse,* p. 109–24. London: Macmillan, 1908.
Designates Thomson, "Master of the vignette."

Spielmann, Marion Harry, and **Walter Jerrold.** Hugh Thomson: his art, letters, humour and his charm. London: Black, 1931.

N. C. Wyeth

Hunt, Dudley. "N. C. Wyeth, 1882–1945," *Horn book magazine* 22:332–38 (October, 1946).
Written at his death.

Smith, James Steel. "Painted adventure: N. C. Wyeth and his children's books," *School librarian* 17:45–50 (Summer, 1968).
"An author-artist-educator discusses the influence of illustration upon the printed work by recalling his childhood memories of Wyeth."—introduction.

Wyeth, Stimson. "My brother: N. C. Wyeth," *Horn book magazine* 45:29–36 (February, 1969).
Discusses the family, home life, education, training, and work of N. C. Wyeth.

AUTHOR AND TITLE INDEX

Prepared by Nancy H. Knight

This index includes authors and titles appearing in the text. An author, as a subject, can be located in the classified arrangement used in the text. Articles appearing in journals are indexed by the title of the article. Articles or chapters within a larger work are indexed by article title when the author of the article is not responsible for the entire work (e.g., an anthology) or by title of the entire work when the author is also responsible for the whole work.